"Adebanwi's unparalleled skills as a scholar, researcher, and social commentator are on full display in this book. *How to Become a Big Man in Africa* is a remarkable and eye-opening study on the concept and practices of the Big Man in Africa. Adebanwi weaves together robust scholarship and lucid prose to explore the intersections of ethnicity, youth development, and political elites in Nigeria. The book is also a thoughtful and intelligent assessment of class mobility and political strategy in Nigeria. Through groundbreaking archival and ethnographic research and magnificent social and cultural analysis, *How to Become a Big Man in Africa* offers a tour de force in African Studies. The author closely and intimately examines and reimagines the categories of subalternity and political elitism to construct what I believe is to become one of the most critically acclaimed and cited political biographies in African Studies. *How to Become a Big Man in Africa* is a seminal contribution to anthropology, political science, and ethnic studies in Africa."

—Jacob K. Olupona, Professor of African Religious Traditions, Harvard University, author of *City of 201 Gods: Ilé-Ifè in Time, Space, and the Imagination*

"*How to Become a Big Man in Africa: Subalternity, Elites, and Ethnic Politics in Nigeria* is an authoritative book in African political studies. Drawing on theoretical works across the humanistic social sciences and extensive primary research, and firmly anchored on Africanist scholarship, this path-breaking book animates critical issues in African politics—neo-patrimonialism, statism, communalism, military despotism, democratic transition, underdevelopment, youth culture, elite aspiration, demographic shifts, and neoliberalism. This impressive book on the charismatic Gani Adams and Yoruba populist politics in the context of the exigencies of Nigerian state formation will have an enduring impact on Nigerian political studies for many years to come. This is the most engaging and compelling book in African politics I have read in the last decade."

—Olufemi Vaughan, Alfred Sargent Lee '41 & Mary Ames Lee Professor and Chair of Black Studies, Amherst College, author of *Letters, Kinship, and Social Mobility in Nigeria*

"This is an amazing study of the rise of a Nigerian Big Man. The author, a distinguished scholar, has followed the ascent for more than twenty years, from his subject's humble beginnings to the present. Rarely are we privy to the personal rivalries and friendships among the nation's political elites in such detail, such authenticity. The author adds to the richness of the story a large and compelling collection of photographs showing from start to finish how one of the country's most famous leaders, a man with initial three years of high school, has orchestrated his career. The book is filled with marvelous insights of wide political and human interests."

—Sandra T. Barnes, Professor Emeritus of Anthropology, University of Pennsylvania, author of *Patrons and Power: Creating a Political Community in Metropolitan Lagos*

"The notorious figure of the 'Big Man' in Africa typecasts those social actors who rise to great heights through guile, cunning, and a preternatural ability to transgressively self-aggrandize with impunity. In what is the first intensive ethnography of an African Big Man, Wale Adebanwi focuses on the extraordinary career of Gani Adams in Nigeria as he rose from wanted fugitive to become one of the nation's preeminent power brokers. This path-breaking study of agency and 'self-actualization' based on more than two decades of research, locates Adams's remarkable story within the liminal pathways and festive arenas which he negotiated to gain access to the Nigerian state. *How to Become a Big Man in Africa* is a must read for all students of Nigerian cultural politics and African political economy."

—Andrew Apter, Professor of Anthropology and History, UCLA, author of *Black Critics and Kings: The Hermeneutics of Power in Yoruba Society*

"A magnificent exploration of how one becomes a man of consequence in employment-challenged Nigeria. With considerable acuity and empathy, Adebanwi traces the—anomalous yet also exemplary—trajectory of a high school dropout who 'seizes history' to become a key political actor and a celebrated 'big man.' *How to Become a Big Man in Africa* is a must read for anyone interested in youth culture, subalternity, elites, and African politics."

—Adeline Masquelier, Tulane University, author of *Fada: Boredom and Belonging in Niger*

HOW TO BECOME A BIG MAN IN AFRICA

HOW TO BECOME A BIG MAN IN AFRICA

SUBALTERNITY, ELITES, AND ETHNIC POLITICS IN CONTEMPORARY NIGERIA

WALE ADEBANWI

INDIANA UNIVERSITY PRESS

This book is a publication of

Indiana University Press
Office of Scholarly Publishing
Herman B Wells Library 350
1320 East 10th Street
Bloomington, Indiana 47405 USA

iupress.org

 The paper used in this publication meets the minimum requirements of the American National Standard for Information Sciences—Permanence of Paper for Printed Library Materials, ANSI Z39.48–1992.

Manufactured in the United States of America

First Printing 2024

Library of Congress Cataloging-in-Publication Data

Names: Adebanwi, Wale, author.
Title: How to become a big man in Africa : subalternity, elites, and ethnic politics in contemporary Nigeria / Wale Adebanwi.
Description: Bloomington : Indiana University Press, 2024. | Includes bibliographical references and index.
Identifiers: LCCN 2023055983 (print) | LCCN 2023055984 (ebook) | ISBN 9780253070357 (hardback) | ISBN 9780253070364 (paperback) | ISBN 9780253070371 (ebook)
Subjects: LCSH: Adams, Gani, 1970- | O'odua People's Congress—History. | Power (Social sciences)—Nigeria. | Nigeria—Politics and government—1993-2007. | Nigeria—Politics and government—2007- | BISAC: POLITICAL SCIENCE / World / African | SOCIAL SCIENCE / Anthropology / Cultural & Social
Classification: LCC JC330 .A22 2024 (print) | LCC JC330 (ebook) | DDC 303.3309669—dc23/eng/20231204
LC record available at https://lccn.loc.gov/2023055983
LC ebook record available at https://lccn.loc.gov/2023055984

For
Sunday Ojukwu Ibekwu, Taiwo Ogunsola,
and Lawrence Adegoke,
three great teachers in high school who
helped to clear my path;

Jacinda Ardern,
a leader who showed unceasing kindness, decency,
and integrity—and knew when there was no longer
"enough in the tank to do the job justice";

and, again, for Temitope,
who agglutinates the verses of my life.

Living and surviving in the moment . . . often necessitates an extreme (mental and physical) flexibility as well as a mastery of the tricky skills of improvisation, a capacity . . . describe[d] as "mathématiques." And indeed, to steer your life unharmed through all the pitfalls, all the possible parameters of your daily existence, seems to demand an advanced knowledge of higher mathematics and of topics such as chaos, fractals, mobility, and dynamics. Generated in the moment and therefore rarely knowing where they will end up, the meandering lines of local lives constantly generate conjunctures and conjectures of sudden action and passivity, power and powerlessness, expectation and disappointment, rise and fall, dream and nightmare.

Filip de Boeck, "Local Futures and the Future of the Local"

Not everything is possible, not everything is feasible. So, people have to have an understanding of what is feasible in order to move, and they have to have a system of intelligibility to which they can refer in order to determine the logic of effective action. These three things, then, *causality, possibility,* and *efficacy,* explain the rationalities at work.

Achille Mbembe, "Everything Can Be Negotiated: Ambiguities and Challenges in Time of Uncertainty"

CONTENTS

ACKNOWLEDGMENTS

This book is the outcome of more than two decades of research. It is part of what I hope will be a tetralogy on the elites and (ethno-national) power formations in Nigeria. The first in the series, *Yorùbá Elites and Ethnic Politics in Nigeria: Ọbáfemi Awólọ́wọ̀ and Corporate Agency* (Cambridge University Press, 2004), examines about six decades of the formation of a power elite around the leadership and figure of Awolowo, the statesman and first premier of the Western Region of Nigeria. The present work examines a sociocultural figure who transformed himself from a subaltern into a member of the elite. I watched that transformation happen over two decades. It is therefore understandable that I owe a debt of gratitude to many people.

At first, I did not intend to write this book. As a student of society who was just transitioning from journalism to academia in late-1990s Nigeria, at the same time as Nigeria was transitioning from late military rule to democratic governance, I was interested in studying the Oodua People's Congress (OPC) in the context of ethno-nationalist politics, democratization, and violence in the hope of publishing one or two journal articles. In 1999, I started monitoring and collecting media coverage of the group while discussing the OPC with journalists, public intellectuals, and politicians who knew the leadership of the group well or followed the group's activities closely. My interest in the group was partly also fueled by the need to understand its relationship with the Yorùbá power elite whom I was also studying. However, the tone and tenor of my research changed when I received the New York–based Social Science Research Council (SSRC) grant under the auspices of the "African Youth in a Global Age Fellowship" (2001–2). For this fellowship, I focused on the OPC in the context of youth, culture, and violence.

For facilitating the SSRC fellowship, I thank Ron Kassmir and Funmi Vogt, both then at the SSRC. Ron directed the fellowship program while Funmi administered it. Both were kind and helpful. I am also grateful to the resource persons who commented on the initial proposal and the final research report in Dakar, Senegal, and Maputo, Mozambique: Alcinda Honwana, Jean Comaroff, Filip de Boeck, Mamadou Diouf, and the late Beverlee Bruce.

I thank my teachers and colleagues in Lagos, Ibadan, Cambridge, and Davis whose intellectual and professional guidance and support helped me along the way. To different degrees, there are traces of their efforts in this book. At the University of Lagos, Adidi Uyo, Victor Ayedun-Aluma, and the late Delu Ogunade; at the University of Ibadan, Adigun Agbaje, Egbosa Osaghae, Rotimi Suberu, and the late Kunle Amuwo; at Cambridge, Dame Marilyn Strathern, Stephen Hugh-Jones, Paul Sant Cassia, and the late Sue Benson; and at the University of California–Davis, Moradewun Adejunmobi. The late J. D. Y. Peel, a most thoughtful and methodical supervisor, provided watchful intellectual guidance during the latter part of my time at Cambridge and until his passing in 2015.

I am grateful to the good people of the Oxford African Studies Centre, the Oxford School of Global and Area Studies (OSGA), St. Antony's College, and the Africa Oxford Initiative (AfOx). My time in Oxford was made rewarding and remarkable by the collegiality, support, and friendship of David Pratten, Miles Larmer, Jonny Steinberg, William Beinart, Carly Coetzee, Anne Makena, Stephen Tuck, Roger Goodman, Peter Tufano, Ricardo Soares de Oliviera, Kevin Marsh, Kalypso Nicolaïdis, and Eugene Rogan. I thank them all. At Penn, my colleagues in the Africana Studies Department, Michael Hanchard, Camille Charles, Heather Williams, Tim Rommen, Tukufu Zuberi, David Amponsah, Eve Troutt Powell, and Barbara Savage, as well as our administrative staff, particularly Carol Davis and Teya Campbell, have been of immense assistance. Michael Hanchard and his wife, Zita Nunes, welcome me into their home regularly, for which I am thankful. I thank Theodore Roger Ajluni, for excellent proofreading, and Rosie Poku and Chukwudi Mathias Isiani, who both provided research assistance during the revisions stage.

Many friends and colleagues (in academia and journalism) did their best in different contexts to support the research for this work throughout many years or at certain critical points. They are too numerous to mention here. However, I must express my gratitude to Olu Daramola, Ebenezer Obadare, Kunle Ajibade, Laolu Akande, Segun Adeyemi, Sina Babasola, Babafemi Ojudu, Dele Momodu, Kunle Bakare, Waziri Adio, Martin Oloja, Simon Kolawole, Kemi Rotimi, Olufemi Vaughan, Olúfẹ́mi Táíwò, Simeon Ilesanmi, Gbemisola

Animasawun, the late Yinka Odumakin, Akin Osuntokun, Festus Adedayo (who proofread the initial draft of the manuscript), Edward Dickson, and Lasisi Olagunju. I thank the chair of the African Newspapers, publishers of the *Nigerian Tribune*, Ambassador Tokunbo Awolowo Dosumu and Uncle Tokunbo Ajasin. My friend in Oxford Nana Lily Owusu-Darkwa was particularly generous with her suggestions. She read the entire manuscript carefully and commented on it insightfully. Nana's scholarly keenness and interventions and the sacrifice of her time are immensely appreciated. William Ojo and Femi Anjorin provided useful research assistance at various points, for which I am grateful.

My gratitude goes to the two anonymous referees whose insightful comments not only challenged me to explore some illuminating and critical paths but also helped to improve the arguments tremendously. I thank Jacob K. Olupona, who read one of the key chapters and gave generous comments; Andrew Apter and Emmanuel Akyeampong, for their critical comments when I presented a part of this work at the weekly seminar in African Studies at Harvard University; Jean Comaroff, for the invitation to present the work at Harvard; and the students in Jean's class, for the important questions they raised about the work. The graduate students in the proseminar of my department at UPenn read a few chapters, raised some interesting points, and asked useful questions. I thank them and my colleague Grace Sanders Johnson, who coordinated the seminar in the 2022–23 academic year. The Association for Africanist Anthropology (AfAA) invited me to give the annual lecture during the American Anthropology Association (AAA) annual conference in 2021, where I presented a part of this work. For the honor, I am deeply grateful to the association, Richard Werbner, the gracious *living ancestor* in Africanist anthropology (who initiated the process); the president of AfAA, Yolanda Covington-Ward; and Omolade Adunbi.

In the many years I was working on this book, the man at the center of the research, Gani Adams, the leader of the OPC and now the *Ààrẹ Ọ̀nà Kakaǹfò* of Yorubaland, exercised a lot of patience—even when he wondered why this research was going on "forever." At one point—I think in the nineteenth year—he asked, partly in exasperation and partly out of curiosity, "Where is the book you have been writing all these years?" I did not have an answer for him, partly because I was not sure if I was going to write it. Given the sheer volume of material I had gathered, even at that point, and Adams's continuous generation of more and more data, I was wondering where to start. At the same time, I had a strong conviction that I must get to it someday. In the first decade of my research for this book, Adams was most welcoming and even indulgent toward me. He gave me as much access to him and the group's events as I requested, and he responded to every question—sometimes with "Let's leave that aside for now!" As he became bigger and more influential in the second decade of my research, he, perhaps understandably, had less and less time and patience for my intrusions into his social and personal lives. Yet, even in this context, when I had to see him or when we met at public events, he always accorded me the kind of regard that was critical for my inquiry—which could be vexing for him, at times, given the nature of the relationship we had developed and, perhaps, also because of my own career trajectory. I decided against a more elaborate preface that would have located both of us in the social history of contemporary Yorubaland and Nigeria, given that we belong to the same generation and were nurtured in the same socioeconomic, cultural, and political contexts—because of, and/or despite, the (dis)similar familial opportunities and challenges related to the structural context that intervened in our personal trajectories. There may be another opportunity for this in the future.

The late Dr. Fredrick Fasehun, the founding leader of the OPC, also afforded me the access I needed in the early years of my research and allowed me to attend a few meetings of his faction—before I decided to focus on the Adams faction. Other members of the OPC also deserve my appreciation. As I interacted with them over the years, sought their opinions, or asked for specific information, they were often eager to be of help. I cannot even attempt to mention all of them. But I must record my special gratitude to some of the key members of the group: Rasaq Arogundade Balogun (Saddam), Sunday Adebayo, Monsuru Akande, Maruff Olanrewaju, Musiliu Amusa (Big Fish), Kayode Ogundamisi, Lateef Olawale Oshodi, the Honorable Oluwayemi Shiyanbola, Evangelist Kunle Adesokan, Omolara Raliat Adaranijo (Lara), and Bose Omolaoye. My special gratitude to Segun Akanni and Wale Adedayo, who provided critical insights into the OPC. The candid illumination provided by Segun, who was a personal aide to Adams for many years, made it possible for me to understand different dimensions of the transformation that I tried to reflect in this book. I also thank Sunday Adeyemo (Sunday Igboho) and Professor Adebanji Akintoye, who both welcomed me warmly in Cotonou during my research trip to the Republic of Benin.

The late *Aláàfin* of Oyo, *Oba* Lamidi Adeyemi III, and Archbishop Ayo Ladigbolu were both generous with their time and insights, particularly regarding the installation of Adams as the *Kakañfò*. The staff of several libraries in Nigeria, the United States, and the United Kingdom assisted me in many ways; these include the staff of the *Nigerian Tribune* library in Ibadan, *TheNEWS* library in Lagos, *TELL* library in Lagos, Kenneth Dike Library (University of Ibadan), the University of Cambridge Library, Peter J. Shields Library

(University of California–Davis), the Bodleian Library (University of Oxford), and Van Pelt-Dietrich Library (UPenn). I thank them all. As I mentioned earlier, initial funding for this work was provided by the SSRC. Since the end of the fellowship in 2002, I have received support through the Bill and Melinda Gates Cambridge Trust, and Higher Studies Fund (OSGA, Oxford). In the last couple of years, the generous funding provided by the College of Arts and Sciences of the University of Pennsylvania made it possible for me to complete this work. I thank all these institutions for committing their resources to an uncertain project—by which I mean the author.

The support and enthusiasm that my editor at Indiana University Press, Bethany Mowry, showed for this work is remarkable. She offered encouragement at every turn, for which I am very grateful. I also thank Anna Francis, the assistant acquisitions editor.

Parts of chapters 1 and 2 were published as "The Carpenter's Revolt: Youth, Violence, and the Reinvention of Culture in Nigeria" (*Journal of Modern African Studies* 43, no. 3 [2005]: 339–65). I thank Cambridge University Press for permission to republish the article in a new form here.

I wrote the first draft of this book during the COVID-19 pandemic in Oxford and Kidlington in the UK. The lockdown provided me the opportunity, time, and solitude to contemplate confronting the massive data that I had been carrying around three continents for two decades. It is important to note that those of us who survived the pandemic owe our lives and well-being to the many scientists, medical personnel, essential workers, administrators, and leaders around the world who did what was necessary to preserve our individual and collective lives. But for these people, it would have been impossible for me to even contemplate writing a book in that gravely uncertain era. During this period, whether I was holed up in my study or not, my wife, Temitope, and children, Liberty and Demilade Jayden, gave me so much joy and hope despite the medical peril that our world was facing and despite our own individual and collective anxieties—not to talk of the peripatetic life across three continents that I have subjected them to for almost two decades. Temitope's love and unremitting sacrifices have sustained me and our children. I owe her an inestimable debt—a small part of which is rendered with the dedication of this work.

I also dedicate this book to Jacinda Ardern, the former prime minister of New Zealand (2017–23). In a contemporary global context increasingly devoid of decent, dignified, and deliberate leaders, Ardern, in a reversal of the Žižekian take on a different kind of leader, systematically reinforced the dignity, decency, and concern associated with being a head of state. In addition to Temitope and Jacinda, this book is similarly dedicated to Sunday Ojukwu Ibekwu, Taiwo

Ogunsola, and Lawrence Adegoke—three great teachers, who taught me government, literature, and English language, respectively, in high school (the first in Lagos and the other two in Lalupon, Ibadan) and thus helped me to form my path. Mustafa Kemal Atatürk must have had these three in mind when he stated that "a good teacher is like a candle—it consumes itself to light the way for others." I can only hope to follow their examples.

A NOTE ON ORTHOGRAPHY

Tone marks and subdots are important in understanding the Yorùbá language. However, the tone marks are the most critical. In this book, I use tone marks and subdots mainly for three key words: Yorùbá, *Ààrẹ Ọnà Kakañfò,* and *Aláàfin.* I use them in some other instances when they are critical for the reader to understand certain words, phrases, or sentences in Yorùbá.

PRAELUDIUM

THE POLITICS OF ELECTORAL (NON)SENSE

It was Monday, March 16, 2015. Nigeria's general elections would be held in two weeks. Lagos, the most populous metropolis in Africa and the commercial capital of Nigeria, often described as the nation's heartbeat, experienced a tumultuous event early that morning. Traffic in Lagos on any day, and especially on Monday mornings, is the definition of chaos. In his paean to Lagos, "Laaro Monday, Eko o ni gbagba ku gba o"[1] (On Monday morning, Lagos does not tolerate nonsense), Fela Anikulapo-Kuti, one of Africa's most famous musicians and a Lagosian, reflects the city's ceaseless energy and its impatience with obtuseness.[2]

In a way, this was perhaps the most appropriate day of the week for Gani Adams, the national coordinator of the Oodua People's Congress (OPC), to reject what he and his followers regarded as the "political nonsense" that would, in their view, be consolidated by the proposed general elections, which would be supervised by the Independent National Electoral Commission (INEC) under the leadership of Professor Attahiru Jega. While those Adams was protesting also regarded his action as "utter nonsense," the Lagosians, whose (vehicular and other) movements and businesses were temporarily disrupted by the protests, were the first to dismiss the action as such. The protest led to "almost complete paralysis of the day's activities"[3] in central Lagos. But wherever anyone stood in Lagos—or elsewhere in the Nigerian federation—that day, on the most important political question of the moment, Gani Adams had again, even if only momentarily, defined the issues at stake in the fractious polity. The main question was whether the general elections that threatened to sweep out

Figure 0a.1. Adams leading other protesters during the rally on March 16, 2015. Since he first acquired a new status, as Otunba (chief) around 2004–5, this was the first time Adams allowed himself to be seen in public while not wearing traditional clothes. Photo courtesy of *Nigerian Tribune.*

Nigeria's ruling party, the People's Democratic Party (PDP)—along with its presidential candidate and incumbent president, Goodluck Jonathan—should be held as scheduled.

Acting under the auspices of the Coalition for Concerned Nigerians (CCN)—which he described as "a broad-based organisation that cut[s] across the country"[4]—the OPC leader marched alongside hundreds of people in central Lagos to demand the removal of Jega, the chair of the electoral body, INEC.

When he spoke to the press, Adams articulated Jega's sins, which provoked him to lead the protest:

> We are doing that [putting Lagos at a standstill] to register our displeasure against the activities of Professor Jega on the election of January 28.[5] We realize about six million [in the] Southwest have not got their PVC [Permanent Voters Card]. In the Southeast, about 22 percent haven't got their PVC. South-South, about 25 percent. And the election is just eleven days to go. So, we are calling on President Goodluck Jonathan to remove him [Jega] immediately. He should proceed on terminal leave on the twenty-fourth of this month. So that [a] credible person can organize this election.[6]

Figure 0a.2. Adams and others holding a banner at the protest. Photo courtesy of *Nigerian Tribune.*

Sahara Reporters and other media outlets and opposition parties dismissed Adams and his CCN as tools of President Goodluck Jonathan, who "sponsored the protest."[7]

It was a terrible indictment for Adams, who had always emphasized that his group was nonpartisan and once even accused the group's founding leader, Frederick Fasehun, of using the OPC as "a ready tool for his own political advancement" and of promising highly placed politicians and businessmen "massive electoral support and patronage from the OPC in defiance of the congress['s] laid-down principle."[8]

It was obvious to political observers that the president and the ruling party had access to intelligence indicating that they would lose the national elections and most of the state elections if they were held, as earlier scheduled, on February 14 and 28, 2015. Many believed that this was why the ruling party forced the major security agencies to lean on INEC to postpone the elections. Jega announced the postponement on February 8, 2015. Reuters described him as "caving in to pressure from the ruling People's Democratic Party in a move likely to enrage the opposition."[9] However, Jega's decision was understandable given that all the security agencies had warned him that they were "not available to support the elections planned for February 14 and 28" because "they were

Figure 0a.3. Adams at the press briefing to further clarify the position of the CCN and defend himself and the group against accusations of sponsorship by President Jonathan. Photo courtesy of *Nigerian Tribune.*

commencing a six week special operations against Boko Haram insurgents in the north eastern corridors of the country and would rather not be distracted by the elections."[10] Because of this lack of security, Jega postponed the presidential and national assembly election until March 28 and set the governorship and state assembly elections for April 11, 2015.[11]

A week before the Lagos protest, Adams, foreshadowing the planned protest, had asked President Jonathan to dismiss Jega.[12] In reporting this initial call, *Premium Times* described Adams as "an ally of President Goodluck Jonathan."

Most public commentators were convinced that Gani Adams was Jonathan's puppet—pretending to mobilize and raise popular public objections to Jega's continued leadership of INEC, to which a responsive president would be expected to respond.

For all of his public life, Adams had claimed that he was neither "a politician" nor a man beholden to any political party, insisting that his fundamental goal was to protect the democratic and cultural rights and interests of the Yorùbá of Nigeria. Why, then, was Adams thrusting himself so deeply and decisively into the partisan rancor between the ruling party, PDP, and the main opposition, All Progressives Congress (APC)—and between their two presidential candidates, President Goodluck Jonathan and General Muhammadu Buhari?

What was at stake for him? Was it just his concern with fairness in electoral politics and the stated possible disenfranchisement of his people? Or was it the multimillion-naira pipeline contract previously awarded to the OPC leader by the Jonathan government? Was Adams defending his group and personal economic interests?[13] Or was this about his opposition to the current most valuable player (MVP) in Yorùbá politics, Governor Bola Tinubu, who was the chief promoter of Buhari's presidential bid in the country, particularly in Adams's and Tinubu's mutual (Yorùbá) home region in Southwestern Nigeria?

STATUS QUO ANTICS

About a decade before the protest, most people would never have envisioned Adams upholding the (federal) status quo in Nigeria by supporting the ruling party and a non-Yorùbá president. It must have been particularly galling for him to be accused of "acting against Yoruba interests"[14] and having "deliberately dismounted from the great height of fame to that of infamy" while abandoning "a well-laid table of greatness to dine in the sewers."[15] For many years, the Nigerian press described Adams as the "leader of [the] militant faction" of the OPC. The congress, a plebeian social movement, sociocultural group—or "Yoruba self-determination" group, as Adams often described it—one of the most consequential phenomena in Nigeria's political life in the first decade of the twenty-first century, was founded by the medical doctor and civil rights activist Dr. Fredrick Fasehun[16] and a few other people. Adams said in 2007, "The Congress had at its inception resolved to be non-partisan. Consequently, no member of the congress was allowed . . . to be part of any political association of party."[17] Five years before what many regarded as a pro-Jonathan rally that he led, Adams stated, "Our group is not involved in pro-government activities . . . I [had stated that] 'I will never compromise.' So, by and large, I have never involved myself in any pro-government rally."[18] That is, until 2015.

When, as a twenty-nine-year-old artisan, he first burst into public consciousness through a spate of violent intra- and interethnic clashes in Lagos in 1999, the media described Adams variously as a "criminal," a "vagabond," and an "illiterate." In the early years of his public life, a section of the Yorùbá elite regarded Gani Adams's OPC as a "vulgar," though tolerable, form of Yorùbá neonationalism. Adams has since moved through different social, cultural, political, and even economic registers and processes of maturation to become the man who wanted to preserve the government in power in 2015—a man of such great reckoning that a sitting president (Jonathan) and many governors coveted his support and counsel. Adams's transformation is the stuff of dreams. He grew from a "young man" who saw Nigeria as a "slave camp" from which to liberate his Yorùbá constituents to a man who dines and wines with the most powerful in Nigeria, someone who is received in council by leading traditional rulers, state governors, senate presidents, retired generals, and the wealthy, as well as the most accomplished intellectuals and scholars. Once dismissed by the British Broadcasting Service (BBC)—when he was arrested by the police and charged with murder, robbery, firearms offenses, and incitement in 2001[19]—as a "notorious leader of a banned ethnic militia group,"[20] he was later invited to the National Peace Forum in 2004. And he became a high chief who was "assured of [the movement's] continuous love and prayers"[21] by "*the* revered man of God"[22]—the powerful general overseer of perhaps the largest Pentecostal movement in Africa, the Redeemed Christian Church of God (RCCG), Pastor Enoch Adejare Adeboye.

Adams has also risen from one dismissed as a "vandal" to the position of *Ààrẹ Ọ̀nà Kakaǹfò* (generalissimo/field marshal), one of the most important sociocultural offices among the Yorùbá, a people who constitute one of the most populous ethnic nationalities in Africa. The Yorùbá are spread across Nigeria, Benin, and Togo in West Africa. Their old and new diasporas are also spread all over the Americas, Europe, and Asia, while their traditional religion (orisa worship), arts, and culture have become part of religious practices in North, Central, and South America and the Caribbean.[23]

Adams's remarkable transformation is also evident in his growth from a young man whom many would not even grant the title of "mister" to one who had earned more than fifty chieftaincy titles and was, ultimately, installed as the *Ààrẹ Ọ̀nà Kakaǹfò* of Yorubaland, succeeding to the coveted position held by the supremo of the imperial army of the old Oyo Empire—which survived from the mid-seventh century to the late eighteenth century. For a man forced by his material circumstances to drop out of school in the third year, this is an unprecedented and remarkable rise in the sociocultural world of the Yorùbá, who have produced some of the most educated and highly skilled professionals in the world, including a Nobel laureate in Literature. However, Adams's emergence and authenticity as a leader is based, in part, on some of the contradictions of his rise and the ways in which he has sustained his new status. But the contradiction, as I demonstrate in this book, is no surprise, because, as Archie Mafeje has argued, "authentic subjects are never formed but in contradiction."[24]

(TRANS)FORMATION

In less than two decades, Gani Adams has moved from someone derided as an "illiterate young man," a "carpenter," and a man "of no fixed address," as the police chief stated when he was arrested in 2001, to one of the "eminent people"

Figure 0a.4. Adams in handcuffs after his arrest in August 2001 for alleged involvement in the murder of a police officer. Photo courtesy of *Nigerian Tribune.*

at events, a "Big Man" who also sits at the coveted high table, where the most important dignitaries sit at public events in Nigeria.

The monumental change in Adams's fortune—politically, socially, economically, and, most crucially, culturally—arises from many factors, structural and agential, at the heart of which is the genius he has exhibited in the management of the agential and structural dynamics in his immediate constituency, Yorubaland; in Nigeria, in general; and even in the Yorùbá diaspora across the world. Adams's monumental rise, I will show, is a product of his keen awareness of how to seize history and press it in the service of his own personal agenda and cultural vision. In *How to Become a Big Man in Africa: Subalternity, Elites and Ethnic Politics in Nigeria*, I hope to show why Adams's support for President

Jonathan in the 2015 election was only incidental to his larger strategic vision of how to leverage his assets and consolidate his position as one of the most important Yorùbá and Nigerians of his age. Adams utilizes such personal ambition, I will argue, in pursuit of a larger cultural agenda of placing the "Yoruba race" or "Yoruba nation," as he variously uses the terms, at an advantageous position, in Nigeria and in the comity of nations.

I intend to use this personal-cum-cultural project as the background for an analysis of youth—specifically as a social process, and as a particular form of social experience involving the process of social maturation[25]—subalternity, elites, and ethnic and cultural politics in a postcolonial context. Descriptions of the process of social maturation in Africa have often been "truncated" in extant literature by a focus on the youthful stage, with insufficient interest in the stages when particular young persons are transformed into adults while mobilizing that very process of social maturation, even in adulthood, to build power and expand their socioeconomic and political leverage—both as individuals and as members of a corporate group,[26] such as an ethnic group. In a sense, the literature on youth in Africa, in its legitimate and robust engagement with the "waithood" that afflicts young people on the continent,[27] understates the ways in which particular young people turn the conditions that impose waithood into resources as they take a leap into the spaces and circumstances from which they have been structurally excluded.[28] By approaching waithood as representing "a prolonged adolescence or an involuntary delay in reaching adulthood, in which young people are unable to find employment, get married, and establish their own families,"[29] even while acknowledging that such waithood does not imply "passively lingering," because young people use "their creativity to invent new forms of being and interacting with society,"[30] the extant perspective essentially sidesteps the fact that the waiting period can be used not just to wait for a chance—"eking out a living," "making do," or "just getting by"[31]—but to deliberately bide one's time. The active agency that is implied by *biding one's time* (i.e., awaiting an opportune time)—the conversion of precarity (vulnerability, insecurity, uncertainty, defenselessness) into invulnerability and a level of socioeconomic certainty—turns what extant literature might approach as waithood into what I would describe as *awaithood*. I suggest, therefore, that waithood[32] as "a liminal, neither-here-nor-there state"[33] (that is, a period of suspension between childhood and adulthood)—in the literature that "explores the lives of young people struggling with unemployment and sustainable livelihoods in the context of widespread social and economic crisis" produced by "failed neo-liberal economic policies, bad governance and political instability"[34]—does not adequately account for the potential resources these structural limitations constitute for personal self-fulfillment for particular young people in Africa, such as Adams.

Against this backdrop, waithood, theorized as fundamentally a function of generalized immobility, is not adequate. I am more interested in the process in which generalized immobility becomes the very condition and instrument of mobility for particular young people. Thus, *awaithood,* in this context, is about biding your time, about lingering purposefully because you know something (potentially) transformative is on the horizon. *Awaiting* involves a particular form of active agency that embraces what is on the horizon as it gradually approaches. Therefore, for those engaged in awaithood, there is no "arrested adulthood" in the long term. Indeed, they use the strategy of awaiting to challenge and surpass the existing structural constraints that would otherwise have "arrested" their adulthood. This is the sense in which I think Filip de Boeck's illuminating take in the opening epigraph to this book on "an advanced knowledge of higher mathematics and of topics such as chaos, fractals, mobility, and dynamics"[35] challenges us to study agential mobility even within the context of structurally conditioned immobility.

No doubt, the conditions that predispose most young people to waithood in Africa are formidable. As scholars have pointed out, "a chronic state of waiting emerged in the aftermath of neoliberal structural adjustment policies that accelerated inequality, poverty, unequal resource access and marginalization."[36] Yet some young people—the subaltern—in some admittedly rare circumstances, use these conditions to turn themselves into socially, culturally, economically, or politically consequential persons. This is particularly interesting when such young people mobilize the challenges and opportunities of subalternity in becoming putative and (eventually) actual members of the elite.

In this book, I explore the possibilities for social analysis that emerge when the theoretical rigor of subalternity does not merely contend but is also reconciled with the theoretical dynamism of elitism in the study of ethnocultural politics in Africa. How might we profit from a congruence rather than dissonance between the two fascinating sociological and anthropological analyses of contemporary social formations—subalternity and elitism?

This book confronts this question and demonstrates the value of the potential answers for understanding contemporary social forces in Africa.

NOTES

1. Fela Anikulapo-Kuti, "Monday Morning in Lagos," YouTube, https://www.youtube.com/watch?v=evPv4vYAZiY.

2. The popular saying in Lagos in Yorùbá is "*Eko o f'osi*" (Lagos detests nonsense). It is commonly assumed that you cannot survive in Lagos if you are not smart—even

if the actions that make you come across as sharp sometimes border on the mendacious or are of questionable legality.

3. Yemi Adebisi, "Nigeria: As Gani Adams Joins the 'Jega Must Go' Campaigners," *Daily Independent*, March 21, 2015, https://allafrica.com/stories/201503230794.html.

4. See SaharaTV, "Our Anti-Jega Rally Most Peaceful Ever, Says Gani Adams; Accused APC of Manipulating the Media," YouTube, March 24, 2015, https://www.youtube.com/watch?v=wkehDSna7HA.

5. He meant March 28.

6. See SaharaTV, "OPC Militia Leader Gani Adams Leads Anti-Jega Protest in Lagos," YouTube, March 16, 2015, https://www.youtube.com/watch?v=BTfbNqA9o-o.

7. Sahara Reporters, "OPC Militia Leader Gani Adams Leads Anti-Jega Protest in Lagos, Says Jonathan Recently Awarded Pipeline Contract to Him," New York, March 16, 2015, http://saharareporters.com/2015/03/16/opc-militia-leader-gani-adams-leads-anti-jega-protest-lagos-says-jonathan-recently.

8. Gani Adams, *My Life and Struggle* (Lagos: Publishers Express, 2007), 50.

9. Julia Payne, "Nigeria Postpones Feb. 14 Presidential Election to March 28," Reuters, February 8, 2015, https://www.reuters.com/article/us-nigeria-election/nigeria-postpones-feb-14-presidential-election-to-march-28-inec-idUSKBNoLBoTL20150208. Jega, however, said, "Nobody has coerced us . . . to take this decision."

10. *Premium Times*, "Why We Can't Proceed with Elections—Jega," February 8, 2015, https://www.premiumtimesng.com/news/headlines/176422-cant-proceed-election-jega.html.

11. The announcement caused a lot of consternation both locally and internationally. See Will Ross, "Nigeria Postpones Presidential Vote over Security," BBC, February 8, 2015, https://www.bbc.co.uk/news/world-africa-31221545. See also Payne, "Nigeria Postpones."

12. Michael Abimboye, "Sack Jega Now, Gani Adams Tells Jonathan," *Premium Times*, March 8, 2015, https://www.premiumtimesng.com/news/top-news/178158-sack-jega-now-gani-adams-tells-jonathan.html.

13. In 2013, the Adams-led faction of the OPC "secured a lucrative contract from the [Jonathan-led] federal government to secure crude oil pipelines in the Southwest." Ben Ezeamalu and Michael Abimboye, "OPC Factions Clash after Anti-Jega Protest," *Premium Times*, March 17, 2015, https://www.premiumtimesng.com/news/top-news/178602-opc-factions-clash-after-anti-jega-protest.html.

14. Adams's entire public life, or what he calls "my struggle" (Adams, *My Life and Struggle*), is predicated on fighting to defend the Yoruba. Ezeamalu and Abimboye, "OPC Factions Clash."

15. A member of a breakaway faction of the OPC, Adeshina Akinpelu, so denounced Adams. Akinpelu Adeshina, "Gani Adams: Two Years on the Road of Infamy," *Nigerian Voice*, accessed April 12, 2021, https://www.thenigerianvoice.com/news/247428/gani-adams-two-years-on-the-road-of-infamy.html.

16. There is a controversy over the founding of the OPC. See chap. 1.

17. Adams, *My Life and Struggles*, 50.

18. *Vanguard*, "Why Obasanjo Should Not Be Allowed to Kill Labour, by Gani Adams," October 8, 2004, 17.

19. BBC, "Nigerian Vigilante Leader Charged," August 24, 2001, http://news.bbc.co.uk/1/hi/world/africa/1507846.stm.

20. BBC, "Nigerian Vigilante Leader Arrested," August 22, 2001, http://news.bbc.co.uk/1/hi/world/africa/1505010.stm.

21. See Friday Olokor, "Adeboye Hails Gani Adams, Regrets Absence from Installation," *Punch*, January 23, 2018, https://punchng.com/adeboye-hails-gani-adams-regrets-absence-from-installation/; *Nation*, '"Adeboye Salutes Adams on Installation as *Ààrẹ Ọ̀nà Kakaǹfò*," January 23, 2018, https://thenationonlineng.net/adeboye-salutes-adams-installation-aare-ona-kakanfo/.

22. Eagle Online, '"Pastor Adeboye Salutes Adams on Installation as *Ààrẹ Ọ̀nà Kakaǹfò*, Regrets Inability to Attend," January 22, 2018, https://theeagleonline.com.ng/pastor-adeboye-salutes-adams-on-installation-as-aare-ona-kakanfo-regrets-inability-to-attend/.

23. Tracey E. Hucks expands "the geographical, ideological, and theological landscape of Yoruba locales across the globe" by examining how "Yoruba Americans framed new discourses of how Africa could be . . . envisaged as the transubjective center of a religio-nationalist movement in the New World." Hucks, *Yoruba Traditions and African American Religious Nationalism* (Albuquerque: University of New Mexico Press, 2012), xviii. For more on orisa worship in the Americas, see Jacob Kẹhinde Olupona and Terry Rey, eds., Òrìṣà Devotion as World Religion: The Globalization of Yorùbá Religious Culture (Madison: University of Wisconsin Press, 2008).

24. Archie Mafeje, "South Africa: The Dynamics of a Beleaguered State," *African Journal of Political Economy/Revue Africaine d'Economie Politique* 1, no. 1 (1986): 95.

25. Johanna Wyn and Rob White, *Rethinking Youth* (London: Sage, 1997), 8, 9, 21.

26. I use this in the Parsonian-Weberian (Max Weber, *The Theory of Social and Economic Organization*, trans. A. Henderson and T. Parsons [New York: Free Press, 1947], 145) sense of *Verband*—that is, a group that is closed or that admits outsiders only subject to rules enforced by a "chief." For more on this, see Wale Adebanwi, *Yoruba Elites and Ethnic Politics in Nigeria: Obafemi Awolowo and Corporate Agency* (Cambridge: Cambridge University Press, 2014), 19–21.

27. See Alcinda Honwana, *The Time of Youth: Work, Social Change and Politics in Africa* (Boulder, CO: Kumarian, 2012); Adeline Masquelier, "Teatime: Boredom and the Temporalities of Young Men in Niger," *Africa* 83, no. 3 (2013): 470–91; Masquelier, *Fada: Boredom and Belonging in Niger* (Chicago: University of Chicago Press, 2019); Karen T. Hansen, "Getting Stuck in the Compound: Some Odds against Social Adulthood in Lusaka, Zambia," *Africa Today* 51, no. 4 (2005): 3–16; Daniel Mains, *Hope Is Cut: Youth, Unemployment, and the Future in Urban Ethiopia* (Philadelphia:

Temple University Press, 2012); Mains, "Too Much Time: Changing Conceptions of Boredom, Progress, and the Future among Young Men in Urban Ethiopia, 2003–2015," *Focaal: Journal of Global and Historical Anthropology* 78 (2017): 38–51.

28. Though, for instance, Masquelier "consider[s] . . . what is produced, and in particular how value, exchange and affect emerge in the context of daily routines at the *fada*" in Niger, rather than focusing on "what is lost under conditions of crisis and privation" in the context of waithood, I don't think this reflects the kind of active agency I focus on in this book (Masquelier, *Fada*, 31).

29. Honwana, *Time of Youth*, 4.

30. Ibid.

31. Ibid.

32. For an exploration of the different perspectives of youth waithood, see Anne-Marie Peatrik, "Towards an Anthropology of Youth in Africa," trans. Matthew Cunningham, *Ateliers d'anthropologie* 47 (2020), https://doi.org/10.4000/ateliers.12620. My departure point is in a sense hinted at by Peatrik's suggestion that "waiting" can be "a particular way of projecting oneself" that signals an "active time of metamorphosis."

33. Honwana, *Time of Youth*, 3.

34. Alcinda Honwana, "'Waithood': Youth Transitions and Social Change," in *Development and Equity: An Interdisciplinary Exploration by Ten Scholars from Africa, Asia and Latin America*, ed. Dick Foeken, Ton Dietz, Leo de Haan, and Linda Johnson (Leiden: Brill, 2014), 28.

35. Filip de Boeck, "Local Futures and the Future of the Local," in *African Futures: Essays on Crisis, Emergence, and Possibility*, ed. Brian Goldstone and Juan Obarrio (Chicago: University of Chicago Press, 2017), 165.

36. Michael Stasik, Valerie Hänsch, and Daniel Mains, "Temporalities of Waiting in Africa," *Critical African Studies* 12, no. 1 (2020), 1, following James Ferguson, *Global Shadows: Africa in the Neoliberal World Order* (Durham, NC: Duke University Press, 2006).

INTRODUCTION

"SUBALTERN ELITE": YOUTH, VIOLENCE, SUBJECTIVITY, AND ETHNIC POLITICS IN A NEOLIBERAL AGE

Do subalterns have the capacity to transform themselves into members of the elite? If so, how can this (trans)formation be accomplished? What strategic improvisations are critical in the process of profound transformation from membership in a ("violent") underclass to a ("peacemaking") elite status? How do the subalterns, in effecting their social climbing, appropriate and instrumentalize the elements of culture propagated by the hegemonic classes? I suggest that these questions have not been raised and answered sufficiently in the Africanist literature. If they have been raised at all, they have not been answered through an ethnographic study that follows the subjects over a very long period (in this case, more than two decades), paying close attention to the tissues and contours of the particular *life in transition and transformation* and also locating the particular life in the broader sociocultural, economic, and political (trans) formations within which it unfolds over the long term.

While subalternity would appear to be a fixed condition, in its emic and etic guises, elite status is an ongoing, as well as aspired-to, status. This book uses the practices and materiality of violence and "culture" as a way of opening up an interesting discussion on social hierarchies, exploring the ways in which subalterns, in their interactions with the elite and their encounters with the state, can mobilize violence and culture to create or alter the processes of social hierarchization.[1] However, given that violence can ultimately be a strategy used to generate *dissensus*[2] and attract *recognition,* this book explores how, in the postviolence stage, the subaltern can mobilize cultural resources to (re) negotiate and consolidate *achieved recognition*.[3]

How to Become a Big Man in Africa focuses on subaltern youth, acting within the context of a plebeian social movement, and their praxis—and particularly on the leader of a group of subaltern youths and his praxis. It explores what Gani Adams's evolution over two decades reveals about how this category of young people in Africa reflect, reflect on, and respond to their precarious conditions in the neoliberal age. Extant literature on the youth in Africa has not considered the evolution of particular youths over the long term, especially of youth leaders, who are often critical in determining how young people respond to social, economic, or political tension on the continent. Accordingly, I hope to interrogate what particular young people do with the constraints of their age, including their conversion of constraints to opportunities for self-realization. The leaders I approach as strategic improvisers are useful for examining the trajectory of youth in the late neoliberal era and the specific ways of negotiating the transition from youth to adulthood while concomitantly transforming from the *deprived* to the *privileged*, from the *undesirable* to the *desirable*.

THE BEATIFICATION OF A LUMPEN

Extant academic literature on the Oodua People's Congress (OPC) is rich and robust. Scholars interested in the phenomenon have published many critical journal articles, book chapters, and working papers.[4] The apparent robustness and richness of the extant literature, however, belies a certain poverty—the exiguity of the biographical, particularly regarding the leadership of the "militant faction," a dimension that constitutes one of the most powerful lenses for understanding the group's relative durability and relevance in all of its different dimensions: violence, vigilantism, festival promotion, and involvement in electoral politics, among others.

While some of the literature have either identified the movement exclusively as a subaltern revolt against the elite and the state or pointed to the imbrication of the subalterns' activities in the OPC with elite politics, none has focused deeply on how this apparent break or link was transformed in the long term by individual efforts toward material (personal) gain for the leadership of the OPC as well as for a significant portion of the following. This book combines a focus on the biographical (which provides a powerful illumination of the activities of the congress) with a social analysis of the (tensions inherent in) subaltern-elite interface, through which we can account for how collective self-determination morphed into personal self-determination in the elaboration of group activities and agenda. Against this backdrop, the book develops some general statements about the intersection of subalternity and elitism in the analysis of ethno-nationalism in contemporary Africa.

It is also significant that this book is the first scholarly monograph on the group. This is surprising given that OPC-inspired (intra- and interethnic) violence, to a great extent, defined—and, therefore, attracted a lot of local and international attention in—the early years of Nigeria's Fourth Republic. Comparable violence provoked by the imposition of Sharia in the northern states of Nigeria has attracted a lot of monographs and edited volumes.[5] Perhaps the disparity is dictated by the fact that, comparatively, religion and religious crises attract greater attention in the post-9/11 era than ethno-nationalism, ethnicity, or ethnic crises do. Another reason could be the fact that the OPC and OPC-related violence were subsumed, in some cases, under the categories of ethnicity and ethnic violence in the academic literature. While there are books that discuss the OPC, they do so as part of a wider focus on ethnicity rather than using the group as a lens for understanding ethno-nationalism, ethnicity, or ethnic violence in relation to subalternity and elitism in contemporary Africa. Yet another reason for the disparity could be that most scholars working on the OPC have limited access to key leaders of the group, particularly over a long period. Unlike this author, who was able to gain access to the group and its leadership over a long period, most scholars who have worked on the OPC engaged with the group only for a brief period and had limited access to the leadership. They therefore could not have gained the insight evident in this book, which is largely a function of long-term participant observation and the fact that the author, like Adams, is also a Yorùbá.

However, in comparison to the academic literature, the lay literature on the OPC is rich. There are innumerable articles, news reports, and special reports on the OPC in the Nigerian press and some foreign publications. One of the most comprehensive lay publications is a 2003 report by the New York–based Human Rights Watch. But it focuses largely on OPC-inspired violence.[6] Also, though the two antagonistic leaders of the group, Frederick Fasehun and Gani Adams, have both published partly autobiographical books,[7] their accounts, while useful and illuminating, are mostly self-serving. They present narrow narratives that sometimes muddle the facts or offer interpretations that only support what they would like the public to believe. As the following chapters show, their accounts need greater contextualization, as well as some contention.

Thus, this book, the first scholarly monograph on the OPC—particularly the first focused on what was described for many years as the "Gani Adams faction" or the "militant faction" of the OPC—represents an important lens for understanding one of the most significant social movements in Nigeria's

Fourth Republic. The Adams faction has since become *the* dominant faction of the OPC,[8] especially since the death of the group's founding leader, Fasehun, in December 2018. And it has done so despite the fact that, in the last few years, the dominance of the main group (Adams's) has become a matter of contention and contestation.

How to Become a Big Man in Africa focuses on a specific context in which a subaltern, a young artisan, Gani Adams, used the strategic agency of violence; the leveraging of the social processes of maturation; the challenges of interethnic and intercultural relations, including actual and symbolic suffering; and the dynamics of cultural politics to transform himself, within the space of a decade, from a working-class foot soldier for the leaders of the democratic struggle and the Yorùbá ethnic group in Nigeria into a member of the regional and national elite with considerable power, influence, and relative wealth. My ethnographic research on the OPC was conducted over a period of two decades beginning in 1999. In addition to benefiting from constant interactions with my principal subject, members of his group, and the subaltern and the elite associated with him and others over a long stretch of time, I was also able to reflect on the implications of these interactions over a lengthy period. I literally watched my subject grow from an "insignificant" subject, a radical lumpen[9] dismissed by some as an "area boy,"[10] into a "big man" who continues to struggle—and reflect, in both private and public—over (the significance of) his role as a cultural subject. Adams's initial and intermittent experiences of pejorative judgments based on his background are not solely a consequence of his background; they are also a function of the widespread attitude toward young people in Africa. Harry Blatterer suggests that the arguments that serve to legitimize such negative judgments are sometimes ("not always unwittingly") supplied by social scientists.[11] I do not hope to supply the "evidence" for such arguments here. Rather, I am hoping to present a nuanced account of a life course that is "characterized by several contradictory forces" and that reflects the "greater onus" that contemporary neoliberal societies, particularly those in transition, place "on the [young] individual, as opposed to the collective, to adjust to anomalous and contradictory social conditions."[12]

My initial interest in the OPC, and later the Gani Adams faction, was related to violence and youth agency and, subsequently, the implications of the group's formation and activities for the Yorùbá political elites I was simultaneously studying.[13] I later elaborated my interest beyond the violence perpetrated by and attributed to the OPC and, ultimately, focused my interest on the Adams faction as it became a metropolitan, regional, and national phenomenon critical to an understanding of youth agency, urban and ethnic violence, cultural

Figure ob.1. *Left:* Adams at an event, a few years before his new life as a chief began. Photo courtesy of *Nigerian Tribune.*

politics, and the democratic struggle in Nigeria. Though I started studying the group in 1999, between 2001 and 2002, under the auspices of the New York–based Social Science Research Council's fellowship (the African Youth in a Global Age program), I conducted ethnographic research on the Adams faction of the OPC. This was when I first met Adams; the founding leader, Dr. Frederick Fasehun; and other members of the group. I have since focused on the Adams faction, meeting Adams and members of faction countless times, attending some of the events organized by, around, and in conjunction with Gani Adams (or in which he played a critical role). From my attendance at OPC's meetings and activities in 2001 to my presence at the formal installation of Gani Adams as the Ààrẹ *Ọnà Kakaǹfò* of Yorubaland in January 2018, my vantage point has allowed me to observe the evolution of the subject and the ways in which his

Figure 0b.2. Adams at his installation as *Ààrẹ Ọ̀nà Kakaǹfò* in 2018. Photo courtesy of *Nigerian Tribune.*

(mis)fortunes have provided a critical window into the (mis)fortunes of the Nigerian state, the Yorùbá (and their relationships with other ethnic groups in Nigeria), and urban youth. I have also observed how his life reflects the nature and dynamics of the democratic struggle that preceded and attends Nigeria's Fourth Republic—including the social bases of (youth and ethnic) violence and the challenges and opportunities of cultural politics in the Fourth Republic. The research ended in 2023. In the latter part of the process, I relied on a series of telephone interviews and online research (focusing on reports on the emergent factions of the group and Adams's activities) as the COVID-19 pandemic ravaged the world and made it impossible for me to travel to Nigeria between 2020 and 2021.

At the center of the processes I describe in this book is the "exemplary" life story and fascinating (trans)formation of Gani Adams. However, Adams's life story is not exemplary in the sense of being a model (to be followed) or a consummate life.[14] His story is, in fact, a challenge to the typical exemplar in modern Nigerian[15] (and African) context. For the Yorùbá, the typical exemplar—such as Obafemi Awolowo, the late Second Republic presidential candidate of the Unity Party of Nigeria, who is regarded as the leader of the Yorùbá, and Moshood Abiola,[16] the winner of Nigeria's June 12, 1993, presidential election, which was annulled by the military—struggles against all odds to attain education and uses that leverage to achieve political or economic eminence.[17] In Gani Adams's case, his exemplarity is not based on his ability to pull himself up by his bootstraps—as the old cliché goes—to attain education and achieve eminence. Rather, it is the *lack* of (complete) formal education that gave him the opportunity to become, initially, a foot soldier for the democratic movement in urban Lagos and, later, a critical participant in a cultural struggle (for self-determination). Perhaps given this peculiar route to eminence, Adams represents his own life story as "exemplary." Ultimately, he has successfully encouraged many others to accept, repeat, and elaborate this self-representation. While his initial range of choices was culturally and economically limited[18] because he dropped out of secondary (high) school, Adams was able to surpass the social and economic limits this act imposed on him. This is particularly important among the Yorùbá who value Western education as the best, if not the only, means of *becoming somebody* in modern times. He has also succeeded in considerably reducing, if not eliminating, the impact of these limitations on the process of social achievement.

Thus, this book explores the intertwined and violent social and political trajectories of a state (Nigeria), an ethnic nationality (Yorùbá), and a subaltern youth (Adams) to come to an understanding of subjectivity and social maturation in cultural and political spaces that are immersed in violence—both material and immaterial—in Africa. I attempt to use the transformation of this lumpen into an elite to (1) interrogate the largely ignored interface between the ethnographic studies of the subaltern and the anthropology of the elite and (2) point to new ways in which, by exploring how the literature on subaltern studies and the theory derived from it speak to theories on the elite, we can transcend the limitations of the (arbitrary) divergence in the understanding and analysis of ideological and material subordination, resistance, and domination in a postcolonial context.

I should quickly note that the unique opportunity to watch my subject grow up and then flourish in personal, social, cultural, political, and economic (he will claim also spiritual) terms, and additionally to *grow up alongside him*, afforded me the opportunity for a certain kind of reflexivity about my research (see the praeludium).

SUBALTERNITY AND ELITISM

The famous Subaltern Studies School has provided innovative and useful ways of interrogating the historiography of postcolonial societies in the context of the subaltern experience, particularly, as Gareth Williams puts it, "of its moments of violence, of suffering, and of many of the scars left behind by the histories of domination."[19] As Daniel Clayton[20] states, "An influential formulation—implicit in Gramsci and pronounced in Spivak's work—is of the subaltern as 'cut off' from society and history—'removed from all lines of social mobility,' unable to be 'generalised according to hegemonic logic.'"[21] The historians and political scientists who formed the Subaltern Studies Group set out to write history "from below," in the context of the development of nationalist consciousness in India, thus shifting the focus from the study of elites to that of the "politics of the people."[22]

However, foregrounding the Gramscian provenance of this concept, as some scholars have argued,[23] provides a more robust template for understanding particular manifestations of subalternity—as group formation as well as a condition.[24] Gramsci's articulations of the concept point to greater diversity and inclusivity[25] and "[apply] to the relations of force and power beyond the terrain of social-economic relations"[26]—which is emphasized in the traditional Marxist concept. Two of Gramsci's applications of the concept of subaltern/subalternity are critical for my approach to Gani Adams (in his initial public life) and his group, the OPC. The first regards subalterns as a group, in "reference to disaggregated sections of the population, politically (and therefore, culturally) marginalized," whom Gramsci considers to be "at the margins of history."[27] The second approaches them as "individual subjects, either in relation to their social setting or their cultural limitations."[28] For Gramsci, as Liguori reminds us, "subalterns" were not "simply an undifferentiated mass combination." On the contrary, "they were subjects of diverse capacity in terms of their self-consciousness and organization."[29] I find some of the dimensions of Gramsci's construction of subalternity and subalterns illuminating against this backdrop: (1) identification of the political life of such groups—such as Adams OPC (like the Davide Lazzaretti movement in nineteenth-century Italy)—as constituting "a subversive-popular-rudimentary tendency";[30] (2) identification of "a distinction between marginal and advanced subaltern groups, with varying levels of consciousness, leadership and organization," with the marginal groups "inclined to act according to an incoherent conglomeration of ideas drawn from 'common sense,' such as everyday experience . . . folklore, traditional conceptions of the world and religion";[31] and (3) emphasis on the fact that subaltern classes "are subject to the initiatives of the dominance class, even when they rebel,"[32] though they can also constitute an "autonomous formation . . . even if [they] are only aiming to achieve partial demands."[33] In relation to the last two points, Gramsci argued that it was only through the transformation of their "common sense" into "good sense" in coordination "with 'organic intellectuals' and 'democratic philosophers' that emerge from the struggle" that subalterns can hope to achieve their revolutionary potential.[34] In the case of the OPC, though some "organic intellectuals" and "democratic philosophers" (elites) were part of the group—as represented by the founding leader, Frederick Fasehun, a medical doctor—these intellectuals emerged from the wider democratic struggle in Nigeria and, thus, only sought to use the group to achieve their larger nationalist-democratic goals. Therefore, it is important to understand the relationship between subalternity and elitism in this context.

Ranajit Guha's inversion of the subaltern and the elite in his analysis of the subaltern subject, approaching the latter as one whose *politics* operate in "an autonomous domain"[35] free of elite politics,[36] has been criticized by others writing within the tradition of subaltern studies.[37] The literature on the subaltern largely assumes irreconcilable differences in the interests of the subaltern and the elite. For Gayatri Chakravorty Spivak, for instance, "the elite [often] rob subalterns of their own voice."[38] Thus, "the subaltern cannot speak" and cannot represent themselves "because they are always spoken *for* by those in power."[39] Spivak argues that the problem is not so much that the subalterns cannot speak but that the subaltern position in society implies that they will not be heard.[40] As this book on a key subaltern—who not only spoke and speaks for himself, his group, and his generation but also was and is heard by society—shows, subalterns can *seize* the space for a voice in society even while leveraging that voice to transform their personal status. There is a theoretical-practical paradox in this case, though. While the example of Gani Adams contests[41] Spivak's assumption that the subalterns are "removed from all lines of social mobility,"[42] it can be argued that Spivak was right to conclude that "if the subaltern could speak—that is, speak in a way that really *mattered* to us—then it wouldn't be subaltern,"[43] given that Adams's capacity to speak transformed him from a subaltern into an elite.

In the literature on elites, the subaltern are assumed to be condemned to a certain intractable lack of "rationality" (given that their lives are regarded as an "embodiment of myths and superstitions"), while, conversely, the elite are presented as the very epitome of "modernity" and "reason."[44] As the term *subaltern* traveled out of the Southeast Asian studies context where it was originally popular, the importance of examining how one signifies "critical positions in relation to power"[45] in different contexts increased. As one of the key theorists of the subaltern, Spivak has argued the status is "totally situational."[46] Nevertheless, most of the scholars who have attempted to transcend the contraposition of the subaltern and the elite are often still not mindful of the possibility that or the processes by which some members of the subaltern may gain elite status. Gyan Prakash exemplifies this when he suggests that "subalternity erupts within the system of dominance and marks its limits from within, that its externality to dominant systems of knowledge and power surfaces *inside the system of dominance,* but only as an intimation, as a trace of that which eludes the dominant discourse."[47] He concludes then that "it is this partial, incomplete, distorted existence that separates the subaltern from the elite."[48] The iconic account of the subaltern—as exemplified in Gramsci's writings[49]—as a class whose members struggle to fully recognize the dynamics of their oppression while being "always subject to the activity of ruling groups, even when they rebel and rise up,"[50] elides the question of when and how some members of the subaltern can become members of the ruling group and free themselves, as individuals, from such subjection to (re)gain their own subjectivity. Indeed, as Edward Said averred in his foreword to Guha and Spivak's coedited volume, *Selected Subaltern Studies,* "no matter how one tried to extricate subaltern from elite histories, they are different but overlapping and curiously interdependent territories."[51]

In their analysis of the social process, even while giving the title *elite* to "a class of the people who have the highest indices in their branch of activity,"[52] elite theorists, from Pareto[53] and Mosca[54] to Lasswell[55] and Bottomore[56] and contemporary theorists like F. G. Bailey,[57] George E. Marcus,[58] and John Higley,[59] fail to recognize that, by this definition, an elite could also exist within the ranks of the subaltern and that members of the subaltern can transition to elite status. Among anthropologists studying the elite, despite the illuminating perspectives provided by the intimacies with the elite through ethnography, there is little recognition that, if elite groups are defined by the "control [of] specific resources by means of which they acquire political power and material advantages,"[60] then we need to exhaust the range of resources that society makes available for the acquisition of political power and material advantages. Though violence has been recognized as one such resource,[61] anthropologists are yet to fully explore how such a resource can be used, through what F. G. Bailey[62] calls "private wisdom" and "pragmatic rules," especially under the rubric of culture and in the transformation of the subaltern into the elite.

For too long, the anthropological literature on "elite formation," "the politics of elite cultures," and elite "cultural practices" has focused largely on how elites maintain or sustain their power,[63] without considering how those who lack the regular means of becoming elite, particularly those who are members of the subaltern, can destabilize or unsettle this process and transform themselves into members of the elite. Relatedly, extant public anthropology on youth elite often focuses on elite reproduction and circulation,[64] without investigating how the nonelite, such as young subalterns, engage in the processes of reproduction that turn them into elites.

Thus, Cris Shore's important question in the work he coedited with Stephen Nugent, *Elite Cultures: Anthropological Perspectives*—"How do elites in different societies *maintain* their position of dominance over subaltern groups?"[65]—has, for a long time, dominated the anthropological and sociological scholarship on elites. This book slightly inverts the question by asking, "How do members of the subaltern groups in different societies transform themselves into elites?" This question precedes that of how the elites maintain this (trans)formed position and their dominance in their new identity as members of the elite—even as they retain the latent or manifest identification with the subaltern. Against this backdrop, this book attempts to redress a lacuna in the anthropological literature by focusing on how a key subaltern (trans)formed[66] himself into a member of the elite and by examining the resources used in this self-(trans) formation as well as the structural and agential circumstances under which it was accomplished.

Using the perspectives of scholars on structure and agency, elite and subaltern studies, and based on an ethnographic study of the *acting subject*, I examine the neoliberal context of declining state authority and rising socioeconomic insecurity. Additionally, I examine a specific form of mobilization for democratic freedom and political and socioeconomic equity used by subaltern youth. This form of mobilization shaped and provoked violent youth agency. I attempt to relate the concept of habitus to those of hegemony and subjectivity while seeking to explain the workings of power in the construction of emergent forms of subjectivity and agency.

The study spanned more than two decades (1999–2023)—coinciding with Adams's transformation from "youth"[67] to adulthood—that is, from ages twenty-nine to fifty-three. I interacted with and interviewed Adams, as well as his supporters and constituents, over this period. In the first four years of this study, I lived in Nigeria, particularly around Lagos and Ibadan, in close observation of the group. In this period, my methods of data gathering included participant observation, interviews, and archival research. After my initial couple of years of observing the OPC, I first met Adams in 2002—after his release from his first spell of detention and trial. He was approaching thirty at that point. After this, I attended some of the gatherings for the National Coordinating Committee (NCC) of the OPC in different parts of Lagos, including some public events. Since relocating abroad (to the United States and United Kingdom), I have visited Nigeria many times for my research. Between 2004 and 2008, I spent several months in Nigeria conducting fieldwork, observing the group and interviewing Adams. From 2008 until the outbreak of the COVID-19 pandemic in early 2020, I spent several weeks in Nigeria gathering more data. During these earlier periods of fieldwork in Nigeria, I met Adams intermittently at formal and informal events and in his home. I was invited to several events he was involved in—festivals, installations, meetings, and other public events. We also met at events to which we were both invited or in which either of us was directly involved. In the COVID-19 era, my research took a more digital approach—involving telephone interviews, interactions, and WhatsApp exchanges and chats, even research-grade gossip[68] with members of the different factions of the OPC.

The data from the ethnographic interactions with Adams and members of his group and the interviews with several others, including members of the elite in Yorubaland in particular and Nigeria in general, were supplemented with library and archival materials. In embedding myself in the cultural (old and new) universe from which Adams emerged and in which he thrives, I have used every medium of (mass) communication mobilized by Adams, members of his group, and others, including songs, proverbs, and social media. To ensure a robust interpretation of the phenomenon I studied over such a long period, I followed Fred W. Clothey's path, employing a method he described as the "hermeneutical spiral."[69] In this spiral, suggests Clothey, "the stance of the interpreter is made self-conscious, 'deconstructed' and reconstructed again and again so that still other meanings can be sought at other focal points and in wider contexts." Thus, this method is "concerned [with] the phenomenon's placement in its appropriate contemporary context, its cultural history, and its universe of morphological significance"[70] in an attempt at a "wholeness" that gathers many individual and collective perceptions and reflections into a configuration containing the many parts, including microhistory and cultural history in which [micro-history] is contained and the ways in which both relate to the larger human enterprise of *being in the world*.[71]

Around 2004 and 2005, my focus changed from understanding the OPC through Adams to understanding Adams's emergence against the backdrop of the structural processes of the OPC and the wider social and political dynamics in Nigeria. I examined how Adams's life and activities mirror the particular constellation of forces that define the contours of the subaltern-elite interface in the context of ethnic politics in Nigeria. In relation to this, two issues arise: one is methodological, and the other is concerned with the presentation of my data in this book. Regarding the method of research, it is important to state that I relied heavily on media reports (including the news press, in both hard copies and online articles, and the social media) in studying the OPC in general, and Gani Adams. In the last two decades in Nigeria, the OPC has been one of the most widely reported-on organizations, alongside political parties. Adams also has attracted high levels of media coverage among those who are not public officeholders or, strictly speaking, major political figures. Given the centrality of the Nigerian press in the understanding of ethno-regional relations and conflicts and the fact that the OPC and Adams are based in the home of the dominant Lagos-Ibadan media axis, perhaps it should come as no surprise that media reports on both would be critical to any scholarly analysis. In addition, as will become evident in the following chapters, Adams is very conscious of the power of the media. He encourages and provokes constant media coverage by building an impressive network of contacts (some of whom are beholden to him in one way or another) and granting interviews regularly. After the initial few years of my research, on many occasions when we met for interviews, he had already addressed in the media many of the issues I wanted to raise. I often had to seek further clarification of or probe behind his advertised positions to explain, understand, confirm or contradict, and interpret what he said regularly in the media.

VISUAL ETHNOGRAPHY, CRITICAL ICONOGRAPHY, AND AESTHETIC SELF-MAKING

In this book, I use hundreds of photographs. This is deliberate and necessary, for three reasons. First, though there has been an explosion of anthropological interest in ethnographic photographs in the last two to three decades,[72] I think that ethnographic studies of elites in Africa have not employed a sufficiently visual approach in the analysis of eliteness. Yet I think that visual representations of different dimensions of elite life, both as "memory practice"[73] and as projections of the future,[74] are useful for understanding particular manifestations of elitism, which involve self-presentation and self-creation,[75] particularly in this context, given the long tradition of "photographic self-making" in West Africa.[76] Drawing from philosophers influenced by Nietzsche who, reflecting on the ethics of self-fashioning, have developed useful perspectives such as "the art of living," "perfectionist techniques of self-enhancement," and "aestheticist practices in the arts of narrative self-writing,"[77] anthropologists have pointed to the ways in which a "visual public"[78] is constantly the target of certain members of the elite, particularly in the display of their "highly explicit consciousness" of what Richard Werbner succinctly describes as "aestheticized self-fashioning."[79] Self-fashioning is as critical to the elites as it is to aspiring elites, particularly those, like Adams, who are shrewd about the crucial role of visuality in the process of self-presentation and self-transformation that is necessary for social climbing. Thus, as the rich pictorial illustrations that reflect Adams's self-presentation in this book show, visual ethnography constitutes an important approach to analyzing and understanding the process of transformation to, and maintenance of, elite status.

Second, a visual approach is even more useful for ethnographic work involving personal transformation, particularly in a context, such as in this book, where the subject goes through a long process of transformation from a subaltern to an elite. Thus, there is a central role for photographic archives in the presentation of the process of both personal and group transformation.

Third, visual accounts of subalternity and elitism—especially where both are connected or converge in the life story or history of particular subjects—constitute both a narrative and an archive on their own, and they also reinforce textual narratives. When text alone proves insufficient, photographs can tell powerful stories. As Susan Sontag states, a photograph helps in "putting oneself into a certain relation to the world that feels like knowledge—and therefore, like power," partly because there is a "presumption of veracity that gives all photographs authority, interest, seductiveness."[80]

Against this backdrop, I use plentiful photographs in this book because (1) I believe that *image* is central to what it means to be elite; (2) for Adams, images, particularly photographs, are crucial for representing and cementing[81] his personal, social, cultural, and class transformation and status (thus, he takes self-presentation and the control of his image very seriously); and (3) Adams's attitude to photography can be inserted into the Yorùbá's general attitude toward photographs. Since they began their embrace of modernity in the nineteenth century, the Yorùbá have "integrated photography into both traditional and contemporary aspects of their culture." For them, photography eventually became "a genuine expression of the culture with unique symbolic meanings and functions and with an implicit set of culturally determined conventions governing proper subject matter and formal coding of the visual image."[82] In light of this, in reflecting on Adams's *personal* metamorphosis—material and immaterial—I show that the visual is as valuable as the textual. Though Adams, when publicizing his "'front stage' public persona"[83] in the era since he became a Big Man, attempts to distance himself from his previous image and public persona, I have tried here to reflect, through both text and photographs, the contours of his personal transformation over time. Most of the photographs used in this book were sourced from the media houses that covered the OPC activities and Adams's endless public and private engagements or from the archives of Adams and other members of the OPC.

—~—

Over the past two decades, Adams—or President, as I called him for many years (because he initially declared himself "the president" of his faction of the OPC[84])—has made a phenomenal move through different (im)material stages, which I have the opportunity to observe either directly or indirectly. I have been in contexts in which he was, at one end, casually dismissed by members of the elite (political and intellectual) in Yorubaland and, at another end, spoken about with a measure of awe or dread. In the early stages, when we had to meet outside of the weekly NCC meetings, he would choose to meet me at a place not too far from where he lived. I assumed that, in the aftermath of his first trial, this was for security purposes. But a few well-placed friends and colleagues in Lagos insisted that it was because he did not live in the kind of house he wanted me to visit. After a few years, he had become prosperous enough to own a house in Soba, near Abule Ado in the Amuwo Odofin Local Government Area of Lagos. He painted it all white; it soon became widely known as the "White House." That was the first house in which he hosted me. I remember noting to myself when I first entered the premises that he was on his way to a better social standing. A few years ago, he moved again, this time to an upscale part of Lagos, Otedola Estate, Gbagada Phase II, an upper-middle-class area in mainland Lagos. When I first visited him in his current home in 2015, I concluded that he had arrived at that better social standing. When I visited him again in late 2017, a couple of months before his installation as Ààrẹ *Ọ̀nà Kakaǹfò*, the "president,"[85] I noted, was now genuinely presiding over a miniature empire of his own.

His has become one of the most storied transformations in both personal and public profiles that I have witnessed in Nigeria in the last four decades, first as a journalist and later as a student of society. Adams's current home is a multimillion-naira house befitting the big man he had become. Security people outside the compound questioned me before letting me enter for the first time. One enters a waiting room before proceeding to his living room. When I first visited him in the new home, there were a few people, aides and other hangers-on, waiting for the big man. Unsurprisingly, the duplex was also painted white. Significantly, a few years earlier, Adams had chosen white as the exclusive color of his clothes.[86]

Again, one of my aims in this book is to use the Gani Adams case to reflect on questions of ethnocultural politics, power, social class, social maturation, social achievement, and accumulation. I also interrogate the means and methods of social climbing—that is, becoming a big man—through gained cultural significance. Daniel Jordan Smith's fascinating book *To Be a Man Is Not a One-Day Job* addresses the "broader concerns about the shifting meanings of masculinity amid changing expectations and practices of intimacy" underlying the "economic worries" of young men who want "to be a man" in Nigeria.[87] Tim Gibbs's interesting article on "Becoming a 'Big Man' in Neo-liberal South Africa" focuses on similar questions, including the "crisis of masculinities" related to "becoming a big man"—such as among minibus-taxi owners and bosses in Johannesburg, South Africa.[88] However, this book goes beyond *becoming* by also reflecting on *being* a (big) man through an exhaustive interrogation of the process of transformation as well as the sustenance or maintenance of the status over the long term.

Interestingly enough, even in lay literature, "the Big Man is back in politics," as Alexander Schuhr declared in late 2017.[89] However, even Schuhr admits that the big man never left the African scene, though the uses of the concept, in both popular representations and social scientific research, have not been precise.[90] This book does not focus on the typical African big man in much of the scholarly[91] and lay literature—that is, a man in (mostly) top political office. My focus is on a big man in a nonpolitical office, or indeed offices. (I will elaborate on this later in the book.)

In examining the means and methods of becoming and being a big man in this context, I am not suggesting that Gani Adams's are the only ways to gain cultural—and therefore social, political, and economic—significance and thereby *become* (as process, method, or progression) and also *be* (i.e., maintain or sustain a status) a big man in contemporary Africa. Rather, I use what may be called the "Gani Adams franchise" to point to crucial examples of how cultural entrepreneurs gain and maintain power, prominence, influence, and cultural authority in Africa. Furthermore, I reflect on the questions that the means and methods of gaining and sustaining social and cultural significance raise for our understanding of contemporary postcolonial formations. I argue that, to paraphrase Marshall D. Sahlins,[92] Adams, with an eye on his own life goals, presents an anthropologist with "a generous . . . gift": "an extended series of experiments in cultural adaptation" and personal advancement.[93] Adams has squeezed together various elements of dynamic institutional processes within and beyond the boundaries of his cultural context and, at the same time, expanded these processes to create (re)new(ed) institutional practices that magnify his role in society and augment his power.[94] He has "created with the means history gave" him a sociocultural narrative adapted to the (ir)realities and mentalities of his age. He has used all these as tools (based on his cultural genius[95]) to manage and manipulate many variables (some of them even countervailing). Thus, I show why and how Adams now exemplifies what it means to become and be a big man in Nigeria. I believe that such a cultural experiment as Gani Adams, as Sahlins argues, constitutes a laboratory for anthropology.[96]

OUTLINE OF CHAPTERS

Following this introduction is chapter 1, "The Carpenter's Revolt: Subaltern Youth, Democratic Struggle, and Ethno-national Politics," which examines the formation of the OPC, the group's leveraging of subalternity and youth identity, and the conditions under which it splintered into two. Against the backdrop of Nigeria's history of military rule, ethno-national rivalries, and the process of re-democratization witnessed in late twentieth-century Nigeria, the chapter approaches the formation of the OPC and the group's aims, objectives, and activities as constituting challenges to democratic rule in the context of the bifurcation of tradition and modernity as the group appropriates "culture" in negotiating Yorùbá identity while retaining democratic rhetoric. The chapter also argues that the rituals mobilized in the group's claim to cultural authenticity can be interpreted both as an instrumentally rational strategy of power struggle and as a form of symbolic action with cultural meaning. The chapter concludes that the activities of the OPC constitute not a stable, bounded manifestation of culture but rather a fluid, ambivalent, and paradoxical appropriation of culture in both organizational and personal struggles for power.

Chapter 2, "Social Anomie, Vigilantism, and the Leveraging of Violent Habitus," focuses on both the intra-OPC, intraethnic, and interethnic violence provoked by the OPC and the (il)legitimate vigilante activities of the group in urban Southwestern Nigeria. The violence perpetrated by and against the members of the group and the group's vigilante activities are linked by a specific kind of urban social anomie in late twentieth- and early twenty-first-century Nigeria. The social anomie provides a basis for reflection on the social world in contemporary Nigeria: how this social world was perceived by Adams, the youthful members of his group, and urban dwellers in Southwestern Nigeria and how this perception determined the reactions of all, including the holders of the legitimate means of violence in Nigeria. This chapter reveals how violence ultimately became, for Adams, a means of self-realization and a tool for gaining social distinction.

Chapter 3, "Becoming Elite: Distinction, Destiny, and *Self*-Determination," focuses on how Gani Adams reconciled both the opportunities and the limitations of his personal-cultural agency with the structural conditions of his age in working toward dominating his environment by gradually moving away, or directly dissociating himself, from the socially generalized violence for which the OPC had become (in)famous. His recognition of the need for personal transformation involved the initial processes of achieving distinction, including a form of self-presentation that signaled his strategic personal-cultural ambitions, manifesting in festivals, religious (Christian, Islamic, and traditional) practices, chieftaincy titles, formal education, and other cultural activities. In this chapter, I examine the specific processes of becoming elite, analyzing the means, methods, and resources that Adams mobilized in his project of self-actualization—including money, vehicles, houses, birthday celebrations, sartorial elegance, public events, beauty pageant, and media or publicity.

Perhaps the greatest affirmation of Adams's transformation was his installation as the Ààrẹ *Ọ̀nà Kakañfò* (generalissimo/field marshal) of Yorubaland, the highest military office in the defunct Oyo Empire. This position, in the postcolonial era, had been held only by two of the most prominent Yorùbá of their generations, Chief Samuel Ladoke Akintola (1910–66), a lawyer, aristocrat, and orator who became the premier of the Western Region (1960–66), and Chief Moshood Kashimawo Olawale Abiola (1937–98), a billionaire businessman, publisher, and philanthropist who won the June 12, 1993, presidential election—which was annulled by the military regime.

Chapter 4, "The Acme of Distinction: (Pre)Eminence and the Rituals of Power," uses this major turning point in Gani Adams's rags-to-riches trajectory to account for the ritual element of the big man in contemporary Africa and to reach an understanding of the critical role that the combination of violence (both manifest and latent) and cultural performances can play in the consolidation (and the unending negotiation) of power and prominence in the Nigerian context. Adams's various rituals of performing his acquired big man status are tracked through different religious affiliative practices.

The big man status is simultaneously a potent and potentially dangerous position, for the individual, his friends and enemies, and the larger community. Using the relationships between Adams and some leading politicians in Nigeria, including Governors Bola Tinubu and Gbenga Daniel as well as Presidents Olusegun Obasanjo and Goodluck Jonathan, in the context of democracy and electoral politics, chapter 5, "Playing (with) Big Men: Elites, Ethno-regional Competition, and Electoral Politics," reflects on the empirical and theoretical implications of the big man thesis in contemporary African politics. Returning to the original anthropological reflections on the big man in relation to contemporary political and sociological literature that focuses on the deformation of African politics, this chapter captures the ebbs and flows of political life in a postcolonial context while analyzing the fate of the political in its terrific and terrible interface with the cultural.

Chapter 6 considers a recent challenge to Adams's position, eminence, and dominance by another "young man," Sunday Adeyemo (Sunday Igboho). Adeyemo attempts to appropriate the Adams franchise in a renewed effort to challenge the Nigerian state through a revival of Yorùbá ethno-nationalist aspirations for statehood. Adams's response to this challenge is analyzed in an exploration of the question of the defense of elite status, power, and privileges.

In the coda, in providing a particular form of social history from below that ambles into a social history from above by anatomizing the transformation of a certain sociocultural agency, I make a case for a way to insert this specific process of becoming and being a big man—that is, of making a particular way through the world—into a more holistic, comparative understanding of the intersection of the process of social maturation (including the reflexivity that this entails or provokes), subalternity, elites, and ethno-nationalism in contemporary Africa.

NOTES

1. For a specific examination of the OPC encounters with the state, see Omobolaji Olarinmoye, "The Subaltern Encounters the State: OPC-State Relations 1999–2003," in *Encountering the Nigerian State*, ed. Wale Adebanwi and Obadare Ebenezer (New York: Palgrave Macmillan, 2010).

2. For an elaboration of this concept, see Jacques Rancière, *Dissensus: On Politics and Aesthetics*, ed. and trans. Steven Corcoran (London: Bloomsbury Academic, 2010); Rancière, "The Thinking of Dissensus: Politics and Aesthetics," in *Reading Ranciere*, ed. Richard Stamp and Paul Bowman (London: Continuum International, 2011). For a brilliant use of this concept in the analysis of a particular postcolonial formation, see Danny Hoffman, "Disagreement: Dissent Politics and the War in Sierra Leone," *Africa Today* 52, no. 3 (2006): 3–22.

3. For an extreme case of an elite-subaltern relationship that produced state collapse, see Jimmy D. Kandeh, "Ransoming the State: Elite Origins of Subaltern Terror in Sierra Leone," *Review of African Political Economy* 26, no. 81 (1999): 349–66. Kandeh argues that "massification in Sierra Leone, especially lumpenisation, was the product of both elite pillage and subaltern banditry." While this case does not exactly parallel the Sierra Leonian case examined by Kandeh and did not involve the extremity that he describes as "subaltern banditry," what he calls "elite pillage" was certainly one of the conditions that produced the OPC—and also one of the conditions that Adams leveraged when becoming a member of the elite.

4. R. T. Akinyele, "Ethnic Militancy and National Stability in Nigeria: A Case Study of the Oodua People's Congress," *African Affairs* 100, no. 401 (2001): 623–40; Akinyele, "The Involvement of the Oodua People's Congress in Crime Control in

Southwestern Nigeria," in *Gouverner les villes d'Afrique. Etat, gouvernement local et acteurs privés*, ed. Laurent Fourchard (Paris: Karthala, 2007); Insa Nolte, "Identity and Violence: The Politics of Youth in Ijebu-Remo, Nigeria," *Journal of Modern African Studies* 42, no. 1 (2004): 61–90; Nolte, "Ethnic Vigilantes and the State: The Oodua People's Congress in South-Western Nigeria," *International Relations* 21, no. 2 (2007): 217–35; Nolte, "'Without Women, Nothing Can Succeed': Yoruba Women in the Oodua People's Congress (OPC), Nigeria," *AFRICA* 78, no. 1 (2008): 84–106; Wale Adebanwi, "The Carpenter's Revolt: Youth, Violence and the Reinvention of Culture in Nigeria," *Journal of Modern African Studies* 43, no. 3 (2005): 339–65; Yvan Guichaoua, "The Making of an Ethnic Militia: The Oodua People's Congress in Nigeria" (CRISE Working Paper 26, University of Oxford, November 2006); Guichaoua, "Who Joins Ethnic Militias? A Survey of the Oodua People's Congress in Southwestern Nigeria" (CRISE Working Paper 44, University of Oxford, March 2007); Guichaoua, "Self-determination Group or Extralegal Governance Agency? The Multifaceted Nature of the Oodua People's Congress in Nigeria," *Journal of International Development* 21 (2009): 520–33; Guichaoua, "How Do Ethnic Militias Perpetuate in Nigeria? A Micro-level Perspective on the Oodua People's Congress," *World Development* 38, no. 11 (2010): 1657–66; Laurent Fourchard, "A New Name for an Old Practice: Vigilantes in South-Western Nigeria," *Africa* 78, no. 1 (2008): 535–58; Olarinmoye, "Subaltern Encounters the State."

5. See, for example, Johannes Harnischfeger, *Democratization and Islamic Law: The Sharia Conflict in Nigeria* (Frankfurt: Campus, 2008); Brandon Kenghammer, *Muslims Talking Politics: Framing Islam, Democracy, and Law in Northern Nigeria* (Chicago: University of Chicago Press, 2016); Abdul Raufu Mustapha and Kate Meagher, *Overcoming Boko Haram: Faith, Society & Islamic Radicalization in Northern Nigeria* (Woodbridge: James Currey, 2020).

6. Human Rights Watch, "The O'odua People's Congress: Fighting Violence with Violence," *Human Rights Watch* 15, no. 4A (February 2003), https://www.hrw.org/node/255663/printable/print.

7. Fasehun was the first to publish two books in succession, which provoked Gani Adams's first book—and eventually an edited volume about him. See Frederick Fasehun's eponymous first book, *Frederick Fasehun: The Son of Oodua* (Lagos: Inspired Communications, 2002), and the second, *OPC: Our History, Our Mission* (Lagos: Inspired Communications, 2005), and Adams's *My Life and Struggle* (Lagos: Publishers Express, 2007) and *Leadership Challenge: Gani Adams and the Oodua People's Congress*, ed. Michael M. Ogbeidi (Laos: Publishers Express, 2005). See also Adams, "Politics and Agenda of Ethnic Militias: The Case of OPC," in *Urban Violence, Ethnic Militias and the Challenge of Democratic Consolidation in Nigeria*, ed. T. Babawale (Lagos: Malthouse, 2003).

8. There are a few breakaway groups, such as OPC New Era, which is led by Rasaq Arogundade, but they have limited leverage. See chaps. 1 and 2 on the breakaway groups.

9. Instructively, Achille Mbembe also describes Adams's parallel in South Africa, Julius Malema, as someone who "embodies . . . the dark and troubling undercurrents of a long South African tradition of lumpen radicalism." Mbembe approaches lumpen radicalism as "a political tradition of unruliness—and at times resistance—in which fantasies of male power, control and desire have always been deeply entangled with '*war envy*' and an *almost insatiable appetite for money, luxuries and women.*" Mbembe, foreword to *An Inconvenient Youth: Julius Malema and the "New" ANC*, by Fiona Forde (Johannesburg: Picador Africa, 2011), vi (emphasis added). For more comparison of Adams and Malema, see the coda to this book.

10. Although Adams was never an "area boy," he was initially dismissed as such by some of his adversaries. Even now, online commentators still dismiss him as such. For instance, when in March 2015 *Premium Times* published a story in which Adams attacked the leader of the All Progressives Congress, Governor Bola Tinubu, one online commentator stated, "How can the Yorubas—who claim to be so sophisticated, educated and learned allow such brainless, illiterate rascal, tout and *area boy* to speak is a mystery!" Taiwo Hassan Adebayo, "Tinubu Using Yoruba for Own Selfish Interest—Gani Adams," *Premium Times*, March 21, 2015, https://www.premiumtimesng.com/regional/ssouth-west/178876-tinubu-using-yoruba-for-own-selfish-interest-gani-adams.html. Area boys in urban cities of Southern Nigeria are adolescents and young men who organize themselves into "survival networks"—or gangs—that are sometimes involved in petty crimes. Abubakar Momoh has argued succinctly that "*Area Boys* culture should be understood, not in the reductionist stigma of crime which it currently carries, but as part of the social and ideological contradictions of class politics played out in the urban context." Momoh, "Youth Culture and *Area Boys* in Lagos," in *Identity Transformation and Identity Politics under Structural Adjustment in Nigeria*, ed. Attahiru Jega (Uppsala: Nordiska Afrikainstitutet, 2000), 183. See also Olawale Ismail, "From 'Area-Boyism' to 'Junctions and Bases': Youth Social Formation and the Micro Structures of Violence in Lagos Island," in *State Fragility, State Formation, and Human Security in Nigeria*, ed. Mojubaola O. Okome (New York: Palgrave Macmillan, 2013).

11. Harry Blatterer, *Coming of Age in Times of Uncertainty* (New York: Berghahn Books, 2007), 112.

12. James E. Cote and Anton Allahar, *Generation on Hold: Coming of Age in the Late Twentieth Century* (New York: New York University, 1994), 29. To draw a parallel, Fiona Forde, author of *An Inconvenient Youth: Julius Malema and the "New" ANC* (Johannesburg: Jonathan Ball Publishers, 2011; Edinburgh: Portobello Books, 2012), reveals that, when she was wavering about writing her book, Achille Mbembe told her, "The register of our humanity extends from cruelty to mercy to love to thuggery, and all of that. The more an individual has all these facets, the more interesting he is as a character." Forde, *Inconvenient Youth*, xvii.

13. See Wale Adebanwi, *Yoruba Elites and Ethnic Politics in Nigeria: Obafemi Awolowo and Corporate Agency* (Cambridge: Cambridge University Press, 2014).

14. Such as the life of Obafemi Awolowo. See Adebanwi, *Yoruba Elites and Ethnic Politics in Nigeria*; Stephen Adebanji Akintoye, *The History of the Yoruba People* (Dakar: Amalion, 2010). For Nnamdi Azikiwe, see Elizabeth Tonkin, "Zik's Story: Autobiography as Political Exemplar," in *Self-Assertion and Brokerage: Early Cultural Nationalism in West Africa*, ed. P. F. de Moraes Farias and Karin Barber (Birmingham: Centre of West African Studies, 1990).

15. In chaps. 1 and 4, to further contradict things, I will show how he is, at the same time, a typical exemplar in the precolonial Yorùbá context.

16. Interestingly enough, Adams was to succeed Abiola as the fifteenth Ààrẹ *Ọ̀nà Kakaǹfò* of Yorubaland ten years after the latter's death.

17. See Obafemi Awolowo's autobiography, *Awo: The Autobiography of Chief Obafemi Awolowo* (Cambridge: Cambridge University Press, 1960). On Abiola, see Bimbo Awofeso, *Abiola: To Make Whole Again* (Lagos: Update, 1990).

18. Cf. Blatterer, *Coming of Age in Times of Uncertainty*, 50.

19. Gareth Williams, "Subalternity and the Neoliberal Habitus: Thinking Insurrection on the El Salvador/South Central Interface," *Nepantla: Views from South* 1, no. 1 (2000): 140.

20. Daniel Clayton, "Subaltern Space," in *Handbook of Geographical Knowledge*, ed. J. Agnew and D. Livingstone (London: Sage, 2010).

21. Gayatri Chakravorty Spivak, "The Trajectory of the Subaltern in My Work" (lecture, University of California, Santa Barbara), aired September 13, 2004, on UCTV, 88 min., http://www.uctv.tv/search-details.aspx?showID=8840. See also Spivak, "Can the Subaltern Speak?," in *Marxism and the Interpretation of Culture*, ed. Cary Nelson and Lawrence Grossberg (Urbana: University of Illinois Press, 1988); Spivak, "Scattered Speculations on the Subaltern and the Popular," *Postcolonial Studies* 8, no. 4 (2005): 475–76.

22. Graham Riach, *An Analysis of Gayatri Chakravorty Spivak's "Can the Subaltern Speak?"* (London: Macat International, 2017), 24.

23. To cite a few examples, Marcus E. Green, "Gramsci and Subaltern Struggles Today: Spontaneity, Political Organization and Occupy Wall Street," in *Antonio Gramsci*, ed. Mark McNally (London: Palgrave-Macmillan, 2015); Guido Liguori, "Conceptions of Subalternity in Gramsci," in McNally, *Antonio Gramsci*.

24. Sonita Sarker, "Subalternity In and Out of Time, In and Out of History," in *Gramsci and Foucault: A Reassessment*, ed. David Kreps (London: Routledge, 2015), 91.

25. Which is different from what is evident in the approaches of Subaltern Studies Groups—Indian and, later, Latin American. See Liguori, "Conceptions of Subalternity in Gramsci," 119.

26. Ibid., 118.

27. Ibid., 129.

28. Ibid.

29. Ibid., 120.

30. Ibid., 122.

31. Green, "Gramsci and Subaltern Struggles Today," 157.

32. Antonio Gramsci, *Prison Notebooks,* Vol. 2, No. 3, §14, ed. and trans. Joseph A. Buttigieg (1971, reprint, New York: Columbia University Press, 1996), 21; Liguori, "Conceptions of Subalternity in Gramsci," 125.

33. Liguori, "Conceptions of Subalternity in Gramsci," 125.

34. Green, "Gramsci and Subaltern Struggles Today," 157. This position has been criticized as "vanguardism" and "elitism."

35. Ranajit Guha, "On Some Aspects of the Historiography of Colonial India," in *Selected Subaltern Studies,* ed. Ranajit Guha and Gayatry Chakravorty Spivak (Oxford: Oxford University Press, 1988), 40.

36. He adds, "For it neither originated from elite politics nor did its existence depend on the latter." Ranajit Guya, "On Some Aspects of the Historiography of Colonial India," in *Selected Subaltern Studies,* ed. Ranajit Guya and Gayatri Chakravorty Spivak (Oxford: Oxford University Press, 1988), 40.

37. See, for instance, Spivak, "Can the Subaltern Speak?," 271–313.

38. Riach, *Analysis of Gayatri Chakravorty Spivak's "Can the Subaltern Speak?,"* 11.

39. Ibid., 12.

40. Ibid., 39.

41. As reported by David Hardiman in *Economic and Political Weekly,* in the original paper, which she presented at a conference (the paper was transformed into the much-cited chapter), Spivak asserted that "it is . . . important to see how the subaltern are *fixed* in their subalternity by the elite." Hardiman, "'Subaltern Studies' at Crossroads," *Economic and Political Weekly* 21, no. 7 (February 15, 1986): 289. Though the elite tried to fix Adams in his subalternity, as the following chapters show, he escaped while deploying his own agency to win some autonomy and to become an elite capable of attempting to fix other subalterns.

42. Spivak, "Can the Subaltern Speak?," 283. However, it must be conceded that Spivak later argued that the subaltern is a shifting identity determined by context, though this did not lead her to revise her position on the absolute absence of social mobility for the subaltern. See Spivak, *The Postcolonial Critic: Interviews, Strategies, Dialogues,* ed. Sarah Harasym (London: Routledge, 1990), 141.

43. John Beverly, *Subalternity and Representation: Arguments in Cultural Theory* (Durham, NC: Duke University Press, 1999), 1.

44. Gyan Prakash, "The Impossibility of Subaltern History," *Nepantla: Views from South* 1, no. 2 (2000): 287–88.

45. Ibid., 287.

46. See Gayatri Chakravorty Spivak, "Theory in the Margin: Coetzee's Foe Reading Defoe's Crusoe/Roxana," in *Consequences of Theory: Selected Papers of the English Institute, 1987–1988,* ed. Jonathan Arac and Barbara Johnson (Baltimore: Johns Hopkins University Press, 1991), 154–80.

47. Prakash, "Impossibility of Subaltern History," 288 (emphasis added).

48. Ibid.

49. Antonio Gramsci, *Prison Notebook* (New York: International Publishers, 1971); and Gramsci, *The Southern Question* (Bordighera: Bordighera Press, 1995).

50. Gramsci, *Prison Notebook*, 55.

51. Edward W. Said, foreword to Guha and Spivak, *Selected Subaltern Studies*, viii.

52. Vilfredo Pareto, *The Mind and Society* (London: Jonathan Cape, 1935), 1422–23.

53. Ibid., 1935.

54. Gaetano Mosca, *The Ruling Class* (New York: McGraw-Hill, 1939).

55. Harold D. Lasswell, Daniel Lerner, and Easton C. Rothwell, *The Comparative Study of Elites* (Stanford, CA: Hoover Institute Studies Series, 1952).

56. T. B. Bottomore, *Elites and Society* (Middlesex: Penguin Books, 1966).

57. F. G. Bailey, *Stratagems and Spoils: A Social Anthropology of Politics* (Cambridge, MA: Westview, 2001).

58. George E. Marcus, ed., *Elites: Ethnographic Issues* (Albuquerque: School of American Research, University of New Mexico Press, 1983).

59. John Higley and Michael Burton, *Elite Foundations of Liberal Democracy* (Lanham, MD: Rowman and Littlefield, 2006); John Higley and Richard Gunther, eds., *Elites and Democratic Consolidation in Latin America and Southern Europe* (New York: Cambridge University Press, 1991).

60. João Pina-Cabral, introduction to *Elites: Choice, Leadership and Succession*, ed. João Pina-Cabral and Antonia Pedroso de Lima (Oxford: Berg, 2000), 2.

61. Jonathan Spencer, *Anthropology, Politics and the State: Democracy and Violence in South Asia* (Cambridge: Cambridge University Press, 2007).

62. Bailey, *Stratagems and Spoils*, 5.

63. Abner Cohen, *The Politics of Elite Culture: Explorations in the Dramaturgy of Power in a Modern African Society* (Berkeley: University of California Press, 1981); Stephen Nugent and Cris Shore, eds., *Elite Cultures: Anthropological Perspectives* (London: Routledge, 2002); Jon Abbink and Tijo Salverda, eds., *The Anthropology of Elites: Power, Culture, and the Complexities of Distinction* (New York: Palgrave Macmillan, 2013).

64. Mattia Fumanti, *The Politics of Distinction: African Elites from Colonialism to Liberation in a Namibian Frontier Town* (Canon Pyon: Sean Kingston, 2016).

65. Cris Shore, "Introduction: Towards an Anthropology of the Elites," in Nugent and Shore, *Elite Cultures*, 1.

66. In the following chapters, I argue and show that the process of *self-forming* occurs before, but also simultaneously with, that of *transformation*.

67. I approach youth as a "social process." See Johanna Wyn and Ron White, *Rethinking Youth* (London: Sage, 1997), 9.

68. This reminds me of one of my old teachers at Cambridge who said during a seminar that "anthropology is elevated gossip." I am persuaded that he offered this as a description of a dimension of anthropology—and did not mean that "elevated gossip" is all that anthropology is about. Indeed, during the COVID-19 era in which I chatted regularly with these members of the OPC via WhatsApp, a significant

portion of the gossip led me to probe further and yielded great insights into the past of the group and the relationships among the leadership.

69. Fred W. Clothey, "Towards a Comprehensive Interpretation of Ritual," *Journal of Ritual Studies* 2, no. 2 (1988): 147.

70. Ibid.

71. Ibid. Clothey adds that the "hermeneutical spiral" makes the interpreter "aware of the distinction between being and understanding."

72. Marcus Banks and Richard Vokes, "Introduction: Anthropology, Photography and the Archive," *History and Anthropology* 21, no. 4 (2010): 337; Elizabeth Edwards, "Anthropology and Photography: A Long History of Knowledge and Affect," *Photographies* 8, no. 3 (2015): 235. Banks and Vokes and Edwards also explore the instabilities, tensions, and complications in the relationship between photography and ethnography. See also Richard Vokes and Darren Newbury, "Photography and African Futures," *Visual Studies* 33, no. 1 (2018): 1–10.

73. Richard Werbner, "Beyond Oblivion: Confronting Memory Crisis," in *Memory and the Postcolony: African Anthropology and the Critique of Power*, ed. R. Werbner (London: Zed Books, 1998). "Memory practice" can involve both individual memory and collective memory. On the latter in the Nigerian context, see Peter Probst, "Picturing the Past: Heritage, Photography, and the Politics of Appearance in a Yoruba City," in *Reclaiming Heritage: Alternative Imaginaries of Memory in West Africa*, ed. Ferdinand de Jong and Michael Rowlands (London: Routledge, 2007), 99–125; Charles D. Gore, "Commemoration, Memory and Ownership: Some Social Contexts of Contemporary Photography in Benin City, Nigeria," *Visual Anthropology* 14, no. 3 (2001): 321–42.

74. Vokes and Newbury, "Photography and African Futures," 2.

75. See Heike Behrend, "'I Am Like a Movie Star in My Street': Photographic Self-creation in Postcolonial Kenya," in *Postcolonial Subjectivities in Africa*, ed. Richard Werbner (London: Zed Books, 2002), 44.

76. Mattia Fumanti, "'Showing-Off Aesthetics': Looking Good, Making Relations and 'Being in the World' in the London Akan Diaspora," *Ethnos: Journal of Anthropology* 78, no. 2 (2013): 201.

77. The anthropological literature on aesthetic self-fashioning is, in part, an homage to the philosophers who have championed these ethics, including Michel Foucault, Richard Shusterman, Alexander Nehamas, Stanley Cavell, and Richard Rorty. See Jerold J. Abrams, "Aesthetics of Self-fashioning and Cosmopolitanism: Foucault and Rorty on the Art of Living," *Philosophy Today* 46, no. 2 (2002): 185. See also Alan Milchman and Alan Rosenberg, "The Aesthetic and Ascetic Dimensions of an Ethics of Self-fashioning: Nietzsche and Foucault," *Perrhesia*, no. 2 (2007): 44–65. Milchman and Rosenberg argue correctly that "Foucault . . . has provided us with the means that will enhance our understanding of how an ethics of self-fashioning can be a powerful response to the cultural crisis through which we are now living." Ibid., 46. I thank one of the reviewers for inspiring me to emphasize this point. However,

it is important to point out, as Paul Allen Miller does, that, for Foucault, the purpose of self-fashioning "was not self-absorption, but to offer new means of resistance to the normalizing structures." This, I think, is helpful still for understanding the self-making of figures of resistance such as Adams. Paul Allen Miller, "The Art of Self-fashioning, or Foucault on Plato and Derrida," *Foucault Studies*, no. 2 (2005): 56.

78. Peter Probst, "Visual Publics: A Matter of Mimicry," *Critical Interventions* 2, no. 1–2 (2008): 7.

79. Richard Werbner, "Introduction: Postcolonial Subjectivities; The Personal, the Political and the Moral," in Werbner, *Postcolonial Subjectivities in Africa*, 2.

80. Susan Sontag, *On Photography* (New York: Picador USA, 1973), 4, 6.

81. Adams's attitude seems to testify to Sontag's apt observation that "after [an] event has ended, the picture will still exist, conferring on the event a kind of immortality (and importance) it would never otherwise have enjoyed." Ibid., 11.

82. Stephen Sprague, "How I See the Yoruba See Themselves," *Studies in the Anthropology of Visual Communication* 5, no. 1 (1978): 11.

83. Kim McNamara, "Publicising Private Lives: Celebrities, Image Control and the Reconfiguration of Public Space," *Social & Cultural Geography* 10, no. 1 (2009): 9.

84. After one of the few "reconciliation" meetings between him and his former leader, Fasehun, he changed his title to national coordinator of the OPC, while Fasehun took the title of founder and leader.

85. Of the OPC, as he named himself when he first announced his breakaway group, in replacement of the founding President of the group, Fasehun. He took the title of national coordinator after the reconciliation with Fasehun.

86. I return to this in chap. 3.

87. Daniel Jordan Smith, *To Be a Man Is Not a One-Day Job: Masculinity, Money, and Intimacy in Nigeria* (Chicago: University of Chicago Press, 2017).

88. Tim Gibbs, "Becoming a 'Big Man' in Neo-liberal South Africa: Migrant Masculinities in the Minibus-Taxi Industry," *African Affairs* 113, no. 452 (2014): 431–48.

89. Alexander Schuhr, "Notes on the African Big Man," Good Men Project, November 14, 2017, https://goodmenproject.com/featured-content/notes-african-big-man-phtz/.

90. Farah Bakaari, Vincent Benlloch, and Barry Driscoll, "Political Scientists Talk about African 'Big Men' Inconsistently," *LSE Blog*, March 22, 2021, https://blogs.lse.ac.uk/africaatlse/2021/03/22/political-science-talk-about-african-big-men-governance-patronage-inconsistently/.

91. See, for example, Barry Driscoll, "Big Man or Boogey Man? The Concept of the Big Man in Political Science," *Journal of Modern African Studies* 58, no. 4 (2021): 521–50; Boniface Dulani, "Big Man Rule in Africa: Are Africans Getting the Leadership They Want?," *African Review* 46 (2019): 275–91; Larry Diamond, "Progress and Retreat in Africa: The Rule of Law versus the Big Man," *Journal of Democracy* 9, no. 2 (2008): 138–49; Mats Utas, ed., *African Conflicts and Informal Power: Big Men and Networks* (London: Zed Books, 2012).

92. Marshall D. Sahlins, "Poor Man, Rich Man, Big-Man, Chief: Political Types in Melanesia and Polynesia," *Comparative Studies in Society and History* 5, no. 3 (1963): 285.

93. Ibid.

94. Such as festivals. See chap. 3.

95. As chaps. 2–5 show, Adams is "astute in manoeuvring," to use Thoden van Velzen's words. See H. U. E. Thoden van Velzen, "Robinson Crusoe and Friday: Strength and Weakness of the Big Man Paradigm," *Man*, n.s., 8, no. 4 (1973): 595.

96. Sahlins adds that such an experiment helps anthropologists to make comparisons. Sahlins, "Poor Man, Rich Man, Big-Man, Chief," 285.

HOW TO BECOME A BIG MAN IN AFRICA

PART I
Becoming a Big Man

1 / The Carpenter's Revolt

Subaltern Youth, Democratic Struggle, and Ethno-national Politics

INTRODUCTION

"And leave all these?" Gani Adams asked as he signed new identification cards for the members of his faction of the Oodua People's Congress (OPC). It was 2002, and we were on the first floor of a building in Amukoko, a low-income suburb of Lagos. Adams was using the living room of the house to conduct some urgent business while he and his comrades prepared for the National Coordinating Council (NCC) meeting. The NCC is the second-highest decision-making body of the OPC after the National Executive Council (NEC) (see table 1.1). The NCC meets every Tuesday for about four hours of festivities and a gathering of the OPC, including all members in the hosting local government and representatives from the other local governments in Lagos and the group's state chapters.

In the building, hundreds of group members were chatting, singing, or dancing while I was alternating between watching them and paying attention to their president, Adams. A majority of those present were young men, but a significant number of young women were participating too.

When I entered the living room, Adams was still signing identification cards. He looked up and asked if I was okay. I responded in the affirmative and took the opportunity to ask a question. A few days before, one of my interlocutors who was close to Adams mentioned an initiative to reconcile the Adams faction and the one led by his erstwhile leader, Dr. Frederick Fasehun. I was eager to know the implications of this effort.

Adams, who was then thirty-two years old, confirmed that such efforts were indeed underway and added that some of those concerned people were

OODUA PEOPLE'S CONGRESS (OPC) ORGANIZATIONAL STRUCTURE

Annual National Conference (ANC)
(Supreme Organ of the OPC)
Membership: All national officers, the chair, the secretary, three other members of each state branch, and co-opted members of NEC

National Executive Council (NEC)
(The Governing Body)
Membership: National officers (president, deputy president, national chairperson, secretary-general, deputy secretary-general, treasurer, publicity secretary, organizing secretary, and finance secretary), chair and secretary of every state branch, head of the Women's League, head of the Youth League, and co-opted members

National Coordinating Council (NCC)
(Carries out the decisions of the NEC)
Membership: President, deputy president, national chairperson, secretary-general, deputy secretary-general, treasurer, and other members elected by the NEC

National Secretariat
Headed by the national secretary-general

State Annual Conference
Membership: All members of the State Executive Committee, delegates representing branches, and leaders of the Women's and Youth Leagues

State Executive Committee (SEC)
Membership: State chairperson, deputy chairperson, secretary, deputy secretary, not more than thirteen persons elected by the State Conference, and two representatives each for the Women's and Youth Leagues

Women's League

Branch Annual General Meeting

Branch Executive Committee

State Branches

Local Government Zones

Ad Hoc Committees

arranging to end the hostilities between the factions. However, when I asked whether reconciliation would cause his faction to merge with Fasehun's, Adams looked up from the identification cards and asked rhetorically in Yoruba, "*Ka fi gbogbo eleyi sile*?" (And leave all these?).

Figure 1.1. Adams addressing members of his faction with Kayode Atanda, Rasaq Arogundade Balogun, Lateef Ogungbayi, and Musa Kilanko standing behind him. Photo courtesy of Rasaq Arogundade Balogun.

Figure 1.2. Marching past: members of the Adams faction of the OPC during a march-past at one of their meetings in Lagos in the early 2000s. The drill instructor, Gbenga Owoyemi (a.k.a. Naheem, late), is in front (*far right*). Photo courtesy of Monsuru Akande.

I realized later that I had asked a silly question. Adams's response suggested that I had failed to grasp the extent of the expansive sociocultural, and potentially political, machine he was building. Though he was not yet set on the path to riches and high society, he had obviously anticipated what would come if he continued to lead and build his own faction. Did I seriously expect Adams to deactivate his faction (whose membership, he claimed, numbered in the millions) and end his presidency, which was increasingly turning him into a household name?

Adams's reference to "all these" as he pointed to the new identification cards did not only refer to the huge following he had acquired since breaking away from the Fasehun-led OPC on March 1, 1999—those whose newly issued cards would further distinguish them from the members, and those pretending to be members, of the Fasehun faction. As I realized in subsequent years, he was also alluding to other matters that marked him as a person of some significance in society: name recognition; increasing media attention; acknowledgment from top members of the political elite (including some governors or governorship candidates) of his relevance and potency, as well as his relationships with them; his considerable and growing influence in the wider polity; financial support; and the resulting change in his personal material circumstances. I was asking if he would abandon *all these* to again take second place to Fasehun, who regarded Adams as "a primary [elementary] school dropout unable to make a success of his carpenter's apprenticeship"[1] and dismissed him as a "Frankenstein [monster]."[2]

In this chapter, I (re)account for the founding of the OPC, including the contested histories of the group's founding; the autobiographies of the leaders of the initial two factions of the group, Gani Adams and Frederick Fasehun; and the emergent different slants in the group's core mission. While exploring the bases and dynamics of the splitting of the group, originally into two factions, I focus on Adams's, exploring the cultural repertoires of this so-called youthful, militant faction, pointing to ways in which its practices can be interpreted as both an instrumentally rational strategy of power struggle and a form of symbolic action with cultural meanings. I argue that, given the group's appropriation of culture in negotiating Yorùbá identity while also retaining the rhetoric of justice, equity, and democracy in its mission and practices, the Adams OPC faction strongly challenges the bifurcation of tradition and modernity. This chapter also makes a case for approaching the activities of the OPC not as stable, bounded manifestations of culture but rather as fluid, ambivalent, and paradoxical manifestations of the (re)construction of ethnic-power relations and formations. In making the foregoing arguments, this chapter provides a basis for understanding how the structural and agential contexts of a mass movement of young, mostly disenfranchised men and women were ultimately mobilized by a strategic improviser, Gani Adams, in leveraging the political challenges of an ascribed identity (Yoruba), the cultural resources of that identity, and the socioeconomic challenges of the process of social maturation (youth) into a personal project of acquired status. The convergence of sociocultural and personal projects in Adams's life story, I argue, represents a compelling illumination of the simultaneous convergence and conversion of subaltern status and/into big man status. This chapter follows the tradition of biography as a means of political, historical, and ethnographic analysis in Nigerian history, as represented by Kenneth Post and George Jenkins's work, *The Price of Liberty: Personality and Politics in Colonial Nigeria*.[3] Post and Jenkins's book is "partly a biography of a man, Adegoke Adelabu; much more though, it tells in a highly personal and intriguing way how a Nigerian politician operated in the last years of colonial rule."[4]

I also draw on Pierre Bourdieu's notion of habitus and Antonio Gramsci's agential conception of culture to explore the construction and activities of the OPC. This chapter points not to stable, bounded manifestations of cultures but to relationships and their capability of creating fluidity and shifts in ethnic-power formations. I do this in a context in which cultural practices are used to reinvent culture and negotiate power. Here, I am sensitive to David Laitin's[5] position that theorists—and, I will add, ethnographers—of culture must embed their analysis more fully in the surrounding social and political realities.

ADAMS: AN EXEMPLARY LIFE HISTORY

In many ways, Adams[6] is a product of the structural conditions of 1970s and 1980s Nigeria, which account for the circumstances of his birth and processes of social maturation. While the structural limitations he faced are important, even more critical and interesting is Adams's mobilization of both personal and organizational agency in reaction to—and in a bid to, alternatively, alter or strengthen—the structural constraints and enablement he faced. Thus, in this section, I interpret, at a broader cultural-cum-political level, "the ways in which particular cultural [and political] formations shape[d] and provoke[d]" Adams's subjectivity.[7] This forms a useful background for exploring (in subsequent chapters) the (re)shaping of Adams's moral imaginations as he encountered the "actual contingencies of [his] life-world"[8] and discerned the "moral possibilities" of that lifeworld. In this context, Mattia Fumanti has suggested that by "bringing agency and subjectivity"[9] into our analysis—of the transformation of a subaltern into an elite, as in this case—we can address Vilfredo Pareto's

Figure 1.3. On the soapbox, Adams addressing members of his faction of the OPC in the early years. Behind Adams (*right*) is Sunday Adebayo, his erstwhile friend and personal assistant. Photo courtesy of *Nigerian Tribune*.

question[10] about "the values, ideals, and moral reasoning behind elite actions." This is crucial for analyzing public lives, such as Adams's, that reflect a particular form of "moral reasoning that persuades and mobilizes people to action."[11]

Born to Lamidi Adams and Dada Adams (née Aduloju) on April 30, 1970, in Arigidi-Akoko, Ondo State, Adams attended many primary schools because his father was constantly moving for his job. His education began in 1976 at the Army Children's School, in Oturkpo, Benue State, in the North-Central Region of Nigeria. In 1978, he moved to St. Thomas Primary School in Erusu-Akoko,

Ondo State. His father moved again with his whole family, to Lagos, shortly after. Adams completed his elementary education at the Municipal Primary School in Surulere, Lagos, in 1981. He attended Ansar-ur-deen Secondary School on Randle Avenue, Surulere, Lagos, but dropped out in the third year, in 1984. He states that he did so because of "the financial incapacity of [his] parents."[12]

"I . . . knew from an early age that an idle mind is the devil's workshop," said Adams. Fearing the dangers of idleness, he took "a course in furniture-making and interior decorating."[13] In 1980s Lagos, though many artisans were using more "elevating" names or phrases to describe their craft (or profession, as they called it),[14] others would have simply referred to Adams as a carpenter, even if he later described himself as a "furniture-maker" and "interior decorator." At any rate, this was how he described himself when he first came into public consciousness. In 2000, in response to accounts of his "illiteracy," he told a reporter, "I am a carpenter by profession, but I am not a stark illiterate as Dr. Fasehun claimed. As I am speaking now, you can draw your own conclusions whether I am a stark illiterate or not. I can address the Queen of England inside the Buckingham Palace and she will understand what I am saying."[15] Therefore, the idea that he was a "furniture-maker" and "interior decorator" came up later as part of his attempt to reconstruct his past to reposition himself publicly.

Adams completed his apprenticeship in 1987 and was later employed at an Italian construction company, Visioni Stabilini, in Apapa, Lagos. He resigned after five years "to establish [his] own furniture-making and interior decorating business."[16] In the early years of our engagement, Adams told me that he had resigned because of the Italians' treatment of Nigerians at the firm. In recalling the hardship he had suffered before he became a "man," Adams once told to me in Yoruba, "Oju ti ri!" (literal translation: "The eyes have seen," which means "I have experienced a lot [of hardship]").[17]

Under the conditions of the Structural Adjustment Programme (SAP) imposed by General Ibrahim Babangida's regime in the second half of the 1980s and early 1990s, many Nigerians lost their jobs. What Eghosa Osaghae describes as "the retrenchment of the state from most areas of individual lives which is consistent with the *destatization* objective of SAP" and the "economic depression or recession, scarcity and immiseration"[18] that followed structural adjustment closed off social and economic opportunities for many young people in Africa, including those in Nigeria. Under this imposition of neoliberal economic doctrines, Adams became underemployed and eventually unemployed. Though he prefers to say that he abandoned his profession for "the struggle," this is not entirely accurate according to many people who knew Adams during this period and suggest that he was barely able to survive. His old friend and

Figure 1.4. "Bony youth." Adams in the early years of the OPC. Photo courtesy of Rasaq Arogundade Balogun.

later personal assistant, Sunday Adebayo, informed me of the hardships they endured while he and Adams lived together: "When he had nothing, I will give him my *okada* [motorcycle taxi] to use for commercial transport to make some money to maintain himself."[19] Indeed, while Adams, in a press interview, challenged Fasehun's description of him as an *okada* rider, his book confirms that he drove an *okada* for survival—even though he claims that he acquired his "motorcycle through the labor of [his] hand."[20] He writes, "My source of income include[d] riding [a] commercial motorcycle popularly called *okada*. . . . Although, at my early life, I did not have the privilege of a formal education, nonetheless, I have never at one time or the other pretended to be what I am not. . . . Thus, I was able to manage myself with the meagre takings from my *okada* business."[21]

Thus, Adams's life history points alternatively to the opportunities and limitations that were offered or imposed on his life by the political and economic conditions or crises in Nigeria. By the time Adams left primary school in 1981, the Yoruba-dominated Unity Party of Nigeria (UPN) was already in power in all the Yoruba-speaking states in Western Nigeria. In line with the UPN policy, state governments instituted a free education program, which supplied school uniforms, books, and other essentials. It is therefore significant that Adams gained admission to high school in 1981 but dropped out in the third year, in 1984—the year the military seized power and reintroduced school fees in the heat of rising inflation and the worsening economic crisis.

Some scholars have linked the economic crisis that led to the imposition of SAP, which in turn worsened the economic conditions in many African states in the 1980s and 1990s, to the resurgence of an identity crisis. For instance, Nigerian political scientist Attahiru Jega argues that, in the decade of SAP, "traditional forms of identities, dubbed as primordial and for long trivialized, have proved to be [not only] resilient" but also resurgent, as they became "popular and of political significance in the contemporary political economy, with all sorts of outcomes and consequences."[22]

Given the conditions that truncated Adams's education in a region of Nigeria where education is perhaps the most valuable means of social achievement and personal enhancement, it perhaps comes as no surprise that he later named a "degenerated educational system" as one of the factors necessitating the founding of the OPC. He also made "qualitative education . . . free at all levels" one of the key points on his group's agenda. Thus, in the early years of his emergence, Adams was sensitive to any reference to his lack of formal education. He responded to the endless vilification based on his lack of formal education by constantly emphasizing that he was not an "illiterate" while also pointing out that "the battle for self-determination does not solely reside in academic prowess."[23]

Apart from education, Adams emphasized another fundamental issue evident in the early years of his rise to significance and in the eventual split in the OPC: his identity as a young man. Adams was twenty-four when the OPC was formed in 1994. Before then, he had been the publicity secretary of the Campaign for Democracy (CD), the coalition of civil society groups that was formed around 1991 to end Nigeria's military dictatorship. He joined the CD in 1993 and became "one of those instrumental to many of the protests [against military dictatorship] that were held in Lagos State at the time."[24] He further explained, "I was one of the vibrant youths who coordinated the struggle in Mushin, with the support of the dependable forces on the Mainland. Anyone conversant with the history of the various protests then would know that Mushin and Mainland were the strategic points where protests took off in Lagos. So, I was the figure that the CD used to signal for protests in Mushin, while Omoyele Sowore, who later founded Sahara Reporters, a popular online media outlet, and Wale Balogun operated from the Mainland front."[25]

Thus, for Adams, his initial subaltern identity was linked as much to the limits of his education and to his work as an artisan as to his experience as a

Figure 1.5. *Left to right:* Adams, Rasaq Arogundade Balogun (Saddam), and Kilanko Oladipupo (popularly called Kila) of the Adams faction around 2000. Photo courtesy of Rasaq Arogundade Balogun.

young man. In light of this, his youthful identity is central to understanding the course of Adams's life and the nature of his relationship with Fasehun and other elders in the OPC. His youthfulness and dynamism also account for his ability to mobilize the youth in the OPC to take over leadership and the manner in which he leveraged this identity for many years.

In the last two decades, Africanist literature has overcome the tendency to oversimplify and trivialize youth as a social category in Africa and criminalize the youths themselves.[26] The burgeoning literature on youth, ethnic militia, vigilantism, child soldiers, and so on has brilliantly located the African youth in nuanced and insightful ways in contemporary social processes.[27] Focusing on youth as a social category and process alerts us to the untenable nature and ambiguity of youth as a universal category.[28] The category and process are shaped differently by the material, objective factors of the cultures and contexts in which youths live and by their subjective encounters with and interpretations of the conditions of their lives.[29] In studies of youths in Africa, particularly those groups who "spearhead contemporary political contests between the politics of identity and citizenship"[30] in response to the "politics of plunder," such as the OPC, it is therefore illuminating to connect our understanding of youth to the intersection of social and physical maturation and perhaps the most salient identity/resource on the continent: ethnicity.

Adams's personal biography illuminates this important connection. He claims to have become "politically inclined" by 1992, the year that Babangida's transition to the democratic rule program was scheduled to end. Toward the end of 1991, hopes for a transition to democracy faded even as the regime's economic program lagged, with the SAP producing economic devastation.

The objective conditions of Adams's own life—conditions shared by many young Nigerians, particularly his fellow Yoruba—predisposed him to activism. His perception of that activism, and others' perception of him, are located within two interlocking legitimating discourses: that of modern democratic politics and that of Yorùbá cultural values. The two perceptions constitute the link between the circumstances of an individual life and those of its wider context. Pierre Bourdieu[31] has reflected on this form of temporality. He argues that practices or actions "cannot be deduced either from present conditions which may seem to have provoked them or from the past conditions which have produced the habitus. . . . They can . . . only be accounted for by relating the social conditions in which the habitus that generated them was constituted, to the social conditions in which it is implemented."[32]

Adams explains that the "contradictions" that produced the OPC include "structural imbalance, the military and repressive decrees, destructive constitutional structure, conscious debasement of ethnic nationalities, insecurity of life and property, ethnic cleansing, degenerated educational system." Much of these he blamed on the "northern (Hausa-Fulani) oligarchy."[33] Therefore, his faction's goals included self-determination and social emancipation for the Yoruba; regional autonomy; self-government and self-management; economic reconstruction and control; a restructured and reconstituted and genuinely federal Nigerian union; the reunion of all Yorùbá in Kwara and Kogi States (in the North-Central Region) with their kith and kin in the Southwest; an independent army, police, and judiciary; and a Sovereign National Conference (SNC).[34] Although the group did not originally include this formally in its list of goals, the members believed that the separation or secession of the Yorùbá nation from the rest of Nigeria was the "last option." Again in 2002 and 2005, some group members repeated to me the desire to secede from Nigeria. On this Adams says: "Definitely. That is the last option. If we cannot have true federalism, nor have a Sovereign National Conference convened by the government of President Olusegun Obasanjo, then we implore all Yorubas to be alert and vigilant, as we shall then have no other choice than to announce the inevitable, a Sovereign Oodua Republic, in the nearest future."[35]

For Adams, the fact that prominent northerners backed the annulment of the 1993 presidential elections reinforced ideas of a "northern conspiracy." He stated in 2000: "The OPC is a child of necessity that came into being after the

Figure 1.6. Adams speaking during an OPC public gathering in the early years. Beside him is Abideen Ige, coordinator, OPC Eti-Osa Local Government Area, Lagos State. Photo courtesy of Rasaq Arogundade Balogun.

criminal and retrogressive annulment of the June 12, 1993, presidential election in which the winner, Chief MKO Abiola, was illegally arrested and detained for more than four years before he was subsequently murdered in July 1998. . . . Generals Ibrahim Babangida, Sani Abacha and Abdulsalami Abubakar who perpetrated this evil against the Yoruba are northerners, representing the northern interest."[36]

Many members of the OPC with whom I spoke over the years reflected similar positions when articulating the reasons they joined the group. Some of them, like Adams, embraced the ethno-nationalist path in response to the Nigerian crisis after initially joining the prodemocracy and human rights groups to protest against the national crisis. For example, Taofik Adeyemi, who was a personal assistant to Fasehun (he left Fasehun's faction later to join a splinter group, OPC Reform), said that he joined the OPC after being a member of the CD under Dr. Beko Ransome-Kuti. He also flirted with the National Democratic Coalition (NADECO), the main opposition group to General Sani Abacha's autocracy. He concluded eventually that the prodemocracy and human rights groups did not have "as much weight as the OPC."[37]

Adams added that the 1959 and 1979 general elections had been manipulated to favor the North.[38] By 2000, the North had ruled Nigeria for thirty-four of its thirty-nine years of existence as an independent state. In these comments, we see both the importance of key events (in this case the annulment of the presidential election) and the weaving of such events into the claims of political actors—that is, the discursive instrumentalization of key events and the ways in which actors make such events meaningful by locating them in broader patterns of historical understanding. As Adams's references to the 1959 and 1979 elections show, the events of 1993–94 and beyond were understood in terms of an enduring pattern of ethnic antagonism and inequality. Therefore, for Adams, the annulment of the 1993 presidential election revealed the enduring agenda of the North to keep the Yorùbá "in subjection."

This narrative that constructed a boundary dividing the Yorùbá from its principal Other, the Hausa-Fulani, apparently understated the internal boundaries within Yorubaland as well as the divisions among members of the OPC—and eventually between the two factions of the OPC in their battle for legitimacy. However, Adams's rendering of the sociopolitical and economic conditions that provoked his activism indicates a reflexive self that, unable to escape the structural forces in society and state, decided which of the forces to act on and which to ignore.[39] As Beverley Skeggs argues, following Ulrick Beck,[40] while such structural conditions or forces do not free individuals (for example, Adams in his agency), such "agency-overloaded selves" become "individuals who live out, biographically, the complexity and diversity of the social relations which surround them."[41] According to Anthony Giddens,[42] individuals like Adams seek to "create a coherent biography,"[43] which becomes the basis of their everyday life as well as the condition for their actions in the world.

Reflecting on the contributions the life history method of inquiry—pioneered by anthropologists and later adopted by sociologists—has made to our understanding of the link between individuals, such as Adams, and the social process, Becker argues that "by providing this kind of voice [such as Adams's, particularly in the early period of his emergence] from a culture and situation that are ordinarily not known to intellectuals generally," we can "improve our theories at the most profound level" because we are able to put ourselves in the individuals' "skin." This helps scholars to "feel and become aware of the deep biases about such people that ordinarily permeate our thinking and shape the kinds of problems we investigate."[44] As Ivor Goodson commented more than four decades later, the life history approach forces researchers into a "messy confrontation with human subjectivity."[45]

In the resurgence of the life history method for social analysis since the early 1990s, "the notion of a singular, knowable, essential self is judged as part of the social production of individualism, [one that is] linked to argentic selves in pursuit of progress, knowingness, and emancipation."[46] In this context, as partly reflected in this book, "assumptions of linearity of chronological time lines and story lines are challenged in favour of more multiple, disrupted notions of subjectivity."[47] Life stories are never neat and absolutely chronological. Also, those who tell their life stories often "fashion coherence from the disparate and potentially contradictory experiences of their lives."[48] Thus, it is important—as some scholars have suggested, and as reflected in Adams's story—that ethnographers pay attention to silences as well as to what is said and "attend to the tensions and contradictions rather than succumb to the temptations to gloss over these in our desire for 'the' story."[49]

The subsequent narrative and interpretive analysis of Adams's trajectory, in the context of the OPC and beyond, focus on the tensions and contradictions in the encounters between the significant individual and the larger society.

ETHNIC POLITICS AND DEMOCRATIC TRANSITIONS

Ethnicity, as a social phenomenon based on "forms of interaction between the largest possible cultural-linguistic communal groups (ethnic groups) within political societies,"[50] has been central to Nigerian politics and sociocultural life since the two decades preceding political independence in 1960. However, ethnicity or ethnic groups as a significant force in Nigerian politics crystallized from the "modern" kinship and "tribal" associations that emerged in the 1920s in the urban centers.[51] These associations "gave organizational expression to the persistent feeling of loyalty and obligation to the kinship group and the town or village where the lineage was localized."[52] In the early twentieth century, the associations provided "mutual aid and protection" to their members in urban areas dominated by certain indigenous groups while also exporting "the enlightenment, modernity, and civilization they encountered in urban centers" to their rural homelands.[53]

James S. Coleman has explained that these associations developed thorough vertical and horizontal diffusion and integration that eventually led to the formation of "all-tribal federations in a pyramidal structure."[54] This structure became the basis of the "modern" form of ethnicity (as competitive relations)[55] and ethnic groups in Nigeria. The first of these groups was the Ibibio Welfare Union (later Ibibio State Union), formed in 1928. Others, like the Edo National Union, the Ibo Federal Union, and the pan-Yorùbá Egbe Omo Oduduwa, followed after World War II.[56] For Coleman, the exclusion of the educated elements of these associations from the colonial public sphere in the first few decades of the twentieth century significantly contributed to making them the "media for political . . . expression" by the emerging indigenous elites.[57]

In the two decades preceding Nigeria's independence, ethnic or ethnoregional associations blossomed and became the basis of party politics, particularly in the manifestation of such politics as important processes for the articulation and organization of the democratic struggle for power among the ethno-regional or ethnic groups in the immediate pre-independence and the postindependence eras. In these struggles, as Okwudiba Nnoli, one of the leading scholars in ethnic politics in Africa, has argued, a dominant class has often been able to present its own interests—or, I would add, its understanding of the group's interests—"as that of the ethnic community as a whole."[58]

In the last three decades, scholarship on the African social process has transcended the tradition of dismissing ethnicity as an "epi-phenomenon," as was dominant in African Marxist or Marxian scholarship in the earlier era.[59] As Attahiru Jega notes, most Africanist scholars now admit that "primordial sentiments" or ethnic identities "are increasingly creating, recreating and reinforcing centrifugal forms of politics, often check-mating and decisively overcoming those few unifying tendencies engendered by the postcolonial state."[60] It is therefore critical, according to Jega, that, in the context of economic crisis and the "global resurgence of democracy," we "investigate how the resurgence of the politics of identities relates to, or feeds into, the democratisation processes of plural, peripheral and dependent capitalist societies such as Nigeria."[61] Within this framework, Eghosa Osaghae has shown convincingly that "ethnic political mobilization has become more pervasive in Nigeria since the 1990s" in response to the "aggravated crisis of legitimacy that has engulfed the state . . . the weakness of alternative identities and political units, the prevailing milieu of lawlessness that has enveloped the country's political landscape, and the inability of the state to act as an effective agency of distributive justice."[62]

Against this backdrop, Okwudiba Nnoli, despite elaborating on the negative consequences of ethnicity and ethnic groups[63]—which are often the bases, as well as the outcomes, of ethnic politics in most sub-Saharan African states,[64] and in Nigeria, in particular—notes two important elements of ethnicity that are useful for my understanding of ethnic politics in the context of this book. The first is ethnicity's critical "mediatory role in mass societies that are complex, impersonal and alienating."[65] In this context, as is evident in the Gani Adams case, "ethnicity offers a *personal* solution to the generic problems of exploitation, oppression, deprivation and alienation."[66] The second is what Nnoli describes as "a democratic side" to ethnicity in the context of "social struggles . . . concern[ed with] injustice in the distribution of resources" and the "issues of domination, exploitation and oppression."[67] Thus, ethnicity can potentially be "harnessed in the drive for equality, justice, and in the struggle to redress injury caused to a group"[68] or suffered by individuals in society. Nnoli shows that the social struggles in which ethnicity is enfolded "are associated with the demand for democratisaton of the society's decision-making process":[69] "This is part of the overall demand of the masses *to be subjects rather than object of governance.*

Through the use of ethnic solidarity, they hope to bring the government closer to the people. Their demand is part of their search for a structure of government that provides them with unfettered initiative and democracy in the functioning and development of their society, and gives scope to their creative initiative."[70]

I argue that this approach to understanding ethnic politics (as represented, for instance, by the OPC) in the context of the struggle for and sustenance of democratic rule (as it manifested in Nigeria's First,[71] Second,[72] and Third Republics[73]), as well as the democratic transition[74] that led to Nigeria's Fourth Republic,[75] can bring into sharp relief the OPC phenomenon and Adams's own insertion in these processes. This is particularly so given that the formation of the OPC and Adams's own sense of social mission have been driven by a particular reading of the "mediatory" and "democratic roles" of ethnicity in confronting what the late Nigerian economist Bade Onimode regarded as "the persistent domination of the country by conservative winning coalitions from the north—both civilian and military"—that had imposed an "incompetent hegemony" over the country.[76] It is, therefore, illuminating to examine how the OPC and Adams framed the socioeconomic and political challenges of Nigeria—particularly in terms of their effects on the members of the social class that Adams belonged to at the start of his engagement with human rights and prodemocracy groups—in the language of ethnicity and within the context of plebeian nationalism.

Ethnic politics in Nigeria and the democratic transitions are both literally and metaphorically fueled by oil resources. This is why, as explicated in chapter 5, the politics of "resource control" intersects with ethnic and ethno-regional politics as well as the question of democracy. *Resource control* points to the struggle by oil-bearing states in Nigeria for a greater share of the revenues that accrue to the federation purse from the proceeds of crude oil sales.[77] However, as a petro-state, Nigeria is dominated by the politics of consumption, which subsumes even the most elaborate process of equity in resource distribution to the elite struggle for access and accumulation. As Terry Lynn Karl has argued, "Petro-states . . . rely on an unsustainable development trajectory fueled by an exhaustible resource—and the very rents produced by this resource form an implacable barrier to change."[78]

BECOMING YORUBA

The literature on the Yorùbá is vast.[79] The group and its subgroups have attracted and continue to attract a lot of attention from scholars in different disciplines. One of the most interesting dimensions of the study of the Yoruba, as Andrew Apter notes,[80] is that a substantial part of this literature is produced by the Yorùbá themselves. Thus, the process of *becoming Yorùbá* in modern times—that is, the construction of a single Yorùbá identity beginning from the mid-nineteenth century—is as much about how the Yorùbá define themselves as about how they have been shaped in their interactions with others, including encounters with neighboring ethnic groups as well as missionary and colonial contact.[81]

Broadly, among Yorùbá scholars, two axles form the basis of the positioning of the Yorùbá in relation to themselves and to the world from ancient times to the present: the Oyo-centric and the Ife-centric approaches. Though most Yorùbá acknowledge Ile-Ife as being at the center of Yorùbá origin (and the creation myth) and also acknowledge Ile-Ife's Oduduwa as their progenitor, the Oyo Empire, with its capital at Oyo-Ile, was founded by Oduduwa's grandson[82] and became the greatest and most powerful of the ancient Yorùbá kingdoms.[83] The two therefore represent a rival reference point in the evolution of the Yorùbá.[84]

These approaches are illustrated in two histories of the Yorùbá written by major Yorùbá intellectuals of their age, *The History of the Yorubas: From the Earliest Times to the Beginning of the British Protectorate*, authored by the lay historian Samuel Johnson and first published in 1921, and *A History of the Yoruba People*, authored by the academic historian S. Adebanji Akintoye and published almost ninety years later. While Johnson took an Oyo-centric approach, Akintoye's is an Ife-centric history. Johnson considered the most glorious era of Yorùbá history to be the period of "universal peace with prosperity and advancement" and the welding into one of "the disjointed units [of the Yoruba] under one head," under the king of Oyo-Ile, *Aláàfin* Abiodun.[85] However, for Akintoye, the most glorious era, when the kingdom grew and prospered at home and "also became the source of inspiration for major political changes in Yorubaland in general," took place when Oduduwa was the king of Ile-Ife.[86]

The two latest attempts at a comprehensive history of the Yoruba, Aribidesi Usman and Toyin Falola's *The Yoruba from Prehistory to the Present*[87] and Akinwunmi Ogundiran's *The Yoruba: A New History*,[88] sidestep this binary grounding of Yorùbá history as informed by the Ife or Oyo traditions.[89] However, Ogundiran challenges extant literature—and the lay "consensus"—on what is regarded as the *recency*, or the *modern* construction, of collective Yorùbá identity. His approach is therefore useful in understanding how the OPC's sociocultural-political project is based on this identity. I have argued[90] that John D. Y. Peel's and David Laitin's reflections on modern Yorùbá identity[91] can illuminate the rupture that the OPC case represents in the context of the democratic denouement,[92] which constitutes what Laitin describes as "a new arena for democratic action."[93] According to Peel, the modern Yorùbá identity in the twentieth century was facilitated by the reconfiguration of Yorubaness around Christianity and the associated discourses of enlightenment, development, and civilization (òlàjú), despite the violence that dominated the Yorùbá country in the nineteenth century.[94] Peel acknowledges the "unusual vitality, adaptiveness, and tenacity" of Yorùbá indigenous religious culture,[95] yet, on the basis of massive archival evidence, he understands the modern, unified Yorùbá identity to be a product of the imaginative projects of early Christian Yorùbá themselves. The project, Peel argues, was partly a response to the racial discrimination, social exclusion, and disparagement of indigenous culture in the colonial—and, to some extent, the missionary—context that provoked the educated Yorùbá in the late nineteenth and early twentieth centuries to reassert their dignity as a race/nation by returning to their roots. This cultural nationalism, with the simultaneous validation of African tradition and the assimilation of European modernity,[96] raised a paradox that, as Emmanuel Ayandele noted,[97] was obviously overlooked by most of the educated people. There appears to be a parallel in the emergence of the OPC in late twentieth-century Yorubaland.

In the case of the OPC, subaltern Yorùbá youths were responding to perceived ethno-regional domination and discrimination on the part of the Hausa-Fulani North. The disparagement led them to reassert the dignity of their ethnic group through a "return to culture." But, unlike those in the era described by Peel, modern manifestations of cultural nationalism among Yorùbá youths are set against a postcolonial state and its perceived hegemonic ethnic group. Moreover, whereas in the earlier era such assertions and validations paradoxically drew, as Peel shows, on the "liberation theology" of Christianity, the recent "retraditionalization" has taken place, equally paradoxically, within discourses of universal human rights, justice, equity, and democracy. It is important then to see tradition not just as a site of values and identity but also as an active political resource.

Even though he does not contest the role that Peel claims Christianity played in the making of modern Yorùbá identity, David Laitin demonstrates the uses of the Yorùbá cultural identity in the late twentieth century as a marker for collective political action in the context of the "non-politicisation of religious differentiation" among Muslim and Christian Yoruba. Laitin shows that Yorùbá adherents of Christianity and Islam see themselves culturally and essentially as Yorùbá rather than as Muslims or Christians.[98] While Laitin's work does not encompass recent transformations (in the 1990s and beyond),[99] it offers an important perspective by emphasizing the political instrumentalization of Yorùbá culture.[100]

However, in a rejection of Peel's thesis and a possible partial endorsement of Laitin's position, Ogundiran argues that to understand the Yorùbá properly in the *longue durée,* one must approach the category as a "cultural group" rather than as an "ethnic group" or a "nation."[101] He believes this approach can "restore agency, dynamism, and movement" to their "historical experience before the nineteenth century,"[102] which constitutes the departure point for Peel's analysis. Therefore, if the Yorùbá as a "cultural group," rather than as an "ethnic group" or a "nation," is our departure point, Ogundiran advances that the category would become "a marker of practices, networks, self-consciousness, and interconnectedness that constitute our subject's sociological and historical reality."[103] Such practices and networks can be reconstructed from AD 500 to 1840. The archaeologist argues that by avoiding the "encumbrances" of the "atemporal, geographically bounded, static, and tribal model of ethnicity and identity" bequeathed by European colonial ethnography and historiography, we can demonstrate how "individuals and social groups *became Yoruba through learning, and creating and participating in emergent knowledge production, communicative interactions, and regional social networks.*"[104]

While I do not share the rejection of Peel's persuasive and evidence-based argument that the particular understanding and contours of contemporary Yorùbá identity were largely determined by (Yoruba) missionary Christianity in the late nineteenth and early twentieth centuries,[105] as demonstrated by the embrace of modernity, Enlightenment, and civilization[106] (a movement that achieved its zenith in Obafemi Awolowo's project of the remaking of the Yorùbá in the second half of the twentieth century),[107] I take Ogundiran's point about the fundamental nature of the "cultural group." Thus, *becoming* or *being Yorùbá* would, in particular instances, primarily involve everyday "learning, and creating and participating in emergent knowledge production, communicative interactions, and regional social networks." In this way, whatever constituted the trajectory of this identity in ancient times, the specific form of Yorùbá cultural identity that emerged from the late nineteenth and early twentieth centuries and was deployed for ethno-political purposes, particularly from the fourth decade of the twentieth century, remains a daily work in progress. Hence, the members of the OPC, and particularly Gani Adams, mobilize the cultural knowledge learned, created, produced, and reproduced to (re)affirm that identity—as both a cultural and an ethnic group—in their interactions with others and, specifically, in the creation and expansion of Adams's social networks, both within and beyond the cultural/ethnic group.

Importantly, the OPC case presents a strong challenge to the bifurcation of tradition and modernity in the contexts of the group's appropriation of "culture"—as a "tool kit" that "contains diverse, often conflicting symbols, rituals, stories, and guides to action" from which they selected specific pieces[108]—in negotiating Yorùbá identity while retaining a powerful democratic rhetoric of citizenship, rights, equity, and justice. While the primary motive of late nineteenth-century cultural nationalism was to write Christianity into Yorùbá culture and history[109] and thus appropriate the emergent attributes of òlàjú as a precondition for "greater effectiveness and prosperity,"[110] the contemporary task of the OPC can be seen as writing a complicated modernity[111] (rather than Christianity per se) into Yorùbá culture and history, and writing Yorùbá culture into modernity, in the political encounters with other ethnic groups and the Nigerian state. But, as Peel states, "in relating themselves to this heritage, the main strategic choice faced by contemporary Yoruba has been where to place the continuities and where the ruptures from what has gone before."[112]

In this book, I explore some aspects of this "strategic choice" and the attendant reconfiguration of Yorubaness. In particular, I examine the role of ritual and violence in the negotiation of power within a sociopolitical formation that is marked by uncertainties. I proceed from a strong conviction that it is difficult and largely unrewarding in this context to draw a line between polarities such as tradition/modernity and rationality/irrationality. The actions of OPC members, particularly of the group's most significant symbol, Gani Adams, are difficult to understand if we are locked in such antinomies.

POLITICO-PERSONAL CONTENTIONS: ACCOUNTING FOR THE EMERGENCE OF THE OPC

Critical to the formation of the OPC is an account of the political history of Nigeria, especially its long period of military rule, during which mostly northern military officers held sway. This account is generally shared among the Yoruba. A core concern of this account is that the Hausa-Fulani power elite, using the military, made an orchestrated and elaborate attempt to "emasculate" the other ethnic nationalities, particularly the Yoruba. As Gani Adams captures it,

> We of the Oodua People's Congress hereby make it categorically clear to the people of the world that the threat to peace, security and unity [and] the corporate existence of Nigeria today is the handwork of the Hausa-Fulani oligarchs. Of the thirty-nine years of the existence of Nigeria, the North ruled and dominated other ethnic nationalities for thirty-four years. Nigeria's more than 250 ethnic groups have long experienced uneasy relations. The relations between the so-called mega-tribes—the Hausa-Fulani in the North, the Igbo in the East, and the Yorùbá in the West—have been central to Nigeria's postindependence politics.[113]

Frederick Fasehun, the founding leader of the OPC, renders a similar state of affairs by focusing on the annulled election. The OPC, he notes, is "dedicated

Figure 1.7. The OPC (Frederick Fasehun faction) logo

to salvaging our race from the cesspool of disgrace into which the annulment of June 12 [the 1993 presidential election] had collectively cast the children of Oduduwa."[114]

The "mythico-history"—to use Malkki's phrase[115]—constantly rehearsed by the leading voices in the early years of the OPC often simplified the complex history of ethnicity and politics in Nigeria, as might be expected. But, as the literature on ethnicity and nationalism reminds us,[116] the reality is often far more complex than ethnic entrepreneurs are willing to admit.

The annulment of the June 12, 1993, presidential election provided an opportunity, by default, for the public articulation of many of the issues confronting Nigeria. But, as it turned out, this program, succinctly described by Richard Joseph as "one of the most sustained exercises in political chicanery,"[117] was soon exposed as an attempt by the soldiers, particularly the military president, to cling to power. After many twists and turns, presidential elections were held on June 12, 1993. Although there was no official announcement of the total results, Moshood Abiola, a Yorùbá billionaire businessman and publisher, was widely believed to have won. The Babangida regime annulled the elections. The national paralysis that followed the battle to validate the election results pitted southerners, particularly the Yorùbá West, against the Hausa-Fulani North.

The annulment of this election formed the immediate backdrop to the creation of the OPC, which took its name from the shortened form for the mythical progenitor of the Yorùbá people, Oduduwa (also rendered as O'odua or Oodua). From the preceding sociopolitical events, many Yoruba, particularly those who formed or joined the OPC, concluded that the rival Hausa-Fulani had resolved to undermine the other ethnic groups in Nigeria, particularly the Yoruba. What started as a struggle for democratic rule and against autocracy, injustice, and inequity—using what Mamadou Diouf characterizes as "a language of . . . universal rights"—devolved into an ethno-nationalist struggle against what was regarded as an ethno-regional conspiracy against the Yorùbá manifesting as military autocracy.[118] The youthful members of the group under Adams's leadership regarded this as an opportunity for the Yorùbá to secede from Nigeria.

Frederick Fasehun, a medical doctor, civil rights activist, and onetime presidential aspirant, called the annulment of the 1993 presidential election the "last straw" for the Yorùbá:

> The most momentous event in Nigeria's contemporary history, General Ibrahim Babangida's annulment of the June 12 presidential election[119] that Abiola won in 1993, *was an affront and a crime against a Yoruba man*. Yet the Yoruba people, who should have naturally led the vanguard of those resisting that dastardly act, could not do so because,[120] though they felt a common grief, they lacked the unity required to marshal a befitting confrontation. . . . A people numerically strong, educationally powerful and legendarily sophisticated as the Yoruba lost out in the game of wits. No Yoruba man alive was proud of such *a collective display of racial impotence*. . . . But the real tragedy of the June 12 case dwelt not on the fact that we Yoruba had been robbed of an age-long dream to take our place in the country's leadership, but that history appeared likely to repeat itself. . . . It occurred to me that a recurrence must be pre-emptively countervailed.[121]

For this reason, Fasehun formed the OPC.

However, despite Fasehun's narrative of "racial [read ethnic] impotence," Yorùbá politicians, activists, intellectuals, and other professionals were in the vanguard of the struggle against the annulment of the 1993 presidential election and the wider struggle for democratic rule, justice, and equity in Nigeria. At the initial stage, they and other Nigerians pursued the struggle on a common front as a *national* prodemocracy struggle. In fact, both Fasehun and Adams were initially members of the CD, one of the leading prodemocracy organizations, and the Joint Action Committee (JACON), led by famous lawyer Chief Gani Fawehinmi. However, matters came to a head for the OPC founders when General Sani Abacha, Babangida's army chief, seized power from the ambivalent Interim National Government (ING) in November 1993, eighty-four days after

Babangida was forced to hand over power. Abacha appeared ready for a long haul in office, despite initially pretending to have taken power to prepare the grounds for the validation of Abiola's widely acknowledged victory in the 1993 presidential election. When it became clear that Abacha had a long-term plan and was set to become Nigeria's most vicious dictator, Abiola declared himself president in June 1994. He was later arrested, detained, and tried for treason. The Yorùbá, and the OPC in particular, regarded Abiola's arrest and trial as the height of injustice and humiliation.

"The miscalculated attempt of the ruling oligarchy, the power drunk elites, to deal a last blow on the Yoruba's [*sic*]," Adams writes in his book, "was the daylight robbery of the June 12 presidential election. It was a criminal act as well as a retrogressive annulment of the freest and fairest election in the history of Nigeria. . . . And the Yoruba felt enough was enough. Hence, the Oodua People's Congress came into being."[122]

The two factions that emerged four years after the founding of the OPC, the Fasehun and the Adams factions, render different accounts of that founding and of the founding members. These accounts are significant for three important reasons. First, involvement in the founding of a group—especially one that is as successful as the OPC—confers a certain critical legitimacy on anyone involved. Apart from the fact that such legitimacy implies that one cannot be told the story of the group,[123] it also indicates an *original* investment in the group's fate, fortunes, and future. Second, being present at the inception gives one a claim to supreme *priority*; the fight over the founding history is central to claims about which of the two leaders and groups had the more legitimate claim to primacy. Third, given how successful, and even *resourceful* in both material and immaterial senses, the OPC became, a founder would have the additional benefit of being regarded as a visionary and achiever with the capacity to see what is in the horizon and respond to present and future challenges. Therefore, Fasehun and Adams's struggle to determine who was present at the founding of the OPC is both understandable and interesting.

According to Fasehun, he alone conceived of the group and was therefore the sole founder. He claims, "I decided to start a sociocultural organisation that would promote unity among my Yorùbá nationality group."[124] He adds that he then contacted three people, Mrs. Idowu Adebowale (popularly known as Iya-Ijebu), Alhaji Ibrahim (popularly called Baba Oja) and Mr. Taiwo (the latter two have now passed). All three "were popular market leaders" at Asimawu Market in the Mushin area of Lagos. He said that he asked each to bring one person along to the first meeting on August 29, 1994.[125] Therefore, the inaugural meeting, in Fasehun's account, was attended by seven people: himself,

Figure 1.8. The OPC (Adams faction) logo

the three people he invited, and the three people they invited along. Fasehun describes the "foundation members"—with the exemption of Taiwo, "a semi-literate retired military officer"[126]—as people "who did not share the benefit of a good education, [though] each was a leader in his own right." He adds that "what they lacked in didactic education, they made up for in native intelligence, common sense and grassroots understanding."[127] This is significant, as I will show shortly, because Fasehun later dismissed Adams and his comrades on the basis of their "illiteracy" (rather than their lack of "the benefit of a good education"). He also notes that "some more educated individuals [who] expressed the desire to join the organisation . . . felt discouraged by the low literacy of its pioneer members," though two of his educated young friends "saw beyond the superficiality of educational qualifications, and felt attracted by the sheer grassroots nature of the platform and the vision of its Founder."[128]

Fasehun states that he asked the members he recruited to also invite more market men and women to join the group. He adds that four potential names for the organization were proposed at the second meeting and that the majority favored Oduduwa People's Congress. A law undergraduate, Adewole Adebayo, later joined to take charge of the secretariat of the new group. Other prominent civil rights activists and lawyers such as Baba Omojola and Femi Falana (later a senior advocate of Nigeria, SAN) also joined. These new members, particularly Omojola and Falana, were also members of the CD, which had a strong presence in Mushin, the low-income area of mainland Lagos—which, to borrow Henrik Vigh's description of the Aguentas, is dominated by "young, marginal men [and women], inhabiting a social space of restricted possibilities"[129]—where the CD often recruited those who led major prodemocracy and human rights protests. Fasehun acknowledges that, at the inception, it was difficult to distinguish CD members from OPC members.

Adams lived in Mushin at this point. Sandra Barnes, in her compelling account of the creation of a "political community in metropolitan Lagos" that focuses on Mushin between the 1960s and the early 1980s—an area she describes by the mid-1980s as "a recent suburb with a reputation for disorder"[130]—brings attention to a few people in "an African city who began at the bottom of their society's structure of power, acquired resources, and developed political skills."[131] However, unlike those on whom Barnes focused, Adams eventually transcended Mushin in the power structure and political skills he developed and the resources he acquired.

Adams was the publicity secretary of the CD in Mushin Local Government Area and therefore knew the leading activists, including Fasehun, Omojola, Falana, and Beko Ransome-Kuti, Fasehun's close friend and a medical doctor who chaired the CD. Adams's narrative of the founding of the OPC is significantly different from Fasehun's. Though, unlike Fasehun, Adams does not provide a particular date for the first meeting of the people who formed the OPC, he also places the founding in 1994. He claims in his book that he was "a founding member."[132] In the book, which was ostensibly published solely to respond to Fasehun's books (particularly the second, *OPC: Our History, Our Mission*),[133] Adams states that any account contrary to his would be based on the "egotistic reasons" of those who wanted "to manipulate [the] historical record or better still, skew the contents of history."[134] He describes the account of the founding of the OPC in Fasehun's first book as an attempt "to re-write a known history about the OPC."[135]

Adams claims that nine people attended the inaugural meeting of the OPC, not the seven indicated by Fasehun.[136] In Adams's account, only two of those on Fasehun's list, Fasehun and Mrs. Idowu Adebowale, attended the inaugural meeting. Adams's list of founding members includes Dr. Frederick Fasehun, Mr. Gani Adams, Mr. Tony Engurube (deceased; interestingly enough, he was an Ijaw and Fasehun's friend),[137] Mrs. Idowu Adebowale, Mr. Ibrahim Atanda (deceased), Alhaji Ibrahim Abobanawo (deceased), Mr. Silas Atanda, Evangelist Kunle Adesokan (later secretary-general of Adams's faction), and Comrade Olumide Adeniji (later chair of the Welfare Committee, Adams's faction, now deceased).[138] Whereas Fasehun claims that Adams joined the OPC while Fasehun was detained by the military regime, though he knew him earlier as one of the officials of the CD in Mushin who had been "brought along to one of the [OPC] meetings,"[139] Adams claims that he was at "the inaugural meeting [where] Dr. Fredrick [*sic*] Fasehun was unanimously picked as the leader of the Congress."[140]

—⁂—

I will pause here to note the significance of the role of Tony Engurube, a non-Yorùbá (who, according to his comrades, spoke excellent Yorùbá), in the formation of the OPC. Although both Fasehun and Adams have acknowledged that the late Engurube played such a role, neither has conceded its pivotal nature. Also, both men, either in ignorance or by deliberate omission, have failed to insert Engurube's role in the larger social context of the time. As Engurube's surviving comrades revealed to me, Engurube was the one who suggested to Fasehun, on behalf of the members of the Nigerian Left (Marxist thinkers, labor activists, intellectual, ex- and current student union leaders, human rights activists, and prodemocracy campaigners, etc.), that the Yorùbá should form a militant nationalist group in the face of what they regarded as the unrelenting ethno-regional nature of the Nigerian crisis under the northern-dominated military rule. Engurube encouraged the formation of something similar among his Ijaw constituents in the Niger Delta region. Engurube was a member of the Patriotic Labor Movement (PLM), which emerged from and in conjunction with another group, the Forward Group (FG)—the latter formed by former University of Ife (now Obafemi Awolowo University) Marxists and student activists. PLM later merged with Socialists Revolutionary Vanguard (SRV), which was formed by older Marxists.

Engurube was a key member of this leftist movement, and, according to his comrades, his suggestion about forming an ethnic militia for the Yorùbá and the Ijaw emerged in the context of the debates on the nationality/self-determination question among Nigerian Marxists in the late 1990s. According to one member of the group, members were convinced of "the need to build a militia founded on the idea of revolutionary and ideological clarity in its mechanics, actions and organization."[141] My source, who was a member of the PLM and SRV, clarified that Engurube had been given the mandate to discuss the idea with Fasehun, who embraced it. Some of the SRV members had even found a location where the "cadre" would be trained to fight the "hegemony imposed" on the country, another source revealed. However, my source concluded that "unfortunately, after the formation of the OPC, [they] fell short of following through by reining ideological and revolutionary clarity on the group, leading to instinctive actions and ultimately virtual derailment of the initial ideas that led to its formation."[142]

—⁂—

To continue with the debate between Fasehun and Adams about the founding of OPC and those who participated, the fact that Adams, whom Fasehun later described as a "bony youth,"[143] did not provide a particular date for when the group first met would seem to vitiate his account about his presence at that meeting. However, given the limitations of his education and his social conditions at that point, it might be argued that Adams was less able to keep documentary evidence of the meeting. Yet, as the publicity secretary of the CD in the same period, he would have been expected to maintain similar records. Since all the people on Fasehun's list are dead except one, Mrs. Idowu Adebowale, and since she is the only one alive who appears on both lists, she is in a good position to confirm whose claim to priority is valid. Unfortunately, I could not reach her. Everyone who promised to find out how to contact her failed to obtain any useful information. Apart from Adebowale, the only other person on Adams's list who is still alive is Evangelist Kunle Adesokan, the first secretary-general of the Adams faction. Fasehun describes him variously as "a seasoned traditionalist"[144] with a disarming gift with the Yorùbá language,[145] one of those who helped build OPC branches all over Yorubaland,[146] and, later, as "the director of the propaganda laboratory" of the Adams faction.[147] I asked Adesokan about the veracity of the claims of both men.

Adesokan told me categorically that he was not at the initial meetings of the OPC.[148] However, he added that, "if there is a need to 'stretch' the meaning of 'founding members,'" then he and Adams could qualify. Such stretching would not be faithful to Adams's claims that he was present at the founding of the group. Adesokan explained that he could not have been a founding member of the OPC, as Adams claims, because at the time, in 1994, he was a member of the Nigerian Labour Congress (NLC), representing the General Metal Product (GMP), where he was a mechanical craft engineer. "Before OPC was formed, most of those who became the initial members of the OPC were in Campaign for Democracy," Adesokan explained. He continued,

> While still in the CD, Dr. Fasehun formed the Movement for Social and Economic Justice [MSEJ]. Fasehun and Adams knew each other in CD. Fasehun was the national treasurer of the CD [under Dr. Beko Ransome-Kuti's leadership]. But he was like the boss of CD in Mushin where Gani [Adams] was the publicity secretary. Even there, they didn't get along too well. Gani was always questioning why Fasehun would hold meetings with other important people without taking him and others along. Fasehun used to wonder why "this young man" would want to be with him when he [Fasehun] was visiting important people. Anyway, because of the nature of their relationship, Adams swore that he would never join any organization founded by Fasehun. When

Figure 1.9. Adams, evangelist Kunle Adesokan, and other members of the Adams faction during the inauguration of the Agbado-Oke Odo Local Government Area chapter of the OPC around 1999. Photo courtesy of *TELL*.

> Fasehun started the MSEJ, Adams joined the Oodua Youth Movement. But after a couple of years after I left the NLC because I was no longer working for GMP, I joined OPC.[149]

Adesokan added, "Adams later came to me to say that he wanted to join the OPC because he saw a vision that the OPC would be a large and great organization. So I took him to the meeting of the OPC in Pa Taiwo's house. At this point, Dr. Fasehun was in detention. He was not around, so we were meeting in Pa Taiwo's house. When we got there, they didn't want Gani to join the group. Most of the members were in CD, so they knew Gani and didn't want his troubles. I begged them, and they accepted him." Fasehun, he said, was not happy when he found out that Adams had joined the OPC.

Adesokan explained further that Adams's first meeting incidentally coincided with the day the group was debating what to do while Fasehun was incarcerated. At this point, the group had only a few members, was unknown to most people, and was partially underground. The older members did not want the group to be active while the leader was away. Adesokan said he proposed that a committee be set up to plan activities for the group. The elders countered that Fasehun had instructed them not to do anything until he returned. All the young people in the group, including Adams, supported him, Adesokan claimed. There was a split along generational lines. At the end of the contentious meeting, Adesokan said he retired to his Olusoga, Mushin zone, which happened to be the strongest zone in the congress. Most of the young people followed him there and reaffirmed their support for his position. He explains,

> Two weeks later, Papa [Adekunle] Ajasin [the leader of the main opposition coalition, the National Democratic Coalition, NADECO] died. So the youth who were with me mandated a five-man committee to plan for our involvement in the burial of Ajasin. We made white *kembe* [wide-mouthed traditional trousers popular in the past] and *dansiki* [traditional top] and put *ori Olokun* crest on it. There were only about twenty of us in the group. We wore the same white clothes and appeared at the Eko Club on Adeniran Ogunsanya Street. The police had threatened that there should be no lying-in-state for Ajasin in Lagos. *Afenifere* organized the lying-in-state, anyhow. We went there and started dancing and celebrating Ajasin's life. We took the coffin, carried it on our head, and danced around within [the] area, including in front of the police station. The police could do nothing. Everyone in the area saw us and became aware of the OPC for the first time. The press also reported what we did. This was how OPC came out big in public.

Fasehun claims that he gave the order from detention that his followers must participate in the burial plans for Ajasin.[150] Adesokan denied this, insisting that their participation in Ajasin's burial was the initiative of the young people, under his leadership.[151] However, Adesokan conceded that "Gani Adams played a pivotal role in OPC because he saw a vision. He said it will be a big organization, that no other organization in Yorubaland will have as many members." For Adesokan, this vision is important because even Fasehun never imagined the significance the OPC would later gain. He added that the group only had a handful of members in the first four years of existence, until he and Adams mobilized young people all over Yorubaland to join. Adesokan, who claimed to have been the "engine room" of the massive recruitment drive, said he went to every nook and cranny of Yorubaland to recruit members. The former secretary general of the Adams faction said that when Fasehun was released from detention after Abacha's death in June 1998, he was shocked to see the huge increase in the membership. "When Fasehun came back, he was expecting about forty members in the group. But he found that we had grown to more than five thousand members. He was shocked. Even *Afenifere* [the political organization of progressive Yorùbá politicians] was afraid of our strength because we had announced our opposition to the transition [to civil rule] program. We were also working with JACON, which also insisted on 'no transition.' Our position was that Abiola must be released and installed as president," said Adesokan.

However, in Adams's rendering of the pertinent history of the OPC, though Fasehun was the first leader, as a founding member Adams had *primary* belonging in and to the group and, therefore, as much legitimacy to embody the group as any other founding member. He also claimed to have remained faithful to the founding ethos of the group, from which Fasehun purportedly deviated. Contrariwise, Fasehun claimed—and insisted until he died in 2018—that he was the sole embodiment of the group, adding that it was Adams and those who followed him who deviated from the core principles of the congress and betrayed him and the Yorùbá cause. In his book, he wonders why Adams "thought [the] OPC was founded at the time he [Adam] joined."[152]

Curiously, Silas Alani, who claims to be a founding member of the OPC, contests the core narratives of the founding as rendered by both Fasehun and Adams.[153] I discovered him very late in my research. His name was mentioned only in late 2021 by one of my sources. When I contacted him, he insisted that the time was not ripe for the OPC story because the goal of "securing self-determination" for the Yorùbá had not been achieved.[154] He told me a few things that no one else could corroborate, even while insisting that there was no reason yet for anyone to try to write the history of the OPC. Among other claims, Alani insisted that (1) the OPC was not created in 1994, the year that Fasehun and Adams and others have indicated (he said the group was founded in 1995); (2) it is wrong for Fasehun to claim to be the founder of the group; (3) about seven non-Yorùbá were involved in the founding of the OPC; (4) the "founding documents" of the OPC are only in his possession; and (5) there was an inner core of the OPC that many of even the early members were and remain unaware of.

Interestingly enough, I found that Fasehun, in *OPC: Our History, Our Mission*, mentions Alani. Fasehun writes that after he had asked three of his "foundation contacts" to invite one person each to the second meeting of the group on September 12, 1994, he also invited two young people, Wale Adebayo, a law student and his close associate, and Silas Alani, whom he describes as "a motel keeper at Ilasa" in Lagos.[155] He also credited Alani with being among the "major players" who, in the first two years of the OPC, helped the group in "quietly ramifying and penetrating deep into Yorubaland."[156] However, Alani conceded that, like himself, Adams was one of the "founding members." He told me that he left the group shortly after it was formed because the secret police were on his trail. He said he went underground for a while and never participated in the activities of the group publicly again. It would appear that Alani was overdramatizing his role in the foundation of the OPC, although Adams knows him well as one of the earliest members.

The clashing views about the original membership of the group are directly related to the question of who could claim to have remained true to the original ideals that necessitated its founding. Not surprisingly, each accuses the other of violating the original principles of the group in addition to betraying both corporate and personal trusts.

(FR)ENEMIES WITHIN?[157]

What caused the division in the OPC that led to the creation of the Adams faction? In this section, I consider the many dimensions of the split from the perspective of both leaders while offering an analysis of their narratives.

General Sani Abacha, Nigeria's top ruler and the most vicious and murderous dictator in the country's history, died suddenly on June 8, 1998. The country was relieved. Shortly after the new head of state, General Abubakar Abdulsalami, was installed, he announced a short transition program that would return the country to democratic rule within one year, on May 27, 1999. At the time of Abacha's death, Fasehun was in detention in Lagos on false accusations regarding his activities in NADECO. He was released—along with most of the political detainees all over the country—about two weeks later.

After his release, Fasehun argued that the OPC should participate in the new transition program. Given the country's emerging consensus that a Yorùbá man should become the next president, so as to "compensate" the Yorùbá for the annulment of the June 12, 1993, presidential election, and given the eventual emergence of two Yorùbá presidential candidates, Olusegun Obasanjo (of the People's Democratic Party [PDP]) and Olu Falae (All People's Party [APP] / Alliance for Democracy [AD]), Fasehun argued that the group should endorse the transition to civil rule and the electoral process that would lead to the Fourth Republic. As he states in his self-titled book,

> We were all prepared to cooperate with him [General Abubakar Abdulsalami] to see the back of the military and welcome civil rule that would graduate to democracy. Only professional agitators were determined to go on agitating. But the sane knew that a civilian government would be easier to negotiate with, and would be more open to persuasion on the need to hold democratic dialogue at a national conference. . . . OPC was later convinced to give the transition a chance lest people accuse the organisation of not allowing democracy to be ushered into Nigeria. . . . [Yet] As a socio-cultural outfit, OPC should not be partisan. This is why the leadership felt free discussing with Yorùbá politicians despite their sophistry.[158]

As the country's powerful forces organized around General Olusegun Obasanjo (retired)—the former head of state who had been released from

Figure 1.10. Adams and Fasehun at a public event after the truce. Photo courtesy of *Nigerian Tribune*.

Abacha's jail a few months earlier—to ensure that he was elected as the candidate of the PDP and eventually the president, Obasanjo was eager to meet the leader of the OPC, which was emerging as a critical social force in his home region of Southwest Nigeria. According to Fasehun, a woman, Yemisi Akinyeye, who was called Lady B (or Lady Bee) in the OPC circle, approached Fasehun on Obasanjo's behalf to persuade him to meet Obasanjo in his Ota home. Lady B seemed a shadowy figure to Fasehun, though she claimed to be Obasanjo's relative.[159] Adams,[160] Rasaq Arogundade Balogun,[161] and another zonal coordinator of the group, Jubril Ogundimu,[162] alleged that she was a security agent. Fasehun states that he was reluctant to meet Obasanjo and thrice found excuses to frustrate the meetings planned by Lady B. When he told the OPC about the request to meet, he writes, he "was *mandated* [by the group] to see Obasanjo."[163] However, in the second book, he adds that "everyone present at that meeting, *except Gani* [Adams], voted in favour of the meeting [with Obasanjo]."[164] Indeed, Jubril Ogundimu told me that Adams was never happy with Fasehun's habit of meeting important people without taking any of the key members of the group with him. According to Ogundimu, "Adams thought Fasehun should be involving him in these meetings with both local and foreign personalities.

But Fasehun didn't like to share information. He used to say 'three is a crowd.' . . . Fasehun later told us to save him from the harassment of Adams and others. He brought out a book to show us that he has been spending his money on the OPC since 1994. He also showed us where he wrote down every penny he gave to Adams and where Adams signed for the monies."[165]

In his books, Fasehun describes the meeting with Obasanjo on December 7, 1998, in the latter's farmhouse in Ota, Ogun State. He maintains that Obasanjo did not ask for his political support or any favor but wanted to know the aims and objectives of the OPC. When Fasehun told the retired general that the OPC stood for "the welfare and general well-being of every Yoruba," Obasanjo "canvassed the irrelevance of ethnicity nationality platforms."[166] But while in the first book Fasehun says that Obasanjo "never offered me any gift. There was no basis for it,"[167] in the second book, he adds that after he left Obasanjo, the latter's aide, who saw him to his car, "had a white envelope in his hand . . . tucked [it] into [his] driver, Teslim Akanji's hand."[168] However, he adds that he prevailed and did not accept it. When Lady B took the envelope and tried to stuff it into her handbag, Fasehun reportedly insisted that he would not let her drive back to Lagos with him with the money in her bag. She then reportedly opened the bag, only to find that it contained a paltry N2,000, which, Fasehun writes, could not have been meant for him. Lady B then returned the envelope to Obasanjo's aide. Fasehun writes that he reported the meeting with Obasanjo to the group and that the members thanked him "for avoiding partisan political discussions" during the meeting.[169]

A couple of weeks later, in Fasehun's account, a member of the group based in Okitipupa, Ondo State, met him in Lagos and "expressed disgust that [he] had accepted bribe money from Obasanjo." When Fasehun demanded to know how much he was alleged to have collected, the man told him N20 million. Though the man refused to disclose the source of his information, Fasehun recalled that Adams had visited Ondo State shortly before then to deliver a message to members of the group in another town. He concluded that Adams's visit "may have afforded the mischief maker the opportunity to start this bogus lie that spread like a [H]armattan forest fire."[170] To provide the context in which this "bogus lie" spread among the members of his group, Fasehun explains that "members of the organisation at that time were *an embodiment of poverty*. They were people who expected that any accrual through OPC leaders should filter down. If that failed to happen, *they were prepared to go to any length* to show their disapproval and anger."[171]

Though Fasehun states that Adams swore he was not behind the rumor, he did not believe Adams, who, he writes, "told various lies in succession to cover the original lie."[172] "It is far easier to believe a lie than to accept the truth," concludes Fasehun. "Members of the organisation with Gani Adams swallowed his fiction. With him as their model, they started holding clandestine meetings organised for their taking over of OPC."[173]

Adams's rendering of what happened is different from Fasehun's. In *My Life and Struggle,* Adams recalls he was at a meeting of the group when he received an "intelligent [*sic*] report through our information dragnets that one Lady B, 'a middle age woman,' *an infiltrator,* who was to have crept into the OPC[,] was negotiating a meeting between Dr. Fasehun and General Obasanjo."[174] Adams alleges that Lady B was "one of those who coordinated late General Sani Abacha's self-succession bid . . . under the aegis of Youth [E]arnestly [A]sk for Abacha [YEAA]."[175] Contrary to Fasehun's claim that his decision to meet Obasanjo was approved by the group and that only Adams objected, Adams recalls Fasehun bringing the issue "to the belated meeting of all state coordinators," where "everyone rebuffed him."[176] "He took it as an affront instead of cooling frayed nerves of his followers as a leader, an aged 'father.'" Adams then alleges, "We were made to believe at the Congress that at the Ota meeting with General Obasanjo, an undisclosed amount of money exchanged hands between him and our leader."[177]

Adesokan also disputed Fasehun's claims regarding his visit to Obasanjo. "Dr. Fasehun did not tell anyone in the group he was invited by Obasanjo or that he was going to visit him. He went with Lady B, his younger cousin who is a journalist, and another man." Adesokan added that members of the OPC got wind of the meeting from a report in a Lagos evening newspaper, *P.M. News,* written by Fasehun's cousin, McNezer Fasehun, with the headline "Obasanjo Woos OPC with N20 million." In truth, McNezer's story did not have such a headline and did not make any reference to any cash gift. The story was headlined "Obasanjo Woos Oodua Leader."[178] Yet many members believed the rumor that originated within the group that Fasehun's cousin had "betrayed" the truth about the OPC leader's meeting with Obasanjo. More than twenty-two years later, some members of the group still swear by the "revelation" in the *P.M. News.*

In the first few paragraphs of the story in the evening paper, the younger Fasehun reports,

> There are indications that former Head of State and presidential aspirant under the platform of the People's Democratic Party, PDP, General Olusegun Obasanjo has begun talks with Dr. Fredrick Fasehun, leader of pan-Yoruba group, the Oodua People's Congress, OPC. Although the thrust of the Otta farmer's discussion with the OPC leader was [not] clear as at press time,

> sources close to Dr. Fasehun told *PM News* that General Obasanjo invited Fasehun to his Otta farm in Ogun State yesterday for the parley. When the *PM News* learnt of General Obasanjo's invitation to the OPC leader, hours before the scheduled meeting yesterday, we spoke with Dr. Fasehun on the rationale behind the Otta farmer's new-found romance with the Oodua People's Congress which has been the butt of attacks by security agents in Lagos State. Said Dr. Fasehun: "Is General Obasanjo not a Yoruba man? Can we deny him his Yoruba citizenship because of the political party he belongs to?"[179]

In the report, the OPC leader reiterated that the group would have "nothing to do with political parties, the transition programme and whoever is participating or not" but added, "The Yorubas must learn to play safe politics such that if there is any of their own they would not support, they should for God's sake let the sleeping dog lie, *and* should not do anything to injure the interest of their brother."[180] The reporter concluded that "sources close to the Oodua People's Congress . . . revealed that General Obasanjo must have recognised that OPC has very firm control of the grassroots, and wants to capitalise on that to boost his chances in the presidential race."[181]

Perhaps what infuriated some members of the OPC was the indication that the OPC leader was not opposed to Obasanjo's ambition or the insinuation that Obasanjo would like "to capitalise" on the group's "very firm control of the grassroots." Or perhaps it was the fact that, as some of the members claimed, Fasehun did not consult them before meeting Obasanjo, which led to the false rumor about the newspaper headline. Whatever was responsible, some of the disgruntled members still believe that the evening newspaper published a story on the N20 million "gift" that Fasehun allegedly accepted from Obasanjo.

"When I saw it [the newspaper report on the N20 million]," Adesokan told me in 2021, "I ran to Dr. Fasehun, [who] told me that Obasanjo brought out some envelope that was big; however, he didn't know how much was in it, and he turned it down. I take people at their words. So I pleaded with members of the group since he said he didn't take the money."[182]

However, Adesokan said that, despite his intervention, the matter became "a big crisis." Because of the allegation, he added, "Gani started a campaign against Dr. Fasehun in OPC." Even before the subsequent disagreement over whether the group should participate in the transition program and before Fasehun's release, the youth and the elders had already been divided. "The earlier difference with Pa Taiwo and the elders [while Fasehun was incarcerated] was a minor division," stated Adesokan. "With this ideological difference [over participation in the transition program], we had a sharp division. This explains the reason for the other OPC led by Gani Adams."[183]

While Adams does not state categorically in his book that this was why he and others broke away from the Fasehun-led group, it is obviously one of the key reasons for his "rebellion" against the medical doctor. "I knew that since money is the root of all evils, the incident which could not be handled by our leader will either break or mar the Congress," Adams writes.[184]

While there is no way for me to confirm or dismiss the allegation against Fasehun, I initially found it implausible that Obasanjo would offer him any bribe at that point in his bid to be the presidential candidate of the PDP. First, Obasanjo is a notorious miser. Second, my sense is that, at that point in the process, Obasanjo did not yet need to buy the support of any group that was tangential at best, if not irrelevant, to his selection as the party's candidate. Though money later became dominant in the process of building political support among the politicians, at this point, beyond the political parties, and even among the OPC leaders themselves (in both factions, as later chapters will show), particularly after the new civilian administrations at the federal and state levels came into power, the OPC was still relatively insulated from exposure to huge financial inducements. Yet Fasehun's slightly varied accounts of the encounter in his two books, the story he allegedly told Adesokan, the credible confirmation of Adams's claim that Fasehun did not inform the group before meeting Obasanjo, and the subsequent financial exposure and inducements that all the factions were later exposed to and eagerly embraced imply that one cannot dismiss the allegation against Fasehun. Additionally, Jubril Ogundimu, who stayed with the Fasehun faction "because he was an elderly man," told me that Fasehun had died before he discovered that "Fasehun was a very deceitful man." He added, "Gani Adams is a noisemaker. But Fasehun will deceive you, and you will achieve his aims and objectives for him unknowingly. Fasehun will never share money with anyone.... He didn't share money or information. If you discovered that people brought money to him, he will swear that he has never taken money from anyone. He even said this on TV, and I asked him, 'Suppose those people [who gave you money] accused you?' He said they will need to explain what the money was for."[185]

However, Adams seems to link the allegation of Fasehun's financial inducement with the police's incessant attacks against members of the OPC, to which he claims Fasehun refused to respond. He states: "Dr. Fasehun also watched every situation from the rear pretending not to have the resources or the clout to address the ugly situation until matters got out of hand when [on] January 8, 1999, two of our members were attacked and killed by a squad of policemen at Ore." In a slightly incoherent way, Adams recalls a few other incidents to which Fasehun allegedly failed to respond,[186] though he said the members otherwise had the capacity to "repel the forces"—that is, the police "attacks."[187]

Perhaps the final straw for Adams was his kidnapping by the members of the group faithful to the leader. According to Fasehun, the week before Adams announced the former's expulsion, Alhaji Toyin Jimoh, who doubles as the coordinator for the OPC Oloruntosin Zone in Mushin and the *Olori Eso* (head of the Security Guards; similar to a Brigade of Guards)[188] revealed to Fasehun that he was privy to a plan by Adams, Adesokan, and others to expel him from the organization over the alleged N20 million bribe from Obasanjo. Jimoh said all his attempts to persuade them to go to Fasehun's Century Hotel to resolve the matter were ignored.[189] Being loyal to Fasehun, Jimoh then put a plan in motion "to neutralise the threat" from Adams and his "co-conspirators." He suggested to Adams that, given his position in the group, he needed to be guarded. Adams agreed. Jimoh then assigned to Adams six guardsmen who were loyal to Jimoh. "One day," Fasehun recounts, "they threw Gani Adams into the boot of a Peugeot 505 Saloon and brought him to me at Century Hotel. I was in my office when they opened the door and threw him on the floor like a pack of rags. I was shocked. They told me that *the boy was too ambitious* and that before he became too wild for control they should be allowed to go and '*finish him.*' Gani, shaking visibly, pleaded for mercy and offered all sorts of inducements and penances to overt the fate he knew could be dispensed to him at my word. However, I refused to harbour evil."[190]

Fasehun writes that he informed Adams's abductors that as a medical doctor, his duty "[was] to save life, not take life." He told them: "Let this young man go and do according to his conscience."[191] According to Fasehun, Adams's abductors then let him off "reluctantly." The following week, Adams announced Fasehun's expulsion and assumed leadership of a faction of the group. "But much worse than that," adds Fasehun, "this young man, whose life I had saved, began to seek ways to take my life."[192]

Fasehun's rendering of the story raises a few important issues about the nature of the OPC at this point. First, evidently, he did not see anything wrong, let alone illegal, with the kidnapping of Adams. If the members of the group could kidnap a friend turned enemy who, at the time, remained within the group, the fate of other enemies could only be imagined—although not for too long, as captured in the next chapter. Second, although the capacity and willingness of some OPC members to take the law into their hands was beginning to manifest publicly at this point, this incident was an extreme demonstration. Third, the fact that Fasehun acknowledged, without expressing alarm, his followers' capacity and willingness to murder anyone, including a prominent member of the group, also points to the violence that was in the offing when the group finally broke into factions (see chap. 3). It is therefore not surprising that Fasehun also alleged a few times that Adams wanted to have him killed.[193]

Adams's interpretation of the kidnapping was understandably different from Fasehun's. In his book, *My Life and Struggle,* Adams thanks Fasehun, tongue in cheek, for ordering his kidnapping because, as he implies, it led him to create his own faction—which ostensibly set him on the path to becoming a big man himself.[194] "My gratitude . . . goes to Dr. Fasehun," he writes, "who[,] as part of his plans to get rid of *his sworn enemy,* sent his men, headed by Alhaji Toyin Jimoh, to kidnap me for a reason best known to them." Though claiming not to know why he was abducted, Adams says he had discovered that "[his] presence in OPC had continued to generate unquantifiable threat to his [Fasehun's] life and aspirations . . . hence, the order for [his] kidnap." He added, "It was a mission accomplished for Dr. Fasehun and his men as I was confined into the boot of a Peugeot 505 Salon Car and taken to Century Hotel where the grievous plan was to be executed. But for mother luck, *I would have been sent to the great beyond.*" However, Adams admits he was "let off the hook" only "after several pleas,"[195] confirming his suspicions that he could have been killed by his former comrades.

On March 1, 1999, at a press conference, Adams, with the support of most of the youth in the group, announced the expulsion of Fasehun and "the rebirth of [their] political movement, a qualitative leap forward in our struggle for the self-determination of our people and the social and political emancipation of the masses."[196] He read a statement that he signed as the new national coordinator of the OPC. (He later took the title of president.)[197] He also announced Evangelist Kunle Adesokan as the secretary-general of the group.

The press statement raises a few significant points. First, unlike in his book published eight years later, Adams claimed the OPC had five "founding members." In fact, this was the first major point he raised at the press conference after stating that the congress had been established in 1994. According to him, these members included the now late Tony Ugborue and Ibrahim Atanda, Kunle Adesokan, Frederick Fasehun, and Gani Adams. Adams emphasized that "right from inception, [the OPC] was not the idea of a sole individual."[198] Second, Adams reemphasized that "the political and economic domination of Nigeria by the conservative ruling class of the Hausa/Fulani" was the main reason for the formation of the OPC. Third, he also reaffirmed that the annulment of the June 12, 1993, presidential election won by Moshood Abiola—"just because his victory did not go down well with members of this conservative ruling class"[199]—provided the immediate backdrop to the rise of the OPC. Fourth, he reclarified the core purpose of the OPC: "To consciously mobilise the Yoruba and galvanise them into action to stem the tide of the northern domination of both the political and the economic sectors of Nigeria."[200] Fifth, to "stem the tide," he reiterated the group's intention to pursue the convocation of an SNC in Nigeria "to peacefully resolve the crisis of the Nigerian state," even while insisting on "the right to self-determination of this Yoruba race."[201] Sixth, he noted that the Abubakar regime had ignored the calls for an SNC by instituting a transition program, "which begs the question of needed economic and political restructuring of Nigeria." As a result, he stated, the OPC opposed "the transition program tailored to the interest of the Northern oligarchy" and had therefore "embarked on a consistent and systematic mobilisation of the Yoruba people for the exercise of their right to self-determination and independent convocation of the SNC."[202] Seventh, Adams discredited Fasehun's disclaimer on any opposition to the transition to civil rule, adding that "the OPC is opposed to the transition program" because the group had decided rather to "mobilise the Yoruba race for self-determination and to actualise the SNC." He added that Fasehun had "isolated himself from the leadership and followership of the OPC" and had also been "meeting with and taking cues from political contractors who are only interested in beheading our political movement." In this context, the OPC associated itself with JACON, an umbrella group for all prodemocracy and human rights groups led by the famous lawyer and activist Chief Gani Fawehinmi.

Eighth, Adams rejected Fasehun's designation of the OPC as a sociocultural organization and affirmed the OPC as a "political movement which is interested in articulating the interest[s] of the Yoruba race and in struggling for the right to self-determination of the Yoruba race." While Adams conceded that "sociocultural regeneration is part of [the OPC's] mission," he declared, "We are not, in the strict sense, a socio-cultural outfit." Ninth, Adams, who would introduce identification cards for the members of his own faction (as related in the opening of this chapter), condemned Fasehun for announcing that anyone who did not have a card signed by him was not a member of the group. "'Identity card' of OPC members," Adams declared, "are primarily their political beliefs and readiness to work for the actualisation of the program[s] of OPC and not a piece of paper or laminated card." And given "the hostility of the Nigerian state to [the] OPC and its members," Adams announced, the NCC had declared that "it is unwise to make the possession of an identity card a requisite qualification for an OPC membership."[203] Tenth, the new OPC leader stated that when Fasehun, who had "taken the option of collaborating with politicians and military apologists," was "confronted with allegations of clandestinely meeting with General Olusegun Obasanjo and collecting the sum of N20m (twenty million naira) from the general" at a meeting of the OPC on January 4, 1999, he admitted "having met with the general without the mandate of our NCC and that the

Figure 1.11. Oodua People's Congress members at a Heroes Day event. *Left to right:* Tosin, Monsuru Akande, Sade Mama Ola, and Bose Omolaoye. Photo courtesy of Bose Omolaoye.

general attempted to give him the said sum," but he "denied having accepted any money." Adams alleged that "subsequent investigations," however, revealed that Fasehun had "accepted the money and deposited it at a branch" of a named bank. Fasehun was also accused of collecting N5 million each from five other notable Nigerians and companies. On the basis of all these claims, Adams condemned Fasehun's "political degeneration [degeneracy]" and "reprehensible conduct." Eleventh, Adams stated that the outcome of the "so-called presidential election on February 27 [1999] . . . is a clear indication of our position that the transition program was instituted to ensure the 'election' of a stooge of the northern oligarchs [a reference to the president-elect, Olusegun Obasanjo]."[204]

Fasehun describes the "damage done" to his person in Adams's press conference as "incredible."[205] In his two books, Fasehun alleges that Gani Fawehinmi (SAN), a Lagos lawyer, social crusader, and (later) presidential candidate of the National Conscience Party (NCP), manipulated the young men for his selfish political ambition.[206] Fasehun writes, "Gani Fawehinmi . . . had always nursed an ambition to lead a political movement that would send Nigeria scampering whenever he roared, but lacked the temperament to entice followers in the number required to make a mark. . . . He was determined now to associate with OPC capable of forming his long-sought base."[207] He adds that the text of the press conference "aroused [his] curiosity" for two reasons: "First, Adams lacked the educational acumen, political enlightenment, as well as the

Figure 1.12. Adams's men and women. *Left to right:* Comrade Ayodele Akele, chair of Free Gani Adams; Clement Omoyeni; Alhaji Abudu Modiu, the secretary-general of the OPC; Sade Mama Ola (late); Fatimo Iyayi; Wale Ajakaye; Hassan; and Ajibade, posing at the office of the OPC in Alediye in the early 2000s. Photo courtesy of Bose Omolaoye.

intellectual rationalisation which" the text conveyed. Second, "the text of the address was out of tune with the non-partisan nature of OPC."[208] On May 10, 1999, the Fawehinmi-led JACON, made of fifty-two prodemocracy groups, had disassociated itself from the Fasehun faction and embraced the Adams faction. In a press release by JACON's general secretary, Femi Aborisade, the group accused Fasehun of "allowing political differences with Ganiyu Adams faction of the OPC to mislead [him] into abandoning the defence of basic democratic rights."[209] In fact, a few months later, in an interview with *Vanguard,* Fawehinmi stated that "Fasehun is not the leader of OPC," adding that Adams's faction is the "authentic OPC."[210]

There were others in JACON whom Fasehun describes as "our so-called comrade activists" who were "clearly surprised and envious of the phenomenal growth and popularity of OPC" and therefore "were determined to see the demise of the organisation" under his leadership by "secretly and clandestinely [supporting] the dissident group, giving it Marxist indoctrination."[211] Although the men had been friends and Fawehinmi had worked pro bono for

Figure 1.13. Adams greeting Gani Fawehinmi, SAN, at the latter's daughter's wedding. Photo courtesy of *Nigerian Tribune*.

Fasehun when he was detained by Sani Abacha, Fasehun claimed that Fawehinmi regarded him as a stumbling block to his ambition "to fuse OPC with his own platform." (Fawehinmi, a popular and respected attorney and activist, later ran as the presidential candidate of the NCP in the 2003 elections and won only 161,333 votes nationwide.) Fawehinmi's erstwhile friend alleged that the attorney "kept propping up and masturbating the young man's [Adams's] ego intellectually," adding that "the moment Frankenstein stood on his own two legs, the monster jettisoned the control of his maker and went to town on a damaging spree."[212]

Fasehun was particularly galled by Adams's claim that the congress was a "political movement" and not a sociocultural organization. He insisted that the group was "a non-political, non-partisan . . . cultural organisation" that was "seeking cultural regeneration among the Yoruba" and not one "seeking [a] chimeric 'affirmation of self-determination and emancipation,'" as Adams had claimed at the press conference.[213]

It was obvious from this point on that Adams and his faction had put a different but significant inflection on the core purpose of the OPC, transcending its initial sociocultural mission and specific goal of ensuring the validation of the June 12, 1993, presidential election. In the post-Abacha (Abacha died on June 8, 1998), post-Abiola (Abiola died in detention on July 7, 1998) era, while Fasehun fervently clung to the sociocultural mission—seeking to build a Yoruba World Centre in Ile-Ife, the city regarded as the founding place of the ethnic group[214]—Adams redirected the group's focus to the pursuit of "self-determination and emancipation" for the Yorùbá. However, while Adams initially approached the "socio-cultural regeneration" mission of the group as subsidiary, later, in the postviolence stage of his OPC career, it was precisely this sociocultural mission that he focused on (see chap. 3).

According to Fasehun, with Fawehinmi's "weight behind . . . this bony . . . bespectacled, raw-boned youth,"[215] Adams "became openly defiant of [him]."[216] In his books, Fasehun reserves the greatest contempt for Adams, emphasizing his young age and the challenging process of his social maturation, his subalternity (inferior rank), his lowly and artisanal background, his lack of education, his "fascination" with charms and magic, his "betrayal," and his "violence." However, as he discloses in *OPC: Our History, Our Mission*, even while he was in jail, the seed for the factionalization of the group had been sown. Fasehun states that while in Abacha's gulag, he received "disturbing news" that the OPC had split into two camps, one consisting of the "Youth Wing" under Adams—"a band of hotheads . . . [who] laid the foundation of misguided militancy within the OPC"[217]—and the other made up of "mature elders" under the leadership of "Papa" Taiwo. The groups were "mutually hostile and antagonistic."[218] The basis of this tension was also money—as it was again later with Fasehun himself. Adams's followers had been circulating a rumor that when Pa Taiwo and another female member of the group, Mrs. Aniyikaiye, visited Fasehun in detention, he introduced them to another detainee, who gave them N75,000, which the two "misappropriated." This rumor, argues Fasehun, "found fertile ground in the gullible minds of the followers of Gani Adams," whom he also described as "untamed minds,"[219] and additionally ensured that Taiwo, whom Fasehun had put in charge of the group while in detention, lost "effective control of even his own 'branch' of the" OPC.[220]

Although during a visit at the detention center Fasehun counseled Adams that the latter's "indoctrinating [of] the youths to imbibe rudeness, lack of respect for elders and hooliganism" was "detrimental to the future of the youths and the [Yorùbá] Nation," Fasehun states, Adams did not change, as he returned to "cast aspersions on the elders and drench them with vituperations," while also targeting those he regarded as his adversaries in the group with "unrelenting propaganda."[221]

"Gani Adams earned his living taking passengers on a commercial motorcycle, the popular *okada*," Fasehun writes in the chapter of his book entitled

"Enemy Within," beginning a description of the young subaltern follower who became his rival.[222] "He had not had an opportunity for formal education. He immediately struck you as an artless, innocent youth without anxieties, content with the meagre takings from his *okada*."[223] Yet, three years earlier, Fasehun had described the same "innocent youth without anxieties" as an "artisan [who] had hot anger boiling inside his soul."[224]

Fasehun continues his dismissive, disdainful, and class-conscious attempt to locate Adams in the socioeconomic ladder: "[Adams's] *educational deficiencies* would have prevented him from immediately vividly absorbing the operational philosophy behind OPC. This philosophy was not vivid to many literate minds let alone a mind *not primed by formal schooling for the power of reason,* as guaranteed by prior knowledge of class-taught history or socio-political experiences or basic information of the economy and the legal implications. He was, and still is, garrulously and fictionally inventive. His fictional inventiveness bordered on psychopathy. His self-proclaimed courage easily vaporised on the field of action."[225]

This attempt to describe and also define Adams's station in life speaks to an elite-subaltern division that Fasehun struggled with since he formed (according to him), or joined others in forming (according to Adams), the OPC. While he praised the "good subaltern," whether elderly or youthful, and rejected any attempt to define them by their lack of education, lack of civility or cultivation, lowly status, or poverty, Fasehun was always eager to emphasize that the same lack should be regarded as constitutive of the "bad subaltern"—such as Adams. Fasehun describes Adams further as "a primary school dropout unable to make a success of his carpenter's apprenticeship."[226]

In an attempt to totally eliminate Adams's qualification for membership in the OPC after the split, Fasehun points to a factor that "worked against [Adams] and prevented him from *the restricted world of early OPC,*" alleging that although Adams's mother was from Arigidi in Ondo State, "his father was of the Tapa (Nupe) tribe from Niger State in the North Central Nigeria," adding that "these were the very 'enemies' OPC was set against." But curiously, Fasehun writes that this "fact *easily disqualified him from being an early member of the emerging OPC,* an organisation reserved for full-blooded Yoruba people."[227] If Adams's father was indeed not Yorùbá—which would still make him half-Yorùbá, since Fasehun conceded that his mother was Yorùbá—a factor that Fasehun considered "disqualifying," given that the group was only for "full-blooded Yoruba," why did this not disqualify Adams from being "an early member" of the organization as well as from becoming a member much later?[228]

When I asked him in 2020 when his erstwhile comrades raised this accusation again, Adams said it was laughable. He gave a full account of his progenitors in Arigidi-Akoko.[229] He asked if the traditional ruler, the *Zaki* of Arigidi, Oba Mohammed Asunmo Olanipekun, would have made him the Otunba of Arigidi if he were not a native.[230] "No one had been made an *Otunba* in the town before me. The *oba* told me that he consulted Ifa and Ifa told him to wait until the person who would be the *otunba* grew old enough. The *oba* begged me for two years before I agreed to take the title," said Adams.[231]

However, what is important here is that Fasehun was using this allegation about Adams's ancestry to delegitimize his claim to original membership and to the leadership of a group for "full-blooded Yoruba."

Fasehun continues: "[Adams] began to introduce various 'superstitious weapons': fetish practices, *oaths to himself*, brigandage and 'training in militancy.' In order to become a member of his OPC, you had to pay an oath-taking fee, you had to comply with superstitious practices, and you had to submit to black magic orgies. To Ganiyu Adams, OPC became a pot of honey, a veritable source of earning, thanks to the gullibility of his largely illiterate following, who worshipped him and feared him like the plague."[232]

"Gani Adams was at his 'best' demonstrating how to wear charms, how to recite incantations, what to do with a kola nut, how to interpret the positioning of kola nut leaves when randomly thrown down like a dice,"[233] Fasehun adds, describing his former follower. He also relates an experience he had visiting the room where Adams administered oaths of allegiance to new members of the OPC, after being alerted by Lady B. "The fetish I saw was frighteningly barbaric and so intimidating that any novice would voluntarily empty his pocket or her bag to avoid the curse of the gods for being niggardly or thrifty."[234]

When he returned from jail, Fasehun tried to reverse the trend by reorganizing the OPC because the only thing he "shared with the rabble" led by Adams was "their determination not to have anything to do with General Abubakar Abdulsalami's political transition"[235] (a position he abandoned shortly afterward). He sought to "reinvent" the platform quickly by approaching a few people—including popular activist lawyer Femi Falana; Jiti Ogunye, also a lawyer; and Omoyele Sowore, an activist and former student union leader—"to constitute an elite directorate." He also contacted Evangelist Kunle Adesokan to be part of this new "directorate" "as representative" of the Adams group. In an attempt to separate "the rabble" from the "elite" in rebuilding the OPC, Fasehun says, he "made arrangements to place other individuals in positions commensurate with their individual backgrounds."[236]

Not surprisingly, Adams responded to all the strands of Fasehun's attempts to describe and define him. For a man who is sensitive to how he is generally portrayed, particularly in the media, Adams has used every opportunity since 1999 to counter or explain away Fasehun's emphasis on his humble background, pedigree, initial limited education, subaltern status, and lack of participation in the founding of the OPC.

When explaining how he became the national coordinator and later national president of his faction after the decision to expel Fasehun, Adams said he was reluctant to take over leadership, despite being persuaded to do so by the members of the NCC after all the efforts to make Fasehun change course failed. Monsuru Akande, at one point the Welfare Committee chair of the OPC, confirmed this. "We insisted that there must be a break. We decided that Gani Adams was a good mobilizer, helping to take the congress everywhere. We asked him to lead us."[237] Amusa "Big Fish" Musiliu, a member of the OPC who served as the secretary of the National Guard, corroborated the fact that Adams was the great mobilizer in the group but also claimed that he was initially loyal to Fasehun. "Most of us didn't know Fasehun. We knew Gani Adams when we joined. I noticed that he was always referring to '*oga*' [boss], 'Let me ask *oga*.' He was taking instructions from Fasehun."[238] However, when the crisis started, Musiliu said he and the others were "ready to die for Gani Adams. We were loyal to him."[239]

Sunday Adebayo also confirmed that Adams was reluctant to become the leader. He added that, to encourage Adams to accept leadership, he, as his close friend, volunteered to be his personal assistant.[240] Rasaq Arogundade Balogun, a member of the National Squad and coordinator of the Bariga chapter of the OPC in the Somolu Local Government Area of Lagos, spoke in the same vein. He said that some young people in the group pushed Adams to break away and take over as leader. Marruf Olanrewaju, the OPC coordinator in Kwara State, also supported Adams. "We decided that since [the late Obafemi] Awolowo had predicted that a young person will liberate Yorubaland, we picked Adams to lead us."[241] Oluwayemisi Shiyanbola, the first Iya Oodua General, confirmed that they were all convinced that Adams was the manifestation of Awolowo's prediction. The woman, who turned seventy-two in 2021, said "that a young man would save Nigeria in the future. Gani is my son's contemporary."[242]

Balogun disclosed that their first move was to appoint Adams as the deputy national coordinator of the OPC on February 25, 1999. They held a caucus meeting at Isheri-Osun (near Egbeda) to plan their next step. "Adams said he was young. He was only twenty-nine. But we insisted that he must be the president of the OPC."[243] He added that Fasehun was so affronted by their move that in the months after they formed the splinter group, he told the police that members of the Adams faction were "touts, hoodlums and criminals" who should be "dealt with," allegedly encouraging the police to kill and maim Adams's followers. "Fasehun even revealed to the police that, to identify core members of the group, they should ask any suspected OPC member to remove his clothes. We used to have something we called 'Sergeant'—that is, twenty-one *gbéré* (incisions) on our left shoulder. Fasehun revealed this to the police."[244]

In an interview with *Premium Times* in August 2013, Adams accused Fasehun of three core vices and even alleged that Fasehun was capable of the worst crime, murder. He said he tried in vain to persuade his supporters to remain with Fasehun. "I pleaded with them [members of the NCC] to stay and I told them that though they were fighting a genuine cause, Dr. Fasehun was mean, and he could kill, maim, destroy because of money, power and women. I told them I knew him very well and that they should be prepared to make sacrifices."[245]

"Although I decided I would play down the issue of Dr. Fasehun," Adams said while insisting that he cofounded the group, "unfortunately he continues to speak ill of me in the media. And you cannot underrate the power of the media, especially when there is frequency of negative news about you. It is not only the people here who read those publications, they do in the Diaspora, too. How can Dr. Fasehun say that a leader of the OPC cannot speak for the organisation? I must state for the umpteenth time that Fasehun and I founded the organisation together in 1994 and my contribution to the struggle which gave birth to the OPC was about 75 per cent."[246]

He backed up his claim to original membership by explaining the role he played in sustaining the group and adding that the group met in the chambers of Opeyemi Bamidele (now a senator) at 110 Palm Avenue Street, Mushin, Lagos, "where we originally named the organisation OPC on 25 August," and later in the residence of Dr. Esan at Layi Oyekanmi, Mushin.[247] This directly contradicts Fasehun's claim that they met in an apartment he rented in the same area. Adams states,

> At the inception of the OPC . . . Fasehun had expected to gain so much fame and popularity, but he was not happy when, eight months after, he did not get it. Around 1996, he gave us a condition that he would no longer join our meetings if our attendance was not up to 200, but we persuaded him, yet he was reluctant. . . . After holding three to four meetings, Dr. Fasehun was arrested on the allegation that he was a member of the National Democratic Coalition, NADECO, and not OPC. Go and check newspaper publications between 1993 and 1996, hardly will you find any report in which Dr. Fasehun claimed to be representing OPC and hardly anywhere did he say he was an OPC leader. He preferred to call himself a NADECO chieftain or the treasurer of the Campaign for Democracy, CD, rather than a leader of OPC, despite the fact that he was made the convener the day the organisation was formed.[248]

Adams explained that his difference with the elderly Taiwo arose because the man wanted to join one of the political parties set up under General Abacha while Fasehun was in jail. According to Adams, after Fasehun was released from prison in June 1998, he sided with the Taiwo faction even though Taiwo had joined one of the Abacha political parties:

> We later found out that Pa Taiwo and his group were frequenting Alagbon, where Dr. Fasehun had been detained. Upon his release, he attended a meeting with them, but found out that there were not more than 20 people left with Papa Taiwo's group and he decided to attend our own meeting the next day and he was surprised to see about 8,000 of us. That made him declare openly that we were the authentic OPC and he challenged Papa Taiwo that he had been feeding him with wrong information during his detention. But we did not know that Dr. Fasehun still had some evil plans in his mind against us.[249]

Adams also countered Fasehun's claims that he is an ambitious young man, stating, "I am not inordinately ambitious, and I did not think at any time in my life that I would be chosen to lead the organisation." He was happy to confirm his humble background even while claiming that he was a person of fate: "I considered it my destiny to lead the OPC, because at the time I did not even have more than three shirts and trousers, and I was still living with my father at a room apartment at Genedo Street in Itire. I neither had a car nor a motorcycle, even though *Dr Fasehun used to call me an Okada rider and a carpenter.* . . . Was it a crime that I decided to learn *interior decoration* after I dropped out from school?"[250] In his biography, he states, "I have noticed that the way to greatness has little or nothing to do with your detractors in life but [your] destiny according to the will of God. . . . I associate with the lowly and the highly classed people in the society. . . . I became one of the forces to be reckoned with despite my age."[251] As to being unemployed and being an *okada* rider, Adams said, "I abandoned my work to commit myself to the struggle. So, I don't know where Fasehun got all the things he said about me from. During the struggle, I was always borrowing my friend's motorcycle to attend the meetings of the Campaign for Democracy, CD, at Imaria [Dr. Beko's office] and I did not know how that translated to me being an *okada* rider."[252] However, Adams's friend, Sunday Adebayo, told me that, indeed, he sometimes lent his motorcycle to Adams to use as *okada* during the hard times when they lived together in Mushin.

Being sensitive to social status but at the same time eager to be seen as both a "man of the people" and one who relates easily with those at the highest levels of society, Adams asserts, "I associate with the lowly and highly classed people in society."[253]

Even while confirming his humble background, he was at the same time eager to show that he was not the "illiterate," "uncivilised," and "unevolved" person Fasehun was presenting to the world in his books. OPC members, he insists in his own book, "are enlightened." Adams adds that he was committed "to get[ting] our entire members educated with the available resources."[254] He reminds Fasehun that, although at the inception of the OPC he had realized that "all foundation members were not operating at the same educational level, [they] could not be classified as fools, morons or imbeciles. [They] *were leaders in* [their] *own rights*."[255] He even quotes Benjamin Rush, a signer of the US Declaration of Independence, physician, politician, social reformer, humanitarian, and civic leader in Philadelphia, on "extending education to the children of the poor."[256] He asks Fasehun to help the poor rather than casting "aspersions on the *leaders of tomorrow*"[257]—ostensibly himself included—and criticizes the elite for regarding "the poor, the underprivileged as miscreants, only to later turn to them for the realization of their personal political ambition or [aggrandizement]."[258] He then signals that he was evolving socially, politically, and intellectually and therefore would not be or remain anyone's tool, a declaration of active agency that many failed to fully take note of at that point. Adams provides multiple indications of this evolution, including the fact that he had regularly organized "seminars, symposia, conferences and lectures along with the National Coordinating Committee (NCC)" of his faction. He points to the books he donated to schools and provides examples of conferences and seminars, such as the International Conference on Urban Violence, Ethnic Militia and the Challenge of Democratic Consolidation in Nigeria in April 2002, where he delivered a paper on "Politics and Agenda of Ethnic Militias: A Case of the OPC," and a national seminar on "Achieving Violence Free Election in 2003."[259] Adams realized that one of the marks of the "enlightened" and the elites in the public sphere in Nigeria, particularly in the nongovernmental organization–civil society world and the universities, is the regular hosting of conferences or symposia. He sought to use them to prove his evolution when other members of the elite, such as Fasehun, accused him of not being "enlightened."

Adams also defends Fawehinmi against Fasehun's accusations. In the early to mid-2000s, Adams used his relationship with Fawehinmi when responding to his former leader's claim that he was a "low-life." In his book, he states that Fawehinmi, "a notable radical constitutional lawyer and human rights activist" of "international status" associated with him because he "admire[d Adams's] courage."[260] He also drops the names of Nigeria's leading lawyers, including those representing the leading Yorùbá political elite organizations, the *Afenifere* and the Yoruba Council of Elders (YCE), who at one time or another took up his legal briefs pro bono.

To prevent doubt, in *My Life and Struggle*, Adams affirms his evolving status: "Due to the wits of men of valour, *I became one of the forces to be reckoned with despite my age*. The political situation in the country which infuriated me and which I condemned boldly to the admiration of the general public *brought out the heroism in me. The thrust of leadership on me* has *nothing to do with my education, my profession, my family background or friendship association* but [results from] diligence and providence."[261]

By this point in Adams's public trajectory, he was already signaling that he recognized the social and political attention he had gained and that, despite the limitations and disadvantages of his past, he was ready and eager to embrace the potentials of his transformation from a virtual *zero* in society to a *hero.*[262]

The Fasehun-Adams split indicates two possibilities inherent in the Yorùbá habitus that produced the OPC. When the youths removed Fasehun from office and installed Adams as president, they were prepared to change the tempo of the group's activities to make it more "militant." But to Fasehun, Adams—after the split—was a "29 year-old Okada rider who has failed to make headway from being a carpenter" and who had a "very modest and humble background," lacking "educational acumen [and] political enlightenment."[263] This reference suggests class disdain—indicating that Adams is not "a man of substance"—even though Fasehun had worked with the "illiterate" Adams as secretary-general in the past. But more importantly, given the Yorùbá romance with and appropriation of òlàjú (enlightenment, sophistication, civilization, modernity), which is closely linked with *eko* (education) and iwe (book, book learning) as reconditions for individual and communal advancement,[264] Fasehun may be suggesting that Adams does not and cannot represent such a people, because *kò'lajú* (lit. "his eyes are not open") or he lacks òlàjú.

Thus, the ambiguities and paradoxes of the Yorùbá romance with and appropriation of òlàjú within the Nigerian context are revealed by the OPC split's discursive construction. In the "external" dimension, the Yorùbá are constructed as "modern," "educated," "progressive," and "enlightened,"[265] as opposed to the Hausa-Fulani, who are a "backward," "conservative," "irrational" people whose Islamic and "cultural heritage" is marked by "oppression," "tyranny," and "violence." But divisions within the group produce similar discourses, accusations, and counteraccusations internally over what "authentic" Yorùbá ideals are and how they can be legitimately portrayed. Therefore, between the Adams and Fasehun factions, there are also appeals to "modern," and thus "enlightened," ideas, as opposed to "traditional," and therefore "backward," ideas.[266] There is also a split between the old and the young, a struggle over which age group best represents and can best defend Yorùbá culture and interests. While respect for old age is one of the key indices of immersion in Yorùbá culture, the Adams group, which claims to represent this "return to culture" can be said, in their collision with Fasehun and their position on Yorùbá elders, to contradict this assertion. But Adams and his constituents present him not as a hoodlum but as an authentic "man of the people," untainted by "collusion" with some members of the ruling elites like the group's elders. Adams's life and role therefore reveal these ambiguities and paradoxes of the discourses of òlàjú and cultural heritage in the politics of the OPC.

The OPC claims to have three to five million members. Even though the group has some university graduates and many members with high school diplomas, the bulk of the membership comes from the community of artisans, unskilled workers, semiliterate people, and some practicing and ex–area boys who live in high-density and poor areas of Lagos and other major cities. This is partly responsible for the image of (potentially) violent "rabble" that the group had in its early years. But Adams told *TheNEWS* that the OPC members should be regarded as people "standing for truth, justice and equity."[267] He added later that "we are not violent at all but we hate cheating, we hate provocation, we hate people who want to deprive us of our rights. We will surely fight for our rights with the last blood in our body. I don't believe in violence but nobody should say I should not operate the organisation I believe is fighting for the cause of Yoruba in my own land."[268]

A major dimension of the Adams faction's problem with the Fasehun leadership is the generational-cum-class contradiction. Given that most of the membership comes from the socially disadvantaged classes, they are very conscious of the economic and social deprivations they suffer. However, they attribute these to political marginalization caused centrally by the Hausa-Fulani elite, with the collusion of some Yorùbá elders. While one dimension of the OPC rhetoric stresses continuities with the Yorùbá past, a second distinguishes youth from the "selfish," "corrupt," and "collaborative" (Yorùbá) elders. These generational and class dimensions may partly explain the rhetoric of the militant faction and its actions. In their conception, the state is not just the Hausa-Fulani-dominated state but also a quasi-class state, even when it is headed by one of their own—President Olusegun Obasanjo.

Interestingly enough, Fasehun uses the same division to justify his position. He argues that his detention by the Abacha regime and his long absence allowed the "quality control system that we had erected for membership [to] quickly collapse."[269] Fasehun, describing Adams as a "raw-boned youth" and an "artisan [who] had hot anger boiling inside his soul," argues that while he was in jail, Adams recruited, from "various ghettos, garages and highways," members whose confidence "rested in charms and amulets that emboldened them to confront 'enemies'" and who radiated "darkness and spiritism."[270] Fasehun was, however, less disdainful of charms in an interview he later granted to a newsmagazine in 2002, where he said that, "I am a Christian. . . . [T]hey say, self-protection is the first law of nature. Any means available to protect you is what you shall employ. . . . So, if people believe that the charms they use confer some protection, as much as my Bible confers protection on me, so be it. . . . But I can assure you that this also is part of Yoruba culture. And I have seen some of these things. I have seen people shot at, and they just smiled in return. There is a woman here who was shot at eight times and she collected all the bullets and gave them back to the police, and said, 're-load your rifle!' She is here."[271]

With the "gullibility of his largely illiterate following,"[272] Fasehun concludes, Adams turned the OPC into "a pot of honey [and] a veritable source of earning."[273] Fasehun attempted to counter the advance of this "rabble" and reverse the situation in which the "elite class had been scared away" by establishing "an elite directorate" that would place individuals "in positions commensurate with their individual back-ground,"[274] given the fact that the Yorùbá "enjoy age-long reputations of sophistication, intellectual attainment, native wisdom, philosophy, diplomacy, political sagacity, political awareness and economic prowess."[275] Yet according to Fasehun, the same people he wanted to replace, whom he would later describe as "the rabble" and the "hoi polloi," made it possible for the group to take off.[276] However, Fasehun and other well-educated people involved with the OPC accused Adams of having been uncomfortable with and particularly distrustful of highly educated people. Fasehun writes, "Gani Adams had a pathological aversion for intellectuals and never hid it."[277]

Bent on transcending his academic limitations, Adams has since enrolled in the Lagos State University to study for a diploma in history and international studies.[278] However, these rhetorical oppositions—between young men and elders, violent hotheads and measured experience, educated and illiterate people, conservatives and radicals, and violence and statecraft—are blurred in practice.

First, while Fasehun's support for General Abubakar's transition program and Obasanjo's candidacy and eventual presidency were said to have inflamed the Adams group, it should not be assumed that the Adams faction was irrevocably opposed to Obasanjo's presidency, particularly after it began to suffer attacks from northerners. For instance, the Adams faction saw the introduction of Sharia by northern states as a move against a Yorùbá-led government and so opposed it.[279] Also, even though the president would later ask that the members of the group be shot on sight, Adams rose to defend him against "northerners":

> We note with utter dismay the hue and cry of some selfish and mischievous people whose political machinery has for long been exhausted. These gangs of self-centered people always hide under the needless fear of disintegration to oppose restructuring the nation. This same set of criminals are the first to

> complain of being marginalized when the head of the civil rule, Chief Olusegun Obasanjo, was ensuring fairness in federal appointments, which likely may be reversed at the expiration of his regime. . . . President Olusegun Obasanjo's administration is achieving what the so-called born-administrators[280] could not achieve in thirty-nine years of misrule. To this effect, we warn all evil-planners to steer clear of any attempts on the person and life of this emerging patriot.[281]

The Adams faction held this position even while insisting that "the window-dressing attempted with the current democratic arrangement is fragile and shall not offer the long-lasting solution desired to this problem."[282]

Second, prominent Yorùbá elders recognize and acknowledge Adams's leadership of their youth. They consult him on matters relating to "the state of insecurity and matters of inequality in the polity."[283] Even when he was arrested by the police, the secretary-general of the YCE, a pan-Yorùbá sociopolitical organization, Justice Adewale Thompson (ret) stated that "Gani Adams should not be treated as a criminal because the whole of Yoruba nation believes that OPC is out to salvage the bad security situation in Yoruba land."[284] Adams has[285] since he was released from jail received four chieftaincy titles, all denoting that he is a "savior-warrior." Indeed, nothing better exemplifies his importance, at this point in his public career, than his service on the Yoruba Agenda Committee selected by the ad hoc Planning Committee to prepare a position paper for the Yorùbá for presentation at the National Political Reforms Conference. The agenda committee on which Adams served was chaired by Chief Richard Akinjide, eminent lawyer and former Federal Minister of Justice, and included other eminent Yorùbá such as General Alani Akinrinade, former Chief of Staff of the Nigerian Army and civil war hero, Chief Olu Falae, former Secretary to the Government of the Federation and the presidential candidate of the APP/AD alliance in the 1999 presidential election, Professor Bolaji Akinyemi, and former federal Minister of External Affairs.[286]

Third, as Nolte has suggested, the youth-versus-elder rhetoric can be overplayed, as elders mobilize and instrumentalize youth violence, from which they can then keep a safe distance.[287] Even though Yorùbá elders, politicians, and traditional rulers do not ordinarily identify with the group's actions publicly unless challenged by northerners or the federal government, they believe that the OPC will help institute a "balance of terror" against the North, which seemed to have "monopolised terror" for a long time. For instance, according to Adams, during the peace meeting convened to settle the rift between the rival factions of the OPC, the late Chief Bola Ige, eminent Yorùbá politician, presidential aspirant, federal attorney general, and minister of justice, said:

"Kabiyesi, pray for these young men; their generation will be the ones to deliver us from the yoke of our oppressors."[288] At any rate, the youth-versus-elder rhetoric has its limitations, given that Fasehun's faction, even if led by an "elder," is also largely composed of youths. The struggle between Adams and Fasehun over how best to represent and re-present, and who best represents the Yorùbá and their culture and interests in contemporary times, is therefore interesting in many ways.

BECOMING OPC: THE RITUALITY OF BELONGINGNESS

One of the main points of contention before and immediately after the fragmentation of the OPC was what Fasehun describes as Adams's embrace of "oath-taking . . . various superstitious practices, and . . . black magic orgies"[289] and the subsequent "darkness and spiritism that had crept" into the group in his absence.[290] Interestingly enough, after Adams created his own faction, Fasehun, perhaps because he felt betrayed, also started administering oaths. Kayode Ogundamisi told me he had to take an oath when he joined the group, upon Fasehun's invitation, to be the secretary-general. However, oath-taking in the Fasehun faction was not as "fully traditional" as the oath-taking in the Adams faction.[291]

Indeed, Adams strongly believed in the efficacy of African Traditional Religion, in general, and the effectiveness of traditional oaths and charms, in particular.[292] He believed that an organization such as the OPC could not survive without the absolute loyalty of its members. Given that he is habitually suspicious of other people's intentions,[293] he was convinced that making everyone swear an oath of allegiance through the 'traditional' methods would help avert betrayal by members of the group and ensure their loyalty. He believed that most Yorùbá would be warier of betraying an oath sworn through traditional means than with the Bible or the Quran.[294] Therefore, by the time Adams broke away from the Fasehun faction, the oath-taking had become an absolute necessity for joining his group.

While Adams sees his actions and the rituals his group participates in as the best representation of the Yorùbá, their culture, and their past, Fasehun argues that this is not "the way we (were) are" or the best way "to represent us" to the world.[295] While the Adams faction's "return to culture" has been captured as "retraditionalisation" by Patrick Chabal and J.-P. Daloz,[296] I argue that such actions constitute habitus, "a durably installed generative principle of regulated improvisations" that, in a practical sense, "reactivates the sense objectified in institutions."[297] This habitus, which I approach as a reinvention of culture and "which is constituted in the course of an individual history, imposing its particular logic of incorporation, and through which agents partake of the history objectified in institutions, is what makes it possible to inhabit institutions, to appropriate them practically, and so to keep them in activity, continuously pulling them from the state of dead letters, reviving the sense deposited in them, but as the same time imposing the revisions and transformations that reactivation entails."[298]

The understanding, explanations, and activities of Adams and his group produce harmony between "practical sense" and "objectified meaning," leading to the "harmonisation of the agents' experiences and the constant reinforcement each of them receives from expression of similar or identical experiences,"[299] whether individual or collective (such as in rituals and festivals) or improvised or programmed (such as in commonplaces and sayings).

Mamadou Diouf has argued persuasively that the rituals embraced by the Adams faction—besides constituting an attempt at retraditionalization, as some have argued—could also be approached as one of the consequences of the exclusion of African youth from "the arenas of power, work, education, and leisure."[300] With youth as both victims and agents in this economy of exclusion and lack, Diouf suggests, the embrace of rites and rituals could flow "from [a] posture of defiance [that] takes place in the spaces deserted by political power [where] emptiness and indetermination are dominant: places ready to be filled, conquered, and named, and which favor the expression of rites and rituals intended to produce signs of identity."[301]

While the Adams faction's rituals of membership may seem paradoxical in the context of the group's representation of the Yorùbá as a "modern," "progressive," and "peaceful" people, they make sense in the context of their reconciliation of reinvented culture with the defense of Yorùbá interests and the struggle for justice and equity in Nigeria. But Adams sees no contradictions in their appropriation of different religious artifacts and registers because they are all in the service of self-determination. For instance, at one of the open meetings I attended in 2002, I saw the banner of the Islamic Council of Nigeria Prayer Group (formed by the OPC), which reads, "Prayer is the key to success of self-determination." Generally, for Adams, any form of spiritual process, traditional, Christian, or Islamic, constitutes a ritual of sorts. He ignores any contradiction.

The dynamic character of Yorùbá ritual, even though often glossed over in the literature, is recognized by the practitioners.[302] As Margaet Thompson Drewal argues in *Yoruba Ritual*, practitioners of Yorubá religion "often express the need to modify rituals to address current social conditions."[303] This is a function of what she regards as the "sophistication" evident in the "remarkable reflexivity" demonstrated in Yorùbá rituals as a result of the "level and quality of Yoruba exegesis."[304] The malleability of Yorùbá ritual practices enables participants to transform ritual itself[305] and also enables traditional religion in Yorubaland to accommodate Christianity and Islam[306]—as evident in OPC practices.

On one level, Adams and his followers account for the importance of protective magic and ritual practices in the OPC within the context of a "return to culture," which they glorify. Adams considers this a central value: "Definitely, we go back to our tradition. We encourage our members to recognize and accept our tradition and heritage. . . . Not only to recognize but to practice our culture. . . . We have a very rich culture."[307] As Anthony Giddens argues, "Tradition has its greatest sway when it is understood simply as how things were, are (and should be) done."[308] What has shifted, therefore, is not people's convictions but the role of such convictions in publicly expressed ideology. At the same time, according to Adams's assertions, rituals in the OPC context are as prospective as they are retrospective, as much an "invention" of tradition as they are a reiteration. To understand the Adams faction's devotion to using the resources of culture, we have to "return to practice, the site of the dialectic of the *opus operatum* and the *modus operandi*; of the objectified products of the incorporated products of historical practice."[309] This is particularly crucial in understanding not only how Adams mobilized these "incorporated products of historical practice" to empower himself both personally and organizationally in the early years of the OPC but also how he pressed these products into service in his larger project of becoming and being a big man.

Again, to Adams and his followers, the rituals, the charms, and the propitiation of Yorùbá gods do not detract from their practices as Christians and Muslims. For instance, one late evening in April 2021 during the Islamic holy month of Ramadan, I was chatting with Kunle Adesokan, an Evangelist and the founding secretary-general of the Adams faction, when I heard him swallow something as he responded to my question. He apologized and said he was breaking his fast. I asked if he was fasting with the Muslims. He responded that he was. Not surprised, though I knew him to be a Christian, I asked if he was also an adherent of Yorùbá religion (given that Fasehun had described him as a "traditionalist"). He answered in the affirmative. "So, you practice all three?" "*Beeni* [Yes]," he responded. Members of the OPC operate under many (spiritual) registers. Adams, during an interview in his first house in Abule Ado, pointed to a Christian prayer room where he, his wife, and others regularly conducted night vigil—a popular (Christian) overnight prayer session in Nigeria. Muslim *alfas* also visited him regularly to pray for him and the Yorùbá cause. He told me he also uses the "ancient wisdom of our forefathers," including charms and incantations.[310] After the Owo incident (see chap. 3)—about which he stated, "We did everything expected of us. We consulted the oracles. We made sacrifices to appease (the) gods"[311]—Adams thanked the Muslim Prayer Warriors for supporting the group with "spiritual assistance" but rebuked the Christian prayer band for not doing enough. He then disbanded the Christian prayer band and reconstituted it, charging it to meet "regularly to support the organisation with prayers and fasting."[312] When he was arrested after being on the police list of wanted persons for twenty months, charms, other fetish objects, and copies of the Bible and the Quran were found in his car.[313]

It can be argued that these different religious elements, in the Yorùbá worldview, primarily serve as resources through which the OPC members cope with the social, economic, and political conditions they encounter, rather than as totalizing systems of faith or practice. Unsurprisingly, members of the group vehemently reject religious fundamentalism.

RITUALS OF MEMBERSHIP

New members go through a ritual of initiation, which Adams described as "protocol." This initiation takes place with the participation of a "congregation of initiated members." New members swear an oath of secrecy and allegiance and are expected to buy kola nut and other items depending on the requirements of the local group. Initiation is usually into the *eso* (literally, "guard") rank. The *esos* constitute what the group calls the Resistance Wing. The idea of the *eso*, as noted earlier, is an appropriation of one of the key features of the age of warlords in nineteenth-century Yorubaland, when an eso was the epitome of courage and perseverance. During the initiation ceremony, a bowl of water is placed on the ground. Someone in charge of the rite puts a piece of iron, a stone, and a palm frond in the bowl. Initiates swear by Sango (the Yorùbá god of thunder), Ogun (the god of iron and thus of war), or Yemoja (the water goddess), depending on individual preference, through any of the symbols of the gods—such as a knife for Ogun. The initiate places his or her hand on the symbol and swears not to betray the organization or abuse whatever it provides. The new member then confirms allegiance to the group by declaring, "*O'odua ni mi t'okan t'okan*" (I am Oodua with all my heart). The initiation processes do not include swearing by the Bible or the Quran.[314] As I stated earlier, Adams and his constituents believe in the greater efficacy of traditional oaths, particularly in relation to action and consequence.

There is also a more practical and instrumental aspect. Having passed through these rituals, the new member is armed with charms believed to prevent bullet, cutlass, or knife wounds; a handkerchief soaked in a concoction

Figure 1.14. Lateef Olawale Oshodi being readmitted into the OPC by Adams during a gathering of the group. He was suspended for refusing, as a Muslim, to be inducted into *Ifa* religion. Photo courtesy of Lateef Oshodi.

deemed to prevent gun wounds; a small gourd with a black powdery substance; and native rings that have also been soaked (òrùka ère). Incisions (*gbéré*) are made on the new member's body to prevent harm. However, as members climb higher in the group's hierarchy, they take higher oaths.[315] Thus, the rites serve to "reveal further gradations of status to which individuals may aspire."[316] This kind of oath-taking, Adams told me in 2004, made the group "indestructible," despite the efforts of the state and the group's adversaries.[317] However, even core members of his faction who have taken this oath and the higher oaths, such as the members of the National Guard, have since left Adams's faction (see chaps. 2–4).

Members of the group call the charms panadol or phensic—two widely popular analgesics in Nigeria—but Adams describes them as "self-defense drugs" in an attempt to graft "modern" medicinal understandings on "traditional" occult practices. The members also consult oracles regularly to divine the immediate future. If they are traveling or going to meetings, they may ask the oracle to check what might happen and then seek protection;[318] such protection is important because of the centrality of violence—with attacks on, by, and within the OPC (see chap. 2). At one point, it was compulsory for every senior member of the group to *gba Ifa* (be initiated into the *Ifa* religion and system of divination). One of the few exceptions to this rule was Lateef Olawale Oshodi (popularly called Osho).[319] Oshodi refused to be initiated and was, according to him, under a cloud of suspicion for many years but was later readmitted when Adams realized that he had a lot of influence on Lagos Island, particularly regarding the mobilization of the group members.[320]

While the rituals of membership have not prevented the Adams faction from fractionalizing, they have helped to maintain unity and cohesion within the group for many years and to preserve and consolidate Adams's leadership. His word remains law within the group, even after another breakaway group sought to challenge his leadership. As members of his "National Guard" (more about this in chap. 2) told me, once Adams gave them an order, no matter what risks were involved, they carried it out. They only contradicted him in exceptional cases.[321] The membership ritual has also helped to strengthen group members' resolve to devote themselves to the purposes of the group in the belief that they have the necessary spiritual and cultural protection, provided as much by faithfulness to their oath of allegiance to the group and to Yorubaland as by their struggle for justice and equity in Nigeria.

CONCLUSION

"Each time the front runner is vehemently opposed by the subordinate," Fasehun writes in relation to Adams's decision to expel him and create his own faction of the OPC, "those who fail to learn from history always *go uncelebrated, unremembered*, except with ignominy, condemnation and domination."[322] He adds that because of the "treachery [of Adams and his faction]—seasoned with dishonesty, garnished with robbery, looting and paradoxical protection [provided by powerful supporters]"—the Adams faction had become one "of the destructive, poorly informed charlatans" while members of his own faction remained "the truly patriotic and visionary sons and daughters of Oodua."[323]

It is understandable that Fasehun, an accomplished medical doctor and respected prodemocracy activist, would conclude that, in a contest for supremacy with a typical subaltern—a "carpenter," "school dropout," and "*okada* rider" who revolted against him and led a group "comprised of young, brusque men who had been recruited from various ghettos, garages and highways"[324]—he would be adjudged to have chosen the right cause. In addition, he could be forgiven for assuming that the leader of these "young, brusque men" would in the end "go uncelebrated, unremembered, except with ignominy, condemnation."

However, Fasehun could not have been more wrong. Two decades after Fasehun predicted the horrible fate that awaited Adams principally for the revolt against him, the elite, and the Nigerian state, Adams has been celebrated, remembered, honored, and praised. The leader of what Fasehun dismissed as "a rabble"—whom, in contrast, Adams describes as "able-bodied and agile youths"[325]—has rallied his followers and the subaltern in general in Yorubaland, including a wider spectrum of elites in Nigeria,[326] to broaden his appeal, expand his power and influence, enlarge his cultural and socioeconomic estate, and consolidate his hold on the mass of young people in Southwestern Nigeria as well as his electoral appeal to the political elite within and beyond that region while also amplifying the significance of his subsequent achieved and conferred statuses in contemporary society.[327]

As I will show in the next chapter, the disagreement with Fasehun that later devolved into violence between the two factions, a path that eventually also partly accounted for the group's clashes with members of other ethnic groups in the urban areas in Southwestern Nigeria, is inserted into cultural practices within a long chain in Yorùbá history and encounters with other ethnic groups in Nigeria.

However, in the context of the OPC, the entwining of the practice of culture with an interplay between tradition and modernity is particularly interesting, as is the way that a strategic improviser and sociocultural entrepreneur[328] such as Adams employed this entwining in his project of personal transformation from a subaltern to an elite. As an embodiment of his own faction of the OPC—and, after Fasehun's death in 2018, the overall living embodiment of the group—Adams provides a useful reflection of the ways in which culture confronts new complexes of power relations[329] and, in its complexity, is used to negotiate power relations.

This chapter reflects on "hybrid, cosmopolitan experiences [such as the discourses of justice, rights, and democratic freedom] as much as on rooted, native ones [such as tradition, ritual, or identity]."[330] Reading Antonio Gramsci into the prevailing conceptions of culture can give analytical power to the study of its particular manifestations, particularly when it is conflated with political struggles in the social world of subalterns, such as the OPC youths. For Gramsci, first, the cultural world of the subaltern is anything but systematic. Second, the primary object of study is never a specific culture; "it is always power, more specifically particular constellations of power relations in particular times and places."[331] Gramsci consequently alerts us to the importance of focusing not on "stable, bounded cultural wholes, but [on] relationships and how these create fluid and shifting social entities."[332] Third, given the focus on power, for Gramsci, the question is not between the traditional and the modern but between the dominated and the dominant: "Societies are not mosaics of different cultures, hybrid or otherwise, rather they are constellations of different power groups."[333] In this context, culture becomes agency. And for Adams and the subaltern youths in his group, ritual and political struggles geared toward emphasizing and essentializing culture and politico-cultural autonomy constitute a reflection reflection on why certain conditions exist and "how best to convert the facts of vassalage into the signals of rebellion and social reconstruction."[334] Culture, in the way Adams uses it to understand his own historical value, function in life, and rights and obligations, is capable of articulating conflicts and alternately legitimizing, displacing, or controlling the superior force—as de Certeau points out.[335]

My analysis of the Gani Adams "revolt" in this chapter is placed within Gramsci's strongly agential definition of culture. In Adams's approach, culture is as much a process and a space as an institutionalized instrument for defining oneself in relation to others—individuals, group members, and the world in general. During the first few years in which he created and led his own faction of the OPC, Adams's "cultural grammar" was modulated or accentuated by his personal and social (class) circumstances and also entangled in three levels of struggles: with or against (1) the Fasehun faction, (2) Yorùbá elders and elites, and (3) other ethnic groups or the Nigerian state and its institutions. These struggles were all immersed in the ongoing social construction of power relations in Nigeria within which Adams sought to distinguish himself, in the sense of both *separating* himself from the general flow of things (through cultural activities and the use of force) as a committed person fighting for political change and *differentiating* himself (through self-promotion) from the "rabble" as an exceptional individual.

More than any other person, Adams was quick to see the potential for self-actualization within the context of his struggle for Yorùbá self-determination. Perhaps he did not fully realize the challenges he would have to confront to emerge as a man of consequence, but he was prepared to give it all that it would take—as subsequent chapters demonstrate.

NOTES

1. Frederick Fasehun, *OPC: Our History, Our Mission* (Lagos: Inspired Communications, 2002), 33. Contrary to Fasehun's claims, Adams completed primary school education. He dropped out only in his third year of high school.

2. Frederick Fasehun, *Frederick Fasehun: The Son of Oodua* (Lagos: Inspired Communications, 2002), 239.

3. Kenneth Post and George Jenkins, *The Price of Liberty: Personality and Politics in Colonial Nigeria* (Cambridge: Cambridge University Press, 1973).

4. "[Adelabu's] family was not closely connected with the traditional chieftainships of his native city, Ibadan, but he was sufficiently well placed to take advantage of such secondary school education as was available to African boys in the thirties.

After a number of vicissitudes, involving abortive careers as a government official, working for one of the big British trading concerns and on his own account, Adelabu found his role as a popular leader and 'boss' of Ibadan politics." Ibid.

5. David D. Laitin, *Hegemony and Culture: Politics and Religious Change among the Yoruba* (Chicago: University of Chicago Press, 1986), 173.

6. Many of his associates say that his father's name is Adamu and not Adams. Indeed, having been born to a Muslim father, Lamidi, he could not have had a Christian surname. This is not totally implausible in the Yorùbá context, yet since those who knew him long before he became a social phenomenon attest to this, it is likely that, in his quest to be "modern," he found Adams to be better for social acceptance than Adamu, which is the Yorùbá/Islamic equivalent of Adam (without the *s*). See the interview with one of his former aides for a contestation of Adams's rendering of his genealogy, Asabe AfrikaTV, "Why I Fell Out with Gani Adams over Greed—Chief Arogundade, OPC, New Era," YouTube, November 14, 2020, https://www.youtube.com/watch?v=mjO-H9PfntU. Fasehun also contests his genealogy. I will return to the controversy.

7. Sherry B. Ortner, *Anthropology and Social Theory: Culture, Power, and the Acting Subject* (Durham, NC: Duke University Press, 2006), 110.

8. Richard Werbner, "The Poetics of Wisdom Divination: Renewing the Moral Imagination," *Journal of the Royal Anthropological Institute* 23, no. 1 (2017): 82.

9. Mattia Fumanti, *The Politics of Distinction: African Elites from Colonialism to Liberation in a Namibian Frontier Town* (Canon Pyon: Sean Kingston), 7.

10. Vilfredo Pareto, *The Mind and Society* (London: Jonathan Cape, 1935); Pareto, *The Rise and Fall of the Elites*, intro. Hans L. Zetterberg (1968; reprint, Salem, NH: Ayer, 2017).

11. Fumanti, *Politics of Distinction*, 7.

12. Gani Adams, *My Life and Struggle* (Lagos: Publishers Express, 2007), 5.

13. Ibid.

14. Such as furniture maker (carpenter), fashion designer (tailor or seamster), businessman or businesswoman (trader), etc.

15. *Guardian*, January 13, 2000, 1.

16. Adams, *My Life and Struggle*, 5.

17. Gani Adams, in discussion with the author, June 20, 2002, Lagos, Nigeria.

18. Eghosa Osaghae, *Structural Adjustment and Ethnicity in Nigeria*, Research Report 98 (Uppsala: Nordiska Afrikainstitutet, 1995), 6.

19. Sunday Adebayo, telephone interview with the author, December 5, 2020.

20. Adams, *My Life and Struggle*, 7.

21. Ibid., 6.

22. Attahiru Jega, "The State and Identity Transformation under Structural Adjustment in Nigeria," in *Identity Transformation and Identity Politics under Structural Adjustment in Nigeria*, ed. Attahiru Jega (Uppsala: Nordiska Afrikainstitutet and Centre for Research and Documentation, 2000), 24.

23. Adams, *My Life and Struggle*, 6.

24. Folarin Ademosu, "Fasehun Can Kill, Destroy for Power, Money and Women," *P.M. News*, August 21, 2013, https://www.pmnewsnigeria.com/2013/08/21/fasehun-can-kill-destroy-for-power-money-and-women.

25. Ibid.

26. Cf. Abubakar Momoh, "Youth Culture and Area Boys in Lagos," in *Identity Transformation and Identity Politics under Structural Adjustment in Nigeria*, ed. A. Jega (Uppsala: Nordiska Afrikainstitutet, 2000), 181.

27. See, among others, Alcinda Honwana and Filip de Boeck, eds., *Makers and Breakers: Children and Youth in Postcolonial Africa* (Oxford: James Currey, 2005); Deborah Durham, "Youth and the Social Imagination in Africa: Introduction to Parts 1 and 2," *Anthropological Quarterly* 73, no. 3 (2000): 113–20; J. Abbink and I. van Kessel, eds., *Vanguard or Vandals: Youth, Politics and Conflict in Africa* (Leiden: Brill, 2004); D. B. Cruise O'Brien, "A Lost Generation? Youth Identity and State Decay in West Africa," in *Postcolonial Identities in Africa*, ed. R. Werbner and T. Ranger (London: Zed Books, 1996); Mamadou Diouf, "Engaging Postcolonial Cultures: African Youth and Public Space," *African Studies Review* 46, no. 2 (2003): 1–12; Jean Comaroff and John Comaroff, "Reflections on Youth: From the Past to the Postcolony," in Honwana and Boeck, *Makers and Breakers*; Monique Marks, *Young Warriors: Youth Politics, Identity and Violence in South Africa* (Johannesburg: Witwatersrand University Press, 2001); Adeline Masquelier, "The Scorpion's Sting: Youth, Marriage and the Struggle for Social Maturity in Niger," *Journal of the Royal Anthropological Institute* 11 (2005): 59–83; Henrik Vigh, "Youth Mobilisation as Social Navigation: Reflections on the Concept of Dubriagem," *Cadernos de Estudos Aricanos* 18, no. 19 (2010): 139–64.

28. Johanna Wyn and Ron White, *Rethinking Youth* (London: Sage, 1997), 9.

29. E. Liebau and L. Chisholm, "Youth, Social Change and Education: Issue and Problems," *Journal of Educational Policy* 8, no. 1 (1993): 5.

30. Charles Gore and David Pratten, "The Politics of Plunder: The Rhetoric of Order and Disorder in Southern Nigeria," *African Affairs* 102, no. 407 (2003): 212.

31. Pierre Bourdieu, *The Logic of Practice* (Stanford, CA: Stanford University Press, 1990), 56.

32. I will return to a critique of Bourdieu's general formulation on agency and subjectivity in the conclusion.

33. Gani Adams, "Politics and Agenda of Ethnic Militias: The Case of OPC," in *Urban Violence, Ethnic Militias and the Challenge of Democratic Consolidation in Nigeria*, ed. T. Babawale (Lagos: Malthouse, 2003), 97–100.

34. "I'm Not In Hiding," (Interview), *TheNEWS*, January 31, 2000, 16.

35. Gani Adams, interview with the author, May 28, 2002.

36. "I'm Not in Hiding," 15.

37. Taofik Adeyemi, interview with the author, April 1, 2021.

38. "I'm Not in Hiding."

39. Beverley Skeggs, "Exchange, Value and Affect: Bourdieu and 'the Self,'" supplement ("Feminism after Bourdieu"), *Sociological Review* 52, no. 2 (2004): 81–82.

40. Ulrick Beck, *Risk Society* (London: Sage, 1992).
41. Ibid.
42. Anthony Giddens, *Modernity and Self-identity* (Cambridge: Polity, 1991).
43. Skeggs, "Exchange, Value and Affect," 81.
44. H. Becker, *Sociological Work: Method and Substance* (Chicago: Aldine, 1970), 71.
45. Ivor Goodson, "The Story of Life History," in *The Routledge International Handbook on Narrative and Life History*, ed. Ivor Goodson, Ari Antikainen, Pat Sikes, and Molly Andrews (New York: Routledge, 2016). This author engages in a useful history of this method.
46. Ibid., 29.
47. Ibid. See also P. Munro, *Subject to Fiction: Women Teachers' Life History Narratives and the Cultural Politics of Resistance* (Buckingham: Open University Press, 1998), 8.
48. Gelya Frank, "Anthropology and Individual Lives: The Story of the Life History and the History of the Life Story," *American Anthropologist* 97, no. 1 (1995): 145. See also Charlotte Linde, *Life Stories: The Creation of Coherence* (New York: Oxford University Press, 1993). Linde argues correctly that "in order to exist in the social world with a comfortable sense of being a good, socially proper, and stable person, an individual needs to have a coherent, acceptable, and constantly revised life story." Ibid., 3.
49. Munro, *Subject to Fiction*, 12–13. It is important to note that, despite its usefulness in illuminating the personal and the social, the life story method is only about "lives interpreted and made textual." It can, therefore, only represent "a partial, selective commentary on lived experience." Goodson, "Story of Life History," 30.
50. Okwudiba Nnoli, *Ethnicity and Development in Nigeria* (Aldershot: Avebury, 1995), 1. In his earlier and more popular work, *Ethnic Politics in Nigeria* (Enugu: Fourth Dimension, 1978), on the basis of a radical interpretive mode and against overwhelming evidence, Nnoli dismissed ethnicity as "not a critical variable" in African states and societies. According to him, "Its role in African politics, although sometimes considerable, is more apparent than real." Nnoli, *Ethnic Politics in Nigeria*, 12.
51. James S. Coleman, *Nigeria: Background to Nationalism* (Berkeley: University of California Press, 1958), 213. Cf. Nnoli, *Ethnicity and Development*, 1.
52. Coleman, *Nigeria*, 213.
53. Ibid., 214.
54. Ibid.
55. Nnoli, *Ethnicity and Development*, 1.
56. Coleman, *Nigeria*, 215.
57. Ibid.
58. Nnoli, *Ethnicity and Development*, 2. On the "manipulation" of ethnicity by Nigerian elite, see ibid., 92–96. International IDEA, *Democracy in Nigeria: Continuing Dialogue(s) for Nation-Building* (Stockholm: International IDEA, 2000).

59. For a review of the different scholarly perspectives on ethnicity in Nigeria, for instance, see Ukoha Ukiwo, "The Study of Ethnicity in Nigeria," *Oxford Development Studies* 33, no. 1 (2005): 7–23.

60. Attahiru Jega, "General Introduction," in *Identity Transformation and Identity Politics Under Structural Adjustment in Nigeria*, ed. Attahiru Jega (Uppsala: Nordic Africa Institute, 2000), 12.

61. Ibid.

62. Eghosa Osaghae, "Explaining the Changing Patterns of Ethnic Politics in Nigeria," *Nationalism and Ethnic Politics* 9, no. 3 (2003): 54.

63. Ebere Onwudiwe also locates ethnicity along with religion as constituting "the structural roots of the political conflicts in Nigeria." Onwudiwe, "Geopolitical Zones and the Consolidation of Democracy," in *Nigeria's Struggle for Democracy and Good Governance: A Festschrift for Oyeleye Oyediran*, ed. Adigun Agbaje, Larry Diamond, and Ebere Onwudiwe (Ibadan: University of Ibadan Press, 2004), 269.

64. See Victor Azarya, "Ethnicity and Conflict Management in Post-colonial Africa," *Nationalism and Ethnic Politics* 9, no. 3 (2003): 1–24.

65. Nnoli, *Ethnicity and Development*, 4.

66. Ibid. (emphasis added).

67. Ibid. For a contrary view, see Henry Ani Kifordu, "Ethnic Politics, Political Elite, and Regime Change in Nigeria," *Studies in Ethnicity and Nationalism* 11, no. 3 (2011): 427–50. See also Okechukwu Ibeanu, "Ethnicity and Transition to Democracy in Nigeria: Explaining the Passing of Authoritarian Rule in a Multi-ethnic Society," *African Journal of Political Science/Revue Africaine de Science Politique* 5, no. 2 (2000): 45–65.

68. Okwudiba Nnoli, "Ethnic Conflicts in Africa: A Comparative Analysis," in *Ethnic Conflicts in Africa*, ed. O. Nnoli (Dakar: CODESRIA, 1998), 9.

69. Nnoli, *Ethnicity and Development*, 4.

70. Ibid. (emphasis added).

71. See Larry Diamond, *Class, Ethnicity and Democracy in Nigeria: The Failure of the First Republic* (Syracuse, NY: Syracuse University Press, 1988). While noting the "record of chronic and ultimately catastrophic ethnic and regional conflicts" in Nigeria, Diamond argues that "to develop a fuller understanding of the nature of ethnic conflict and the process of conflict polarization, we [need to] see that the development of stable democracy . . . [in] Nigeria depends on much more than the effective management of subcultural cleavage. It may also require basic change in the economy and society and the way these articulate with a rapidly growing state." Ibid., 3.

72. See Richard Joseph, *Democracy and Prebendal Politics in Nigeria: The Rise and Fall of the Second Republic* (Cambridge: Cambridge University Press, 1987). Joseph notes that "the underlying social and political system in Nigeria yields a continuing concern with how interests are represented and benefits distributed." He notes that within this context "Nigerians are compelled to pursue democracy for the very reason that they are unable to rely on a government . . . in which their particular subgroup of the population is not directly and effectively represented." Ibid., 4.

73. Bamidele A. Ojo, ed., *Nigeria's Third Republic: The Problems and Prospects of Political Transition to Civil Rule* (New York: Nova Science, 1998); Emeka Nwokedi, "Nigeria's Democratic Transition: Explaining the Annulled 1993 Presidential Election," *Round Table* 83, no. 330 (1994): 189–204. See also Larry Diamond, Anthony Kirk-Greene, and Oyeleye Oyediran, eds., *Transition without End: Nigerian Politics and Civil Society under Babangida* (Boulder, CO: Lynne Rienner, 1997).

74. Adigun Agbaje and Oyeyele Oyediran, eds., *Nigeria: Politics of Transition and Governance, 1986–1996* (Dakar: CODESRIA, 1999). Like Diamond and Joseph, the editors of this volume also note "the persistent pressures for democratisation and responsible governance in Nigeria." Ibid., 21. See also Abubakar Momoh and Said Adejumobi, *The Nigerian Military and the Crisis of Democratic Transition: A Study in the Monopoly of Power* (Lagos: CLO, 1999).

75. Agbaje, Diamond, and Onwudiwe, *Nigeria's Struggle for Democracy*; Aaron T. Gana and Yakubu B. C. Omelle, eds., *Democratic Rebirth in Nigeria*, vol. 1, *1999–2003* (Abuja: African Centre for Democratic Governance, 2005); A. Carl LeVan, *Contemporary Nigerian Politics: Competition in a Time of Transition and Terror* (Cambridge: Cambridge University Press, 2019).

76. Bade Onimode, "Game Theory and the Politics of Transformation in Nigeria," in *Governance and Development in Nigeria: Essays in Honour of Professor Billy J. Dudley*, ed. Oyeleye Oyediran (Ibadan: Oyediran Consult International, 1996), 83. For a typical example of the question of "Hausa-Fulani hegemony" as articulated in the South of Nigeria, see Okechukwu Okeke, *Hausa-Fulani Hegemony: The Dominance of the Muslim North in Contemporary Nigerian Politics* (Enugu: Acena, 1992).

77. For more on this, see chap. 5.

78. Terry Lynn Karl, "The Perils of the Petro-State: Reflections on the Paradox of Plenty," *Journal of International Affairs* 53, no. 1 (1999): 31–48.

79. While acknowledging this fact in the most recent attempt at writing a comprehensive history of the Yorùbá, Akinwumi Ogundiran argues that "despite the large volume of scholarship in Yoruba studies, and Yoruba history in particular, we still lack an understanding of the events and eventfulness, meanings and motivations, and social actors and processes of social valuation that shaped the ancestral Yoruba experiences in the long term." Ogundiran, *The Yoruba: A New History* (Bloomington: Indiana University Press, 2020), 5.

80. Andrew Apter, *Black Critics and Kings: The Hermeneutics of Power in Yoruba Society* (Chicago: University of Chicago Press, 1992), 3.

81. It is important to note that Akintoye and Akinwumi Ogundiran strongly reject the position in parts of both lay and scholarly that the construction of a single Yorùbá identity is a product of the 19th century missionary (and later colonial) encounter. Stephen Adebanji Akintoye, *The History of the Yoruba People* (Dakar: Amalion, 2010); Ogundiran, *Yoruba*, 8.

82. Robin Law contests this. See Robin C. C. Law, *The Oyo Empire, c. 1600–c. 1836* (Oxford: Oxford University Press, 1977).

83. Ibid.

84. See also Andrew Apter, "The Historiography of Yoruba Myth and Ritual," *History in Africa* 14 (1987): 1–25; Apter, *Oduduwa's Chain: Locations and Culture in the Yoruba Atlantic* (Chicago: University of Chicago Press, 2018), 1.

85. Samuel Johnson, *The History of the Yorubas: From the Earliest Times to the Beginning of the British Protectorate* (Lagos: CMS Nigeria Bookshop, 1921), 646.

86. Akintoye, *History of the Yoruba People*, 70.

87. Aribidesi Usman and Toyin Falola, *The Yoruba from Prehistory to the Present* (Cambridge: Cambridge University Press, 2019).

88. Ogundiran, *Yoruba*.

89. Usman and Falola state that, "while recognizing the pivotal position of Ile-Ife and Oyo in Yoruba history," their book "also considers the tremendous impact of other Yoruba polities and non-Yoruba neighboring groups in the formation of a powerful Yoruba frontier culture in Africa." Usman and Falola, *Yoruba*, xviii.

90. See Wale Adebanwi, *Yoruba Elites and Ethnic Politics in Nigeria: Obafemi Awolowo and Corporate Agency* (Cambridge: Cambridge University Press, 2014).

91. J. D. Y. Peel, "Olaju: A Yoruba Concept of Development," *Journal of Development Studies* 14, no. 2 (1978): 135–65; Peel, *Ijeshas and Nigerians: The Incorporation of a Yoruba Kingdom, 1890s–1970s* (Cambridge: Cambridge University Press, 1983); Peel, *Religious Encounter and the Making of the Yoruba* (Bloomington: Indiana University Press, 2000); Laitin, *Hegemony and Culture*.

92. Wale Adebanwi, "The Carpenter's Revolt: Youth, Violence and the Reinvention of Culture in Nigeria," *Journal of Modern African Studies* 43, no. 3 (2005): 340.

93. Ibid., 99.

94. Peel, *Religious Encounter*.

95. Ibid., 8, 26.

96. Peel, *Religious Encounter*, 280; cf. Peel, "Olaju."

97. Emmanuel A. Ayandele, *The Missionary Impact on Modern Nigeria, 1842–1914: A Political and Social Analysis* (London: Longman, 1966).

98. Laitin, *Hegemony and Culture*, 97.

99. Jacob K. Olupona contends that Laitin's argument no longer holds in the post-1990 era. Olupona, *City of 201 Gods: Ilé-Ifè in Time, Space, and the Imagination* (Berkeley: University of California Press, 2011), 287.

100. cf. Peel, *Ijeshas and Nigerians*, 221–25.

101. Ogundiran, *Yoruba*, 8. Andrew Apter, in exploring "diasporic influences that eventually gave rise to Yoruba ethnicity," also challenges "externalist perspectives," but only "to complicate the very distinction between inside and outside that they presuppose." Apter, *Oduduwa's Chain*, 123.

102. Ogundiran, *Yoruba*, 9.

103. Ibid.

104. Ibid. (emphasis added).

105. J. Lorand Matory, on his part, also presents convincing evidence about the contributions that nineteenth-century Afro-Brazilian travelers to Lagos made to the formation of modern Yorùbá identity. Matory, "The English Professors of Brazil: On

the Diasporic Roots of the Yoruba Nation," *Comparative Studies in Society and History* 41, no. 1 (1999): 72–103. See also Matory, *Black Atlantic Religion: Tradition, Transnationalism, and Matriarchy in the Afro-Brazilian Candomblé* (Princeton, NJ: Princeton University Press, 2005). For an interesting perspective that complicates "the very distinction between 'inside' and 'outside'" in the making of the Yorùbá identity, see David Apter, "Yoruba Ethnogenesis from Within," *Comparative Studies in Society and History* 55, no. 2 (2013): 357.

106. A point articulated in a different direction by Olúfemi Táíwò when describing the project of modernity in African as midwifed by missionary Christianity. See Táíwò, *How Colonialism Preempted Modernity in Africa* (Bloomington: Indiana University Press, 2009).

107. See Adebanwi, *Yoruba Elites and Ethnic Politics*. As N. A. Fadipe also shows, "the label, Yoruba, as that of an ethnic group could not have been long in vogue prior to 1856." Fadipe, *The Sociology of the Yoruba*, ed. Francis Olu Okediji and Oladejo O. Okediji (Ibadan: Ibadan University Press, 1970), 30.

108. Boel Berner, "Manoeuvring in Uncertainty: On Agency, Strategies and Negotiations," in *Manoeuvring in an Environment of Uncertainty: Structural Change and Social Action in Sub-Saharan Africa*, ed. Boel Berner and Per Trulsson (Aldershot: Ashgate, 2000), 99, following Ann Swidler, "Culture in Action: Symbols and Strategies," *American Sociological Review* 51 (1986): 273–86.

109. Peel, *Religious Encounter*, 317.

110. Peel, "Olaju," 144.

111. The fundamental basis of the group is the fight for democratic rights, justice, and equity. Yet the group also approaches its mission through cultural practices.

112. Peel, *Religious Encounter*, 317.

113. Gani Adams, statement issued at press conference, Lagos, October 26, 1999.

114. Fasehun, *OPC*, 14. Many of the OPC members I spoke with over the years represented the same sentiments in different ways.

115. Lissa A. Malkki, *Purity and Exile: Violence, Memory, and National Cosmology among Hutu Refugees in Tanzania* (Chicago: University of Chicago Press, 1995).

116. See Benedict Anderson, *Imagined Communities: Reflections on the Origin and Spread of Nationalism* (London: Verso, 1991); Marcus Bank, *Ethnicity: Anthropological Constructions* (London: Routledge, 1996); Abner Cohen, *Urban Ethnicity* (London: Routledge, 2001); T. H. Eriksen, *Ethnicity and Nationalism: Anthropological Perspectives* (London: Pluto, 1993); E. Gellner, *Nations and Nationalism* (Oxford: Blackwell, 1983); Eric Hobsbawm and Terence Ranger, *The Invention of Tradition* (Cambridge: Cambridge University Press, 1992).

117. Richard Joseph, *"Nigeria: 1993; The Way Forward," Testimony before the Subcommittee on Africa, House Committee on Foreign Affairs, August 4, 1993*, 103rd Congr. (1993).

118. Diouf argues that, because of their "unique" position in speaking "a language of both universal rights and specific African cultures," young people in Africa are involved in a "refashioning of the indices and signs of autochthony and membership,

of inclusion and exclusion," as part of a new trajectory that suggests "new avenues of political action and expression that may be violent or nonviolent." Diouf, "Engaging Postcolonial Cultures," 1, 3.

119. For an insider's reflections on the annulment, see Omo Omoruyi, *The Tale of June 12: The Betrayal of the Democratic Rights of Nigerians (1993)* (London: Press Alliance Network, 1999).

120. Contrary to Fasehun's account here, the Yorùbá were actually in the vanguard of the prodemocracy movement. Fasehun needed to present this picture of a "disenabled" people to further heroize himself. For accounts of the role of Yorùbá activists in the prodemocracy movement, see J. Kayode Fayemi, *Out of the Shadows: Exile and the Struggle for Freedom & Democracy in Nigeria* (Ibadan: Amandla Consulting, 2005); Olawale Oshun, *Clapping with One Hand: June 12 and the Crisis of a State Nation* (Lagos: Josel, 1999); Oshun, *The Open Grave: NADECO and the Struggle for Democracy in Nigeria* (Lagos: Josel, 2002).

121. Fasehun, *Frederick Fasehun*, 159–60 (emphasis added).

122. Adams, *My Life and Struggle*, 13.

123. This is important because the Yorùbá consider the act of telling someone a pertinent history (*pà'tàn fun*) as a crucial way to either put someone in his/her place or intervene powerfully in (inter)personal, communal, cultural, or social crisis.

124. Fasehun, *Frederick Fasehun*, 160.

125. Ibid.

126. Ibid.

127. Ibid.

128. Ibid., 161.

129. Vigh, "Youth Mobilisation as Social Navigation," 139–64.

130. Sandra T. Barnes, *Patrons and Power: Creating a Political Community in Metropolitan Lagos* (Manchester: Manchester University Press, 1986), ix.

131. Ibid., 1.

132. Adams, *My Life and Struggle*. Unlike Fasehun's, Adams's book is not really a biography or a biographical memoir.

133. Fasehun, *OPC*, vii. In fact, Adams states in his own book that he had ignored Fasehun's "first salvo" but decided to respond to the "second straw." Adams, *My Life and Struggle*, 2.

134. Adams, *My Life and Struggle*, vii.

135. Ibid., 42.

136. Ibid., 13.

137. Fasehun, *OPC*, 18. Fasehun describes Engurube as "one of the prominent Ijaw human rights activists that was in the forefront of the agitation for social justice in Ijawland . . . [and] my friend of about 30 years." Fasehun, 17.

138. Ibid., 13–14.

139. Fasehun, *OPC*, 26. It seems unlikely that Owolabi (alias Ikare), whom Fasehun describes as "one of the pioneer OPC members," would have "brought [Adams] along

to one of the meetings" unless Adams had been convinced to join the group at that point.

140. Ibid., 14.

141. Telephone interview and WhatsApp exchanges with two members of the group(s), June 2023.

142. Ibid.

143. Fasehun, *OPC*, 39.

144. Though the Ibadan-born Adesokan is an "Evangelist" and therefore a Christian, he says he is also a Muslim and African Traditional Religion adherent. When we chatted on the phone during Ramadan, the Islamic holy month, in April 2021, he was fasting. He joked that "*ona kan o wo' ja*" (lit. "the market can be accessed through more than one road").

145. Fasehun, *OPC*, 24.

146. Ibid., 20.

147. Fasehun, *Frederick Fasehun*, 229.

148. Kunle Adesokan, telephone interview with the author, April 14, 2021.

149. Ibid.

150. Fasehun, *OPC*, 24.

151. Adesokan, interview with the author, April 14, 2021.

152. Fasehun, *OPC*, 29.

153. In his book, Adams mentioned Silas Atanda as one of the founding members of the group. Is this the same as Silas Alani? Or was the last name an error in Adams's book?

154. Silas Alani, telephone interview with the author, September 5, 2021.

155. Fasehun, *OPC*, 16.

156. Ibid., 20.

157. "Enemy Within" is the title of chap. 2 of Fasehun's second book on the OPC. This is a reference to Gani Adams.

158. Fasehun, *Frederick Fasehun*, 240–41.

159. Ibid., 241.

160. Adams, *My Life and Struggle*, 28.

161. Balogun, telephone interview with the author, November 18, 2020.

162. Ogundimu, telephone interview with the author, December 1, 2020.

163. Fasehun, *Frederick Fasehun*, 241 (emphasis added).

164. Fasehun, *OPC*, 33 (emphasis added).

165. Ogundimu, December 1, 2020. Ogundimu said that later at a meeting in the house of Makinde Omolaja (late), who was the OPC coordinator for Lagos, he had asked Gani for documentary evidence of his claims against Fasehun, but Adams had no documents. He added that he had warned Adams that he should be keeping documents as Fasehun did.

166. Fasehun, *Frederick Fasehun*, 241.

167. Ibid.

168. Fasehun, *OPC*, 35.

169. Ibid.
170. Ibid., 36.
171. Ibid. (emphasis added). This, as became more evident over the years, is a significant description of the state of affairs in the OPC by the founding leader of the group. And, as I show in chap. 3, in the story about the "N10 million boys," Fasehun was right in stating that some members of the group were "prepared to go to any length to show their disapproval and anger."
172. Ibid.
173. Ibid.
174. Adams, *My Life and Struggle*, 28 (emphasis added).
175. Ibid. Led by Daniel Kanu, the Youth Earnestly Ask for Abacha (YEAA) group, which was formed in 1997, campaigned for General Abacha to self-succeed as president of Nigeria. The group organized a Two Million Man March in Abuja to convince Abacha to self-succeed.
176. Ibid.
177. Ibid.
178. McNezer Fasehun, "Obasanjo Woos Oodua Leader," *P.M. News*, December 8, 1998, 1, 5.
179. Ibid., 1.
180. Ibid., 5.
181. Ibid.
182. Adesokan, interview with the author, April 14, 2021.
183. Ibid.
184. Adams, *My Life and Struggle*, 28.
185. Ogundimu, telephone interview with the author, December 1, 2020. Incidentally, another ranking member of the group, Alhaji Maruf Olanrewaju, the OPC coordinator for Kwara State who later formed his own group, Oodua Progressive Care Initiative (OPCI), made a similar accusation against Adams. "Gani Adams did worse than Fasehun," he told me. Olanrewaju, telephone interview, January 8, 2021. Balogun also alleged that the "first big money" they received was from a governor in the Southwest. "He gave us N10 million. But Adams did not share the money," he alleged. He alleged further that after they formed the Adams faction, they received a lot of money from politicians. Akande made a similar claim.
186. See Adams, *My Life and Struggle*, 29–31.
187. Ibid., 29.
188. The *esos*, or guards, were the "guardians of the kingdom" in the old Oyo Empire. The reappropriation of this category by the OPC is a part of their efforts at retraditionalization. In the Oyo Empire, *esos* were also noble men of the second class. See Johnson, *History of the Yoruba*, 73. A popular saying from the Oyo Empire that survives till now has it that "one of two things befits an Eso/The Eso must fight and conquer (or)/The Eso must fight and perish (in war)." Quoted in Toyin Falola and G. O. Oguntomisin, *Yoruba Warlords of the Nineteenth Century* (Trenton, NJ: Africa World Press, 2001), 15.

189. Fasehun, *OPC*, 40–41.
190. Ibid., 41 (emphasis added).
191. Ibid.
192. Ibid.
193. Suspicions or allegations of assassination attempts or murder plots are thrown around among the leaders of the group constantly. For example, Ogundamisi, onetime secretary-general of the Fasehun faction, said Fasehun once accused him, Adams, and Alhaji Toyin Jimoh (the last two of whom were mutual enemies) of also planning to kill him. Adams, over the years, has accused several members of his faction and those he expelled of attempting to assassinate him. These suspicions and allegations may not be true in the particular instance, but there is no doubt that, for many years, there were countless plots for mutual elimination in the group. Ogundamisi mentioned an instance when the police were hunting Adams while the Fasehun faction was also looking for him to eliminate him. Fasehun's faction got wind of where Adams was hiding and decided to storm the place. They were certain that if Adams was eliminated, it could easily be blamed on the police. However, Ogundamisi said he realized that, even with "security" around Adams, the hideout could be bridged. He secretly sent a message to one of Adams's closest aides to ask them to move him to another location. Ogundamisi, interview with the author, November 15, 2020.
194. Adams, *My Life and Struggle*, 21.
195. Ibid.
196. See appendix in Fasehun, *OPC*, 239.
197. Fasehun took note of this, describing Adams as the "self-designated 'President.'" Ibid., 45.
198. "The Rebirth of Our Political Movement: An Affirmation of Self-determination and Social Emancipation," National Leadership and State Co-ordinating Council of the OPC, press conference, office of the OPC, Lagos, March 1, 1999.
199. Ibid.
200. Ibid.
201. Ibid. Initially, they also wanted the "immediate actualisation of . . . Abiola's mandate won in the June 12 19993 presidential election."
202. Ibid.
203. Ibid.
204. Ibid.
205. Fasehun, *OPC*, 39.
206. Ibid., 37–39.
207. Ibid., 38–39.
208. Fasehun, *Frederick Fasehun*, 238.
209. Richard Elesho and Bamidele Adebayo, "Divided It Stands," *TheNEWS*, July 19, 1999, 23.
210. Dayo Benson, "Fasehun Is Not the Leader of OPC—Fawehinmi," *Vanguard*, September 19, 1999, 10.

211. Fasehun, *OPC*, 44.
212. Fasehun, *Frederick Fasehun*, 239.
213. Ibid., 238.
214. I once visited Fasehun's Century Hotel in Okota, Lagos, where he proudly displays a prototype of the center.
215. Fasehun, *Frederick Fasehun*, 228.
216. Fasehun, *OPC*, 38.
217. Fasehun, *Frederick Fasehun*, 228.
218. Fasehun, *OPC*, 27.
219. Ibid., 27–28.
220. Fasehun, *Frederick Fasehun*, 229.
221. Fasehun, *OPC*, 28.
222. Ibid., 25.
223. Ibid.
224. Fasehun, *Frederick Fasehun*, 228.
225. Fasehun, *OPC*, 26 (emphasis added).
226. Fasehun, *OPC*, 33.
227. Ibid., 26.
228. This was raised again in 2020 by Adams's erstwhile comrades who left the Fasehun faction alongside him. See Asabe AfrikaTV, "Why I Fell Out with Gani Adams over Greed—Chief Arogundade, OPC, New Era," YouTube, November 14, 2020, https://www.youtube.com/watch?v=mjO-H9PfntU. If Ogundiran's argument about the cultural group—and therefore what it means to be Yorùbá—holds, then this allegation about Adams's progeny is irrelevant to his being Yorùbá. See Ogundiran, *Yoruba*.
229. He traced his ancestry back to Oyo. He claimed that his progenitors had migrated from Oyo to Epimi and then to Arigidi.
230. Balogun and other erstwhile associates of Adams claimed that Olanipekun's predecessor had told them about Adams's alleged Nupe pedigree.
231. Adams, telephone interview with the author, November 30, 2020. After they fell out with him, Adams's lieutenants, including Balogun and Akande, dismissed this narrative. They asked how someone who was eager to acquire many chieftaincy titles could claim that the traditional ruler of his hometown begged him for two years before he accepted a title. They added that the traditional ruler told them that the title *otunba* was not a *traditional* title in the town and that it had been invented only because Adams wanted a title in the town.
232. Fasehun, *Frederick Fasehun*, 229 (emphasis added).
233. Fasehun, *OPC*, 31.
234. Ibid., 33.
235. Fasehun, *Frederick Fasehun*, 231.
236. Ibid.
237. Akande, telephone interview with the author, November 17, 2020.
238. Anusa Musiliu, telephone interview with the author, December 10, 2020.

239. Ibid.
240. Adebayo, telephone interview with the author, December 5, 2020.
241. Marruf Olanrewaju, telephone interview with the author, January 28, 2022.
242. Telephone interview with the author, May 6, 2021.
243. Balogun, telephone interview with the author, November 18, 2020.
244. Ibid.
245. Ademosu, "Fasehun Can Kill." Adams presented a totally different image of Fasehun in his tribute after the latter's death. Adams stated that Fasehun's passing "was a great loss to the Yoruba race." He added: "I passed through him for a period of five years. Baba deserves all respect and will also be remembered as a distinguished leader in all ramification[s], and one that was greatly admired by the general public and his peers as a straightforward and a complete gentleman. He demonstrated wisdom, honesty and good leadership, established friendship, harmony, and accommodation across the board." Samson Folarin, "Fasehun: My Father, Mentor Is Gone, Says Gani Adams," *Punch*, December 1, 2018, https://punchng.com/faseun-my-father-mentor-is-gone-says-gani-adams/.
246. Ademosu, "Fasehun Can Kill."
247. Ibid.
248. Ibid.
249. Ibid.
250. Ibid. (emphasis added).
251. Adams, *My Life and Struggle*, 19, 20, 26.
252. Ibid.
253. Ibid., 20.
254. Ibid., 24.
255. Ibid., 14 (emphasis added).
256. Ibid., 25.
257. Ibid.
258. Ibid.
259. Ibid., 22–24, 26.
260. Ibid., 21.
261. Ibid., 26.
262. Olugbenga Onasanya, a contributor to a volume that examines the "leadership challenges" that Adams has faced, concludes that "like all . . . great men, Gani Adams is already towing the line of heroism through his activities," adding that "Gani Adams rose to stardom and greatness through hard work and resilience." To further heroize Adams, the author even states, "It is on record that his birth was accentuated by a miraculous experience." Olugbenga Onasanya, "Who Is Gani Adams? A Biographical Sketch," in *Leadership Challenge: Gani Adams and the Oodua People's Congress*, ed. Michael M. Ogbeidi (Lagos: Publishers Express, 2005), 68, 69, 71.
263. Fasehun, *Frederick Fasehun*, 238–39.
264. Peel, "Olaju," 148, 150.
265. Fasehun, *Frederick Fasehun*, 230–31.

266. See, for instance, ibid., 230–33.
267. "I'm Not in Hiding," 17.
268. Muyiwa Akintunde, "Obasanjo Is Not Biased," *Africa Today*, February 2002, http://archive.africatoday.com/secret/feb02/feb02obasanjoisnot.htm.
269. Fasehun, *Frederick Fasehun*, 228.
270. Ibid., 228, 230.
271. Muyiwa Akintunde, "Dr Frederick Faseun: 'Give a Dog a Bad Name,'" *Africa Today*, February 2000, http://archive.africatoday.com/secret/feb00/feb00inter vwdrfred.htm.
272. Fasehun, *Frederick Fasehun*, 221.
273. Ibid., 229.
274. Ibid., 230–31 (emphasis added).
275. Ibid.
276. Ibid., 160–62.
277. Fasehun, *OPC*, 62. In *My Life and Struggle*, Adams seems to attempt to show that he was capable of being an intellectual too. The first part of the book is replete with references to, or quotations from, thinkers, scientists, writers, intellectuals, and scholars from antiquity to contemporary times, including Socrates, Plato, Aristotle, Galileo, Hobbes, Shakespeare, Yeats, Picasso, Nehru, Awolowo, and Soyinka.
278. Adams, interview with the author, July 8, 2004.
279. Chris McGreal, "Nigeria's Ethnic Hatreds Turn Lethal," *Guardian*, October 19, 2000, https://www.theguardian.com/world/2000/oct/20/chrismcgreal.
280. This is a reference to the controversial statement by Maitama Sule, a northern politician and Nigeria's former permanent representative at the UN, that northerners were "born to rule."
281. Gani Adams, statement issued at press conference, Lagos, October 26, 1999.
282. Ibid.
283. Emma Nnadozie, Albert Akpor, and Olasunkanmi Akoni, "Gani Adams: YCE, Gani, Others Seek Fair Hearing OPC Members Protest Arrest in Lagos, Demand Release," *Vanguard*, August 24, 2001, 1.
284. Ibid.
285. This was long before he became the generalissimo. On this, see chap. 4.
286. Jide Ajani, "Regional Govt Tops Yoruba Agenda for Confab," *Vanguard*, February 11, 2005, 14; Clifford Ndujihe, "National Conference: Glimpses of a Likely Yoruba Agenda," *Guardian*, January 24, 2005, https://www.dawodu.com/articles/national -conference-glimpses-of-a-likely-yoruba-agenda-681.
287. Insa Nolte, "Identity and Violence: The Politics of Youth in Ijebu-Remo, Nigeria," *Journal of Modern African Studies* 42, no. 1 (2004): 69.
288. Adams, interview with the author, July 8, 2004.
289. Fasehun, *Frederick Fasehun*, 229.
290. Ibid., 231. See also Fasehun, *OPC*, 32–33.
291. As stated in the OPC Constitution and Bill of Rights (p. 12): "I . . . solemnly declare that I will abide by the aims and objectives of the OODUA PEOPLE'S

CONGRESS as set out in the Constitution, OODUA bill of rights and other duly adopted police, positions, that I am joining the organisation voluntarily and without motives of material advantage or personal gain."

292. However, he says in his book, "I am not in any way fetish. Neither do I wear charms and amulets for protection." Adams, *My Life and Struggle*, 20. See, for example, references to what the police found in his car when he was arrested in chap. 2. Fasehun writes that "Adams was at his 'best' demonstrating how to wear charms, how to recite incantations." Fasehun, *OPC*, 31.

293. Virtually every one of his associates and aides with whom I spoke mentioned this. For example, Ogundamisi told me, "Adams is suspicious of everybody."

294. Even in his personal relations with his aides, as some of them told me, every time he raised a suspicion about them, he asked them to swear an oath to confirm the truthfulness of their claims.

295. Fasehun states that before Adams left his group, he once unexpectedly visited the "oath-taking room" that Adams had set up. What he saw, he claims, "was frighteningly barbaric and so intimidating." This was probably an exaggeration, though. Fasehun, *OPC*, 32.

296. Patrick Chabal and J.-P. Daloz, *African Works: Disorder as Political Instrument* (Oxford: James Currey, 1999).

297. Bourdieu, *Logic of Practice*, p. 57.

298. Ibid.

299. Ibid., 58.

300. Diouf, "Engaging Postcolonial Cultures," 5.

301. Ibid.

302. Margaret Thomas Drewal, *Yoruba Ritual: Performers, Play, Agency* (Bloomington: Indiana University Press, 1992), 8.

303. "Even the deities keep up-to-date," a priestess told Drewal. Ibid.

304. Ibid., xvi.

305. Ibid., xiv.

306. Ibid., 9, 27.

307. Adams, interview with the author, May 28, 2002.

308. Anthony Giddens, *Central Problems in Social Theory: Action, Structure and Contradiction in Social Analysis* (Berkeley: University of California Press, 1979), 200.

309. Bourdieu, *Logic of Practice*, 52.

310. Adams, interview with the author, July 8, 2004.

311. Gbeminiyi, "... Our Men Slept with Women—OPC," *Sunday Tribune*, January 20, 2002, 15.

312. Ibid.

313. Adegbenro Adebanjo and Yemi Olowolabi, "End of the Manhunt," *Tell*, September 3, 2001, 31.

314. Shiyanbola claimed to have secured an exception as a Christian. She said she read a passage from the Bible.

315. Adams, interview with the author, August 8, 2004.

316. L. S. La Fontaine, *Initiation* (Manchester: Manchester University Press, 1985), 16.
317. Adams, interview with the author, August 8, 2004.
318. Gbeminiyi, "... Our Men Slept with Women—OPC," 15.
319. Ironically, though Osho is a shortened form of Oshodi's name, it is pronounced differently by the group members to mean "wizard."
320. Oshodi, interview with the author, July 2, 2021.
321. Balogun, Akande, and Adebayo said that every time this happened, it had to with Adams "hoarding" the money the group had earned.
322. Fasehun, *OPC*, 44 (emphasis added).
323. Ibid.
324. Fasehun, *Frederick Fasehun*, 230.
325. Adams, *My Life and Struggle*, 7.
326. As early as 2005, even Fasehun recognized that Adams was on his way to becoming a big man, writing, "The lowly gave up humility and assumed equality with long-standing national figures." Fasehun, *OPC*, 63.
327. Chapters 3 and 4 examine these achieved and conferred statuses. As far back as 2005, an edited volume had been published on Adams's "leadership challenges." The foreword was written by Professor Sophie Oluwole, a retired professor of philosophy at the University of Lagos. See Ogbeidi, *Leadership Challenge*.
328. I use this in the same sense that Sandra Barnes uses "political entrepreneur." Barnes, *Patrons and Power*, 70, following F. G. Bailey, *Stratagems and Spoils: A Social Anthropology of Politics* (New York: Schocken Books, 1969), 36.
329. James Clifford, *Routes: Travel and Translation in the Late Twentieth Century* (Cambridge, MA: Harvard University Press, 1997), 7.
330. Ibid., 24.
331. Kate Crehan, *Gramsci, Culture and Anthropology* (London: Pluto, 2002), 66.
332. Ibid.
333. Ibid.
334. Ibid., 75.
335. Michel de Certeau, *The Practice of Everyday Life* (Berkeley: University of California Press, 1984), xvii.

2 / Social Anomie, Vigilantism, and the Leveraging of Violent Habitus

INTRODUCTION

In July 2004, Gani Adams and I were chatting by a gas station near the tollgate in the Ibadan end of the Lagos-Ibadan Expressway. He introduced me to his wife, Mojisola, whom he had married about a year earlier. They were traveling from an event in his hometown back to Lagos. Some of the faction members traveling with him were either sitting in the vehicles in his entourage or milling around. A few appeared to be standing guard or keeping watch over their leader.

We had been in touch on the phone a few days earlier. He agreed to stop briefly in Ibadan on his journey back to Lagos so I could ask him a few questions about some recent developments concerning the group. Some of the vehicles bore "OPC Gani Adams Faction" banners. Those who noticed this stopped to watch. By that time, the OPC had achieved both popularity and notoriety in Southwest Nigeria. Members of the group were alternatively—and in some cases, simultaneously—feared and admired for their defense of "Yorùbá interests" and their vigilante activities in urban areas, as well as for their incessant clashes with rival groups, the police, and members of other ethnic groups. Therefore, the presence of members of the "militant" or "Gani Adams faction" of the OPC, and the leader of the group himself, could not but attract attention.

Though Adams was kind enough to break his journey for a brief chat with me, and despite the fame and measure of stardom (or, for his adversaries, infamy) he had achieved in urban social circles, he was not yet a superstar. Therefore, it was not altogether unusual for him to be found standing by the roadside having a chat. Still, his presence attracted attention, given his recent eruption in the sociocultural and political scene and the measure of awe with which

Figure 2.1. Adams, shirtless and in handcuffs, on the cover of *TELL* magazine. It was his first time on the cover of a major newsmagazine in Nigeria. After this, he was on his way with the Nigerian media.

many urban dwellers, particularly the poor and the youth, talked about him. I wanted, above all, to know his reaction to the recent accusations that he and members of his faction had deliberately instigated violent clashes in Lagos and elsewhere in Southwest Nigeria.

It was only around 2004 that I first noticed that he was concerned that he was acquiring a reputation as a "violent" man. Initially, I assumed that he intended to transform his reputation in order to legitimize his faction beyond the context of what he described as "a Yorùbá self-determination group" and to create a new ethos that would turn away from constant clashes with other groups—including the Fasehun-led faction of the OPC. Later events and subsequent reflections indicated that the unease was not merely about repositioning the group. It fed into his vision of his future role as a key player in urban politics and, more widely, in the politics of Southwestern Nigeria and the country at large. Yet the tactical and strategic move to represent himself not as a man of violence but as a man of peace also meant an intricate retention of the generalized acknowledgment of his latent, if not manifest, capacity to mobilize violence when necessary. With a combination of the present status of a "man of peace" with the past yet (under)current image of one who could mobilize and unleash violence, Adams could move to the next stage in his intriguing public career. Thus, unlike in the early days, when he defended his group against accusations of illegitimate violence by insisting that they were protecting the interest of the Yorùbá or defending themselves against the police or rival groups, in the post-initial-arrest era, particularly from around 2004, Adams began to emphasize that he and his group embraced peace rather than violence. Before this stage, he had been eager to dismiss accusations of violence as part of the concerted efforts by the Nigerian state; its dominant ethno-nationalist group, the Hausa-Fulani; its agencies, such as the police; or the Fasehun faction to destroy him by continuing to depict him as a hotheaded and violent young man.

After chatting with me for twenty minutes, Adams jumped into his vehicle to continue his journey to Lagos. I headed back to my car, which was parked at the gas station. A man who sold audiocassettes by the side of the Total Petro Station—from whom I had bought the recordings of leading artists in the past, such as *Yorùbá Ro'nú*, Hubert Ogunde's popular songs on the political crisis in western Nigeria during the First Republic, and also rousing songs about the late Yorùbá leader, Obafemi Awolowo—stopped me to confirm that it was Gani Adams I had been chatting with. In one of the songs blaring from the two speakers in front of the shop, Ogunde praises the *new* "age of violence" (described as the era of *wetie e*—wet it) in the 1960s Western Region of Nigeria, when violence erupted in response to the rigging of elections by an unpopular regional government. The shop owner suggested to me, as if reflecting the historical backdrop of Ogunde's lyrics, that Adams was "brave and dreaded," while referencing both the violent clashes in which the group had been involved in the recent past and their "praiseworthy" vigilante services in urban areas.

"[The] Yorùbá do not believe in being too aggressive," Adams had stated during our roadside chat, reflecting his eagerness to connect or project his position, attitude, actions, and reflections to or onto the cultural whole. "We are a peace-loving race.[1] . . . [The] Yorùbá believe that you cannot achieve anything if you do not have peace; you cannot have good economy, and politics will be unstable. . . . [The] Yorùbá are a very accommodating race. [The] Yorùbá don't believe in discrimination."[2] He added, however, that some "other groups" would want to use these positive attributes of the Yorùbá to "override our race."

—∿∿—

During the first half of the more than two decades of my research for this book (during which I met Adams on many occasions), after his emphasis on his and his group's commitment to "justice, equity, and democratic freedom," perhaps his next most critical refrain was their commitment to peace. Many found it odd that someone who was (in)famous for so much defensive or offensive violence, depending on where you stood, always spoke about peace in his media interviews. Such were the suspicions of others and the ironies that framed the person of Adams, the head of a "militant" group that many regarded as an "ethnic militia." Adams's claim to be "peaceful" met with such disbelief that when he repeated it in the presence of the president of Nigeria at a gathering of eminent people, he drew laughter from the audience.

In February 2004, when asked to introduce himself at a meeting of the National Peace Forum hosted by Rochas Okorocha, the president's special adviser on interparty affairs, and featuring President Olusegun Obasanjo as the special guest, the leader of the OPC said, "I am Ganiyu Adams, man of peace."[3] A reporter described the response: "Well, they all laughed it off as a paradox, knowing the OPC as a Yoruba ethnic militia organisation, whose reputation had been built around series of violence and bloody clashes especially in the South West geo-political zone in the recent past."[4] The National Peace Forum was a federal government initiative to bring together groups involved in violent protests over different national issues—particularly ethnicity, religion, and natural resources—to find a way out of the incessant and widespread clashes in different parts of Nigeria. Some of those invited to join the forum, including Adams, were appointed "Ambassadors of Peace." The designation is interesting in Adams's case given that he once told me, "Although everyone wants peace, but justice and equity [are] the bedrock of peace in any society. Without justice and equity, there can never be peace."[5] Though President Obasanjo did not like part of Adams's contribution at the first meeting of the forum he attended—in which Adams indicated the need for a Sovereign National Conference—it was remarkable that Obasanjo's government was hosting Adams a few years after he had ordered the police and soldiers to shoot on sight in reaction to OPC-inspired violence in Lagos. In fact, Obasanjo had been so displeased with Adams and the activities of his group that he refused to acknowledge Adams's greeting when the young man prostrated himself at the event.[6]

After the meeting, Adams told the press that the convocation of the Peace Forum, which he had initially been reluctant to participate in, was an indication that Nigeria "was ready to move forward":[7]

> [At the meeting] I saw the personalities assigned to manage peace in this country. I saw lots of people who are no longer interested in politics, elder statesmen, the kind of people who are ready to talk to the president about peace in this country, experienced people who fought for the independence of this country. Who know the inside-out of Nigeria. So, my membership is an experience in my life.[8] I met people, who when I was not even born in 1970, were managing the affairs of this country, who believe in peace.[9]

However, again he was eager to contest the association of his group with violence, emphasizing that the group existed to "fight for the interest" of the Yorùbá: "But with all humility, my organisation is not for violence. It is an organisation formed to fight for the interest of our people. And I stand to prove to you with this forum that our organisation stands for peace. We don't want cheating of any side. I come from the Yoruba race. We don't want the Yoruba to cheat the Igbo, neither Hausa the Middle Belt. We equally don't want our race to be oppressed. We want everybody to be first class citizens. We want everybody to have a sense of belonging in Nigeria."[10]

—∾—

Tijo Salverda and Jon Abbink have argued correctly for an approach to elites that avoids moral qualification,[11] because "the manner in which elites acquire prestige or power can be violent, coercive, or benevolent." Whatever form the process of the acquisition of prestige and power takes, these scholars argue, what is important is that those so described have become "societal forerunners"; they are "emulated," and they attract "admiration, rivalry and resistance."[12] In this chapter, I examine how Adams initially acquired power—and later prestige—through the violence associated with the OPC, both illegitimately (intragroup, interethnic, etc.) and legitimately (vigilante). Though, in Gramscian terms, the violence made it impossible for the OPC, as a subaltern group, to be transformed "from a mere egoistic-passional moment to an ethical-political one,"[13] I approach the forms of violence as, essentially, apparatuses and instruments used by the leader of a group, in this case Adams, to create a pathway for the domination of a sociocultural and political space. While my take here does not exhaust the ways in which we can understand the OPC-inspired violence, I argue that, even though the other ways are useful and illuminating, unless we connect them to the central strategic vision of the critical agent in this context, Adams, it will be difficult to fully account for how he methodically mobilized, managed, and maneuvered structural , institutional , and agential processes—though not always with the desired results—to become a person of much consequence in local, regional, and national contexts.

This chapter shows the ethnographic value of the mass media as I consider the major events of the recent past in relation to the ethnographic moment while moving from the front stage of events to their backstage[14]—and vice versa—in an attempt to understand the context of incessant violence and crises that consumed urban Yorubaland at the height of the OPC's activities.

I will show that while violence itself helped the OPC affirm its potency and stamp its authority and relevance in the urban space, for Adams, the greater strategic value of violence—whether directed against rival OPC factions, other ethnic groups in urban areas, or state agents such as the police or mobilized against urban crimes through vigilante activities—lay in its ability to promote him as an important player in two of the most critical aspects of modern life in Nigeria: security and safety. Such importance, he realized, could be converted into social, economic, and political eminence, first in Yorubaland and eventually in the rest of Nigeria. The ways in which he—and his constituents—symbolized and interpreted violence as integral to the defense of "Yorùbá interests," the "integrity" of his faction of the OPC, and the identity of the "youth"[15] are useful for understanding the mobilization of violence for status transformation.

Whether the violence concerned (the reality or imaginations of) ethno-national security regarding territorial claims or matters of personal or communal safety and security among urban dwellers in the light of the failure of state agencies—particularly the police—to adequately protect life and property, Adams recognized a vacuum that his faction of the OPC could fill. He understood that this vacuum, for good or for ill—despite the temporary inconveniences he would suffer as a result of the violence (including arrests, detentions, and prosecutions)—would ultimately transform him into an important player in the determination of some of the most critical social, cultural, economic, and political issues of his time. The visibility, leverage, influence, and power afforded by the postviolence era would, he was quick to anticipate, provide him with opportunities for personal transformation that he could easily convert into a form of personal autarky[16]—that is, socioeconomic independence.

There are two important points that I wish to emphasize in this chapter about Adams and his faction of the OPC, the second of which the authors of virtually all lay and academic literature about the OPC either are unaware of or have yet to capture. This point, largely confidential initially, was revealed to me (1) because I am a member of Adams's ethnic nationality, (2) because I could be described as an *in-out* member of the elite group[17] to which Adams was connected and within which he now fully operates, and (3) because, through my long-term fieldwork, I have developed close relationships with Adams, some of his aides, and key members of the group—including those who later left as a result of differences with Adams.

The first important point, which some have mentioned, if in rather simple ways, particularly in the public media, is the direct and indirect relationships between Adams and the leading members of the Yorùbá elites in Southwestern Nigeria. These relationships often led Yorùbá leaders to make public statements in support or defense of Adams and his group—and the OPC in general.[18] However, many of the media reports have failed to capture the fact that the relationships and connections forged between Adams and the elites are not limited to nonstate institutions or nonstate processes that constitute a response to his problems with the state and its institutions. In fact, some members of the Yorùbá elite in public office, including at the highest level of political power, had critical relationships with Adams and his group—even when he was mostly regarded as an outlaw. These officials are often split between their formal roles as custodians of state power and of the legitimate means of violence and their (in)formal roles as politicians and members of the Yorùbá elite whose personal, communal, and political interests the OPC ultimately defended or extended through its activities, which included even illegitimate violence.[19] Among these officials are state governors who were informal patrons of Adams and his group, lawmakers at the state and federal levels, legal practitioners, and even judges, particularly retired judges who could serve as contact points with active judges, who could help when Adams or members of his group were in trouble with the law.

But beyond the aforementioned officials is an even more strategic relationship that Adams forged with the retired and serving rank and file in the Nigerian

Police Force, particularly senior police officers. The allegations that the OPC had killed police officers—particularly a divisional officer in the Bariga Police Station in Lagos, Afolabi Amao, who was killed during a clash between the police and the OPC—made Adams the target of officers in Lagos, including the Lagos State police commissioner, Mike Okiro. However, elements of every rank within the police force had good relationships with Adams and his group. One set of officers identified with the group's defense of Yorùbá interests. Some in the police force, who share the group's position on the Hausa-Fulani "domination" of others in Nigeria, supported the OPC even when they were uncomfortable with its sporadic violence and direct clashes with law enforcement officials. These officers separated their personal, ethnic attitudes toward the group from their corporate (police) interests as agents of the Nigerian state. The other set, not necessarily separate from the first, consisted of senior police officers whose crime-fighting efforts were assisted in critical ways by the vigilante activities of the OPC in urban areas—which led to a significant reduction in crime at one point. Some of these officers even received commendations and promotions from their bosses because of crime-busting accomplishments that they acknowledged had been aided by the OPC's activities.

Sunday Adebayo, Adams's friend in his early youth and his former personal assistant, revealed to me that when he visited the governor of Oyo State, Rasheed Ladoja, he encountered one such senior police officer who had since been promoted to commissioner of police. "The man was so happy when he saw me. We embraced. The governor was surprised that the police commissioner knew me well. The man told the governor: 'These are the people who got me promotion through their activities.' He even gave me money before he left."[20]

Thus, Adams and the OPC leaders had and still have complex relationships across social, economic, and political groups and across state and civil society that they could tap into during periods of stress—particularly during encounters with state agencies (such as manhunt, arrest, detention, trial, and imprisonment)—and in normal times. Adams's relationships with the police run the whole gamut from hostility to amicability. Among other reasons, this explains how Adams was able to evade police arrest for twenty months, between January 2000 and August 2001, and also why, on one occasion, he decided to voluntarily surrender to the police—though the police, and many in the media, reported, in a sensational way, that he had been "captured."[21]

Beyond this, even when he had no direct relationship with a particular police chief seeking his arrest, such as when Police Commissioner Mike Okiro

Figure 2.2. Sunday Adebayo and his friend and leader, Adams, at the latter's engagement ceremony.

declared him wanted, Adams recognized that such declarations, arrests, detentions, or imprisonments contributed, paradoxically, to his renown and eventually to his prominence, influence, and power. In fact, proving his understanding that every major event in his public life moved him closer to his personal goal of becoming a big man, Adams told the press many years later that, by declaring him wanted in 2000, Okiro had "brought him into stardom."[22] The inspector general of police, the head of the federal police force, had placed a prize of N100,000 (approximately US$770) on his head.[23] Adams responded, "The Hausa-Fulani who have pocketed the military [and] police [are] using them at will to oppress and silence the voice of Southerners."[24] He added, "I am neither afraid nor hiding. . . . (B)ut I will not surrender myself to the enemies of progress, social justice and equity. . . . I am in my fatherland, not wanted by my people."[25] When the Arewa People's Congress,[26] founded by northern elements in response to the OPC, announced that they would raise the ransom to N200,000, Adams said that the northerners should "use [the money] to alleviate the poverty situation of Hausa-Fulani beggars all over the country."[27]

Indeed, becoming "the most wanted man" in Nigeria between 1999 and 2001 was the turning point in Gani Adams's life. From the moment he was declared wanted by the police on January 15, 2000, he became a household name, a hero for many in his homestead of Southwest Nigeria and a villain for some state actors and other ethnic groups, particularly the rival Hausa-Fulani in the North of Nigeria. Yet, between villainy and heroism, Adams was emerging as a man of reckoning who had to be acknowledged almost equally by those who loved and hated him.

"I thank the then Lagos State Commissioner of Police, Mike Okiro, for declaring me wanted and [the] subsequent arrest, because it turned out to be a blessing for me," Adams told *Premium Times* in 2015. "The unnecessary publicity brought me into limelight. . . . I have to give thanks to God and Okiro who God used to turn my story for better."[28] He added that the publicity he gained from this had turned him into a "hero," comparing himself with Obafemi Awolowo, the premier of the Premier Region during the First Republic, the man generally regarded in his lifetime as the leader of the Yorùbá; Wole Soyinka, Africa's preeminent writer, playwright, and Nobel laureate; and South Africa's Nelson Mandela, all of whom had suffered political imprisonment.

Two quick points are apposite here. First, even in the early stage of his public career, Adams made comparisons indicating that he envisioned himself as a visionary and committed leader of the Yorùbá (like Awolowo), a global cultural icon (like Soyinka), and a global icon in the fight for racial equality (like Mandela). Initially, some of Adams's detractors dismissed these kinds of comparisons as examples of his inflationary sense of self-importance. However, as the following chapters will show, Adams has been moving steadily toward these triple targets (in addition to other targets that I will discuss later). In fact, he now considers himself close to achieving the first (as *a* leader among the Yorùbá, though not yet as widely respected, preeminent, or virtually worshipped as Awolowo) and the second (as a cultural icon, even if not yet global, in the manner of Soyinka). Second, Adams's statement indicates that the media have helped him tremendously in his mission of sociocultural self-elevation. Though Adams himself did not use the word *stardom* to describe what he had achieved as a result of the police commissioner's action (he used *limelight*), *Premium Times*, an upscale online newspaper led by one of Nigeria's foremost media intellectuals, Dapo Olorunyomi, was obviously persuaded enough that Adams had become a superstar to use that word.

An example of what Adams described as "unnecessary publicity [that] brought [him] into limelight" was *TheNEWS* magazine's cover story about him, published while he was in hiding, which helped to validate the urban legend that surrounded him. The story, dubbed "exclusive," was headlined "I'm Invincible: 'No One Can Arrest Me'—Gani Adams."[29]

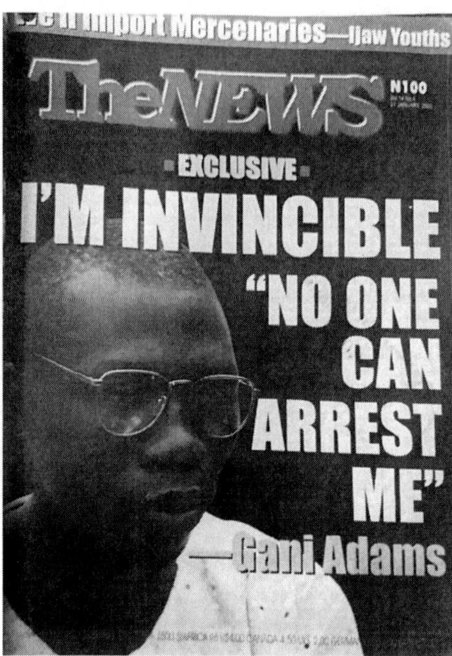

Figure 2.3. The cover of *TheNEWS* magazine in which the first exclusive interview with Adams was published after he was declared wanted.

Though some of the magazine's editors spoke with Adams by telephone, in his note to the cover story, the editor in chief, Bayo Onanuga, acknowledged the "massive manhunt for the bespectacled Yoruba irridentist" and asked, "Where could the man be hiding? What could be his responses to the demonisation of his image and his cause by the police and agents of the central government?" Onanuga explained that while his reporters were searching fruitlessly for Adams in many cities of Southwestern Nigeria, "Nigeria's most wanted fugitive" had called their office "from God-knows-where for this exclusive interview." In the interview, Adams declared that he was "not in hiding." He dismissed the ban placed on the OPC:

> Since it is not possible to separate a child from her mother's womb, because without the womb there will be no child, so it is not possible to ban the OPC from Yorubaland. Those who are agitating for its ban are mostly the Northern feudal lords whose main occupation is feeding fat on the sweat of others. It was their [Northern] governors that first called for the ban and not their legislators. And while they are calling for the ban on the OPC, the Hausa/Fulani are simultaneously equipping their kinsmen with arms, ammunitions, and other dangerous weapons all over the South-West so as to launch attacks on our people.[30]

THE RHYTHM OF VIOLENCE

The blood-dimmed tide is loosed, and everywhere
The ceremony of innocence is drowned;
The best lack all conviction, while the worst
Are full of passionate intensity

—*William Butler Yeats, "The Second Coming"*

In mid-2002, I was at one of the weekly OPC gatherings in Lagos. The meeting of the National Coordinating Committee was ongoing, and I was waiting at the somewhat carnivalesque venue where the larger membership would gather after the meeting. While waiting for their leaders, the OPC members, including young ladies, were singing and dancing, accompanied by the Yorùbá talking drum. The *gangan* drummer beat a certain rhythm that the dancers recognized, and they repeated the drumbeats in words that constituted a highly bigoted reference to the Hausa. Thus, dehumanizing references to members of a "rival" ethnic group were pressed into a song. And the chorus was joined.[31] But the next song was less prejudiced:

Ijangbara ma d'ode o
Omo Oodua e ja de o
Ijangbara ma de o
Awon Hausa ma sa
Awon omo Oodua lo ma leke o.

[The struggle for freedom is on
Oduduwa's children, come out
The struggle for freedom is on
The Hausa will flee
Oduduwa's children will triumph.]

The expression of disregard for the lives of the Hausa (by which they often mean the Hausa and Fulani) in particular, and other non-Yorùbá Nigerians in general, was not an immaterial attitude expressed in pulsating rhythm and melody. It was a material credo that manifested in violent conflicts provoked by the OPC in urban areas in Southwest Nigeria. The reality of the drumbeat in the mindless killings of hundreds of people, including OPC members, in Lagos and elsewhere led *TELL* magazine to describe Adams as one in whom "boils a molten magma of violence" despite his "seemingly harmless exterior" and the fact that he is "painfully frail . . . quiet and fond of wearing safari suits."[32] It also led the *Tribune* columnist Festus Adedayo to warn that Adams's "capacity," as head of a militia group, "to cause havoc is unlimited," while adding that the

Figure 2.4. Members of the OPC Women's Wing during the meeting of the NCC hosted by the Somolu Local Government Area wing of the OPC around 2005. Photo courtesy of Bose Omolaoye.

OPC leader "is a troublesome fly perched on our balls. To scare it off would require tact and wisdom."[33]

I noticed that no one seemed uncomfortable with the prejudice expressed by the drummer and repeated by some of the members. In fact, many of the members laughed while acknowledging the drumbeats. Omolara Raliat Adaranijo (once Omolara Sanni but popularly called Lara), a young lady and the chorus leader, picked up the microphone and, with some relish, sang, "*Ganiyu, oro mi f'amojuto, ko ye ki baba mi j'iya k'e mi omo tun je*" (Ganiyu, my situation calls for remedy, it is not right for my father to suffer and for me to follow his example). Then she substituted the names of some of the group leaders for Adams's name.

Adaranijo was the *Yèyé Oòduá* of the OPC in Lagos Island. In fact, one of the most active members of the group who brought her into the OPC, Lateef Olawale Oshodi, told me that she would have been the *Yèyé Oòduá* National, the overall leader of the women's wing, but for the opposition of some powerful members. She produced a self-promotional narrative about how she "stepped back" from the group at one point so the Honorable Oluwayemisi Shiyanbola could be appointed *Yèyé Oòduá* National. Adaranijo claimed she did this because she was the first "Iron Lady" of the group and a team player.[34] Adaranijo—who also claimed that she "stepped back" from the group for about nine years on the advice of Oshodi, who warned about "conspiracies" against her—has since returned to the fold and remains a member of Adams's faction.

Figure 2.5. Members of the OPC Women's Wing: *Yèyé Oòduá* National, Honorable Oluwayemi Shiyanbola (*fourth from right*) during a philanthropic gathering for the families of OPC members who died in the struggle. Photo courtesy of Bose Omolaoye.

"[Moshood] Abiola's death was the reason I joined OPC," Adaranijo told me in Yorùbá, many years after I first encountered her at an OPC rally in 2001.[35] "Alhaji Oshodi talked to me at Isale Eko [Lagos Island] to join the group. I have been in the struggle since then." Explaining why she led the signing in those years, she said that "Oga" (Adams) had recognized her as a talented singer and decided that she should lead choruses.

"Many songs would come to my mind as I reflected on what the Hausa were doing to us [Yorùbá] in Nigeria. Sometimes others will form the song and pass it on to me to sing because I had a good voice. That was my gift. They realized that I had the talent,"[36] she said as she recalls another song:

O se o Awo, o se Ajasin
Ipo t'awa wa, e to re ma ni
Awon kan j'ogun, awon kan da'le
Ipo t'awa wa, e to re ma ni.

[Thank you Awolowo, thank you Ajasin,[37]
Our position today, it is thy right (effort)
Some fought the battle, some betrayed the cause
Our position today, it is thy right (effort).]

Figure 2.6. Sade (*left*) and Latifat (both late) during an OPC social gathering. Sade died in a motor accident during one of the group's trips. Photo courtesy of Bose Omolaoye.

She discusses some of the sacrifices she made for the group, including having to strip naked publicly to destroy the "powerful *juju*" (magic/sorcery) of the Ijaw fighters during their clash with the OPC in Lagos. This symbolic act is a common counterattack performed in West Africa to curse and punish those who commit evil, dehumanizing acts and traumatic offenses, especially against women.[38] Adaranijo claimed that her sacrifice allowed the OPC to "defeat" the Ijaw during the clashes in Lagos in 1999.

In Fasehun's narrative of the founding of the group, two women were among the first four people he invited. The implication is that the OPC recognized the critical role of women from its founding. Although no woman was on Adams's list of the founders, his faction also recognizes the role of women. The leader of the Women's League of the Adams faction is called *Yèyé Oòduá* (mother of *Oòduá*). The Honorable Oluwayomisi Shiyanbola was the first national *Yèyé Oòduá*. The group also appoints *Yèyé Oòduá* at all levels. This position, as Insa Nolte has explained, "is clearly linked to the perception of women's power that is based on complimentary, rather than egalitarian, gender roles."[39] The

Figure 2.7. OPC members dancing during *odun Ifa* at Abule Ado field. Photo courtesy of Bose Omolaoye.

position, Nolte argues, helps "to contain female agency within the OPC's revalidation of Yoruba political traditions and its wider political struggle."[40] Still, women played prominent, even if at most times supportive, roles in the OPC. As Shiyanbola and Bose Omolaoye, the group's first office secretary, told me, women, particularly in the first few years of the Adams faction, were prominent in the group's activities. Many traversed Yorubaland with Adams, and a few of them even lost their lives to vehicular accidents or to "stray" bullets. One woman who lost her life during a vehicular accident is Sade, who, some disclosed, was very close to Adams at one point. She sold OPC merchandise.

The Women's League at every level of the organization, each with a leader, *Iya Oodua*, was also critical to mass recruitment and mobilization regarding health and sanitation. They also supported the families of those who lost their lives in service to the group, planning events such as "Heroes' Day" ceremonies attended by the families of the deceased.

Some men in the group regarded the role of the women as solely "supportive" because the women did not engage in the many "physical battles" fought in the early days. However, as the first *Iya Oodua* general, Shiyanbola, and the first office secretary for the groups, Bose Omolaoye, disclosed, the role of the women

Figure 2.8. Honorable Oluwayemi Shiyanbola, the first *Iya Oodua General* (*right*), with Bose Omolaoye (*middle*), OPC office secretary, delivering a lecture at an orientation for OPC women around 2000. Photo courtesy of Bose Omolaoye.

was no less critical. Like the men, they also bore the brunt of the group's travails, though they did not enjoy as many of the benefits as the top-placed men. For instance, Omolaoye related her personal experience after the Bariga crisis, when OPC members became targets for the police, and at other times. Such periods were "refugee periods."[41] Many of the women who were known members of the group, including Omolaoye, had to leave their homes and even Lagos to stay with other people to avoid the threat of arrest, harassment, and death.

"I left Lagos for Ibadan after the crisis. Even after I returned from 'refugee' and found a job in Fadeyi [Lagos], I had to use disguises so that I will not be identified on the streets of Lagos as an OPC member," Stainless, as she was called by OPC members, disclosed. "I will cover my head with a shawl like a Muslim woman. I left home before dawn and stayed in the office until dusk."[42]

There were many relationships between the men and women in the group. While a few of the members were eager to gossip about who was dating whom, spreading rumors about which of the female members had relationships with "the president" (Adams), most of the top members avoided discussing such liaisons, especially regarding other top members. As Lateef Olawale Oshodi (Osho) told me, "It was not my business who was involved with who in the group."

During the open celebrations at the weekly meetings of the National Coordinating Council (NCC), the most visible women, apart from the *Iya Oodua* general and other state *Iya Ooduas,* were often the ones who led the singing and dancing.

Songs, dances, drumbeats, and other metaphors of the rituals of celebration and becoming (or what might be more cogently described as cultural cues)—including the bigoted and the culturally or politically rousing songs, the ones focused on singing the praises of Adams, and those that castigated other groups or former members of the group—constituted powerful rival motifs and material forces in the construction of the youth-against-injustice discourses of the OPC in its early years. They also gave form to otherwise formless articulations of goals while providing "reasons" for the group's violence.

Some of the most popular songs in the group can be considered here. The first relates the "history" of the Yorùbá leaders' struggle against "domination" by the Hausa-Fulani, heroizing past leaders but at the same time indicating the need to "complete" the "battle" that they started but did not win:

Awolowo gbiyanju titi
K'ole bawa gbon'ya nu
Baba Ajasin gbiyanju titi
K'ole bawa gbon ya nu
Abiola gbiyanju titi
K'ole bawa gbon ya nu
Oduduwa, o se o
K'owa ba wa gbonya nu / 2x

[Awolowo worked hard
To free us from bondage (literally "to wash off our suffering")
Elder Ajasin worked hard
To free us from bondage
Abiola worked hard
To free us from bondage
Oduduwa, thank you,
Help free us from bondage / 2x]

This song encapsulates the group's specific history of a long ethno-national struggle. Four prominent Yorùbá—the mythical progenitor, Oduduwa; the man regarded as his modern incarnation, Obafemi Awolowo; Awolowo's successor as leader of the Yorùbá, the Second Republic governor of Ondo and the late leader of *Afenifere*, Adekunle Ajasin; and the winner of the June 12, 1999, presidential election, Moshood Abiola, whose electoral victory's annulment directly provoked the creation of the OPC—are symbolically invoked to tell a story that links the experience of the Yorùbá in Nigeria with the struggle against ethno-regional domination and authoritarian rule and the struggle for ethno-regional unity and solidarity rooted in a common progenitor, Oduduwa. It is

Figure 2.9. Adams (with microphone) leading the singing and merriment before the meeting of the NCC in the early 2000s. Sunday Adebayo (*second from left*), Adams's friend and personal assistant, dances as the leader sings. Photo courtesy of Sunday Adebayo.

significant that the song refers to all three modern-era Yorùbá (Awolowo, Ajasin, and Abiola) as leaders who spent their lives struggling against domination and injustice and thus sets them up as forerunners in the current OPC "battle" for freedom from domination, as symbolized by Gani Adams.

Another song describes the police and the Hausa-Fulani as working hard to destroy the OPC. This song is often led by Funke Aderanijo (popularly called Mama Yusuf), one of the lead singers in the OPC:

Olopa lo fe b'egbe yi je
Hausa-Fulani lo fe b'egbe yi je
Gambari lo fe b'egbe yi je
Nibi tan ba joko si o
Ni'be na ma ya'gbe si.

[The police want to destroy this group (OPC)
Hausa-Fulani wants to destroy this group
Gambari[43] (Hausa-Fulani) wants to destroy this group
They will defecate wherever they sit.]

Another of Adaranijo's favorite songs galvanized the members of the group and reminded them that their collective aims were achievable:

Omo odua, e ma ma so jo / 2x
W'ehin wo
Pelu ipinu, yi o se e se.

[Oduduwa's children, don't be afraid / 2x
Look back
With determination, it will be possible.]

—∞—

One of key reasons that critics, including Fasehun, often dismissed Adams and his young constituents as "miscreants" was that they were violent. Indeed, the "militant" OPC was implicated in several violent clashes with other ethnic groups, the Fasehun faction, and the police. This violence was interpreted by some, like Fasehun,[44] as alien to Yorùbá culture and civilization. However, as Bettina Schmidt and Ingo Schroeder[45] argue, "no violent act can be fully understood without viewing it as one link in the chain of a long process of events, each of which refers to a system of cultural and material structure." How, then, can we locate violence in the Yorùbá cultural repertoire?

Figure 2.10. Adams leads others in singing during one of their open gatherings in 1999. On the left of Adams is Olumide Adeniyi. Photo courtesy of Monsuru Akande.

VIOLENCE IN YORÙBÁ HISTORY

For J. D. Y. Peel, the key shift in Yorùbá self- and individual understanding in the late nineteenth and early twentieth century was a shift from the world of warlords to that of Christianity-*olaju* (enlightenment, civilization, civility)—a shift that involved both critique of and reflection on the violence and confusion of the nineteenth-century Yorùbá world.[46] The "age of confusion" ended with the triumph of "civilised, Christian" Yorùbá ethics, which were pitted against the "violent and traditional" warlordism of the earlier era. How then do we account for the OPC phenomenon? Is it a shift back to the values of the world of warlords? I suggest that, rather than a return to that world, the new era is an attempt to inscribe *warlordism*, the "tradition of valor," into the valued triumph of *olaju* among the Yorùbá. The "militant" OPC members therefore imagine the Yorùbá as both strong and civilized, immersed in culture yet modern and progressive, failing to realize that the values and virtues they claim for their culture and the ones they project onto other cultures (ethnic groups) are, to use Peel's words, "aspects of the same political culture" in which they are demonstrably involved—as the physical and rhetorical tussles between the two factions show.[47]

Violence has played a central part in Yorùbá social and political life through the centuries. It can be argued that violence has been on and off, perennial and occasional, normal and abnormal in Yorùbá history. The trajectory from the "war boys" (*omo ogun*) of nineteenth-century Ibadan through the political violence in the First, Second, and Third Republics to the contemporary OPC-inspired violence suggests that the Yorùbá regard violence as both normal, in the sense that it is already allowed for within their cultural horizons, and exceptional, in that it constitutes an understandable response to an abnormal situation, as Peel demonstrates in the case of the Ijeshas.[48]

Despite this history of violence in the nineteenth century—perhaps the longest civil war among any of the major African ethnic nationalities in the precolonial era—and during the three republics (in the 1960s, 1980s, and 1990s), and although the key army generals during the Nigerian civil war were Yorùbá,[49] the Yorùbá have come to acquire the image of easygoing and partying (*owambe*) people at best and of cowards at worst, particularly among the other two major ethnic groups, the Hausa-Fulani and the Igbo. For the OPC, this image was patently wrong and needed to be obliterated.

Adams's articulation of this bears long quotation:[50]

> Yoruba do not believe to be too aggressive. We are . . . a peace-loving race. We believe in justice. Yoruba believe that it is better if you avoid crisis [than] managing crisis. . . . Yoruba is a very accommodating race. . . . But, by and large,

Figure 2.11. Members of the OPC at their office. *Left to right:* Monsuru Akande, chair of the Welfare Committee; Bose Omolaoye, OPC office secretary; Wale Oseni; Sade (late); and Musiliu "Big Fish" Amusa. Photo courtesy of Bose Omolaoye.

> some people want to take it as a chance to override our race.... [They have] an illusion that maybe it is because of our cowardice that... we always accept... [other] people.... So, it got to a stage that our race [was] not being respected. ...After the annulment of the June 12 [1993 presidential] elections ... we heard lots of things from different people; Yoruba cannot do anything, Yoruba is a coward race, Yoruba like parties, we like enjoyment, we don't believe that we can get our rights because we like speaking grammar [meaning English language].... [Those] making this kind of statements ... one day, they will just put fire on our house ... or silence this race [Yoruba] forever. That was the reason we [started] an organization like the OPC. We have it as a sociocultural organization and, at the same time, an organization that will prepare for self-defense.[51]

DEMOCRACY AND POLITICAL VIOLENCE

Violence is regarded as "anathema to [democracy's] spirit and substance"—as democracy's greatest enemy.[52] However, democracies experience violence in different forms. African democratic states, particularly since the "third wave democratisation,"[53] have constantly experienced various forms of violence: low intensity war, electoral violence, ethnic violence, and terrorism, among others. Ordinarily, this would seem paradoxical. Democratization and democratic rule were expected to ensure civil peace at the levels of both state and society.[54] One of the key reasons for the violence experienced by African democracies in the post–Cold War era is the absence of a genuine effort to resolve the fundamental questions of national unity as the states transitioned either from autocratic rule to democratic rule or from a one-party state to a pluralist democracy. While these fundamental questions manifested in different ways in different African states, they became sources of constant tension and regular or occasional violence. And because these fundamental questions were often connected with ongoing or evolving social, economic, or political challenges (such as the scarcity of economic and social goods), they have often provided ready justification for the outbreak of violence.

Because many of these states are not genuine democracies or states in which democratic traditions and institutions have deep roots, they often have limited, constrained, or even compromised institutionalized processes for conflict resolution. "Ideally conceived," argues John Keane, "democracies understand themselves as systems of lawful power-sharing, whose actors are attuned to the dangers of violence—and to the mutual benefits of non-violence."[55] However, in many instances in Africa, the state itself generates violence—both manifest and latent—against certain groups and citizens in the name of law and order.[56] Therefore, violence is often justified by those who employ it as a necessary and unavoidable response to the state, organizations, or the socioeconomic and political arrangements imposed by the nature of the state in Africa. In post-1989 Africa, as democratic rule was revived, some parts of civil society, rather than removing violence from social and political life,[57] reproduced and mobilized it in their struggle—as they claimed—to build a fairer society and state. Against this backdrop, it is useful to examine the contexts in which violence is loosely approached, or even tolerated, as "a developer of noble virtues of heroism and endurance among youth."[58]

In this chapter, I examine a particular case "that illustrate[s] how certain factors do come together that enable us to make sense of patterns of violence within their own contexts."[59] As Pamela J. Stewart and Andrew Strathern argue in their clarification of ethnographic approaches to the study of violence, contextual analysis of violence does not constitute cultural determinism or cultural relativism.[60] It only emphasizes the crucial importance of historical context for explaining the origin, nature, and trajectory of violence. Therefore, I locate the account of OPC violence here within a symbolic approach to violence that investigates the advertised subjective and cultural meanings of violent acts that subvert the existing order but constitute an alternative or imagined order.[61]

David Riches has argued that "the performance of violence is inherently liable to be contested on the question of legitimacy."[62] Below, I examine this question by illustrating how various forms of OPC-related violence—versus police, other ethnic groups, other Yorùbá, and other OPC members—contested the existing forms of order in Nigeria and ultimately provided the context for Adams's emergence as a man of consequence.

However, it is important to emphasize that the forms of political violence inspired by the OPC are not exceptional in Nigeria's history. As "one of the most deeply divided states in Africa," given "its complex web of politically salient identities and history of chronic and seemingly intractable conflicts and instability,"[63] Nigeria has experienced political violence throughout its postcolonial history, including countless inter- and intraethnic conflicts, some of which are recurrent. The worst of these spates was the 1967–70 civil war, in which more than one million people died. Questions of the terms under which the different ethnic groups would live together within the Nigerian federation led to that war.[64] As Osaghae and Suberu argued, "rather than abate, conflicts have become more or less pervasive and intense in the post–civil war period, and disintegration continues to be contemplated by aggrieved segments of society as one of the possible ways of resolving the 'National Question.'"[65] The crisscrossing and recursive ethnic, religious, regional, and subethnic (communal) identities constitute the "most salient and main bases for violent conflicts in the country."[66] The interconnectedness of these identities and their often mutually reinforcing implications are evident, as Osaghae and Suberu show, in the fact that they are sometimes compounded or hyphenated as ethno-regional or ethno-religious because of their historical, geographical, and political origins.[67] The defense of these identities involved contestations over resources, privileges, and sometimes symbols.

The Yorùbá are highly implicated in this, given, as discussed earlier, the role of violence in the constitution of the emergent Yorùbá ethno-national identity in the nineteenth century and also in the consolidation of that identity in the twentieth century, in both intra-Yorùbá struggles[68] and political struggles with other ethnic groups.[69]

VIOLENCE AND THE OPC

In early 2000, the Nigerian police claimed that the OPC was responsible for 60 percent of the two hundred violent clashes recorded nationwide between January 1999 and January 2000. In 2006, while opposing bail requests by Fasehun and Adams, the federal government claimed that the OPC had been responsible for ten thousand deaths and described the two leaders as "callous, murderous, tribal and secessionist" men "whose organisation has no regard for human lives."[70] Though the Nigerian Police Force was (and continues to be) notorious for presenting "facts" that served its purposes, the percentage of OPC-related

Figure 2.12. Adams arriving at an event in the early 2000s as a drummer (*foreground*) heralds him. On both sides of the leader are members of the National Guard, Kayode Atanda *Godogodo* (*Adams's right*), Semiu Ogunrinde (*Adams's immediate left*), and Rasaq Arogundade Balogun (*right*). Photo courtesy of Rasaq Arogundade Balogun.

violence claimed by the police reflects the dominance of the organization in police conceptions of law enforcement, challenges to law and order, crimes, and violence in that era. No other social formation or unit of crime caused greater concern about law and order between 1999 and 2005 than the OPC did.

It is not a coincidence that OPC-related violence skyrocketed in the same period in which the Adams-led faction broke away from the original group headed by the medical doctor and activist Frederick Fasehun. While the younger men led by Adams constituted the lifeblood of the group, as a leader, intellectual guide, and father figure, Fasehun served, initially, as a valve for the searing energy or boiling rage of the young men. With Fasehun out of the way, the distance between contemplation and action was bridged. Consequently, the young men worried less about implications and consequences than about action in itself—that is, the need to intervene, to do something critical about the social, economic, and political issues of the day.

The socioeconomic and political atmosphere provides a troubling context for OPC violence. When Nigeria returned to democratic rule in May 1999, all the state institutions had been wrecked by military autocracy. General Ibrahim Babangida's regime (1985–93), in particular, waged a war of attrition against every national institution, devastating what was left of the main anchors of public culture and morality in Nigeria. In the name of neoliberal economic reforms—some of which were necessary in the light of the state of the economy—the regime imposed a structural adjustment policy (SAP) that was meant to address the deformities of the Nigerian economy.[71] However, the few necessary macroeconomic changes—some of which had already begun—were eventually blocked, weakened, constrained, undermined, or even destroyed,[72] largely because of General Babangida's determination to hold on to power. Babangida turned corruption[73] (euphemistically described as "settlement") into a directive principle of state policy, leading—despite the huge revenue accruing in the national purse from oil owing to the first Gulf War—to a massive balance-of-payment crisis, colossal public debt, weak currency, rising inflation, and massive unemployment. The catastrophic economic woes were worsened by the annulment of the June 12, 1993, presidential elections and the ensuing protest. The annulment provided the immediate backdrop for the creation of the OPC; it catalyzed the violence unleashed by OPC members. Babangida's military successor, General Sani Abacha, made matters worse by narrowing the martial assault on the nation into a regionalized onslaught on Southwestern Nigeria, where the opposition to military rule and the prodemocracy activities were concentrated. The Abacha regime raided the national treasury[74] and unleashed terror on the opposition—and Nigerians in general—assassinating or attempting to assassinate leading prodemocracy activists, including Kudirat Abiola (the wife of the winner of the June 12, 1993, presidential election), who was gunned down in the streets of Lagos by members of Abacha's killer squad on June 9, 1996.

This twin legacy of official corruption and state violence, which disinherited and devastated the members of Adams's generation, led to the fermentation of OPC-inspired violence. When democratic rule was restored, the young people in the OPC used the change to actualize agitations and vent their frustrations. Many of them approached the newly installed president, Olusegun Obasanjo, though a Yorùbá, as only a gentler continuation of the "Hausa-Fulani dominated" military regimes that, they believed, had devastated the country and made the possibility of a better Nigeria arduous, if not impossible. Many of them therefore wanted to be part of a new nation-state that would emerge from the ruin of Nigeria. This was the privately and publicly articulated ideological justification and discursive orientation of their cause. Thus, the Adams faction's attitude toward both socioeconomic challenges, faced especially by urban youth, and political interethnic relations did not change, even under a federal government led by a Yorùbá, Obasanjo.

Given the Hausa-Fulani "domination" of the leadership of Nigeria, despite the presidency of Obasanjo, Adams contended, the Yorùbá have "witnessed unprecedented marginalisation . . . which has brought untold hardship to the citizenry."[75] He added, "For how long are we going to fold our arms and look while all these atrocities are being committed against our people in these [*sic*] civilised age? Hence, the emergence of the OPC as an organisation to make necessary change."

With the soft-spoken Fasehun out of the way, the "militant" OPC was ready to pursue its aims under the leadership of Adams "by any means necessary," even while Adams denied that his organization fomented violence. I suggest that Adams's reaction to the issue of his group's violence largely depended on how the question was posed. In my interactions with him, I found that when the question was posed politically—in terms of, say, the defense of Yorùbá interest and the struggle to restructure Nigeria—he was often proud of the violence perpetrated by his group and glorified it. But when the question was posed socially—in terms of law and order, bloodshed, the loss of life, urban violence—he firmly denied the willful involvement of his group in such violence. Thus, while he told the Human Rights Watch (HRW) that "the OPC has never insinuated or provoked any act of violence. . . . The OPC is not a violent organisation. . . . My own struggle is purely political and cultural,"[76] he had said at an earlier press conference, "More skirmishes can be expected in the future, so much as shall threaten the corporate existence of this country. It is our pertinent desire to see true federalism come to being in Nigeria."[77] In line with his political defense of OPC violence, Adams argues further: "Definitely, you don't expect me to fold [my] arms, when some people want to exterminate our race, they want to turn us into second-class citizens on our own soil."[78] Thus, everywhere that the interest of the Yorùbá was at stake, whether in union matters, markets, kingship, tradition, or even mere symbolism, the militant OPC intervened. A trail of blood followed, as OPC-inspired violence, and threats of violence, became a regular feature in daily life as well as in daily news.

It is important to emphasize that, apart from the socioeconomic and political contexts (including the question of urban security and communal safety), two other critical factors contributed to OPC violence. The first was the attempt to reclaim the tradition of valor to show that the Yorùbá were a courageous group with the capacity and willingness to defend themselves and their territory. The other was the presence of young under- and semi-employed people who were eager to precipitate social disorder or even war,[79] either to bring an end to Nigeria or to ensure the reordering of political relations in the country to give the Yorùbá West greater autonomy. Most of such people in the leadership of the group were eager and battle-ready "combatants" who were convinced about their spiritual and physical fortifications. They feared neither the police nor the Nigerian Army. As some of these elements in the group, including members of the National Guard in the Adams faction of the OPC,[80] boasted to me, they had been "so well-cooked in spiritual potions" (*won ti se wa ji'na*) that no bullet could penetrate their bodies.

"MACABRE DANCE OF DEATH"[81] OR "THE PAINS OF INSANITY"?[82]

"The remains of Sunny, popularly known as Baba Ibeji, lay in the market without his head. His bowels have been ripped open and a pool of blood formed a ring round his lifeless body."[83] Such was the depiction of the gruesome consequences of one of the intra-OPC "wars" in Lagos in late 2000. *The Post Express* described this scene as the "curtain raiser to the gruesome encounter between the members of the [two factions of the] dreaded Oodua People's Congress (OPC)" in Ejigbo, a Lagos suburb. Since Adams announced his splinter group, "violence, arson, wanton destruction of lives and property," reported the *Express*, "had become the trademark of the factions." In its description of what it saw as "the pains of insanity," the *Express* added, "At the end of the battle for supremacy, residents of Ejigbo fled their homes while at least 10 people were reportedly killed by stray bullets from the combatants."[84] One of the victims, Sunny, otherwise known as Baba Ibeji, was reportedly a member of the Adams faction.

The clash was reportedly provoked by members of the Fasehun faction who—"fully armed with deadly weapons that could cow the fire power of an armed regiment"—had been on a "reconnaissance patrol" in a bus but stopped to fill their tank at a gas station owned by the traditional ruler of the town, Oba Morufu Adisa Ojoola. The members refused to pay for the fuel. Unknown to them, Ojoola was affiliated with the Adams faction. When informed about the refusal of the "Fasehun boys" to pay for fuel, the traditional ruler asked his aides to deflate the tires of the offending customers' vehicles. Almost immediately, the whole area reportedly "erupted into a battleground" in which the Fasehun faction had greater firepower. Once dislodged, the Adams faction sent

Figure 2.13. Adams and other members of the OPC, including Monsuru Akande, chair of the Welfare Committee (*left of Adams*). Sitting on a wheelchair is Dr. Oki, a medical doctor who was also a member of the group and who attended to some of the injured members at his clinic at Badagry. Photo courtesy of Monsuru Akande.

for reinforcement. The Fasehun faction reportedly took on the wounded Baba Ibeji, who was the last man standing on the Adams side. They "dragged him to the nearby market constructed by the royal father who was at the centre of it all. There . . . they beheaded him and ripped his bowel open."[85] They consequently stormed the palace and wreaked havoc. They also allegedly gunned down those who refused to surrender and set vehicles and houses on fire as they embarked on a house-to-house search for members of the Adams faction. The traditional ruler fled the town. Still, one week later, the battle continued as members of the Adams faction rallied.

Fasehun claims that the spate of violence was provoked by the Adams faction, though he acknowledges that he lost control of the members of his own faction after preaching restraint for a long time. He further argues that, encouraged by the "Marxist indoctrination" of some older people ("comrade-activists"), the Adams faction was convinced that "if an ideological group disagreed and broke into two, one group must use all methods—orthodox or barbaric—to fight for supremacy in order to annihilate the other":[86]

> Their teachings further fuelled the breeding of a monster. It further encouraged the dissidents to adopt any method in the fighting, including kidnapping, maiming, murder, and genocide. Members of the mainstream OPC [Fasehun's faction] maintained their cool in order not to derail from its original aims and objectives. They avoided provocation to retaliate. . . . [But the] general public began to think that the strength or militancy of the organisation resided in the dissident group. . . . Some of my people thought to break his [Adams's] wings

> and return fire for fire. But I would have none of it. Much as I prevailed on the authentic OPC, some of my members finally broke loose, taking the law into their own hands in wildcat counter-reactionary retaliation to serve as a deterrent to the mouse that was singeing the beard of a father-cat! Provocation and retaliation became a common phenomenon. Soon they made the land unsafe for everybody.[87]

Indeed, as Fasehun admits, the retaliation of his group did not serve as "a deterrent" to the Adams faction; instead, Lagos and other areas in Southwestern Nigerian became spaces of urban warfare. "We killed ourselves [one another]," Taofik Adeyemi, a member of the Fasehun faction, said, summing up that era. "We all regretted the battle. We now ask ourselves, 'What did we gain?'" He concludes, however, that the two leaders, Fasehun and Adams, gained from the mutual battle: "As we were fighting [one another], Gani Adams and Fasehun's names grew bigger. Adams became rich and eminent, and Fasehun, who was already a medical doctor, became even bigger."[88]

OPC-related violence can be grouped into four categories. The first, like the event described above, involves clashes between the rival OPC factions, initially only the Fasehun and Adams factions; the second includes clashes with members of other ethnic groups (including the Hausa-Fulani, the Igbo, and the Ijaw) over spatial, cultural, or economic issues, all with ethno-political undertones; the third includes clashes with the police; and the last comprises vigilante activities. The four are not mutually exclusive.

Media reports and statements by state officials often emphasized the loss of lives and property due to OPC-related interethnic violence and OPC-police clashes. Indeed, even the OPC trumpeted, in the group's massive media campaigns, the countless numbers of its members killed by the police. But Adams's former chief of staff and long-term aide, Segun Akanni, revealed that the group's greatest loss in human lives was a result of factional violence: "We lost far more of our members to OPC factional crises than in our clashes with the police. Internal crisis in the OPC consumed most of our members who are dead. The casualties in the OPC factional wars were more than in the battles with the police."[89] Though Akanni was quick to say that the members were victims of indiscriminate killings by the police, he emphasized that the number of casualties in OPC-police clashes still did not match the number of those who died as a result of the struggle for supremacy between the two factions.

Apart from the Ejigbo clash, before the violent hostilities between the two factions ceased in 2005, at least five other major clashes consumed the lives of many OPC members on both sides: in Mushin, Alimosho, Osodi-Isolo, and Iyana Ipaja (where Fasehun and Adams were arrested and detained for fourteen months), all in Lagos, and in Ibadan.[90]

Figure 2.14. Leader of NURTW (Lagos wing), Musiliu Ayinde Akinsanya, popularly known as M. C. Oluomo (*right*), with Mustapha Adekunle (Mustapha Sego), the treasurer of the NURTW (*left*), during a visit to Adams in his home in 2016. Photo courtesy of *Nigerian Tribune*.

Though the Iyana Ipaja battle was mostly reported as a fight for supremacy between the two factions, it was also a reflection of the OPC's involvement in the internal politics of key civil society groups or cultural processes in urban areas. In this case, the Adams and Fasehun groups supported different factions in the battle for the control of the socially powerful and politically salient National Union of Road Transport Workers (NURTW), which drew its members from a similar socioeconomic class as the OPC. In 2005, two people were struggling for the leadership of the NURTW, one of the richest organizations run by subalterns in Nigeria. The group's strong, efficient, extensive, and well-oiled (but hardly financially accountable) machine for the collection of membership dues and bus-stop levies and its resulting value as a potential tool for political and cultural leaders made its leadership a financial gold mine and provided a route to social and cultural prestige and political leverage. The leadership of the union has always been a matter of great contention, from High Chief Lawani Asani Oluwo (popularly called *Omo Pupa*), the head of the road transport workers in Mushin area[91] and one of the most loyal supporters of the Action Group (AG) in the First Republic (1960–66), to Adebayo Ogundare (alias Bayo Success),[92] the head of the NURTW in Lagos State, who supported the ruling National Party of Nigeria (NPN) in the Second Republic (1979–83), and Musiliu Akinsanya (alias MC Oluomo),[93] the current chair of the NURTW in Lagos, who is allied with former governor Bola Tinubu of the ruling All Progressives Congress (APC). Whoever controls the union wields a lot of influence in Lagos and other parts of Nigeria.

Against this backdrop, when Alhaji Toyin Jimoh and Alhaji Fowler were contesting for the leadership of the NURTW Iyana Ipaja, Lagos, both sought the help of different factions of the OPC. Fasehun's faction supported Jimoh, while Adams's supported Fowler. When the two OPC factions clashed in Iyana Ipaja, with the Adams faction claiming the upper hand, the Fasehun faction, in reprisal, allegedly returned to wreak havoc on the motor park in the area where Fowler held sway. Arogundade Rasaq Balogun, at this point Adams's chief security officer (CSO) and head of the National Guard, accused the Fasehun faction of burning several vehicles belonging to members of the NURTW in Iyana Ipaja while drivers and passengers were inside. However, some of the media reports about the incident differed from Balogun's narrative. According to the *Daily Independent*, while "it was not clear what exactly led to the mayhem," it was "apparent" that a "protracted crisis between the OPC men and members of the NURTW in the area triggered the clash."[94] The newspaper reported that, on October 21, 2005, members of the Fasehun faction allegedly "stormed" the Iyana Ipaja unit of the NURTW, leaving several vehicles torched and eight

Figure 2.15. Emergent big men. Musiliu Akinsanya, or M. C. Oluomo, welcomes *Kakañfò* Adams to the burial ceremony of his mother-in-law in Lagos in February 2018. Photo courtesy of *Nigerian Tribune*.

Figure 2.16. Members of the OPC National Guard. *Left to right:* Monsuru Akande, Rasaq Arogundade Balogun (Saddam), and Musiliu "Big Fish" Amusa. Photo courtesy of Monsuru Akande.

people feared dead. According to the newspaper, members of the Adams faction "suffered defeat" and "subsequently . . . staged a reprisal attack the next day not only in the area but elsewhere in Lagos where the members of the other faction were based." The Fasehun faction also responded on October 25 as the violence spread to other parts of Lagos.[96]

In reaction to this violence, the inspector general of police (IGP), Sunday Ehindero, ostensibly on the orders of President Obasanjo, ordered the arrest of Fasehun and Adams. The Lagos State police commissioner, Adewole Ajakaiye,

Figure 2.17. "Free Gani Adams Now!" Members of the OPC protesting the detention of Adams, including his aide, Segun Akanni (*second from left*), and former labor leader and activist Comrade Ayodele Akele (late; *second from right*). Photo courtesy of Segun Akanni.

with whom the Adams faction claimed to have very good relations, called both factional leaders to his office at the command headquarters, Adekunle Fajuyi Road, Ikeja, Lagos, to inform them that he had orders to arrest both men and take them to Abuja. Sunday Adebayo, Adams's erstwhile right-hand man, told me that he was with Adams when Ajakaiye called the OPC leader to inform him of the orders from Abuja. Adams and Fasehun reported to the police on Saturday, October 22, 2005, and were subsequently flown to Abuja, where they were detained.[96] Five days later, on October 27, they were flown back to Lagos and arraigned, alongside nine others,[97] before a chief magistrate court at Igbosere, Lagos. They were charged with various offenses, including conspiracy to commit murder, malicious damage to property, rioting, causing fear to members of the public by carrying firearms, arson, and managing an unlawful organization.[98]

Both were later remanded to Kuje prison in Abuja without trial. However, Fasehun was released on medical grounds, while Adams remained in prison for fourteen months.

After Fasehun's release, Adams's comrades and friends organized the Free Gani Adams Now movement. Comrade Ayodele Akele, a veteran of activist movements who was described as "the ageless giant fighter for social justice,"[99] and Professor Kolawole Raheem provided the impetus for the movement. As a student at the Yaba College of Technology, Lagos, in 1980, after the proscription of the National Association of University Students (NUNS) by the military regime of General Olusegun Obasanjo, Akele had played a key role in the formation of the National Association of Nigerian Students (NANS) as the founding secretary-general. He later became a human rights activist and joined the Campaign for Democracy (CD), led by the medical doctor and activist Dr. Beko Ransome-Kuti. (Akele died in June 2020.)

Raheem had been a special researcher at the Institute for Educational Research and the Department of Biological and Environmental Science, University of Jyvaskyla, Finland, before he moved back home. He told me that his mentor, Ambassador Segun Olusola, a cultural activist and Nigeria's former ambassador to Ethiopia, introduced him to Adams during one of his visits to Nigeria in 2003, before he moved back to West Africa. Olusola had been educating Raheem about the activities of the OPC because he was close to Adams, who even addressed him as "Daddy," an indication that the older man commanded fatherly respect.

"I was with Ambassador Olusola one day when Adams called to say he was coming to see him. He came over with two of his lieutenants. He was very respectful when I met him. He came to discuss Yorùbá culture. He said he wanted to ensure that Yorùbá culture was well-preserved and nurtured,"[100] disclosed Raheem, who is now the head of the Centre for School and Community Science and Technology Studies (SACOST) at the Institute for Educational Research and Innovation Studies (IERIS), University of Education, Winneba, Ghana. He added that Olusola had queried Adams about the violence in which the group was implicated but that Adams had explained the group's position.

"After he left, Ambassador Olusola asked for my opinion. I told him that Adams was someone who needed a mentor like the ambassador. I saw the young man as a Yorùbá diamond. You get the rock, and then you polish it to become a diamond," stated Raheem. He accompanied Olusola to the Olokun Festival organized by the OPC in 2003. It was his first public identification with Adams. He has not looked back since then.

When Adams was detained at Kuje prison between 2005 and 2006, Raheem joined others in campaigning for his release. He revealed that, while deliberating with others about what to do about the detention, one Abudu, a draftsman and a volunteer in charge of information technology for the OPC, suggested

Figure 2.18. Professor Kolawole Raheem, who was based in Finland (and later moved to Ghana) and who sympathized with the cultural revival championed by the OPC, making a call in the Onipanu, Lagos, office of the Adams OPC. Some of the posters of the "Free Adams" campaign are on the floor beside him. Photo courtesy of Bose Omolaoye.

that they invite Akele, who was well known among activists in Lagos, to lead the campaign. Akele accepted the invitation.

Apart from campaigning to free Adams, Raheem became an intellectual guide, helping to draw other intellectuals—who would have been reluctant to associate with Adams—to the OPC leader. "I did not join the OPC. I remain an adviser to Gani Adams," Raheem told me. In his post-Ààre era, Adams installed Raheem as one of his chiefs as the *Parakoyi* Ààrẹ *Ọ̀nà Kakañfò*. However, the professor said he regarded himself less as a chief than as one of the "special assistants" of the *Aare*. "The *Parokoyi* is one of the closest advisers to the *Aare*," he added.

Adams's return to Lagos on December 21, 2006, after the Federal High Court Abuja ordered his release, was "triumphant."[101] Hundreds of members of the OPC reportedly laid siege to the domestic wing of the Murtala Mohammed Airport, Ikeja, Lagos, to welcome him. According to newspaper reports, when he was "ushered out of the VIP lounge of the airport . . . the crowd exploded in ecstasy, falling over themselves to catch a glimpse, and this continued for more than 15 minutes. Clad in complete white Guinea Brocade with a pair of black shoes to match, Mr. Adams managed to speak with the press for just five minutes in the midst of the surging crowd, as his efforts to even bring the crowd under control failed."[102]

The clashes between the rival OPC factions eventually abated after the July 2, 2005, reconciliation. But that reconciliation happened three months before both warring OPC leaders were arrested and detained in Abuja for several months. Otunba Gbenga Daniel, the governor of Ogun State, reconciled the two factional leaders. Five earlier attempts—by the *Afenifere* leader, Abraham Adesanya, in September 1999 at Ibadan; by the *Ooni* of Ife, *Oba* Okunade Sijuade, Olubuse II, on December 10, 1999, followed by the Oodua Self-Determination Group (COSEG); by Governor Bola Tinubu; and by Kayode Ogundamisi and Evangelist Kunle Adesokan, the secretary-generals of the Fasehun and Adams factions, respectively—had failed. As Adams himself admitted to the press, "Since the reconciliation, there has never been any serious factional crisis within the group. The Ogun State governor, Otunba Gbenga Daniel, during the reconciliatory meeting, told us to embrace peace and the positions were shared."[103]

As part of the truce, Adams took the position of "national coordinator" of the group, while Fasehun accepted the position of "founding father and spiritual

Figure 2.19. Adams and Fasehun embrace after the reconciliation. Photo courtesy of *Nigerian Tribune*.

Figure 2.20. Fasehun and Adams join hands after the reconciliation. Photo courtesy of *Nigerian Tribune.*

leader." Attempts to merge the two groups, however, failed. As onetime Welfare Committee chair of the OPC Monsuru Akande told me, some younger elements from the Adams faction disrupted a meeting to ensure the merger.[104] After this, the groups never attempted to restart the process. A few believed that neither of the leaders, particularly Adams, was committed to a merger. Neither wanted to expose his fiefdom to any contestation by the other, given how incredibly powerful and rich they had both become.

Three of the most fatal clashes involving Adams's OPC and other ethnic groups occurred at the popular Alaba International Market, between the OPC and Igbo traders; in Ajegunle, a suburb of Lagos, between the group and the Hausa community; and in Idi-Araba, between the group and members of the Hausa community in February 2002.

The Alaba market violence reportedly started in mid-July 2000 as a minor disagreement between a Yorùbá landlord and his Igbo tenant, Ike, who sold electronics at the market.[105] The landlord allegedly tried to eject the tenant through the courts and then, when that failed, sought the help of OPC members by labeling the tenant a criminal.[106] The OPC members threw the tenant's property out of the house and waited for him. When he returned, the OPC members accused him of being a criminal and attacked him. They ignored the man's denial and pleas and allegedly beat him into a coma, from which he never recovered. He died from his injuries.[107]

In retaliation, the victim's neighbors set fire to the landlord's building. Other Igbo traders mobilized to protest the death of their colleague. When they went to the *Baale* (the Yorùbá traditional head of the area), the OPC were standing guard and reportedly attacked the protesting traders. Tension rose as the traders ran back to marshal their ethnic constituents, only to find that the OPC had sent for reinforcement. The traders took up arms to defend themselves, only to suffer further attacks.[108] The market area became "a war zone" for two days as the clashes extended beyond the OPC and Igbo traders to include the Igbo in general.[109] Before the mobile police unit, the Rapid Response Squad (RRS), brought the situation under control, some Igbo and Yorùbá, OPC members, and police officers, among others, were killed, and property worth millions was destroyed. As the HRW reported, the violence worsened "ethnic polarisation in the area." An Igbo trader told the HRW, "It was after this crisis that we initiated another association, the Alaba United Traders' Association, for the Igbo traders alone. The former association had comprised every trader in Alaba, irrespective of tribal affiliation. . . . It was a good thing that peace was restored because at a time, we were thinking of acquiring arms and even declaring the Alaba area a Biafran territory."[110] The trader added that "a prominent Yoruba leader had come to apologize" for the actions of the OPC.

It is significant, however, that this clash happened after the OPC had been outlawed and its factional leader had been declared wanted.

The clash between the OPC and members of the Hausa community in Ajegunle in the Ajeromi-Ifelodun Local Government Area of Lagos, an incident the *New Nigerian* described as the "macabre dance of death,"[111] led to the loss of more lives than was witnessed in Alaba about three months earlier. It was described as "the bloodiest" in recent years in Lagos at the time—even without consideration of the retaliatory killings in the North of Nigeria. (A retaliatory attack on Yorùbá and southerners occurred in Kano a few days later, in which more than one hundred lives were lost.)[112]

In mid-October 2000, what started as a "verbal disagreement" between the OPC members and the Hausa community in Ajegunle—a low-income suburb of Lagos popularly called Jungle City—over the alleged killing of a Hausa man who was mistaken for a fleeing thief by the OPC snowballed into full-scale interethnic "war."[113] About one hundred people reportedly died as the crisis spread to other parts of Lagos that hosted significant populations of the Hausa community, including Mushin, Idi-Araba, Ijeshatedo, Abule Egba, Ketu, Mile 12, Yaba, Ikotun, Agege, Amukoko, Ijora, Agege, and Idumota and Apongbon on the island.[114] A lady who witnessed the mayhem in Lagos Island told journalists, "There is no government in this country. Life is worth nothing here. I was

Figure 2.21. *TheWeek* magazine cover from February 2002, featuring the OPC-Hausa clashes.

frozen by the number of corpses I saw yesterday."[115] The voice of the North, the *New Nigerian* newspaper, later described the violence as an "October Lagos massacre of the people of the north by blood-thirsty OPC."[116]

Another violent clash reportedly also started as a minor problem in which a man of Hausa extraction refused to pay to use a public convenience on Karimu Street in Idi-Araba. This led to a scuffle between him and the keepers of the facility. The matter reportedly drew the attention of the man's kinsmen and eventually other Yorùbá and the OPC in the area. The two groups reportedly engaged in a "fierce duel in which knives, clubs, daggers, charms and guns were freely used."[117] Between Saturday, February 2, 2002, and Tuesday, February 5, when the battle raged—spreading to Lawanson, Mushin, and Ilasamaja areas and subsequently Agege, Palmgrove, Onipanu, and Mile 12 areas, where there were considerable populations of the Hausa community—about sixty lives were lost.[118] The media reported "huge debris of burnt houses, property and human bodies that lined virtually all the streets, from Sadiku Street on the Oshodi-Apapa Expressway to the Lagos University Teaching Hospital (LUTH), whole streets were burnt or destroyed and the entire area deserted."[119]

In response to the clashes, the Yorùbá political group *Afenifere*, after an emergency meeting on February 4, stated that "enemies of democracy and the Yoruba race" were responsible for the violence. The statement read in part, "Information at our disposal after extensive consultation suggests that the massacre was part of a programme to truncate the nascent democracy and destabilise the Yoruba nation."[120]

Between 1999 and 2002, there were clashes between the "militant faction" of the OPC and members of the Ijaw community in Ajegunle, Lagos[121] (October 1999); Hausa traders in Mile 12 and Ketu, Lagos (November 1999);[122] and members of the Hausa community in Sagamu, Ogun State (1999).[123]

Given the spate of OPC-inspired violence in Lagos, President Obasanjo wrote to Governor Bola Tinubu, threatening to declare a state of emergency if the situation was not brought under control. Tinubu challenged the president, stating that the situation did not warrant such a threat.[124] The Alliance for Democracy (AD) governors of the other five Yorùbá states supported Tinubu. In reaction, some northern senators asked for the removal of the IGP, Musiliu Smith, a Yorùbá, and the minister of police affairs, retired major general David Jemibewon, also a Yorùbá. Jemibewon described this call as an "ethnically and politically motivated open display of immaturity and regional sentiment." By this time, the OPC crisis had taken critical national dimensions, polarized the political elite, and worsened interethnic relations. The Senate and the House of Representatives set up fact-finding committees. But while the recriminations and investigations were going on, several other violent clashes involving the OPC occurred.

Against the backdrop of its reading of Nigeria's political history, the OPC identifies the Hausa-Fulani as its principal Other. The OPC believed that the violence this Other constituted needed to be countered both discursively and physically. However, the reality was more complicated than this. The OPC, as evident here, was involved in more intra-Yorùbá struggles for power and prominence than interethnic clashes. Yet Adams argued that if any violence could be associated with the group, it was the violence unleashed on them, particularly by the police. This violence, he argued, was a manifestation of the violence instituted by the Hausa-Fulani. He claimed to have been fighting hard to end the violence of the Other.[125]

A northern intellectual, Abubakar Jika,[126] captured the reaction of the Hausa-Fulani elite to the OPC activities, stating that the group's activities defined how the rest of Nigeria saw the Yorùbá: "Many Nigerians are no longer confident that Nigeria as we know it could survive the next decade, let alone millennium, unless the Yorubas turn a new leaf. They are pushing other tribes to their ethnic shells. The question is, were the Yorubas looking for political power to preside over the balkanization of Nigeria? Were they looking for power to hold the knife in the final sharing of Nigeria? Why do the generality of Yorubas appear to be contented with the separatist agenda of the OPC?"

Another commentator from the North stated that "events . . . in Lagos have clearly shown once again that the Federal Government of Nigeria of today [led by a Yorùbá] is either unwilling or incapable of protecting the lives and property of Northerners living in Lagos. . . . Probably the OPC feel nothing is going to happen to them because their 'brothers' are the ones in charge of the whole national security apparatues. . . . (T)he OPC feel they have the license to kill, maim, and destroy and nothing would happen."[127] He added, "We have seen times without number through its numerous acts of omission of commission that the [Lagos State] Government is not only a strong supporter of OPC, but also its strongest financiers."[128] Alhaji Abubakar Rimi, former governor of the northern state of Kano and former People's Democratic Party presidential aspirant, alleged that the ban the Obasanjo government had placed on the OPC was "a hoax" because there was a "conspiracy between the government and OPC to kill other Nigerians in Lagos."[129] Also, Rimi accused Obasanjo of "hypocrisy" on OPC violence. He stated that "OPC is flourishing because there is government hypocrisy in dealing with them because they are from the southwest." He added, "When there was trouble in Odi, in Bayelsa State (south-south Nigeria), Obasanjo sent troops to level down the whole village. When there was problem between Jukun and the Tiv (central Nigeria), Obasanjo sent soldiers and they levelled structures standing in the area. When OPC killed people and burnt mosques and killed [M]uslims and killed the Hausa/Fulani and people from other parts of Nigeria, killed the Ibo and so on. . . . There was even a façade of an order that OPC members should be shot at sight, nobody up till today, no member of the OPC since that order was given two years ago was shot at sight. . . . How can any sincere leader of a country reason like this?"[130] The fact that the OPC was not involved in violent clashes with other ethnic groups in Nigeria from its inception in 1994 until a Yorùbá man became the president in 1999 supported the accusation that Obasanjo could not be trusted to end the OPC "menace."

Indeed, members of the Yorùbá progressive elite, represented mainly by *Afenifere* and the breakaway group Yoruba Council of Elders (YCE), came to the defense of the OPC.[131] The *Nigerian Tribune*,[132] a Yorùbá-owned paper, also disagreed with the northerners' reading of OPC-inspired violence, arguing that "the OPC was created to break an existing violence. In its political dimension, it has sought to break the violence of irresponsible and inefficient power that has been integral to the logic of the Nigerian state. There have been official and other (particularly from rival ethnic groups) attempts to quarantine this dimension in the present circumstances; an attempt to ignore the core reasons that inform the dark rage and the sterile madness that enacted itself in Lagos."

The pressures and accusations of "complicity" perhaps provoked President Obasanjo to issue a shoot-on-sight order against the OPC.[133] The president, threatening to declare a state of emergency in Lagos, accused the Lagos governor of losing control of the security situation in his state. In Nigeria's peculiar federal system, though the governor is the CSO of the state, the police force is a federal organization. There are no state police. President Obasanjo accused Governor Tinubu of making statements in support of the OPC and added, "There is evidence of increasing disorder, loss of lives and property and general sense of fear among the citizens of Lagos State."[134] Tinubu responded by telling the president that he had no evidence for his allegations while blaming Obasanjo for ignoring his request for a ten-thousand-man police force to respond to the security challenges in the state.[135]

The OPC deliberately pursued the major "war" to retake Ilorin, a northern Yorùbá city that the Fulani jihadists captured in the mid-nineteenth century after killing their Yorùbá ally, Afonja, the Ààrẹ *Ọnà Kakańfò* (generalissimo and head of the imperial army),[136] who was rebelling against the head of the Oyo Empire, the *Aláàfin*. Since then, the "traditional" ruler of the town has been a Fulani emir, although its population is predominantly Yorùbá. The OPC swore

Figure 2.22. What next? Adams looking at a document while Rasaq Arogundade Balogun (*second from right*) and his other lieutenants look on. Photo courtesy of Rasaq Arogundade Balogun.

to appoint a Yorùbá *oba* (traditional ruler) for the city. This has also occasioned clashes with law enforcement agents. The Ilorin Emirate Chiefs Forum reacted to the OPC's move by describing the members as "Yoruba hoodlums" while calling on their own Hausa-Fulani kith and kin from the North and Kwara State to assist them in protecting the emirate system.[137]

"THE POLICE IS YOUR FRIEND": ENMITY AND AMITY IN POLICE-OPC RELATIONS

In June 2019, the head of the federal police in Nigeria, the IGP, Mohammed Adamu, sent a delegation to the Ààrẹ *Ọ̀nà Kakañfò* of Yorubaland, Gani Adams. The team was led by the IGP's chief of staff, Jude Nwakor, a superintendent of police (SP). The visit followed a seven-day ultimatum issued by the OPC against Fulani herdsmen to leave Southwestern Nigeria or face the organization's wrath.[138]

In the previous year, the security threat to lives and property posed by herdsmen in most parts of the country had reached a boiling point. Apart from creating security challenges in Southwestern Nigeria, the indiscriminate killings, kidnappings, wanton destruction of farmlands, and banditry allegedly perpetrated by the herdsmen threatened to provoke interethnic clashes. The governors of the six Southwest states, reacting to pressure from their people, decided

Figure 2.23. The Ààrẹ *Ààrẹ Ọ̀nà Kakañfò, Iba* Adams, being welcomed by the Lagos State commissioner for police, Zubairu Muazu, during Adams's visit to his office. Photo courtesy of *Nigerian Tribune*.

to set up a state security outfit, named *Amotekun* (named after the leopard), in each of the states.[139] It was in this context that Adams issued his threat.

Rather than committing himself directly to resolving the security problems in the region—given that Nigeria, despite being a federation, operates a federal policing system with no other level of formal policing—or responding to the illegality of the threat issued by the Yorùbá generalissimo, the IGP decided to send a delegation of senior police officers from Abuja to Lagos to meet Adams and seek his "assistance and support in solving the security challenges in the country."[140] The action indicates that the police regarded Adams's threat as credible and that the IGP considered him a critical player in the security sector in Nigeria.

Nineteen years earlier, one of Adamu's predecessors had placed a N100,000 ransom on Adams's head for alleged complicity in the murder of Afolabi Amoa, a divisional police officer of the same rank as the IGP's representative, Nwankor. Perhaps nothing symbolized the radical transformation in the IGP's view of the OPC leader (and now Yorùbá generalissimo) better than the shift from placing a ransom on Adams's head for alleged murder about two decades earlier

Figure 2.24. Police officers meeting Adams in his Lagos home. Photo courtesy of *Nigerian Tribune.*

to seeking his "assistance and support" in resolving Nigeria's security challenges. Except perhaps the fact that, while in police custody in August 2001, Adams had been, as he told the *Guardian* at the time, "tortured with the butt of the gun, chained and handcuffed to the door."[141] In organizational and personal terms, the police force and the OPC, as well as the leadership of both organizations, had, by 2019, totally altered the terms of their engagement, moving from a torturer-victim relationship to a partnership.

"We are happy to relate with you as a prominent voice in Yorubaland," the IGP's representative told Adams in his Lagos home. "We know there is no way we can secure the grassroots without local intelligence. The IG has indicated interest in seeking your assistance and support and that is why we are here to tell you that the Nigeria Police Force, as an institution, is ready to partner [with] you."[142]

Adams told the police that as the Ààrẹ *Ọ̀nà Kakańfò* of Yorubaland, he had been under pressure to act on the security situation in Southwest Nigeria. He therefore commended "the Inspector General of Police on this move." He added, "The visit, as far as I am concerned, is a welcome development and it goes a long way in solving the menace."[143] Boasting that the OPC "has a history of winning war against kidnapping, banditry and other social vices,"[144] Adams indicated his support for the police initiative while presenting a letter to the IGP through his emissaries that proffered solutions to the pervasive insecurity in the country.[145]

A few months later, Adams also paid a courtesy call to the Lagos State commissioner of police, Zubairu Muazu, and announced that he was ready "to support the Lagos state Police authority in strengthening the security architectures in the state."[146] He reportedly noted that "the partnership between the police and the Oodua People's Congress (OPC) is beginning to yield positive results with other relevant groups coming on board as partners in progress." Instructively, he informed the police commissioner of "the various efforts he had put in place since the Inspector-General of Police, Muhammadu Adamu, and the southwest governors [announced that] *they were ready to work with the OPC under his leadership* in combating insecurity across the southwest."[147]

The call was Adams's subtle but significant way of reminding the state police boss that he had the mandate of the latter's boss in Abuja and of the governors of the region, who acted as the chief security officers of their states. The media quoted Adams as further stating,

> So far, we have made significant progress since the IGP had expressed the readiness of the police to work with the OPC under my leadership. It is on this note that I said *the OPC and the Nigerian Police are partners in progress*. . . . We have started work in earnest and everybody can attest to the fact that our efforts are beginning to yield positive results. . . . We have set the pace and the signs are there for everybody to see that we are ready to secure the southwest and make the region safe for Nigerians.[148]

Police commissioner Muazu repeated some platitudes about the significance of the police and their efforts regarding the current security situation in the country. He said, "I think Aare Gani Adams' visit is timely and it is a positive sign that things are taking good shape in the country."[149]

There has not been any major clash between the OPC and the police since Adams's entry into high society in Nigeria became a generally acknowledged fact. The two courtesy calls mentioned previously appear to signal a new era in the relationship between the OPC and the police. While that relationship has indeed been transformed, in part by the transformation of the leader of the group, Adams,[150] the popular impression in the media that the OPC and the police had been sworn enemies did not fully capture the reality, particularly between 1999 and 2008. Indeed, of all the relations of violence that the OPC has had with the state, state agencies, political and civil society, and different social formations, the relations with the police were perhaps the most complicated, even intriguing. As the encounter between a police chief and Monsuru Akande, then the Welfare Committee chair of the OPC and a member of the group's National Guard, which I related earlier, shows that, despite the mutual hostility at the height of OPC-related violence, particularly between 1999 and 2008, some in the police force had confidential, but sometimes open, tactical, strategic, personal, and institutional relationships with the OPC leadership, particularly Gani Adams.

However, these relationships did not preclude the incessant killings of OPC members by police officers and vice versa or the various other forms of human rights violations perpetrated by the police against members or suspected members of the group.[151]

In the early years of the OPC, especially when the group became visible in urban areas, the police attitude was not unlike its general attitude toward most social formations in Nigeria. However, when the OPC initially acquired the image of an organized group of area boys,[152] or social miscreants, some police officers tried to exploit the group and its members, and when this failed, they brutalized them. As the OPC's visibility increased, the police became more violent in reaction to the members' actual or suspected gatherings or activities. Many police officers saw the group's attempt to respond to urban social anomie—particularly the frequent incidents of armed robbery—as an affront. The OPC members too believed that a significant percentage of police officers were collaborating with criminals. Yet they identified some police officers whom they believed to be honest, committed to law enforcement, and eager to collaborate with members of the civil society to fight crime.

Still, the relationship with the police in general was worsened by the OPC's reputation for violence, magic, and the occult. During arrest attempts, many officers who themselves believed in the efficacy of magic were eager to shoot on sight or brutalize OPC members to prevent them from deploying their magic against the police.

When President Olusegun Obasanjo gave a shoot-on-sight order, the police became even more emboldened to kill suspected OPC members before ascertaining whether they belonged to the group. A newsmagazine asserted that "the men in black [police] savoured the order and wherever they came across members of the congress, they opened fire."[153] Criminals and criminal gangs—including those assumed to be in police uniform—also seized on the police attitude toward the OPC, as the group was becoming a far more formidable enemy, particularly in certain areas of Lagos. Given that most of the members of the OPC were unemployed, underemployed, or working as artisans, apprentice artisans, and *okada* riders—with a significant percentage being reformed delinquents or even thugs—they possessed local knowledge of the criminals and the criminal networks in their areas. As some key members of the group revealed to me, this knowledge proved critical when the OPC decided to root out armed robbers from the low-income areas of Lagos. This often meant that the group had to contend with both good and bad cops even as they took on criminals. The complex process of managing multiple challenges of (il)legitimate law enforcement often resulted in messy situations—and the loss of lives.

The murder of the divisional police officer (DPO) in charge of Bariga, SP Amos Afolabi Amao, is a case in point. As stated earlier, the hostility of the police toward the OPC preceded the president's shoot-on-sight order. That order only worsened things. There are different versions of what happened to Amao—even in Nigerian newspapers. Two of the leading newsmagazines of that era, *TheNEWS* and *TELL*, published different details. According to *TheNEWS*, "On Monday 9 January, Mr. Afolabi Amao, a superintendent of police in charge of the Bariga Station was allegedly killed by the OPC and his body dumped in the lagoon. . . . Trouble began on Sunday when a man was brought to the Bariga police station for possession of arms and ammunition. The DPO reportedly waded into the matter and followed the suspects to where others could be found. A bus, loaded with some civilians, intercepted, overpowered, and seized the senior officers and his men."[154]

While admitting that "there are several accounts of the incident that led to the killing of Amao," *TELL* reported,

> Amao was abducted by men suspected to be members of the militant Oodua People's Congress, OPC, on the night of January 10, a few metres from the Bariga police station, a Lagos suburb. The abduction followed a fresh violence at Ilaje area of Bariga, in Somolu [local government] council. . . . Sources told

> the magazine that earlier, information reached the police that Ganiyu Adams . . . who had been declared wanted by the police, was in the area, holding a meeting of his group. The DPO and his men then launched a search for him. They did not search long before they stumbled on the OPC meeting in session on Odunsi Street. Amao, it was said, ordered the meeting to stop and demanded to search the house. The OPC members reportedly resisted. . . . During the shoot-out that followed, two OPC members were killed. Amao then withdrew to the station. . . . But infuriated by the loss of their two colleagues, the OPC men were said to have quickly mobilised and went after Amao. They met him a few metres from the police station and abducted him.[155]

TELL also later reported that Amao was "killed in the wake of Police-OPC clash in Bariga," adding that "Adams absolved himself of complicity in Amao's murder."[156]

However, according to the key members of the OPC with whom I spoke, in early January 2000, while the Somolu Local Government chapter of the OPC was holding its meeting in the Bariga area of Lagos, the RRS suddenly arrived and started shooting at the members. Alhaji Rasaq Arogundade Balogun, whose sobriquet in the group is Saddam,[157] told me that because of incessant "police harassment and attacks, we were always ready for them."[158] According to the OPC leaders, they had greater firepower than the RRS. Saddam added, "We beat them back. We forced them to flee to the Bariga Police Station."[159]

The members of the squad could have fled to the station to seek protection or reinforcement against the OPC members. However, confident of their relationship with the DPO, Balogun, who was also the coordinator of the OPC in the local government and a member of the OPC Squad (also named the National Guard), stated that the OPC members went inside to see the DPO, Amao, to demand that the RRS members be ejected from the station. However, Amao was not around. According to the OPC members, when Amao later heard about the incident, he visited the scene. Amao was killed near the area. His body was never found. In the OPC version, after the murder of Amao, a contingent of heavily armed police officers descended on the whole Shomolu-Bariga area to "retaliate" against the OPC and others for the murder of Amao.

"We were close to the DPO," stated Balogun. He described the relationship:

> He was sent to head the Bariga Police Station to be able to handle the OPC in the area.[160] When he resumed, he asked to meet us. We used to exchange information about crimes with him. We had a good relationship. If any of our members was arrested by his men just for being members of the OPC, we will approach him. He will release them without demanding money for the

> release.[161] When the DPO came back and heard the report of what happened between the RSS and the OPC, he came to see us with some of his men. So how did he die? Where is his body? How could we kill him?[162]

While the police believed that they had answered Balogun's first and third questions by successfully prosecuting some members of the OPC, no one has been able to provide a conclusive answer to the second question: Where is Amao's body?

Regarding the first and third questions, the police stated that Amao was kidnapped and murdered by the OPC because the group's members always conspired to kill police officers. They also stated, regarding the second question, that Amao's body was dumped into the lagoon near the Oworonshoki Bridge.

But the leaders of the OPC in Bariga alleged that the failure to find Amao's body points to police complicity in his murder. However, even the OPC leaders could not agree on who was directly responsible for the murder. While Balogun (Saddam) stated categorically that "the OPC had no hand in Amao's murder," he theorizes that Amao was a victim of an amorous contestation between the officer and his men. He alleged that a woman who sold clothes on credit to the police in Bariga became the amorous interest of one of the junior officers. He said that the OPC members were later informed that the junior officer had discovered that Amao was having an affair with the same woman. The DPO supposedly incurred the wrath of the junior officers, who believed he was abusing his position by starting the affair. Balogun believed that the junior officers must have shot Amao as he was leaving the scene of the clash in Bariga because they knew they could claim that he was killed by the OPC.

Another key member of the OPC—the former chair of the Welfare Committee and Adams's erstwhile right-hand man, Monsuru Akande—also said the OPC members "had close contacts with Amao."[163] However, his version of why Amao went to the scene of the incident was slightly different. According to him, Amao intended to "settle some disagreements" between his men and the OPC members who had complained that the officers were "disturbing" them. Akande alleged that an armed robbery gang whose operations had more or less been made impossible by the OPC used the opportunity to kill Amao and took his corpse with them so that the OPC could be accused of killing him. He added that the effective banning of the operation of the OPC in the Somolu-Bariga area after the murder indicated that the armed robbers achieved their aim. But Akande could not say whether the armed robbers were conspiring with some of Amao's men or had insider information about Amao's movements.

Again, Balogun's narrative was different: "He [Amao] was killed around the [police] station. There were policemen with him. How could armed robbers kill him and take his body away without the police knowing [about it]? Whenever the government has an interest in a matter, they always use the law."[164]

Both Akande and Balogun were members of the dreaded OPC Squad (National Guard), members of the group's NCC, and close aides of Adams at the point of Amao's death. Thus, one would expect that their narratives would be the same, or at least similar. However, since Balogun was the head of the Somolu-Bariga chapter of the OPC, it could be assumed that he would know the intricate details better than Akande. Still, Akande, as one of those closest to Adams, should also know the group's "official" line regarding the incident, given that it was the single most important event that transformed the OPC into a national phenomenon—which led to their leader being declared wanted and subsequently becoming a figure of national attention.

A seemingly more credible story in the local and international press contains elements of the different versions of the event by the OPC and the police, claiming that Amao was abducted by OPC members. However, the totality of the narrative, when related to the members' renditions, leaves room for the possibility that Amao was abducted by people only pretending to be affiliated with the OPC.

According to the media, the day before Amao's murder, the police in Bariga arrested a man for theft and armed robbery. The *Guardian* quoted Lagos State police commissioner Mike Okiro as stating that, after the arrest and detention of the suspect, "a group of about 300 men stormed Bariga police station [the next day, Monday] . . . claiming they were members of the OPC and were there to effect the release of the member who was arrested by the police."[165] The police claimed that these were the people who had kidnapped and killed Amao. However, the media reported that an "unofficial source linked the reported killing of Amao to the disruption on Sunday [January 9, 2000] of an OPC meeting by police, who allegedly shot dead one militant."[166]

The "official" version of this report contains some elements of Akande's claim involving armed robbers, though in his own story, the OPC members were not seeking the release of the robbers. The "unofficial" version has elements of Balogun's claim that the police (RRS) attacked the OPC during their meeting on Sunday, January 9.

Yet the disparity in the stories given by the two leading OPC members and the police raises questions. In what context was Amao killed—after a clash between the OPC and the RSS (as Balogun claimed), after he tried to settle a rift between his men and the OPC (as Akande claimed), or during a clash between the police and the OPC (as the police claimed)? If Amao indeed had a good relationship with OPC members, particularly in Bariga, as Balogun and Akande claimed, why would the OPC members kill him? If Amao was killed

Figure 2.25. Members of the Women's League of the OPC Somolu Local Government presenting an award to Mudasiru Aderibigbe, the chair of the OPC in the local government. Aderibigbe was convicted and sentenced to fourteen years over the murder of police DPO Amao. Bose Omolaoye, the OPC office secretary, is to the right of Aderibigbe. Photo courtesy of Monsuru Akande.

by the OPC in a clash with the police, where were his men? Why were there no casualties among Amao's men? If the police were sure—as they claimed—that Amao's body had been dumped in the lagoon, why did the marine police and divers who were "ordered to recover the body from the lagoon"[167] not find the body or any trace of it? If the police could deploy so much manpower to invade Bariga in response to the killing and to hunt down OPC members, why did they not attempt to search for the body of their comrade?

The answers to these questions remain open to contestation. However, as far as the law is concerned, the case is closed. A few men were convicted for Amao's murder. Though Adams, who was declared wanted for the murder, among other alleged crimes, was arrested and prosecuted, the case was eventually dismissed. Other OPC members who were convicted for Amao's murder included Mudasiru Aderibigbe, coordinator for the Shomolu Bariga chapter (jailed for fourteen years); Najeem (jailed for fourteen years);[168] and Lawrence (jailed for seven years).[169]

As the confusion over the context of Amao's killing shows, the clashes between the police and the OPC, as local and international human rights organizations concluded, involved criminality and human rights violations on both sides. As the HRW reported,

> There has been a pattern of arbitrary and indiscriminate arrests of suspected OPC members by the police. Waves of arrests were especially common following the major outbreaks of violence, for example the clashes in Ketu/Mile 12 in November 1999 and Ajegunle in October 2000, and after the killing of DPO Amao in January 2000. The OPC has repeatedly claimed that its members have been targeted by the police purely on the basis of their membership of the organization, not because they were involved in any criminal offense. While there is no doubt that many OPC members have been responsible for grave human rights abuses and a range of criminal offenses, Human Rights Watch found credible evidence to support the OPC's claim that in many cases, the arrests carried out by the police were arbitrary. These arbitrary arrests were sanctioned by and sometimes carried out on the orders of senior federal government officials.... In some cases, OPC members have been arrested not because they were suspected of any act of violence, but to prevent them from meeting.... Frederick Fasehun claimed that when he was detained in Ikoyi prison in October 2000, there were 814 OPC members detained in that prison alone, and that at the time of his release at the end of November 2000, there were a total of between 2,000 and 3,000 OPC members detained.... When Human Rights Watch spoke to Gani Adams in May 2002, he said that around 150 members were still detained in Ikoyi prison and about fifty in Kirikiri prison (both in Lagos). He claimed that some had been detained for about two years.[170]

Adams was still in hiding in early 2000 when *TheNEWS* magazine asked him, supposedly in a telephone interview,[171] if he had any message for "the families who have lost their children to the OPC-inspired violence." He countered,

> An observation, please. The OPC has never insinuated or provoked any act of violence. If I must remind you, in September 1998, it was the police that came to disrupt our peaceful meeting in which a school boy, Azubuike, was shot in the eye. Did the OPC provoke this? On 8 November, 1998 at Bariga, policemen descended on another peaceful meeting where so many people, including Kolawole Arowosaiye, were shot. Is that OPC-provoked violence? Three days later, at an all-states meeting at Olusoga Street in Mushin, the police came with an armoured tank and other vehicles to bombard another peaceful meeting, where many people were shot. Will you label this an OPC-insinuated attack?[172]

Adams read out a litany of police attacks against the OPC in different parts of Lagos and elsewhere in Southwest Nigeria.[173] He added an accusation that sought to reconstruct the crisis not as one between the OPC and the police but as one between the Yorùbá and the Hausa-Fulani, who, according to him, used the state and its agencies against other groups. Adams alleged, "Our investigations revealed that the Lagos State Deputy Police Commissioner, M.D. Abubakar, has been in charge of these cold-blooded killings of the Yoruba under the guise of law enforcement."[174]

In what the press described as "an eye for an eye,"[175] a "reign of terror,"[176] or an "all-out-war,"[177] even as some senior police officers and highly placed officials of the state collaborated and kept in touch with the OPC leaders, police officers and OPC members targeted one another on the streets. The newspapers constantly reported that officers had been killed by OPC members or were missing in action, while the OPC's own massive information machinery[178] reported several cases of police killings and brutality against its members. Newspaper headlines that captured the nature of the relationship between the police and the OPC include "War in Lagos as OPC Loses 50 Men in Police Execution,"[179] "The Road to War,"[180] "War without End,"[181] "Police vs OPC,"[182] and "No peace agenda for Nigeria."[183]

"Don't fight *o*!" Gani Adams shouted at the OPC members who had been pushed back by the police as they struggled to catch a glimpse of him as he emerged from the Ikeja Magistrate Court on Friday, August 24, 2001, where he was facing a twenty-three-count charge including culpable homicide, attempted murder, and armed robbery.

Dressed in a green safari suit, the same clothes he had worn on the day of his arrest a few weeks earlier, Adams raised the victory sign as he acknowledged cheers from the members of his group. The sign was not a mere symbol of his optimism about his current travail, nor was it specific to the current struggle. No other Nigerian politician or political movement has been associated with the victory sign more than the late Obafemi Awolowo and his defunct political parties, the AG (First Republic) and the Unity Party of Nigeria (UPN). The victory sign was one of the most recognized gestures of the Awolowo political movement, both in times of tribulation and in times of victory, personal and political. It was the sign Awolowo raised in 1962 while coming out of the Black Maria—the infamous police vehicle for transporting those on trial to and from prison—to acknowledge the support of his teeming admirers during trial; it was the same sign he raised to acknowledge the adulation and celebration of his people when he was released from jail in 1966; it was the sign he raised countless times in 1979 when he campaigned around the country to become

INTERVIEW/P8

ISSUE/P27

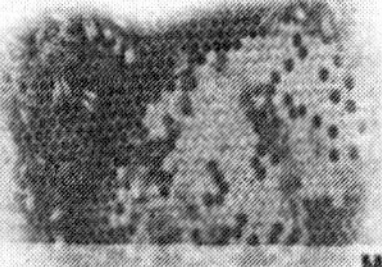

MONEY GUIDE/P29

THE GUARDIAN
CONSCIENCE, NURTURED BY TRUTH
VOL 18 NO. 8,304 SATURDAY, AUGUST 25, 2001 EIGHTY NAIRA

Adams: 'I'm a Freedom Fighter'

• Court Rules on September 14

BY MUSTAPHA OGUNSAKIN

"I AM a freedom fighter and I have been a freedom fighter for more than 10 years."

These were the words of the factional leader of the Oodua People's Congress (OPC) Mr. Ganiyu Adams, who was yesterday arraigned with three others by the police at the Ikeja Chief Magistrate Court over a 23-count charge that borders on culpable homicide, attempted murder and armed robbery. It was also a day of solidarity, as a large crowd of spectators invaded the hallowed precincts of the court in support of the embattled activist on hearing that his trial was holding there.

Adams, in the same green *Safari* suit he had worn the day he was arrested and paraded, spoke with *The Guardian* despite the medley of activities, for some minutes, while he was in the dock.

See Page 14

"I am not a hired killer," he said emphatically, refuting the offences with which he was charged by the police.

On the day of his arrest, he had had no opportunity to react to the allegations levelled by the Police, as he was allowed to only confirm his identity before journalists. Also yesterday, he hardly had an opportunity to defend himself, save replies to the charges preferred against him by the police, when his reaction was sought.

Speaking with *The Guardian* while in the dock, he accused the police of torturing not only himself, but also many others in detention, with whom he was detained.

Of himself, the self-assigned defender of Yoruba interests said: "I was tortured with the butt of the gun, chained and handcuffed to the door. They removed all my clothes despite the fact that I told them that I am asthmatic."

CONTINUED ON PAGE 2

Anxiety As Adams Is Arraigned

James Dadzie, Godwin Ijediogor, Yinka [illegible], Charles Coffie Gyamfi, Tolu Olanrewaju, Julius Alabi

IT was an admixture of the grief, disbelief and anxiety that reigned at the premises of the Ikeja Chief Magistrate Court yesterday as the factional leader of the Oodua Peoples Congress (OPC), Ganiyu Adams, was arraigned amidst tight police security.

Adams who was driven to the court premises at about 10.40 a.m. in a white Mazda pick-up with registration number AS 505 EKY appeared in the same green safari suit he wore on the day of his arrest (Wednesday). He was hemmed in by two equally armed policemen in mufti, in the middle seat.

About eight other heavily armed policemen, mainly in mufti occupied the rear seats of the vehicle.

The vehicle was escorted to the court by a Rapid Response Squad Mazda Pick-up van with registration number DM 650 KJA filled with armed uniformed policemen and with registration number PF 5123 LA also loaded.

On the whole, about 30 heavily armed policemen mostly at mufti were on standby in the court premises.

There was a hushed silence among the crowd gathered in the court premises as Adams alighted from the police vehicle with leg cuffs.

Adams who looked tired and unkempt shuffled slowly into the courtroom. He appeared to be moving with a limp.

No sooner had the court proceedings begun at about 10.45 a.m. than a large crowd thronged the outside of the courtroom.

Occasionally, the police had a hectic time keeping the anxious crowd at bay.

Shouts of "action", "action" however filled the air as Adams emerged from the courtroom after the proceedings.

With a bread smile, the OPC factional leader acknowledged the cheers, waving his right hand in a victory (V) sign.

And all the while, he enjoined the crowd: "Don't fight O!"

However, reactions continued to trail Adams arrest. A chieftain of the Yoruba Council of Elders Dr. Kunle Olajide said the group's position is that the factional leader must be dealt with according to the laws of the land.

Fielding questions in a telephone interview with {The Guardian}, Olajide said Adams must be arraigned in a proper court of law within the specified period of time and his charges made known to him.

He said, "we believe he should not be tortured or treated as a criminal until the charges levelled against him have been proved by a competent

CONTINUED ON PAGE 2

Adams at the Ikeja Chief Magistrate Court, Lagos ... yesterday

Adams' alleged offences, by police

"THAT you Ganiyu Adams (m) on the 20th of July, 2000 between the hours of 0010 and [illegible] Under the Bridge Ijora Lagos in the Lagos Magisterial District did conspire with others still at large to commit felony to wit: – Murder/Unlawful possession of firearms and thereby committed an offence punishable under Section 324 of the Criminal Code of Lagos State 1994 and contrary to Section 5(b) and punishable under Section 3(1) of the Robbery and Firearms Special Provisions Act. Cap. 398 Vol. 22 Laws of the Federation of Nigeria 1990.

Count II: That you Ganiyu Adams (m) and others still at large on the same date and place, in the aforesaid Magisterial district did unlawfully kill one Inspector James Ebiloma by hitting him [illegible] and also gave him matchet cuts, and thereby committed a offence punishable under Section 319 of the Criminal Code, Cap.32 Vol. II Laws of Lagos State, 1994.

Count III: – That you Ganiyu Adams (m) and others still at large, on the same date and place in the aforesaid Magisterial district without a valid licence granted by the Inspector General of Police had in your possessions two single barreta shot guns and thereby committed an offence punishable under Section 3(1) of the Robbery and Firearms (Special Provisions) Act, Cap. 328 Vol. 22 Laws of the Federation of Nigeria, 1990.

Count IV: — That you Ganiyu Adams (m) being the leader of the proscribed (O.P.C.) Odudua Peoples Congress Lagos State between 1999 and the year 2000 at Lagos State at the aforesaid Magisterial

CONTINUED ON PAGE 2

Figure 2.26. The cover of the *Guardian* the day after Adams first appeared in court.

the president of Nigeria. In raising and parting his index and middle fingers in this gesture, Adams was indicating that he hoped to be victorious against the police and the state prosecuting him; he was also linking his struggle to that of the dominant progressive movement in Yorubaland and Nigeria, led in the past and enduringly symbolized by Awolowo. As would become evident later, the strategic improviser that he is, Adams identified the moment of his trial as one that would transform him in the estimation of the Yorùbá people, as a similar moment did for Awolowo—and, after Awolowo's passing, for Moshood Abiola, the winner of the June 12, 1993, presidential election.

In the light of the potential for self-transformation that his trial offered, the OPC factional leader was quick to warn his lieutenants and members against violence in the court. He knew the firepower his group possessed. It was not for nothing that they had confronted and repelled the police, including its dreaded mobile unit. However, he realized that this was not the moment for such tactics. Thus he shouted "Don't fight" to his lieutenants. Violence would be counterproductive on a day like this.

Contrary to the image of an unthinking man of violence who knew no moderation or measure, Adams, despite his limited education at this point, was a tactical and strategic thinker when it came to opportunities for self-actualization. Unlike his restless and teeming followers that day, he knew that his arraignment in court and subsequent trial could catapult him to a higher status in Yorubaland, and in Nigeria in general. This was therefore a moment to nurture the *figure of suffering*, embrace and even luxuriate in the image of "the embattled activist," as a newspaper described him—a man who was being "unjustly persecuted" by the state for standing up for the rights of his people and for the causes of justice, equity and liberty.

In fact, as some newspapers and newsmagazines later hinted, at a proposed press conference where he was billed to surrender but that was aborted by the police (see details below), Adams was scheduled to read a press statement, "Beyond Human Endurance," that would have pressed this theme of the figure of suffering. *TELL* magazine reported that "the tone of the statement showed that Adams was prepared to cast off the wanted stigma at whatever cost."[184] Gani Adams appropriate the figure of suffering (and sacrifice) and presented it as the core of his moral imagination. It thus became the basis of his "norm and the attribution of moral values"[185] to his activities in ways that were and remain central to the (re)making of the self.

"I am a freedom fighter and I have been a freedom fighter for more than 10 years," he announced to the *Guardian*, Nigeria's newspaper of record, as he sat on the dock waiting for his arraignment to begin in August 2001. The newspaper took its main headline the next day from that claim. It was the first time Adams's words and photograph made the lead story of the *Guardian*. The erstwhile carpenter could not have hoped for a better opportunity to begin simultaneously making and repairing his image—not as a violent young man, a "bloodthirsty" and "destructive" youth, but as a man who was fighting for all the best values of the modern era. Many members of the Nigerian elite would have done anything to be on the front page of the *Guardian*, with their statement and photograph to boot. The former *okada* rider was riding his way to stardom.

A few weeks earlier, Gani Adams had been arrested in what the police described as a "capture." Given the way Adams had been taunting the police for twenty months, the Lagos State police commissioner, Mike Okiro, was eager to advertise the arrest as a major accomplishment and a demonstration of a combination of factors, including the deployment of police "intelligence" assets.[186] Okiro's statement to the press included some misrepresentations and exaggerations, as well as some truths. He said that the immediate catalyst for Adams's arrest was the OPC's attack against a police station in Owutu village on August 20, 2001. He added that the police had arrested some armed robbers the previous day and that OPC members attacked the police station because of that arrest. As the officers themselves acknowledged before and after the arrest of Adams, the OPC constituted a menace to armed robbers, even more than the police, in some cases. At least, this was what many people in urban areas believed at the time. Therefore, except for those who attacked the police station claiming to belong to the OPC, real members—though there were some who did, from time to time, perpetrate crimes—would not have attacked the police to release armed robbers. But since Okiro specifically clarified that "Adams released the men [armed robbers] and their arms. . . . [He] led the operation,"[187] the OPC could easily dismiss his allegation as untrue.

However, when Okiro claimed that he had "found out that he [Adams] was still somewhere in Ikorodu and he was due to address a meeting" the next day (August 21), he was stating the truth. Indeed, Adams addressed a huge crowd that day. According to the police chief, Okiro and his men were on hand but, to prevent "bloodshed," decided not to arrest Adams there. No doubt, if the police had tried to arrest him at that gathering, there would have been a bloodbath because the OPC Squad was on hand and heavily armed. Therefore, the police waited till the next day.

However, Okiro exaggerated the nature of the "intelligence" that led to Adams's arrest. Unknown to him—although it is not unlikely that he received at least some hint—the leaders of the two main Yorùbá sociocultural and political organizations, *Afenifere* and the YCE, and other Yorùbá leaders, including state governors, had convinced Adams to come out of hiding. They had assured him that his alleged crimes were state crimes and that since he would be tried by the Lagos State attorney general, whose government was controlled by the AD, he should have no fear of an unfair trial. At any rate, since the members of the progressive Yorùbá elite in the two groups were convinced that Adams had committed no crimes and was not responsible for the murder of Superintendent Amao, they assured him that the charges would be dropped in the end. However, to regain his freedom, he would need to surrender to the police and go through the motions of arraignment and trial.

As Adams himself, members of his group, and the Yorùbá leaders who persuaded him on this score revealed to me, once he was convinced of the need to surrender, he decided to relax his arrangements for hiding and protection. He moved more freely around Lagos. In fact, at one point, the group decided to host a press conference to announce that Adams would come out of hiding.

"We made arrangements with Olaide Agege, who we called 'Big Boss,' who was then the head of the National Guard [also called the Squad] to make the arrangements at Olusoga," revealed Akande, Adams's erstwhile close aide. "We then announced to the press that the press conference will be held in Olusoga, even though the conference was scheduled for Olateju. We knew the police would go to Olusoga rather than wait for Adams to surrender. So, the members of the National Guard waited at Olusoga so that the conference would not be interrupted at Olateju. But while we were there, the police came and started shooting at us. The bullets didn't hit any of us because we were protected by magic. Unfortunately, it hit Laide, who died that day. We escaped when Laide was killed."

Akande could not explain how the magic protected the rest of them but not Laide. But since he had given many examples of OPC members immersed in magic who had escaped police and rival members' bullets, he was convinced that the magic worked for the most part. After this attack, Akande revealed that the NCC had decided that Adams should draft a statement to be released to the press about his preparedness to surrender. An OPC think tank comprising three well-educated men, including a journalist, drafted the statement.

Thus, contrary to what Okiro told the press, Adams was prepared for his arrest, as Sunday Adebayo, Adams's childhood friend and former personal assistant, revealed. He was "virtually no longer in hiding," as they were going around Lagos in a Honda that was gifted to him by a supporter, a sitting local government chair in Oyo State. "The police didn't even know Gani," said Adebayo, who was with Adams when he was arrested.[188]

Other members of Adams's group were following him. Akande, who was in another vehicle, revealed that they were coming from Ori-Okuta on the outskirts of Lagos, where they had met with Alimi, the chair of the Ori-Okuta chapter of the OPC.

"I was with him [Adams] along with Sunday Adebayo and Segun Amao. We were prepared for the arrest," stated Akande, the former chair of the OPC Welfare Committee. He agreed with Adebayo that most of the police officers did not know Adams but added that one policeman was able to identify him. However, despite the resolution that Adams should surrender to the police, Akande revealed that Adams panicked when they asked him to park the car. Adams stopped and tried to flee.

In his narrative of the arrest, Okiro confirmed that Adams had been driving the car and that he tried to escape when the police identified him—contrary to Adebayo's claim that they could not. "We pursued him. You see, when you are looking for a big fish, you forget about the small ones. By the time we came back, the others had gone. Everybody's attention was on Gani Adams," Okiro told the press.[189]

Akande confirmed that the attention was on Adams and that therefore the ladies and the aides, including Akande himself, were able to escape from the scene. Adebayo added that when they ran into the police, they recalled that "the [Yorùbá] leaders had asked him to surrender."

Indeed, after he was convinced that he should surrender to the police, Adams embarked on a tour of Southwest cities, ignoring the police dragnet. He held rallies and "spoke in glowing terms about his commitment to the struggle for the emancipation of the Yoruba race." Three weeks before his arrest, he held a rally in Ondo State and in Ilorin, the Kwara State capital. At the latter rally, which was held in a school, he reiterated the group's commitment to ensuring that a Yorùbá oba would be crowned in the city alongside the Fulani emir.[190]

The police found "some charms, Bible and Quran" in Adams's car when he was arrested. In fact, they displayed the charms, ostensibly in an attempt to show that the fetish objects had failed to protect him from arrest. To emphasize their depiction of Adams as a "vagabond," the police chief also told the press that it was initially difficult to formally charge Adams because they needed the suspect's address: "Unfortunately, he does not have a home. When we interviewed him, he said he was moving from hotel to hotel. Wherever he held a meeting, he would sleep."[191]

Indeed, Adams did not have a place of his own at this point. While in hiding, he moved from place to place. His aides revealed that he was initially in Lagos.

He later moved to Ijero, in Ekiti State, for a few months and then returned to Lagos when he was convinced to surrender.

"Once we left the scene [of the arrest], we went to Gani Fawehinmi's chambers," revealed the former head of the OPC Welfare Committee. Fawehinmi was Nigeria's leading activist lawyer. A senior advocate of Nigeria and the nation's most vocal oppositional legal mind, Fawehinmi met Adams during the antimilitary, prodemocracy struggle and had brought him under his wing.[192] He served as an unpaid legal adviser to the OPC. According to Akande, Fawehinmi asked one of the lawyers in his chambers, Ebun Adegoruwa, to assist them pro bono. Adegoruwa became Adams's lawyer during the trial. He also secured his release on bail first in Lagos and later in Abeokuta. Adams was rearrested after being released on bail in Lagos and was then taken to Abeokuta to stand another trial.

(OUT)LAW ENFORCEMENT: SELF-DETERMINATION AS VIGILANTISM

Three male members of the OPC were holding an impromptu discussion as we waited for the end of a monthly meeting of the NCC held on the outskirts of Lagos in mid-2002. One young man, who had a deep wound on the back of his hand, appeared to have more experience in the group's actions than the others. He had apparently been wounded in some battle in the recent past. He was clarifying matters for the other two and instructing them on the leadership's attitude toward some issues they were debating. "Look," he said emphatically in Yorùbá, "it is possible for the government to integrate us into the law enforcement. All they need to do is to put a number on the guns they give to us and hand them over collectively to a sectional commander. Once we return from vigilante activities, we will hand them back to our leader."

One of the other two disagreed: "I don't think it is in the interest of government to do that. If they gave us guns, you mean when the final battle is here, I will surrender the gun? I will not."

The "final battle," as I was to learn from the group leaders, was the expected catalyst that would lead to the disintegration of Nigeria, most likely preceded by a war between the constituent ethnic groups, particularly the rest of the country—led by the Yorùbá—against the Hausa-Fulani North.

But the first speaker insisted that the "final battle" would be another matter entirely. At the moment, he was concerned with the organization's role in crime prevention. Hadn't his comrades paid attention to how effective the OPC men were when they were involved in crime fighting, before the police and government's actions made them abandon the task? He mentioned the regime of discipline in the group and gave the example of three members who had been chained for hours for acts contrary to the rules of engagement.

After a while, their discussion moved to political matters. The first one regretted that Yorùbá elders did not seem to appreciate their sacrifice and role. "If not for the OPC," he stated, "the Yoruba nation would have been in serious trouble by now."

The young man was referring to the "political trouble" with the other major ethnic groups, particularly the dominant Hausa-Fulani. However, beyond what the OPC member regarded as the fundamental justification for the group's existence, the members also took up vigilante duties all over Southwest Nigeria. As incidents of armed robbery and other crimes increased in the last couple of years of the twentieth century and the first few years of the twenty-first, the police force, which apart from its own internal challenges had been decimated by long years of military rule, could not respond adequately. The minister for police affairs in the first postmilitary democratic administration, retired major general David Jemibewon, acknowledged that the Nigerian Police Force was "a destroyed organisation" that needed time "to bring itself back on course."[193]

The post–Second Republic military regimes (1984–99) disregarded the police as an institution of law enforcement, using it primarily for regime sustenance and enhancement. It could be said that the military feared the idea of an efficient, effective, and well-resourced police force. This fear was partly a response to the incipient militarization of the police under the former inspector general, Sunday Adewusi, who led the Nigerian Police Force in the Second Republic. Under the President Shehu Shagari administration (1979–83), IGP Adewusi became powerful within the ruling party in an effort to hold on to power against all odds. With the party's suspicion of the military, as well as of the opposition, the police force was so well funded that it acquired all sorts of sophisticated machinery to put down any form of insurrection. It did more. Adewusi deployed the police so effectively to help the ruling party steal the general elections of 1983, particularly in opposition areas, that he was reportedly one of the first people whom President Shagari thanked when he was declared the winner. Thus, one of the first institutions to be demobilized when the soldiers seized power on the eve of the New Year in December 1983 was the police force, whose mobile unit had been built in a fashion similar to that of the army.[194] With the police weakened, the military responded to social anomie by relying more on soldiers to perform policing functions, with the police serving merely as support.

In addition to internal institutional rot, including corruption and the distrust of the police as institution and as agents,[195] the neglect by successive military regimes resulted in an ineffective and inefficient police force that could not respond adequately to widespread crimes in the early years of the Fourth Republic (roughly 1999–2005). In many urban areas of Nigeria, the people had taken charge of their own security by building high fences, locking themselves behind steel or chained doors, recruiting night watchmen, and installing gates that sometimes closed off one or more entries to connecting streets or roads.

This was the context in which vigilante groups became crucial in the late twentieth and early twenty-first century. The OPC was a godsend for many urbanites. In light of the state institutions' structural and operational weaknesses in protecting lives and property, and as a group aiming for "self-determination" by the Yorùbá people of Southwestern Nigeria, the OPC considered the security and safety of its people to be a necessary part of its overall mission—hence the group's embrace of vigilante duties. There was a correlation between the group's view of its mission and the attitude of poor urbanites who saw the OPC as their protector.[196] This was not so much the "transformation from a self-determination group ready to use violence into an agency of local extra-legal governance" that Yvan Guichaoua describes.[197] The OPC saw its vigilante activities as part and parcel of its core mission of ensuring security and safety in the "fatherland," described in the group's founding constitution as "the protection of [the] interests" of Yorùbá people.

The post–Cold War era of democratization in Africa also brought a resurgence of vigilantism in Africa.[198] From Nigeria to South Africa, the phenomenon of vigilantes under the democratic order has raised questions about "state failure" and "civic failure."[199] Different explanations have been advanced for the phenomenon in different African countries.[200] For some scholars, it appears counterintuitive that vigilante activities would increase in the atmosphere of greater freedoms and respect for law and order that pluralist democratic rule was expected to promote.[201] In the Nigerian context, the increase in vigilante activities at the end of military rule did not appear surprising for a myriad of factors, including what happened to the police force during the long years of military rule (as mentioned above), as the military dictators mismanaged the economy and threw millions of young people into economic misery while fostering social anomie. The endemic nature of vigilantism[202] in all parts of Nigeria[203] in the postmilitary era, therefore, intersects with and is provoked or nourished by Nigeria's fundamental political, economic, and social crises.

Though vigilante activities were incidental to the reason for the OPC's existence, at one point it was among the most important duties of the group. I suggest that the group was eager to take on this task for some years for two critical reasons: (1) the work presented the group as socially relevant and socially responsible, thus improving its image among urban dwellers, and (2) it provided both employment for the members and income for the group. These benefits were important to Adams and his faction when they were struggling to find outlets for the youthful members, many of whom were unemployed.

Because of its vigilante actions from 1999 until around 2003, the OPC was very popular among urban dwellers, especially Lagosians. Regarded as an "answer to crimes" and a "terror to robbers,"[204] the OPC and Adams acquired the image of "invincible" social forces. Even the excesses of the group were, for some time, condoned by the public. For instance, when the OPC beheaded some suspected bandits, a newspaper reported that "Despite the gory nature of the killing and the rampage of the suspected OPC members, they were hailed by members of the public."[205] Someone told the *Guardian* that "Despite the renewed effort by the police, the robbers seemed to have been more emboldened as they are inflicting deaths, pains and disposing their victims of property without let or hindrance." He said that "all known robbers in the metropolis would not last many days, if the police allowed the OPC to assist them in fighting the bandits."[206]

At the beginning of this "social service" vigilantism, or informal law enforcement, members of the group provided security for communities, businesses, and individuals.[207] Though many of these services involved payments from the concerned parties to OPC leaders or individual members, the group's overall unofficial investigations and arrest of armed robbers and other miscreants were done gratis. It was a form of community service. Because a significant portion of its members were disenfranchised and dispossessed young people who could have ended up as criminals themselves, in recruiting them into its ranks, the OPC enjoyed a double advantage over the police. First, these young people knew their communities very well and often possessed intelligence about local criminals and criminal networks, information they then used to bust gangs and crimes. Second, because of the OPC's system of traditional oaths, which were believed to impose powerful esoteric penalties if violated, most members had greater ethical and spiritual imperatives not to be compromised by criminals—perhaps unlike some police officers, whose oath of office was imposed by secular authorities and therefore carried no spiritual sanctions when violated. Yet the OPC, while it did not directly sanction, harm, or kill criminals, worked with the police, particularly when OPC zonal sections found the leadership of the law enforcement in their areas to be trustworthy and genuinely committed to crime fighting. In fact, such was the "legitimacy" of the group's vigilante activities that Adams admitted that members of the group carry arms.[208]

Between 1999 and 2005, newspapers regularly published articles and features on the "gallantry" and "heroic exploits" of OPC members in crime prevention. Some of these stories are the stuff of urban legends. Two good examples come to mind, the first in Mushin, Lagos, and the other in Ayete, Oyo State. In December 1999, the Adams faction was meeting in Mushin when news reached them that armed robbers "had gone on [the] loose" in the area, killing one Biola Lamoji, a female member of the group. The faction declared "total war" on the criminals and gathered no less than one thousand members to seek out criminals in the area. Mushin is notorious as "a haven of ruthless armed robbers, miscreants, motor park touts and other criminals."[209] Incidentally, Adams and some of the initial core members of the group had emerged from the same area. Akala Street was the most notorious of the areas in Mushin as it had "a large concentration of the criminals." The first victim of the OPC vigilante justice was Kayode Oyeleke, a thirty-four-year-old jobless man who was hacked to death.[210] Subsequently, the group reportedly went on "a week's orgy of macabre killings and arson." On January 4, 2000, the group "intensified their cleansing acts against criminals [as] Akala and its environs were turned into a theatre of war." The next day, no fewer than thirty-five alleged criminals and others had been killed, with forty houses torched. When reporters arrived on the scene, four bodies were still smoldering and "corpses littered . . . the streets."[211] Some locals reportedly applauded the OPC "for ridding the area of certain elements considered a nuisance." One stated that "although the action of the OPC was illegal, it was a welcome development," adding that "there are robbery cases around here every day and both the people and the police are helpless in doing anything about the perpetrators."[212] The police reportedly avoided the clashes between the OPC and the alleged criminals even though two police stations were located in the area. In fact, the press reported that "the police could have been glad [that] its dirty job was done for it by the OPC."[213]

This particular case illustrates a striking paradox. While the OPC's actions were ostensibly "illegal," the police ignored the vigilante activity because they were reluctant to or could not use the same illegal means to combat the crime. This is an example of where, as a vigilante organization, the OPC served as the police force's "friend," even as both continued their rivalry and clashes on other fronts.

Another example is the story of "How [an] OPC Boy Wrestled and Subdued Four Armed Bandits" who had robbed "forty market women."[214] The *Tribune* reported that some members of the OPC later joined Koosi Ahmadu in arresting two of the armed robbers and handing them over to the Divisional Police Headquarters in Ayete, Oyo State, which was confirmed by the police. The coordinator of the OPC in Ibarapa Zone, Comrade Lanre Ogedengbe, told the newspaper that he was not surprised by Ahmadu's action. He boasted that the members of the group "have been taught how to face such ordeal," adding, "The simple message to be drawn from this young man's experience is courage and faithfulness. He is very courageous and faithful to OPC's oath. . . . We can still do better as a vigilante group if the government could provide us with patrol cars to make the job easier for us."[215]

In some cases, the OPC claimed that the suspects they handed over to the police were released only to then attack OPC members. Consequently, extrajudicial killings of suspected armed robbers increasingly became the norm. When the number of such killings rose, the police became worried, even as people hailed the OPC. In a few instances, robbery suspects were either publicly nailed to a cross[216] or beheaded.[217] A newspaper reported that people praised the OPC "despite the gory nature of the killing and the rampage of the suspected OPC members."[218] At one point in 2001, because of the police's official opposition to the group's activities and the arrest of Adams, the OPC eventually asked its members to "halt all its vigilante activities."[219] It was neither the only nor the last time that the OPC would announce the discontinuation of its vigilante services. A couple of months after the arrest of Fasehun and Adams in October 2005, the group again announced that it was "withdrawing from vigilance [*sic*] services."[220] Adams's aide, Segun Akanni, told the press that the two factions were united on the matter, adding, "We have since realized that nobody appreciates what our group has been doing in the area of protecting lives and property. If they do, at least, people would have risen in defense of our leaders and seek their release."[221]

CONCLUSION

In *Notebook 3*, §48, Gramsci argues that because subalterns "act according to a restless impulse or 'instinct' to revolt, due to crises or unacceptable conditions . . . subaltern political struggles are often characterized by spontaneity, a factor that contributes to the ineffectiveness and, at times, regressive aspects of subaltern political activity."[222] Though the forms of violent "spontaneity" examined in this chapter eventually proved ineffective in transforming the conditions of the subalterns as a group (OPC), it eventually helped in transforming the conditions of the leadership, particularly of Adams—as subsequent chapters will show. Against this backdrop, John Higley and Michael Burton offer an instructive definition of *elite* that is relevant to an understanding of how Adams mobilized all the foregoing violent clashes and vigilante activities of the OPC to transform his social status. "Put most simply," Higley and Burton argue, "elite are persons and groups who have the *organized capacity to make real and continuing political trouble*."[223] However, the OPC-related violence had no predetermined outcome in relation to Adams's personal trajectory. As is evident in the past two chapters, he could even have lost his life on a few occasions. Therefore, the element of luck cannot be ruled out in his process of becoming a big man.

Yet, what is important is how Adams capitalized on his situation in the context of the structural opportunities and challenges presented by violence in late twentieth- and early twenty-first-century Nigeria. He was quick to recognize that his group's "organised capacity to make real and continuing political trouble" gave him national name recognition and that once he was free from trial and detention (in 2000 and later in 2006), he could harness the actual (as well as the potential) capacity for political troublemaking to build a public career for himself in society. Though this public career was initially based on the image of a "violent man," Adams adroitly but gradually moved away from this depiction and transformed himself—as I will explore in chapter 3—from an *actual* warrior to a symbolic warrior, one whose distinction initially might have been based on the capacity to mobilize (il)legitimate violence but could now be based on sociocultural leadership and activities.

NOTES

1. Adams often describes the Yorùbá as a race rather than an ethnic group. It is partly a way of indicating the uniqueness of the Yorùbá in Nigeria and pointing to their spread in West Africa and the diaspora—both old and new—in the Americas, Europe, and Asia. See chap. 3 for his attempt to harness this through the founding of the Oodua Progressive Union (OPU).

2. Gani Adams, interview with the author, July 8, 2004, Ibadan.

3. Richard Eghaghe, "I Am a Man of Peace—Gani Adams," *Daily Independent*, February 18, 2004.

4. Ibid.

5. Adams, interview, July 8, 2004.

6. Monsuru Akande, telephone interview with the author, November 28, 2020.

7. Eghaghe, "I Am a Man of Peace."

8. Indeed, as I will relate in chap. 3, Adams's experience at the Hilton Hotel Abuja, then Nigeria's most prestigious and most expensive five-star hotel, during this visit was so transformative that it helped to orient him toward becoming a big man.

9. Eghaghe, "I Am a Man of Peace."

10. Ibid.

11. Tijo Salverda and Jon Abbink, "Introduction: An Anthropological Perspective on Elite Power and the Cultural Politics of Elites," in *The Anthropology of Elites: Power, Culture, and the Complexities of Distinction*, ed. Jon Abbink and Tijo Salverda (New York: Palgrave Macmillan, 2013), 1.

12. Ibid.

13. Alex Demirović, "The Politics of Truth: For a Different Way of Life," in *Gramsci and Foucault: A Reassessment*, ed. David Kreps (London: Routledge, 2015), 26.

14. I thank one of the readers of the manuscript for pushing me to articulate this.

15. For a comparative view of such processes, see Monique Marks, *Young Warriors: Youth Politics, Identity and Violence in South Africa* (Johannesburg: Wits University Press, 2001), chap. 8.

16. Although *autarky* denotes the self-sufficiency of political states, societies, or economic systems that can survive without depending on external assistance, I use it here to capture a similar process at a personal level, in which an individual works toward a state of social and economic freedom in which she or he would ultimately need little or no help from others for sustenance.

17. See my description of my role as a "native" ethnographer as "someone who is a product of the same culture as those he is studying, and one, who through many years of ethnographic interactions with the elite, became 'one of them'" in Wale Adebanwi, "Elites, Ethnographic Encounters and the 'Native' Ethnographer in Contemporary Africa," in *Postcolonial African Anthropologies*, ed. Rosabelle Boswell and Francs Nyamnjoh (Cape Town: HSRC, 2016), 153.

18. See, for instance, the *Week* magazine's condemnation of the "open endorsement" of the OPC by Chief Abraham Adesanya, lawyer and leader of the *Afenifere*, the preeminent sociocultural and political group of Yorùbá progressives, because he held "the hands of the leaders of the OPC factions in the 'spirit of reconciliation.'" The magazine accuses Adesanya of not understanding "the full implications of the message he is passing to the public." Indeed, the *Afenifere* leader did that precisely because he understood the message he was passing to the public. "Enough Is Enough," editorial, *Week*, February 18, 2002, 3.

19. I will explore these relationships further in chaps. 3–5.

20. Sunday Adebayo, telephone interview with the author, November 11, 2020.

21. Dimeji Kayode-Adedeji, "Nigeria Police Made Me Famous—Gani Adams," *Premium Times*, June 27, 2015, https://www.premiumtimesng.com/news/more-news/185751-nigeria-police-made-me-famous-gani-adams.html. Indeed, though Adams had been persuaded to surrender to the police, he panicked when the police discovered that he had been driving the vehicle. He tried to flee.

22. Ibid.

23. See Anayochucwu Agbo, "Who Knows Him from Adam?," *TELL*, September 3, 2001, 30. Ademola Adegbamigbe, "The OPC Bogey," *TheNEWS*, January 31, 2000, 14.

24. Gani Adams, "I'm Not in Hiding" (interview), *TheNEWS*, January 31, 2000, 15.

25. Ibid., 16.

26. *TheNEWS* described the formation of Arewa People's Congress (APC) as a "balance of terror." See Henry Ugbolue, "Balance of Terror," *TheNEWS*, January 10, 2000, 14.

27. Adegbamigbe, "OPC Bogey."

28. Kayode-Adedeji, "Nigeria Police Made Me Famous—Gani Adams."

29. "I'm Invincible: 'No One Can Arrest Me'—Gani Adams," *TheNEWS*, January 31, 2000.

30. Adams, "I'm Not in Hiding," 15.

31. Although members of the Fasehun faction would argue that this was the forte of the Adams faction, Kayode Ogundamisi, onetime secretary-general of the Fasehun faction, told me that by the time he joined, the members were tending toward a "Yorùbá supremacist" attitude, especially in their songs. He said he finally left the faction because of the "rhetoric of anti-Igbo and anti-Hausa in Lagos" dominant among the members, though Fasehun supported some northerners and Igbo, even against the Yorùbá in Lagos. Ogundamisi insisted that "Lagos was open to all." Ogundamisi, telephone interview with the author, November 15, 2000.

32. Anayochukwu Agbo, "Who Knows Him from Adam?," *TELL*, September 3, 2001, 30.

33. Festus Adedayo, "Gani Adams: Fly Perched on Our Balls,"*Sunday Tribune*, August 26, 2001.

34. Adaranijo, telephone interview with the author, July 9, 2021.

35. Ibid.

36. Ibid.

37. Adekunle Ajasin, Second Republic governor of Ondo State, was the leader of the Awolowo movement after Awolowo died in 1989.

38. I thank Lily Nana Owuso-Darkwa for pointing this out.

39. Insa Nolte, "'Without Women, Nothing Can Succeed': Yoruba Women in the Oodua People's Congress (OPC), Nigeria," *Africa* 78, no. 1 (2008): 85. See Nolte's article for more on the Women's League.

40. Ibid.

41. Bose Omolaoye, telephone interview with the author, May 6, 2021.

42. Ibid.

43. *Gambari* is used among the Yorùbá as an ethnic slur for the Hausa-Fulani, though a famous and illustrious Fulani family in Ilorin bears that name.

44. Frederick Fasehun, *Frederick Fasehun: The Son of Oodua* (Lagos: Inspired Communications, 2002), 230–31.

45. Bettina Schmidt and Ingo Schroeder, eds., *Anthropology of Violence and Conflict* (London: Routledge, 2001), 7.

46. J. D. Y. Peel, *Religious Encounter and the Making of the Yoruba* (Bloomington: Indiana University Press, 2000).

47. Ibid., 253.

48. J. D. Y. Peel, *Ijeshas and Nigerians: The Incorporation of a Yoruba Kingdom, 1890s–1970s* (Cambridge: Cambridge University Press, 1983), 193.

49. Including Brigadier (later General) Olusegun Obasanjo, who as the head of the Third Marine Commando initially accepted the Biafran surrender; Brigadier Benjamin Adekunle, Obasanjo's predecessor and the dreaded head of the Third Marine Commando, whose division was largely responsible for defeating the Biafran forces; and Lt. Colonel (later Lt. General and Defense Chief) Alani Akinrinade, who headed key sections of the Third Marine Commando.

50. As in the original—notwithstanding the infelicities.

51. Gani Adams, interview, July 8, 2004.

52. John Keane, *Violence and Democracy* (Cambridge: Cambridge University Press, 2004), 1.

53. Samuel Huntington, *The Third Wave: Democratization in the Late Twentieth Century* (Norman: University of Oklahoma Press, 1991). See also Julius O. Ihonvbere, "Where Is the Third Wave? A Critical Evaluation of Africa's Non-transition to Democracy," *Africa Today* 43, no. 4 (1996): 343–67.

54. Cf. Mark Ungar, Sally Avery Bermanzohn, and Kenton Worcester, "Introduction: Violence and Politics," in *Violence and Politics: Globalization's Paradox*, ed. Mark Ungar, Sally Avery Bermanzohn, and Kenton Worcester (New York: Routledge, 2002), 1.

55. Keane, *Violence and Democracy*, 3.

56. Ibid., 2.

57. Ibid., 4.

58. Ibid., 11.

59. Pamela J. Stewart and Andrew Strathern, *Violence: Theory and Ethnography* (London: Continuum, 2002), 2.

60. Ibid.

61. Cf. ibid.

62. David Riches, "The Phenomenon of violence," in *The Anthropology of Violence*, ed. David Riches (Oxford: Basil Blackwell, 1986), 11.

63. Eghosa E. Osaghae and Rotimi T. Suberu, "A History of Identities, Violence, and Stability in Nigeria" (CRISE Working Paper 6, Queen Elizabeth House, University of Oxford, 2005), 4.

64. John De St. Jorre, *The Nigerian Civil War* (London: Hodder and Stoughton, 1972).

65. Ibid.

66. Ibid.

67. Ibid., 7.

68. See Andrew Apter, *Black Critics and Kings: The Hermeneutics of Power in Yoruba Society* (Chicago: University of Chicago Press, 1992); Dare Babarinsa, *House of War: The Story of Awolowo's Followers* (Ibadan: Spectrum Books, 2003).

69. See Remi Anifowose, *Violence and Politics in Nigeria: The Tiv and Yoruba Experience* (New York: NOK, 1982).

70. Malachy Uzendu, "OPC Kills 10,000—FG," *Daily Champion*, March 8, 2006; Ise-Oluwa Ige, "FG Accuses OPC of Killing 10,000 People," *Vanguard*, March 8, 2006.

71. See Yusuf Bangura, *Crisis, Adjustment and Politics in Nigeria* (Uppsala: AKUT, 1989); J. O. Aderibigbe, "The Current Austerity Measures and Their Impact on the Nigerian Economy," *African Development* 10, no. 1–2 (1985): 217–35; Adebayo O. Olukoshi, "Introduction: From Crisis to Adjustment in Nigeria," in *The Politics of*

Structural Adjustment, ed. Adebayo Olukoshi (London: James Currey, 1993); Nils Borje Tallroth, "Structural Adjustment in Nigeria," *Finance & Development* 24, no. 3 (1987): 20–22; Julius O. Ihonvbere, "Economic Crisis, Structural Adjustment and Social Crisis in Nigeria," *World Development* 21, no. 1 (1991): 141–53.

72. See Wale Adebanwi, "Comparative Politics of Austerity in Nigeria" (background paper for the World Bank Group, June 2017).

73. See Wale Adebanwi, *Authority Stealing: Anti-corruption War and Democratic Politics in Post-military Nigeria* (Durham, NC: Carolina Academic Press, 2012).

74. A perceptive newspaper intellectual stated that when the "arithmetic of graft" became too complicated for Abacha, he literally moved the tanks to the national exchequer and emptied it. Also, following Fela Anikulapo Kuti's popular song, *TELL* magazine was succinct in describing Abacha, in a cover story, as a "Vagabond in Power." *TELL*, August 10, 1998.

75. Adams, "I'm Not in Hiding," 15.

76. Human Rights Watch, "The O'odua People's Congress (OPC): Fighting Violence with Violence," *Human Rights Watch* 15, no. 4 (January 2003), https://www.hrw.org/report/2003/02/28/oodua-peoples-congress-opc/fighting-violence-violence.

77. Gani Adams, Statement issued at press conference, Lagos, October 26, 1999.

78. Adams, interview, July 8, 2004.

79. All the OPC members that I spoke with in the early years of the Adams faction were convinced of the "imminence" of a war of independence (or succession) from Nigeria by the Yorùbá.

80. Members of the National Guard included the head and Adams's chief security officer, Rasaq Arogundade Balogun; the secretary, Amusa "Big Fish" Musiliu; Yar Lateef; Ranti Akande ("Otepa"); Monsuru Akande; Semiu Tatan; Lai Ogunsolu; Toba Ajiboye ("Ijaya"); Kirogo Adu; Layiwola Ogunsola ("Burger"); Segun Amurat; Kayode Atanda ("Godogodo"); and Kola Arowosaye. Musiliu told me, "All of us were volatile members of the group. Nobody could confront us. We intimidated and subdued every member for Gani Adams. We built an empire for him. . . . He then misused the empire when he became an authoritarian. We were his enforcers." Musiliu, telephone interview with the author, December 10, 2020.

81. This was one of the phrases used to describe OPC clashes with the police and members of other ethnic groups in Lagos in the *New Nigerian*. Sunday Ode, "Return of the Evil Days," *New Nigerian*, July 22, 2000, 6.

82. This was the title of a feature piece on intra-OPC violence in *Post Express*, October 22, 2000, 19.

83. Ibid.

84. Ibid.

85. Ibid.

86. Frederick Fasehun, *OPC: Our History, Our Mission* (Lagos: Inspired Communications, 2005), 44.

87. Ibid., 45–46.

88. Taofik Adeyemi, telephone interview with author, April 1, 2021.

89. Segun Akanni, telephone interview with the author, November 14, 2020.

90. See Tunde Oladipo, "Carnage in Ibadan," *TheNEWS*, January 24, 2000, 23–24. For reports of other clashes, see Juliana Francis and Kelechi Ngboji, "Blood Flows as Area Boys, OPC Clash," *Sun*, May 24, 2005; Yemi Akinsuyi, "12 Killed, 30 Vehicles Burnt in OPC Rival Clash," *ThisDay*, October 23, 2005.

91. Omo Pupa (1890–1977) was the "militant leader" of the Action Group in the First Republic. He and a friend formed the National Union of Road Transport Workers (NURTW). See Wole Adegoke Adedoyin, "Before MC Oluomo, There Was Lawani Asani Oluwo alias Omo Pupa ni Mushin," *Opera News*, accessed May 8, 2021, https://ng.opera.news/ng/en/crime/9edaaa31b32c08fb40d4ad83e70e7c0c. See also "Egba History of Past and Present Heroes: Action Group (AG) Militant Leader," Facebook, accessed May 7, 2021, https://hi-in.facebook.com/egbanations/posts/action-group-ag-militants-leader-he-started-collecting-garage-taxes-nurtw-in-fro/1706986759431291/; Sunday O. Ajai, "Politicians and Thuggery in Nigeria," *Daily Trust*, June 6, 2017, https://dailytrust.com/politicians-and-thuggery-in-nigeria. See also Sandra T. Barnes, *Patrons and Power: Creating a Political Community in Metropolitan Lagos* (Manchester: Manchester University Press, 1986).

92. Bayo Success (1941–2002) was also the leader of the NURTW in the 1970s and 1980s. He was an ally of the ruling National Party of Nigeria (NPN) in the Second Republic and even attempted to contest for the Federal House of Representatives under the NPN's banner. See Ajai, "Politicians and Thuggery in Nigeria." See also Festus Adedayo, "Oluomo, Bayo Success and the Curse of Lagos Motor Park Kingpins," *Cable News*, January 20, 2019, https://www.thecable.ng/mc-oluomo-bayo-success-and-the-curse-of-lagos-motor-park-kingpins.

93. MC Oluomo (1975–) is the current chair of the Lagos State chapter of the NURTW. He is an ally of the leader of the All Progressives Congress (APC), Governor Bola Tinubu. See BBC, "MC Oluomo Book: Di Book *My Service to Humanity* Na about Im Life," February 2, 2021, https://www.bbc.com/pidgin/tori-55910593. See also Jude Egbas, "This Is the Full Story of How MC Oluomo Was Stabbed with a Poisoned Knife at Lagos APC Campaign Rally," Pulse Ng, January 9, 2019, https://www.pulse.ng/news/politics/mc-oluomo-how-notorious-nurtw-official-was-stabbed-with-poisoned-knife/1gh9279; Adedayo, "Oluomo, Bayo Success."

94. Femi Ogbonnikan, "OPC: An Organisation Shooting Itself in the Foot," *Daily Independent*, November 11, 2005, E4.

95. Ibid.

96. For reports on the arrest, see Wale Akinola and Emma Nnadozie, "Lagos Bloodbath: Fasehun, Gani Adams, 9 Other OPC Leaders Held. Flown to Abuja," *Vanguard*, October 23, 2005.

97. Including Edward Ajayi, Mudashiru Adeniyi, Chief Oyinloye Awe, and Chief Wahab Isiaka.

98. Akinola and Nnadozie, "Lagos Bloodbath."

99. Kayode Oladele and Sina Loremikan, "Good Night, Comrade Ayodele Akele—the Bridge Builder of the 'Have Nots,'" Sahara Reporters, June 26, 2020, http://saharareporters.com/2020/06/26/good-night-comrade-ayodele-akele-bridge-builder-%E2%80%9Chave-nots%E2%80%9D-kayode-oladele-and-sina.

100. Kolawole Raheem, telephone interview with the author, September 16, 2021.

101. Kenneth Ehigiator and Bukola Oduyoye, "OPC Members Besiege MMA as Gani Adams Returns to Lagos," *Vanguard*, December 21, 2006, https://allafrica.com/stories/200612210313.html.

102. Ibid.

103. Sulaimon Olanrewaju and Saka Gbeminiyi, "Why the Police Do Not Want OPC's Assistance in Providing Security—Gani Adams," *Nigerian Tribune*, April 30, 2008, 26.

104. Monsuru Akande, telephone interview with the author, July 17, 2020.

105. See Human Rights Watch, "O'odua People's Congress."

106. Ode, "Return of the Evil Days," 6.

107. Human Rights Watch, "O'odua People's Congress."

108. Ibid.

109. Ode, "Return of Evil Days."

110. Human Rights Watch, "O'odua People's Congress," 16. Biafra was the name of the Igbo-led secessionist republic that collapsed in January 1970 in what had been the Eastern Region of Nigeria.

111. Sunday Ode, "Return of the Evil Days," *New Nigerian Weekly*, July 22, 2000, 6.

112. Barnaby Phillips, "Africa: Kano 'Tense' after Ethnic Riots," BBC News, July 23, 1999, http://news.bbc.co.uk/2/hi/africa/401888.stm; Tajudeen Suleiman, "Nigeria: Massacre in Kano," *TheNews*, August 2, 1999, https://allafrica.com/stories/199908020234.html; Bamidele Johnson, "Nigeria: Horror! Tales from Kano Killing Fields," *Tempo*, August 11, 1999, https://allafrica.com/stories/199908110228.html; BBC News, "Nigeria: More Divided Than United?," November 26, 1999, http://news.bbc.co.uk/2/hi/africa/538133.stm.

113. Zebulon Agomuo, "96 Hours of *Madness*," *Post Express*, October 21, 2000, 10. There is another version of the story about a disagreement over the price of an item between a Yorùbá buyer and a Hausa seller. See Joseph Aimienmwona, "OPC: The Pains of Insanity," *Post Express*, October 22, 2000, 22.

114. Agomuo, "96 Hours of *Madness*." See also Aimienmwona, "OPC," 19; Human Rights Watch, "O'odua People's Congress," 16–19.

115. Agomuo, "96 Hours of *Madness*."

116. Shittu Obassa, "OPC, Fasehun: Our Stand," *New Nigerian*, January 27, 2001, 22. This was partly in reaction to Fasehun's release on bail by a Lagos High Court for "want of evidence" in relation to the clashes.

117. Vincent Obia, "Hate Thy Neighbour," *TheWeek*, February 18, 2002, 12–15; see also Human Rights Watch, "O'odua People's Congress," 20–22.

118. Obia, "Hate Thy Neighbour," 12.

119. Ibid., 12, 14.

120. Ibid., 14.

121. See Victor Oladinni, "Fury of the Men of War," *TheNEWS*, November 15, 1999, 30–31.

122. For a detailed report on this violence that turned the area into "a most mindless, ruthless volume in killing field" during which, for "hours on end, the toll was rising speedily and innocent blood was being savagely spilled," with "mangled bodies, some roasted beyond identification still [dotting] street corners" two weeks after the clashes, see Obiora Chukwumba, "An Eye for an Eye," *TELL*, December 13, 1999, 14–20. Even Gani Fawehinmi, the famous Lagos lawyer and supporter of the Adams faction, released a statement after the Mile 12-Ketu violence to denounce the group, stating, "I thought OPC was a peaceful organisation but recent events in Lagos proved conclusively that it is not." Chukwumba, 19.

123. On July 18, 1999, in Sagamu, Ogun State, a clash between the Hausa and their Yorùbá "hosts" over a Hausa woman who died mysteriously after flouting the compulsory curfew order for the Oro (the Yorùbá ancestral spirit, which no female can witness—on pain of death) festival attracted the OPC, who defended their kinsmen. Adams said his group could not be blamed for this since it was a "case of lack of respect or disregard for indigenous cultural values." See Insa Nolte, "Identity and Violence: The Politics of Youth in Ijebu-Remo, Nigeria," *Journal of Modern African Studies* 42, no. 1 (2004): 61–90. Over fifty people lost their lives.

124. Bamidele Johnson, "The Plot against Lagos," *Tempo*, January 21, 2000, https://allafrica.com/stories/200001210303.html; Chris McGreal, "Nigeria's Ethnic Hatreds Turn Lethal," *Guardian*, October 19, 2000, https://www.theguardian.com/world/2000/oct/20/chrismcgreal.

125. Gani Adams, interview with the author, April 16, 2002, Amukoko.

126. Quoted in R. T. Akinyele, "Ethnic Militancy and National Stability in Nigeria: A Case Study of the Oodua People's Congress," *African Affairs* 100, no. 401 (2001): 623–40, 632.

127. Ujudud Shariff, "OPC: The Limis of Tolerance," *Daily Trust*, February 12, 2002, back page.

128. Ibid.

129. *Daily Trust*, "I Will Support Military Strike—Ex-Minister," February12, 2002, 1.

130. Muyiwa Akintunde, "The Rimi Interview," *Africa Today*, February 2002, http://archive.africatoday.com/secret/feb02/feb02therimiinterview.htm.

131. See *Daily Champion*, "OPC Not Murderers—*Afenifere*," March 9, 2006, front page; Bolade Omonijo, "Afenifere Berates FG over Comments on OPC," *Vanguard*, March 9, 2006.

132. *Nigerian Tribune*, "The OPC and the Rest of Us," (editorial), October 25, 2000, 10.

133. *Vanguard*, "Obasanjo Orders Clampdown on OPC," November 26, 1999, front page.

134. Adegbamigbe, "OPC Bogey," 19.

135. Ibid.

136. Adams later succeeded to this position in January 2018. See chap. 4.

137. *Nigerian Tribune*, October 25, 2000.

138. Esther Oluku, "Insecurity: IG Sends Emissaries to Gani Adams over OPC's Threats to Herdsmen," *ThisDay*, June 19, 2019, https://www.thisdaylive.com/index.php/2019/06/19/insecurity-ig-sends-emissaries-to-gani-adams-over-opcs-threats-to-herdsmen/.

139. See Queen Esther Iroanusi, "Amotekun: Don't Back Down, Nigerians Tell South-West Governors," *Premium Times*, January 26, 2020, https://www.premiumtimesng.com/regional/ssouth-west/374375-amotekun-dont-back-down-nigerians-tell-south-west-governors.html; Modestus Aneasoronye, "Five Things You Need to Know about Operation Amotekun," *Business Day*, March 4, 2020, https://businessday.ng/news/article/five-things-you-need-to-know-about-operation-amotekun/; Adeola Badru, Dayo Johnson, Adeola Badru, Rotimi Ojomoyela, Shina Abubakar, and James Ogunnaike, "How South West Gave Legal Teeth to Amotekun," *Vangaurd*, March 7, 2020, https://www.vanguardngr.com/2020/03/how-south-west-gave-legal-teeth-to-amotekun/.

140. Oluku, "Insecurity." See also Dapo Akinrefon, "IG Parleys Aare Adams on Security," *Vanguard*, June 19, 2019, https://www.vanguardngr.com/2019/06/ig-parleys-aare-adams-on-security/.

141. Mustapha Ogunsakin, "Adams: 'I'm a Freedom Fighter,'" *Guardian*, August 25, 2001, front page.

142. Oluseye Ojo, "IGP to Partner Gani Adams to Tackle Rising Insecurity," *Sun*, June 18, 2019, https://www.sunnewsonline.com/igp-to-partner-gani-adams-to-tackle-rising-insecurity/.

143. Oluku, "Insecurity."

144. Ibid. See also Wale Odunsi, "Security in Lagos: Details of OPC Leader Gani Adams' Meeting with Police Boss," *Daily Post*, September 22, 2019, https://dailypost.ng/2019/09/22/security-lagos-details-opc-leader-gani-adams-meeting-police-boss/.

145. Oluku, "Insecurity."

146. *National Insight*, "We're Partners in Progress, Gani Adams Tells Lagos CP," September 22, 2019, https://nationalinsightnews.com/were-partners-in-progress-gani-adams-tells-lagos-cp/.

147. Ibid. (emphasis added).

148. Ibid. (emphasis added).

149. Ibid.

150. I will discuss other factors in subsequent chapters.

151. For example, see *Guardian*, "Panel Urges Police to Stop Indiscriminate Arrests," February 8, 2000, 80; *Punch*, "Lagos Clashes: Scores of Youths Still in Detention," November 5, 2000, front page; *Daily Times*, "OPC Cries Out over Police Attack

on Members," September 26, 2001, 5; *Monitor*, "Police Hold 22 OPC Men," September 26, 2001, 32.

152. For more on the area boy phenomenon in Lagos, see Abubakar Momoh, "Youth Culture and Area Boys in Lagos," in *Identity Transformation and Identity Politics under Structural Adjustment in Nigeria*, ed. Attahiru Jega (Uppsala: Nordic Africa Institute, 2000); Olawale Ismail, "From 'Area-Boyism' to 'Junctions and Bases': Youth Social Formation and the Micro-structures of Violence in Lagos Island," in *State Fragility, State Formation, and Human Security in Nigeria*, ed. Mojúbàolú Olúfúnké Okome (New York: Palgrave-Macmillan, 2013).

153. Alex Ogundadegbe, "The Evolution, the Revolution," *TheWeek*, February 18, 2002, 16.

154. Adegbamigbe, "OPC Bogey," 14.

155. Stepp Offi, "An Eye for an Eye," *TELL*, January 24, 2000, 24.

156. Adegbenro Adebanjo and Yemi Olowolabi, "End of the Manhunt," *TELL*, September 3, 2001, 31.

157. He was named after Saddam Hussein, who, after the First Gulf War (August 1990–February 1991), was regarded among the youth in Nigeria as someone who had stood up to the world's sole superpower, the United States. Hussein was, therefore, considered a symbol of fearlessness and bravery.

158. Alhaji Rasaq Arogundade Balogun, telephone interview with the author, November 18, 2020.

159. Evangelist Kunle Adesokan, at the time the secretary-general of Adams's OPC, according to media reports, accused Tunde Sobulo, the head of the Lagos RRS, of involvement in "some questionable acts and called on the Lagos State government to investigate the acts." See Offi, "Eye for an Eye," 24.

160. The Shomolu-Bariga area hosted one of the original chapters of the OPC in Lagos.

161. Saddam regards this as an important example of the strength of the relationship between the OPC and Amao. Police officers almost always demand bribes for any and all things in Nigeria—even from the injured party. Therefore, stating that a police officer did not demand money to do his official duty, let alone an obligation, is a great testimony to either the integrity of the concerned officer or the nature of the relationship between the concerned person and the officer.

162. Offi, "Eye for an Eye," 24.

163. Monsuru Akande, telephone interview with the author, November 17, 2020.

164. Balogun, interview.

165. New Humanitarian, "Abducted Policeman Murdered," January 11, 2000, https://www.thenewhumanitarian.org/report/11648/nigeria-abducted-policeman-murdered.

166. Ibid.

167. Ibid.

168. Balogun claimed that Najeem was in the NURTW and not the OPC.

169. Some claimed that Lawrence was in the "transport business" and was not an OPC member.

170. For some details of the arrests, detention, torture, and extrajudicial killings of OPC members, see Human Rights Watch, "O'odua People's Congress." See also Adegbamigbe, "OPC Bogey," 19.

171. Although the magazine claimed this was a "telephone" interview, it must have done so to avoid giving the impression that it knew the whereabouts of a man wanted by the police. Most likely, the magazine sent written questions to Adams, who then asked some of his well-educated members to send written responses. The answers appear too articulate and considered (and include the data and names of people killed, including some police officers acting in their official capacity) for Adams—who at this time had only three years of high school education—to have said them in a telephone interview.

172. Adams, "I'm Not in Hiding," 18.

173. Ibid. He also alleged that the police "unleashed terror" on the members of the group in Ode-Irele, Isheri-Olofin, and Egan Townships and at Sango-Ota. Adams alleged that ninety-four members of his group were killed in Bonny Camp (a military camp) in Lagos on March 6, 1999. Adams, interview, Amukoko. He accused the Rapid Response Squad (RRS) of murdering some of his members because it consisted of "bizarre Hausa policemen" with the alleged encouragement of the Lagos State deputy police commissioner, M. D. Abubakar, a northerner who "has been in (charge of) these cold-blooded killings of the Yoruba under the guise of law-enforcement." Adams, "I'm Not in Hiding," 18. In all, Adams said, the group must have lost about nine hundred members to police "terror." The press has also reported a "reign of terror" by the police in reaction to the "perceived excesses" of the OPC. Over one thousand people were arrested, and many fear that the police killed some of them. Adegbamigbe, "OPC Bogey."

174. Adegbamigbe, "OPC Bogey."

175. Chukumba, "Eye for an Eye," 14–20.

176. Adegbamigbe, "OPC Bogey," 19.

177. Gabriel Orok and Moses Uchendu, "War in Lagos as OPC Loses 50 Men in Police Execution," *P.M. News*, July 17, 2000, https://allafrica.com/stories/200007170472.html.

178. For more on this, see chap. 3.

179. *P.M. News*, July 17, 2000.

180. *TheNEWS*, January 31, 2000.

181. *Saturday Champion*, August 19, 2000.

182. Ibid.

183. *New Nigerian on Sunday*, February 20, 2000.

184. Adegbenro Adebanjo and Yemi Olowolabi, "End of the Manhunt," *TELL*, September 3, 2001, 31.

185. Beverley Skeggs, "Exchange, Value and Affect: Bourdieu and 'the Self,'" supplement, *Sociological Review* 52, no. 2 (2004): 76.

186. Dele Agakameh, "His Offence Is Heinous—Okiro," *TELL*, September 3, 2001, 32.

187. Ibid.

188. Sunday Adebayo, telephone interview with the author, November 9, 2020. Adebayo, ex-personal assistant to Adams and a member of NCC, added that he and Adams were with their girlfriends and that Adams was driving though he had no driver's license and was just learning how to drive. When the police demanded his driver's license, he could not show one. The police asked them to park their car. Adebayo said he and their girlfriends were not charged.

189. Agakameh, "His offence Is Heinous—Okiro."

190. Adebanjo and Olowolabi, "End of the Manhunt," 31, 33.

191. Ibid.

192. As related in chap. 1, this caused some friction between him and Fasehun, his friend and comrade, after Adams created his own faction of the OPC.

193. Adegbamigbe, "OPC Bogey," 19.

194. For a useful history of the Nigerian Police Force, see Kemi Rotimi, *The Police in a Federal State: The Nigerian Experience* (Ibadan: College Press, 2001).

195. See I. Olawale Albert, T. Awe, G Hérault, and W. Omitoogun, *Informal Channels for Conflict Resolution in Ibadan, Nigeria* (Ibadan: IFRA, 1995).

196. As demonstrated, for instance, in a cartoon in the *Punch* (January 18, 2002) newspaper where, after a head-on collision between two vehicles driven by a rich man and a poor man, both bring out their phones to call for help, and the poor man says, "You think you can intimidate me by calling the police. . . . Me too. Let me call OPC." Cited in Guichaoua, "Self-determination Group or Extra-legal Governance Agency? Multifaceted Nature of the Oodua People's Congress in Nigeria," *Journal of International Development* 21 (2009): 530.

197. Guichaoua, "Self-determination Group," 520–33.

198. This is generally true of the late twentieth- and early twenty-first-century Global South. See Eduardo Moncada, "Varieties of Vigilantism: Conceptual Discord, Meaning and Strategies," *Global Crime* 18, no. 4 (2017): 403–23.

199. For a review of the literature that dwells on either explanation, see Nicholas Rush Smith, *Contradictions of Democracy: Vigilantism and Rights in Post-Apartheid South Africa* (Oxford: Oxford University Press, 2019), 4–6.

200. See ibid.; David M. Anderson, "Vigilantes, Violence and the Politics of Public Order in Kenya," *African Affairs* 101, no. 405 (2002): 531–55; Lars Buur and Steffen Jensen, "Introduction: Vigilantism and the Policing of Everyday Life in South Africa," *African Studies* 63, no. 2 (2004): 139–52; Lars Buur, "Democracy & Its Discontents: Vigilantism, Sovereignty & Human Rights in South Africa," *Review of African Political Economy* 35, no. 118 (2008): 571–84; R. G. Abrahams, "Vigilantism: Order and Disorder on the Frontiers of the State," in *Inside and Outside the Law: Anthropological Studies of Authority and Ambiguity*, ed. Olivier Harris (London: Routledge, 1987); Abrahams, "Sungusungu: Village Vigilante Groups in Tanzania," *African Affairs* 86, no. 343 (1987): 179–96.

201. Cf. Smith, *Contradictions of Democracy*, 4.
202. David Pratten, "Introduction: The Politics of Protection; Perspectives on Vigilantism in Nigeria," *Africa: Journal of the International African Institute* 78, no. 1 (2008): 1.
203. For discussions of the different vigilante groups, see Akinyele, "Ethnic Militancy and National Stability in Nigeria"; Bruce Baker, "When the Bakassi Boys Came: Eastern Nigeria Confronts Vigilantism," *Journal of Contemporary African Studies* 20, no. 2 (2002): 223–44; Conerly Casey, "Policing through Violence: Fear, Vigilantism, and the Politics of Islam in Northern Nigeria," in *Global Vigilantes: perspectives on justice and violence*, ed. David Pratten and A. Sen (London: Hurst, 2007); Laurent Fourchard, "A New Name for an Old Practice: Vigilantes in South-Western Nigeria," *Africa: The Journal of the International African Institute* 78, no. 1 (2008): 535–58; Johannes Harnischfeger, "The Bakassi Boys: Fighting Crime in Nigeria," *Journal of Modern African Studies* 41, no. 1 (2003): 23–49; Adam Higazi, "Social Mobilization and Collective Violence: Vigilantes and Militias in the Lowlands of Plateau State, Central Nigeria," *Africa: Journal of the International African Institute* 78, no. 1 (2008): 107–35; Kate Meagher, "Hijacking Civil Society: The Inside Story of the Bakassi Boys Vigilante Group of South-eastern Nigeria," *Journal of Modern African Studies* 45, no. 1 (2007): 89–115; Insa Nolte, "Ethnic Vigilantes and the State: The Oodua People's Congress in South-western Nigeria," *International Relations* 21, no. 2 (2004): 217–35; Daniel Jordan Smith, "The Bakassi Boys: Vigilantism, Violence and Political Imagination in Nigeria," *Current Anthropology* 19, no. 3 (2004): 429–55; Ukoha Ukiwo, "Deus Ex Machina or Frankenstein Monster: The Changing Roles of Bakassi Boys in Eastern Nigeria," *Democracy and Development: A Journal of West African Affairs* 3, no. 1 (2002): 39–51.
204. Anayochukwu Agbo, "Who Knows Him from Adam?," *TELL*, September 3, 2001, 30.
205. Lekan Sani, Ben Akparanta, Eno Bassey, and Tunde Alao, "Suspected OPC Members Re-launch War on Bandits, Behead Four," *Guardian* (Lagos), August 17, 2001, 2.
206. Ibid.
207. OPC members also participated in picketing and acted as security guards at events, including even major religious crusades—such as a five-day crusade in Ijebu-Ode, Ogun State, by the German American Pentecostal evangelist Reinhard Bonnke. See Toba Suleiman, "OPC to Provide Security for Bonnke," *ThisDay*, February 13, 2004; Prisca Egede and Emmanuel Onwubiko, "Labour May Invite OPC for Picketing: 500 Lawyers to Defend Detained Labour Men," *Guardian*, October 18, 2003.
208. Human Rights Watch, "O'odua People's Congress."
209. Tayo Odunlami, "Unending Mayhem," *TheNEWS*, January 24, 2000, 14.
210. Ibid.
211. Ibid.

212. Ibid. Some objected to the actions of the OPC, accusing them of also killing innocents.
213. Ibid.
214. Rotimi Omole, "How OPC Boy Wrestled and Subdued Four Armed Bandits," *Nigerian Tribune*, November 23, 2005, 19.
215. Ibid., 20.
216. "OPC Nails Robbery Suspect to the Cross," *Vanguard*, August 17, 2001, front page.
217. Lekan Sani et al., "Suspected OPC Members Re-launch War on Bandits," 1.
218. Ibid.
219. The New Humanitarian, "OPC Faction to Stop Vigilante Activity," September 5, 2001, https://www.thenewhumanitarian.org/report/25930/nigeria-opc-faction-stop-vigilante-activity.
220. Oluseto Olatuyi, Kunle Adeyemi, and Semiu Okanlawon, "OPC Withdraws Vigilance Services," *Punch*, December 28, 2005, front page. For other times when the group withdrew from vigilante service, see The New Humanitarian, "OPC Faction to Stop Vigilante Activity," September 5, 2001, https://www.thenewhumanitarian.org/report/25930/nigeria-opc-faction-stop-vigilante-activity; Olanrewaju and Gbeminiyi "Why the Police Do Not Want OPC's Assistance in Providing Security." After the group first withdrew its vigilante services, a few OPC members told me informally that they would have succeeded in drastically reducing the spate of armed robbery in the urban areas if the police had not stopped them. They alleged that some police officers aid the robbers. Informal discussions, May 2002.
221. Olatuyi, Adeyemi, and Okanlawon, "OPC Withdraws Vigilance Services," 2.
222. Marcus E. Green, "Gramsci and Subaltern Struggles Today: Spontaneity, Political Organization and Occupy Wall Street," in *Antonio Gramsci*, ed. Mark McNally (London: Palgrave-Macmillan, 2015), 156. See Antonio Gramsci, *Prison Notebooks*, vol. 2, ed. and trans. Joseph A. Buttigieg (New York: Columbia University Press, 1996), N3 §48.
223. John Higley and Michael Burton, *Elite Foundations of Liberal Democracy* (Lanham, MD: Rowman and Littlefield, 2006), 7 (emphasis added).

3 / Becoming Elite

Distinction, Destiny, and Self-*Determination*

INTRODUCTION

Against the background of how Adams achieved distinction through OPC-inspired crises and violence, this chapter focuses on how he sought to transform that achievement into a form of personal sociocultural distinction.[1] As scholars have noted, ethnographic studies of elite distinction are well placed to present the diversity of cultural representations of distinction in opposition to the illusion that there are universal categories.[2] For instance, Jean-Pascal Daloz argues correctly that "it is a reasonable goal to seek to identify divergent patterns to social distinction . . . in order to account for significant variations." In light of this, interpreting the divergent patterns in different contexts "requires inductive work aimed at deciphering contextually meaningful codes."[3] Analyzing forms of elite distinction, particularly "contextually meaningful codes," requires that (1) our conception of elite be broad, given the different properties that those who are at the apex of society bring to bear on their position, and (2) we avoid "casting moral judgements" based on ideals.[4]

In this chapter, I examine the specific means of differentiation Adams employed to separate himself from the "rabble" in his group, to become more *distinct,* and hence acquire sociocultural eminence and prestige. This process involved forms and practices of aestheticized self-fashioning[5] that served to facilitate his social ascendancy and the acquisition and exercise of cultural power. Here, I explore how Adams created an "axis between the apparently apolitical terrain of aesthetics and decidedly political" project of self-determination (examined in chaps. 1 and 2) through consumption,[6] an intersection between what Jonathan Friedman has described as "broader strategies of self-definition and self-maintenance."[7] Thus, this chapter is a modest contribution to the comparative study of elite distinction,[8] especially where this manifests as what Clifford Geertz, in his groundbreaking work on the Balinese, describes as a fundamental "dramatization of status concerns."[9]

This dramatization of status, particularly of emergent status, occurs through publicly staged recognition, as evident in the following vignette that captures such recognition of Adams.

When the master of ceremonies announced the presence of *Otunba* Gani Adams at the fifteenth anniversary of the founding of *TheNEWS* magazine, held at the prestigious Planet One Events Place in Ikeja, Lagos, on March 27, 2008, everyone paid attention. Some clapped to acknowledge his presence, as they did for all the other special guests who had been recognized. Some expressed hushed surprise that he was not only attending the gathering but also being recognized. No other recognition had attracted a similar mixture of applause, laughter, and murmurs. For a moment, the master of ceremonies stopped, seeming to gauge the audience's reaction to the announcement.

TheNEWS is an activist publication founded by a group of journalists who had resigned from a similar newsmagazine that was muzzled by the military regime under General Babangida. Editors and reporters for *TheNEWS* had since been repeatedly harassed and jailed by successive regimes for exposing the military's human rights violations and the sit-tight plot of Generals Babangida and Sani Abacha. Two events stand out as examples of *TheNEWS* journalists' travails under the military. One was the jailing of one of its founding editors, Kunle Ajibade, for alleged complicity in a plot that was widely acknowledged as a phantom coup. The second was the assassination of one of the reporters, Bagauda Katho, by those believed to be agents of the Abacha regime. The newsmagazine's editors, thus, were eager to celebrate their personal and corporate survival beyond the era of military rule.

I had been asked to write the company's history. The book *Trials and Triumph: The Story of "TheNEWS"*[10] was the highlight of the fifteenth anniversary celebration.

I was sitting at one of the front tables at the event and therefore saw the reaction at the high table (the dais) where the most distinguished guests, including the vice president, Dr. Goodluck Jonathan; the former governor of Lagos State, *Asiwaju* Bola Tinubu; and the former governor of Osun State, Chief Bisi Akande, were seated. I noticed that the vice president seemed to be asking the other distinguished guests about Adams.

The murmuring went on for a couple of minutes. Then the master of ceremonies announced a request from the high table for Gani Adams to approach the

Figure 3.1. Screenshot of Adams making his way through the crowd to approach the high table at the fifteenth anniversary of *TheNEWS* magazine in Lagos, March 27, 2008.

stage. He was sitting a fair distance from my seat. I watched the gangling, six-foot-two man walk to the stage and shake hands with the distinguished guests. He was the only one whose presence was acknowledged not merely by the audience in general but specifically by the high table. It was a form of distinction, or at least an acknowledgment that Adams was *distinct* from the rest of us who were not sitting at the high table.

According to the editors, the special guest of honor at the event, Vice President Jonathan, requested to meet Adams once he was recognized by the master of ceremonies. It seems the vice president was also affected by the Adams mystique. As *TheNEWS* magazine details in its narrative of Adams's rise to prominence, a few years earlier "it would even have been unthinkable and laughable

Figure 3.2. Screenshots of Adams bowing to greet the then vice president Goodluck Jonathan, who requested that he approach the high table at the fifteenth anniversary of *TheNEWS* magazine in Lagos, March 27, 2008. Sitting beside Jonathan is Bayo Onanuga, the editor in chief of *TheNEWS*.

for a 29-year-old secondary school drop-out" to move "from the dark alley of obscurity" to the height of such acknowledgment—thus "act[ing] his script into the history book[s]."[11] In the preface to a cover story on Adams shortly after he was declared wanted, Tayo Odunlami of *TheNEWS* had observed that "only two years ago, [Adams] was an unknown quantity. On the streets, [he] was just another anonymous figure, an innocuous passer-by."[12]

In December 2017, after I asked Adams about this first experience with Jonathan, he narrated a glowing encounter in which the vice president seemed to be in awe of him. "Gani, how are you?" Jonathan reportedly asked while shaking his hand. "You are doing well. Keep it up."[13] Adams recalled the vice president saying he was impressed with how Adams had "built his organization [the Oodua People's Congress (OPC)]."

Approximately two years later, Jonathan became president, succeeding President Umaru Yar'Adua, who had died in office. His rise in prominence turned what had been a chance meeting into an opportunity that would transform

Figure 3.3. Adams and his aides walking toward his vehicle around 2014. Segun Akanni, then his spokesman, is first on the left. Photo courtesy of *Nigerian Tribune*.

Adams's fortune and help to propel him into national reckoning as an officially recognized and compensated negotiator in security and election matters.

This vignette is an example of how Adams's fame and notoriety helped to make him distinct and thus elevated him to high society in Nigeria, creating opportunities for critical relationships with well-placed members of the highest level of cultural, economic, and political elites in Nigeria. With this, Adams strategically and shrewdly (re)appropriated and leveraged the OPC's clamor for Yorùbá self-determination to create a form of personal *self-actualization*.

In a manifestation of Adams's success in transforming himself from a "violent" subaltern into a "peaceful" member of the elite, key members of the ethnic groups that violently clashed with the OPC in the past, such as the Hausa-Fulani, the Igbo, and the Ijaw, now associate with him, regularly attend his events, or have become his friends. I have provided the example of President Jonathan, an Ijaw. Other examples include retired rear admiral Ndubuisi Kanu (1943–2021), a former Igbo military governor of Lagos State and later a leading prodemocracy activist; former governor of Abia State Orji Ozor Kalu (to whom Adams, in June 1998, presented an award for his "financial and moral support

Figure 3.4. Adams and Rear Admiral Ndubuisi Kanu (late) at one of the anniversaries of the June 12, 1993, presidential election, which was annulled by the military. Photo courtesy of *Nigerian Tribune*.

Figure 3.5. Adams presenting an award to Senator Orji Ozor Kalu, former governor of Abia State, on behalf of the OPC for Kalu's "financial and moral support to the Yoruba organisation" at the twenty-fifth anniversary of the June 12, 1993, presidential election in 2018. With Kalu are Rear Admiral Ndubuisi Kanu (retired; *far left*); chairperson of the Campaign for Democracy, Joe Okei-Odumakin; and Senator Shehu Sani. See Chukwudi Nweje, "True Story of June 12 Annulment'll Still Be Told—Kalu," *Sun*, June 13, 2018, https://www.sunnewsonline.com/true-story-of-june-12-annulmentll-still-be-told-kalu/. Photo courtesy of *Nigerian Tribune*.

to the Yoruba organisation" [OPC] at the twenty-fifth anniversary of the June 12, 1993, presidential election); and Senator Shehu Sani, an activist and former senator from the northern state of Kaduna.

In this chapter, I hope to demonstrate that Gani Adams's *ogbon ori* (genius)—what AbdouMaliq Simone would describe as his "cognitive proficiency"[14] and what Richard Werbner, following Deborah Durham, would describe as "effective pragmatics in the face of moral puzzlement"[15]—is made manifest in his cultivation of an image of an important player in contemporary Yorùbá/Nigerian society and politics. Perhaps more importantly, his genius also manifests in his exploitation of the tactical and strategic advantages offered by his newfound fame—or infamy, as his adversaries would insist. In addition, I hope to show that violence perpetrated by or against the OPC members (see chap. 2) gave Adams recognition and made him a person of reckoning. Along with that came even more sociocultural, political, and economic leverage. Additionally, I account for how Adams subsequently mobilized that leverage to ensure that, while he remained the personification of the OPC, he also became increasingly distinct from the group that originally gave him distinction. Thus, he recognized, and later mobilized, different personal and sociocultural capacities to achieve further distinction—to transform himself into the elite of the subaltern and, eventually, into a *genuine* member of the elite.

It is important to note here that, while the stages of *becoming* and *being* a big man are generally traceable, at some point in Adams's trajectory it became difficult to clearly or absolutely mark when *becoming* ended and *being* started. Thus, the accounts in this and following chapters are not chronological. Owing to this, readers might find that some aspects of the process of *being* appear to foreshadow the process of *becoming*, or vice versa. Again, this is because, as Adams achieved success in *becoming*, the process of *being* was simultaneously taking place. At the same time, the earliest moments of *being* also involved some forms of *becoming*.

STRADDLING AND STRATIFICATION

Among a people such as the Yorùbá for whom, particularly since the second half of the twentieth century, distinction has become less about ascription and more about achievement through education—as already explained in chapter 1—Adams suffered many disadvantages that would have made it difficult for him to become *an* elite. Yet, in particular ways, he resolved the contradictions between the old tradition of *omo ogun* (war boys) / *oga ogun* (war lord) in nineteenth- and early twentieth-century Yorubaland—described by J. D. Y. Peel as the "age of confusion"[16]—and the modern trajectory of the neo-Yorùbá. This modern trajectory began with the spread of missionary Christianity[17] organized around the Enlightenment project, as initially embraced by returnee slaves and locals around Lagos and Abeokuta and eventually rearticulated, elaborated, and generalized by Obafemi Awolowo[18] through the free education program of his Action Group in the 1950s. Adams embraced the core ideals of the neo-Yorùbá, including education, democracy, freedom, and egalitarianism, which were generally accepted as the post-early-twentieth-century ways of becoming modern and elite. Yet he retained some of the elements of the old order, such as violence and superstition,[19] which the cultural whole had projected itself as moving away from. In this context, Adams seems to have reflected in a practical way on questions raised by Richard Werbner: "How do people place each other in terms of prestige, rank, rather than class? How do they mark or signify that placement, and how responsive are their rankings and ratings to changing circumstances?"[20] While Adams did not present an entirely new route to elite reckoning by a partially educated subaltern in modern Yorùbá history,[21] he is perhaps the first to force himself into central reckoning as a member of the dominant elite from such an initial position of disadvantage. In the neo-Yorùbá context of competition and individuality,[22] others who followed a similar trajectory before Adams were peripheral to the dominant elite, who largely used them as a tool for their own political ambitions. The subaltern elites were mere enforcers of the political and cultural interests of the dominant elites. Those who preceded Adams in his role can be grouped into two categories. The first comprises direct violent enforcers of party or political ideology, including High Chief Lawani Asani, popularly known as *Omo Pupa ni Mushin*, and Adebayo Ogundare, popularly known as Bayo Success, who were leaders of the road transport workers in Lagos. While both were popular and feared in Lagos and were connected to regional or national political parties—(Action Group in the First Republic in Asani's case and the National Party of Nigeria in the Second Republic in Ogundare's case; see chap. 2), neither acquired the leverage, resources, and national recognition that Adams has since achieved. The second category comprises (in)direct political coercers, including Busari "Eruobodo" Adelakun, the late grassroots politician in the Second Republic, and Lamidi Adedibu, the late "strong man of Ibadan politics" whose activities spanned from the First to the Fourth Republic.

The main difference between the enforcers and coercers is that the latter were politicians and, in time, became political godfathers in their own rights. Adelakun, a semiliterate influential Ibadan politician, even became a commissioner under the Governor Bola Ige administration in Oyo State in the Second Republic. Unlike Adelakun, Adedibu, also a semiliterate but astute Ibadan politician, never sought political office; he was content to be a political godfather in charge of coercion to ensure the victory of his favored candidates in local, regional, and later national elections. Adedibu, also unlike Adelakun, became influential beyond Ibadan and Oyo State because both state and national office seekers needed his support. However, these two coercers, even though they, like Adams, achieved greater political leverage than the enforcers and even became nationally prominent (particularly in the case of Adedibu), they, unlike Adams, operated only within political parties. The coercers, even though they were members of political parties, differed from Adams in their lack of an organizational framework that was largely under their personal control—as Adams had with the OPC.

The enforcers also differed from Adams. Although they took chieftaincy titles, they never sought to become cultural leaders. Therefore, they did not acquire Adams's cultural leverage, nor were they regarded as pan-Yorùbá activists who sought to protect the collective interests of the Yorùbá.

Against this background, Adams, at some point in his public career, recognized that, to obtain a measure of political reckoning and personal economic prosperity, as the enforcers and the coercers had done, and then add to that political leverage, sociocultural prominence, and *authentic* membership in the dominant elite, he needed to achieve two things his predecessors had failed to achieve: cultural status and higher education—or at least educational certificates.[23] Therefore, the next stage for Adams, particularly after he was released from his final and longest spell of detention in 2006, was to pursue these twin goals and to harness them alongside other organizational, aesthetic, agential, and relational tools to achieve self-transformation. And he intended to do it while still publicly pursuing self-determination for the Yorùbá. Through a calculated and perhaps cynical process, Adams enfolded self-determination for the Yorùbá into his own adroitness, thus solidifying the process of his personal transformation, which he needed in order to join the ranks of the elites.

With this project of *self*-determination, starting around 2006 (when he was released from jail), Adams began his transformation from a "warlord," a man with a remarkable command of violence, as had been common in nineteenth- and early twentieth-century Yorubaland, to an elite in Yorùbá's age of modernity, which had started in the early twentieth century. While Adams had always intended to use his involvement in, first, the human rights and democratic struggle, and then, the ethno-nationalistic struggle, to transform his social circumstances, his repeated personal triumphs over every obstacle inspired him to enlarge his ambitions. His serial victories also encouraged him to trust that his initial extravagant claims to sociocultural, economic, and political importance were not just credible but also realizable. Becoming a big man was difficult, though, as shown by his repeated risks of death, police manhunt, harassment, and detention, in addition to the scorn he endured from sections of the existing

Yorùbá elite and the aversion he attracted from other groups. Yet he realized that, ultimately, he could leave behind his long years of deprivation—which began when he was a carpenter in Mushin, scrounging out a bare life by borrowing his friend's (Sunday Adebayo's) *okada*—for a life of abundance.

I need to quickly clarify how this chapter is different from the next (chap. 4). While this chapter examines how to *become* a big man, the next chapter examines how to *be* (maintain the status of) a big man. I emphasize this relative distinction to show that, while *becoming* a big man is an unavoidable process connected with *being* a big man, there are important differences between the two stages—despite the difficulty of marking, in absolute terms, where one ends and the other begins. Though the attributes and the apparatuses needed to *become* a big man correlate with those needed to sustain, nurture, or keep that status, there are ostensibly other processes, aesthetics, performances, and modes of being that become necessary when one is already a big man.

LUMPEN-BOURGEOIS?

Gani Adams and two of his lieutenants, Monsuru Akande, the chair of the Welfare Committee, and Olumide Adeniji, the organizing secretary, were standing in front of their allocated rooms at the Nicon Noga Hilton Hotel, Abuja, in February 2004. At the time, the Hilton in Abuja was Nigeria's most prestigious and expensive hotel. The porter who took the suitcases to their floor, strangely, left them all by their doors and gave them their card keys.[24] They thought they could figure things out, though none of them had ever stayed in such a prestigious hotel and had never seen a card key until that day. According to Akande, the three—whom Karl Marx would have dismissed as *Lumpenproletariat* but who had, contrary to Marx's prediction, become the leaders of a "revolutionary" vanguard[25]—fumbled with the keys for a while.

"Our three rooms were beside one another," revealed Akande. "We all stood by the door and didn't know how to use the card key. We had never seen anything like that before. We were laughing and making fun of one another. Then I think the hotel people were able to see us from their CCTV, so they sent someone to help us open the doors."[26]

Adams, Akande, and Adeniji, three leaders of the OPC, were attending the National Peace Forum convened by Rochas Okorocha, the federal minister of special duties.[27] Akande said that when they went to the hotel restaurant for dinner, they were surprised to see such a variety of food and drinks and to find that guests could eat as much as they wanted. It was a buffet. They had never experienced such gastronomic excess.

Akande, recounting the scrumptious buffet, revealed that Adams had come to his room and exclaimed, "I will never suffer again!" adding, "So, this is why

Figure 3.6. Olumide Adeniji, OPC organizing secretary; Monsuru Akande, chair of the Welfare Committee; and Adams at an event. Photo courtesy of Monsuru Akande.

Figure 3.7. *First Row:* Adams (*second from left*) and his men, including Rasaq Arogundade Balogun (*far left*), Monsuru Akande (*left of Adams*), and Musa Kilanko, a member of the OPC National Guard, at an event in the early years. Photo courtesy of Monsuru Akande.

these politicians don't like to leave power." Akande told me, "I think this was one of the moments when Gani's mentality changed."

The former OPC Welfare Committee chair added that the three were booked into the hotel for three nights to attend a two-day conference and so expected to check out on the third day. But they decided not to leave after the three days. The other two agreed with Adams that they should spend the week enjoying the "bliss." Akande disclosed that they called one of their supporters, a serving senator representing Osun State, to ask him to cover the cost of three additional nights after the conference. The senator, according to Akande, asked if they knew how much it cost to stay at the Hilton per night. When he revealed the sum, the three OPC men retorted, "Just to sleep for one night!"

They packed their bags and left the hotel the third day.

Adams sometimes contests such narratives of his past, often speaking generally about how he had "paid his dues" before rising to prominence. Such stories about the conditions of his poverty, many of which I heard from his lieutenants and a few of which came from Adams himself, constitute a past that he was eager to move away from as he climbed the social ladder. Afraid to return to his former life of precarity, Adams resolved to press on with his steep rise to the upper-middle class, taking important steps in response to the structural and agential possibilities and limitations of his environment—some of which Niccolò Machiavelli, the late Italian theorist of cynical power, propounded in his sixteenth-century political treatise *The Prince*.[28] Adams did more than that; he also transformed himself in many ways.

POST-JAIL MANEUVER: RESTRUCTURING AND REPOSITIONING THE OPC

After fourteen months in jail, Gani Adams was released from Kuje prisons in December 2006. Fasehun, along with whom he was arrested and detained after the two factions clashed in Iyana Ipaja in 2005, had been released on bail on health grounds in April of the same year.

When the police commissioner Okiro pursued him and eventually arrested him in 2001, Adams's long incarceration between 2005 and 2006 enhanced his image by boosting his reputation as a freedom fighter. It did more. His estranged lieutenants[29] explained that while he was in detention, Yorùbá leaders, including politicians and officeholders, worked hard to ensure his release, and some also provided financial support. Surviving in Nigerian prisons can be very expensive, especially for highly placed people, so the provision of some form of financial support is quite common. The conditions of Nigerian prisons are appalling. Those who have the means must fund their own feeding, utilities, and sanitation while also bribing prison officials for access to certain coveted facilities and supporting other prisoners whose help they need. Realizing this, Adams's well-wishers sent large sums of money to ensure his survival in jail and allow him to fulfill his ongoing obligations outside the prison walls. Arogundade Rasaq Balogun, a member of the National Guard; Sunday Adebayo, Adams's personal assistant and childhood friend; Monsuru Akande, chair of the Welfare Committee; and Segun Akanni, initially Adams's protocol assistant, later special assistant (media), and eventually chief of staff, in separate interviews, told me that they had collected money from those who were eager to support Adams while he was in jail, including former and serving governors. Some gave money weekly; others did so occasionally.

In addition, some public figures, including the serving governor of Ogun State, Gbenga Daniel,[30] visited Adams while he and Fasehun were still detained at the guest house of the inspector general of police before they were transferred to Kuje prison. Rauf Aregbesola, former commissioner for works under Governor Tinubu and later governor of Osun State, also visited Adams in Kuje prison.[31] The visits to the prisons and Adams's welfare there were coordinated by the OPC coordinator in Abuja, Wole Adedeji.

Before he was arrested in 2005, Adams realized that no one without a house in his hometown was regarded as a person of consequence in Yorubaland.[32] Therefore, he decided to build a house in Arigidi. He bought a plot of land and asked Balogun to supervise the construction. Not long afterward, he was arrested. According to his aides, the construction would have stalled but for their efforts.

While Adams was in jail, Balogun lost his wife, which forced him to temporarily abandon his supervisory role in the construction of Adams's house. Akande said that when he visited Adams in jail, Adams instructed him to take over the project, to Balogun's displeasure. The latter felt that the leader was insensitive to the reason he had temporarily returned to Lagos.

"I used to collect money from those who supported him," stated Akande. "I suggested to Adams that we should use the money to build the house in Arigidi, and he agreed. We did the foundation about two months before he was arrested and then continued after his detention."

Balogun and Akande were members of the OPC National Guard.[33] The National Guard, also called the Squad or Entourage, was an elite group of protectors and fighters. They regarded themselves, along with Adebayo, Adams's boyhood friend, as some of those closest to Adams. Therefore, when Adams returned from jail and convened a meeting of the National Executive Council (NEC) and the National Coordinating Council (NCC) to announce that he

Figure 3.8. Adams receiving a plaque presented by members of the OPC Meiran Caucus. He is surrounded by members of the National Guard. Photo courtesy of Rasaq Arogundade Balogun.

wanted to restructure the OPC, they were initially surprised and eventually disappointed.

The meeting was held in Adams's first home, instructively called the "White House," in Abule Ado in the suburbs of Lagos. Adams, his erstwhile aides told me, announced that he was dissolving the National Guard.[34] All members of the guard were to return to their local government areas, where they would become group coordinators.

The members of the guard saw this as a power grab. These were the people who had a voice at the highest level of the group. They also knew him well and knew many of the group's secrets.

"This was at the first meeting in 2006 after he returned," disclosed Akande. "Everyone was happy that he was back from jail. He greeted us warmly at the meeting and even announced that I was his favorite in the group. Then he added that though I was his favorite, we would no longer be together from that day. He wanted to reconstitute the National Executive Council and the National Coordinating Council. He said I would become an ex-officio of the NEC. I said no to him."[35]

However, with the edict from the leader, Akande lost his position as the Welfare Committee chair of the national OPC and, in addition, lost his place as the coordinator of his local government, which would have entitled him to direct membership in the NCC. Akande said Adams had the majority of the members behind him, especially the junior ones, who thought that getting rid

Figure 3.9. Adams talking with Senator Tokunbo Afikuyomi at a public event. Adams's friend and first personal assistant, Sunday Adebayo, is in the middle. Photo courtesy of Sunday Adebayo.

of the "caucus" members would pave the way for them to "also enjoy" all the benefits of the group.

"There is too much poverty in the OPC. This is why most of the members were ready to do whatever he wanted," Akande alleged. Balogun agreed with Akande that Adams's return from jail in 2006 was a turning point.

"After he returned, he said he had served the OPC, and it was now time for him to serve himself. This was at the meeting in his house. All of us in the Entourage were at the meeting," said Balogun. "Until that day, I was his chief security officer [CSO]. As CSO, I didn't have time for my family. Even when my wife was sick [before she died], I couldn't be with her because Gani said 'order is order.' But with his return from prison, he turned the OPC to a dictatorship. He asked me to go back to Somolu Local Government as coordinator. He asked Otepa, another member of the National Guard, to go back to Ejigbo Local Government. He dispersed all of us."

Balogun said Adams's main target was his kitchen cabinet, which included six people and sometimes a seventh. The constant members included Balogun, Monsuru Akande, Rasaq Arogundade Balogun, Lande Banjoko (now late), Sunday Adebayo (Adams's friend and first personal assistant), Segun Akanni,

Figure 3.10. Kitchen cabinet. *Left to right:* Segun Akanni, Monsuru Akande, Adams, Razaq Arogundade Balogun, and Segun Olusanya.

and Segun Olusanya (initially Adams's protocol assistant). Musiliu "Big Fish" Amusa was the inconstant member, according to Balogun. He added that "of all the members of the cabinet, only Akanni and Banjoko were retained."

Adams's estranged comrades wanted to make clear that Adams had adopted a strategy of divide-and-rule that left them all stranded as he consolidated power in his post-jail life. As a result of this strategy, according to his erstwhile comrades, when Adams took total control of the group, no one questioned his authority. This was at a time when the group was amassing a lot of money—allegedly hundreds of millions—as the country prepared for the 2007 elections, which would herald the first civilian-to-civilian change of government in Nigeria's history. These former comrades of Adams may not have realized that, as social identity theorists have pointed out, "the dissociation with one's former group" is one way to gain distinction while achieving individual mobility.[36]

The group's first major conflict over money happened after the 2007 elections. According to Monsuru Akande, having become aware of how much politicians of different ideological persuasions needed them, they decided on a policy of nonalignment, which they described as *a la'tan* (keeping our options open). This policy, as Balogun and Adebayo confirmed, brought in several millions of naira as politicians in the two major political parties, the ruling People's Democratic Party (PDP) and the main opposition party in the Southwest, the Action Congress of Nigeria (ACN), led by Tinubu, courted the OPC. The group was crucial for the politicians in terms of both its numerical strength and its control of unofficial policing powers. They were particularly needed to guard (or *not* guard) the electoral process, especially the ballot boxes, which were often snatched and stuffed with ballots during elections.

Against this backdrop, in the 2007 elections, the group became allied with disparate politicians and different parties, including Governor Bola Tinubu in Lagos State (ACN), Governor Gbenga Daniel in Ogun State (PDP), and Governor Olusegun Agagu in Ondo State (PDP). According to Balogun, Akande, and Adebayo, after the elections they met in Adams's house to demand sharing the tens of millions they had collected from politicians for the elections. At a meeting of the NCC, attended by about eighty members, Sunday Adebayo said he stood up to ask Adams to declare the amount of money the group had made. Musiliu Amusa said Adams had allegedly offered Adebayo N5 million to keep quiet, which the latter refused.[37] Akande, Balogun, and Amusa confirmed that Adebayo raised the matter at the meeting. Amusa added that Adebayo and Adams grew up together in Mushin and that this explained their closeness. In addition, he stated that Adebayo and himself (Amusa), were always with the OPC leader. Therefore, Adebayo knew about all the money that was coming in.

Adebayo told me that, at the meeting, Adams denied that they had made tens of millions. He put the figure around N3 million. According to the three, a fight broke out over this claim. Obviously, some of the group members were hoping to become very rich as a result of the elections and were disappointed that their boss had decided that this would not happen.

"We made money during the 2007 elections," Musiliu Amusa, the secretary of the National Guard, told me. He alleged that they had received money from the gubernatorial candidates of all the major political parties in Lagos State and elsewhere in Yorubaland.[38] The figures that the different members of the group I spoke to mentioned were between N140 and N200 million.

According to Akande, "Adams stated that OPC will use the money we made to build hotels in all the states of the Southwest. And members will buy shares in the hotel. But we asked him to share the money." Musiliu confirmed that Adams had promised to build six hotels in Yorùbá State as a form of "empowerment" for the members of the group. Akande and Balogun revealed that, at one point during the meeting, the leading members threatened to manhandle Adams in his home. According to the group, Adams then went into his room, and the door was blocked by a member who did not want the leader assaulted. Amusa Musiliu told me that he was the one who had led Adams to his room and "controlled the situation." A negotiation ensued. When Adams asked how much the angry members wanted, Akande said someone suggested N10 million. Because of this suggestion, all who insisted on sharing the money were subsequently named the "N10 million boys." However, Adams, according to the four members of the National Guard, refused the request for N10 million. There was no resolution that day. The aggrieved members, according to Amusa, "left the meeting in anger." Marruf Olanrewaju, then the coordinator of the OPC in Kwara State, supported Adams against the N10 million boys at that point. But in 2021, he told me that he realized he had made a mistake.[39]

At the next meeting of the NCC, the group had split into camps, the N10 million boys (who numbered about ten) and their supporters against Adams and his own. Amusa told me that Adams called him and Balogun to the room and told them that if he acceded to the N10 million request, "he would have lost authority." He added that Adams allegedly offered N400,000 to each of the N10 million boys. "Money was not our priority," Amusa said without any sense of irony. "We didn't want outsiders to know that we were fighting over money. That was the organization the Yorùbá were looking up to."[40] Indeed, the members kept this dispute within the group for many years. Though, over the years, some people close to Adams hinted at what they regarded as his "lack of transparency," no one mentioned the disagreement that led to the phenomenon of the N10 million boys. It was not until the late 2010s that some of the members started mentioning the issue publicly. They only informed me of the details in 2020.

However, Amusa and Akande concluded that the organization was never the same after that day. The N10 million boys became less powerful after this and left the group some years later, some of them forming their own faction. Interestingly enough, some of the regular members of the group who remained with Adams believed that the N10 million boys actually received that amount from Adams. As recently as June 2021, Omolara Adaranijo, the *Yeye Oodua* of Lagos Island, "reaffirmed" that the "conspirators took the money from Adams."

"Saddam [Balogun] and the rest of them ['conspirators'] made a lot of money through *Oga* [Adams] in the past," Adaranijo alleges. "They will vomit all they have eaten. The 10 million boys, they made so much money from *Oga* before betraying him. Saddam, Big Fish [Amusa Musiliu], Otepa [Ranti Akande], and the rest of them. *Oga* gave them big money. . . . He gave them 10 million naira. All of them, including Kila [Musa Kilanko]. They keep smearing him, yet they can never be a great as *Aare*."[41]

Adaranijo, however, regrets that Lateef Olawale Oshodi, with whom she has a good relationship, decided to join one of the splinter groups, OPC New Era. She says that, rather than make money from the OPC like those she condemned, Oshodi spent his own resources for the OPC and its members.[42]

When in late 2020 I asked Adams about the allegations of his ex-comrades, he dismissed them as "people [he] brought up."[43] He added that they were being sponsored by Governor Bola Tinubu to tarnish his name. "When I was in detention in 2005, they didn't want me to return. So, when I returned, I removed them when I heard about what they had done. Tinubu was using them. So I removed them from my cabinet and *spread them out* so they were no longer close to me. It was when they were with me that the OPC had the biggest trouble."[44]

Why would Adams "spread out," his closest aides, rather than sack them, if he was sure they were conspiring against him?

Without reading Machiavelli, Adams might have adopted one of the options the Italian theorist recommended; yet it was evident that he also realized he did not need to dispense with these men completely to augment his power and give himself the freedom to advance to the next stage in his public career. Under his leadership, they had done their part to take the OPC to the next level. They were not critical to the next stage, which, he envisaged, would demand less violence and more sociocultural and political networking to make him a more important figure in the approaching post-Obasanjo era. He needed to consolidate his assets, improve his image, and mobilize and concentrate cultural and financial resources for self-transformation.[45] He did not need the National Guard for that. But dispensing completely with the old guard would let them loose, and they could potentially cause him harm. So, he kept them—*at length*.

THE AESTHETICS OF ELITENESS: MATERIALIZING PERSONAL TRANSFORMATION

The acquisition and display of prestige goods are critical in the process of personal transformation. This is particularly so for those wishing to mark or signal their transformation from lower social classes to the middle or upper classes. As Jean-Pascal Daloz argues, "Dominant [persons] often tend to define themselves—and to judge others—in terms of material symbols. Elegant clothes, vast houses, luxury cars . . . function as badges of social rank, denoting superior status of elites against the groups below or vis-à-vis outsiders."[46] For someone like Adams, who had generally been regarded as a (violent) *lumpen,* in both its specific (class) and general (sociological) meanings, this was especially urgent. While what is regarded as prestigious within "hierarchies of esteem" has varied in different cultures, Graham Clark has observed that, since classical antiquity,[47] "the transmission of precious substances . . . or other objects of display has at all times . . . served the same purpose the world over, that of signalling and enhancing status."[48] Clark's observation can be regarded as applicable to prestige goods of all kinds.[49]

Prestige is defined as "respect and deference freely conferred on an individual by others, not compelled through violence, threat or coercion."[50] Therefore, prestige goods are "valuables [that] are critically important in establishing a person's social position . . . and in gaining personal prestige"[51] or "material items whose primary function in most contemporary societies is to signal elevated social status as well as to assist in augmenting status."[52] From early history, prestige goods have helped would-be elites to establish and maintain their elevated positions, authority, and privilege without resorting to force or violence.[53] Ambitious people, or "aggrandizers," as John Clark and Michael Blake describe them,[54] have been the subject of ethnographic and historical analyses. Ethnographers and historians ask different questions, such as why some people are more willing than others to expend effort to gather prestige goods and how goods confer prestige on their owners.[55]

While contemporary ethnographic and sociological studies of prestige goods focus on material goods such as adornment, money, wealth, and vehicles, earlier studies focused on both property and cultural objects as prestige goods. Building on the earlier tradition, Simon Harrison, focusing on Melanesia, argues, "It would therefore have appeared quite natural to actors to regard, let us say, a myth or magical spell as thing-like, equivalent perhaps to a prestige good such as a pearl shell or boar's tusk ornament not just in worth but, as it were, ontologically."[56] Harrison, however, notes that cultural objects and practices that were once "reified as transactable prestige goods now . . . tend increasingly to be reified as an inheritance or legacy from the past."[57]

In this chapter, I argue that, as he sought to transform himself into a proper member of the elite, Adams recognized the changes in the attitude toward prestige goods in contemporary Yorùbá society and also realized that, beyond violence, what I will call the *cultural prestige goods* (both material and immaterial, such as rituals, ritual knowledge, ritual bulletproofing, charms, bravery, oratory, etc.) he used in becoming recognizable would need to be augmented by, if not exchanged with, *solid* prestige goods,[58] such as wealth, houses, luxury vehicles, and adornments like clothing and jewelry. Doubtless, violence had helped him to command some social rank with a measure of dominance.[59] In contrast, prestige goods would afford him authority and privilege freely offered by others.[60] Therefore, in the process of striving for status, Adams was fervent about the acquisition of prestige goods.

THE SOCIAL CONSTRUCTION OF SELF-AGGRANDIZEMENT

"Elites," Daloz observes, "usually have a rather active social life."[61] In fact, *becoming* and *being* elite are determined by and connected to particular forms of social life. Therefore, the ways in which those who wish to be or already are members of the elite make and live their social lives can constitute affirmations of—or challenges to—their eminence. For this reason, members of the subaltern, such as Gani Adams, who are in the process of transforming themselves into elites and wish to achieve social eminence display "ostentatious affirmation *vis-à-vis* long standing elites"[62] and pay particular attention to both the material and immaterial assets, displays, and deportments that can affirm their membership in the elite ranks. Beyond universalist typologies of elite distinction that lead to "ethnocentric generalisations,"[63] ethnography is critical in accounting for the specific ways in which individuals in different cultural contexts approach the processes of achieving distinction. Therefore, the contributions of ethnographers to the understanding of the process of becoming and being elite include investigating "observable variations [in self-affirmation] without instantly referring to ready-made schemes of explanation."[64]

Below, I discuss the material and immaterial assets, displays, and deportments—some of which Daloz would describe as "*defensive* forms of conspicuousness"[65]—mobilized by Adams to achieve distinction and to become a big man.

"WHITE HOUSE": A HOME FIT FOR A "PRESIDENT"

In 2004, I went to see Adams in his new home in Suba, Abule Ado, a low-income suburb in Lagos. When I first met him in 2002, he had asked his aides to take me to a small church, where we sat and chatted under a tent out front. I learned many years later that at that point he had been living with his then fiancée, Mojisola, in her parents' home in Ijanikin, another suburb of Lagos. While in Ijanikin, Adams considered renting an apartment in Surulere because, according to his former chief of staff, Segun Akanni, he had always wanted to live in Surulere. Mushin, the low-income area where he grew up, shares borders with greater Surulere, which is a middle-class area of mainland Lagos. For Adams, who grew up in a congested area with inadequate sanitation and low-income housing, Surulere was a "prestigious" area to live as he moved up the social ladder.

After Adams moved out of Mushin when he was being hunted by the police, he never had a place to call his own. He and his followers pretentiously called his first house in Lagos the "White House" because it was painted white and because Adams was and remains a self-described "spiritual person" to whom the color white is significant. In fact, he was and is invested in all sorts of spirituality, including those of two world religions, Islam and Christianity, and African Traditional Religion. He believes in the permanent intervention of the esoteric realm in the physical and in the efficacy of prayers, rituals, and charms. Painting his house white—and wearing only white clothes from a certain point in his life—was part of his acknowledgment of the role of color in his spiritual and physical life. However, the building was also called the White House to signal that it was an important and stately dwelling for a big man who led an important group with millions of members. When they first broke away from the Fasehun faction, Adams was named the president of the OPC's militant faction. In fact, for many years, I called him president too in acknowledgment of his position in the group—even after he was named the national coordinator as a result of the rapprochement between his faction and Fasehun's. Therefore, as president, Adams named the White House as a parody of the official residence of the president of the United States.

"Building and expanding one's home," argues Tim Gibbs, "continues to be one of the preeminent forms of displaying prestige in a patriarchal society."[66] This is true in South Africa, the context of Gibbs's observation, as it is elsewhere in Africa, including Nigeria. As soon as the OPC leader made some money, he needed a house of his own that befitted his emerging status. Daloz has argued that "beyond their fundamental function as a shelter, dwelling places have often been essential indicators of social standing."[67] The White House—a one-story building in a relatively large compound that has enough space for large meetings and sufficient rooms for his aides and is situated among the community of subalterns and the urban poor—helped Adams "to demonstrate [his] dominance vis-à-vis subordinates and to exhibit at least as much supremacy as [his] peers."[68]

Although Adams did not provide the details of how he was able to build such a grand house after his first experience of detention, his former aides revealed that Governor Bola Tinubu was largely responsible for financing the construction.[69] The former governor's close aides confirmed this. Other anonymous supporters and group members also contributed their lot to the building project, which Akanni revealed was supervised by Akeem Adio (Adu), then the head of the OPC in Amuwo Odofin Local Government Area.[70]

Perhaps Adams abandoned his dream of renting a place in Surulere because of Tinubu's offer to help him build a house of his own. According to his close aides, the offer was extended at a time when the people of Suba in Abule Ado were facing increasing cases of armed robbery. The *Baale*, the head of the community, offered Adams some land on which he could build his house because the community leader and his people believed that the armed robbers would cease their attacks once they realized that the head of the OPC lived in the area. They were right.

The construction of the house started after Adams was released from his first spell of detention. It was completed in 2002, and he moved in shortly afterward. His aides, including Sunday Adebayo (personal assistant), Monsuru Akande (welfare chair), Segun Olusanya (protocol officer 1), and Segun Akanni (protocol officer 2) all moved in with him, some of them leaving their families behind to serve the president. The four shared two rooms in the new "presidential palace."

In addition to the White House, Adams also built a house in his hometown of Arigidi in Ondo State. It is expected in Africa that any man of consequence must have a house in his village. Adams bought land in Arigidi shortly before he was incarcerated in 2005. As explained earlier, his close aides ensured that the building was completed before he was released from jail in December 2006. With the house in Arigidi, he was ready to confirm his status as a big man, both at home and abroad.

With the first two houses built in Lagos and Arigidi, Adams confirmed Daloz's argument that, in Africa, "local 'Big Men' do indeed try to distinguish themselves by constructing the most impressive edifice, but generally in the very place where they have their roots, that is, among their community and followers, even if this is a miserable village or an overcrowded suburb."[71]

IN PRAISE OF THE BIG CHIEF: SPECIAL OCCASIONS AND THE SOCIALITY OF PRESTIGE

"Ààre, Ààre, *olo'un ma je n s'Ààre* Ònà *Kakaǹfò*" (Ààre, Ààre, may God help me, so I never run afoul of the *Ààre*).[72] One of Nigeria's most popular musicians, K1 De Ultimate (Wasiu Ayinde), sings Gani Adams's praise as the recently installed Ààrẹ *Ọ̀nà Kakaǹfò* of Yorubaland mounts the stage to "spray" money on the musician.

"Spraying" money on a musician (or any other performer) and dancers during a performance is a common practice in Yorubaland (and the rest of Nigeria, by extension). It started with putting naira notes on their foreheads. But in recent years, the superrich have taken things to a higher level. Bundles of money are often too big for pasting on the forehead; therefore, the superrich just hand it over in stacks to the musician or the musician's aide as they dance—or even stand—by the musician to relish the high praise.

One of the markers of *eliteness* is participation "in several types of prestigious gatherings throughout the year"—including one's "home performances,"[73] such as birthdays, naming ceremonies, and burials.[74] Therefore, in Nigeria, particularly in Yorubaland, those who wish to climb the social ladder are compelled to attend several social gatherings and ceremonies. One distinguishes oneself by selecting which invitations to accept and when, where, and how to appear at such events. Specifically, spraying money is a critical marker of self-presentation and self-aggrandizement. Reflecting on Yorùbá society before European contact, Karin Barber argues that a "driving dynamic" of the society "was the competitive self-aggrandizement of individuals."[75] In this context, Gani Adams mirrors the big men who emerged in the era described by Barber. The period, particularly in the context of nineteenth-century Yorùbá wars, provided a fertile ground for the emergence of entrepreneurial warlords in Yorùbá city-states like Ijaye and Ibadan. For example, Kurunmi,[76] a self-aggrandizing military entrepreneur in Ijaye, made vast investments in commercial farms, slaves, and artisanal production and indulged in the conspicuous consumption of wealth and displays of generosity.[77] Such self-aggrandizing individuals attracted *oríkì* (praise poetry), which, "by representing in concentrated form the gaze of recognition by adherents, [becomes part of] the ultimate basis of big men's power in an achievement-oriented society." Therefore, in contemporary Yorùbá society, musicians' praise singing of eminent and rich people like Adams constitutes a form of *oríkì*.

When Adams stands in front a musician to spray—whether it is K1 De Ultimate or another Fuji star (such as Alabi Pasuma, Adewale Ayuba, or Saheed Osupa) performing for him and almost deifying him with praise—he hardly ever dances.[78] While he occasionally moves briefly to the beat, most times he stands still and intermittently takes money from his aide (Segun Akanni until he was replaced), who holds the stacks of cash in an accompanying bag, to give to the musicians. The aide hands the stacks to his boss as he stretches out his hand to indicate that he wants more. Usually, the higher denominations of currency (preferably in mint, as brand-new notes are called in Nigeria) have been preselected for the task.

It was the fiftieth birthday of Prince Temitayo Adeolokun (popularly called Tasman)—the CEO of the Mushin-based House of Heavy Sounds, a company that rented out musical instruments in Lagos. Many top musicians patronized the company. In attendance at the birthday party were Pasuma (Wasiu Ajibola Alabi), a popular Fuji musician who is a personal friend of Adeolokun,[79] K1 De Ultimate (Wasiu Ayinde), and several other musicians and socialites. Gani Adams was also invited to the party, which was held at the Grandeur Events Centre on Billings Way, Ikeja, Lagos. At some point during the party, K1 De Ultimate, the leading Fuji music star and perhaps the most resourceful and adaptive of all the Yorùbá musicians of his era, took the microphone. Adams was so moved as K1 sang his praises that he decided to show the musician and all present how far he had come materially. As Segun Akanni told me, Adam

Figure 3.11. Fuji musician Alabi Pasuma bows to greet Adams at the Olokun Festival. Sitting on Adams's right is Sally Mbanefo, director general of the Nigerian Tourism Development Corporation (NTDC). Adams's aide, Segun Akanni, is standing beside Pasuma. Photo courtesy of Segun Akanni.

asked his aide to call someone in his home to quickly bring over three stacks of hundred-dollar notes. One of his aides claimed that the notes amounted to about US$30,000. Not long after, according to Akanni, the bearer arrived with the coveted currency. Given that everyone in Nigeria is able to spray money, the elite with access to foreign currency differentiate themselves from others by spraying hard currency. Thus, a few members of the elite monopolize this special criterion of social distinction.

Adams collected the stacks of money and rose to his feet as his aides and bodyguards scrambled to flank him. He then marched to the stage. As he approached, K1 raised the tempo in praise of the OPC leader. Adams took hundred-dollars bills intermittently and handed them over to the musician. K1 De Ultimate was so impressed that he started to eulogize Adams as "*Olokun to n po* dollar" (the water spirit/god that vomits dollars). It was obvious from the reaction of most people present that Adams had made a great impression.

In February 2018, barely a month after his installation, Adams was at the burial ceremony for the mother-in-law of MC Oluomo, the head of the Lagos National Union of Road Transport Workers (NURTW). Such special

Figure 3.12. "Money Speaking Gani Adams over Spend for K1 De Ultimate @ MC Oluomo Mother-in-Law Burial." This is the description of a video of an event where Adams spent a lot of money for popular musician K1 De Ultimate (Wasiu Ayinde). See Facetv Africa, YouTube, February 13, 2018, https://www.youtube.com/watch?v=5PtivpDJK84. Screenshots (*clockwise*): *Aare* takes a stack of money from the bag held by his aide, Segun Akanni; Adams hands over a stack to K1's assistant as K1 sings his praise; Adams takes another stack as K1 watches; the *Kakaǹfò* listens to his praises as the musician's aide (*middle*) holds the five stacks of money already handed over.

occasions constitute some of the most important means for aspiring big men and women, including the nouveaux riches and the superrich, to show their financial strength and announce their status.

At another event nine months later, in November 2018, once K1 noticed Adams's arrival, he started to sing his praise. Adams walked up to the stage but did not climb it. He stopped in front of the musician and handed stacks of cash directly to him. When K1 took the first stack, he placed it in front of his own head to acknowledge the *Aare*'s generosity. Adams handed over five stacks of ₦1,000 notes, totaling ₦500,000 (at that time about $2,000). He then waved to the musician and walked away.[80]

At yet another event, the opening of Chillers Hotel and Suites in Abule Ado, Lagos, in January 2022, Adams again made it clear that he could now spend dollars superfluously. He was raining ₦500 notes into a box held by K1's assistant.

Figure 3.13. Screenshots (*clockwise*): Adams's aide, Segun Akanni, pulling bundles of money from a bag to hand over to Adams as he prepares to spray money on K1 De Ultimate, who was singing his praise; Adams savoring K1's praises; Adams handing over a bundle of money to K1; KI bowing to receive another bundle from Adams. Screenshots from Facetv Africa, YouTube, November 4, 2018, https://www.youtube.com/watch?v=Yg4IuotFs54&t=308s.

Figure 3.14. Screenshots (*clockwise*): Adams arrives on the stage to spray K1 De Ultimate; Adams sprays naira notes into the money box as K1 sings his praises; moved by particular lines in K1's song of praise for him, Adams reaches into his pocket and hands over dollar notes to the musician; the musician puts some of the dollar notes under his cap as he reaches out to collect more. Screenshots from GoldMyne TV, YouTube, January 24, 2022, https://www.youtube.com/watch?v=Yk3XrScksyM.

As the musician started to pray for him along with singing his praises, Adams abandoned the naira notes he was dropping into the box and reached into his pocket. He brought out a pile of hundred-dollar notes, which he handed to K1. K1 bent and danced in front of Adams to appreciate the coveted currency, which he hung by the side of his cap so the dollars would not be mixed with the naira notes in the box. "*Aare* se kini yen fun mi, o mun dollar wa" (Aare has done it for me, he brings dollars), he sang.[81]

As stated earlier, one of the most important markers of status in contemporary Yorùbá high society is the amount of money one can spray on musicians and others during ceremonies.[82] Money spraying is a critical means of image making and a way for those who are just entering into, or hoping to join, high society to show that they have the material means or capacity *to belong*. There are sensory-emotional values inherent in being considered someone who has the capacity to spray well in high society. There is also an erotic aspect to the process, as some of those who engage in the practice have told me over the years. There is a chemistry between or among the people present during spraying (including mutual spraying among those celebrating particular events). Spraying or being sprayed makes people both *solid* and *liquid*, and therefore sexually appealing. This, I understand, happens with both sexes in many complicated ways. When a woman is dancing, especially if she is unattached or vulnerably attached, the men spraying her can potentially drop sexual cues. Those who can spray a lot of money, thus affirming their wealth, could also potentially be dropping cues, intentionally or unintentionally, about how *liquid* they are and thus become points of attraction for prospective licit or illicit relationships. This is particularly true of men who can spray musicians with a lot of money in hundreds of thousands or even millions of naira. Their display of wealth often makes them attractive to or targets of society women. While the erotic aspect of spraying at social events is part of a larger cultural practice, this capacity to announce one's wealth and status always carries the potential to announce one's economic and therefore social distinction, which can be mobilized or exploited for erotic liaisons—as well as other relationships.

BIRTHDAYS AND THE RITUAL OF PRAISE

In July 2010, the accomplished and the eminent came together with the subaltern to celebrate Gani Adams's fortieth birthday. *Akogun* Tola Adeniyi, a journalist, playwright, and former managing director of the *Daily Times*, previously the biggest print media conglomerate in Africa, was the guest speaker. He spoke to the theme "The Yoruba Race: Forging a Common Front." Before charting a new course for the Yorùbá based on the concept of *omoluabi* (good character), he identified the crises facing the Yorùbá "race": "Our collective failures are in four core areas: first our dwindling, almost vanishing political relevance, our bastardization, vulgarization, subjugation, and outright liquidation of our cherished cultural values, our loss of sense of history of who we really are, as well as the loss of our pride of place in the comity of nation."[83]

Adeniyi's audience and Adams's guests included Professor Ibidapo Obe, mathematician, engineer, former president of the Nigerian Academy of Science, and former vice chancellor of the University of Lagos; Ambassador Segun Olusola, Nigeria's former envoy to Ethiopia; *Ogbeni* Rauf Aregbesola, the gubernatorial candidate of the ACN and later governor of Osun State; and Mohammed Fawehinmi, son of Nigeria's late feisty lawyer and activist Chief Gani Fawehinmi. Apart from criticizing the state of affairs in Yorubaland, Adeniyi also celebrated the "valour, heritage, cultural superiority and trail-blazing spirit of the [Yorùbá] race."[84]

Figure 3.15. Adams and his wife with (*left to right*) Ambassador Segun Olusola (former ambassador to Ethiopia); Dr. Joe Okei-Odumakin, chairperson of Campaign for Democracy; and Dr. Pat Utomi, former adviser to President Shagari and former chief operating officer of Volkswagen Nigeria, at one of Adams's birthday ceremonies in his late thirties. Photo courtesy of *Nigerian Tribune*.

Figure 3.16. Adams and his wife cut another of his birthday cakes as Ambassador Segun Olusola (with microphone) officiates the process. Photo courtesy of *Nigerian Tribune*.

Figure 3.17. Adams's wife, Mojisola, dancing as Alabi Pasuma sings. Adams is spraying her. For the video, see GoldMyne TV, "Pasuma Thrills Audience at Otunba Gani Adams' 47th Birthday Celebration," YouTube, May 3, 2017, https://www.youtube.com/watch?v=pn4fr-S49nU. Photo courtesy of *Nigerian Tribune*.

Adams also uses the annual celebration of his birthday to simultaneously negotiate and affirm his eminence and elite status. The celebration, which is an example of what Adélékè Adéèkó describes as the "ever-growing pursuit of self-commemoration,"[85] usually involves attempts at showcasing his own intellectual[86] concerns and displaying his sociocultural rank.[87] Therefore, an intellectual, cultural icon, or someone politically important often gives a lecture, and a musician provides entertainment. Birthday celebrations also constitute opportunities for the high and mighty, the powerful who recognize Adams's position in society or those who need his support, to show him that he matters to them. For instance, a source told me that, for Adams's fortieth birthday, one governor gifted him a bulletproof sport utility vehicle (SUV). I could not confirm this, although around that time Adams was driving a new SUV.

Adams's fortieth birthday was celebrated not just as a personal but as a cultural milestone. It was a weeklong event that included a cultural night, a lecture, a media luncheon, a novelty football match, thanksgiving services (one in a mosque on Friday and another in a church on Sunday), and a grand reception. Adams always makes a grand entrance with his beautiful wife at his birthday ceremony, particularly during the lecture or grand reception. For instance,

Figure 3.18. Adams spraying Fuji musician Adewale Ayuba as his wife, Mojisola (*far left*), dances. Photo courtesy of *Nigerian Tribune*.

at his fortieth birthday celebration, a social commentator described his entry thus: "Otunba Gani Adams, the Oodua People's Congress generalissimo, breezed into the venue of his own birthday gathering with the confident swagger of a decorated war hero. Unlike the archetypal war commander in full combat gear and walking stick, Adams wore a flowing white *agbada* while two strands of chunky, long white beads sat on his neck. You could detect an air of 'no shaking' in his demeanour. No war songs but all smiles."[88]

"It is part of my destiny," Adams once told me about his decision to wear only white clothes and paint his houses white.[89] "That was what my guardian angel wants."

He described his birthday celebration as an "annual ritual."[90] Indeed, this annual ritual is grander every year, though the milestones, such as the fortieth, are grander still. The thirty-ninth was also grand. It included representatives of the *Ooni* of Ife and of the governors of Lagos[91] and Oyo States. As a reporter noted, at the birthday celebration on April 30, 2009, "the class of automobiles which parked in and around the vicinity of the events centre, owners of which were around to grace the celebration evidently pointed out that Gani, as he is called by his followers, was a man held in high esteem by not a few ordinary people."[92] The "splendour, gaiety and exuberance" that attend Adams's birthday celebrations often form a backdrop to "the multi-titled culture advocate's" monumentalisation—showcased at the celebrations. A reporter described an example of this:

> In fact, the aura of the larger-than-life importance that enveloped Gani Adams, who with no extra prompting ignited the hall which some minutes earlier was in a shadow of itself, could be equated to that of a nation's president. Indeed, Adams was a president of the OPC nation. The picture painted by his arrival at the venue vis-a-vis the caliber of the already seated traditional rulers, obas, rights activists from across Nigeria, entertainers, media representatives and of course the hordes of OPC stalwarts, even from outside the shores of this country surely made further attestations to Adams' rising profile both as a national ethnic leader, and also an activist of national repute.[93]

The birthday celebration is as much an annual ritual of praise as a ritual of power and distinction. Adams told journalists in 2018 that "the annual event is to appreciate God's blessings in his life."[94] He added, "It is my usual tradition to celebrate it in a big way. I often tell people that each year, I celebrate my birthday to receive more blessings from God. Over the years, God has been so good to me and the rest of my family. I can't thank God enough for the inestimable blessing bestowed on me, annually. I always have reasons to celebrate my birthday anniversary. That is why I invite people from across the world to celebrate with me."[95]

Indeed, the annual birthday celebrations serve many purposes. They constitute a regular reaffirmation of his status, given the caliber of people who attend. Every year an assortment of governors (sitting or former), traditional rulers, businesspeople, famous artistes, and other celebrities show up. The presence of such dignitaries at a birthday celebration confirms that the celebrant is a dignitary too. Beyond that, the dignitaries who attend have to speak, either at the event or with journalists thereafter, about Adams. They are often full of praise for his role in the Yorùbá region and Nigeria at large, thus reinforcing his self-projection as an important person. The celebrations also provide an opportunity for him to speak about the state of the nation, including matters that are of private concern to him. He usually holds a press conference in his home before the celebration, which is then followed by journalists interviewing him and his famous guests during the event. Through the celebrations, Adams also displays his social status in a myriad of ways, including the quality of the venue, aesthetic features such as lavish decorations, the quality of the food and drinks served, and his and his wife's appearances—which combine to pass, in a

Figure 3.19. Adams and friends. *Left to right:* Gani Kayode Balogun (once the advertising manager of African Newspapers PLC, publishers of the *Nigerian Tribune,* and later appointed by Adams as the *Osi* Ààrẹ *Ọnà Kakaǹfò* of Yorubaland); Adams; Wale Adedayo, Adams's friend and adviser; and Ambassador Segun Olusola (late). Photo courtesy of *Nigerian Tribune.*

Bourdieusian sense, the "judgement of taste" of the members of high society.[96] In addition, the crowd of regular people who attend the event constitute an audience; they also help to reaffirm his commitment to the subaltern. However, some of his old comrades have criticized his penchant for throwing parties, arguing that Adams "is no longer in the struggle," as his friend and journalist (and later the chief press secretary to Governor Gbenga Daniel) Wale Adedayo told me in 2012.[97] He added that at one point after the post-jail era when there was tension between an Ijaw group and the Yorùbá, Adams was asked if the OPC would intervene. Adedayo said Adams queried those asking for his intervention in Yorùbá, "You want me to go back [to jail]?"

IMPRESSION MANAGEMENT[98]

On December 13, 2012, I was the book reviewer at the public presentation of Professor Jacob Olupona's book *City of 201 Gods: Ilé-Ifè in Time, Space, and the Imagination.*[99] Olupona is a Nigerian American professor at the Harvard Divinity School with a joint appointment at the Africa and African American Studies Department at Harvard. The *Ooni* of Ife and billionaire businessman

Oba Okunade Sijuade, Olubuse II, was the chief host of the event, which was chaired by Sir Olaniwun Ajayi, the London School of Economics and Political Science–trained lawyer and elder statesman and one of the leaders of *Afenifere*. Special guests included the governors of Ekiti and Osun States, Dr. Kayode Fayemi and *Ogbeni* Rauf Aregbesola, respectively, and the *Olowo* of Owo, *Oba* Folagbade Olateru Olagbegi III, a UK-trained lawyer, former law teacher, and senior advocate of Nigeria. These six people and other distinguished Nigerians were at the high table, as the rostrum where dignitaries are seated is called in Nigeria.

Gani Adams arrived almost three hours into the program and went straight to the high table. As he approached, they struggled to find a seat for him. He greeted Professor Olupona, Sir Olaniwun, the *Ooni*, and others and took his seat as the compere, a lady lecturer at the Obafemi Awolowo University, Ile-Ife, quickly introduced him, welcoming him as "*baba wa*" (our father, meaning "our elder"). Some people who were seated beside me were surprised that Adams headed straight for the high table, despite arriving late. At any rate, they were confused as to why Adams would think he deserved to sit at the high table when more important people, including first- and second-class traditional rulers, were seated in the first two rows of the audience.

Olupona later told me that as Adams climbed the raised platform, the *Olowo*, a first-class chief from Adams's home state of Ondo, gathered his robes to exit the platform to provide a seat for the OPC leader. Olupona's wife, Dupe, a US-based nurse, stopped the Owo monarch, insisting that it was against tradition and protocol for a traditional ruler to concede his seat to Adams. She persuaded *Oba* Olagbegi to stay in the hope that another chair would be found. Indeed, the organizers brought another chair so Adams could sit at the high table. Olagbegi was apparently trying to avoid trouble. For four years (between 1999 and 2003), the OPC and his supporters were involved in violent clashes that claimed several lives after the Olowo's installation because Adams and his members, along with the then Alliance for Democracy (AD) governor of the state, Adebayo Adefarati, were opposed to his installation.[100] They had tried to dislodge him from the palace.

In the summer of 2010, I stepped out of a postmortem meeting of the Trustees Board of the Obafemi Awolowo Institute of Government and Public Policy (OAIGPP), only to run into Gani Adams. He wore his new signature attire: a flowing white *agbada*, complete with an *abetí ajá* cap (a traditional cap favored by the Oyo-Yorùbá, which is folded back up in dog-ear) and long heavy beads adorning his neck and dropping below his navel. Although he arrived well past the end of the opening ceremony (all the dignitaries, including the wife of the

Figure 3.20. Adams and the author standing in front of Awolowo's bust at the OAIGPP Museum in Lekki, Lagos, in 2010. I did not realize that a photographer had captured this moment until much later, when the coordinator of the institute sent us the photographs taken at the opening ceremony of the institute. Author's photo.

late leader, Chief HID Awolowo; the state governor, Raji Fashola; his predecessor, *Asiwaju* Bola Tinubu; and others had left), he was still being conducted around the museum inside the complex. The members of the trustees board were still there only because the board had decided to have a postmortem meeting long after we had bidden goodbye to the dignitaries who attended the formal opening. I stopped to engage in a brief chat with Adams before returning to the board room.

In later years, as Adams became bigger and bigger in society, I realized that lateness to events was not a character flaw; it was an important modus and indicator of his *bigness*, or his claim to eminence. I have never since met him at any event where he arrived on time.

"He always comes late to a loud ovation," said one of his closest former aides. "He likes the MC [master of ceremonies] calling his name and praising him as he enters the stage."[101]

As the examples of the book launch and the opening of the institute show, and as his close aides confirmed, Adams was convinced that, in Nigeria, the big man must come later than other attendees. Generally, people with comparatively "smaller" personalities have to wait for the big man to arrive. Even if you are not the *biggest* man in a particular context, you can use your lateness to negotiate your bigness relative to other big people at the event. In fact, the later you are, the more it reflects your importance—or your sense of your own importance—relative to others. Although this is not an absolute or unconditional measure of bigness (because a few big men are often punctual), Adams regarded lateness as a critical modus of playing the big man.

To give another example, a meeting of distinguished Yorùbá from all walks of life was convened on November 7, 2017, in Abeokuta. It was the first Southwest Stakeholders Summit organized by the Southwest Patriots Movement. As usual, Adams arrived late. *Aare* Afe Babalola, octogenarian university proprietor, senior advocate of Nigeria (SAN), and perhaps the most distinguished lawyer in Nigeria at the time, a man who also held the *Aare Bamofin*[102]—generalissimo of law—conferred by the *Aláàfin* of Oyo, was delivering his talk when Adams came in with his retinue of aides. Rather than feel insulted by the disruptive entry of the much younger and far less distinguished man, Babalola paused his address as Adams took his seat to lay to rest the rumors about the friction and acrimony that could occur between the two as a result of Adams's planned installation in a few months. The revered advocate stated,

> The Chairman, Ladies and gentlemen, I have been watching with keen attention the many questions being asked and the many comments being made about the nomination of *Otunba* Gani Adams as the 15th Ààre Ònà *Kakaǹfò* of Yorubaland by the *Aláàfin* of Oyo, *Oba* Lamidi Olayiwola Adeyemi III. The truth and the reality of the matter is that both of us are occupying different seats of honour in the Yoruba nation. He has been most deservedly nominated as the Ààre Ònà *Kakaǹfò* of Yorubaland while I had long been installed as the Ààre *Baamòfin* of Yorubaland. Whereas *Otunba* Gani Adams is the Generalissimo of Yoruba race, the Field Marshall for all descendants of Oduduwa, I am the *Aare Baamofin* of Yorubaland, the Generalissimo of Law, a title which was bestowed on me by the *Aláàfin* in appreciation of my using the instrumentality of law to ensure that the late Bashorun M.K.O. Abiola was made the Ààre Ònà *Kakaǹfò*.[103]

Rather than excoriating Adams for his tardiness, the disciplined and time-conscious octogenarian was acknowledging that the younger man would soon occupy, as he did, a "seat of honour in the Yoruba nation." It was yet another confirmation that Adams was big enough to arrive late and still have his presence recognized.

Figure 3.21. Adams in the white clothes, long necklace, and *abetí ajá* cap that have become his signature attire. Photo courtesy of *Nigerian Tribune* library.

However, beyond strategically and carefully deciding which events deserve his august presence or whether his time of arrival is critical for his status, perhaps one of Adams's most important tools for image management has been fashion—the totality of his adornment, including clothing and jewelry. In fact, his transformation and the long process of gaining social distinction can be mapped by the changes in his wardrobe and the "aestheticized self-fashioning," to use Richard Werbner's phrase,[104] that this transformation reveals. From T-shirts and jeans or native clothes—that is, *buba* and *sokoto* without cap—he moved to wearing cheap French suits and later *buba* and *sokoto* with cap (which is what it means to be formally dressed in traditional clothes). By the time he started wearing *buba* and *sokoto* with cap, he had become conscious of his outfit. This was immediately before and immediately after he was detained for the longest period (2005–6). As he became more financially comfortable, Adams graduated to wearing *agbada* on top of the *buba* and *sokoto*, the full traditional regalia. Then he stopped wearing the regular Yorùbá cap and adopted the *abetí ajá* cap, the unique Oyo-Yorùbá cap that is worn by the *Aláàfin*. This was an indication of sartorial distinction. Ultimately, the full flowing white *agbada* and *abetí ajá* cap with long strands of large beads around his neck and a beaded bracelet became his insignia. Over the last decade, he has worn white clothes, now sewn by high-price fashion designers, thus achieving a uniqueness in his sartorial appearance and tastes.

Another critical dimension of his image management is his acute understanding of the role of the media in society. From the outset, Adams recognized the power of the Nigerian press—and eventually of all forms of media, including social media (as it became dominant in the second decade of the twentieth century). Therefore, building on his media contacts in the early days of his rise, he befriended or recruited journalists to serve as his contacts with other journalists and the media in general. Some of these journalists were young Yorùbá who believed in his cause, others were eager for news sources, and still others were interested in the pecuniary benefits that came from a relationship with him as he became solvent. A few developed relationships with him through their friends or family who were either members or supporters of the OPC, while others were eager to support him and his group because they were challenging those in power.

But in the end, even for some of his aides, these relationships with journalists became somewhat incestuous. One of his erstwhile low-level members of the OPC used disparaging terms to describe the reporters who covered the group and Adams's activities in the early years. "They just write what he asked them to write," she said.

Whatever the reason for their support and their relationship with him, Adams became a subject of constant media attention in his own right. This was partly why he was able to trounce the Fasehun faction in the media war. Whatever happened, his version of events received greater coverage and therefore greater public attention. He so enchanted the most critical section of the Nigerian press that even when there were infelicities in his interviews or in the ceaseless press releases, unless the reporter and editor did not know better, they mostly corrected the errors or did not publish his words verbatim. However, there were significant exceptions to this pattern of coverage—particularly in the newspapers based in the north of Nigeria.[103]

The media also eagerly played along as he transformed his self-presentation. His evolving images are displayed only in their current iteration. Therefore, few stories about Adams illustrated at each evolving stage contain images of an

Figure 3.22. Adams and his wife, Mojisola, in the early years of their marriage. Photo courtesy of *Nigerian Tribune*.

earlier stage when he had not yet started wearing full traditional regalia with the *abetí ajá* cap.

One of those who was instrumental to Adams's media blitz in the early years was the erstwhile *Punch* journalist Wale Adedayo, who later served as an aide to Governor Gbenga Daniel—and also facilitated a closer relationship between the governor and Adams. Adedayo told me that, at one point, he and two other senior journalists working with the *Comet* newspaper and *P.M.* News formed a trio that constituted the Adams's "media council." Adams had (and still has) countless other journalists at his beck and call.

However, because stories about Adams are also good copy, often complete with the conflictual or the dramatic—whether he is denouncing important personalities or raising critical public issues; proffering solutions to local, regional, and national challenges; making pronouncements on future political configurations; suggesting knowledge of those behind consequential public events, such as the assassination of Bola Ige; accepting chieftaincy titles; getting married; or even having babies (twins) after trying unsuccessfully with his wife for many years—the media are also eager to publish them.

Figure 3.23. Adams and the leading members of the OPC at his traditional wedding. On Adams's immediate left is Monsuru Akande. Photo courtesy of Monsuru Akande.

Thus, in my more than two decades of research, I gathered an almost overwhelming amount of information from the media. Indeed, few other Yorùbá of his generation, other than high political officials or entertainers, have come close to the level of reporting and general media attention that Adams has attracted. And in an age transformed in unprecedented ways by information and communications technology and social media, an entrepreneur of Adams's status and gift can, more than ever before, put almost everything in the service of his enhanced public image and personal eminence.

With his beautiful wife, Mojisola, further cementing his public image as an accomplished family man—as the musicians who praise him acknowledge in Yorùbá, *"aponle o si f'oba ti o l'olori"* (there is no honor for a king without a queen)[106]—it is no longer just an *impression* (notion) that he is a superb impression manager; the *impression* (perception) has become reality. On Saturday, November 29, 2003, Adams married Dorcas Mojisola in Lagos. The following Monday, his and his bride's wedding photo was on the front page of *P.M. News*. Governor Bola Tinubu of Lagos attended the wedding. In fact, he played the role of the father of the groom (see chap. 5). At the traditional wedding in Ondo, Chief Gani Fawehinmi, SAN, one of Nigeria's most eminent lawyers and human rights activists, was in attendance.[107] The traditional wedding was also reported in the newspapers. Marrying a beautiful young lady was, for Adams and his admirers, a way of "marrying well," to use Kristin Mann's phrase for the phenomenon of elite marriages in late nineteenth- and early twentieth-century Lagos,[108] and also a way of consolidating his emergent status and privileges as a responsible and famous *adult*. A newspaper described Mojisola as "the jewel behind the lion."[109]

When Mojisola celebrated her birthday in 2018, Adams serenaded her on his Facebook page thus: "To a beautiful woman and a loving wife Ayinba Mojisola Adams, the light of my house; May this day, and all the days for the rest of her life be showered by blessings from God. May all your wishes and desires be fulfilled this day and the days to come, May you always remain loving, charming and adorable throughout your life as you always are. . . . Happy Birthday My Dear Wife, many happy returns. . . . Congratulations."[110]

Since 2001, when she experienced trepidation as the police stopped and later arrested her then fiancé at a checkpoint in Owutu, Ikorodu, and when she was audacious enough to allow him to live in her mother's house while he was on trial for alleged grievous crimes, Mojisola herself has gone through a significant transformation, becoming a prominent face in the media. When she had her babies, especially the twins she delivered in 2020,[111] her personal life was a subject of media attention.

FROM THE MOB TO THE MOBILE: THE SOCIAL FACILITY OF MOBILITY

The elaborate and several-hour-long installation ceremony of Gani Adams as the Ààrẹ *Ọ̀nà Kakaǹfò* (the generalissimo) of Yorubaland in January 2018 had just ended. He made his way to the fleet of vehicles that would take him, his family, and his entourage back to their hotel in Oyo. Police officers and other security personnel struggled to form a cauldron around him and his wife as hundreds of people attempted to catch a glimpse of the new *Aare*. Adams had arrived at the event in a spectacular manner along with the *Aláàfin* of Oyo, the king of Oyo town, the heir to the ancient throne of the Oyo Empire: in a horse-drawn carriage. Perhaps the people who were following wondered if his exit would be similarly dramatic.

However, the exit of the new *Aare* was not as dramatic as his entrance. This time, he was leaving in one of his SUVs, a Toyota Land Cruiser. While the entry was more dramatic, the exit was also regarded as befitting someone of Adams's latest status. His admirers and members of his group struggled with security to hail him as his car drove out of the venue. Three other SUVs followed, and his personal protective aides mounted the sides of the SUV as the *Aare* exited Atiba Stadium, Oyo.

Figure 3.24. The crowd hailing the new *Aare* in his car as he prepares to leave the venue of the installation. Photo courtesy of *Nigerian Tribune*.

"In Nigeria," states the French sociologist Jean-Pascal Daloz, "the type of automobile you drive or, better, that you entrust to your driver, sometimes classifies you ruthlessly."[112] Gani Adams's first car was a gift from a chair of a local government council in Oyo State who secretly supported the OPC. It was a 406 Peugeot. Moving from the *okada* (motorbike) he had used for occasional commercial transportation in Mushin and other low-income areas of Lagos to the *molue*, the notorious, large, and then ubiquitous Lagos commercial buses, and then to a private car of his own was a major shift in Adams's life. But it was nothing in comparison to what was to come. At a time when many regarded Adams as the leader of a mob, the lack of a *respectable* means of transportation confirmed his status as a *lumpen*. Therefore, as he transformed his means of transportation, every point in the process also signaled his social mobility.

In urban areas of Nigeria, if someone does not know whether you have a personal car but does not want to embarrass you when discussing how you will get to a particular destination, they are likely to ask, "Are you *mobile*?" This metaphor for the ownership of a personal vehicle indicates that the car is also a mark of social mobility. Even more important is the *type* of car. The bigger, more expensive, and rarer the vehicle, the more it symbolizes the owner's

Figure 3.25. The *Aare* is inside the SUV, with his personal security details mounting the sides. Photos courtesy of *Nigerian Tribune*.

level of distinction and wealth—and also conspicuous consumption.[113] Adams started with a Peugeot, which was near the bottom of the vehicular pyramid in Nigeria at the time.[114] However, he later graduated to the SUV class when another benefactor of the group, a member of the National Assembly, according to his former aides, bought him one. The SUV is a must-have in the fleet of any big man in Nigeria. Stepping into and alighting from an SUV exhibits the big man's taste in automobiles; it is also an important announcement of both the literal and metaphoric *arrival* of the big man (or big woman)—particularly at important events. Although this also depends on the class of the SUV (Prado is a favorite, but Mercedes Benz, BMW, and Jeep are good too), generally any brand-new SUV will do.

What Marxists call "commodity fetishism," as Daloz has argued, is a symbolic aspect of power and prominence that, in Marxian intellectual tradition, is dismissed as an epiphenomenon.[115] This aspect of power and prominence, as exemplified in vehicles, has always been central to the purchase of distinction throughout the ages. As Daloz reminds us, "From ancient rulers . . . to aristocrats . . . to the 'jet set' participating in high life activities across continents . . . the ability to travel rapidly, comfortably and in style has been a priority." He concludes that this "is why elites frequently attach great value to vehicles which prove to be a primary object of competitive display"—from chariots in antiquity to gorgeous coaches and elegant carriages in more recent history.[116] Other scholars have linked the performance of cars to "social hierarchies on the road,"[117] and still others, following Bourdieu, have emphasized that "aggressive overtaking" on the road can be interpreted as a form of "symbolic violence."[118] In Nigeria, such aggressive overtaking, while common, is performed most conspicuously by the powerful, who use the siren. The extravagance of the acquisition of a fleet of SUVs and other expensive vehicles, as the Adams case illustrates, shows that "consumption becomes increasingly social as incomes rise" and also becomes a matter of "positional competition" among the elite.[119]

In line with the expectations inherent in the process of becoming a big man, when he became relatively rich, Adams acquired his own SUVs. It was a bold assertion that his life of poverty had been transformed into a life of plenty. As Achille Mbembe stated when reflecting on the transformation in the life of South Africa's former leader of the ANC Youth League, Julius Malema, "A life of shame, social humiliation and dishonour is thought to be retrieved from abjection through conspicuous display and consumption of wealth."[120] Indeed, in a process that has been described as "emulatory consumption,"[121] by the time Adam was being considered for the ultimate chieftaincy title, the Ààrẹ *Ọnà Kakañfò*, he had acquired his own entourage of SUVs, complete with a lead vehicle outfitted with a siren to clear the road ahead of him and to confirm

Figure 3.26. The *Kakaǹfò* has arrived: Adams, with his staff of office, steps in front of his SUV as he arrives at an event in 2019.

his status as a very important person (VIP). Though the police repeatedly announced that people who do not have official approval to use sirens in Nigeria should desist from doing so, many big men and women in Nigeria use them on either their personal vehicles or the vehicles that lead or follow them. This practice both allows them to beat traffic and also affirms their statuses. The police usually stop those who are not *genuinely* big but who use sirens to pretend to the kind of license that *truly* big people in Nigeria have.[122]

HALLOWED BE THY STATUS

In their introduction to a recent edited volume, *The Politics of Custom: Chiefship, Capital, and the State in Contemporary Africa*,[123] John L. and Jean Comaroff ask, "How do we explain the so-called resurgence . . . in contemporary Africa, of figures who were supposed to disappear with modernity but are a rising force in many places across the continent today?" The editors and their contributors provide insightful analysis, in different countries in Africa, of how "so-called 'traditional' offices, and the culturally distinctive species of authority they presume, continue to manifest themselves in a vibrant array of forms across the continent, coexisting in various ways—sometimes in collaboration, sometimes in contestation, sometimes in creative confusion, always in reciprocally transforming interplay—with dominant regimes of power, governance, knowledge, and capital accumulation in the late modern world."[124] The Comaroffs conclude that what chieftaincy—or chiefship—is depends "both on circumstance and on the angle of vision from which it is regarded."[125] One of the critical "angle[s] of vision" for understanding chieftaincy in contemporary Africa is the capital—cultural, social, economic, political, and even spiritual or psychic—that it constitutes for those who seek and acquire it. And almost no two chiefs have entirely the same needs, motivations, and uses of their chieftaincy. This is particularly true of chiefs who are not customary *sovereigns*—that is, both "traditional" and honorary chieftaincies.

In many parts of Africa, and particularly in Nigeria, one of the most critical ways of being a person of consequence, of affirming distinction, is to have an honorific besides the *common Mr.* or *Mrs.* An "ordinary Mr. or Mrs." is an ordinary person. So, to be more than ordinary—to be *extraordinary*—one needs a title, any title, although the grander the better. From formal titles (Excellency, Honorable, Sir, Dame, Lady, Madam) to academic or professional titles (Professor, Doctor, Barrister, Architect, Surveyor); military titles (General, Lieutenant General, Major General, Brigadier General, Rear Admiral, Commodore, Colonel); religious titles (His Lordship, His Eminence, His Grace, Father, Reverend, Pastor, Elder, Senior Apostle, Venerable, Imam, Sheik); and traditional titles (Chief, High Chief, *Otunba, Aare, Basorun, Yeye, Iba, Ayinba*), there is hardly any Mr. or Mrs. left who can claim to have much distinction.[126] In fact, the more honorifics, the better. Therefore, you have "Prof. (Barrister)," "Dr. (Chief)," "Rev. (Dr.)," "Prof. (Rev.)," "Lady Evangelist (Dr.)"—or as Gani Adams was at a point, "*Otunba* (Dr.)" or "Chief (Dr.)"—and many other combinations that express the outrageous search for esteem, respect, and rank in contemporary Nigeria.

This backdrop is important to understand why Adams had to become more than a Mr. as he moved up the social ladder. But his need for a title was even more crucial given the ways in which his detractors, particularly Dr. Frederick Fasehun and some sections of the media, had dismissed him over the years as "an illiterate," "a carpenter," "an *okada* rider," and "a nobody." To become *somebody* in society, he needed a title. Even among his contemporaries in the OPC, particularly his old friends, he needed a title beyond the one conferred on him in the group. When he created his own faction, he became president of the OPC militant (or Gani Adams) faction. Still, a few of his old friends in the group, sometimes within earshot, called him his old nickname, *ganga*—a reference to the gangling frame. Other members just called him *ogu*, or boss. When I first met him, and for many years afterward, being sensitive to the obsession with titles in Nigeria, I used his formal title in the group, *president*.

Eventually, as he became more prominent, he and his closest associates felt he was due for a traditional title to affirm his new cultural and social status in

Figure 3.27. Adams after he was awarded his first chieftaincy, *Ajagungbade* (warrior), by the Meiran Caucus of the OPC. Photo courtesy of Monsuru Akande.

Yorùbá society. But since the relevant traditional authorities would not be conferring one soon, the Meiran caucus of the OPC organized a title for him: *Ajagungbade* (a war victor, who won the crown). On the basis of this title, though he did not follow the typical process to obtain it, he started to answer to *chief*. The media picked this up and stopped describing him as "Mr. Gani Adams," instead calling him "Chief Gani Adams." He was on his way to solidifying his chiefdom.

Figure 3.28. Adams's installation as Akogun of Badagry by the Oba of Badagry, Oba Claudius Dosa Akran. Photo courtesy of *Nigerian Tribune*.

As time went on and he became richer, the coveted traditional titles flooded in. The first was the title of *Otunba* (right-hand principal—chief—of the king). From this point, his preferred honorific, particularly in the media, became *Otunba* Gani Adams. Many more chieftaincies came later all over Yorubaland: *Akogun of Badagry, Aare Mayegun of Ira,* and others. By the end of 2017, he had garnered fifty-two titles.[127]

Figure 3.29. Adams (*right*) kneeling before the *Zaki* of Arigidi, *Oba* Mohammed Asunmo Olanipekun (*left*), during his installation as the *Otunba* of Arigidi. Photo courtesy of *Nigerian Tribune*.

Figure 3.30. Adams at his installation as *Aare Mayegun* of Ira in Kwara State. Photo courtesy of *Nigerian Tribune*.

Despite this flood of chieftaincies, given that virtually every member of the elite had a chieftaincy title, after many years Adams saw an opportunity to become more distinct from the countless chiefs in Yorubaland. There is only one title for the nontraditional head of a village, town, or city that is nonpareil in Yorubaland: the title of Ààrẹ *Ọ̀nà Kakaǹfò*, the generalissimo or field marshal of the imperial army of the old Oyo Empire. This title, in the post-empire age, remains highly coveted. In the postcolonial era, it had only been held by two prominent Yorùbá, one a lawyer, politician, and premier of the old Western Region, Samuel Ladoke Akintola, and the other a billionaire businessman and politician and the winner of the June 12, 1993, presidential election, Moshood Kashiwano Olawale Abiola. Abiola, the last holder of the title, died in 1998. The position had been vacant since then. Adams, who had a warm relationship with the king, the *Aláàfin* of Oyo, Oba Lamidi Adeyemi II, who appointed the *Aare*, thus trained his eyes on the position. (This is the subject of the next chapter.)

DOCTORING THE WARRIOR: EDUCATION AS DISTINCTION

On Friday, June 1, 2007, a story appeared in the Lagos-based *Nation*. It was published in other newspapers too, but the *Nation*'s reporting, headlined, "Varsity Packed as OPC's Adams Gets Doctorate Degree," is particularly instructive and bears full re-presentation:[128]

> Traffic literarily [*sic*] grounded at the entrance of the Obafemi Awolowo University (OAU), Ile-Ife, Osun State due to the large number of vehicles stirring to drive into the ivory tower.
>
> There was a large crowd of well-wishers, essentially die-hard members of the Oodua People's Congress (OPC). Also in the crowd were local musicians and dancers who added colours to the historic event.
>
> They were at the ancient city of Ile-Ife, reputed to be the cradle of the Yoruba race to celebrate Gani Adams, OPC National Co-ordinator.
>
> The Conference Centre of the University seemed so small for the crowd as the Bradley University, United States awarded Otunba Gani Adams, the National Coordinator of the OPC[,] a doctorate degree. The award came barely a week after Adams and his lieutenants received diplomas in Tourism Management from the Ghana-based International Institute of Aviation.[129]
>
> Decked in a cream Giorgio Armani suit, the recipient was accompanied by Erelu Mojisola, his wife, whose designer sunshade added colour to a memorable affair.
>
> Expressing delight at Adam's recognition, Prof Paul Kunle Jegede thanked God for granting guests journey from Lagos and other parts of the country.
>
> "We are here to honour the excellence of an illustrious Nigerian. May I also add that there is no time limit to celebrate or recognise excellence because

Figure 3.31. Adams being presented with the certificate of his honorary doctorate awarded by Bradley University. Professor Paul Kunle Jegede, reportedly an alumnus of Bradley, presented the degree. Photo courtesy of *Nigerian Tribune*.

every time, people embark and disembark from the bus of life," he said. Jegede explained that the choice of Ife as the venue of the occasion was based on its unquestionable spiritual and cultural significance as the cradle of the Yoruba race.

He said owing to his pedigree as a PhD student at the Bradley University, "the university authority gave me the honour to represent her in honorary doctoral awards by recommending notable and outstanding achievers to the university."

"What we should realise is that there are men and women of high societal standings who could be honoured. However, many are called but few are chosen and among the chosen ones are the people sitting in front of you today," he told the ecstatic audience who thundered shouts of Odua. Lives of great men who reached immense heights, in Prof Jegede's view, were not attained by sudden flights.

"Such attainments mean that while their companions slept, they toiled even in the night. Surely, we can make our lives sublime and at our departure, leave behind footprints on the sands of time. Therefore, we are here today to make

> history by honouring somebody who deserves all the encouragement he can get," he added. Jegede urged the recipient to live up to the responsibility of his new status. . . . Jegede urged Adams to continue to show the light as Nigeria strives for freedom from all manner of oppressions. His praise for Adams was described by Mr. Tunde Ilesanmi as weighty "because the man is widely regarded in the Ife academic circle as a man whose little words carry a lot of weight."
>
> Adams confessed to *The Nation* that words could hardly describe his feelings. He expressed joy over the show of solidarity displayed by a teeming gathering of friends and well-wishers. He stated that the event was, indeed, significant in the annals of the history of the Yoruba emancipation group.
>
> "Today, I am recognised for my contributions to human and social development. As a freedom fighter and ardent defender of social rights, I am impressed that my modest inputs have not gone unnoticed," he said. Adams explained that the presence of many Nigerians was a testimony of their affection for his person and cause.
>
> "With the conferment by Bradley University, it has become clear that service to humanity is worthwhile and rewarding, not necessarily in terms of financial benefits but in a more elevated form of appreciation."
>
> "May I state at this point that the OPC is doing all it can afford to promote education because of its power to strengthen the body and mind, hence our involvement in the annual celebration of International Literacy Day and other literacy promoting programmes," he added.

"People at the top often prove to be exceedingly worried about possible deficiencies," argues Daloz.[130] Focusing on Big Men in Nigeria, Daloz alerts us to the fact that "lacunae are quickly interpreted [by the Big Man] as denoting a lack of substance," adding that "it is so in the eyes of competitors, and in those of supporters within the community or faction one claims to represent. Typically, Big Men with little education will thus attempt to buy an *honoris causa* degree and will happily add the qualification 'Dr' to their business card."[131]

As discussed earlier, the conferment of an honorary doctorate on Adams illustrates the quest for distinction through titles. But Adams's search for, and obtainment of, an honorary doctorate from an American university was not just another example of his quest for titles—in this case, an "academic" title, which he described in the story above as an "elevated form of appreciation"—it was also a demonstration of his astute conclusion that, in the long term, he would not be treated with much respect among his Yorùbá constituents in particular, and the rest of the country and the world in general, if he did not acquire (educational) *certificates*. He recognized that while *true* education was useful, in his current station in life, he might have difficulty obtaining much

Figure 3.32. Adams and his wife, Mojisola, at the ceremony for the conferment of an honorary doctorate at the Obafemi Awolowo University, Ile-Ife. Photo courtesy of *Nigerian Tribune*.

formal—particularly tertiary and perhaps also (post)graduate—education.[132] However, it was possible and necessary for him to acquire the *certification* that came from some form of formal education—no matter how that was achieved. Thus, the honorary doctorate was both a fast-tracking of his *education* (or more functionally, *certification*) as well as a socioacademic affirmation of his journey toward social distinction.

The media understandably avoided a few questions that could be raised about this award. Thus, the nature of the reporting raises some interesting points. First the questions: Why was a man whose "service to humanity," to use his own words, in reference to his provisions for his community in Southwest Nigeria, not attracting honor from the many universities in his homeland but rather being recognized by an American institution? Was it a case of "a prophet is without honor among his people"? Or was an honor from a foreign university "a more elevated form of appreciation," to use Adams's words? How did an American university become aware of his "service to humanity"—given, at that point, the existing negative reports on past OPC-inspired violence in the foreign media; state, foreign, and international departments of major countries;

and the annual Human Rights Watch reports? Why did no representative of the American institution attend the event, and why was Bradley reportedly represented by its alumnus, an OAU professor?

Beyond the questions are some interesting points about the conferment. Not one of the newspapers that reported the event mentioned the city or state where Bradley is located. The only Bradley University in the United States is in Peoria, Illinois. It is significant that the *Nation*'s editorial adviser, star columnist and communications professor Olatunji Dare, was then teaching at Bradley. The newspaper reporter would be expected to know this and therefore be able to locate Bradley more precisely on the map than to report only that it is based in the United States. Moreover, none of the newspapers that reported the event bothered to confirm the award from Bradley, not to indicate that they doubted its authenticity but in fact to confer further authenticity through their reporting, given the gale of certificate forgery and fake claims to academic certification that had been witnessed in Nigeria among the elite, particularly since the return to democratic rule in 1999.[133] None of the newspapers noted that the award was honoris causa, which would have emphasized the fact that such an award involved the waiving "of [all] the usual requirements, such as matriculation, attendance, course credits, a dissertation, and the passing of comprehensive examinations." The newspapers also neither sought to confirm Professor Paul Kunle Jegede's claim that a Bradley "university authority gave [him] the honour to represent her in honorary doctoral awards by recommending notable and outstanding achievers to the university" nor gave any indication of Jegede's own status at the OAU (or at any other university, let alone his discipline), where the event was held. They only mentioned "his [Jegede's] pedigree as a PhD student at the Bradley University," without indicating whether that meant he was an alumnus of Bradley or, at that time, a current PhD student. But all of these would be dismissed as needless nitpicking, particularly given that Tunde Ilesanmi, another person whose status was not stated in the story, gave credence to Jegede's lavish praise of Adams by describing it as "weighty 'because the man is widely regarded in the Ife academic circle[134] as a man whose little words carry a lot of weight.'"

I describe Adams's pursuit of tertiary education certificates as a form of *fast-tracking* because, once he settled down after the era of incessant violence involving the OPC and his incarceration, he sought postsecondary education as soon as possible. He did so as much to gain social distinction as to end the incessant derogatory references to him as an "illiterate." But since he did not finish high school, the only way he could seek admission for postsecondary education was to get the school leaving certificate—either through the standard

Figure 3.33. Adams's aides whiling away the time by playing an *ayo* game when they accompanied their leader to Iseyin to take the GCE exams. Photo courtesy of Monsuru Akande.

West African Examination Council (WAEC) exam with formal registration in a high school or through the General Certificate of Education (GCE) exam, which could be taken as an external student. To do this without attracting attention from the press in Lagos, he went to the north of Oyo State to register for the exam. While I could not gain access to the results, it is obvious that he passed enough subjects to register for a diploma in tourism management in the International Aviation School, Tema, Ghana, in 2003. In a process described by one of his admirers as a "drive for self-improvement" and an attempt to "further sharpen his academic capabilities,"[135] Adams later registered for a diploma in international relations and strategic studies at the Lagos State University (LASU) and then used both diplomas for admission into the degree course in political science at LASU. He earned a bachelor's degree in political science from LASU on May 24, 2018.

There is no doubt that Adams's effort to gain formal education is impressive. He also encouraged other members of the OPC, particularly the top members who did not have formal education, to go back to school. A few of his lieutenants also studied for diplomas.

Figure 3.34. Adams wearing his bachelor's graduation gown in his home on May 24, 2018. Photo courtesy of *Nigerian Tribune*.

However, what is most crucial is the recognition of, action toward, and *successful* accomplishment of educational certification for someone who desired to become a big man in contemporary Nigerian society. Indeed, it can be argued that Adams succeeded in his bid to gain respect for his academic accomplishment, as reporters and interviewers in the media (print, broadcast, and online) constantly reference his degrees and also use the honorific *Dr.* to refer to him. The honorific is also usually boldly displayed in event programs and in giant posters for his anniversaries, particularly birthdays.

It is important to raise a few issues here. Even before Adams attained postsecondary education, and despite the attacks on his limited literacy, he was demonstrably a smart person who probably would have done very well in high school if his education had not been truncated. He spoke sufficiently comprehensible, or perhaps passable, English at this point, even before he furthered his education. And since then, he has improved considerably. Also, in the same era—that is, before going back to school—Adams showed remarkable knowledge of Nigeria's history (though his take on that history could be contested by his adversaries) and of the most pertinent history of global struggles for democracy and human rights. Finally, as he stated at the conferment, the OPC, under his leadership, was "doing all it [could] afford to promote education because of its power to strengthen the body and mind." For example, Adams—in the immediate postviolence stage of the group's history—encouraged all his aides, mostly artisans, who had not completed secondary school or did not have postsecondary education to go back to school. His erstwhile aide Monsuru Akande told me that he "asked everyone to go to school, to get diplomas and degrees." Adams recognized that it was not sufficient for him to shed the image of an illiterate; those among his ranks who were not educated also needed to do so to raise the general literacy level in the group—which already included a few university graduates and some professionals—thus ensuring that his image as the leader was enhanced.

PAGEANTRY, FESTIVALS, RELIGIOUS PLURALITY AND CULTURAL 'EXEMPLARITY'

Gani Adams was in an especially jolly mood one mid-October morning in 2019. As the activities for the annual *Olokun* Festival were set to commence, he radiated warmth. No one can say exactly why he was so happy, but his excitement was infectious among his aides, members of the OPC, and guests. At this, the seventeenth year of the festival, he told the audience, "It is the only festival that has been consistent since we started in 2002. Even when I was in jail, it held."

A line in Adams's speech points to the importance of the Olokun Festival as the first of the festivals he and his group organized, coordinated, or participated in: "These [festivals] are parts of our struggles."[136]

Figure 3.35. In the midst of beauty queens. Adams and the winners and runners-up of various beauty pageants. Photo by Dapo Adeseko. Courtesy of *Encomium* magazine.

Figure 3.36. Misses Kwara, Abuja, Lagos, Ekiti, and Osun at the Miss Olokun 2015 contest. Photo courtesy of *Encomium* magazine.

Figure 3.37. Adams crowns Miss Olokun 2015. Photo by Dapo Adeseko. Courtesy of *Encomium* magazine.

Figure 3.38. Adams arriving at the Olokun Festival in 2006. On the right is Segun Akanni, his aide. Photo courtesy of *Nigerian Tribune*.

Figure 3.39. Miss Olokun 2014 poses with Adams and his wife, Mojisola. Photo by Dapo Adeseko. Courtesy of *Encomium* magazine.

He lamented the financial challenges of hosting the festival and the 2019 edition's inability to meet previous festivals' standards because he could not attract sponsorship from the relevant organizations. However, he concluded, "But we will continue to promote our cultural heritage. Through our activities that are widely reported, we are telling the world that Nigeria is peaceful for foreigners to come and invest. But we will not want the Lagos government to take it over and relegate us to the back bench."[137]

The description of the festivals as part of the OPC's struggles—for the promotion and defense of Yorùbá cultural and self-determination, among others—indicates that, though the celebrations were not part of the OPC's specific remit for the first eight years of its founding, in the immediate postviolence era, Adams, as a strategic improviser, started thinking about what to do next with a group that had become so visible and powerful yet needed redirection and a new mission. He realized that the incessant clashes with Fasehun's faction and other ethnic groups, the vigilante activities, and the general violence would not sustain the group in the future. He had achieved name recognition; now he needed to leverage that to become someone of consequence in society. Violence and unofficial policing (vigilantism) were an insufficient even if initially useful means of *self*-transformation. Therefore, as the embodiment of the OPC, to ensure *self*-transformation, Adams first needed to transform the group's image,[138] including its essential and practical purpose. To do this, he needed to capitalize on the revalorization of culture and thus "create new sources of identity, income, [and] empowerment."[139]

Among the Yorùbá, the secularization of religious culture that started in the era described by J. D. Y Peel as *aye oyinbo* (the age of the white man—from missionary contact to the colonial era), which then became *aye olaju* (the age of Enlightenment, civilization, progress, and development), has meant that the majority of the Yorùbá, regardless of their conversion or adherence to either Christianity or Islam, embrace cultural practices that they often approach as separate from, or not completely immersed in, traditional Yorùbá religion. Even where some of these practices are deeply embedded in orisa worship (Yorùbá religion), many Yorùbá still participate in these practices in one form or another because they approach it as practicing culture rather than religion. Therefore, an elaborate organization of the celebration of the Yorùbá gods can be packaged and received as a *cultural festival* rather than as a form of traditional religious worship. Jacob K. Olupona has described this phenomenon as "civil religion."[140] It is therefore understandable that a number of clerics from both the Christian and Islamic religions participate in the Olokun Festival annually by praying for its success. Thus, the festival also unites the Yorùbá across

Figure 3.40. An Islamic leader visits Adams in his Lagos home. In the background, Islamic and Christian symbols are prominently displayed in his living room. Photo courtesy of *P.M. News*.

Figure 3.41. Adams with a Celestial Church of God cleric at a church service. Photo courtesy of *TheNEWS*.

religions, emphasizing their identity as Yorùbá as more important than their religious identities.

This is the background in which Adams created the Olokun Festival Foundation and the Gani Adams Foundation as instruments of "promoting culture" and engaging in sociocultural activities. He recognized that most Yorùbá embrace cultural festivals despite their religious affiliation. Even the most fervent Yorùbá Christians and Muslims (excepting the deeply conservative "fundamentalists") can tolerate deep *cultural* celebrations. Therefore, elaborate cultural celebrations opened up endless possibilities for Adams. Cultural festivals had the potential to turn him into a cultural ambassador and even icon, as well as to create avenues for relationships with a variety of traditional institutions, social groups, and highly placed individuals who might not otherwise be eager to associate with him and the OPC. Corporate organizations might want to tap into the tourism potential of annual festivals. Thus, both government and corporate sponsorships could offer opportunities for financial support for his group.

In the light of these potentials, and in his quest to become a *cultural exemplar*[141]—and to use this status to promote Yorùbá culture and further leverage himself within the Yorùbá nation and among the Yorùbá diaspora in Africa and beyond—Adams, in his postviolence life, decided to concentrate on cultural activities.

When he first started the Olokun Festival, it garnered limited support. But as the years rolled by, it became a major point on the cultural calendar. In Yorùbá religion, Olokun is an *orisa*. It is regarded as the god of all bodies of water and as the highest god among all water deities, but it is particularly identified with the deep sea (*okun*). It is also the parent of *Aje*, the god of wealth. It is represented as either male or female or as both. But there are two sides to this *orisa*: there is a positive, beneficial, or benign part that holds the potential for wealth and the mysteries at the bottom of the ocean, and there is the negative or dangerous part that can sink ships, cause flooding, and swallow people. In a sense, it can be an ambivalent spirit, captured by the Yorùbá belief that money and wealth are related to Olokun—*awo Olokun*. Thus, this spirit can determine both wealth and want, and thus it needs to be worshipped or appeased.

"The move to establish Olokun Festival foundation was really actuated by the [pace] at which we were fast losing the value of our festivals and culture," Adams told the tourism editor of the *Nigerian Tribune* in 2017. "I was provoked to inaugurate Olokun Festival when our people were being overrun by the terrible indoctrination that our festivals were fetish, diabolic and of no economic value. In [many towns] the indoctrination nearly led to the abandonment of some of the precious festivals which were . . . reminders and preservers of values,

Figure 3.42. Promoting Culture: Contestants for Miss Olokun 2015 performing like Olokun worshippers. Photo by Dapo Adeseko. Courtesy of *Encomium* magazine.

Figure 3.43. Cultural performance by some young people during one of the editions of the Olokun Festival. Photo courtesy of Segun Akanni.

Figure 3.44. Adams with some traditional rulers as the national anthem is rendered at the Olokun Festival. Photo courtesy of Segun Akanni.

norms, unique entertainment, songs, dances, chants and mores. I cannot just stand there [and] allow this to happen during my life time. So, we decided to inaugurate the foundation and the promotion of these 18 festivals in Yoruba land."[142]

At one of the annual celebrations, Adams stated, "We spend our personal money and sacrifice our time and efforts for the good of all Nigerians. But we will continue to promote our cultural heritage. Through our activities that are widely reported, we are telling the world that Nigeria is peaceful for foreigners to come and invest. But we will not want the Lagos government to take it over and relegate us to the back bench. We cannot deny the economic benefits that our host community, Lagos and Nigeria have been enjoying since we started the festival some years ago. Apart from the *spiritual blessings*, it has brought tourist attraction to Lagos," Adams told the audience.[143] The media also reported that Adams "vowed that despite the lack of sponsorship and other hurdles, nothing would stop him from hosting the annual Olokun Festival."[144]

Apart from the "spiritual blessings" he mentioned and the cultural and economic benefits, hosting the festival annually has provided immense personal benefits for Adams. Perhaps part of the reason he was happy, despite the low-key activities of the festival in 2019, was that it was the second year of the celebration since he was installed as the *Kakañfò*. And as the *Aláàfin* of Oyo, Oba Lamidi Adeyemi II, who appointed him to the position, told me, Adams's promotion of Yorùbá culture was one of the reasons he considered appointing him as the

Ààrẹ *Ọ̀nà Kakaǹfò*. Tayo Ogunbiyi, the chair of the Publications Committee of the Nigerian Union of Journalists, Lagos State Council, stated that Adams's appointment as *Kakaǹfò* attested to his "undying and conscientious passion for the promotion of Yoruba culture and tradition."[145]

Beyond this, organizing the Olokun Festival and other festivals has expanded Adams's network widely among the Yorùbá both at home and in the diaspora. For instance, until he died in 2012, one of the constant notable figures in virtually every one of Adams's events was Ambassador Segun Olusola, former TV producer, broadcaster, cultural ambassador, and envoy to Ethiopia. With such credible people around Adams, others felt comfortable enough, over time, to show up at his events.

Organizing the festivals also connects Adams culturally to many Yorùbá communities and their traditional rulers and guardians of culture, thus presenting him with another powerful network of relationships that are strong and enduring. It has also served as a link between him and non-Yorùbá and even non-Nigerian institutions, groups, and individuals promoting culture and tourism around the world. Additionally, the festivals' opening ceremonies provide a platform for Adams—and sometimes other dignitaries he invites to the events—to make statements about himself, the OPC, and the state of the nation that usually receive wide coverage in the media. For instance, during the 2020 *Eledumare* (Almighty God) Festival, Adams urged the governors of the six Southwest states to declare an annual two-day public holiday to celebrate across the region to "promote the core values of the Yoruba race." He also noted that the festival "has transformed the image of OPC, it has brought peace and tranquillity to us. Eledumare has rewarded all our efforts, [both] physically or spiritually, by transforming the image of OPC from bad to good patriotic Nigerians and thus becoming the most vibrant organisation in the South-West."[146]

After the initial success of the Olokun Festival, Adams revived more festivals, attracted greater media attention to still others, and joined other people in celebrating their own. Because of this, he is constantly in the news as a cultural ambassador and responsible cultural citizen of the Yorùbá world, home and abroad. Some of these festivals also include beauty competitions among young women for titles such as Miss Oodua, Miss Olumo, Miss Okota, Miss Olokun, and Miss Oya.

The addition of beauty contests also widened the appeal of the festival among young women and even attracted other dignitaries, such as Sally Mbanefo, the director general of the Nigerian Tourism Development Commission.

The Olokun Festival Foundation, in conjunction with the Gani Adams Foundation, celebrates the *Okota* Festival in Adams's hometown of Arigidi (Ondo State) in June every year. They also join in the celebration of the *Osun*

Figure 3.45. The winner of one of the earliest editions of Miss Olokun with female members of the OPC. Adams in the background, behind the second woman on the right. Photo courtesy of Monsuru Akande.

Figure 3.46. Adams (*second from left*) with Miss Olokun 2016, Sally Mbanefo, director general, Nigerian Tourism Development Commission, and Miss Oodua 2015. Photo courtesy of Segun Akanni.

Figure 3.47. Miss Olokun 2004 with Miss Okota 2015, Miss Oodua 2014, and Miss Oya 2014. Photo by Dapo Adeseko. Courtesy of *Encomium* magazine.

Osogbo Festival and Oodua Festival in Ile-Ife (Osun State) and *Oke* Ibadan Festival (Oyo State), among others.

During the 2019 edition of the Oodua Festival, the *Ooni* of Ife, Oba Adeyeye Enitan Ogunwusi, Ojaja II, the powerful king of Ile-Ife who presently occupies the stool of Oduduwa (Oodua), the Yorùbá progenitor, acknowledged Adams's role in promoting the cultural identity of the Yorùbá. He added that the annual Oodua Festival constitutes "a pleasant homecoming for all members of the Oodua Progressive Union (OPU) across all the 79 countries in the world, and the Oodua People's Congress in Nigeria." He stated, "The Oodua festival we are celebrating today provides a big opportunity for everybody present to meet and relate with one another." Then he added, "As great sons and daughters of the Yoruba race, we must not fail in our duty to project the cultural identity of the Yoruba race as it is being promoted by *Aare* Adams, through the Olokun Festival Foundation and the OPC."[147]

All these festivals and the affirmations and acknowledgments that he garners from them consolidate Adams's public image as an exemplary man and leader in Yorubaland.

MEDIATIZATION AND MEDIATION

Gani Adams was reveling in the approaching glory as he drove out of the palace of the *Aláàfin* in Oyo, *Oba* Lamidi Adeyemi III, in late 2017. He had just secured the much-awaited official letter from the monarch appointing him as the fifteenth Ààrẹ *Ọ̀nà Kakaǹfò* of Yorubaland. His chief of staff, Segun Akanni, posted the letter on his Facebook page. A few minutes later, Adams's phone rang. It was Lasisi Olagunju, the editor of the *Saturday Tribune* and former chief press secretary to the governor of Osun State, calling to congratulate Adams. He had just seen the post online and wanted to quickly celebrate with the *Kakaǹfò*-designate. Adams thanked him.

"He [Adams] is fantastic with media relations," his erstwhile friend Wale Adedayo told me in 2012. Some top members of the OPC disclosed that, in the early years of his emergence, Adams even organized transportation for journalists to wherever he was hosting an event, apart from also "taking care of them." A close associate volunteered, "He even knows the positioning of stories in newspapers. He persuades journalists to place his stories and photographs in particular pages in the newspaper." The associate added that some big men who had issues with the media sometimes sought Adams's intervention because they recognized that he "understands the press."

Figure 3.48. Adams being interviewed by Sunday Olajide of the *Nigeria Tribune* around 2002–3. Olajide later became editor of *Saturday Tribune*. Photo courtesy of *Nigerian Tribune*.

Figure 3.49. Adams being presented a copy of the *Nigerian Tribune* during a visit to the newspaper's Lagos office by John Awe, one of the reporters, around 2004. By this time, Adams had jettisoned the French suit in the photograph above for *buba* and *sokoto* with a cap. Photo courtesy of *Nigerian Tribune.*

"You cannot underrate the power of the media," Adams stated in an interview, "especially when there is frequency of negative news about you."[148] By the time he became the *Aare*-designate, Adams worried less about negative news. Most of his depictions in the media, particularly in print and broadcast, were positive, until around late 2020, when Sunday Igboho emerged to contest his primacy in Yorùbá nationalism (see chap. 6). They generally reinforced his position as a person of consequence. He had succeeded, after many years of obsessive but methodical cultivation of the media, particularly the print platforms, in turning himself, his activities, and even his family into perpetual news items. He has a phalanx of reporters, line editors, and broadcasters as personal or social friends—some even at his beck and call. Many editors, publishers, and even media managers are also a phone call away. Adams did not need to attend a media and communications class or read a book that explains mediatization theory to understand that the media shapes the processes of political

Figure 3.50. Adams, the Àare Ònà *Kakaǹfò* of Yorubaland, is interviewed by reporters.

communication and society or the resultant "influence [the] media exert[s] on society and culture."[149] He already understood these in practice.

The editor's swift response to the post on Adams's social media page was not unusual. It fell into the pattern created by the extensive media contacts that Adams had built over time and that helped to sustain and defend his status and even propel him into greater heights—as the new appointment as Àarẹ *Ọ̀nà Kakaǹfò* attested.

As the unceasing coverage of Adams and his group (including OPC press activities and press releases, and festivals as well as Adams's political interventions, wedding, birthday ceremonies, and birth or naming ceremonies for his children)[150] shows, Adams himself became what old-time editors would call "good copy"—that is, interesting news. There is always something about him that can be published or broadcast. Adams's total investment in all means of

Figure 3.51. Evidently, appearing in a photograph in which he is seated beside Africa's first winner of the Nobel Prize in Literature, Wole Soyinka, is a major achievement for a man who was dismissed as an "illiterate" only a few years earlier. Photo courtesy of *Guardian*, July 21, 2012.

communication—from traditional to social media, with a particular emphasis on visuality, both still and moving—and the mediation that is central to his unceasing elaboration of rank and dignity invoke the kind of entanglement of the media "with [the phenomenon or processes] they contribute to mediate" that Birgit Meyer captures in her study of the Pentecostal churches in Ghana.[151] Ebenezer Obadare's study of Pentecostal pastors in Nigeria reflects a similar investment in mediatization and mediation.[152]

When, in 2002, Adams and Monsuru Akande jumped on an *okada* to go to the African Independent Television (AIT) premises in Alagbado, a distance of about twenty-seven kilometers, for his first television interview, the OPC leader could not have anticipated a life of such ceaseless media attention. But once he recognized the media's value for his sociopolitical and personal projects, Adams deployed everything in his power to court journalists and broadcasters—and later bloggers and entertainers—to, directly or indirectly, shape his own image and also validate his status as a newsmaker and part of the cultural crème de la crème.

Although he appeared in the newspapers as a wanted criminal between 1999 and 2001 or on the cover of *TELL* magazine in handcuffs in 2001, in the post-2006 era, newspaper stories about Adams have mostly concerned his interventions in political, economic, social, cultural, and religious life in Nigeria and beyond.

Figure 3.52. Adams, Okei-Odumakin, and Wole Soyinka at a public event in 2007. Photo courtesy of *Nigerian Tribune.*

At his and other major public events, he is joined by the leading lights of the public sphere in Nigeria, as well as the biggest names in the country. There is hardly any category of high society that Adams does not associate with, both in public and in private. His name and statements also appear in headlines beside those of statesmen, governors, retired generals, professors, diplomats, leading experts, and other respected Nigerians, such as Professor Wole Soyinka, the first Black Nobel laureate in literature.[153]

He has also mobilized the power of visuals as a crucial component of his overall processes of self-aggrandizement and his specific practices of impression management. He always has a photographer or videographer with him. No public engagement—or even important private engagement, as when a VIP visits his home—escapes the camera lens. When I visited him at his home in December 2017, a few weeks after the announcement of his pending installation as the *Aare*, a photographer was on hand to take the photographs of all consequential people who visited him—or whom he visited or met at a public event.[154]

From statesmen, politicians, traditional rulers, captains of industry, scholars, and public intellectuals to cultural icons, celebrities, popular musicians, and other entertainers, the who's who of the Nigerian society have appeared in photographs with Adams.[155] To use Susan Sontag's words, these "photographs furnish evidence" of his eminence and thus become "a social rite" as well as "a

Figure 3.53. Dr. Joe Okei-Odumakin, president of Campaign for Democracy, visiting Adams at home in the late 2000s. Photo courtesy of *Nigerian Tribune*.

tool of power."[156] And through the display of these photographs (both in his home and in the media), Adams "translates into photography the panegyric tendency that pervades popular self-projection arts in the Yoruba cultural environment."[157] Generally, among the Yorùbá, as Stephen Sprague has argued, the photograph is a "literal record and memory device" and "an object symbolizing respect and status."[158] Adéèkó identifies the particular subgenre of the Yorùbá panegyric that helps one to understand the passion for photography as *oríkì bọ̀rọ̀ kìní* (chants in praise of the eminent).[159] As *bọ̀rọ̀kìní* (the eminent, or elite), Adams is in constant need of the *visual praise poetry* that photographs of his eminence, and his photographs with the eminent, constitute. Though Adams told the press that his name "rings louder" than those of many governors—which is true—he still needs visual appearances with these governors to further affirm his elite status. Through these images, Adams "shines in prominent circles, in which it is important to be seen."[160] As Goffman argued many decades ago, "The social identity of those an individual is with can be used as a source of information concerning his own social identity, the assumption being that he is what others are."[161]

As he socializes with the rich and powerful within and beyond Nigeria, some of his erstwhile comrades argue that Adams has been transformed from someone who was committed to the liberation of the subaltern to a protector

Figure 3.54. Adams meeting Dr. Bukola Saraki, the president of the Senate, in the latter's office in Abuja. Photo courtesy of *Nigerian Tribune*.

Figure 3.55. Adams in conference with the Senate president, Dr. Bukola Saraki. Photo courtesy of *Nigerian Tribune*.

Figure 3.56. Adams and Governor Aminu Tambuwal, former Speaker of the Federal House of Representatives and current governor of Sokoto State. Photo courtesy of *Nigerian Tribune*.

Figure 3.57. Adams visiting General Theophilus Danjuma, billionaire businessman and former defense minister. Photo courtesy of *Nigerian Tribune*.

Figure 3.58. Adams with Governor Abiola Ajimobi of Oyo State. Photo courtesy of *Nigerian Tribune.*

Figure 3.59. Adams with Governor Akinwumi Ambode of Lagos State. Photo courtesy of *Nigerian Tribune.*

Figure 3.60. Adams visiting former governor Gbenga Daniel of Ogun State in his Sagamu home. Photo courtesy of *Nigerian Tribune.*

of privilege. Rather than succeeding in his initial project of "restructuring" Nigeria to make it a better federation, Adams himself, some of his critics say, "has been *restructured.*"[162]

Mediatization is further leveraged through (inter)nationalization. After the years of violent clashes with other ethnic groups in Lagos and elsewhere in Yorubaland, Adams developed strategic relations with leaders or key members

Figure 3.61. Adams; Smart Adeyemi, the president of the Nigerian Union of Journalists and later the senator representing Kogi West (*immediate left of Adams*); members of the Arewa Consultative Assembly; and others in Minna in 2003. Photo courtesy of *Nigerian Tribune*.

of these groups in Nigeria. Since around 2009, many of his events have been attended by leaders of the Hausa, Igbo, Ijaw, and other ethnic groups in Lagos. He also meets and plays host to political leaders of these ethnic groups. In these other power mongers' quest for different forms of advantage or leverage on a range of issues, there is a mutual agreement to leave the interethnic violent clashes of the past behind as they forge relationships with Adams, who has quickly become a power broker in Southwest Nigeria. With labor leaders who need to mobilize people for picketing or protests and ambitious politicians who wish to appear popular with the masses in Yorubaland, Adams negotiates a system of mutual benefits that often redound in his favor. For instance, one of Adams's aides revealed that a journalist, Smart Adeyemi (later a senator from Kogi State), sought Adams's help when he felt threatened during his bid for the leadership of the Nigerian Union of Journalists. The aide claimed that Adeyemi rewarded Adams by introducing him to a rich and influential retired general who became a huge source of financial support.

With the OPC boasting chapters in thirty-three of Nigeria's thirty-six states,[163] many politicians, including President Goodluck Jonathan, saw a potential for huge electoral support. This, a source told me, was part of what convinced Oronto Douglas, the late environmental rights activist and Ijaw nationalist who later became President Jonathan's close aide, to provide Adams access to the president, who, at any rate, knew Adams by reputation (see chap. 5).

THE CULTURAL AMBASSADOR AND (INTER)NATIONALIZATION

Eventually, Adams decided to internationalize his influence. Recognizing the huge population of the Yorùbá diaspora, he created the Oodua Progressive Union (OPU), an organization separate from the OPC that is open to all Yorùbá descendants abroad. With the OPU, he had a reason to tour the world in a bid to establish chapters in different countries, from Africa and Asia to Europe and the Americas. He also created a huge network of relationships that further burnished his image as the custodian of Yorùbá values and a propagator of culture. By 2017, he could boast of OPU chapters in seventy-nine countries. When I visited him in 2016 at his Omole Phase II home, he introduced me to the head of the chapter of one of the East Asian countries, who was visiting Nigeria and staying in his house. Adams regularly travels around the world to either inaugurate new chapters or visit existing chapters, from southern Africa and East Asia to the UK and Canada. During such "world tours," as he describes them, Adams is received at the Nigerian consulates and by major institutions such as the British Broadcasting Corporation (BBC) in London.

Figure 3.62. Adams and others at the Oodua Progressive Union World Congress in 2019, held in Akure. Photo courtesy of *Nigerian Tribune*.

Figure 3.63. Adams and others at the launch of OPU Canada. Photo courtesy of Segun Akanni.

Early in 2019, delegates from the OPU chapters around the world converged in Akure, Ondo State, for the Fifth OPU World Congress, hosted by Adams, who is the global convener of the organization. The media described the meeting as "a perfect mixture of pure Yoruba tradition, royalty, rich culture, intellectual discussions, fashion and glamour."[164] In February 2022, the OPU celebrated its ten-year anniversary, where a book entitled *OPU: Globalizing Yoruba Value and Culture* was presented. "Since its inception, [the] OPU has morphed into a global brand with a diaspora organization in 96 countries across six continents of the world. But we still have about 40 countries that are yet to be launched officially. In the coming years, all these countries will be inaugurated officially," Adams said at the event.[165] The chair of the OPU Tenth Anniversary Planning Committee and European Coordinator of OPU, Chief Victor Adewale, echoed Adams [166]

Adams has perfected an important technique of self-aggrandizement: the public discourse. It has helped him tremendously in gaining further traction in the media and in becoming an elite. The technique has two interconnected aspects: the discourse of the *good* Yorùbá and that of the *bad* Yorùbá.

Obafemi Awolowo, the late statesman, politician, and philosopher who was regarded as the leader of the Yorùbá, remains Adams's number one exemplar and ultimate signifier of the *good* Yorùbá.[167] Adams often refers to Awolowo.[168]

Figure 3.64. Adams, hosted by the Nigerian high commissioner to South Africa (*sitting right of Adams*) at the Nigerian House in Johannesburg. Owa Ajero of Ijero-Ekiti, Oba Joseph Adebayo Adewole Arojojoye II (*sitting far left*), and Onigbaye of Igbaye, Oba Joseph Moronfoye Okunlola-Oni, Ejiolu IV (*sitting far right*), accompanied him on the visit. Standing behind them are OPU members in South Africa. Photo courtesy of Segun Akanni.

But he also references others, including the late Moshood Abiola, a billionaire businessman, publisher, and politician and Adams's predecessor as *Aare*; the late Bola Ige, a lawyer, author, and federal attorney general and the Second Republic governor of Oyo State; and the late Gani Fawehinmi, SAN and social critic. For Adams, "the transcendent accomplishments of [these] predecessors act as long-lasting model[s] of reference."[169] By constantly invoking the names

Figure 3.65. Adams with the Nigerian high commissioner to the UK, Ambassador Oguntade, and the traditional ruler of his hometown, *Zaki Arigidi* of Arigidi-Akoko, *Oba* Yisa Olanipekun, at the Nigerian House in London. Photo courtesy of Segun Akanni.

Figure 3.66. Adams with Dr. Onabanjo, a Nigerian based in Atlanta, Georgia. Photo courtesy of Segun Akanni.

Figure 3.67. Adams with Germany's consul general in Nigeria. Photo courtesy of *Nigerian Tribune*.

Figure 3.68. Adams visiting Awolowo's widow, Mrs. HID Awolowo. Photo courtesy of *Nigerian Tribune*.

Figure 3.69. Adams with Dr. Mrs. Tokunbo Awolowo Dosumu, daughter of Chief of Obafemi Awolowo, at a ceremony. Photo courtesy of *Nigerian Tribune*.

of these exemplars, Adams discursively presents himself as someone in their image[170]—one who could succeed to their position of eminence (as he eventually did with Abiola). Indeed, one Pius Oyeniran Abioje, writing from the University of Ilorin, indicates that Adams's self-reflection has worked on some of his audience. Abioje published a letter to the editor in which he states inter alia:

> Gani Adams is now a Yoruba traditional chief. He shares his Gani with Chief Gani Fawehinmi, and his Adams with the Comrade Governor [of Edo State], Adams Oshiomhole. Like those he shares his names with, uneasy lies on the head that wears a crown, not just silver and gold, but serious responsibility for Chief Gani Adams: *he has been tipped for the position of Deputy Yoruba Leader*, by a cross section of his followers and admirers across Yorubaland. . . . I don't know his age either, except to say that the Yoruba monarchical system and the *tender age at which Pa Obafemi Awolowo became the Yoruba Leader indicates that age is no obstacle to leadership* in the land.[171]

ADAMS WITH YORÙBÁ ROYALTY: A VISUAL REFLECTION

Then there is the obverse. Adams constantly inveighs against those he regards as the *bad* Yorùbá, as an indirect way of contrasting them with himself, the *good* Yorùbá. Through the constant glorification of some good Yorùbá leaders (almost always those who are dead—Awolowo, Abiola, Ige, Fawehinmi), Adams rhetorically creates a vacuum in Yorùbá leadership that he could occupy

Figure 3.70. Adams kneeling in front of Oba Okunade Sijuade, Olubuse II, the Ooni of Ife (late). Photo courtesy of *Nigerian Tribune*.

Figure 3.71. Adams with the current Ooni of Ife, Oba Adeyeye Enitan Ogunwusi, Ojaja II. Photo courtesy of *Nigerian Tribune*.

Left, Figure 3.72. Adams and Owa of Ilesa, Oba Adekunle Aromolaran II. Photo courtesy of *Nigerian Tribune*.

Above, Figure 3.73. Adams with the Alake of Egbaland, Oba Michael Adedotun Gbadebo III. Photo courtesy of *Nigerian Tribune*.

Figure 3.74. Adams with the Deji of Akure, Oba Aladetoyinbo Ogunlade Aladelusi, Odundun II. Photo courtesy of *Nigerian Tribune*.

Figure 3.75. Adams with Osemawe of Ondo, Oba Adesimbo Victor Kiladejo. Photo courtesy of *Nigerian Tribune*.

Left, Figure 3.76. Adams with the Ayangburen of Ikorodu, Oba Kabiru Adewale Shotobi. Photo courtesy of *Nigerian Tribune*.

Left, Figure 3.77. The *Kakaǹfò* visits the *Ayangburen* of Ikorodu, *Oba* Kabiru Adewale Shotobi. Photo courtesy of *Nigerian Tribune*.

in the present or near future. He also—apart from practically toppling Fasehun, a Yorùbá elder—rhetorically topples living Yorùbá leaders (such as President Olusegun Obasanjo and *Asiwaju* Bola Tinubu),[172] thus presenting "the exemplary youth" (as he initially imagined himself) as the one who is most committed to the welfare of the Yorùbá people.

CONCLUSION

BIG MAN, RICH MAN, CHIEF:[173] A CULTURAL TYPE IN AFRICA

The different aspects, processes, and stages of *becoming* a big man described in these chapters are geared toward, as Paul Roscoe has argued, making "visible in concrete and comparative terms [the big man's] organizational and manipulative talents, allowing them to be calibrated against those of other Big Men in the perpetual competition for pre-eminent status."[174] As Adams became more and more successful in his effort to display the characteristics of a big man and so become one,[175] he transformed the nature of his wealth[176]—that is, something of value that his power and influence depended on—including wealth in things and wealth in people. Initially, his power and influence had depended entirely on the OPC, including both the latent and manifest violence the group commanded and the resulting clout and capacity he acquired through their activities and their sheer number of members (wealth in people). By the stage described in this chapter, Adams had acquired considerable material possessions, including money, houses, land, and cars (wealth in things), which allowed him to act with relative autonomy, or greater freedom and less restraint, in relation to both OPC members and others outside the group.

As he amasses more and more wealth in things, he also continues to rely on his wealth in people—both initial (OPC members) and acquired (his social, cultural, economic, and political networks, including relationships with leading politicians, public officeholders, traditional rulers, cultural icons, leading activists, top academics, and popular musicians). By combining both, he has been able to "tighten the connection between [wealth in people and wealth in things]"[177] (see fig. 3.78). However, there remains a tension in reconciling both forms of wealth and sustaining this reconciliation. As Peter Geschiere reminds us in his work on the challenges facing African chiefs in the "post–Cold War moment," the challenges of the sociocultural context "oblige chiefs to walk a tightrope between seductive new forms of enrichment and empowerment on one hand and on the other, the need to retain their moral prestige as protectors of their communities in the eyes of their followers."[178] Despite the many challenges Adams has faced and continues to face in the context of his transformation in social status, for a long time Adams seems to have walked this

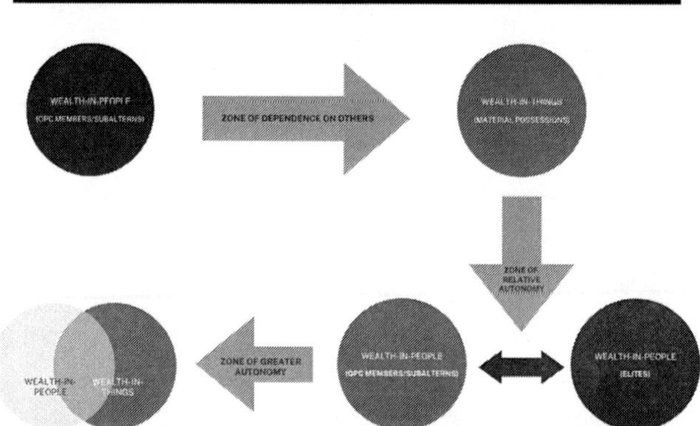

Figure 3.78. Transformation and *Self*-Determination: The transitional process of wealth in people and wealth in things for Adams. Designed by Shaan Pattni.

"tightrope" well and used the consequences to his own advantage. (The most recent challenge is discussed in chap. 6.)

Though he is often quick to remind people of the sacrifices that earned him his current acquired status, at the same time, Adams acknowledges the role of destiny in his rise. One could say that he was a man destined for greatness who had to work hard to embrace his fate. "I was so young when I made my name," he told a journalist. "I started making my name through a crisis in [the] OPC. But then, many people did not understand what I stood for then."[179] He told another journalist, "Assuming I got my education right from the beginning, I may not likely be the leader of the OPC today. God has already set an agenda for my life. . . . What I realized in all these is that God designed my destiny to be where I am."[180] As he often told me over the years, where he came from and what that meant provide an important context for his meteoric rise. "It is not easy," he would say, meaning that it was no mean feat for him to come this far and that no *ordinary* person could accomplish it. Adams has pointed out that his *extraordinariness* is a function of destiny, yet it has still demanded huge sacrifices from him. His transformation from a subaltern to an elite, he often implied, is as much a generalizable historical phenomenon as it is a factor of singular devotion to certain ideals. "All over the world," he said, "history has always favoured underdogs, somebody who is lower to another person in personality, in everything, in financial capacity."[181]

However, once he reached the point where he could no longer be described (or describe himself) as an underdog, how would Adams respond to history, which, according to him, only favors the underdog? How would he manage the impending *disfavor* of history? As the next chapter shows, Adams seems to believe that constant upward movement and the unceasing exploration of new vistas will ensure that his "destiny," or luck, will hold and allow him to continue to be in charge, to determine his own fate even as he champions self-determination for his people. Yet, while his rise in the sociocultural world of the Yorùbá continues, as the next chapter shows, his ascendancy also makes him vulnerable as the changing tides of regional and national politics open up opportunities for other ethnocultural entrepreneurs to challenge him.

NOTES

1. Daloz has warned that differentiating between "intentional and less conscious ground of social distinction" is not an easy task. I do not make a case for distinguishing between them in this chapter because, as I argue later, even when he is not consciously making a choice, Adams is quite adept at seizing any opportunity presented by circumstances. Jean-Pascal Daloz, *Rethinking Social Distinction* (New York: Palgrave Macmillan, 2013), 6.
2. Jean-Pascal Daloz, *The Sociology of Elite Distinction: From Theoretical to Comparative Perspectives* (New York: Palgrave Macmillan, 2010), 115.
3. Ibid., xiv.
4. Ibid., xii, xiii.
5. See Richard Werbner, "Introduction: Postcolonial Subjectivities; The Personal, the Political and the Moral," in *Postcolonial Subjectivities in Africa*, ed. Richard Werbner (London: Zed Books, 2002), 2.
6. I draw on the particularly succinct way in which Martin Travers captures a dimension of politics and aesthetic self-fashioning in a fascist context. Travers, "Fascism and Aesthetic Self-fashioning: Politics and the Ritualised Body in the Poetry of Stefan George," *Culture, Theory, and Critique* 42, no. 1 (1999): 21.
7. See Jonathan Friedman, "The Political Economy of Elegance: An African Cult of Beauty," in *Consumption and Identity* (London: Routledge, 2004).
8. As Daloz argues, the "chief merit of [such] field studies on elite distinction [as I attempt here] lies precisely in avoiding the temptation to generalise *a priori* on the basis of grant theories held to be universally valid." Daloz, *Sociology of Elite Distinction*, 53. See also Daloz, *Rethinking Social Distinction*, 15.
9. Clifford Geertz, "Deep Play: Notes on the Balinese Cockfight," in *Interpretation of Cultures* (New York: Basic Books, 1972), 412–53.
10. Wale Adebanwi, *Trials and Triumphs* (Lagos: West African Book, 2008).
11. Tayo Odunlami, "The Road to War," *TheNEWS*, January 31, 2000, 12.
12. Ibid.

13. Gani Adams, interview with the author, December 14, 2017.

14. That is, "the ability to assess information and adapt to new conditions." AbdouMaliq Simone, "Some Reflections on Making Popular Culture in Urban Africa," *African Studies Review* 51, no. 3 (2008): 86.

15. Werbner, "Introduction," 13. Deborah Durham, "Uncertain Citizens: Herero and the New Intercalary Subject in Postcolonial Botswana," in Werbner, *Postcolonial Subjectivities in Africa.*

16. J. D. Y. Peel, *Religious Encounter and the Making of the Yoruba* (Bloomington: Indiana University Press, 2000), 48.

17. See Olúfemi Táíwò, *How Colonialism Preempted Modernity in Africa* (Bloomington: Indiana University Press, 2009).

18. At the start of his political career, Awolowo described the Yorùbá as "a highly progressive people but badly disunited group." He identified both the disadvantages and the assets of their cultural history (which he called their "long history") and then resolved to mobilize them to deemphasize and reduce these disadvantages, if not obliterate them, and then emphasize and increase the assets—by raising "their morale," "rehabilitat[ing] their self-confidence, and imbu[ing] them with confidence." Awolowo, *Awo: The Autobiography of Chief Obafemi Awolowo* (Cambridge: Cambridge University Press, 1960), 166.

19. Instructively, one of aims of the *Egbe Omo Oduduwa* (Society for the Descendants of Oduduwa), a Yorùbá group that Awolowo founded in London in 1945, was to "combat the cankerworm of superstition and ignorance" in Yorubaland. See Awolowo, *Awo*, 169.

20. Richard Werbner, *Anthropology after Gluckman: The Manchester School, Colonial and Postcolonial Transformations* (Manchester: Manchester University Press, 2020), 103.

21. See Ayokunle Olumuyiwa Omobowale and Akinpelu Olanrewaju Olutayo, "Chief Lamidi Adedibu and Patronage Politics in Nigeria," *Journal of Modern African Studies* 45, no. 3 (2007): 425–46; Ebenezer Obadare, "Being Adedibu: On Contracting (Out) the state in Nigeria," trans. Vincent Foucher, *Politique Africaine* 106, no. 2 (2007): 110–27.

22. Andrew Apter, *Black Critics and Kings: The Hermeneutics of Power in Yoruba Society* (Chicago: University of Chicago Press, 1992), 93.

23. Daloz raises a critical but general question regarding how such manifestations of distinction constitute part of cultural continuities or represent discontinuities—or rupture. Therefore, he encourages researchers to "always wonder to what extent distinction reflects an arbitrary power or depends instead on the dictates of cultural universes that are handed down from generation to generation—and in which all actors, including prominent ones, are embedded." Daloz, *Rethinking Social Distinction*, 70.

24. This is unusual, especially in a five-star hotel in Nigeria. Adams had no recollection of this event. However, given Akande's credibility and the fact that the only other person who could have confirmed this, Adeniji, was dead at the time Akande

told this story, I suspect that the porter, as sometimes happens in hotels in Nigeria, calculated, on the basis of their appearances, that the three would offer no pecuniary benefits if he accompanied each of them into their rooms. At any rate, there would most likely be other potential benefactors waiting to be assisted.

25. In *The Communist Manifesto*, Marx referred to the "lowest stratum of the industrial working class" as *Lumpenproletariat* (rabble proletariat), who are "not only disinclined to participate in revolutionary activities with their 'rightful brethren,' the proletariat, but also tend to act as the 'bribed tools of reactionary intrigue.'" See *Encyclopaedia Britannica*, s.v. "Lumpenproletariat: Marxism," last modified December 3, 2014, https://www.britannica.com/topic/Lumpenproletariat.

26. Monsuru Akande, telephone interview with the author, November 28, 2020. Akande largely spoke in Yorùbá.

27. See chap. 2.

28. Machiavelli argues that "in general men are ungrateful, inconstant, hypocritical, fearful of danger, and covetous of gain." Niccolò Machiavelli, *The Prince*, trans. George Bull (London: Penguin, 1961), 79.

29. Including Arogundade Rasaq Balogun (Saddam), Sunday Adebayo, Monsuru Akande, and Segun Akanni.

30. In his book on his boss, Segun Akanni writes, "Governor Gbenga Daniel too was there for Oga [meaning 'boss,' but it was also an acronym formed from Adams's chieftaincy title and his name: Otunba Gani Adams]. He supported his group and ensured that Oga's members in Ogun State were not intimidated. He . . . was Oga's real friend. He also, in the company of the Inspector General of Police, Mr. Sunday Ehindero, visited Oga when he was in the custody of the police." Akanni, *The Volunteer of the Savannah: A True Picture of Gani Adams* (Lagos: Prince Genesis Concept, 2015), p. 7.

31. Akanni writes, "We talked to Mr. Rauf Aregbesola, who had been visiting Oga in detention to console him. Oga often said that Mr. Aregbe (as he used to call the current governor of Osun State) had been coming to give him help. He would offer money to buy food and water for Oga and other inmates. He was really a helper when his friend needed him." Ibid., 7.

32. For a useful take on the attitude toward owning a house in Yorubaland—particularly in relation to Mushin, where Adams started out—see Sandra T. Barnes, *Patrons and Power: Creating a Political Community in Metropolitan Lagos* (Manchester: Manchester University Press, 1986), 68–69.

33. The idea of the National Guard is interesting because it is a parody of sorts of President Ibrahim Babangida's pet military project, which did not endure. Babangida envisioned the National Guard as an elite military formation that would be loyal only to him and could suppress attempts (either within the military or from the civil society) at subverting his self-perpetuation project.

34. Members included Balogun, Akande, Musa Kilanko, Idowu Akintunde (Warrior), Laide (late), Muyiwa Stevie, Akeem Adu, Kayode (Godogodo), Lai Ogunsola, Semiu Ogunrinde, Gbenga (Major), Ayangbenro (late), Gbenga Egunnusi.

35. Monsuru Akande, telephone interview with the author, November 17, 2020.

36. See Jean-Pascal Daloz, *Rethinking Social Distinction* (New York: Palgrave Macmillan, 2013), 40.

37. Musiliu Amusa, telephone interview with the author, December 10, 2020.

38. Amusa put the total figure at N140 million.

39. Marruf Olanrewaju, telephone interview with the author, January 28, 2021.

40. Amusa, telephone interview with the author, December 10, 2020.

41. Omolara Adaranijo, telephone interview with the author, July 9, 2021.

42. She disclosed that Oshodi had paid for her to observe the pilgrimage to Mecca when he was still with the Adams faction.

43. Adebayo was particularly insulted by Adams's statement that he had "brought him up." When I asked him to respond, he asked, "How can he say he brought me up?" He claimed that in the early 1990s he used to lend his motorcycle to Adams to use as *okada* to earn money. He conceded, though, that it was Adams, and not OPC, who had encouraged him to join the Beko Ransome-Kuti–led Committee for the Defence of Human Rights (CDHR). "When we joined OPC, he had two clothes. What is 'brought up'?" he asked. Adebayo, telephone interview with the author, December 5, 2020.

44. Adams, telephone interview with the author, November 29, 2020.

45. Cf. Barnes's argument, in the context of Mushin, that "people who wished to move ahead . . . found it necessary to display their entrepreneurial talents in another direction—by amassing economic resources. . . . It was even possible to convert political gains into economic assets." Barnes, *Patrons and Power*, 96.

46. Daloz, *Sociology of Elite Distinction*, 61.

47. Between the eighth century BC and the sixth century AD. The cultural history of the era so designated is around the Mediterranean Sea—that is, the Greco-Roman world. See Wikipedia, s.v. "classical antiquity," accessed February 22, 2021, https://en.wikipedia.org/wiki/Classical_antiquity#:~:text=Classical%20antiquity%20(also%20the%20classical,as%20the%20Greco%2DRoman%20world.

48. Graham Clark, *Symbols of Excellence* (Cambridge: Cambridge University Press, 1986), 82.

49. Aimée M. Plourde, "Prestige Goods and the Formation of Political Hierarchy: A Costly Signalling Model," in *Patterns and Process of Cultural Evolution*, ed. Stephen Shennan (Berkeley: University of California Press, 2009).

50. Ibid.

51. A. W. Johnson and T. K. Earle, *The Evolution of Human Societies: From Foraging Group to Agrarian State* (Stanford, CA: Stanford University Press, 2000).

52. Aimée M. Plourde, "The Origins of Prestige Goods as Honest Signals of Skill and Knowledge," *Human Nature* 19 (2008): 374.

53. Plourde, "Prestige Goods and the Formation of Political Hierarchy."

54. John E. Clark and M. Blake, "The Power of Prestige: Competitive Generosity and the Emergence of Rank Society in Lowland Mesoamerica," in *Factional*

Competition and Politics Development in the New World, ed. E. M. Brumfiel and J. W. Fox (Cambridge: Cambridge University Press, 1994).

55. Plourde, "Prestige Goods and the Formation of Political Hierarchy."

56. Simon Harrison, "From Prestige Goods to Legacies: Property and the Objectification of Culture in Melanesia," *Comparative Studies in Society and History* 42, no. 3 (July 2000): 662–79, 668.

57. Ibid., 676.

58. See Daloz, *Sociology of Elite Distinction*, 61–62. Harrison argues that, in Melanesia, "the two types of goods were often so closely linked [and] were combined together as unitary valuables." Harrison, "From Prestige Goods to Legacies," 668.

59. It has been argued that while ranking is ubiquitous in all social species, prestige is unique to human beings. This explains why even though animals can use violence to achieve ranking, they cannot gain prestige among their kind. See Plourde, "Origin of Prestige Goods," 375.

60. Ibid.

61. Daloz, *Sociology of Elite Distinction*, 96.

62. See Daloz, *Rethinking Social Distinction*, 20.

63. See Daloz, *Sociology of Elite Distinction*, 115.

64. Daloz, *Rethinking Social Distinction*, 40.

65. Ibid., 26–27.

66. Tim Gibbs, "Becoming a 'Big Man' in Neo-Liberal South Africa: Migrant Masculinities in the Minibus-Taxi Industry," *African Affairs* 113, no. 452 (2014): 444.

67. Daloz, *Sociology of Elite Distinction*, 68.

68. Daloz, *Rethinking Social Distinction*, 69.

69. Monsuru Akande (telephone interview, November 17, 2020), Rasaq Balogun (telephone interview, November 18, 2020), and Sunday Adebayo (telephone Interview, December 5, 2020) provided details of this in interviews with me.

70. Segun Akanni, telephone interview with the author, November 7, 2020.

71. Daloz, *Sociology of Elite Distinction*, 70.

72. The line is from an old Yorùbá folk song in the defunct Oyo Empire that acknowledges the awesome powers of the Yorùbá generalissimo. Anyone who ran into trouble with the often-volatile generalissimo in the ancient times risked it all—including life and limb. While those who held the position in the postcolonial era did not pose similar risks, the description still speaks in some measure to the huge influence of the contemporary generalissimos, particularly Adams, who had considerable command of firepower.

73. Daloz, *Sociology of Elite Distinction*, 96.

74. In the sections below, I will discuss such "home performances" as birthdays and naming ceremonies.

75. Karin Barber, "When People Cross Thresholds," *African Studies Review* 50, no. 2 (2007): 115.

76. For more on Kurunmi, see Dare Oguntomisin, *Kurunmi of Ijaye, 1831–1862: A Biography of a Militant Yoruba Ruler* (Ikeja: John West, 1986).

77. I thank Emmanuel Akyeampong for alerting me to this specific comparison.

78. One exception was when he moved briefly to the beat as Adewale Ayuba sang his praise during the second anniversary celebrations of his installation as *Aare* in January 2020. See GoldMyne TV, "Ayuba Dazzles Fans with Bonsue Vibes at Gani Adams' 2nd Anniversary as Aare Kakanfo of Yorubaland," YouTube, January 26, 2020, https://www.youtube.com/watch?v=mLwVHJERMJE.

79. See "Pasuma Biography," *Opera News*, accessed June 4, 2021, https://ng.opera.news/ng/en/entertainment/98446bf60d14bca776f0448c77d6ebc1.

80. For another occasion when Adams "sprayed" K1, see "Money Speaking Gani Adams over Spend for K1 De Ultimate @ MC Oluomo Mother Inlaw Burial," February 13, 2018, https://www.youtube.com/watch?v=5PtivpDJK84.

81. See GoldMyne TV, "K1 De Ultimate Serenades Are Ona Kankanfo of Yorubaland, Gani Adams, as Her Rains Dollars on . . ." YouTube, January 24, 2022, https://www.youtube.com/watch?v=Yk3XrScksyM.

82. Although pioneered by the Yorùbá in Nigeria, it has since been embraced by other Nigerians, particularly the Igbo.

83. Taju Tijani, "Banjo Akintoye: Beyond Yoruba Triumphalism as UNPO Member," *Guardian*, May 29, 2020, https://guardian.ng/opinion/banji-akintoye-beyond-yoruba-triumphalism-as-unpo-member/.

84. Ibid.

85. Adélékè Adéèkó, *Arts of Being Yorùbá: Divination, Allegory, Tragedy, Proverb, Panegyric* (Bloomington: Indiana University Press, 2017), 166.

86. Some would say pseudo-intellectual.

87. I gathered that at every stage of his public career, intellectuals were providing support, coaching him in Marxian ideas, writing statements for him, and advising him on how to present the image of a thoughtful and reflective emerging leader. At this stage, I was informed that a University of Lagos professor who headed a cultural institution and the leading head of a civil society organization were his key intellectual props.

88. Taju Tijani, "Hard Talk on Yoruba Race," *TT Soundings*, August 13, 2011, https://tajutijani.wordpress.com/2011/08/13/hard-talk-on-yoruba-race/.

89. Adams, interview with the author, December 14, 2017.

90. "Why I'm Celebrating My Birthday—Aare Gani Adams," *Independent*, April 30, 2018, https://www.independent.ng/why-im-celebrating-my-birthday-aare-gani-adams/.

91. Lagos governor Babatunde Fashola, in the speech delivered on his behalf, "described Adams as an individual with rare leadership sagacity." Oba Adeoye, "Nigeria: Celebrating Gani Adams' Day of Honour," *Daily Independent*, May 4, 2009.

92. Ibid.

93. Ibid.

94. Ibid.

95. Ibid.

96. See Pierre Bourdieu, *Distinction: Social Critique and the Judgement of Taste*, trans. Richard Nice (Cambridge, MA: Harvard University Press, 1984).

97. Wale Adedayo, interview with the author, June 30, 2012, Lagos.

98. This phrase was popularized by Erving Goffman in *The Presentation of Self in Everyday Life* (Garden City, NY: Doubleday Anchor Books, 1959). Daloz argues that Goffman "has a tendency to equate everything with 'impression management.'" Daloz, *Sociology of Elite Distinction*, 34.

99. Jacob Olupona, *City of 201 Gods: Ilé-Ifè in Time, Space, and the Imagination* (Berkeley: University of California Press, 2011).

100. For the details of the four-year-long clashes, see the Human Rights Watch, "The O'odua People's Congress: Fighting Violence with Violence," *Human Rights Watch* 15, no. 4A (February 28, 2003), https://www.hrw.org/reports/2003/nigeria0203/nigeriaopc0203-04.htm. In one of the clashes, on January 12, 2002, between thirty and forty-five OPC members were reportedly killed by the police and palace boys who had mobilized in in response to earlier attacks by the OPC members, which led to the loss of many lives among the *Olowo*'s supporters.

101. Anonymous, telephone interview with the author, November 14, 2020.

102. Unlike Adams's *Aare* position, the *Aare Baamofin* is of no historic significance. It was invented in recent years to honor distinguished lawyers.

103. Tunde Olofintila, "Between Aare Baamofin and Ààre Ònà *Kakaǹfò* of Yorubaland," *Vanguard*, November 21, 2017, https://www.vanguardngr.com/2017/11/aare-baamofin-aare-ona-kakanfo-yorubaland/.

104. Werbner, "Introduction," 2.

105. For instance, Nosa Osaigbovo, writing in the *Nigerian Tribune*, dismissed Adams as a symbol of "outlawry." He states further: "Mr. Adams was a carpenter before he became the leader of ethnic militants. He was completely unknown. Now the former fugitive is famous, at least in his own part of the country. He is a chief and also a 'doctor.' And he is immensely rich. Mr. Adams built himself a mansion and married a pretty woman. It seems wrongheaded militancy is a lucrative line of business. Mr. Adams is respectfully received by governors and traditional rulers in the South-West. Mr. Adams must see himself as the new Yoruba leader." Nosa Osaigbovo, "The Outlaw as Hero," Friday, April 23, 2010, http://www.tribune.com.ng/index.php/mosaic/4427-the-outlaw-as-hero. A piece in the Kaduna-based newspaper, *New Nigerian*, dismissed Adams and his colleagues as "tribal gangsters and moronic" people. "OPC Activities: The North Is Watching," *New Nigerian*, December 14, 1999, 5. See also *New Nigerian on Sunday*, "No Peace Agenda for Nigeria," February 20, 2000, 10.

106. Daloz argues that "because of the prominence of sexual desire in human life, the display of fine-looking (mainly female) companions frequently plays a primordial symbolic role in strategies of distinction. Of greatest importance here is the fact that gorgeous spouses . . . not only suggest sensual pleasures but often carry added enhancements (dress, jewels, etc.) that contribute to the vicarious assertion of the wealth of their husband." Daloz, *Sociology of Elite Distinction*, 100. Some of Adams's aides told me that he has attracted a lot of attention from ladies, including some of

the actresses in Nollywood. Perhaps he was hinting at this when he said upon release from a long spell in jail, "My stay in prison taught me that one can actually stay off women." Olusola Fabiyi, "My Stay in Prison Taught Me That One Can Actually Stay Off Women," *Saturday Punch*, December 23, 2006, A9.

107. Femi Adepoju, "Gani Adams' Wedding: The Role of Masquerades," *P.M. News*, December 3, 2003, 7.

108. Kristin Mann, *Marrying Well: Marriage, Status and Educated Elites in Colonial Lagos* (Cambridge: Cambridge University Press, 1985).

109. Ronke Kehinde, "Jewel behind the Lion," *Compass*, May 21, 2011, 26.

110. Quoted in "Ààre Ònà *Kakañfò*, Gani Adams Share Top Secret as Wife Celebrates Birthday," De Reportorial TV, November 14, 2018, https://www.de-reportorial.com.ng/2018/11/aare-ona-kakanfo-gani-adams-shares-top.html.

111. Temidayo Akinsuyi, "Gani Adams' Wife, Ayaba Mojisola Gives Birth to Twins," *Independent*, May 27, 2020, https://www.independent.ng/gani-adams-wife-ayinba-mojisola-givers-birth-to-twins/.

112. See Jean-Pascal Daloz, "Voitures et prestige au Nigeria" [Cars and prestige in Nigeria], *Politique Africaine* 38 (1990): 148–53.

113. Nkem Nwankwo's popular novel, *My Mercedes Is Bigger Than Yours* (Ibadan: Heinemann, 1975), is a cautionary tale about the lives of the nouveaux riches and the centrality of the car to their glamorous lives. Incidentally, though Mercedes Benz was the ultimate symbol of wealth in Nigeria in the decade the book was published, the protagonist, Onuma Okude, drives a Jaguar.

114. In an earlier era, between the early 1970s and the late 1980s, the German-made Volkswagen Type 1 car, a two-door, rear-engine economy car popularly called a Beetle, was at the bottom of the car ladder in Nigeria. Next in line was the Peugeot series, including the 504 and later 505 series. When the local Volkswagen plant closed in Nigeria, a variety of secondhand cars replaced the Beetle as the signal of the lowest ranks of the middle class.

115. Daloz, *Sociology of Elite Distinction*, 27, see also 73–76. As Daloz also points out, Marxist theory emphasizes "the relative autonomy of prestige in relation to material conditions." Ibid., 28. Yet, in the reality of the Nigerian social context, such autonomy is hardly practical. Material conditions are, for the most part, sine qua non for prestige.

116. Ibid., 73–74.

117. Ibid., 75, following Henri Lefebvre, *Everyday Life in the Modern World* (London: Allen Lane, 1971), 101–102.

118. Daloz, *Sociology of Elite Distinction*, 75. See also Luc Boltanski, "Les usages sociaux de l'automobile: Concurrence pour l'espace et accidents," *Actes de la recherché en sciences sociales* 1, no. 2 (1975): 25–49.

119. Fred Hirst, *Social Limits to Growth* (London: Routledge, 1977), in Daloz, *Sociology of Elite Distinction*, 41.

120. Achille Mbembe, "Everything Can Be Negotiated: Ambiguities and Challenges in Time of Uncertainty," in *Manoeuvring in an Environment of Uncertainty:*

Structural Change and Social Action in Sub-Saharan Africa, ed. Boel Berner and Per Trulsson (Aldershot: Ashgate, 2000), vii.

121. Quoted in Rick Tilman, *Thorstein Veblen and His Critics, 1891–1963: Conservative, Liberal and Radical Perspectives* (Princeton, NJ: Princeton University Press, 1992), 223.

122. Even such people, for the most account, will be able to bribe their way through.

123. John L. Comaroff and Jean Comaroff, *The Politics of Custom: Chiefship, Capital, and the State in Contemporary Africa* (Chicago: University of Chicago Press, 2018), vii.

124. Ibid., 1.

125. Ibid., 2.

126. Paradoxically, a few people of high distinction in Nigeria maintain what may be described as their *distinct distinction* by remaining just Mr., Mrs., or Ms. However, this is rare.

127. Dapo Akinrefon, "With 52 Titles Already, I Didn't Think I Would Become the Ààre Ònà *Kakaǹfò*—Gani Adams," *Vanguard*, October 22, 2017, https://www.vanguardngr.com/2017/10/52-titles-already-didnt-think-become-ona-kakanfo-gani-adams/.

128. *Nation*, "Varsity Packed as OPC's Adams Gets Doctorate Degree," June 1, 2007.

129. It is surprising that the newspaper did not reconcile the claim that Adams had just received a diploma in tourism with his previous claims that he had received this diploma in 2003. Obviously, such details were irrelevant to the emphasis on this "historic" achievement.

130. Daloz, *Rethinking Social Distinction*.

131. Ibid. See also Jean-Pascal Daloz, Élites et *représentations politiques: La culture de l'échange inégal au Nigeria* (Pessac, France: Presses Universitaires de Bordeaux, 2002).

132. In terms of formal instruction complete in its breadth, length, and complexity.

133. The most infamous being the certificate forgery by the first Speaker of the Federal House of Representatives in the Fourth Republic, Salisu Buhari, who claimed to have graduated from Toronto University, for which he was prosecuted and found guilty. See "The Face of Liar," *TheNEWS*, July 19, 1999.

134. Does this mean the Obafemi Awolowo University community? I cannot say. It is a rather nebulous description of Jegede's constituency—particularly given that there is no reference to his discipline, his department, or the university where he was based.

135. Abisoye Gbadamosi, "Biography of Otunba (Dr.) Gani Adams," *Otunba Gani Adams Cares for Nigerians* (blog), July 2011, http://otunbaganicares.blogspot.com/2011/07/biography-of-otunba-dr-gani-adams.html.

136. Seventeen such festivals from across Yorubaland are listed in the program of his installation as Ààrẹ *Ònà Kakaǹfò*. Apart from the Olokun Festival, these include the Eledumare, Oodua, Obatala, Ajagunmale, Osun Osogbo, Oke-Ibadan, Olumo, Obatala, Elegbara, Ogun, Oranmiyan, Aje, Oro, Ife, and Grandmothers Festivals.

137. Job Osazuwa, "Olokun Festival Is Here to Stay, Says Gani Adams," *Sun*, October 15, 2019, https://www.sunnewsonline.com/olokun-festival-is-here-to-stay-says-gani-adams/.

138. For instance, after two public disturbances in two areas of Lagos in 2004, the Media Relations Office of Adams' faction issues a press release condemning the "uncultured, undisciplined and uncivilized members of [Fasehun'] group," adding that the recent violence was perpetrated by the other faction as "part of a grand plot aimed at rubbishing the name of [the Gani Adams faction]." The statement concluded that each of the recent disturbances by the Fasehun faction "coincides with [Adams faction] climbing another rung in our constant strife for development," given that "The OPC led by Gani Adams has taken it upon itself, to extricate the group from the pigeon-hole of negativity to which it had been consigned." The statement then provided a few examples of the group's "non-violence" turn including organizing, in 2003 and 2004, "successful Violence-Free Seminar[s] as our contribution [toward] an enduring democracy in Nigeria." See Abiodun Adesina, "Call Fasehun to Order," Press Release by OPC, March 14, 2004.

139. John Comaroff and Jean Comaroff, "Chief, Capital, and the State in Contemporary Africa: An Introduction," in Comaroff and Comaroff, *Politics of Custom*, 16.

140. See chap. 4.

141. This also included a new dressing style, which will be discussed below.

142. Wale-Ojo Lanre, "Why We Sponsored 18 Festivals in Yoruba Land—Gani Adams," *Nigerian Tribune*, October 25, 2017, https://tribuneonlineng.com/sponsored-18-festivals-yoruba-land-gani-adams/.

143. Osazuwa, "Olokun Festival Is Here to Stay" (emphasis added).

144. Ibid.

145. Tayo Ogunbiyi, "Gani Adams and the Preservation of Indigenous Culture," *BusinessDay*, January 6, 2019, https://businessday.ng/analysis/article/gani-adams-and-the-preservation-of-indigenous-culture/.

146. *Vanguard*, "Declare 2 Days Holiday for Eledumare Festival, Gani Adams Urges Governors," March 13, 2020, https://www.vanguardngr.com/2020/03/declare-2-days-holiday-for-eledumare-festival-gani-adams-urges-governors/. See also Segun Kasali, "Eledumare Festival: Gani Adams Urges Southwest Governors to Declare 2 Days Holiday," *Nigerian Tribune*, March 12, 2020, https://tribuneonlineng.com/eledumare-festival-gani-adams-urges-southwest-governors-to-declare-2-days-holiday/.

147. Dapo Akinrefon, "Ooni of Ife, Aare Adams Task INEC on Credible Polls," *Vanguard*, January 29, 2019, https://www.vanguardngr.com/2019/01/ooni-of-ife-aare-adams-task-inec-on-credible-polls-2/.

148. Folarin Ademosu, "Fasehun Can Kill, Destroy for Power, Money and Women," *P.M. News*, August 21, 2013.

149. See Stig Hjarvard, "The Mediatization of Society: A Theory of the Media as Agents of Social and Cultural Change," *Nordicom Review* 29, no. 2 (2008): 105–34.

150. For instance, see Dapo Akinrefon, "Aare Gani Adams' Wife Gives Birth to Twins," *Vanguard*, May 27, 2020, https://www.vanguardngr.com/2020/05/aare-gani-adams-wife-gives-birth-to-twins/.

151. Birgit Meyer, "Mediation and Immediacy: Sensational Forms, Semiotic Ideologies and the Question of the Medium," *Social Anthropology/Anthropologie sociale* 19, no. 1 (2011): 23–39.

152. Ebenezer Obadare, *Pastoral Power, Clerical State: Pentecostalism, Gender, and Sexuality in Nigeria* (Notre Dame, IN: University of Notre Dame Press, 2022).

153. There are countless examples. See, for instance, Olayinka Olukoya, Adebayo Waheed, and Olalekan Olabulo, "Declare MKO Ex-president, Family Tells FG," *Nigerian Tribune*, June 13, 2012; Seye Olumide, "Utomi, Adams Task FG on Corruption, Security," *Guardian*, November 12, 2019, https://guardian.ng/news/utomi-adams-task-fg-on-corruption-security/.

154. I guess that, as an "Oxford don," as the Nigerian press are wont to describe someone like me, I qualified too. Therefore, the photographer took a photo of the *Kakanfo*-designate and me.

155. Foran interesting take on the "valorization of objects, persons, and status" through "adulatory . . . photographs," see Adéèkó, *Arts of Being Yorùbá*, esp. chap. 6.

156. Susan Sontag, *On Photography* (New York: Picador USA, 1973), 5, 8.

157. Adéèkó, *Arts of Being Yorùbá*, 122.

158. Stephen Sprague, "How I See the Yoruba See Themselves," *Studies in the Anthropology of Visual Communication* 5, no. 1 (1978): 11.

159. Adéèkó, *Arts of Being Yorùbá*, 122.

160. Daloz, *Sociology of Elite Distinction*, 97.

161. Erving Goffman, *Stigma: Notes on the Management of Spoiled Identity* (Englewood Cliffs NJ: Prentice Hall, 1963), 47.

162. Adams's old friend and former adviser Wale Adedayo, in a discussion with me in June 2012, used this phrase to describe Adams's new status.

163. Some of his critics doubt that the group has a presence in as many states of the federation. But the politicians buy the claim. At any rate, for them, whatever the number of states, the OPC had sufficient chapters for Adams to be politically useful for their ambitions.

164. *ThisDay*, "At OPU World Congress 2019, It Was Glitz and Glamour in Akure," February 3, 2019, https://www.thisdaylive.com/index.php/2019/02/03/at-opu-world-congress-2019-it-was-glitz-and-glamour-in-akure/.

165. Sahara Reporters, "Nigerians in Diaspora Don't Want to Come Home Because of Insecurity—Gani Adams," February 6, 2022, http://saharareporters.com/2022/02/06/nigerians-diaspora-dont-want-come-home-because-insecurity%E2%80%93gani-adams.

166. Gabriel Olawale, "Insecurity Preventing Nigerians in Diaspora from Coming Home—Gani Adams," *Vanguard*, February 7, 2022, https://www.vanguardngr.com

/2022/02/insecurity-preventing-nigerians-in-diaspora-from-coming-home-gani-adams/.

167. For an analysis of Awolowo as the *ur*-Yorùbá, see Wale Adebanwi, *Yoruba Elites and Ethnic Politics in Nigeria: Obafemi Awolowo and Corporate Agency* (Cambridge: Cambridge University Press, 2014), 21.

168. Though one could say that Adams has "a vague, idealised knowledge" (Daloz, *Rethinking Social Distinction*, 69) of Awolowo's political philosophy and moral vision, he really wished to acquire what he regarded as the man's "spiritual powers." An aide alleges that Adams once went into a one-month trance in consultation with a spiritualist to acquire Awolowo's capacity to "predict the future." He believed that the ability was one of the reasons people respected Awolowo. Odia Ofeimun dismissed such "myth and mysticism" as capable of "drowning the secular import" of Awolowo's life. Cited in Adebanwi, *Yoruba Elites and Ethnic Politics*, 86. See another reference to Adams going "into a trance" in the book by his aide Segun Akanni, *Volunteer of the Savannah*, 26.

169. Daloz, *Rethinking Social Distinction*, 69.

170. He even spoke about his "premonition for greatness," stating, "I have a divine role in the liberation of the Yoruba." Tunde Thomas and Henry Omafode, "How We Toppled Fasehun—Gani Adams," *Spectator*, December 16–22, 2009, 16.

171. "Gani Adams' New Status and Outlook," *Nation*, April 21, 2009 (emphasis added).

172. For example, see Taiwo-Hassan Adebayo, "Tinubu Using Yoruba for Own Selfish Interest—Gani Adams," *Premium Times*, March 21, 2015, https://www.premiumtimesng.com/regional/ssouth-west/178876-tinubu-using-yoruba-for-own-selfish-interest-gani-adams.html. See also "OPC Will Reject OBJ's Third Terms Agenda—Gani Adams," *Saturday Tribune*, August 30, 2005, 32; "Obasanjo Presidency Was a Disaster to the S/West—Gani Adams," *Saturday Tribune*, October 27, 2007, 18; "Abiola's Death: Yoruba Leaders Were Induced, Gani Adams," *National Mirror*, August 5, 2011; "I'm Not Satisfied with the State of the Yoruba Nation—Gani Adams," *Nigerian Tribune*, April 29, 2010, 23.

173. This is a parody of the title of Sahlin's famous 1963 work, "Poor Man, Rich Man, Big-Man, Chief: Political Types in Melanesia and Polynesia."

174. Paul B. Roscoe, "Before Elites: The Political Capacities of Big Men," in *Before Elites: Alternatives to Hierarchical Systems in Modelling Social Formations*, ed. Tobias L. Kienlin and Andreas Zimmerman (Bonn: Rudolph Habelt, 2012), 1:43.

175. Victoria J. Baker has argued that these characteristics, in the Melanesian context, include "ambition, intelligence, charisma, persuasiveness, generosity, and managerial as well as rhetorical skills." As this and the preceding chapters show, Adams had not only all these but also many more that are fitting for the Yoruba/Nigerian context. See Victoria J. Baker, "Elders in the Shadow of the Big Man," *Bijdragen tot de Taal-, Land- en Volkenkunde* Deel 139, *1ste Afl., Anthropologica* 25 (1983): 2.

176. In an important analysis of "wealth in people" and "wealth in things," Jane I. Guyer argues that "one of the guiding lodestones for social theorists and social

historians across the entire theoretical spectrum has been 'wealth': the things people imbue with value, the caches they collect up by every means from prestation to predation, the performative displays they orchestrate, the treasures they store and eventually leave behind, and all the complex cultural constructions whereby such things are counted, praised and imagined as sources and instruments of power." Guyer, "Wealth in People, Wealth in Things: Introduction," *Journal of African History* 36, no. 1 (1995): 83. Guyer and Samuel M. Eno Belinga argue that wealth in people can also be wealth in knowledge. See Jane I. Guyer and Samuel M. Eno Belinga, "Wealth in People as Wealth in Knowledge: Accumulation and Composition in Equatorial Africa," *Journal of African History* 36, no. 1 (1995): 93.

177. Sara Berry, "Questions of Ownership: Proprietorship and Control in a Changing Rural Terrain—a Case Study from Ghana," *Africa* 83, no. 1 (2013): 52.

178. Peter Geschiere, "African Chiefs and the Post–Cold War Moment: Millennial Capitalism and the Struggle over Moral Authority," in Comaroff and Comaroff, *Politics of Custom*, 74.

179. Shola Oshunkeye, "People Who Ignore Me, Do So at Their Peril," *Sunday Sun*, December 4, 2011, 32. See also, NBF News, "Gani Adams: My Name Rings Louder Bell Than Some Governors," *Nigerian Voice*, December 4, 2011, https://www.thenigerianvoice.com/news/76834/gani-adams-my-name-rings-louder-bell-than-some-governors.html.

180. Okorie Uguru, "Gani Adams: Interview," ("Weekend Treat"), *Nation*, September 11, 2009.

181. Oshunkeye, "People Who Ignore Me, Do So at Their Peril," 32.

PART II
Being a Big Man

4 / The Acme of Distinction

(Pre)Eminence and the Rituals of Power

INTRODUCTION: BEING A BIG MAN

As we drove through the "ancient"[1] town of Oyo on the morning of Saturday, January 13, 2018, the town was in a festive mood. A once-in-a-generation ceremony was to be hosted there in a few hours. I was in a convoy with a few friends and old colleagues in journalism, including Adeolu Akande, a university teacher, politician, and gubernatorial aspirant on the platform of the ruling All Progressives Congress (APC), heading to the palace of the Oyo monarch, the *Aláàfin* of Oyo, Oba Lamidi Adeyemi III. We intended to head to the palace first before going to Durbar Stadium, the venue where Gani Adams would be installed as the fifteenth *Ààrẹ Ọ̀nà Kakañfò* of Yorubaland. My politician friend had to be at the event to give some visibility to his political aspirations.

A few weeks earlier, while I was visiting the *Kakañfò*-designate, he had mentioned that a few governors from the Southwest states had yet to reach out to him directly as he prepared for his installation. *Reaching out* in this context, I understood, included congratulating him personally and offering financial support for the forthcoming ceremony. Since I knew that my politician friend, Akande, was close to one of the governors Adams was expecting to hear from—and that Akande would be glad to facilitate the contact between Adams and the governor[2]—I called him. I mentioned that the *Kakañfò*-designate had not yet received a message from his governor friend. Did he mind speaking directly with Adams and arranging the link? Akande said he would be pleased to do so. I handed my mobile phone to Adams. Akande later confirmed that the governor had reached out to Adams.

When we arrived at the gate of the *Aláàfin*'s palace, I noticed that the usually wide-open, big gates of the palace had been shut, with security men standing guard. They allowed only those qualified into the palace. Behind the gates, the soon-to-be-installed *Ààrẹ Ọ̀nà Kakañfò* was going through the final rites before the public ceremony that would follow at the Oyo stadium. I later headed to that site.

Undoubtedly, the installation of Adams as the *Ààrẹ Ọ̀nà Kakañfò* (generalissimo or field marshal) of Yorubaland was the highest and grandest affirmation of his recently acquired status as an elite and, in fact, as a member of the Ur-elite in Yorubaland and, by extension, Nigeria. As Sandra Barnes has shown, in the area of metropolitan Lagos from which Adams emerged, "The goal of many of Mushin's top leaders was to perpetuate their position of power."[3] Since the post-jail-era, Adams had realized the huge potential for self-actualization through systematic (or cynical, as his critics would say) social climbing—using the necessary guises and disguises of social power and cultural influence—he had set his eyes on the highest level of cultural and political offices attainable. As he acquired one chieftaincy title after another, as well as social and cultural acknowledgment, Adams craved a nonpareil position that would remove any doubt about his eminence.

The *Ààrẹ Ọ̀nà Kakañfò* was that position. While during the precolonial era the title had belonged to daredevil war heroes (those the Yorùbá called *Akikanju*),[4] the previous two occupants of the office, Samuel Ladoke Akintola and Moshood Kashimawo Olawale Abiola, were distinguished Yorùbá civilians, though they fought their own political wars. Akintola (1910–66) was a politician, a lawyer, and the premier of the Western Region of Nigeria (1960–66),[5] while Abiola (1937–98) was an accountant, businessman, and politician. As the candidate of the Social Democratic Party (SDP), Abiola won the June 12, 1993, presidential election, which was annulled by the military regime. Given the status and accomplishments of the two immediate past holders of the title, some critics argued that Adams was undeserving of the position. But the critics were mistaken. Akintola and Abiola were the exception to the rule. As Olufemi Vaughan has shown, in Yorubaland and beyond, "chieftaincy structures are continuously regenerated in rapidly shifting sociopolitical and economic contexts."[6] Thus, while the appointment of Akintola and Abiola redefined what it meant to be a field marshal or generalissimo, in the postcolonial era in Yorubaland, Adams's background and life trajectory as the leader of the Oodua People's Congress (OPC) were the closest in modern times to those of the martial men who held the position of *Kakañfò* in precolonial Yorubaland.

Figure 4.1. *Left:* Chief Samuel Ladoke Akintola as the thirteenth *Ààrẹ Ọ̀nà Kakaǹfò*. *Right:* Chief Moshood Abiola and the *Aláàfin* of Oyo, *Oba* Lamidi Adeyemi III, at the latter's installation as the fourteenth *Ààrẹ Ọ̀nà Kakaǹfò* in 1987. Photos courtesy of *Nigerian Tribune*.

Figure 4.2. Chief Samuel Ladoke Akintola and his wife, Faderera, with *Aláàfin* Bello Gbadegesin Ladigbolu II (*middle*) at Akintola's installation as *Ààrẹ Ọ̀nà Kakaǹfò* in 1962. Photo from Adams's installation booklet.

Part II (chaps. 4–6) of this book is devoted to examining how Adams has preserved and entrenched his achieved status. In this chapter, I examine what I describe as "the acme of distinction" in Adams's life: his ascension to the position of the *Ààrẹ Ọ̀nà Kakaǹfò*, the highest traditional title that a commoner (as opposed to those with a royal pedigree) can attain in Yorubaland. In this exceptional rags-to-riches trajectory, Adams's ascension to the status of Yorùbá generalissimo is used here to (1) reflect on the process and performances of rituals in the sustenance of the position of a big man in contemporary Africa; (2) foreground the critical role that the mobilization of violence (both manifest and latent) and cultural activities play in specific forms of the elaboration and consolidation (and the unending negotiation) of self-actualization, power, and prominence in the Yorùbá context; and (3) illuminate the processes by which one who is already eminent can mobilize that eminence, or particular forms of it, in a bid to gain even greater eminence—or preeminence—in society.

RITUAL OF ASCENT

As I was ushered into the presence of the *Ààrẹ Ọ̀nà Kakaǹfò*–designate by his chief of staff, Segun Akanni, in December 2017, I noticed that something had changed about him. Just ahead of me in greeting Adams was the Honorable Kehinde Ayoola, the former Speaker of the Oyo State House of Assembly.[7] Ayoola and I had never met, but we shared mutual friends. When Adams introduced us, Ayoola mentioned that he had just been talking about me with our mutual friend on his way to Adams's house. Ayoola, who died in May 2020, was from Oyo and was close to the *Aláàfin*.

At this time, I had known Adams and studied his group for about eighteen years. Even in the last few years, during which he became a big man, the new aura around him had never felt as strong as it felt that morning. As he spoke, I noticed that there was a new authority tinged with a measure of excitement in his voice. He spoke animatedly about the plans for the installation ceremony. I assured him that I planned to fly back to Nigeria from the UK in a few weeks to attend the event. He asked his aides to bring some invitation cards. I noticed that there were at least two types: there was a "regular" version, and though that card was impressive, another was reserved for the VIPs. The latter version had some of the letters written in gold and blue threads with a piece of metal at the base tied to the card. The card was then inserted into a glossy envelope with a floral motif in gold. This indicated both elegance and rank. In Nigeria, invitation cards demonstrate the status of the invitee and the invited.

He gave me one of the VIP invitation cards and asked if I wanted an additional one for a guest. I answered in the affirmative since I intended to bring

Figure 4.3. Akoko chiefs visiting the *Kakañfò*-designate at home. Photo courtesy of Segun Akanni.

along a friend. The card, which contained the images of the *Aláàfin* and the *Kakañfò*-designate, also had the name of President Mohammadu Buhari as the "Chief Guest of Honour" and Vice President Yemi Osinbajo as the "Special Guest of Honour." All the governors of the six Southwest states were listed as "Special Guests."

Before the Honorable Ayoola left, Adams asked that they take a photograph together. An obvious resident photographer quickly readied his camera. At that point, I thought it was an odd request for him to make of such a casual visitor to his home. I did not realize that he did this with everyone of some consequence who visited him during this period. He also asked me to join him for a photograph before we started a short interview. We stood in front of the TV. Behind us were symbols of both Christianity and Islam, the image of Jesus Christ and the popular Islamic affirmation *la ilaha illallah huwa lahu* (There is no God but *Allah*, and Muhammad is his messenger. He is *Allah*). On the floor around the TV stand were photographs of leading traditional rulers, either alone or with Adams, including the *Aláàfin* of Oyo and the *Ooni* of Ife.

I later realized that the photographs taken with visitors to his home formed an archive of those who came to pay homage to him after he was announced as the *Kakañfò*-designate. But beyond those visitors, his media team, led by his new chief of staff, Segun Akanni, encouraged the aides of the most prominent people in the country to ensure that their bosses issued congratulatory messages in the media. The team also methodically channeled into the media any congratulatory messages from the high and mighty. To give a few examples, President Muhammadu Buhari's special adviser on media and publicity,

Femi Adesina, issued a statement on behalf of the president congratulating the *Kakaǹfò* designate, while encouraging him to "use his new position to pursue worthy goals of security, peace and national unity."[8] The president, who commended the *Aláàfin* for the appointment of a new *Kakaǹfò* "who will assist him in the arduous task of leading the illustrious Yoruba people," also urged Adams "to bring quintessential courage, wisdom and astuteness to bear on his new office for a more secured life for the weak, vulnerable and voiceless in the country."[9]

Chief Ayo Adebanjo, one of the leaders of *Afenifere*, the apex Yorùbá political organization, also congratulated Adams while describing him as "a true Yoruba son." Adebanjo added, "He should bring the Yoruba nation together. The people of Yorubaland need to be united now more than ever." For Adebanjo, Adams's new role was even more critical because Adams could help to ensure that "*people who are not on [Adebanjo and Adams's] level of civilisation* [would] not be allowed to dominate [them]."[10] Even those who had major differences with Adams were forced to acknowledge the monumental achievement that his appointment as the *Kakaǹfò*-designate represented and, to concede, even if grudgingly, the über-affirmation of his status as a big man that the appointment constituted. One such example was Adams's former patron, the former governor of Lagos State and the national leader of the ruling APC, Bola Tinubu, who, in his congratulatory message, noted that Adams came to the position "with . . . extra youth, vigour and vitality." Tinubu stated that Adams "had never left anyone in doubt over his resolve to fight for the interest of Yoruba race." He added, "I congratulate you on your appointment as the next *Àárẹ Ọ̀nà Kakaǹfò* of Yorubaland. With this, you have joined the elite rank of generalissimos in Yorubaland. You deserve this honour. You have a heart of steel. You have never left anyone in doubt about your resolve and readiness to fight for and defend the interest of Yoruba race."[11]

Former governor of Ogun State Gbenga Daniel described Adams's appointment as "God-ordained."[12] Daniel added, "The courage, bravery and patriotic acts in the areas of promotion of culture values, security and overall development of Yoruba nation are the exemplary virtues of Otunba Adams that stood him out as a true son of Oduduwa who the region needs at this particular moment of our national history."[13] The governor of Ekiti State, Ayo Fayose, while wishing Adams "a fruitful and successful tenure," added that the "title of the *Àárẹ Ọ̀nà Kakaǹfò* of Yorubaland is for that bold, courageous, exemplary man who burns with the zeal to defend our land and protect her interest. All these are not lacking in the character of *Otunba* Gani Adams."[14] Even Adams's estranged former leader, Frederick Fasehun, gave a grudging congratulations by stating, "The *Aláàfin* can give *anybody, whether young or old, altruistic or otherwise* [the title]. I congratulate him (Adams) and I hope he will behave true to his title."[15] The Yorùbá community in the South-South and Southeast, with their headquarters in Port-Harcourt, raised the stakes by describing Adams's appointment as "an act of God" because Adams "was divinely ordained to save the Yoruba people."[16]

Pastor Enoch Adejare Adeboye, the general overseer of the biggest Pentecostal church in Nigeria—and probably in Africa—the Redeemed Christian Church of God (RCCG), could not attend the installation due "to the work of evangelism both within and outside Nigeria." However, he sent a congratulatory letter to Adams, which Akanni released to the press: "Grace be unto you and peace from God our Father. We greet you in the name of our Lord Jesus Christ of Nazareth. We congratulate you on your installation as the 15th Ààre Ònà *Kakaǹfò* of Yorubaland."[17] Adeboye "assured" Adams "of [their] continuous love and prayers." Another famous Pentecostal cleric, the senior pastor of Daystar Christian Centre, Pastor Sam Adeyemi, in his congratulatory message, expressed regrets that he would not be able to attend the installation but commended Adams while acknowledging his "passion to protect the interests of all Yoruba people."[18]

More than any of the other statements from Nigeria's most prominent clerics, the words of the sedate Adeboye, currently the primus inter pares among the Christian clergy, confirmed the high status that Adams, who claims to be "liberal with the three prominent religions we practice in the country,"[19] had achieved.

KAKAǸFÒ AND THE KING'S "PROGRESS"

On January 14, 2018, *Oba* Lamidi Adeyemi III, the *Aláàfin* of Oyo, said,

> [Adams] has been poignantly consistent in fighting for the protection of Yoruba. He was for many times humiliated, disgraced, manacled and jailed. It is natural for you either to hate, love and dislike him. However, the truth must be told that he was there when the Yoruba needed a person who is bold, strong and ready to lay his life for the defence of the heritage. . . . The role of an Ààre Ònà *Kakaǹfò*, both in the peace and war period is not a deal for the lilly- or jelly-livered or for a spineless fellow. It is the consignment of a man with a lion's heart and an eagle spirit which we have found in Aare Gani Adams.[20]

On the morning of Monday, December 10, 2017, as we entered the large reception room that also served as the state room for the *Aláàfin* of Oyo, *Oba* Lamidi Adeyemi III, we were welcomed to the palace by drummers and courtiers who praised us in the expectation that we would give them some money—as is the practice in the culture of praise. I was accompanied by my old schoolmate and former colleague (in journalism) Festus Adedayo. Adedayo was now a communications consultant and editorialist at the end of his term as the special adviser on public communication to Governor Abiola Ajimobi. We had both had access to the monarch for many years since the period of our shared careers in journalism, particularly at the Ibadan-based *Nigerian Tribune*. Adedayo had alerted *Oba* Adeyemi on the phone as we set out from Ibadan. The monarch told him that he would be receiving some traditional rulers from Adams's home state, Ondo State, who would be visiting to thank him for appointing someone from their area of Yorubaland as the *Kakaǹfò*, the first in their history. We were advised that we had to wait.

After a little while, one of *Kábíyèsí*'s assistants informed us that he was ready to receive us. Festus and I made our way out of the large reception room and headed for a smaller room where the *Aláàfin* hosts fewer guests. We met Archbishop Ayo Ladigbolu, who had been appointed the chair of the installation ceremony. The retired cleric and prince was just exiting the monarch's inner reception room. We exchanged pleasantries. When we were finally in the presence of the *Aláàfin,* we prostrated ourselves to greet him.[21] He greeted us familiarly and blessed us.[22] It is always a pleasure to be in the presence of the cerebral monarch. He is one of the most widely read and studious traditional rulers in Nigeria. Before we came into his presence, I reminded Festus of an interesting encounter with the *Aláàfin* about a decade earlier, in April 2008. I had accompanied my former supervisor, J. D. Y. Peel, then of the School of Oriental and African Studies (SOAS), to interview the *Aláàfin* for the book he was working on.[23] In the course of the interview, to illustrate a point, *Oba* Adeyemi launched into British history. Peel was so impressed that he said, "*Kábíyèsí,* you are telling me my own history!" In the book, Peel reflects on the attitude of *Oba* Adeyemi—whom he would later describe as "a genial and widely respected *ọba,* and at least a third-generation Muslim"[24]—regarding Yorùbá religion and Islam. Peel states,

> [*Oba* Adeyemi] is also regarded as the earthly successor to Sango, the thunder god, whose cult is central to Oyo kingship. Well practiced in expounding Oyo history and culture to visitors, he was not at all fazed or embarrassed when I asked him how he reconciled the discharge of his traditional duties with his personal identity as a Muslim. He did it by means of an ingenious two-way assimilation between Islam and Yoruba culture. First, he read Islam a long way back into Oyo history, maintaining that even Sango, deified after his death for his magical powers, had been a Muslim and was actually given the epithet

> *Akewugbẹru* (One given a slave for reciting the Koran). At the same time, he interpreted Islamic conversion as an expedient policy of self-protection against the Fulani jihadists that at the same time allowed it to be subordinated to Yoruba values: "The Yoruba never allowed other religions to destroy their identity." The *Alafin's* vision of Yoruba history, in fact, has more in common with the Rev. Samuel Johnson's.[25]

"I have been thinking about this matter since [*Kakañfò* Moshood] Abiola died [in 1998]," *Oba* Adeyemi began while explaining to me why he chose Adams as the *Kakañfò*-designate.[26] "Abiola was not able to fully accomplish the mission for which I appointed him. He accomplished some. [Therefore,] I have been thinking since his death about his successor. I had about fifteen people in mind."[27]

Oba Adeyemi then discussed the most prominent four he had considered, aside from Adams. All four were among the most prominent and accomplished Yorùbá of their era: President Olusegun Obasanjo, retired general and two-time head of state; Governor Bola Tinubu, former governor of Lagos State and national leader of the ruling APC and later the president of Nigeria (2019–); General Alani Akinrinade (retired), chief of defense staff in the Second Republic and minister of defense in the General Ibrahim Babangida regime; and *Aare Bamofin*, Afe Babalola, senior advocate of Nigeria, perhaps Nigeria's most respected living lawyer, philanthropist, and the founder of the eponymous Afe Babalola University, Ado-Ekiti. The *Aláàfin* then explained why each of these people, who would ordinarily be considered far more qualified for the position than Adams, did not emerge as his choice.

President Obasanjo, the *Aláàfin* said, "is not for the Yoruba; he is always thinking only about Nigeria." As for Governor Tinubu, *Oba* Adeyemi conceded that "he had the courage and the wherewithal" for the office. However, he concluded that since Tinubu "is very political and partisan," with a lot of responsibilities for his political party, the APC, he might not be able to discharge the responsibilities of the office of the *Kakañfò*. General Akinrinade, a Civil War hero, was already a warrior and would have been fit for the office. But, according to the *Aláàfin*, he was too old. The retired general would have been nearing seventy-nine by the time of his installation and would therefore lack the energy needed for the position. At any rate, I knew that Akinrinade would have rejected the offer. The famed lawyer, Babalola, is even older than Akinrinade. By the time the monarch was considering selecting a new *Kakañfò*, Babalola was eighty-eight. He was the closest to the *Aláàfin* among the four. He was also the king's lawyer in most of his critical legal battles over the decades. In fact, the monarch had installed him as *Ààrẹ Bamòfin* (roughly, legal generalissimo;

a latter-day honorary title). With these considerations in mind, the *Aláàfin* had a clearer choice. *Oba* Adeyemi stated, "So I thought of Gani Adams. There are a few qualities I was looking for. Someone who had both internal and external networks to help Yorubaland. The OPU [Oodua People's Union, which Adams created as an international cultural arm of the OPC][28] has branches in about seventy-six countries. He is also very devoted to Yoruba culture. He is very brave and therefore very suitable. When you look at the attributes of the earlier *Kakaǹfòs*, he has them. And he is able to defend Yorubaland."[29]

The monarch added that the political and security situation in Nigeria at this point necessitated that someone who was courageous and committed to the welfare of the Yorùbá and had the organization and network to defend Yorùbá interests should take the title of *Kakaǹfò*. The progress of Yorubaland, he reasoned, would depend on the appointment of such a "strategic leader."

However, before the *Aláàfin* came to this conclusion, Adams was making his own move to realize his ambition. Adams told me a few days after I spoke to the *Aláàfin* that the idea was first broached by a lady (whose identity was not revealed) bearing a message from the *Aláàfin* on an unrelated matter. The lady suggested to him in early 2017 that he should approach the Oyo monarch to ask to be considered as the next *Kakaǹfò*. I could not confirm from either the *Aláàfin* or Adams whether this lady had picked up the thinking of the monarch.

"I dismissed the idea," said Adams. "But after much persuasion, I did spiritual consultations. After I got some green light from the spiritual consultation, I spoke to a few key individuals in Yorubaland, such as Chief Ayo Adebanjo [one of the leaders of *Afenifere*], Chief Olu Falae [former secretary to the federal military government, the presidential candidate of the All People's Party–Alliance for Democracy alliance in the 1999 presidential election, and one of the leaders of *Afenifere*], Yinka Odumakin [the spokesman of *Afenifere*], and others."[30]

Because of the positive feedback from these consultations, Adams said he then approached the *Aláàfin*. He explained that even though the monarch did not initially make any commitment, *Oba* Adeyemi acknowledged that, in addition to Adams's dedication to promoting Yorùbá culture, he has the "organization, bravery, perseverance and persistence." The king also acknowledged that the OPC had chapters in twenty-eight states in Nigeria, claiming to have six million members.[31] In addition, according to Adams, when the monarch was informed that the OPU had branches in seventy-eight countries around the world,[32] he was impressed—as was evident in what he had told me three days earlier.

The *Aláàfin*, according to Adams, promised to consult widely, both within the *Oyo Mesi* (his cabinet) and among the prominent traditional rulers in

Figure 4.4. Adams with Chief Olu Falae (*second from left*), former presidential candidate of the APP-AD, former secretary to the federal military government, and one of the leaders of *Afenifere,* at a public lecture. Photo courtesy of *Nigerian Tribune.*

Yorubaland. He also added that he had to do spiritual consultation. This would take at least two months, the *Aláàfin* said. However, while warning that the position comes with heavy responsibilities, *Oba* Adeyemi disabused Adams of the general belief that *Kakaǹfòs* do not live long and always die violently.[33] He gave examples of ancient *Kakaǹfòs* who lived very long, such as Ojo Aburumaku.

A waiting game followed this initial discussion between the *Aláàfin* and Adams. Some who became Adams's informants in the king's palace fed him with information on when the monarch would likely make up his mind about the title. When the *Aláàfin* eventually verbally informed Adams that he had decided to appoint him the fifteenth *Kakaǹfò,* the waiting period became even more exasperating. Adams had to wait for the *Aláàfin* to make a public proclamation and present him with an official letter. Nothing was guaranteed before then.

The OPC leader was later credibly informed by palace sources that the letter would be ready on *Oba* Adeyemi's birthday on October 15, 2017. He therefore showed up at the birthday celebrations. But he was disappointed when the *Aláàfin* made no reference to the letter. He was prepared to return to Lagos, but some of his supporters who were close to the monarch persuaded him to pass the night in Oyo. Later in the evening, the monarch sent for him and handed over the proclamation letter announcing Adams's selection as the *Kakanfò*-designate. Adams was beside himself with joy. This would be the ultimate game changer in his life.

I asked Adams in December 2017 whether this was the fulfillment of his destiny. He agreed but added, "People say I am a good organiser, a good mobilizer . . . coming from grass to grace."[34] It was his way of saying that, though this was his destiny, he had also earned it.

As he and his aides left the Oyo palace that evening and headed for Lagos, his closest aide, Segun Akanni, tweeted a copy of the proclamation by the *Aláàfin*. As the news reached those on Adams's Twitter page, it was picked up and disseminated across social media and eventually appeared in newspaper and broadcast media.

There were some dissenting voices, particularly on social media, shortly after the announcement. Some argued that the *Aláàfin* had vulgarized the position by appointing Adams. The debates about whether Adams was qualified for the position dominated the sociocultural discourse among the Yorùbá both at home and abroad for a few months. I spoke to a number of people, and some called me to ask for my opinion. Such was the nature of the debate about Adams's qualification for the position that the *Aláàfin* had to defend the choice.

Oba Adeyemi told the press that he had picked Adams "based on his antecedents in the promotion of culture."[35] He described Adams as "equipped by God with the vitality of youth, agility of the long-distance runner, unblemished patriotism, and the wisdom of Solomon. His antecedents in the promotion of Yoruba culture are unquestionable, and he has a clear vision of where the nation should be in its cultural reawakening both at home and overseas."[36]

The monarch further defended himself, stating that "he did not receive money from" Adams before appointing him.[37] *Oba* Adeyemi added, "Money or material wealth is not considered before choosing an *Ààrẹ Ọ̀nà Kakanfò*. Abiola [Adams's predecessor] promoted everything that had to do with Yoruba race. He was popular among his people, and he was close to traditional rulers. So, Adams may not be as rich as Abiola, but I can tell you he has all the qualities an *Ààrẹ Ọ̀nà Kakanfò* should possess. He leads an organisation that is ever ready to defend the cause of the Yoruba race. *Is there any Yoruba man that has such clout as Adams without being a politician today?*"[38]

Again, at the thanksgiving service held at the Catholic church the day after the installation, *Oba* Adeyemi defended his decision. He told the congregation that twenty-five candidates had been shortlisted for the title[39] but that Adams had been selected because he was "found to have paid dearly and earnestly for the interest of Yorubaland."[40] The monarch indirectly responded to critics' emphasis on the violence perpetrated by the OPC under Adams's leadership:

> The benchmark of selection was not hung at the sentinel of political engagement, solidity in terms of gold, wealth or fortune, neither was it on the number of properties acquired on global pedestal but on agrarian and blind engagement of those who have abused and abusing, those who have infringed and infringing on the territorial and cultural territory of Yoruba. Whatever methods employed by [Adams] and his association, the fact still remains that there was a counter balance check valve which sent jitters down the spines of the irrational irredentists, who hitherto thought that they can make mince-meat of Yoruba land. . . . [Adams] has been poignantly consistent in fighting for the protection of Yoruba. He was for many times humiliated, disgraced, manacled and jailed. It is natural for you either to hate, love and dislike him. However, the truth must be told that he was there when the Yoruba needed a person who is bold, strong, and ready to lay his life for the defence of the heritage.[41]

As the "bold, strong and ready" prepared to be installed as the fifteenth *Ààrẹ Ọnà Kakaǹfò* of Yorubaland in January 2018, much of the dissension against Adams's appointment had been drowned out by the celebration of his imminent elevation. Thus, only the voices of affirmation and acclamation registered in the public media.

RITUAL AND TRANSFORMATION[42]

According to Meyer Fortes, "An unoccupied politico-ritual office endangers the stability of social life. . . . Ritual represents office to the individual as the creation and possession of society or a part of society into which he is to be incorporated through the office. Ritual mobilizes incontrovertible authority behind the granting of office and status and thus guarantees its legitimacy and imposes accountability for its proper exercise."[43]

One of the key questions raised in the anthropology of rituals is whether ritual is really capable of effecting transformation.[44] This question arises often, specifically in terms of rituals of initiation. While there are a myriad of approaches in anthropology about the nature, purpose, and place of ritual, here I emphasize two features that are crucial for my analysis of *becoming* and *being* a big man in contemporary Africa and the mobilization of tradition, custom, and culture in these processes. These are the formal structure of ritual—which those who engage in ritual must participate in and conform to—and the necessity of performance.[45] I suggest that, for strategic improvisers such as Adams (and many of those who impose, supervise, and perform "traditional" rituals, especially on chiefly matters in contemporary Africa), assenting and conforming to the formal structure of ritual is not as crucial as the *performance* of ritual. Thus, the structure of ritual is *formal* because it is *ceremonial*, not because it requires strict observance of "immemorial" rules. More crucial is the *performance* (of what is regarded as the formal structure of the ritual), both solitary and public. Given that the core purpose of chiefly rituals in contemporary Africa is power and control (over resources, people, institutions, and the social process, in general), both the structure and performance of such rituals, even where they remain exceedingly elaborate, have been liquefied, emptied of as much of their content as possible to make them serviceable to the performance of power and control, as grandly as possible.

While the potential *integrative* role of rituals that some anthropologists[46] have emphasized is useful for the elite—who give and take chiefly offices as they often glibly enunciate this role—in reality, because of the unrestrained commitment to the grandeur of performance in the struggle to seize and expand power, this role no longer gains much attention among those who wish to use chiefly positions for greater prominence and social power. As David Apter argues, contemporary "Yoruba ritual is a *critical practice* that is based on a hermeneutics of power."[47] Against this backdrop, Edmund Leach's insight about the fact that ritual primarily conveys the dynamics of already existing power relations in society[48] is illuminating, though it could be rendered even more strongly in light of contemporary experience. Ritual predominantly suggests the nature of the existing power relations in society; it can also indicate emergent forms of power—including even the rupturing of preexisting power relations.

As argued in chapter 1, the transformation of the structure and agency of human possibilities in what the Yorùbá call *aiye oyinbo* (the era of the white man or European)—or what can be called the age of modernity, particularly since the late colonial era symbolized by the ascendancy of Obafemi Awolowo, the first premier of the Western Region of Nigeria and the man regarded as the modern leader of the Yorùbá[49]—has meant that the highest form of self-actualization is achievable through Western education. Since the 1940s, with very few exceptions, people of consequence were those who had a good education. The ethos of this new age affected all facets of public life in Western Nigeria (Yorubaland), and since the late 1950s, even most of the prominent traditional rulers who lacked education have, upon their deaths, been replaced by the educated. Hence, since the start of the post–Oyo Empire era in the early twentieth century, and particularly since the colonial era, the only two men who have been *Ààrẹ Ọ̀nà Kakañfò,* Akintola and Abiola, were reflections of this new age—and thus were figures of the *neo*-Yorùbá, men of means who were educated in the United Kingdom: one a lawyer, the other a chartered accountant. Though both were men of *valor* in the "modern" Yorùbá sense, in that they were self-made, accomplished, and courageous, both were also departures from the rule in that they were not *professional* soldiers (*omo ogun*) as were all the other *Kakañfòs* who were appointed since the time of *Aláàfin* Ajagbo, who created the title of *Ààrẹ Ọ̀nà Kakañfò* in the seventeenth century. Thus, Adams's eruption into public consciousness as a neo–*omo ogun,*[50] a daredevil young man who had command of violence, is the closest approximation in contemporary times to the kind of men who held the title between the seventeenth and early twentieth centuries.

Consequently, the transformation of the office and role of the *Aare,* as symbolized by Akintola and Abiola and the attempt to approximate the original precept through the appointment of Adams, have forced the transformation of the ritual surrounding the installation.

J. L. Austin, the British philosopher of language, made an indirect contribution to the study of ritual by alerting us to the possibility that ritual may act as a vehicle of *transformation*.[51] Though this position of transformation is articulated through the rubric of performance theory with an emphasis on the dramatic and aesthetic qualities of rituals, I approach it here in terms of specific changes that the ritual of the *Kakañfò* is expected to invoke in the person who occupies the office—particularly the sociocultural and personal elevation in his status and the attendant benefits and responsibilities. Thus, ritual transforms, in this context, through the elevation of the officeholder.

Unlike all the previous officeholders, Akintola and Abiola were not adherents of *orisa* religion; Akintola was raised a Christian, and Abiola was raised a Muslim. Unlike the two, Gani Adams was raised a Muslim and now practices both Christianity and Islam, as well as Traditional African Religion. In the light of this, and because of the transformations wrought by the encounter with missionary Christianity and Western modernity, including the transformation in the nature, causes, and means of intra- and interethnic warfare in the postcolonial era,[52] the nature of the ritual process for the installation of the *Kakañfò* has also changed. What is left are traditions invented in the attempt to reappropriate the hallowed aspects of the institution and title of *Kakañfò*-ship in the old Oyo Empire so as to ensure and preserve the power, prominence, or eminence of the *Ààrẹ Ọ̀nà Kakañfò* in the new Yorùbá society. As Fortes argues, the contemporary ritual for the installation of *Ààrẹ Ọ̀nà Kakañfò* is designed to mobilize "incontrovertible authority behind the granting of office and status" and therefore ensure the legitimacy of the office and impose "accountability for its proper exercise."[53]

In approaching the ritual around the installation of the *Kakanfò* in contemporary Yorùbá society, I follow Barry Stephenson, who agrees with Clifford Geertz's postulation that the study of ritual is basically a hermeneutical endeavor.[54] Stephenson adds—as I hope to reflect in this chapter—that "one way to avoid reductive kinds of interpretation is to offer detailed descriptions of ritual events, from their preparation, through enactment, and aftermath, while also situating rites in their sociohistorical contexts."[55]

BECOMING KAKAǸFÒ

According to tradition, before an *Ààrẹ Ọ̀nà Kakanfò* is installed, he has to go through an elaborate ritual process that roughly corresponds to Arnold van Gennep's famous three-stage rites of passage: *separation, liminality,* and *incorporation*. However, two important caveats are necessary here. The rituals of installation have been modified or adapted in the postcolonial era—since the installation of Ladoke Akintola in 1962—because, as Margaret Thompson Drewal has argued, "improvisational interventions" are central to Yorùbá rituals.[56] "Like the larger society in which it operates, [Yorùbá ritual] is shaped by the competitive pulls and tugs of a multitude of manipulators"; therefore, it is never rigid.[57] A leading scholar of transatlantic *orisa* religion, Jacob Olupona, argues that Yorùbá religious culture "is remarkably adaptable . . . and open to creative meanings and interpretation."[58] Drewal also asserts that Yorùbá ritual is "continuously under revision" and is thus "molded and remolded by creative performers/interpreters who, acting both independently and in concert, reformulate it."[59] The ritual process for the installation of the current *Kakanfò* reflects this adaptability and creative (re)interpretation,[60] as well as the preservation of the myth through the ritual of installation.[61]

The first of the three stages of the ritual of installation, the *preliminal* stage, is called *ipebi* (seclusion). In the centuries when the Oyo Empire held sway, and even in the immediate post-Fulani invasion era in the nineteenth century,[62] the *Kakanfò*'s seclusion involved certain traditional processes. The modifications that began with *Kakanfò* Akintola and Abiola seem to have been fully realized by the time of Adams's installation.[63] In the past, as reported by the foundational (modern) historian of the Yorùbá, Reverend Samuel Johnson, in his *History of the Yorubas*, "at the time of taking office, [the *Kakanfò*] is first to shave his head completely and 201 incisions (*gbéré*) are made on his occiput, with 201 different lancets and specially prepared ingredients from 201 viols are rubbed into the cuts, one for each."[64] This process is "supposed to render him fearless and courageous." After shaving during the rites, in the postliminal period, the *Kakaǹfò* is allowed to grow his hair long only on the "inoculated part" (where the incisions have been applied). When the hair is fully grown, he will then plait it to form a tuft or a sort of pigtail.[65]

However, in what van Gennep describes as "the rites of separation from a previous world,"[66] Adam's *ipebi* ritual process, the preliminal stage, was unlike the ancient practices. He went into seclusion for three days in a hotel in Oyo. His head was not shaved, and no incisions were made on his occiput. In a *reconstituted, reinvented* process of detaching him from his "earlier fixed point in the social structure,"[67] to "cut him away" from his former self, all three religious practices in Yorubaland were involved, as demonstrated below. Against the context of such practices, Olupona has argued for the concept of "civil religion"[68] as a way of understanding the contemporary evolution of Yorùbá religion and the "very loose boundaries"[69] that Yorùbá (traditional) religion, Christianity, and Islam maintain in many dimensions of Yorùbá social life. Instructively, he advances the idea that "although indigenous *orisa* traditions have vigorously infiltrated Islam and Christianity, the *orisa* traditions have co-opted Islamic and Christian frameworks and interpretive models to make sense of their own plausible structures." This is evident in the contemporary process of the installation of a *Kakaǹfò*—as, to use Olupona's words, "traditional actions, rituals, and mythologies remain part of the Yoruba psyche and cultural identity."[70]

The headship of the Installation Committee also points to the transformation that has taken place in the appointment of the *Kakaǹfò*. The *Aláàfin* appointed the seventy-nine-year-old Ayo Ladigbolu, the retired Methodist archbishop of Ilesa and Ibadan Diocese, as the chair of the Installation Committee. Ladigbolu's biography reflects the religio-cultural transformations in Yorubaland in the last century. He is a prince born into the Muslim family of the late *Aláàfin* of Oyo, Oba Bello Gbadegesin Ladigbolu II, who reigned between 1956 and 1968. As a young man, Ayo Ladigbolu was a fiery Muslim preacher before, according to him, he "met [Jesus] Christ."[71] When he converted to Christianity, the king and his family were so displeased with the young man, who was expected to succeed his father as king, that he had to flee Oyo. Many years later, he reunited with his family. By that time, his father, *Aláàfin* Ladigbolu, had acknowledged the conversion of his first son and welcomed him back to the family. Thus, Archbishop Ladigbolu was well versed in the traditions of all three religions, Christianity, Islam, and African Traditional Religion. He was also very close to the *Aláàfin, Oba* Adeyemi, and was widely respected in Yorubaland and Nigeria.[72] In addition, his father, *Oba* Ladigbolu II, installed the first *Kakaǹfò* of the postcolonial era (Akintola). Ladigbolu was thus in an

Figure 4.5. Archbishop Ayo Ladigbolu, chair of the Installation Committee. Photo courtesy of *Nigerian Tribune.*

advantageous position to be appointed by the reigning *Aláàfin* as the head of the Installation Committee.

How did the retired Methodist priest, prince, and Yorùbá elder handle the ritual process for the installation of the *Kakaǹfò*?

"In the first place, there are still some ancient men and women left in our communities, people who knew all that were involved in preparing the *Kakaǹfò* by the way of the ritual," stated Ladigbolu. However, Ladigbolu recognized the great transformations in the ritual process: "Things are changing; times are changing. When a person like me is made to head the committee that plans this kind of [installation], I will have to be *true to the culture* as well as *try to be proactive* in terms of changes in the trend. All these were put together into the event."[73]

Although I met with Archbishop Ladigbolu—whom I had known for many years, particularly when I started my research on the Yorùbá power elite—at the installation ceremony, it was only afterward that we were able to discuss his involvement in the process. Navigating a ritual process that was "true to the

Figure 4.6. Adams during a visit to Archbishop Ladigbolu's home in Oyo. Photo courtesy of *Nigerian Tribune*.

culture" and that also compelled the ritual managers to be "proactive in terms of change" involved a lot of compromises between tradition and modernity.

Ladigbolu explained, "There were a number of incisions that were supposed to be made on the head, but that was for the [*Kakaǹfò*] going to the battlefield. Times have changed. The Ààre [*Ọ̀nà Kakaǹfò*] doesn't need a million incisions on his head to fight the kind of battle that we have to fight today."[74] However, Ladigbolu conceded that many Yorùbá still expected that the ritual process would involve incisions on the head as in the past.

"But people have forgotten that [times have changed]. [Therefore] a lot of people were still thinking in the mode of the previous ancient [*Kakaǹfò*] who needed to be fortified with such powers that comes from traditional medicine and concoctions to get them ready to do what they had to do. But then they needed to do [that] because of the need of the era."[75]

Indeed, the process adopted by Ladigbolu and the Installation Committee with the approval of the *Aláàfin* was a confirmation of the malleability of rituals in general and of Yorùbá rituals in particular.[76] The rites of the new age, according to the retired Methodist priest, are tailored to aid the *Kakaǹfò* in the challenges of the current times:

> Here is an era where the Ààre has to be intelligent, to be articulate, has to be courageous and be able to have wealth of his own to boost the prestige of the position. He has to be respected by members of his community and other communities. So, what do you need? How do you prepare this kind of Ààre [*Ọ̀nà Kakañfò*]? Do you just depend on the incisions? How many incisions you put on his head, how many charms and armlets you wrap him up with? No. So that really is the philosophy that guided me and my committee in prescribing what kind of preparation the Ààre Ònà *Kakañfò* of today needed.
>
> [On the basis of this,] we recommended that there must be seclusion because that falls in line with the traditional format in preparing anybody for a position of power. Even when you become an *oba*, you are put in seclusion, which gives you time to relax and reflect. That period gave the [*Kakañfò*-designate] time to be taught the rudiments of his new responsibility and help him focus and refocus ahead of the ceremonies that will put him in that position.[77]

In line with this philosophy of change, the *preliminal* and *liminal* stages, as explained by Ladigbolu, blended into each other in the three days of seclusion in the hotel, where the *Kakañfò*-designate was not allowed to see anyone apart from his closest family and aides. At the beginning of the first day, Adams was *separated* from his old self as he was welcomed into seclusion by the chief ritual manager, Ladigbolu. The second half of the first day through to the end of the third day represented a *threshold* stage, the liminal stage, where he was no longer the Gani Adams he had been but had not yet assumed a new status. Four specially selected persons took him through this period of liminality. Each spent about half a day with him. The first was a "knowledgeable, foremost Yoruba elder," as Ladigbolu described him, who spent time with Adams instructing "him about the history of the Yoruba race and all he needed to know and all he needed to be reminded of. Where did we [come from]? How come we are identified as we are? Where are we going? So that he can be part of that [history and tradition] and that can be part of him and can help him in planning how he wants his reign as *Ààrẹ*."[78]

There was a break after this instruction. The elder was followed by a Muslim cleric, who told him what "God require[s] of a leader of his status." The cleric also told Adams what "God requested [the cleric] to tell" the *Kakañfò*-designate: that "to be a leader at this level," he must perform the actions that "God expects of him, whether they are acceptable to the society or not." The next was a Christian cleric, who followed the same pattern as the Muslim. The last was a practitioner of Yorùbá religion, who also went through the same process. All three also prayed for the success of Adams's tenure as the *Kakañfò*.

Figure 4.7. After the rites on the eve of the installation. The *Kakaǹfò*-designate, with Sango ritual officials in red behind him, emerging from a three-day seclusion and meeting the *Aláàfin*, who hands over the staff of office to him. Standing next to the woman behind the *Aláàfin* is his senior wife, called Iya Koto. Photo courtesy of Segun Akanni.

Ladigbolu defended this eclectic approach to the ritual of installation. For him, this was not a subversion of tradition; rather, it represented a reconciliation of old practices with new realities. "It doesn't matter, if you believe in God, whoever your God is, whether *Olodumare, Allah* or *Yahweh,* the priests all told him what is expected from God's point of view."

On the third day, the seclusion process was completed. Ladigbolu then took Adams from the hotel to the palace of the *Aláàfin*. He handed him over to the palace aides and the *ayaoba* (*Aláàfin*'s wives). That evening, the king's aides took Adams through lessons in what was expected of the *Kakaǹfò* in general, including his obligations to the *Aláàfin*, the *Ọyọ Mẹsi* (the *Aláàfin*'s cabinet of chiefs), and the Yorùbá people. During the latter stages in the evening, he spent time with only Yorùbá traditional religion adherents, including Sango (the Yorùbá god of thunder) worshippers. Though deified as a god, Sango is also a past *Aláàfin*.

The Sango priests took him to one of the old houses within the palace premises to perform the final rites. The priests and the Sango adherents were all dressed in red, while Adams wore white *buba* and *sokoto* with a red sash wrapped around him and tied at the left side of his neck. A folded cloth was placed over the red sash to cover some parts of his head. Adams and the Sango worshippers did not disclose the details of the rites inside the old house. However, when they emerged, Adams held a staff of the *Kakaǹfò* rites and walked barefoot toward the *Aláàfin* with the Sango priests, other adherents, and the women (all wearing white) beside and behind him. The drummers accompanied them, beating the rhythms associated with Sango worship. As he walked, some in the small crowd within the palace said, "*o ti d'oosa*" (he has become a deity), thus pointing to the end of the liminal period and Adams's transformation. Technically, by this point, he had become the *Ààrẹ Ọ̀nà Kakaǹfò*. The women sang of his triumph over the dangerous liminal stage by congratulating the new *Kakaǹfò*: "Gani Adams *o ku ewu* o, *ewu ina kii p'awodi, Awodi o ku ewu*!" (Gani Adams, congratulations on your survival. The danger of fire does not kill the hawk [or bird of prey]. Hawk, congratulations on your survival!). The traditional hunters fired shots from their dane guns (long-barreled flintlock muskets) into the air.

When he approached the *Aláàfin*, who himself is the heir and personification of *Aláàfin* Sango (the god of thunder), the new *Kakaǹfò* knelt before the monarch, handed over the staff, and raised the traditional gesture of salutation among the *awo* (initiates), a clenched fist with the right hand raised and the left palm resting on the elbow. The *Aláàfin*'s aide took out the staff's white cloth covering and handed it to the monarch, who then handed it to Adams while he stood, thus confirming that he had successfully passed through the liminal process and was about to be publicly installed as the *Kakaǹfò*. The rites completed, and the *Aláàfin* returned to his palace as the women sang the praises of the new generalissimo.

When the process, which Ladigbolu described as "the balance of his tutoring before installation," had been completed, though the seclusion was officially over, Adams returned to the hotel to prepare for the next day.

CEREMONY AS RITUAL

As the horse-drawn carriage in which the *Aláàfin*, Oba Lamidi Olayiwola Adeyemi III, and the *Kakaǹfò*-designate, Gani Adams, were riding arrived at Durbar Stadium for the installation, at 12:52 p.m. on January 13, 2018, the arena erupted in cheers. Some shouted the praises of the *Aláàfin* while others screamed "*Aare*!" *Oba* Adeyemi, dressed in full traditional regalia, the three-piece Yorùbá *aso-oke* and his signature Oyo cap, the *abetí ajá*, stepped out of the carriage with Adams in tow. Adams had donned full white Yorùbá attire. He also wore a matching *abetí ajá* cap. Two long red strands of beads hung from his neck and wrist. Both the king and his field marshal–designate made their way to the state box—the

Figure 4.8. The horse-drawn carriage that brought the *Aláàfin* and the *Kakaǹfò*-designate to the venue of the installation, Durbar Stadium, Oyo. Photo by Tommy Adegbite.

elevated platform where the most important dignitaries, particularly high state officials, sit at open-air public events—in the capacity-filled stadium.

I was sitting in that state box in Nigeria. Festus Adedayo had asked one of the facilitators of the event to lead me there so I could have a better view. This ensured that I could interact with the dignitaries, many of whom I knew, either personally or through other acquaintances. By the time I arrived, many of the most important dignitaries were already seated. We were all waiting for the arrival of other dignitaries and the two most important figures of the day: the *Aláàfin* and the *Kakaǹfò*-designate.

Several politicians, officeholders, prominent lawyers, and traditional rulers were seated in the five rows on the raised platform. I sat in the third row. The first row was reserved for the *Aláàfin*, the *Kakaǹfò*-designate, his wife, the vice president (or his representatives), the governors (or their representatives), and the first-class traditional rulers. Adams had told me earlier that the *Ọ̀ọ̀ni* of Ife, *Oba* Adeyeye Enitan Ogunwusi, Ojaja II—who, like the *Aláàfin*, occupies one of the two most important thrones in Yorubaland—was also planning to attend the event. Although there had been some rapprochement between the two competing thrones,[79] I suspected that the current *Oòni* would have been advised against attending the installation of a chief, even one as significant as the *Kakañfò*, in the *Aláàfin*'s domain. When I called the *Oòni* to ask if I would see him at the event, he said no.

But the *Olubadan* of Ibadan, *Oba* Saliu Adetunji, was already seated when I arrived at the state box. In the nineteenth century, the *Olubadan*'s city became the "Yoruba Sparta."[80] It rescued the crumbling Oyo Empire and the Yorùbá from further incursion by the Fulani by defeating them in the late nineteenth century. The city also produced Latosa, the last *Kakañfò* of the precolonial era. Also present were the *Owa Obokun* of Ijesaland, *Oba* Adekunle Aromolaran; the *Alake* of Egbaland, *Oba* Adedotun Gbadebo; the *Deji* of Akure, *Oba* Aladetoyinbo Ogunlade Adelusi; the *Timi* of Ede, Oba Adesola Lawal; and several other traditional rulers.

The state box also held the representatives of the governors of all the Yorùbá states (except Ekiti); one of the leaders of the most important Yorùbá progressive political group, *Afenifere*, Chief Ayo Adebanjo; the daughter of Awolowo, Dr. Tokunbo Awolowo Dosumu; and the former governor of Ondo State Dr. Olusegun Mimiko. Such "political presence at enstoolments and ceremonies awarding . . . customary titles," as Michael Schatzberg argues in *Political Legitimacy in Middle Africa: Father, Family, Food*,[81] constitutes a critical aspect of the "acts of presence" that help to create and consolidate legitimacy in Africa.

The event could not start on time because the organizers had to wait for the habitually late governor of Oyo State, Abiola Ajimobi. This meant that the *Aláàfin*, the *Kakañfò*-designate, and their entourage had to wait at the palace much longer than planned. The program was scheduled to start at 11:00 a.m. As the time was approaching 1:00 p.m., the governor was still expected. Not long after the monarch was informed that the governor had set out from Ibadan, he and Adams headed for the stadium. Governor Ajimobi arrived shortly after the *Aláàfin* and the *Kakañfò*-designate were seated. Subsequently, the installation formally began with the singing of the national anthem and the Oyo State anthem.[82]

There were speeches by the chair of the Installation Committee, Archbishop Ladigbolu; the host governor, Ajimobi; and the *Aláàfin*. These were punctuated by "cultural displays"—that is, performances by different cultural groups. The installation followed.

Though the rites for installing Adams had been completed by the morning of Saturday, January 13, the public ceremony formalized the position. Thus, it also needed to be ritualized to give it cultural authenticity. As Victor Turner has argued, "a chief or similar functionary in any African society is invariably

Figure 4.9. The *Aláàfin* speaking at the start of the public rites. Adams is holding his own calabash, with his wife, Mojisola, beside him. Photo by Dare Fasube.

installed in office by a public ceremony."[83] Even though the public installation was more of a ceremony than a ritual,[84] it was staged as a *ritualized ceremony*, one that carried a sense of the sacred, even though the actual sacred part of the process had already been performed in secret, during the three-day seclusion. Yet, in such "ceremonies around rites," as Meyer Fortes, following Van Gennep, has explained, "the 'politico-legal' and 'social' elements are more important than the magico-religious."[85] While ritual is expected to *transform*, ritualized ceremony is expected to publicly *confirm* the transformation.[86] The presence of the political authorities and the sociocultural community of people of consequence in Yorubaland and the Nigerian polity was crucial at this stage to confer generalized legitimacy on the earlier ritual process, the installation, the office, and the occupant of the office.

To begin the public rites, Adams, accompanied by his wife, Moji, and the *Aláàfin*, left the platform and moved to the designated area in the center of the arena. There, a long red carpet had been laid. The ritual aides, wearing only white robes tied around their waists with nothing on top, accompanied both men. One held a microphone for the *Kakaǹfò*-designate so everyone could hear him as he repeated the chants for the rites. A ritual calabash was handed to Adams, and he carried it as he walked with the *Aláàfin* toward the calabashes representing all fourteen preceding *Kakaǹfò*—from the first, Kokoro Ngangan,

Figure 4.10. The new *Kakaǹfò* with his own calabash. The *Aláàfin* (*second from left*) is standing in front of Adams, while Adams's wife, Mojisola, watches from behind the *Aláàfin*. Photo by Tommy Adegbite.

to the fourteenth, M. K. O. Abiola.[87] As he stepped nearer to the calabashes, he stopped at intervals to recite chants, while some intoned, "*Ase*" (amen). The *Kakaǹfò* then handed his own calabash to one of the ritual aides.

Subsequently, Adams touched each of the calabashes of his predecessors and repeated a chant that had been written down: "*Iba Eledumare; iba gbogbo irunmole ile Yoruba; iba gbogbo irunmole Oyo; iba Eleda Kábíyèsí Olayiwola Lamidi Adeyemi III; Iba* [the name of each past *Kakaǹfò*]; *e je ki igba temi o tu gbagbo Yoruba l'ara o*" (Hail to the Almighty; hail to the divinities of Yorubaland; hail to the divinities of Oyo; hail to the Creator of His Majesty, Olayiwola Lamidi Adeyemi III; hail to [name of each of the past field marshals]; let my reign be a peaceful era for the Yoruba). After he had repeated the chant while touching Abiola's calabash, the *Aláàfin* pronounced him the new *Ààrẹ Ọ̀nà Kakaǹfò*.

At the completion of this process, the fifteenth *Ààrẹ Ọ̀nà Kakaǹfò* stood beside *Oba* Adeyemi as the monarch addressed the crowd. Adeyemi said the new *Kakaǹfò* would ensure unity among the Yorùbá and all the traditional rulers in the land to guarantee the progress of the Yorùbá in Nigeria. All the traditional rulers were invited to surround the new *Kakaǹfò* and the *Aláàfin* as they prayed for a successful tenure for the new field marshal.

Figure 4.11. The calabashes of the past fourteen *Kakan`fò*s. Photo by Tommy Adegbite.

Figure 4.12. One of the ritual aides inserts the *awe akoko* under the *Kakaǹfò*'s cap at the installation Photo courtesy of Segun Akanni.

Figure 4.13. The *Aláàfin, Oba* Lamidi Adeyemi III, holding the staff of office and describing the meaning of its parts before handing it over to the new *Kakaǹfò*. Photo by Tommy Adegbite.

The ritual aides then took the *ewe akoko* (akoko leaf) from a big *ikoko* (pot). The leaves are a necessary element of any installation into traditional office in Yorubaland. They are usually inserted into the traditional cap on each side of the face of a new chief or king. The ritual aides also brought the *amotekun* (leopard)-skin garb,[88] a symbol of the bravery of the *Kakaǹfò*, which Adams wore over his *agbada*. He took off the *abetí ajá* cap and donned the ritual cap of the *Kakaǹfò*, the *Akoro* (coronet),[89] to which ostrich feathers and bits of cheetah skin had been attached, with a longer strip at the back dropping to his neck like a tail. The *ewe akoko* was inserted into either side of the coronet. This completed the public ritual, the process of installing Adams as the fifteenth *Ààrẹ Ọ̀nà Kakaǹfò* of Yorubaland.

As *Oba* Adeyemi and *Kakaǹfò* Adams—with his wife, Mojisola, beside him—mounted another high platform, the master of ceremonies formally introduced Adams to the world as the new *Kakaǹfò*: "*Baba wa, Iku Baba Yeye, alase ekeji orisa*, Adeyemi III, *won ti fi baba wa je Ààrẹ Ọ̀nà Kakaǹfò*, Dr. (*Otunba*) Gani Adams" (Our father [with the *Aláàfin's* honorifics,] Adeyemi III, has made our father the *Ààrẹ Ọ̀nà Kakaǹfò*, Dr. [*Otunba*] Gani Adams). A new staff of

Figure 4.14. The new *Kakaǹfò*; his wife, Mojisola (*right of Adams*); Governor Abiola Ajimobi (*left of Adams*); the *Aláàfin* of Oyo, *Oba* Lamidi Adeyemi III (*left of Ajimobi*); the *Olubadan* of Ibadan, *Oba* Saliu Adetunji; and other traditional rulers at the installation. Photo courtesy of Segun Akanni.

office was then unveiled by a ritual aide and handed to the *Aláàfin*. The *Aláàfin* held the staff and made a small speech, telling the guests and the crowd that the three arrows in the staff represent the three moments in the life of a human being: morning, afternoon, and night. He added that the morning of the life of the new *Kakaǹfò* has been good, and he prayed that the afternoon and night of his life would be prosperous. The crowd shouted "*Ase*!" (amen). *Oba* Adeyemi then looked at the top of the tall staff (which had a sphere on the top) and said, "This is the earth. May the earth not break in your hand. The calabash will not break in your hand.... You will succeed." The crowd shouted "*Ase*!" He handed the new staff of office to the new *Kakaǹfò*. The crowd hailed the new *Kakaǹfò*.

A *Sango* priest took the microphone and handed the *ose Sango* (Sango's axe) to the new *Kakaǹfò* on behalf of the descendants of Sango. He added that by that token, the new *Kakaǹfò* had also acquired the power and authority of the god (Sango).

Archbishop Ladigbolu, the chair of the Installation Committee, was elated as Adams was publicly installed. He told me later that "God must have chosen [Adams] for divine purpose which is meant to be our common benefit. I felt elated to be part of that history unfolding itself."[90]

Many people regarded the moment of Adams's installation as significant in the context of the interethnic relations in Nigeria. Late 2017 and early 2018 brought times of much political rancor to Yorubaland. Internally, there was a grave division among the dominant progressive elites, who had controlled the politics of Yorubaland for about sixty years, despite strong challenges from local conservative forces, who were often allied with the dominant Hausa-Fulani politicians in the North of Nigeria. However, in this era, a major faction of the progressive political elite, led by Governor Bola Tinubu and others, was now allied with President Muhammadu Buhari. The older progressive elites believed Buhari bore the banner of the Hausa-Fulani elites under the guise of progressive politics. Even the Tinubu camp, at this point, was fractured. Therefore, the progressive political tradition of Awolowo had no strong leader who commanded the respect of all the factions in Yorubaland, as Awolowo once did.

In addition, a wave of expanding crime, including armed robbery, kidnapping, hostage taking, and rape, posed a threat to the social order and the territorial security of Yorubaland. The crime wave was particularly troubling in its links to the Fulani herdsmen (pastoralists), who many believed were "invading" Yorubaland and taking over its forests. As the clashes between Yorùbá farmers and Fulani herdsmen intensified, with media reports of kidnapping, ransoming, and rape allegedly perpetrated by the herdsmen, the Yorùbá wished for a leader who would respond forcefully to the sense of siege that many felt.[91] A few people told me they believed that the "blunting of the sharp edge" of the OPC by the *elitization* of its leader, Adams, made it impossible for the group to stop the upsurge of criminality in the Yorùbá states. Yet others felt that given his antecedents, Adams was also well placed to mobilize the forces needed to respond to the challenge. In fact, a newspaper editor told me that a colleague in the North, when Adams's appointment was announced in October 2017,[92] had said that the appointment reflected the Yorùbá's collective resolve to "take the battle to the herdsmen" who were allegedly behind the rampant crime in the Yorùbá states. They needed an arrowhead, a "generalissimo . . . on a gallant horse," as captured in a poem written by Akeem Lasisi for the *Kakañfò*'s installation, to meet the challenge of an era in which "our homeland is crying for cover." Lasisi, acclaimed poet and journalist, tells the new *Kakañfò*, "You will need to fight wars, Gani. . . . To awaken the sleeping giant in our enviable race."[93]

—∾—

After completing the public rites of installation, as scholars of ritual have argued, Adams assumed the new identity and reentered society with a new status, as he also acknowledged. He had been incorporated into a far higher rank than

Figure 4.15. The new *Kakaǹfò*, in the full regalia of office, thanking the crowd after his installation. Photo courtesy of Segun Akanni.

he had ever imagined, though in the last few years he had already become a man of great reckoning in Yorubaland and beyond.

The new *Kakaǹfò* mounted the rostrum to deliver his inauguration address. "There cannot be a more humbling occasion for me as the one we are in today,"[94] he stated after saluting all his predecessors in the five-and-half-century-old office.

Indeed, for an *Okada*-riding artisan who started his public life at twenty-seven derided as a mere "carpenter," "thug," and "vagabond," Adams's ascent to the position of *Ààrẹ Ọ̀nà Kakaǹfò* two decades later was the stuff of dreams. As he surveyed the crowd, Adams must have felt truly fulfilled.

"Against the backdrop of the size of the office . . . [that] has been bestowed on me," he said, "and the larger-than-life image of my predecessors, my installation as the 15th *Ààrẹ Ọ̀nà Kakaǹfò* is a challenge that has made all past challenges [in my life] seem like a child's play." He noted that the last two *Kakaǹfòs*, Akintola and Abiola, "brought so much power and glamour to the office . . . [and] raised the profile of the office." He added that, despite the changes in the circumstances in the post–Oyo Empire era, the core duties of the *Kakaǹfò* "still stand": "protection of the interests of Yoruba race, both within the country and everywhere else." He then promised, "The preservation of the culture of the [Yorùbá] race will occupy my attention."[95]

Significantly, he noted his own transformation from what he described as "the heady days of the Oodua People's Congress (OPC)" to his present status, which, he believed, "has unwittingly forced the *stature of a statesman* on [him]."[96] On this basis, he promised to use the new office to "project the Yoruba culture and tradition . . . globally," in addition to ensuring the "unity of all Yoruba sons and daughters all over the world." He also promised to ensure through his activities that most people would acknowledge "that a child born of humble beginning like me can make it."

As is usual with all of Adams's events since he became very comfortable, popular musicians were on hand to entertain guests. He invited three, including two Fuji musicians, Adewale Ayuba and Wasiu Alabi Pasuma, and a Juju musician, Shina Peters, to perform at the installation.

PERFORMING KAKAǸFÒ-SHIP

In this section, I examine the ways in which Adams mobilized his new status as *Ààrẹ Ọ̀nà Kakaǹfò*—which he regarded as one of personal, cultural, and sociopolitical preeminence—to redefine his position within and beyond Yorubaland and accelerate his project of self-actualization through self-aggrandizement. I will use two cases to illustrate why, for him, this new position, though it compels him to ensure "the protection of the interests of Yoruba race, both within the country and everywhere else"—as he stated in his inauguration speech—also affords him the opportunity to match, if not surpass, the "power and glamour" that his last two predecessors brought to the office while also attaining their "larger-than-life image."

In this renewed project and process of self-actualization and self-aggrandizement, for Adams, as evident in earlier chapters, the spiritual (specifically, mystical) element has always been as crucial as the practical acquisition of power, influence, and wealth—and the public projection of these. Both are tied, though.[97] In fact, I suggest that the title of *Kakaǹfò* was part of the strategic process of *acquisition* (both symbolic and concrete—of wealth, titles, and other prestige goods, as well as cultural capital and Yorùbá mystical powers), which, when combined with spiritual capital acquired from Christianity and Islam, would make Adams an indestructible warrior. Because Adams is a man who considered himself permanently vulnerable because of his background and who constantly questions the motives of everyone, allies and foes alike, over the last decade he has shown considerable interest in acquiring the spiritual powers that would make him indestructible and capable of predicting the future. As

Figure 4.16. In the shadows of the Sage: Adams standing by a giant portrait of Obafemi Awolowo at the late leader's country home in Ikenne. Photo courtesy of *Nigerian Tribune*.

one of his aides told me, Adams constantly wishes to be like Awolowo, who he believes had the "mystical power" to "see visions."[98] In Adams's mind, in addition to fortifying Awolowo, the ability to "see visions," or predict the future, also helped him earn the respect of the Yorùbá and the rest of Nigeria.

"There is a spiritualist that he went to in Ikare for this [quest for clairvoyance]," reveals one of his former close aides.[99] "He told the man that one of the reasons people respect[ed] Awolowo was that Awo could prophesy. He said he wanted such powers." The aide claimed that, as a result of the engagement with this spiritualist, Adams once went into "a trance" for weeks. I could not confirm this, as Adams was generally dismissive of anything that his former aides had told me. But all those aides and ex-comrades I interviewed spoke about his commitment to "spiritual potency." Indeed, Adams's craving for spiritual powers is not unusual among big men in cultures in which such men play important roles. The "ritual element, or [the] reputation of the big man as a magician and spiritual leader," as Paula Brown describes it,[100] is a crucial dimension of what it means to be a big man. Brown adds, "In some areas, big men, and the Baruya 'great men' . . . were thought to command powerful supernatural forces in themselves, or to hire sorcerers, to destroy their enemies and punish offenders, thus supporting their control of the community." According to Adams's former comrades, in the aftermath of his "trances," he would claim to have received "revelations" about the plots of some of his lieutenants. However, such "revelations," though critical for his survival as a vulnerable leader, are less important to his ambition to acquire the power to predict the future of the Yorùbá and Nigeria.

Thus, for Adams, his earlier investment in the potency of fetish objects as the leader of the OPC, his embrace of the Christianity and Islam as well as the Yorùbá religion, his devotion to the annual public worship of Yorùbá gods through cultural festivals, and his successful bid for the title of *Ààrẹ Ọ̀nà Kakañfò* are different parts of one of the key cornerstones of being a big man: the need to *sacralize* oneself to be distinguished and distinguishable from most people, including even many in the elite circles in Yorubaland and Nigeria. Thus, Adams approaches being installed to a chieftaincy through the rites of Yorùbá religion, being ordained in a church, and participating in Islamic prayers as different rituals that are necessary and useful, in different but connected ways, for the affirmation of his sociocultural preeminence.

TOWARD SELF-SACRALIZATION: BETWEEN INSTALLATION AND ORDINATION

In December 2020, I was inundated with messages from friends and colleagues about the "breaking news" of *Iba* Gani Adams's ordination as an apostle by the Saviour's Ministry World Wide, a Cherubim and Seraphim Church (popularly called C&S) in Nigeria. The C&S Church is one of the second-generation African Independent Christian Churches, popularly called *Aladura* (prayer churches).[101] Early scholarship on these churches described them as "prophet-healing churches,"[102] given their "preoccupation with both direct revelation and therapeutic prayer."[103] Interestingly enough, one of the earliest students of the *Aladura* churches, H. W. Turner,[104] focused on their "use of ritual symbols which might well be susceptible to a magical interpretation."[105] It is understandable that a church with such "weakened doctrinal emphasis on Christ" and "considerable liturgical inventiveness"—to use Eva Krapf Askari's phrases[106]—would appeal very much to the multireligious Adams.

Colleagues and friends who knew that I was not on social media forwarded the postings and reactions on Facebook, Twitter, Instagram, and blogs to me. I also googled the stories and comments.

The leader of the Saviour's Ministry World Wide (C&S), also called *Baba Aladura*, His Eminence (Dr.) Prince Solomon Adeniran Aluko (JP), approved Adams's ordination. The event was held on December 13, 2020, at the church auditorium located in Alausa, Ikeja, Lagos.

Figure 4.17. "Ordinations and installations exhibit . . . a common order." *Left: Kakañfò*-designate Adams at the final rites on the morning of his formal installation in January 2018 with Sango worshippers behind him. Photo courtesy of Segun Akanni. *Right:* Two years later in December 2020, Adams and his wife at the ceremony where he was made an apostle, with the "Lord's army" standing guard as he marches into the church. Photo courtesy of *Nigerian Tribune*.

Figure 4.18. Adams praying with other Muslims at the *Jumat* thanksgiving service after his installation in January 2018. Photo courtesy of Segun Akanni.

Figure 4.19. Apostle Adams receiving his ordination certificate from one of the leaders of the C&S Church in December 2020. Photo courtesy of *Nigerian Tribune*.

While I was not surprised that the ordination (as an apostle) came two years after the installation (as *Kakaǹfò*), given that van Gennep alerted anthropologists to the fact that "ordinations and installations exhibit . . . a common order,"[107] many appeared to be shocked that Adams would take on a Christian priestly position and title after he had become the *Kakaǹfò*. This, for some of the commentators, was a profane act made more egregious by the "sacred" context in which this happened—an *Aladura* church. An online news forum reported that the ordination "has started generating some debate on social media."[108]

One of the commentators on Facebook, Emmanuel Femi Oyeniyi, described the ordination of Adams as "an abomination on the altar!" and "an apostasy."[109] He continued: "[Adams is a] Muslim and Traditionalist yet he was ordained last week by a Church as an 'apostle.' Till now, I've not seen our Pastors or Prophets to speak out against this abomination on the altar. Perhaps they are afraid of their lives or they see the ordination as the Church's strategy to show love and win his soul for Christ. Or they see it as one of the new normals in the Church. Whatever the case may be, the Gospel Truth is that many things have gone wrong in the Church." Oyeniyi concluded that "we cannot all fold our arms and watch sheepishly as these agents of darkness turn the Church bought with Christ precious blood into *witchcraft coven*."[110] One commentator with the name Ezekiel123 on Opera News described the ordination as "from shrine to church" while posting the photograph of Adams during the ritual ceremony for his installation with Sango priests in Oyo and that of Apostle Adams side by side. He asked what the church "is actually turning to now"[111] and added,

> Both believers and unbelievers seems to be given one post or the other in the church this days, the position of Apostle, Bishop e.t.c seems to be ceremonial post now and no proper check and balance before giving out posts in church, the Bible clearly stated in Matt 6:24, No man can serve two masters: for either he. will hate the one, and love the other; or else, he will hold to the one, and despise the other, Ye cannot serve God and mammon, i wonder how the *Aare Ona Kakanfo* of Yoruba land fortified with charms will become an Apostle. I think the (C&S) churches needs to be called to order, the way they handle Christianity and give out post is alarming and dangerous which could cause a lot of damages to the body of Christ sooner or later.[112]

Such commentators regarded Adams, because of his embrace of Yorùbá religions and his installation as the *Kakańfò*, as having been inducted into a "witchcraft coven,"[113] a coven that the *Baba Aladura* of the Saviour's Ministry World Wide had now brought into the church to "pollute" the "precious blood" of Christ.

But while many on social media were concerned about the question of "pollution"[114]—implied in a traditionalist becoming an apostle—in their reactions to the ordination, the traditional media, the Nigerian newspaper press, did not find anything strange or unusual about the event. For them, Adams's ordination was not an important news angle. They had been reporting his adherence to some aspects of the three religions for several years, covering the festivals he organized regularly, as well as his attendance at church services and prayers at mosques. In fact, as both Adams and the reporters recognized, being a practicing adherent of the three religions was another aspect of his distinction. Thus, the newspaper press focused on Adams's condemnation of President Mohammadu Buhari's handling of the security situation in the country, referencing the ordination itself only to state the context in which Adams spoke.[115]

However, the fact that the press approached Adams's ordination as regular news while focusing on what he said at the event reflects two dimensions of his private and public life. The first is his immersion in the Yorùbá religious world, and the other is his success in adroitly managing and manipulating the media over the years. As to the first, Adams's ordination (as apostle), following his installation (as the *Kakaǹfò*) and his participation in an Islamic (*jumat*) thanksgiving, are only reflections of what Olupona describes as "civil religion" among the Yorùbá,[116] which the Lagos-Ibadan press understands too well to report as anything abnormal or outrageous.[117] Thus, the "ritual man" we see in Adams approaches different religious rituals as "adaptable," and hence as "events of origination, of innovative construction and reorientation"—*pace* Victor Turner[118] and Olupona.[119] The second dimension is Adams's skillful management of the media; several reporters defer to him, and some senior editors either are his friends or have been his beneficiaries in the past—including, at one point, the national chair of the Nigerian Union of Journalists, whose election Adams supported by providing security.[120] Almost every news report about Adams takes his viewpoint. In fact, the "bad press" he has attracted in recent years comes almost exclusively from columnists or news reports in which other eminent Nigerians say negative things about him. Even when this happens, either he is given the right of reply within the same report or he responds with good coverage within twenty-four hours. Thus, negative reports or comments about him appear mostly on social media and blogs or in the comment sections of online reports. As I pointed out in chapter 3, the near-total control of the news concerning him in the press, including, in some respects, the broadcast media, ensures that his status, influence, power, and prestige are carefully managed. Thus, ultimately, what comes across in the reportage of both the installation and the ordination is the elevation of Adams's status in society.

—∾—

On Sunday, January 14, 2018, the day after his installation in Oyo as the *Kakaǹfò*, Adams joined the *Aláàfin*, Oba Adeyemi, who is a Muslim as well as the "offspring" and personification of Sango, at the special thanksgiving service at the St. Mary's Catholic Cathedral, Asogo, Oyo. The thanksgiving service was for the installation and for the commemoration of *Oba* Adeyemi's forty-seventh year on the throne. As with Adams, *Oba* Adeyemi's attitude to the three religions is in line with the tradition of toleration and cross-religious or multireligious practices dominant among the Yorùbá.[121]

In *Oba* Adeyemi's speech at the service, he articulated this attitude in regard to the selection and installation of Adams: "After he came first at the examination and scrutinisation *by men and earthly beings*, his appointment as the 15th

Figure 4.20. Catholic Bishop of Oyo praying for the *Aláàfin* and the new *Kakaǹfò* at the thanksgiving service in January 2018. Photo by Bolaji Ibraheem Akewusola.

Figure 4.21. Group photograph after the service at the Catholic Church Cathedral, Asogo, Oyo. The *Aláàfin* (*third from left*); *Aláàfin*'s queens (*second and fourth from left*); the new *Kakaǹfò* and his wife, Mojisola (*third and second from right*); and others, including the Catholic priests. Photo by Bolaji Ibraheem Akewusola.

Figure 4.22. *Ayin'ba* Mojisola and *Iba* Gani Adams (*both in the middle*) with the *Aláàfin*'s queens at the thanksgiving service at St. Mary's Catholic Cathedral, Oyo, the day after the installation. Photo courtesy of Segun Akanni.

Figure 4.23. The new *Kakańfò* bowing to greet the *Aláàfin* at the thanksgiving service in Oyo. Photo courtesy of Segun Akanni.

Figure 4.24. *Kakańfò* Adams exchanging pleasantries with a Catholic priest at the thanksgiving service at the Catholic cathedral, Asogo, Oyo. Photo by Bolaji Ibraheem Akewusola.

Àárẹ̀ Ọ̀nà Kakańfò was also subjected for approval and subsequently *sanctioned by the gods and all the elemental forces in the firmament.* We also ensured that the *three religions* being fervently practiced by the Yoruba prayed and endorsed his appointment. Thus, we find it expedient to be here today not only to give and pray to God through Mother Mary, the Holy Virgin for my 47th year on the

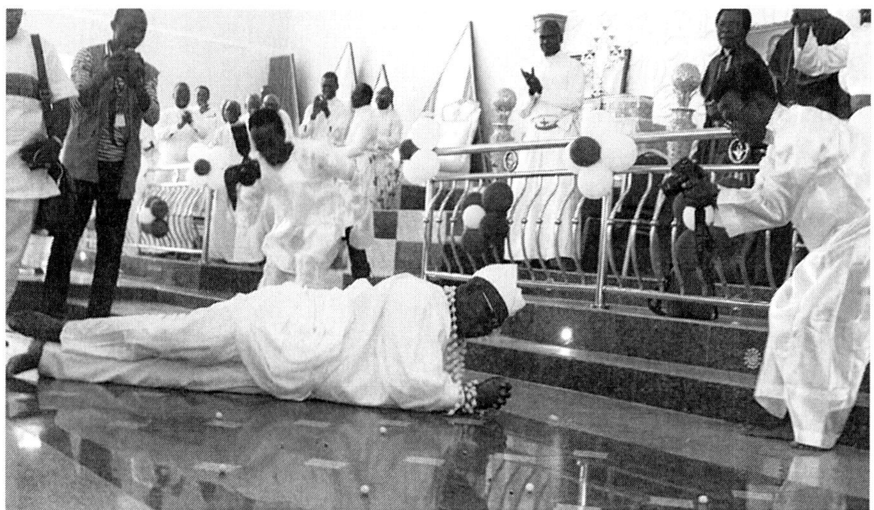

Figure 4.25. To the God of Transformation: Adams rolling on the floor at the altar of the Celestial Church of Christ to acknowledge the massive transformation of his fortune after his installation as *Kakaǹfò*. Photo courtesy of *Nigerian Tribune*.

throne, but also for the successful installation ceremony of the 15th *Ààrẹ Ọ̀nà Kakaǹfò* of Yorubaland."[122]

It can be argued that a Muslim traditional ruler and descendant of the god of thunder invoking the "Mother Mary, the Holy Virgin" in a church is as normal in Yorubaland as a Christian-Muslim-Yorùbá religious adherent[123] who is also the *Ààrẹ Ọ̀nà Kakaǹfò* being installed as an apostle in an *Aladura* church.[124] What some of those venting their anger against the newly installed apostle and *Kakaǹfò* did not know was that Adams felt that the "prophesy" and prayers of a Christian cleric were crucial to his being appointed the *Kakaǹfò*. To demonstrate his gratitude for the "spiritual intervention" of Pastor Israel Ogundipe, the senior pastor of the Celestial Church of Christ (CCC), Genesis Model International, Alakuko, Lagos, the new *Kakaǹfò* went to Ogundipe's church for another thanksgiving on Sunday, January 22, 2018, the next weekend after his installation. At the service, he rolled on the floor in gratitude to Ogundipe's God.[125] In Yorubaland, this act is the highest form of submission to God—or to any higher authority, including a very powerful individual. Adams told the congregation,

> Pastor Israel Ogundipe predicted my emergence as the *Ààrẹ Ọ̀nà Kakaǹfò*. That is one of the reasons I respect him as a man of God. He was at my former office at Palmgrove and he made three predictions which all came to pass in

> less than two weeks. I saw humility and the holiness of God in him. He is one of the few pastors that I respect. When we started jostling for the post, I told him to pray along with me and promised him that I would do my thanksgiving in his church if the Lord answered my prayers. Twenty-five of us contested for the position and I was the least wealthy among them. *The Lord imposed me on all of them.*[126]

Ostensibly, for Adams, Senior Pastor Ogundipe, and his congregants, there was nothing abnormal in an eminent man, no matter his religious affiliation, going to the church to thank God for fulfilling a prophesy, especially one that involved defeating twenty-five wealthier and more powerful rivals. The trope of struggle against, or triumph over, (evil or other) forces has become dominant in the worldview of contemporary Pentecostal Christianity—as well as the first-, second-, and third-generation African Independent Churches, such as the Celestial Church—as is reflected in Adams's statement that God "imposed" him on the more powerful people interested in the position.[127] Beyond the sacred imposition, this statement also reflects Adams's profane attitude toward the exalted positions he attained in comparison to his humble beginnings, particularly in relation to those more eminent people in the Yorùbá society who still looked down on him or who had not yet reconciled themselves with the eminence he had acquired. The use of the word *imposed* again betrays the fact that he is constantly looking over his shoulders to be sure about the *universal* acceptance and acknowledgment of his arrival.

It was perhaps not lost on Adams that Samuel Bilehou Oschoffa, who founded the CCC in Porto Novo (Republic of Benin) in 1947 and then in Nigeria in 1950, was a carpenter-turned-prophet.[128] The church—which, as Afe Adogame argues, was "nurtured within [the] religio-cultural context" of the founder and his immediate subethnic group, the Gun (Egun)-Yorùbá—has now gained worldwide fame with membership in the several millions and has been rechristened the Celestial Church of Christ Worldwide.[129] Despite this spread, as Adogame shows, the CCC's "cosmology . . . its belief system and ritual form in a sense remain tied largely to the 'apron strings' of the [Gun-Yorùbá] cultural matrix."[130] Adogame argues that "the CCC has consciously and unconsciously created a synthesis of Christian and Yoruba belief paradigms and ritual forms as a new rationalization, a new ordering of the cosmos by the adherents."[131]

Therefore, in both Prophet Oschoffa and the CCC, Adams could see mirrors of himself and his OPC, including the melding of religious adherences, which is central to his public and private lives.

Before his installation, Adams had planned to celebrate the title at the three religions' places of worship.[132] About a week after the thanksgiving service at the Celestial Church, Adams attended another thanksgiving service, this time

Figure 4.26. Adams with an Islamic cleric and other Muslim leaders after the thanksgiving service at the Festac Mosque. Photo courtesy of *Nigerian Tribune*.

at an *Ifa* temple (*Ifa* is a Yorùbá religion and system of divination).[133] The *Ijo Orunmila Ato* (Indigenous Faith of Orunmila)[134] in Ebute Metta, Lagos, is a modernized—for want of a better word—gathering of Orunmila (Yorùbá god of divination) adherents. Adams said at the service that he was fulfilling the instructions given to him during the installation rites to respect all religions, particularly traditional religion.[135] He added that he had been told by *Ifa* to always put *Eledumare* (God Almighty) first in everything. The prayer session for the new *Kakaǹfò* was led by the *Akoda* (chief priest) of Ijo Orunmila, Chief Demola Fabunmi, and his *Aseda* (assistant chief priest), Chief Awodiran Agboola.

Before the thanksgiving services in the church and the *Ifa* temple, on the Friday after his installation, January 19, 2018, a special *Jumat* service and thanksgiving was organized at the Central Mosque in Festac Town, Lagos, for the new *Kakaǹfò*. In his sermon, the mosque's chief imam, Sheik Sakariyah Adewale, described Adams as "a worthy son and blessing to Nigeria and the Yoruba race as a whole" while praying that "Allah should continue to bless you with long life, so that you can fulfil all your dreams in life." He added that, as Muslims, the community was "happy to celebrate [Adams's] new status with [him]."[136] Describing the newly installed generalissimo, without any sense of irony, as "a symbol of peace," Adewale urged him "to continually preach unity across the country."[137]

Adams, who reminded the *jamaah* at the mosque that he has been worshipping there for over seven years, particularly during his birthday celebrations, added that he was attending the prayer service on the first Friday of his installation to give thanks to Allah. However, he alerted the congregation that he would also attend a church service and a service at an *Ifa* temple to give thanks: "I am a highly liberal person when it comes to the issue of religion and as a Yoruba man, I have to be liberal with the three prominent religions we practice in the country."[138]

DISTINCTION THROUGH RECONSTITUTION: THE ÀÀRẸ ỌNÀ KAKAŃFÒ-IN-COUNCIL

As part of the second anniversary of his installation as the *Ààrẹ Ọnà Kakańfò*, on January 15, 2020, Adams installed seventeen of his own chiefs who would constitute the *Ààrẹ Ọnà Kakańfò-in-Council.*[139] Like many of his actions and statements, the installation attracted wide media coverage; it also generated a lot of controversy. Many asked why Adams, who was himself a chief, though one holding a unique position as *Eso* of *Esos* (generalissimo), could also install chiefs. Was Adams assuming traditional powers that he did not possess? Was this an indirect challenge to the authority of the *Aláàfin* who appointed him?

Those who were outraged by a chief making chiefs did not realize that they were helping to affirm Adams's status as a particular kind of eminent person: a constant generator of controversies, and therefore a person featured on the front pages of newspapers as well as in online forums and social media. In fact, Adams constantly hosts events in part because it keeps him in the news, given that he regards being out of the news as one of the quickest ways to risk a form of social death.[140] Since intruding on the public space about two decades earlier, and especially since starting his steady climb into social reckoning about five years later, Adams has done everything to avoid reverting into a *social nonperson*, as most people would have regarded him before he became the arrowhead of the OPC.

Though the controversy over whether Adams was qualified to appoint chiefs is understandable, many of the critics did not know the basis of the *Kakańfò*'s power of appointment. As Adams explained at the installation of his own chiefs, twelve of the *Kakańfòs* before him had war cabinets. As the field marshal of the old Oyo Imperial Army, the *Kakańfò* needed a group of commanders and field officers—or chiefs, as they were called. In that sense, Adams was correct to state that he was acting in concert with past practices. "The stool of the *Ààrẹ Ọnà Kakańfò* of Yorubaland [is] historic," he said at the installation of his chiefs. "It was created in 1530 and dedicated to the head and king of all warriors in Yorubaland. Once installed, the *Ààrẹ Ọnà Kakańfò* is mandated to have his chiefs and Council of Chiefs. And all *Ààrẹ Ọnà Kakańfò*, since 1530, had Chiefs and Council of Chiefs."[141]

Figure 4.27. The *Kakaǹfò*-in-Council: Adams and his wife (*middle*) with his new chiefs. *Left to right:* Former director general, News Agency of Nigeria, Akin Osuntokun (*Ajagun-Nla Ààrẹ Ọ̀nà Kakaǹfò*); retired banker, Segun Sanni (*Basorun Ààrẹ Ọ̀nà Kakaǹfò*); former World Bank consultant, Dr. Gboyega Adejumo (*Gbonka Ààrẹ Ọ̀nà Kakaǹfò*). Photo courtesy of *Nigerian Tribune.*

Though he conceded that "the only two exceptions in the long history of the institution were the late S.L.A. Akintola [and] M.K.O. Abiola," the reason he offered for his immediate predecessors' lack of a council of chiefs was disingenuous. Adams said that Akintola and Abiola "could not constitute their councils due to the political developments of their respective periods."[142] In fact, since the end of Oyo's sovereignty and the beginning of the colonial era, the title had effectively become an honorary or titular title rather than an actual office. Thus, when *Aláàfin* Ladigbolu installed Chief Akintola as the *Kakaǹfò* in 1962, it was meant to honor him and rally the Yorùbá around an ancient and valued title. The "war" of the modern era at this point was the struggle between the Yorùbá and other ethnic nationalities in Nigeria. Given the realities of the modern era, neither *Aláàfin* Ladigbolu nor Akintola thought that a council of chiefs was necessary for a post–Oyo Empire *Kakaǹfò*. The same was true of Abiola, an accountant and international businessman who was installed in 1988 by the current *Aláàfin, Oba* Adeyemi. The selection of a council of chiefs did not occur to Abiola, and no one thought that it was necessary or even useful during his time. At any rate, Akintola and Abiola were already eminent men by the time they were installed as *Kakaǹfò*. While the position brought them honor, it did not dramatically change their status in the larger Yorùbá society or beyond. In fact, Abiola was generally referred to by his earlier (and far less eminent) title of *Basorun* (roughly, general)—a title he held in Ibadan. However, for Adams, though he too had achieved a measure of eminence by the time he was installed as the *Kakanfò*, the title greatly transformed his status, enhancing and affirming his achievement in a spectacular way. Thus, he was eager to use the grander eminence invested in him by the new title to further enhance his power, influence, and resources, unlike the last two occupants of the position.

While it is true that Adams was returning to (or reinventing) the imperial-era tradition by appointing his own chiefs, it is evident that he did so because it fitted his own specific project of self-aggrandizement. Yet, because he was the nearest approximation of the warriors who had been named *Kakanfò* in the past, Adams was more likely than his two immediate predecessors to try to revive or reinvent the past practices of the *Kakanfò*, especially those that would further enhance his status.

Apart from generating more activities around Adams and his new status, the installation of the chiefs also helped him energize his twin project of incorporation and subordination. As part of his larger project of self-actualization, he elaborates and employs particular cultural endeavors to incorporate cultural enthusiasts and others who wish for social recognition. Adams's efforts are made easy by the excessive craving for honor and recognition in contemporary African societies.[143] By incorporating people of social or cultural substance (many of whom are significant in their own rights), Adams subtly subordinates them to his own social standing. By culturally elevating these people, as when investing them with cultural titles, he further elevates himself in relation to such accomplished men and women. This would make him the big man of big (wo)men. In fact, at the ceremony, he described himself as "the king of all warriors" in Yorubaland.[144]

The installation ceremony of the *Ààrẹ Ọ̀nà Kakanfò*-in-Council was held at 10 Degrees Events Centre in Ikeja, Lagos. As with most public events organized by Adams, the day was festive, with music, heavy drumming, and cultural performances, including dancing, singing, and praise singing. The *Kakanfò* wore his trademark white *agbada*. For this special occasion, as if to assert the authority of his office, he put on his *official* cap, the *Akoro* (coronet).

Adams invited many traditional rulers. Those who attended were largely lower-class rulers, yet their presence lent greater traditional authority to the event. Hundreds of people attended, including the family members of those being honored. The title of each new chief included "[of] *Ààrẹ Ọ̀nà Kakanfò*" because their titles are formally subordinate to his. But the addition of *Ààrẹ Ọ̀nà Kakanfò* also affirmed that these were the *Kakanfò*'s chiefs and therefore were not the rivals of those who held similar titles, such as the *Aláàfin*'s chiefs. Adams reiterated this at the ceremony in response to rumors that he was rivaling the *Aláàfin* by giving these titles.

Adams installed the chiefs in batches of two or three. He hung long white beads with their titles around their necks and placed the chieftaincy caps (also with the titles) bearing the *ewe akoko* on their heads. He then handed over the small *opa ase* (staff of office) and the certificate of appointment to each chief. These processes included both past and invented practices. Ostensibly, the past *Kakañfò*s did not give any of their warrior chiefs a certificate.

The seventeen new chiefs,[145] who are all people of substance in their own rights, some of them already holding chieftaincy titles, included Mr. Akintola Osuntokun (*Ajagun'nla Ààrẹ Ọ̀nà Kakañfò*), former special adviser to President Obasanjo, former managing director of the News Agency of Nigeria (NAN), and leading newspaper columnist; Mr. Segun Sanni (*Basorun Ààrẹ Ọ̀nà Kakañfò*), former general manager at Stanbic IBTC Bank Nigeria and former director with the Standard Bank of South Africa Group; Mr. Gboyega Adejumo (*Gbonka Ààrẹ Ọ̀nà Kakañfò*), former World Bank consultant and one of the leading members of the *Afenifere*; Hon. Adegboyega Salvador-Adebayo (*Otun Aare Ààrẹ Ọ̀nà Kakañfò*), former special adviser in Lagos State; Chief Abiodun Adewale Kuku (*Otun Balogun Ààrẹ Ọ̀nà Kakañfò*), a US-based tax consultant; Kuku's wife, Hon. Chief Mrs. Bolanle Kuku (*Erelu Ààrẹ Ọ̀nà Kakañfò*); Otunba Obafemi Arowosola (*Agbaoye Ààrẹ Ọ̀nà Kakañfò*); Barrister Babajide Tanimowo[146] (*Atoloye Ààrẹ Ọ̀nà Kakañfò*), a barrister and solicitor of the Supreme Court; Mrs. Esther Oyebola (*Yeye Opeluwa Ààrẹ Ọ̀nà Kakañfò*); Chief Victor Mobolaji Adewale (*Akingbayi Ààrẹ Ọ̀nà Kakañfò*), a Sweden-based businessman; Mr. Ibrahim Adeleke (*Otun Baaregunwa Ààrẹ Ọ̀nà Kakañfò*), a security consultant; Alhaji Gani Oshidele Wahab (*Tunaarese Ààrẹ Ọ̀nà Kakañfò*); Alhaji Fatai Adeshina (*Opo-Akin Ààrẹ Ọ̀nà Kakañfò*); his wife, Mrs. Adeshina (*Yeye Opo-Akin Ààrẹ Ọ̀nà Kakañfò*); Chief Bolaji Thomas Jaji (*Ikolaba Ààrẹ Ọ̀nà Kakañfò*); Hon. Mutiu Olakunle Okunola (*Jagun Ààrẹ Ọ̀nà Kakañfò*); and Sweden-based Mrs. Bisi Tapere Wahab (*Yeye Tunaarese Ààrẹ Ọ̀nà Kakañfò*).

Adams later appointed another round of twenty-one chiefs,[147] expanding and consolidating his power to appoint. This power is crucial for anyone at the apex of an organization, particularly when the power is *singular*—that is, when it does not require another person's approval or oversight. This was the kind of power Adams had exercised as the leader of OPC. Now, he was using it at a much higher level, for the purposes of incorporation and subordination.

At the second installation ceremony for his new chiefs, which was attended by such dignitaries as Titi Atiku Abubakar, wife of former vice president Atiku Abubakar (1999–2007), and *Otunba* Gbenga Daniels, former governor of Ogun

Figure 4.28. The *Kakaǹfò* installing Mrs. Esther Oyebola as the *Yeye Opeluwa Ààrẹ Ọ̀nà Kakaǹfò*. Photo courtesy of *Nigerian Tribune*.

Figure 4.29. The *Kakaǹfò* and two of his chiefs. Mrs. Bisi Tapere Wahab, *Yeye Tunaarese Ààrẹ Ọ̀nà Kakaǹfò,* is on the right. Photo courtesy of *Nigerian Tribune*.

State, Adams said, "I appointed these 21 chiefs to help me to succeed. As the *Ààrẹ Ọ̀nà Kakañfò*, my job covers the entire Yorubaland, but I cannot be everywhere at the same time. The people I am installing today as chiefs [are] from everywhere we have indigenous Yoruba people, including Kogi and Kwara, [and] will act for me in their respective domains and handle issues. They will interface with their local *obas* and traditional chiefs to ensure peace and development in Yorubaland."[148] Those installed in this round included a Labour Party chieftain, Dr. Kayode Ajulo (*Maiyegun Ààrẹ Ọ̀nà Kakañfò*); journalist and former newspaper editor Shola Oshunkeye (*Baaroyin Ààrẹ Ọ̀nà Kakañfò*); Ademola Ige (*Baameto Ààrẹ Ọ̀nà Kakañfò*); and Prof. Taofeek Raheem (*Parakoyi Ààrẹ Ọ̀nà Kakañfò*).

At the ceremony, Adams hinted, without prejudice to the traditional rulers present, that the *Kakañfò* is greater in some respects than many traditional rulers. While this was true in the past, in Yorùbá culture, no one says categorically that his position is greater than that of any traditional ruler. Thus, quite a few people were shocked by the statement. Adams recognized this, and shortly after making the statement, he turned to the traditional rulers present to say that he was not indicating that he was higher in status than them; however, that was what he had implied. It was a reminder to all that, with his new status, especially given that it was a title for the whole of Yorubaland, Adams considered himself not just as primus inter pares but as numero uno.

In the months after the announcement of his appointment and his installation, Adams ensured that eminent people visited him at home to congratulate him or consult with him. As he told one of his close associates who was trying to arrange a meeting in the home of a nonagenarian Yorùbá leader, because he is the *Kakañfò*, with few exceptions, people must visit him at home. Given his new status, he had to choose where and whose homes he visited. Though he visited a few people to formally present himself as the new *Kakañfò*, indeed, most highly placed Nigerians obliged him by visiting him or sending their emissaries to his home. Envoys of some of the most significant countries in the world also visited him. Three examples would suffice here. For the first category of visitors, the then federal minister of solid minerals and former governor of Ekiti State Dr. Kayode Fayemi, who could not attend the installation ceremony, later visited Adams at home. Though Fayemi, in the company of Senator Ibikunle Amosun, then the governor of Ogun State, arrived early enough for the ceremony, neither could show up at Durbar Stadium because the host governor, Senator Abiola Ajimobi, did not arrive on time. They left town before Ajimobi's arrival.

Figure 4.30. The federal minister of solid minerals and former governor of Ekiti State, Dr. Kayode Fayemi, visiting the new *Ààrẹ Ọ̀nà Kakaǹfò* in his home. Photo courtesy of *Nigerian Tribune*.

Figure 4.31. Senator Babafemi Ojudu visiting Adams at home on behalf of Vice President Yemi Osinbajo. Photo courtesy of *TheNEWS*.

Figure 4.32. A two-person delegation from the Canadian Embassy in Nigeria (*on Adams's right and left*) visited the new *Kakaǹfò* at home to celebrate with him. Photo courtesy of *Nigerian Tribune*.

I spoke to Fayemi on the phone while they were waiting at the palace. After a while, he and Amosun had to leave because it was "against protocol" for them to be at the event when the host governor was not yet there—or on his way. To affirm his good wishes toward the new *Kakaǹfò*, Fayemi, who was planning to run again for the governorship of his state in 2019, visited Adams at home after the installation.

In the weeks before the installation, Vice President Yemi Osinbajo sent his special adviser on political affairs, Senator Babafemi Ojudu,[149] to greet Adams at home on behalf of himself and President Buhari. During the visit, Ojudu congratulated Adams on his appointment and assured him that the presidency "would be fully represented at the installation."[150] Visits like that of the vice president's aide—to use Michael G. Schatzberg's words—extend "recognition to a newly empowered player in the field of power."[151]

The second category of visitors included a delegation from the Canadian Embassy in Nigeria that visited Adams at his Lagos home to congratulate him on his installation as the *Kakaǹfò*.

In the years after his installation, Adams celebrated the event annually. The fifth anniversary was in January 2023.

"SECOND HOME OF THE YORUBA RACE": THE KAKAŃFÒ RENEWS AN "ANCESTRAL LINK" IN BRAZIL

In the early hours of Friday, December 9, 2022, a plane carrying the *Ààrẹ Ọ̀nà Kakańfò* and his entourage landed at the Guarulhos International Airport in São Paulo, Brazil—the most populous "Black nation" outside of Africa. He was received at the airport by "the Yoruba fraternity King," Oba (Ogboni) Adekunle Aderonmu; the executives of the OPU in Brazil; and Santos Football Club (FC; Pele's former club) supporters. A delegation from the club had visited Adams in Lagos in November. Adams's entourage included Babajide Tanimowo, the *Atoloye Ààrẹ Ọ̀nà Kakańfò* of Yorubaland; Mr. Yinka Oguntimehin, *Asoju Ààrẹ Ọ̀nà Kakańfò* of Yorubaland and OPC national publicity secretary; and Ambassador Ibraheem Lawal, chair of the Textiles Mills Association of Nigeria.

Adams, as the *Ààrẹ Ọ̀nà Kakańfò* of Yorubaland, was visiting the South American country as part of the internationalization of his role as a cultural ambassador, which, a few years earlier, had been expanded with the formation of the OPU. This internationalization process is central to Adams's project of appropriating the narratives and practices of what Andrew Apter has described as "transatlantic cultural origins and continuities"[152] of the people of Yorùbá descent in the New World. The visit to Brazil was also part of Adams's efforts to tap into what Tracey E. Hucks has described as "the geographical, ideological, and theological landscape of Yoruba locales across the globe"[153]—in this case, in the New World.

During the visit, Adams attended the international summit of the OPU in South America, held between December 9 and 15. At this meeting, he addressed the Assembleia Legislativa do Estado de São Paulo (Legislative Assembly of the State of São Paulo) on the state of the Yorùbá worldwide and held other cultural events. Oba Adekunle Aderonmu, the president of the African Cultural Center in São Paulo, told *Ancestral News*, "The arrival of a significant authority like [the] *Ààrẹ Ọ̀nà Kakańfò* from Yorubaland to Brazil is a divine compliment of ancestral link between Nígeria and Brazil. The Yoruba race is same worldwide. Aare is the warrior of all Yoruba race, including the Yoruba Brazilians. We wish him the very best throughout this historic visit."[154]

Present at the summit were OPU representatives from South American countries including Argentina, Bolivia, Chile, Colombia, Ecuador, Guyana, Paraguay, Peru, and Suriname. Aderonmu described the *Ààrẹ Ọ̀nà Kakańfò* as "a blessing to the Brazilian people" and wished that he would visit Brazil regularly.[155] It was reported that "the Yoruba warrior elevated Yoruba culture

Figure 4.33. The *Kakañfò* walking with Oba (Ogboni) Adekunle Aderounmu and others to the State Parliament in São Paulo. Photo courtesy of Adeyinka Olaiya.

Figure 4.34. Adams with his hosts in Sao Paulo in December 2022. Photo courtesy of Adeyinka Olaiya.

and tradition"[156] when he addressed the Legislative Assembly and the Brazil Bar Association. "The Yoruba culture and tradition is important in Brazil. It has helped Brazil a lot. It has made Brazil a rich environment culturally. I implore the Bar Association to continue condemning racial and religious intolerance. I

Figure 4.35. The *Kakańfò*, his entourage, and members of the Bar Association, São Paulo, during Adams's visit to their office. Photo courtesy of Adeyinka Olaiya.

Figure 4.36. The *Kakańfò* with Chief Pedro Maximiano during a visit to the Santos Football Club, legendary Pele's former club. Photo courtesy of Adeyinka Olaiya.

Figure 4.37. The *Kakaǹfò* with his new chief in Brazil, Pedro Maximiano (*second to the left of the Kakaǹfò*), and others in São Paulo, December 2022. Photo courtesy of Adeyinka Olaiya.

am happy with Brazil. It's lovely to see how the Yoruba culture is taken serious here," Adams reportedly said.[157]

Apart from addressing the Legislative Assembly and the bar association, visiting African museums, and being "received in grand style at the arena of King Pele's eternal club, Santos FC," the *Kakaǹfò* was also honored with African songs and dances. The director of Drums Caverna and founder of Samba Paulistano, Cosmo Damião, presented the generalissimo with an official jersey of Santos FC autographed by Pele. The visit, according to the Board of Directors of Santos, "will further promote the Ancestral link between Brazil and Nigeria."[158]

Another high point of the visit was the *Kakaǹfò* exercise of his power of installation. He installed a new chief in Brazil, Pedro Maximiano, as the *Otunba Amofin Ààrẹ Ọnà Kakaǹfò*. With great excitement and pride, Maximiano declared, "I am happy to be the *Otunba Amofin Aare Ona Kakanfo* in Brazil. It is a reward for all I have contributed to *Isese* [cultural activities] in Brazil."[159]

Before traveling to Brazil in December 2022, as part of his mission to become the global embodiment of the transnational Yorùbá identity, Adams paid a courtesy visit to the Brazil Embassy in Lagos. Speaking with Flavio R. Bonzanini, the consul general of Brazil, Adams said he was ready to use his office to foster better relationships between the two countries.[160] Extolling his own attributes, Adams stated that "he has all it takes to promote the cultural identity and tradition of the [Yorùbá] race beyond the shores [of Nigeria]." While describing Brazil as "a second home of the Yoruba race in South and North America," the *Kakaǹfò* said, "As the *Ààrẹ Ọ̀nà Kakaǹfò* of Yoruba land, it is my plan to use my office to enhance business relationship[s] with the international world, by creating various platforms for growth and capacity building, especially for the youth. This is to create a better synergy for the benefits of the two countries."[161] In his remarks, Consul General of Brazil Bonzanini said, "I am delighted to meet with you because your visit is certainly the beginning of a lasting relationship and I hope it will be of great benefit to the two countries."[162]

CONCLUSION

In the last four centuries of the Oyo Empire, people sang a popular song to emphasize the preeminence of the *Ààrẹ Ọ̀nà Kakaǹfò* and his awe-inspiring power, both physical and mystical: *Ààrẹ, Ààrẹ, Olo'un ma je'n s'Ààrẹ Ọ̀nà Kakaǹfò* (*Aare, Aare,* may God prevent me from crossing the *Ààrẹ Ọ̀nà Kakaǹfò*). Indeed, crossing the *Kakaǹfò,* in the distant past, was an invitation to death and destruction. Except with reference to the *Aláàfin,* the *Kakaǹfò* was a person who lived in a state of exception,[163] with the capacity to transcend the rules in the name—or even guise—of defending the collective good of the empire. Since his installation, Adams has tried, often subtly, to invite everyone to ratify what he assumes to be his exceptional status as a *Kakaǹfò.*

While the three postimperial era *Kakaǹfòs* no longer possess the excessive powers, including the power over life and death, that belonged to the *Kakaǹfòs* of the earlier centuries, unlike his two predecessors, Adams is eager to reinvent the dread—and the measure of exception—in which the *Kakaǹfò* was held in the defunct Oyo Empire. He is the only post-nineteenth-century *Kakaǹfò* to take his staff of office with him wherever he goes. He sometimes even holds it when taking photographs in his home during visits by eminent people.

Adams feels that he has earned this title, as well as the power and privileges that come with it. Indeed, he has taken so many risks over the last two decades—and escaped death a few times through sheer luck—to arrive at his present status. Apart from the public demonstration and elaboration of his current status, the people around him in his private life are either eager or forced to reconcile themselves with his transformation. For instance, one of those close to him revealed that the people in his orbit now (have to) kneel before him when

Figure 4.38. Adams during a visit to the *Ooni* of Ife, *Oba* Adeyeye Enitan Ogunwusi, Ojaja II, before his installation as the *Kakañfò*. Photo courtesy of *Nigerian Tribune.*

they address him. I cannot confirm this because I have not visited him at home since his installation. However, it is understandable that—as a man who is sensitive to the needs and privileges of his status and also vigilant about how people observe what he considers to be the *required* prerogatives of this status—Adams would expect that, in every way, his life and relationships would be completely reconditioned by his installation as *Kakañfò*—a title and office that he had invested more than two decades of struggle and invested plenty of resources to attain. Huge expenses are involved in sustaining the status of a big man in Nigeria, and the installation ceremony for the *Kakañfò*, according to sources close to him, must have cost him about N60 million (roughly US$166,000).[164] However, it is obvious that, for Adams, this was *a truly worthy* financial investment. As the Yorùbá say, *"owo la a fi pe'na owo"* (Money is mobilized to make more money). In his new position, he would attract even far greater resources than he had in the past.

Because it decisively confirmed his preeminent status in Yorubaland and Nigeria, both in the present and in the future, and placed him on a pedestal that he considers comparable to those of leading monarchs, former and serving high officials of the Nigerian state,[165] and accomplished professionals, the *Kakañfò* title is the acme of distinction for Adams, as well as the fulfillment of what he considers his manifest destiny. He had warned those who either did not pay sufficient attention to his rise or disparaged him on his way to the top: "You don't expect reasonable, thinking people to underrate or ignore somebody like me, somebody with my antecedents, a very good organiser, a very good mobiliser, somebody that has heavy leadership potentials, somebody leading about five million people. No reasonable Nigerian will underrate that kind of a person. If you see anybody who says: 'who is he?' definitely that person is a political illiterate. Definitely that person is ignorant; the person is not current; and the person lacks the vision to know what will happen in the future."[166] As explained in the previous chapter, Adams believes that "destiny plays a very vital role in whatever you become in life." He says that "for you to be famous, it must be ordained [by] God."[167]

Thus, in his reckoning, God brought him this far, and there will be no going back.[168]

NOTES

1. Though the current Oyo town (initially called Ago d'Oyo—Camp became Oyo) is the second settlement so named after the destruction of the original Oyo (Oyo-Ile—home Oyo), the capital city of the Oyo Empire, the inhabitants still like to describe it as an "ancient town." The second Oyo was Oyo Igboho—where four *Aláàfins* reigned. The current Oyo became the city of the *Aláàfin* around 1837. See Robert Smith, "The *Alafin* in Exile: A Study of the Igboho Period in Oyo History," *Journal of African History* 6, no. 1 (1965): 57.

2. Linking up important people in Nigeria in this way is one of the means of building social capital and consolidating one's leverage in the processes of networking. As a researcher on elites, I confess that I am implicated in this process myself.

3. Sandra T. Barnes, *Patrons and Power: Creating a Political Community in Metropolitan Lagos* (Manchester: Manchester University Press, 1986), 183.

4. This is both a singular and plural noun. It was in this sense that the *Aláàfin* described war heroes in his proclamation of October 14, 2017, when announcing his choice of Adams as the next *Ààrẹ Ọ̀nà Kakañfò*.

5. He was removed when the federal government declared a state of emergency in the Western Region on May 29, 1962, but returned to power in 1963.

6. Olufemi Vaughan, *Nigerian Chiefs: Traditional Power in Modern Politics, 1980s–1990s* (Rochester, NY: University of Rochester Press, 2000), 1. Vaughan elaborates further on "the interplay of chieftaincy politics, elite formation, communal identities and the struggle for state power in colonial and postcolonial Nigeria." Ibid., 2.

7. He was later appointed commissioner for environment and natural resources by Governor Seyi Makinde in 2019. Unfortunately, he died in May 2020.

8. *Vanguard*, "Buhari Congratulates Aare Ona Kakanfo, Gani Adams, Tasks Him on National Unity," January 12, 2018, https://www.vanguardngr.com/2018/01/buhari-congratulates-aare-ona-kakanfo-gani-adams-tasks-national-unity/.

9. Ibid.

10. Dapo Akinrefon, "Why I Picked Gani Adams as New Aare Ona Kakanfo—Alaafin," *Vanguard*, October 17, 2017, https://www.vanguardngr.com/2017/10/picked-gani-adams-new-aare-ona-kakanfo-alaafin/ (emphasis added).

11. *Vanguard*, "Aare Ona Kakanfo: Tinubu Congratulates Gani Adams," October 17, 2017, https://www.vanguardngr.com/2017/10/aare-ona-kakanfo-tinubu-congratulates-gani-adams/.

12. *Vanguard*, "Conferment of Aare Ona Kakanfo of Yorubaland on Adams God-Ordained—Daniel," October 20, 2017, https://www.vanguardngr.com/2017/10/conferment-aare-ona-kakanfo-yorubaland-adams-god-ordained-daniel/.

13. Ibid.

14. *Vanguard*, "Aare Ona Kakanfo Cap Fits Adams—Fayose," October 18, 2017, https://www.vanguardngr.com/2017/10/aare-ona-kakanfo-cap-fits-adams-fayose/.

15. Akinrefon, "Why I Picked Gani Adams" (emphasis added).

16. Davies Iheamnachor, "Gani Adams Divinely Chosen to Save, Strengthen Yoruba Nation—SS/SE Communities," *Vanguard*, December 24, 2017, https://www.vanguardngr.com/2017/12/gani-adams-divinely-chosen-save-strengthen-yoruba-nation-ssse-communities/.

17. Friday Olokor, "Adeboye Hails Gani Adams, Regrets Absence from Installation," *Punch*, January 23, 2018, https://punchng.com/adeboye-hails-gani-adams-regrets-absence-from-installation/. See also *Nation*, "Adeboye Salutes Adams on Installation as Aare Ona Kakanfo," January 23, 2018, https://thenationonlineng.net/adeboye-salutes-adams-installation-aare-ona-kakanfo/; Eagle Online, "Pastor Adeboye Salutes Adams on Installation as Aare Ona Kakanfo, Regrets Inability to Attend," January 22, 2018, https://theeagleonline.com.ng/pastor-adeboye-salutes-adams-on-installation-as-aare-ona-kakanfo-regrets-inability-to-attend/.

18. Dapo Akinrefon, "Daystar Pastor, Sam Adeyemi Congratulates Him," *Vanguard*, January 9, 2018, https://www.vanguardngr.com/2018/01/aare-ona-kakanfo-final-rites-gani-adams-installation-begins/. The congratulatory messages from leading Christian clerics, especially Adeboye, attracted condemnation by some critics who argued that "he should not have had any dealing with [a] traditionalist." Akanni responded in the press that the critics were ignorant of Adams's "Christian background." "If you see where Gani Adams prays to God with his Holy Bible, you will fear and ask, 'Is this Gani Adams?' He has his Christian temple in his room. . . . You see, majority of our critics cannot serve God the way Gani Adams serves God. . . . He is a prayer warrior; the man prays a lot. He can pray for two hours non-stop. Gani Adams will lock himself inside his room and start praying. What some people don't know is that he has a Christian background. People see him based on his past but it was due to the circumstances [when] the OPC was under serious attacks by the police, armed robbers and other criminal elements [at the beginning of] the struggle." Friday Olokor, "Gani Adams Is Prayer Warrior, Says Chief of Staff," *Punch*, January 25, 2018, https://punchng.com/gani-adams-is-prayer-warrior-says-chief-of-staff/.

19. See *Festac News Online*, "Festac Mosque Hosts Special Jumat Service for Gani Adams," accessed November 3, 2020, https://festaconline.com.ng/festac-mosque-jumat-service-gani-adams/.

20. Dapo Akinrefon and Gbenga Olarinoye, "Courage, Commitment Earned Adams *Aare Ona Kakanfo* Title—Alaafin," *Vanguard*, January 16, 2018, https://www.vanguardngr.com/2018/01/courage-commitment-earned-adams-aare-ona-kakanfo-title-alaafin/.

21. For both of us as Yorùbá, this is the normal practice for greeting a monarch.

22. It is a common practice in Yorubaland that when you greet an older, particularly an elderly, person, he or she will respond with some prayers.

23. J. D. Y. Peel, *Christianity, Islam, and Orisa Religion: Three Traditions in Comparison and Interaction* (Berkeley: University of California Press, 2015).

24. Ibid., 169.

25. Ibid. Johnson's *The History of the Yoruba* is widely regarded as Oyo-centric, in that it gives primacy to the Oyo (both the empire and the subethnic group), even while regarding Christianity as a vehicle for the creation of a modern Yorùbá future. Peel has also argued that Johnson hoped for Ibadan, as the "New Oyo" from the nineteenth century onward, "to become the crucible of Christian enlightenments and civilisation" through "a strategy [of] reconciling Ibadan and Christianity.'" See Wale Adebanwi, *Yoruba Elites and Ethnic Politics in Nigeria: Obafemi Awolowo and Corporate Agency* (Cambridge: Cambridge University Press, 2014), 46–47; J. D. Y. Peel, *Religion and the Making of the Yoruba* (Bloomington: Indiana University Press, 2000), 307.

26. Oba Lamidi Adeyemi III, interview with the author, December 10, 2017, Oyo.

27. Ibid.

28. See chap. 3 for a discussion of the OPU.

29. Adeyemi, interview with the author, December 10, 2017.

30. Gani Adams, telephone interview with the author, December 13, 2017.

31. The number of states in which the OPC has branches keeps changing. When Adams tried to persuade President Jonathan to provide "empowerment" for the OPC, he allegedly told him that the OPC was represented in thirty-three of Nigeria's thirty-six states.

32. I have no independent confirmation of the number, but the OPU obviously has branches in many countries. I have on occasion met visiting representatives of the group from Asian and European countries while visiting Adams's house.

33. This popular view that every *Kakańfò* dies violently is fueled by only two recent examples, Afonja and Akintola. Although many people believed that Abiola was poisoned and died suddenly, he did not die a violent death as Afonja and Akintola did—the first by arrows from his Fulani "guests" and the other through the bullets of soldiers in the January 1966 coup.

34. Adams, interview with the author, December 14, 2017, Lagos.

35. Akinrefon, "Why I Picked Gani Adams."

36. Ibid.

37. Oladehinde Olawoyin, "Why I Made Gani Adams Aare Ona Kakanfo—Alaafin," *Premium Times*, October 19, 2017, https://www.premiumtimesng.com/regional/ssouth-west/246600-i-made-gani-adams-aare-ona-kakanfo-alaafin.html.

38. Ibid. (emphasis added).

39. When I interviewed him, the monarch told me that he considered fifteen people.

40. Akinrefon and Olarinoye, "Courage, Commitment."

41. Ibid.

42. I like to quickly note, following Barry Stephenson, that "a discourse of primitivism and racism is part of the history of ritual theory." Barry Stephenson, *Ritual: A Very Short Introduction* (Oxford: Oxford University Press, 2015), 104. Stephenson goes on to elaborate on the evolutionary thinking that informed this discourse in relation to the non-West, and Africa in particular, especially in the discipline of anthropology. States Stephenson, "The slow march of the Enlightenment meant giving up irrational and repressive group rites for an emancipated reason and individual autonomy. The important point here is that early theories of ritual were yoked to an evolutional perspective, which was often little more than a thinly veiled expression of cultural superiority. The pejorative language and images of 'ritualism' and 'ritualistic' entered the vocabulary and worldview of the modern West." Ibid., 105. Yet I think it is important to examine the continued practices of "traditional" rituals in contemporary Africa despite their massive transformations, even in the context of the claims by those involved that these practices belong to "ancient" customs and "cultures." These rituals help us to understand the ongoing struggles for power and privilege as they are tied to claims to "cultural" authority and knowledge in the unending competition for resources.

43. Meyer Fortes, "Ritual and Office in Tribal Society," in *Essays on the Ritual of Social Relations*, ed. Max Gluckman (Manchester: University of Manchester Press, 1962), 68, 86.

44. Stephenson, *Ritual*, 56 (emphasis added). For van Gennep, the most important thing about ritual is not its meaning but its efficacy. Thus, he argues that "initiation is principally an instrument for the transformation of an individual's social status." Cited in ibid., 57.

45. Roy Rapport, *Ritual and Religion in the Making of Humanity* (New York: Cambridge University Press, 1999).

46. Malinowski described this role as part of "the very cement of social fabric" (Bronislaw Malinowski, *Magic, Science and Religion and Other Essays*, intro. Robert Redfield [Glencore, IL: Free Press, 1948], 50). This emphasis on the integrative role of ritual also leads some scholars, such as Fortes, to stress an "invariably moral component" of ritual in that, as he argues, it "represents the mutual commitment to [the] roles of person and society focussed in status and office." Fortes, "Ritual and Office in Tribal Society," 83. However, the normative assumptions of a "moral component"

do not translate to the actual moral attitude of the person who is ritually prepared for office.

47. Andrew Apter, *Black Critics and Kings: The Hermeneutics of Power in Yoruba Society* (Chicago: University of Chicago Press, 1992), 213.

48. Edmund Leach, *The Essential Edmund Leach: Anthropology of Society* (New Haven, CT: Yale University Press, 2001), 168.

49. See Adebanwi, *Yoruba Elites and Ethnic Politics*, esp. chaps. 1–2.

50. See chap. 1.

51. Stephenson, *Ritual*, 87.

52. In fact, the end of such warfare as it was conducted before the encounter with European domination.

53. Fortes, "Ritual and Office in Tribal Society," 86.

54. Stephenson, *Ritual*, 61.

55. Ibid.

56. Margaret Thomson Drewal, *Yoruba Rituals: Performers, Play, Agency* (Bloomington: Indiana University Press, 1992), 98.

57. Ibid., 28.

58. Jacob K. Olupona, *City of 201 Gods: Ilé-Ifè* in Time, Space, and the Imagination (Berkeley: University of California Press, 2011), 8.

59. Drewal, *Yoruba Rituals*, 27, 29.

60. The Comaroffs, while not responding directly to Drewal, seem to argue that this is true of rituals everywhere when they state that ritual is often "a vital element in the processes that make and remake social facts and collective identities. Everywhere." Jean Comaroff and John Comaroff, introduction to *Modernity and Its Malcontents: Ritual and Power and Postcolonial Africa*, ed. Jean Comaroff and John Comaroff (Chicago: University of Chicago Press, 1993), xvi.

61. Cf. Andrew Apter, "The Historiography of Yoruba Myth and Ritual," *History in Africa* 14 (1987): 5.

62. For details on the invasion of the empire by the Fulani, starting with the seizing of Ilorin, the capital of the *Ààrẹ Ọnà Kakañfò* Afonja, see Samuel Johnson, *The History of the Yorubas from the Earliest Times to the Beginning of the British Protectorate* (Lagos: CMS Nigeria Bookshop, 1921), esp. chap. 7.

63. Though, as evident in Samuel Johnson's authoritative account in *The History of the Yorubas*, the officeholders in the precolonial era were called *Kakañfò* both as an honorific (such as *Kakañfò* Afonja) and as a shortened form of the title, Adams chose *Ààrẹ* as the shortened form and *Iba*—which was used in the past for the regular Èsós, and not the Èsó of *Èsós*, the Ààrẹ *Ọnà Kakañfò*—as his honorific. His wife uses *Ayin'ba* (wife of *Iba*).

64. Johnson, *History of the Yorubas*, 71.

65. Ibid.

66. Arnold van Gennep, *The Rites of Passage* (London: Routledge and Kegan Paul, 1960).

67. Ibid.

68. See Jacob K. Olupona, *Kingship, Religion, and Rituals in a Nigerian Community: A Phenomenological Study of Ondo Yoruba Festivals* (Stockholm: Almqvist and Wiksell International, 1991). He describes "civil religion" as "the incorporation of common myths, history, values, and symbols that relate to a society's sense of collective identity." Olupona, "Bonds, Boundaries, and Bondage of Faith," *Harvard Divinity Bulletin*, 41, no. 2 (2013), https://wcfia.harvard.edu/publications/bonds-boundaries-and-bondage-faith.

69. Olupona, *Kingship, Religion, and Rituals*, 84.

70. Olupona, *City of 201 Gods*, 11, 12.

71. Deji Okegbile, "Archbishop Ayo Ladigbolu at 80: A Prince and a Muslim Evangelist to a Methodist Archbishop," *Deji Okegbile Blog*, June 27, 2018, http://dejiokegbile.com/archbishop-ayo-ladigbolu-80-a-prince-and-a-muslim-evangelist-to-a-methodist-archbishop/.

72. For details of his place among the Yoruba elite, see Adebanwi, *Yoruba Elites and Ethnic Politics*, esp. chaps. 5–6.

73. Ayo Ladigbolu, interview with the author, April 2019, Oyo (emphasis added).

74. Ibid.

75. Ibid.

76. See Drewal, *Yoruba Rituals*, 27.

77. Ladigbolu, interview with the author, April 2019.

78. Ibid.

79. The *Ooni*, after his installation, and for the first time in the history of the two thrones, visited the *Aláàfin* in his palace in January 2016. See Gbenga Olarinmoye and Ola Ajayi, "Ooni Visits Alaafin, as Monarchs End 79-Yr-Old Supremacy Battle," *Vanguard*, January 18, 2016, https://www.vanguardngr.com/2016/01/ooni-visits-alaafin-as-monarchs-end-79-yr-old-supremacy-battle/.

80. K. W. J. Post and G. D. Jenkins, *The Price of Liberty: Personality and Politics in Colonial Nigeria* (Cambridge: Cambridge University Press, 1973), 1.

81. Michael Schatzberg, *Political Legitimacy in Middle Africa: Father, Family, Food* (Bloomington: Indiana University Press, 2001), 79.

82. For video of the installation, see Flow Entertainment, "Coronation of Gani Adams as Aare Ona Kakanfo of Yoruba Land," YouTube, January 16, 2018, https://www.youtube.com/watch?v=fNpuVTSGve4; Kilarigbo Live, "Watch Gani Adams Becomes Aare-Ona-Kakanfo of Yorubaland," YouTube, January 19, 2018, https://www.youtube.com/watch?v=WTClxajxk5U.

83. Fortes, "Ritual and Office in Tribal Society," 67.

84 Ibid., 56. Cf. Victor Turner, *The Forest of Symbols: Aspects of Ndembu Ritual* (Ithaca, NY: Cornell University Press, 1967), 95.

85. Van Gennep, *Rites of Passage*, cited in Fortes, "Ritual and Office in Tribal Society," 56.

86. Turner, *Forest of Symbols*, 95.

87. The list of the past *Kakaǹfòs* and where they came from in the old Oyo Empire and contemporary Yorubaland includes Kokoro Ngangan (Iwoye Cotonou—in the present-day Republic of Benin), Oyatope (Iwoye Cotonou), Oyebi (Ajaa Cotonou), Adeta (Jabata), Oku (Jabata), Afonja (Ilorin), Toyese (Ogbomoso), Edun (Gbogun), Amepo (Abewo Cotonou), Kurunmi (Ijaiye), Ojo Aburumaku (Ogbomoso), Latosa (Ibadan), Samuel Ladoke Akintola (Ogbomoso), and Moshood Kashimawo Abiola (Abeokuta).

88. *Amotekun* (cheetah) translates to "similar to a leopard," the Yorùbá word for leopard being *ekun*. *Amotekun* is generally mistranslated as "leopard."

89. This was worn by the *Esos*, guardians of the kingdom, in the old Oyo Empire. See Johnson, *History of the Yorubas*, 73. However, when he was installing his own chiefs, Adams claimed, "I was installed with a beaded crown called *Ade Idikoko*, a sacred crown used to install any *Aare Ona Kakanfo*." See Segun James, "Gani Adams Installs 16 New Chiefs," *ThisDay*, January 17, 2020, https://www.thisdaylive.com/index.php/2020/01/17/gani-adams-installs-16-new-chiefs/. No one except a king can wear a crown in Yorubaland. Not even all the traditional rulers wear crowns. No other source described his installation cap in this way.

90. Ladigbolu, interview with the author, April 2019.

91. The *Aláàfin* spoke to this in explaining why he appointed Adams.

92. Lasisi Olagunju, editor of *Saturday Tribune*, telephone conversation, January 11, 2018.

93. Akeem Lasisi, "*Aare Ona Kakanfo*" [For Aare Gani Adams], installation program, December 18, 2017, 35.

94. For the full speech, see "What Gani Adams Said during Installation as Aare Ona Kakanfo," *Premium Times*, January 14, 2018, https://www.premiumtimesng.com/regional/ssouth-west/255466-%E2%80%8Ewhat-gani-adams-said-installation-aare-ona-kakanfo-full-speech.html.

95. Ibid.

96. Ibid. (emphasis added).

97. It might seem paradoxical that this wish for the sacred goes along with a passion for the profane. While Adams wishes to sacralize himself through the possession of spiritual powers, he also enjoys the profane performances of his eminence, which comes with praise singing by musicians and spraying money.

98. Indeed, many people in Yorubaland and Nigeria believed that Awolowo had "supernatural powers," including the power to "appear in the moon." Poet, public intellectual, and Awolowo's former private secretary Odia Ofeimun has dismissed this view as "myth and mysticism [that could] drown the secular import of [Awolowo's] life." See Adebanwi, *Yoruba Elites and Ethnic Politics*, 86. For a discussion of Awolowo's alleged "supernatural powers," see ibid., esp. chaps. 2, 6.

99. Telephone interview with the author, November 14, 2020.

100. Paula Brown, "Big Man, Past and Present: Model, Person, Hero, Legend," *Ethnology* 29, no. 2 (1990): 99–100.

101. These included the Church of the Lord, the Cherubim and Seraphim and the Christ Apostolic Church (CAC). For details of the evolution and doctrines of these *Aladura* denominations, see H. W. Turner, *History of the African Independent Church*, 2 vols. (Oxford: Clarendon, 1967); J. D. Y. Peel, *Aladura: A Religious Movement among the Yoruba* (London: Oxford University Press, 1968).

102. H. W. Turner, "A Typology for Modern African Religious Movements," *Journal of Religion in Africa* 1, no. 1 (1967): 1–34.

103. Eva Krapf Askari, review of *History of an African Independent Church*, by Turner, and *Aladura*, by Peel, *Bulletin of the School of Oriental and African Studies, University of London* 32, no. 3 (1969): 662.

104. Turner, *History of the African Independent Church*.

105. Askari, review, 663.

106. Ibid.

107. Max Gluckman, "*Les Rites de Passage*," in *Essays on the Ritual of Social Relations* (Manchester: Manchester University Press, 1962), 2.

108. Segun Adeyemo, "Confusion as OPC Leader, Gani Adams Becomes C&S Ordained Apostle," *City People*, December 16, 2020, https://citynewsng.com/opc-leader-gani-adams-becomes-c-s-ordained-priest/.

109. *Globagist Nigeria*, "Aare Gani Adams Ordained as an Apostle: An Abomination on the Altar-Femi Oyeniyi," December 17, 2020, https://globalgistng.com/2020/12/17/aare-gani-adams-ordained-as-an-apostle-an-abomination-on-the-altar-femi-oyeniyi/.

110. Ibid. (emphasis added).

111. Ezekiel123, "Shrine to Church: Checkout Photos of Gani Adams Installation & Ordination in 2017 and 2012," Opera News, n.d., https://ng.opera.news/ng/en/religion/97484e2c9f6e6e4b379f120cc719fde2.

112. Ibid. I deliberately quoted this without noting the infelicities in the language.

113. Oyeniyi, "Gani Adams Becomes Apostle."

114. This attitude returns us to Mary Douglas's argument that ideas of pollution work at two levels in the "life of society," one instrumental and the other expressive. Those who approach Adams's ordination as a form of "pollution" of the church (and of Christianity) are reflecting the instrumental sense, in that they are trying to influence the actions of others through "social pressure." At the background of this pressure is a belief that "the ideal order of society is guarded by dangers which threaten transgressors." See Douglas, *Purity and Danger: An Analysis of Concepts of Pollution and Taboo* (Abingdon: Routledge and Kegan Paul, 1966), 3.

115. *Premium Times* provided the context: "Adams, who spoke on Sunday after his Ordination as an Apostle at the Saviour's Ministries in Lagos." See Adejumo Kabir, "Growing Insecurity in Nigeria Shows Buhari Has Failed—Gani Adams," *Premium Times*, December 14, 2020, https://www.premiumtimesng.com/news/more-news/431112-growing-insecurity-in-nigeria-shows-buhari-has-failed-gani-adams.html. See also Dapo Akinrefon, "Buhari Lacks Courage to Tackle Insecurity—Gani

Adams," *Vanguard*, December 13, 2020, https://www.vanguardngr.com/2020/12/buhari-lacks-the-courage-to-tackle-insecurity-in-nigeria-%E2%80%95-gani-adams/.

116. Olupona, *Kingship, Religion, and Rituals*, 84; Olupona, *City of 201 Gods*, 8.

117. The dominant newspapers and newsmagazines in Nigeria are located in and around Lagos and Ibadan (almost exclusively in Lagos since the late 1990s). For more on this, see Odia Ofeimun, "The Ngbati Press," *Premium Times*, June 11, 2018.

118. Victor Turner, *The Ritual Process* (London: Routledge, 1969). See also Bruce Kapferer, "Beyond Symbolic Representation: Victor Turner and Variations on the Themes of Ritual Process and Liminality," *Suomen Antropologi: Journal of the Finnish Anthropological Society* 33, no. 4 (Winter 2008): 6. I think Turner's groundbreaking work on rituals is more useful for reading this case (and others) than Robin Horton's take in "Ritual Man in Africa," *Africa: Journal of the International African Institute* 35, no. 2 (1964): 85–103.

119. Olupona, *Kinship, Religion, and Rituals*, 84; Olupona, *City of 201 Gods*.

120. This was revealed to me by some of Adams's former associates who provided "security."

121. As explained in chap. 1, for the Yorùbá, the ethnic identity often trumps religious identity—despite the recent challenges to this tradition by doctrinaire or fundamentalist Yorùbá Muslims and, more recently, Yorùbá Pentecostal Christians. See J. D. Y. Peel, *Religious Encounter and the Making of the Yoruba* (Bloomington: Indiana University Press, 2000); David D. Laitin, *Hegemony and Culture: Politics and Religious Change among the Yoruba* (Chicago: University of Chicago Press, 1986).

122. EnviroNews Nigeria, "Why Gani Adams Was Chosen out of 25 Shortlisted as Aare Ona Kakanfo, by Alaafin," January 15, 2018, https://www.environewsnigeria.com/gani-adams-chosen-25-shortlisted-aare-ona-kakanfo-alaafin/ (emphasis added). See also Akinrefon and Olarinoye, "Courage, Commitment."

123. For an interview in which Adams asserted that he is Muslim, Christian, and traditionalist, see Facetv Africa, "I'm a Muslim, I'm a Christian and also Traditionalist. Gani Adams," YouTube, July 14, 2020, https://www.youtube.com/watch?v=6lZ9lMq6Wj8. He added that though his father was a Muslim, his mother was a Christian who then became a Muslim when she married his father, even though his father was "very liberal" and thus allowed his mother to take him to church. "So, in the beginning, I was in between Christian and Muslim." He said he became involved in traditional religion after he joined OPC.

124. For the phenomenon of Muslim Yorùbá Fuji musicians being invited to perform at Pentecostal churches in recent years, see Ebenezer Obadare, *Pastoral Power, Clerical State: Pentecostalism, Gender, and Sexuality in Nigeria* (Notre Dame, IN: University of Notre Dame, 2022).

125. Dapo Akinrefon, "25 People Contested for Aare Ona Kakanfo Title—Gani Adams," *Vanguard*, January 22, 2018, https://www.vanguardngr.com/2018/01/25-people-contested-aare-ona-kakanfo-title-gani-adams/. See also Zovoe Jonathan, "Photos: Aare Ona Kakanfo Rolls on Floor during Church Thanksgiving Service,"

Punch, January 22, 2018, https://punchng.com/photos-aare-ona-kakanfo-rolls-on-floor-during-church-thanksgiving-service/; Igbokwe John, "Aare Ona Kakanfo, Otunba Gani Adams Rolls on the Floor during Thanksgiving Service," *City People*, January 22, 2018, http://www.citypeopleonline.com/aare-ona-kakanfo-otunba-gani-adams-rolls-floor-thanksgiving-service/.

126. John, "Aare Ona Kakanfo" (emphasis added).

127. As I learned from the *Aláàfin*, among others, only a few people had directly expressed interest in the position at the time of Adams's selection. The other wealthier, more influential, and more prominent people the *Aláàfin* considered and decided against did not directly solicit for the title.

128. Afe Adogame, "*Aiye loja, orun nile*: The Appropriation of Ritual Space-Time in the Cosmology of the Celestial Church of Christ," *Journal of Religion in Africa* 30, no. 1 (2000): 4.

129. Ibid.

130. Ibid.

131. Ibid.

132. A newspaper reported that Adams is "liberal with the three prominent religions in Nigeria" (Friday Olokor, "Adeboye Hails Gani Adams, Regrets Absence from Installation," *Punch*, January 23, 2018, https://punchng.com/adeboye-hails-gani-adams-regrets-absence-from-installation/).

133. *Nation*, "Adams Holds Thanksgiving at Ijo Orunmila," February 7, 2018, https://thenationonlineng.net/adams-holds-thanksgiving-ijo-orunmila/.

134. Orunmila is regarded as the grand priest of *Ifa*, the one who revealed "divinity and prophecy to the world."

135. Ibid.

136. *Festac News Online*, "Festac Mosque Hosts Special Jumat Service for Gani Adams," accessed March 3, 2021, https://festaconline.com.ng/festac-mosque-jumat-service-gani-adams/.

137. Ibid.

138. Ibid.

139. For parts of the installation ceremony, see Facetv Africa, "Oloye Gani Adams Installed New Chiefs in Lagos," YouTube, January 16, 2020, https://www.youtube.com/watch?v=di3WOOejSDI.

140. I do not use this concept in the strong way Orlando Patterson does in his acclaimed work *Slavery and Social Death*, although Patterson's usage illuminates the way in which I employ the concept here, particularly in terms of how social existence is exclusively tied to a referent (for Patterson, "the master," but in this context, "the master" is social relevance, prestige, and respect). Jana Králová, in examining the different senses of the concept, argues that it is used "too broadly" by scholars. Here, I use it strictly in the sense of the loss of social traction. See Patterson, *Slavery and Social Death: A Comparative Study* (Cambridge, MA: Harvard University Press, 1982),

esp. 38–42. See also Jana Králová, "What Is Social Death?," *Contemporary Social Science* 10, no. 3 (2015): 235–48.

141. Segun James, "Gani Adams Installs 16 New Chiefs," *ThisDay*, January 17, 2020, https://www.thisdaylive.com/index.php/2020/01/17/gani-adams-installs-16-new-chiefs/; Bola Badmus, "Gani Adams Celebrates 2nd Anniversary, Installs New Chiefs," *Nigerian Tribune*, January 16, 2020, https://tribuneonlineng.com/gani-adams-celebrates-2nd-anniversary-installs-new-chiefs/; Dapo Akinrefon, "No Comparison between Alaafin, Aare Ona Kakanfo Chiefs—Gani Adams; Installs New Chiefs," *Vanguard*, January 16, 2020, https://www.vanguardngr.com/2020/01/between-alaafins-chiefs-and-that-of-aare-onakakanfo-%E2%80%95gani-adams/.

142. Badmus, "Gani Adams Celebrates 2nd Anniversary."

143. It is important to add a caveat here. Because of the structure of many of these societies in Africa, with Nigeria as an egregious example, even the few who are reluctant to be part of this surfeit of "honors"—or the unceasing passion for "awards for (often faux) excellence"—are sometimes forced by the nature of relationships (including friendship, kinship, political relations, ethnic allegiance, etc.) to accept the "honors."

144. James, "Gani Adams Installs 16 New Chiefs."

145. *ThisDay* reported that Adams installed "16 new chiefs." However, when I counted the number of chiefs from all the reports, I found that there were seventeen. Some reports failed to list all the names. See James, "Gani Adams Installs 16 New Chiefs"; Badmus, "Gani Adams Celebrates 2nd Anniversary"; Akinrefon, "No Comparison."

146. The use of *barrister* as a regular honorific for lawyers in Nigeria is one example of the society's craze for titles. No other country that I am aware of uses such an honorific for lawyers. The practice started around the late 1980s. Before then, lawyers who had no other title were happy to be addressed as *Mr.*

147. *Vanguard*, "Aare Ona Kakanfo Instals 21 Chiefs across Yoruba Land," January 12, 2019, https://www.vanguardngr.com/2019/01/aare-onakakanfo-instals-21-chiefs-across-yoruba-land/.

148. Ibid.

149. Ojudu, formerly a famous journalist and managing editor of *TheNEWS* magazine, knew the younger Adams before he became popular and had assisted him in the past. He was thus used to calling Adams by his first name. He told me in Abuja in July 2021 that when he visited Adams on this occasion and called him by his first name, Adams categorically told the vice president's special adviser that he had to refer to him as *Ààrẹ* subsequently and not Gani.

150. Femi Adewale, "Ojudu Visits Gani Adams," Freedom Online, December 8, 2017, https://freedomonline.com.ng/ojudu-visits-gani-adams/.

151. Schatzberg, *Political Legitimacy in Middle Africa*, 78.

152. Andrew Apter, *Oduduwa's Chain: Locations of Culture in the Yoruba-Atlantic* (Chicago: University of Chicago Press, 2018), 4.

153. Tracey E. Hucks, *Yoruba Traditions and African American Religious Nationalism* (Albuquerque: University of New Mexico Press, 2012), xviii.
154. Adeyinka Olaiya, "Aare Gani Adams in Brazil, Set to Address Parliament, Holds Convention," *Ancestral News*, December 9, 2022, https://ancestrals.com.ng/2022/12/09/aare-gani-adams-in-brazil-set-to-address-parliament/.
155. Adeyinka Olaiya, "Gani Adams in Brazil Bar Association, Grace OPU Summit, Task Parliament," *Ancestral News*, December 15, 2022, https://ancestrals.com.ng/2022/12/15/gani-adams-address-brazil-bar-association-grace-opu-summit-task-parliament/.
156. Ibid.
157. Ibid.
158. Adeyinka Olaiya, "Gani Adams in Pele's Santos, Appoints Chief, Applauds Brazil," *Ancestral News*, December 12, 2022, https://ancestrals.com.ng/2022/12/12/gani-adams-in-peles-santos-appoints-chief-applauds-brazil/.
159. Ibid.
160. *Vanguard*, "Gani Adams Visits Brazilian Embassy: Seeks Collaboration on Cultural Tourism," April 27, 2018, https://www.vanguardngr.com/2018/04/gani-adams-visits-brazilian-embassy/.
161. Ibid.
162. Ibid.
163. For an exposition of the concept of the "state of exception," see Giorgio Agamben, *State of Exception*, trans. Kevin Attell (Chicago: University of Chicago Press, 2005).
164. The figures he gave in an interview about donations from the governors in the Southwest give some credence to this. He told an interviewer that the host governor, Abiola Ajimobi of Oyo State, "spent almost N40 or N50 million on my installation. He gave me 15 million naira cash three days to the installation. He [also] asked every local government in Oyo environ to give the planning committee 3 or 4 million naira each . . . about 4 or 5 local government. . . . The Ministry of Information and Culture, I know he gave them up to 20 or 25 million naira for their own planning." He added that three of the other governors in the zone, including the governors of Lagos, Ogun, Ondo, and Osun, with the exception of the governor of Ekiti State, gave him money—although he volunteered the amount only for the Ondo governor, who gave him N2.5 million after the installation and gave the same amount to those who organized a reception for him in Akure, the capital of his home state. See "Hear What Gani Adams Says about Late Biola Ajimobi. Ajimobi Gave Him over 50 Million for My Coronation," YouTube, December 6, 2020, https://www.youtube.com/watch?v=lSuZA33GYHs (Accessed 4 February 2021).
165. Even before he became the *Kakañfò*, Adams told the press that his name "rings louder bell than some governors." He explained why: "For years, I have been leading a group that cuts across about 33 states in Nigeria and have members in more than 34 countries around the world. As governor, you are only leading a state, and some

states near you may not even know your full name. But talk of Gani Adams, it's synonymous with OPC. Talk of OPC, you are talking of Gani Adams." *Nigerian Voice,* "Gani Adams: My Name Rings Louder Bell than Some Governors," December 4, 2011, https://www.thenigerianvoice.com/news/76834/gani-adams-my-name-rings-louder-bell-than-some-governors.html.

166. Ibid.

167. Sulaimon Olanrewaju and Saka Gbeminiyi, "Why the Police Do Not Want OPC's Assistance in Providing Security—Gani Adams," *Nigerian Tribune,* April 30, 2008.

168. He once told a reporter that his accomplishments constitute the work of God: "This is the power of God, not of any man. This can only happen through the intervention of God Almighty. It's beyond my own intervention." *Nigerian Voice,* "Gani Adams."

5 / Playing (with) Big Men

Elites, Ethno-regional Competition, and Electoral Politics

INTRODUCTION: THE BIG MAN IN EXCELSIS

It was a gathering of "the high and mighty of the Nigerian society,"[1] as a newspaper described it. The wedding of Neya, the daughter of the former governor of Abia State Orji Uzor Kalu, was held at the Catholic Church of Assumption in Ikoyi, Lagos, on Thursday, December 21, 2017. After the service, the guests headed for the five-star Oriental Hotel on Lekki-Epe Expressway in Lekki, Lagos, for the reception—"a show . . . delivered with glitz and glamour"[2] where it was "a herculean task for anyone" to "take an accurate register of the notable people that were at the event."[3] In fact, so many distinguished people were in the audience that the master of ceremonies begged not to observe protocol, which would otherwise have constituted an outrage in Nigeria's high society. Dr. Bukola Saraki, the Senate president and former governor of Kwara State, and many sitting and former governors, political heavyweights, business tycoons, technocrats, religious leaders, professionals, and media chiefs, including foreign guests, were present.

As usual with such society events attended by the heavyweight of the Nigerian state and society, the celebration provided "an opportunity for the exchange of pleasantries" between the chief host, Kalu, and his friends and associates from across the country.

It was a few weeks before the installation of Gani Adams as the *Kakaǹfò*. Adams did not attend the church service. That was not necessary because the *real* venue for the Nigerian elite to flaunt their distinction was the reception. As usual, Adams came in late, well after the event was underway. As he entered the reception hall, the guests, even among these elite of elites, offered glances and

Figure 5.1. Former governors Bola Tinubu (*left*) and Saminu Turaki (*right*) stand to greet Adams at the wedding reception for ex-governor Orji Kalu's daughter's wedding at Oriental Hotel, Lagos, on December 21, 2017. Photo courtesy of Segun Akanni.

nods to acknowledge his presence. The *Kakanfò*-designate acknowledged greetings from the high and mighty. Among the distinguished guests was *Asiwaju* Bola Tinubu, the former governor of Lagos State (1999–2003), once described by a fellow governor as the "governor-general." As Adams approached the table where he was seated, Tinubu stood up to greet him. Sitting with Tinubu was Ibrahim Saminu Turaki, the two-term governor of the northern state of Jigawa. He also stood up to greet Adams.

Photographers were quick to record the moment. They even asked for the three to pose for more images. The three big men obliged.

Other big men and women at the event posed for photographs with Adams, including the chief host, Governor Kalu; the famous Pentecostal leader and the founder and president of LoveWorld Incorporated—popularly known as Christ Embassy Church—Pastor Chris Oyakhilome; Senate president Saraki; the chair of the ruling party, Chief John Oyegun; and the recently released former governor of Delta State who was convicted and jailed of fraud in the UK, Mr. James Ibori. The managing director / editor in chief of the *New Telegraph* and president of the Nigerian Guild of Editors, Funke Egbemode, also posed for a photograph with the OPC leader.

As members of the national political and cultural elite stood one after another to shake Adams's hand at the wedding, they were reaffirming the fact that

Figure 5.2. Adams exchanging pleasantries with Governor Orji Kalu (*left*) as Pastor Chris Oyakhilome (*next to Kalu*) watches at the wedding. Photo courtesy of Segun Akanni.

becoming elite in Yorubaland was only the first step in his journey to become a member of the national elite. Adams had become not merely one who *played* at the regional level but a veritable member of the national elite.

Tinubu standing to greet Adams not only acknowledged Adams's ascendancy in the Nigerian sociopolitical scene but also confirmed it; it was also a moment that could have reassured Adams about the relative autonomy he had achieved among the Nigerian superelite even while still dependent on particular members of this elite. In the two preceding years, Adams, who supported President Jonathan's reelection against Tinubu's favored candidate, Mohammadu Buhari, had been embroiled in a media war with Tinubu because of Adams's campaign to remove the chair of the Independent National Electoral Commission, Attahiru Jega (see the praeludium). Adams believed that the removal would ensure that Jonathan did not lose the 2015 presidential election to Buhari. The media war between him and Tinubu at that point even threatened to spill into a street brawl among their supporters.[4] The fact that Adams could walk up to one of most powerful Nigerians of the contemporary era, whom he had been attacking in the media for a couple of years, and expect Tinubu to stand to greet him was not lost on observers.

It meant, in part, that Adams had learned not only how to play *the role* of a big man but also how to play *with* big men—including even bigger men. Such

Figure 5.3. Adams and Chief John Oyegun, the ruling party's chair, at the wedding. Photo courtesy of Segun Akanni.

Figure 5.4. Adams with Dr. Bukola Saraki, the Senate president, at the wedding. Photo courtesy of Segun Akanni.

intertwining of subjectivities, or what Richard Werbner describes as "the actual intertwining of subjectivity with intersubjectivity,"[5] points to the fact that Adams is "compelled to be aware [of] and concerned about [his] interdependence, even . . . mutual entanglement" with other big men.[6]

Adams appreciates the fact that he must act strategically to enhance and sustain his own achieved and conferred status, even in the context of this mutual entanglement with the superelite in Nigeria. His power—what Foucault has described as "a set of actions upon other actions"[7]—depends on recognizing this reality and acting it out. Against this background, an analysis of the manifestations and challenges of intersubjectivity and interdependence, as Francis Nyamnjoh instructively argues, is critical in addressing the question of how "individuals [are] able to be who they are—agents—through relationships with others."[8]

However, I suggest that the manifestations of intersubjectivity and interdependence in the context of Adams's insertion into the networks of the superelite in Nigeria challenge Abner Cohen's argument that at the center of such relationships is a "network of amity" and "a system of channels for collaboration."[9] As Cohen argues, "A man aspiring to identify with the elite may succeed in acquiring such external markers as accent, housing, clothing and other item of conspicuous consumption"[10] but cannot, on the bases of these, "become automatically affiliated with the power elite and partake of their privileges."[11] However, the "much more difficult task of 'grafting' himself onto the inner network of primary relationships which link the members of the group together,"[12] as I demonstrate below, is not based only on relations of amity, as Cohen assumes. Such "grafting" is possible through both relations of amity and those of enmity with existing members of the elite[13]—as the Adams case shows. Thus, in his attempt to, in some cases, turn patrons into peers, he tests relations of amity and, in some cases, turns them into relations of enmity.

In this chapter, I do not use *play* in the sense of *pretense*, though it does sometimes involve a measure of disguise and pretense. I use it more in the sense of a performance (enactment) of something that could be either real or faux—or sometimes both.

THE ELECT AND THE ELECTED

Adams started his public life as a "small man" who, because of his participation in the prodemocracy and sociocultural movements, was "linked through a multiplicity of capillaries of patronage and influence" to some big men.[14] He operated within a dynamic cultural setting that allows, as Karin Barber reminds us, "a man in a small position to enlarge it by his own efforts" and that, at the same time, provides "a lot of scope for self-aggrandizement."[15] Thus, Adams was able to mobilize and appropriate the capillaries of patronage and influence to transform himself into the actual or symbolic equal of those who, wittingly or unwittingly, helped to pave the way for him. In doing so, he concretized his strivings for personal elevation and socioeconomic and political eminence. This illustrates a dimension of the limitations of the position of the Guha-led subaltern studies group[16] that seems to freeze the location of the subaltern in the immediate and the long term, as Fred Cooper hinted in arguing that "the problem in this rich and varied approach to history is the concept of subalternity itself: subalterns are to be autonomous and agents of their lives, yet to remain subaltern. Are not the structures of power and the idioms in which power is expressed forged and reforged in relationships—unequal as they may be—and does not this give-and-take test, at the very least, the boundaries of groups?"[17] In Adams's (eventually successful) attempt to be an autonomous agent of his own life, he could not remain a subaltern—as the relationships he forged and reforged within existing structures of (unequal) power helped him to transcend the boundaries of subaltern life. Thus, as he came fully into his own, acknowledged far and wide as a man of eminence and consequence, Adams seemed, as hinted in earlier chapters, to have settled in his mind that he is an uncommon person and, as such, potentially part of the elect,[18] someone chosen by God—and the Yorùbá gods—to play a pivotal role in Yorubaland as well as in the relationships between the Yorùbá and other ethnic groups in Nigeria. Therefore, in his relationships with key members of the highest echelon of Yorùbá and Nigerian elite, particularly elected political leaders, he started demonstrating this consciousness of his *chosen-ness*, which, assumedly, privileges him in these relationships, despite the awesome formal powers of the political leaders. Adams's relationships with members of the Yorùbá elite also demonstrate what Andrew Apter describes as "the intense individualism in Yoruba society," which "encourages power competition between all men, without as well as within the formal framework of government." Apter adds, "Through their public records of deeds and misdeeds, Big Men *sui generis* illustrate how . . . power is available to those who are strong and bold enough to seize it."[19] Against this backdrop, I hope to illustrate how *being* a Big Man and *maintaining* the distinction that is integral to the status, for Adams (the *elect*), involve engaging or contending with those who have already accomplished distinction (the *elected*). As a form of public (*dis*)*play* of distinction, Adams accomplishes (further) distinction by cultivating different kinds of relationships with *the already distinct* in society or, through particular methods and practices, by compelling the distinct to relate with him. He recognizes that being a Big Man in the African context involves a strong understanding of "the ways that people actively negotiate or play off" subjectivity and intersubjectivity.[20]

Even though Adams started with limited leverage in his personal and public relationships with some powerful people at the apex of political, economic, and social spheres in Nigeria (including those who provided him with initial financial support), he gradually seized his autonomy from them in various ways. He has ensured multiple, even rival, patrons; regularly acquires new benefactors or methods of receiving patronage; and displays his newly acquired wealth and status in ways that give the public impression of self-sufficiency. The affirmation of his relative autonomy has also included speaking boldly in the media about his previous patrons or benefactors (sometimes even verbally attacking them) and constantly augmenting his own status to *become* the social, cultural, or economic—and if not also the political, certainly the symbolic—*equal* of his erstwhile benefactors or his powerful tormentors.

There are three principal ways through which Adams deals with relationships with people who are superior to him in the social, cultural, economic, and political pecking order. The first is to *socialize* or *culturalize* certain relationships—that is, to ensure that they become serviceable to his agenda of cultural ascension and social viability. This is the mode of his engagement with cultural figures, such as traditional rulers, and society figures, such as celebrities or leading civil society activists. The second way is to *politicize* certain relationships by leveraging, for himself, the political standing and symbolic resources of certain persons holding high office through his association with them. Though such officeholders are often seeking to use him temporarily or situationally for their own political agenda or ambitions, by *politicizing* these relationships, Adams deepens them. He also attempts to reverse things by making such high officeholders beholden to him—with the risk of sanctions if they attempt to exclusively determine the terms of the relationship, cut him off, or cut him loose. This is a viable way to understand his relationships with high officeholders, such as Governor Bola Tinubu. The third way is to *commodify* certain relationships. By turning them into actual economic resources for which he provides particular forms of services, Adams expands his financial capacity to determine and (re)define particular relationships, such as those he has with President Jonathan and Governors Tinubu and Gbenga Daniel. Where such potentially commodifiable relationships are not immediately commodified, he uses them to consolidate the images and appearances that solidify relational commodities—which subsequently support or augment the relationships.

However, these three ways of governing relationships are not mutually exclusive, as the relationship with Governor Tinubu shows. They sometimes operate simultaneously or reinforce one another, depending on Adams's reading of the nature and dynamics of a specific relationship and the moment in the larger and long-term processes of self-actualization. However, there are a few relationships that might represent outliers because they do not easily fall into any of these three categories. One such—and perhaps the only—outlier is with President

Olusegun Obasanjo. Though Obasanjo wanted to use Adams and the OPC at some point immediately before and during his presidency, something about Obasanjo's role in Yorùbá and Nigerian history and the man's own idiosyncrasies (not to talk of his famed miserliness) made it impossible for Adams to be reconciled to him—even long after Obasanjo left office as president. And, in a departure from virtually all his other relationships with people with greater power and leverage, Adams has no capacity to sanction or punish Obasanjo in any significant way. The best he could do, and has done, is to support those opposed to Obasanjo's interests.

Against the backdrop of his capacity to socialize/culturalize, politicize, or commodify interactions with other big men, Adams's relationships with the four examined in this chapter demonstrate his facility for multivalent engagements with—or disengagement from—other big men. In light of this, the chapter brings into play two of Adams's most significant relationships with powerful men—Governor (*Asiwaju*) Bola Tinubu and Governor (*Otunba*) Gbenga Daniel—to illustrate the intricate processes through which he *played* (i.e., performed what it means to be) *a* big man, *played with* big men, and also *played* (maneuvered) *the* Big Men. I use *play* in the third sense as "maneuver" rather than "manipulate" because I think that *maneuvering* captures the element of play involved in these relationships better than manipulation does. This is more so since the big men could be said to have set out to manipulate the initially "small man" (Adams). Therefore, I suggest that where attempts at manipulation cancel out each other, what results is maneuvering; thus, *maneuvering*, in this sense, provides us with a better analytical lens than *manipulation*.[21]

To buttress my argument that Adams *plays* (including both performance and actuality) *a* big man and *plays with* (including maneuvering around, relating to, or messing with) big men to maintain or nourish his big man status, I also reflect briefly on two of his less intimate but no less significant relationships: (1) with President Olusegun Obasanjo, Nigeria's two-time head of state and the first elected president in Nigeria's Fourth Republic, and (2) with President Goodluck Jonathan, the first president from a minority ethnic group in Nigeria's history and the first to be defeated in his bid for a second term.

This chapter also indicates that the study of democratic politics in Africa needs to pay greater attention to nonformal, including public and private, relationships between and among state actors and between and among those assumed to be nonstate public actors. Such relationships are critical for understanding electoral politics and the more formal processes involved in the (un)democratic struggles for power on the continent, as well as for understanding the role of ethno-regional politics in these struggles. In focusing on a certain process of the *(de)formation of politics,* I also hope to capture some aspects of the ebbs and flows of political life in a postcolonial context that reveal how the political, in its *terrific* and *terrible* interface with the cultural, may lead to a more illuminating understanding of actually existing modes of struggles for personal power in the continent.

BETWEEN "THE GENERAL" AND THE GENERALISSIMO

Asiwaju[22] Bola Tinubu had just arrived at the eightieth birthday of Chief Rasaq Akanni Okoya, the Lagos billionaire, industrialist, and founder of the Eleganza Group. The birthday celebration, held on January 12, 2020, was one of the most lavish in the recent history of Lagos, attended by the topmost level of the Lagos and national elite. Vice President Yemi Osinbajo and former president Olusegun Obasanjo were also in attendance at some point in the day. All the top Yorùbá musicians in Lagos performed during the all-day celebrations. At the bandstand later in the evening was K1 De Ultimate, who is regarded as the contemporary king of Fuji music. The music superstar, who was known in the early part of his career simply as Wasiu Ayinde, was singing the praise of the octogenarian celebrator shortly after Tinubu arrived at the venue. Along with Tinubu was his political ward, the governor of Lagos State, Babajide Sanwo-Olu, and his

Figure 5.5. Former governors Bola Tinubu (*left*) and Saminu Turaki (*right*) pose for photographs with Adams at the wedding reception for ex-governor Orji Kalu's daughter. Photo courtesy of *Ovation* magazine.

Figure 5.6. *Left to right:* Governor Bola Tinubu, President Olusegun Obasanjo, Vice President Yemi Osinbajo, and Chief Razaq Okoya at Okoya's eightieth birthday in Lagos. Photo courtesy of *Ovation* magazine.

deputy, Obafemi Hamzat. After singing the praises of Okoya, K1 switched to singing Tinubu's, initially in relation to Okoya. After a little while, the musician, who is Tinubu's favorite—and the "official" musician of his political camp—asked his band to stop the music while he prayed for Tinubu. He asked "all the Yoruba" to listen to him: "Tinubu is a person of pride to his people," he affirmed. Then he prayed that Tinubu's exertions would never be in vain, adding, "*Asiwaju . . . awa soja e a o ni ku. T'alaafia ba kan e . . . igbadun wa ni*" (*Asiwaju*, we, your soldiers, will not die. Your well-being[23] . . . is our delight).[24]

K1 returned to singing as he stepped down from the stage to stand before the table Tinubu shared with other dignitaries, including the governor; his deputy, Okoya; another billionaire businessman and Okoya's friend, Adebutu Kessington; and others: "*Jagun-jagun lo n bo o . . .* [Tinubu] General politician *ni. . . . Iya o gbodo je wa . . . Iwo pelu Buhari, owo yin l'owa o*" (The warrior is coming . . . [Tinubu] is the general of politicians. . . . We must not suffer. . . . You and [President] Buhari, it is in your hands).

The former governor danced in joy along with the host and other distinguished guests. Before he began praising other guests, K1 made references to two matters that are relevant in this context. First, while standing in front of Tinubu, he stated, "*Ota e ota awa ni. Ore re l'ore awa . . . Awa ni soja e . . . B'eyan kan ba f'oju di e o, iya ni o j'oluwa re o*" (Your enemy is our enemy. Your friend is our friend. . . . We are your soldiers. . . . Anyone who affronts you will suffer). Thus, the popular musician was indirectly affirming that Tinubu was beyond reproach by his enemies and that anyone who was opposed to him or insulted him risked the wrath of all of Tinubu's "soldiers." Second, he broached Tinubu's rumored presidential ambition by singing "*Yoruba l'okan o, oro to wa n'ile yi, Yoruba l'okan o*" (It is the turn of the Yoruba, the matter at hand, it is the turn of the Yoruba). This is a reference to the debate about whether, after President Buhari's second term ends in 2023, a Yorùbá (meaning Tinubu) should succeed him.[25] Taken together, these references to Tinubu's enemies and his presidential turn[26] constitute the musician's direct response to those opposed to Tinubu's ascendancy in Yorubaland, his political dominance and national leadership, and his rumored presidential ambition. At this point, those "enemies" would ostensibly include a prominent Yorùbá who had been "affronting" Tinubu in the newspapers: Gani Adams.[27]

In December 2020, about twelve months after K1 De Ultimate described Tinubu as "*the general* of politicians" and insisted that the Yorùbá "must not suffer" in Tinubu's (and President Buhari's) hands, he was again performing at a wedding party. However, Adams attended this one. As Adams sprayed him with money, K1 sang, "*Gbogbo n to ba jo m'ogun, e p'Aare . . . Iya o ni je Yoruba, l'oju* generalissimo [Adams]. *Gbogbo Yoruba mbe leyin e*" (Everything that has to do with battle, call on *Aare*. . . . The Yoruba will not suffer in the era of the generalissimo [Adams]. All the Yoruba are with you).[28] He also added a popular song that in the old Oyo Empire was used to acknowledge the awesome powers of the *Kakaǹfò*, "*Ààrẹ, Ààrẹ ooo, ori mi ma je n s'Ààrẹ Ọnà Kakaǹfò*" (*Ààrẹ, Ààrẹ ooo*, may I never offend the *Ààrẹ Ọnà Kakaǹfò*).

Perhaps the irony was lost on a musician whose professional duty was to sing the praises of people, especially the highly placed people. But K1 De Ultimate is not just any musician. Apart from being one of the most prominent musicians in Yorùbá (with crossover appeal), as mentioned earlier, he is also very close to Tinubu. He regularly sings about the imminence of Tinubu's presidency and invokes curses against anyone who has stood in Tinubu's way. At the same time, he regularly sings the praises of Adams when the latter appears at society gatherings. As discussed in chapter 3, Adams once showered him with thousands of dollars at an event.

That K1 regularly sings the praises of these two prominent Yoruba—one he describes as *the general* (of politicians) and the *Asiwaju* (leader) of the Yoruba, and one he acknowledges as *the generalissimo* (of the Yoruba)—is not what I find particularly interesting here. Instead, I focus on the musician's use of similar metaphors or tropes to describe two ambitious men whose years of collaboration or mutual patronage had since given way to many years of mutual recrimination, political antagonism, and media war. He described both as warriors (one a general, the other a generalissimo) and referenced the reality and potential for both to attract enmity and enemies because of their statuses and accomplishments, while calling any actions against or criticisms of them as "affronts" and threatening their enemies with "suffering." Of course, K1 has never had to address what happens to either or both in the context of their mutual hostility.

Against the backdrop of K1's praise singing of the general and the generalissimo, I argue that the contours of the relationship between Tinubu and Adams over the last two decades can be used to map Adams's transformation. What started as a convivial patron-client relationship based on mutual interests—but involving a lot of maneuvering—about two decades earlier has morphed into a competitive, even rivalrous, relationship defined by personal ambitions and outsize egos. Therefore, tracing the Adams-Tinubu relationship as an example of Adams's transformed status also captures the ebbs and flows of political life in metropolitan Lagos in particular, Yorubaland in a wider context, and Nigeria in general.

What turned Adams into the adversary of Tinubu, the man who symbolically played the role of the groom's father at his wedding in 2003 and, some of Adams's aides claimed, provided funds for the wedding?

According to those close to both men, when the OPC emerged as a major social force in Lagos at the start of Nigeria's Fourth Republic in 1999, Tinubu, as the governor of the state, was concerned about this at two levels.[29] First, he was interested in peace and security in the state, which is a microcosm of Nigeria's multiethnic diversity—and tensions. He wanted to ensure that the OPC, which was becoming increasingly involved in interethnic clashes, as well as clashes with the police, did not destroy the peace of the state—or provide an excuse for President Obasanjo to declare a state of emergency. Second, he wanted to convert such a powerful social force, with a membership potentially in the millions, into political capital. Given his ambition—at the initial point of contact with Adams—not only to secure a second term in office but also to link up with politicians in other parts of the country in his bid to run for president in the near future, Tinubu needed an organization with a massive membership, like the OPC. Conveniently, the OPC could also constitute a potential vanguard of enforcers. At this point, Tinubu was planning to dominate Yorubaland and Yorùbá politics. Therefore, he needed to have influence over all important organizations, institutions, and social movements while ensuring that every critical social force was subjected to his strategic ambition. For that reason, Tinubu was strategically open to the OPC's leadership. According to some of the former key leaders of the OPC, Tinubu's initial target was the founder and leader of the group, Dr. Frederick Fasehun. Fasehun, himself a wily power monger, was

Figure 5.7. Governor Bola Tinubu, Adams, and his wife at their wedding in 2003. Photo courtesy of *Nigerian Tribune* library.

happy to associate with the governor of Nigeria's richest state. When the OPC split into two and Adams emerged as the leader of a faction, Tinubu decided to stick with Fasehun. However, as intragroup and interethnic clashes proliferated, it became clear that the Adams faction had the upper hand and a greater number of members in the chapters spread across Yorubaland.

This is where Rauf Aregbesola, Tinubu's political right-hand man and former commissioner for lands, came in. (He was later governor of Osun State, 2010–18, and federal minister of interior, 2019–23.) According to members of the OPC, Aregbesola was the Adams faction's link to Tinubu. Even Fasehun has acknowledged this without mentioning Aregbesola's name. "Further investigation," he writes, "showed that an influential Marxist-inclined Commissioner in [Lagos] state was sympathetic to Gani's cause and has even gone as far as taking him to see the Governor. His reason? Dr. Fasehun was too rigid and might not be pliable to manipulation during elections."[30]

Aregbesola, a consummate grassroots politician who controls the most populous political district in Lagos, had been involved in one of the Yorùbá self-determination groups and the prodemocracy movement in the late military

Figure 5.8. Screenshots of Adams bowing to greet Bola Tinubu, then the governor of Lagos State, at the fifteenth anniversary of *TheNEWS* magazine in Lagos on March 27, 2008. Sitting on either side of Tinubu are Oluremi, then the First Lady of Lagos State, and Chief Bisi Akande, former governor of Osun State and national chair of the Action Congress of Nigeria.

Figure 5.9. Governor Rauf Aregbesola playfully adjusting the metal snap of Adams's *buba* at a public event around 2014. Photo courtesy of *Nigerian Tribune*.

era. As a member of the Oodua Liberation Movement (OLM), he had relationships with some of those who eventually became either the core members of the OPC or the close associates of the core members. Adams's former closest aides, including members of the National Guard, Monsuru Akande, Arogundade Rasaq Balogun (Saddam), and Sunday Adebayo, as well as Adams's former chief of staff, Segun Akanni, confirmed that Aregbesola had facilitated Adams's relationship with Tinubu.

"[Rauf] Aregbesola was the link to *Asiwaju* [Tinubu]. *Asiwaju* was there for him [Adams]," stated Akanni.[31] "He obliged every time we knocked at his door for financial assistance. Whatever we needed, he facilitated it. We would go to Aregbesola, and he would take us to *Asiwaju* [who was then the governor of Lagos State], wherever he was."

Monsuru Akande, a former Welfare Committee chair of the OPC, told me that when they were having problems getting sureties for Adams's bail after his first arrest in 2001, it was Governor Tinubu who gave his approval to two traditional rulers in Lagos to stand surety for Adams.[32] Akande added that Tinubu, and later Governor Gbenga Daniel of Ogun State, regularly gave financial support to the group. Akande revealed that he collected the financial support regularly while Adams was in detention in 2005–2006. According to him, Tinubu wholly supported Adams's wedding to Mojisola in 2003 and also intervened when the couple had difficulty finding a pastor who would allow the wedding to be held in his church. Tinubu, Akande said, contacted the state chapter of the Christian Association of Nigeria (CAN) to find pastors to conduct the service and also got the Lagos Television Service (LTV) to allow the use of their premises for the wedding.

Beyond that, Adams's former aides claimed that Tinubu offered to give Adams two blocks of houses in the Meiran Millennium Housing Estate, which was built by the state government, and that when Adams rejected the offer, Tinubu asked him to find a piece of land anywhere in Lagos. When the community leaders in Soba, Abule Ado, offered Adams a plot, his former aides claimed, Tinubu almost single-handedly provided the funds and materials to build what Adams later named the White House.[33]

"Tinubu gave us money every week to ensure that we finished the building," Akande said. He added that he and Adams's other top aides built the house while Adams was in jail. "We became so close to Tinubu at a point that we would be in the vicinity anytime Tinubu was having meetings, including during the weekly State Executive Council meetings."[34]

However, during yet another media war, Adams's supporters denied this patron-client relationship between Tinubu and Adams. Olajide Odumosu, the director of communication of the *Ààrẹ Ọ̀nà Kakañfò* Strategic Intervention Group (ASIG), told the press, "He [Tinubu] said *Aare* [Adams] was an ingrate. Let him justify this. Has he built a house for *Aare* Gani Adams? Did he buy a car or sponsor *Aare*'s education? Or did he spend any money for the development of the OPC as organization? When Okiro arrested him in 2001, did he pay for his legal fees?"[35] Odumosu stated, "In 2005, Tinubu offered *Aare* Adams a two-bedroom apartment at Lagos State Low-Cost Housing Estate, Ojokoro, Meiran, Lagos but he rejected it. The last time *Aare* met with him was in 2009. So why is he after *Aare*?"[36]

What happened between the men?

Adams once told me that his problem with Tinubu was that the latter liked to be in "total control" of those whose relationship with him involved using his resources. He alleged that Tinubu wanted people to keep coming back for more money so they would continue to depend on him. Perhaps Adams was frustrated because he had reached a point where he wanted to be his own big man. He did not want financial support "in installments," as one of his former aides put it.

But someone close to Tinubu claimed that Adams had an exaggerated opinion of "his status and usefulness" for Tinubu and made "excessive requests." This source, as well as a former aide of Adams, claimed that the problem could have started when Lagos State received its allocation from the federation account seized by President Obasanjo. Since he had been involved in canvassing for the release of the money, these sources alleged, Adams asked for a "major cut" of the funds, a request that Tinubu dismissed. Razak Arogundade Balogun (Saddam), one of Adams's former closest comrades and now leader of the OPC New Era, also made this allegation in a press release in which he condemned Adams's attack against Tinubu. According to the report, Balogun "disclosed that the only crime Tinubu committed against Adams was his refusal to give him a chunk of Lagos State funds seized by President Olusegun Obasanjo's administration and which was later released by President Yar'Adua's government."[37]

Adams has denied making such requests. Yet he makes it clear that he expected Tinubu to "empower" him and members of his group, even accusing Tinubu of "deliberately . . . *starving*" him of funds. "Deliberately Tinubu instructed all the governors (South-west governors) [']don't work with OPC, don't *empower* OPC, don't associate yourself with OPC.['] Ask our people from the South West, if you treat[ed] us very well, why should we get an opportunity from your enemy? If you gave us jobs, if you *empower* us, we [will] turn down the offer from the federal government. Because you neglected us, you don't want the organization to exist anymore."[38] Therefore, the question of financial empowerment was critical to what a journalist describes as the "cat and mouse game"[39] between Adams and Tinubu.

When their relationship was good, the Adams faction of the OPC fully supported Tinubu's reelection in 2003. Adams confirmed this. The 2003 governorship election was bitterly fought, and Tinubu had to contend with the "almighty" federal power under President Obasanjo, who deployed every available force at his disposal to defeat all the opposition governors in the six Southwest states. Only Tinubu survived the onslaught. This meant that he also had to mobilize every force possible to resist the huge electoral heist that the ruling People's Democratic Party (PDP) perpetrated across the country. When Tinubu returned to office for his second term, Adams felt that the role of the OPC was so critical to the victory that the group deserved to have a commissioner and a special adviser in Tinubu's cabinet.[40] Some of my interlocutors claimed that Tinubu had no intention of ceding political initiative to Adams, whom, he felt, he had already rewarded "massively financially" for his support. Thus, Adams was sorely disappointed that he could not gain political leverage in a government he felt he had helped return to office. When describing his role in Tinubu's reelection, Adams even sounded as if he were Tinubu's benefactor:

> As a matter of fact, we supported (*Asiwaju* Bola) Tinubu . . . in his bid to become governor at the time. Then, the People's Democratic Party wanted to take over the South West and we realised that he was our ally. I was the one who went to Ibadan to seek Baba Adewale Thompson's[41] support. That was when I connected Baba Thompson to Rauf Aregbesola (now Osun State Governor). *I played a lot of roles for them to succeed in 2003*. When you have followers, you may not be fully partisan, but you will have a role to play to elect a leader.[42]

Even while conceding that Tinubu had also helped the OPC, Adams placed primacy on the help he and his group had rendered to support Tiubu's reelection. However, he argued that he supported Tinubu primarily because of the collective interests of the Yorùbá and not because of pecuniary gains. He added that he even suffered personally for this reason:

> Before 2003, we saw Tinubu as a Yoruba hero and we thought that he would be a future Yoruba leader *if Yoruba people could groom him*. We dissipated all our resources. In the process, he helped us too. Anytime [President] Olusegun Obasanjo . . . wanted to hit us, he would lend his voice and he also refused to say any negative thing about us. But we contributed a lot. In the process of supporting him, *we paid the price* because one of the reasons that PDP took us as its staunch enemy was because the party members felt Gani Adams and Tinubu were inseparable. So, most of our arrests at the time were politically motivated. They felt by arresting us, they would clip the militant wing of Tinubu so that they could get to him. I remember vividly in 2005, when people went to Obasanjo to ask "why are you detaining this boy? The crisis that occurred at Iyana Ipaja had nothing to do with Oodua People's Congress, and a Lagos court had freed them. Why then did you arrest them?" He said, "I want to clip his wings." He said he didn't know what was wrong with me. At the time, I had only one house, so he felt, why was I supporting Tinubu and not him?[43] He wondered how much Tinubu could be giving to me that he couldn't do 10 times. So that was one of the reasons Obasanjo kept me in detention in 2005. [Obasanjo's] plan was to keep me [in jail] until the end of the election in 2007. But miraculously, there was a court judgement on December 19, 2006.[44]

Adams contended that, despite the sacrifices, Tinubu refused to share some of the benefits of his political victory with the group. Worse still, he accused the Lagos governor of curtailing his access:

> We just saw a certain change of attitude in Tinubu; *he didn't want to empower us*. Anytime we had a programme and we sent him a proposal, he had a nonchalant attitude to it. When we wanted to see him, he started closing his

> doors. And I'm not a politician or a regular visitor to the government house. I may not see the governor of the state I live in for two years because I'm not a contractor, but we realised that if we suffered for them to get a mandate, by the time they were sharing positions, they would not take us into consideration. Although I may not need an appointment, but I have some of my friends or followers that say, "*oga,* if there is a political position, please kindly give to us."[45]

Adams then compared Tinubu's refusal to "empower" him with his experience with the PDP governors of Ondo (his home state) and Ogun State. The group also supported both politicians in the 2003 and 2007 elections.[46]

> I remember we supported Olusegun Agagu . . . and he promised to give me a position as special adviser if he won for second term. I was in Brazil when he was being sworn in in [2007]. His brother called and asked for the CV of the representative I wanted for the appointment. I sent the CV of one of my friends who was not even a member of the OPC. Something similar happened in Gbenga Daniel's government too. But no matter what you do for Tinubu, he will not empower you or give you the benefit of your struggle. There was an election period, I think 2007, we sent a proposal to him. Politics is about local interest. If anyone says he's in politics without thinking of his interest, he's a liar and a product of deceit. . . . So *we wrote a proposal saying, if you win this election, give us a commissioner, special assistant or adviser.* He threw the proposal away. He would only call you to go and support his party. So we realised that he was not keen to support this organisation anymore. We got information authoritatively that his late mother told him not to empower our group because the group would go to a higher place in future. Yes, quote me.[47]

Apparently, Adams was hoping to increase his status by becoming a political godfather[48] himself, with at least two of his nominees (not necessarily OPC members) holding political offices in Lagos State—and with others in Ogun and Ondo States. If he could repeat this in the other three Yorùbá states, where he also supported governorship candidates, then he would soon become a major political godfather himself. As Larry Diamond observes in his study of Nigeria's First Republic, access to the state or a position within state structures is critical to "both those who aspire to high class standing and those who wish to consolidate [wealth and status]."[49] Unsurprisingly, the man in charge of guarding and determining access to the state did not want the one with limited access to seek more.

When the relationship between the two men got worse in 2012, Adams's former chief of staff told me that he and Wale Adedayo, Adams's friend and initial freelance strategic thinker, planned an intervention.[50] Akanni asked Aregbesola—Tinubu's former commissioner for works, who was the initial link between Adams and Tinubu—to intervene. By this time, Aregbesola was the governor of Osun State. Governor Aregbesola asked Adams to see him in Osogbo, the state capital. He knew Tinubu would be there at the same time; therefore, he wanted to use the opportunity to settle the rift. Tinubu was in the Osun State Government House for a different matter. When Adams arrived in the governor's living room, he found Tinubu there and greeted him. Aregbesola asked about the problem between the two men, for whom he had acted as a bridge in the past.

According to Akanni, Tinubu expressed surprise that Adams had forgotten all that he had done for him in the past, including saving his life when he could have been killed—which Adams indirectly acknowledged in the quotation above. Tinubu told Adams that he had always obliged him when he needed help. Tinubu's only problem with Adams, he reportedly stated, was Adams's political ambition: "If you want to be in politics, then join politics. But we don't want you to be in politics. We can call on you to be there if there is any attack against our people in Lagos or the rest of Yorubaland."[51] Tinubu was ostensibly referring to Adams's request for two positions in his cabinet.

However, during the truce in Aregbesola's official home, Tinubu reportedly made Adams a fresh promise of help. But because this new promise allegedly involved a transaction that would take a while to manifest, Adams, a former aide of Tinubu said, could not wait. "It didn't take a long time before he started attacking Tinubu again in the press," said the source. Even Akanni, according to him, later became a victim of an alleged "surreptitious work" for Tinubu. (I will return to this below.)

In an interview with the Sunday edition of the *Sun* newspaper in December 2011, Adams took another shot at Tinubu, stating that the former Lagos State governor "lacks the charisma to be a Yoruba leader."[52] When the reporter expressed surprise at his dismissal of Tinubu, Adams added, "He is a socialite. Apart from that, he doesn't have the *spiritual means*. Awolowo did not spend money for people to follow him before they followed him blindly." He continued,

> *Asiwaju* Bola Tinubu does not have the spiritual means to be Yoruba leader. . . . You can't be a *psychedelic*[53] leader and you are claiming to be a Yoruba leader. You can't be a Yoruba leader to the extent that you can say go and give someone N500m because you want to capture a state. You don't buy people's conscience to be a leader in Yorubaland. It's a matter of time. And you don't

> impose people to be a leader in Yorubaland. In those days, if you wanted to contest, Awolowo would say go to primaries. Even though he had interests in certain persons, he would not say it. He would tell you to go to your local government, your ward. . . . It's not that someone will just sit down in one place and give an order that go and impose him, and nothing will happen because the party is in power. It's unfortunate. It's giving us sleepless nights because *he was a person we trusted before and many people have known us as very close allies.* So, such a person doesn't have the quality to be a leader of Yoruba land.[54]

Comparing contemporary leaders in Yorubaland with Awolowo, the gold standard, was a way of either declaring them as worthy of leadership or dismissing them. Adams ostensibly believed that, by comparing Tinubu negatively with the man everyone accepted as the standard, he had "irrefutably proved" Tinubu's limitations. When the reporter reminded Adams that he once "believed so strongly in *Asiwaju* Bola Tinubu," asking "What has changed?" Adams deftly equated himself with Tinubu, who, at this time, could be described as the most valuable player (MVP) in party politics in Yorubaland. Yet Adams inadvertently admitted their mutual maneuvering: "It's not as if we believed strongly in each other, we only happened to have shared the same antecedent. He was a leader in NADECO, and he played his role then. He paid his dues in the struggle. But when he got to power, he made money and he became another thing. . . . He became another thing because most of the things he said, the ideologies he professed, he couldn't follow them through."[55]

By 2015, Adams felt sufficiently politically significant to pronounce himself someone Tinubu needed to consult before making any major decision, especially one as important as supporting a candidate for the presidency. He contended that it was Tinubu's failure to empower him that Jonathan exploited:

> Now people will blame me for not supporting Tinubu, *did Tinubu tell me when he was endorsing Buhari as his candidate? Did he consult me?* Have I had interactions with him in the last three years? *He underrated me because I shied away from politics. He underrated my charisma and strength. . . .* Was I not close to him before? But now that he has made money, he's so arrogant to relate with his old friends and [President] Jonathan hijacked that. . . . I have paid my dues and I never got this opportunity in my life. I had never got a job from the government. *When your brother fails to give you a job and somebody from South-South* [Jonathan's home region] *gives you a job, then your brother should be ashamed.* The budget of Lagos State is a lot and *we never benefited any kobo from the Lagos State Government*; meanwhile, our presence here is a security advantage to the state.[56]

In the Yorùbá cultural context, someone of Tinubu's age and status would be regarded as a father to someone of Adams's age and status—especially before he became the *Ààrẹ Ọnà Kakañfò*. This is how Tinubu and Adams would have related in the years when they had a close (patron-client) relationship. However, by 2014, Adams had started calling Tinubu "*egbon wa*" (our brother) in media interviews. Adams's description of Tinubu as a brother or friend was an important way of bridging the (sociocultural) gap between them. The Yorùbá would capture this by saying, "*A tó baba, má p'enìkan ní baba*" (One who is eligible to be a father/patron should call no one else a father/patron).

Adams's erstwhile aide Monsuru Akande told me that Adams "wanted to compete with governors and senators."[57] If Fasehun had been asked for his reaction to the hostility between Adams and Tinubu, particularly against the backdrop of Tinubu's shift in alliance from the Fasehun faction to the Adams faction, Fasehun would most likely have pointed to his dismissal of Adams's initial ascendancy in his book: "Gani Adams certainly enjoyed the limelight. Politicians in search of mercenary services patronised him. With money—solicited and unsolicited—being upturned on to his laps and his bank accounts. . . . *The lowly gave up humility and assumed equality* with long-standing national figures."[58]

Adams's supporters claimed that Tinubu's ambition to dominate Yorubaland while also running for the presidency caused the generalissimo's friction with the political general. In 2005, Adams said that Tinubu was using the Yorùbá for his own "selfish interest."[59] He said to the *Premium Times*, "How can you claim to be a Yoruba leader or love Yoruba when you have never been part of any socio-cultural organisation? [Tinubu] became governor with the support of *Afenifere,* but immediately he was elected he divided the group. He wants to use the Yoruba to negotiate for his selfish interests."[60]

Adams, who was a delegate at the National Conference convened by President Goodluck Jonathan, added that the former Lagos governor's "pro-federalism advocacy was a subterfuge":

> Tinubu has always criticised the National Conference convoked by President Jonathan last year. National Conference report includes much of the principle and content of true federalism which has always been the wish of every true Yoruba socio-cultural group. But Tinubu criticised [the] Confab before it started. Even till now, he continues to criticise the report. True federalism as well as restructuring inter-governmental relations in the country to make the constituent units more buoyant and enable them to develop their own resources for the betterment of their people involves process. And the process is the Confab. How do you then want true federalism without supporting the Confab?[61]

The recurrent recriminations between Adams and Tinubu continued over the years. At different points, their mutual associates would intervene, particularly with Adams, to dissuade him from further attacking Tinubu. I recall on one occasion, when Adams had just attacked Tinubu in a newspaper interview, I called him a couple of days later to discuss the issue. He told me he did not want to talk about the latest attack. I later learned from other sources that a few people had intervened. He knew that I could easily reach out to Tinubu[62] and feared that if he doubled down on the attack in the interview, I might ask Tinubu for a reaction; it was obvious that he did not want to break the agreement he had with the interceders.

However, this truce could not last, given that the personal issues at stake remained unresolved: Adams wanted Tinubu to oblige him on whatever he demanded without submitting his *personal* (sociocultural and political) agency to Tinubu's strategic ambition. Conversely, Tinubu wanted to decide and determine when and how to support Adams based on Adams's total or near-total submission and on his ability to fit into Tinubu's strategic pursuit of his ultimate political ambition (becoming president). But for Adams, who wanted to retain his freedom of action—to be able to *l'atan*[63] (keep his options open) among disparate, even conflicting, political interests and ambitions—and had also come to see himself as a potential kingmaker, Tinubu's quest for absolute control, as a condition for continued financial support, was unacceptable. In the light of these irreconcilable interests and ambitions, it was not long before the two clashed again.

Segun Akanni, Adams's chief of staff and long-term aide, told me that he became the victim of the clash between the generalissimo and the general. In late 2020 from his Canadian base, Akanni revealed that before he asked Aregbesola to intervene in the "war," Adams had accused him of working for Tinubu. He also told the story to a general-interest magazine after Adams fired him. "I recall a similar thing happened in 2012 when I was also alleged [to have been] romancing [*Asiwaju* Bola] Tinubu, alongside one of his former friends, Mr Wale Adedayo. That time, he said *Asiwaju* Tinubu gave me a poison to put in his food. I was out of office for two months. He eventually called me back to resume because the allegations were not true."[64] The second time, in December 2018, Akanni was gone for good, as he claimed, after "[he] diligently served [Adams] wholeheartedly for almost 17 years as well as followed [him] blindly for about 22 years with . . . [my] life being put at risk."[65] Akanni adds further detail to his story:

> It all started on Monday December 3rd, 2018. I was in his house at Omole Phase II. As usual, we were preparing to go to Ajah for a meeting. I was chatting in the lobby of his house with a popular Nollywood actor. *Aare* [Adams]

> just came to where we were and asked me to leave his house and pack all my things. He alleged [that I held] a meeting with Chief Femi Davies on Wednesday November 28th, 2018, and another one on Sunday December 2 at 1am. . . . I've never met with *Asiwaju* Bola Tinubu . . . only *Ogbeni* Rauf Aregbesola, former governor of Osun State, knows me. [Adams] said we agreed in the said meeting to plant an explosive in his house and at the OPC's National Coordinating Council meeting slated for Ajah later that day . . . I was dumbfounded!!!
>
> Before then, I [had] not seen Chief Femi Davies for over four months. *Aare* Adams stated further that I had alliance with and allegiance to *Asiwaju* Bola Tinubu and that some of his men and I were also revealing his secrets to Tinubu; that Asiwaju gave us N200m, a house in Canada and in Lekki. He claimed that I used to visit Asiwaju Tinubu's house in Bourdillon in Ikoyi, Lagos at night after leaving his house. All the allegations against me were baseless, frivolous and unfounded. I didn't have any meeting whatsoever with Asiwaju Bola Tinubu, Chief Femi Davies or any of their representatives. Everything was just like a dream to me.[66]

Interestingly enough, Akanni had a more charitable account of the first time he was sacked by Adams in his book *The Volunteer of the Savannah,* where he eulogizes Adams. He appears to believe that Adams had the spiritual means of discerning any plot against him, particularly by his followers. As Akanni writes, "One day in 2012, Oga went into a trance when he was praying. We could not decipher how God revealed to him the innermost thoughts of many of his followers."[67] He cited an example that "got [him] scared,"[68] while stating, "All he [Adams] was saying had meaning to me personally because I had stayed with him, and was aware that most things he had said to people usually came to pass." He even explained away his first firing by his boss: "One of Oga's proclamations saved me. Some people were bent on killing or attacking him. Oga unintentionally sacked me as his personal assistant, and he went for a spiritual retreat. I was away and he was away. I read later from an article by Wale Adeoye, former media assistant to Gov. Gbenga Daniel, that Oga sent me away because I had forged an alliance with the former governor of Lagos State, Asiwaju Bola Tinubu. I laughed, 'Is this how people want to destroy my relationship with Oga?' I asked myself in solitude."[69] Akanni added that, after Adams's return from the spiritual retreat, while he was attempting to get Ambassador Segun Olusola to intervene on his behalf, he realized that Adams was already expecting him back. His boss reportedly told him, "You did not offend me. Go on with your job."[70]

"I first drove him [Akanni] away in 2012," Adams stated when I asked him about Akanni's allegations concerning the threat to his life in December 2018.

Figure 5.10. The Boss and His Aide: Adams and Segun Akanni, personal assistant and later chief of staff to Adams, in the early years of the OPC (*left*), and later in the "good old days" at the BBC's office in London. Photos courtesy of Segun Akanni.

"Everyone came to beg me, even the king of my town. Everybody begged me. Segun [Akanni] was going to cause a rift between me and my wife. I eventually sacked him in 2018. I accused him of meeting with Tinubu's emissary the night before I sacked him. I asked him to pack his things and leave immediately. . . . [These] same kinds of people betrayed Awolowo. It is the same with me. Awolowo had political power to fight his enemies. God just created me specially. There are traitors in every group."[71]

Akanni, in turn, denied his boss's allegations. He said he had never met Tinubu except while accompanying his ex-boss. But because he had supposedly been working for Tinubu against Adams, Akanni said, even months after his sack, on June 5, 2019, he was physically attacked, allegedly by members of the OPC on the orders of his former boss. He said he escaped death and was hospitalized for a few days. Photographs of his hospitalization were published in *Global Excellence*.[72] He subsequently fled to Canada, where his family was based.[73]

As the country moved toward the 2015 general elections, a realignment of political forces primarily engineered by Tinubu had convinced a coalition of disparate ideological forces under the faux banner of "progressives" to challenge the ruling PDP, which had been in power for sixteen years at the federal level and in a majority of the states in Nigeria. Tinubu's Action Congress of Nigeria (ACN); Buhari's erstwhile party, All Nigeria People's Party (ANPP); Buhari's latest party, the Congress for Progressive Change (CPC); and the All Progressives Grand Alliance (APGA) came together to form a new party, the All Progressives Party (APC), announced in February 2013. The new party also merged with a faction that broke away from the ruling party, called the New PDP, in November of the same year. As this new party became a formidable force that could impede President Goodluck Jonathan's second-term ambition, especially when the group selected General Mohammadu Buhari as its presidential candidate and a Christian Yoruba, Professor Yemi Osinbajo (Tinubu's nominee), as his running mate, Jonathan started desperately seeking new alliances to ensure his victory in the 2015 presidential race.

As I will discuss below, Jonathan had met Adams earlier and had developed a relationship with him. President Jonathan's supporters and the ruling party targeted Professor Attahiru Jega, the chair of the Independent National Electoral Commission (INEC), in the lead-up to the elections in early 2015. Both local and international observers believed that the attacks on Jega's credibility were engineered by the ruling party, which was afraid of the outcome of a free and fair election. As it became evident that Jonathan might suffer a defeat, his supporters filled the airwaves with desperate calls for Jega's removal. This was the basis of the anti-Jega protests led by Gani Adams in 2015—as related in the praeludium. The APC supporters in Lagos accused Adams's OPC of destroying the party's campaign billboards, particularly those of their presidential ticket, in Lagos.

Adams later claimed that his support for Jonathan was based "on principle." He told the Second World Congress of Oodua People's Union (OPU) in January 2016, "Let me say it clearly that we supported the immediate past President Goodluck Jonathan purely on principle of true federalism and towards the implementation of the outcome of 2014 National confab in Abuja, if he emerges as the president in 2015."[74]

Adams's actions in support of Jonathan, particularly the anti-Jega protest, again led to a clash between Adams and Tinubu. Tinubu, seeing Adams's efforts as an attempt to scuttle his party's potential victory, which would clear the path for his own presidential ambition in the near future, spoke about Adams in extremely disparaging ways, asking his supporters to defend themselves against the OPC. In a combination of standard and pidgin English, Tinubu told them, "Don't be scared; don't be afraid. They [ruling party] sent *one boy* out, recently. *Dem call 'am Gani Adams,* right? And they asked him to be fighting poster. *Na poster dem say make he fight.* If he dares fight any of you, you know what to do. You have my endorsement. You know what to do. Defend yourself. It is the rule."[75] He added in Yoruba, "This ballot [election], we will cast it fully."[76]

Calling Adams "one boy" could be Tinubu's way of reminding Adams that he was "a tool" that he had used in the past—even though anyone else (Jonathan) could use, or may be using, him at this point. It was also a slur meant to remind Adams of his humble beginnings and the fact that Tinubu was his onetime benefactor. Adams is particularly sensitive to such expressions of contempt from his (erstwhile) social superiors, especially those who have benefited from formal education. Such slights always alert him to his worst fears of not being considered a bona fide member of the elite. And, as his close aides revealed, he has a long memory about such slights.

Despite this friction, the nature of the complexities and paradoxes of electoral politics, politicians' commitment to win at all costs, and the complications of elite incorporation were again evident in the communication between Adams and some key leaders in Lagos—within both Tinubu's APC and the traditional institution—even after the presidential election. Between the presidential election on March 28 (which Jonathan lost) and the gubernatorial election in Lagos on April 11, the *Oba* of Lagos, *Oba* Rilwan Akiolu, a Tinubu ally; the state chair of the APC, *Otunba* Henry Ajomale; and others "intervened on behalf of the APC" to ensure that the party and Tinubu's candidate won the governorship, as Adams's spokesperson revealed. On the basis of this intervention, according to the spokesperson, "Gani Adams and [the] OPC [were] not partisan in any manner"[77] in the 2019 gubernatorial elections in Lagos State—in which Tinubu's candidate emerged victorious.

The Lagos monarch and Ajomale's intervention is important. Even after his party had won the presidential race, Tinubu still faced a perhaps more strategically critical election in Lagos. Since he became governor in 1999, all sorts of local, regional, and national forces in different combinations have tried to dislodge him from his expanding supremacy over the politics of Lagos. As explained earlier, Tinubu won his reelection in 2003 against all odds, while his contemporaries in the party across the region were defeated by the PDP. Since he left office in 2007, Tinubu has handpicked all his successors (Babatunde Fashola, 2007–15; Akinwumi Ambode, 2015–19; and Babajide Sanwo-Olu, 2019–). He has used his Lagos base to expand his political kingdom to all the other states in the Southwest—at a point being responsible for ensuring the victories of all the governors in the other five Southwest states—and to negotiate for national leadership and alliances. Tinubu's adversaries also realized that, by defeating his candidate in Lagos, they would likely truncate not only his political hegemony in Lagos but also his presidential ambition. Tinubu was more aware of this than anyone else. Therefore, whatever else happened to him, the possibilities of his political survival or revival (whenever he suffered setbacks regionally or nationally) depended on the control of Lagos. This was why, ostensibly with Tinubu's approval, his close allies, the *Oba* of Lagos and the chair of the party, reached out to Adams after the presidential election—despite the mutual antagonism—if not to secure the latter's support for the gubernatorial elections, at least to ensure that the ruling PDP did not use the OPC in an attempt to "hijack" Lagos. Thus, despite his anger at the "*boy*" (Adams), the *man* (Tinubu) realized the limits of his antagonism toward the former in the context of electoral politics. Though this did nothing to end the cat-and-mouse game between the two, for Tinubu, as the Yorùbá say, "*Bí a bá nsun'kún,* àámáa *rí'ran*" (Even when one is weeping, one can still see).

Barely two months after the general elections, a couple of weeks before the inauguration of President-Elect Buhari, Adams announced an alleged plot to assassinate him "by suspected hoodlums sponsored by *a top Lagos based politician.*"[78] Many believed this allegation was a veiled reference to Tinubu. Adams claimed that "the plot, aimed at causing chaos and painting him bad, would unfold shortly after the May 29 presidential inauguration ceremony."[79] In a statement by an OPC spokesperson, Adams also linked the plot to "expelled members of the OPC"—that is, his erstwhile close associates, who had formed splinter groups such as OPC New Era and the Oodua Progressives Care Initiative (OPCI)—whom he accused of being "sponsored" by Tinubu. The statement added, "This is to alert concerned Nigerians that after several failed attempts to remove the leader of the Oodua People's Congress by expelled members of the congress, security reports at our disposal revealed that a top Lagos based politician has devised ways to create chaos and attack the convoy of Otunba Gani Adams soon after the handover of government to Gen. Buhari."[80]

This was not the first time Adams alleged that Tinubu was attempting to eliminate him. According to Wale Adedayo, a journalist, former chief press secretary to Governor Gbenga Daniel of Ogun State, and erstwhile close associate of Adams, in 2012, the OPC leader accused his personal aide, Segun Akanni, and Adedayo of having been paid N10 million by Tinubu to get rid of him. In his reaction, Adedayo stated, "I need to make these few clarifications concerning OPC's Otunba Gani Adams' unfounded claims that former Lagos State Governor, Asiwaju Bola Ahmed Tinubu, gave his Personal Assistant,

Segun Akanni, and me, N10m to kill him."[81] He added, "It is our ancestors and the gods of Yorubaland who have problems with Adams."[82]

Adams did not formally report the alleged threat to the police. And he seems to have dropped the allegations, as Akanni continued as his personal assistant after this and was even promoted to chief of staff in 2017.[83]

Two months after the allegation of the assassination plot, the OPC issued a statement asking Tinubu "to be wary of some expelled members of the group who are bent on removing Otunba Gani Adams as the President/National Coordinator of OPC." The Adams faction alleged that these "dismissed members," who included former members of the group's National Guard, such as Rasaq Balogun (Saddam), Monsuru Akande, and Musiliu Amusa (Big Fish),[84] "had written a letter to the former Lagos State governor, seeking his support to remove Adams."[85] The statement added, "The dismissed members in a letter dated 4th August, 2015 and signed by all of them appealed to the former Governor to help them with their plans to remove or get rid of Otunba Gani Adams as the National Coordinator of OPC. The names, hand writing and signatures on the letter tallies perfectly with the information available in our archives."[86]

Adams was fighting a rearguard war within his faction of the OPC. Shortly after his anti-Jega, pro-Jonathan protest, leading members of his group, whom he claimed to have dismissed from the congress, accused him of collecting N1.6 billion from Jonathan to support his reelection bid. In a statement, Adesina Akinpelu, an Ibadan-based member of the National Coordinating Council of the OPC, stated that though they were not "in any way against President Jonathan," what they were "against is [Adams's] mortgaging the future [of] Yorubas . . . for pecuniary gains."[87] Akinpelu added, "One of the factors that contributed to President Jonathan's defeat in the South-west was his romance with characters like Gani Adams."[88] Adams again denied that he had collected any money from Jonathan to support him or to organize the protest in Lagos,[89] insisting that Akinpelu and the others, who were no longer members of his faction of the OPC, were being "sponsored" to attack him, ostensibly by Tinubu.

However, despite the mutual recriminations, when the *Aláàfin* proclaimed Adams as the *Kakaǹfò* designate, Tinubu publicly congratulated him. Although *Ọba* Adeyemi said he had considered Tinubu for the same position, a few people close to Tinubu claimed that, after seeking the position for many years without success, by 2017, he was no longer interested in the title, given that he was now consumed with running for president. In the past, they claimed that he needed the title for politico-cultural "ascendancy" in Yorubaland. He had since transcended this need. Whether or not it was true that he wanted the title, the fact that the *Aláàfin* considered Tinubu before settling for Adams must have reassured Adams that he was now on par with his erstwhile benefactor turned adversary. Despite this, Adams still valued Tinubu's endorsement of his selection. In fact, Tinubu's congratulatory message was one of the three (the other two being that of Senate president Saraki and Governor Ajimobi) that appeared in Adams's installation program. Indeed, Tinubu was very generous in his congratulatory message, partly because prominent people publicly congratulating other prominent Nigerians for any accomplishment is an important public ritual in Nigeria. In addition, congratulating Adams was a way for Tinubu to honor the *Aláàfin*, who was one of the most prominent Yorùbá traditional rulers with whom he shared a close relationship.

In his message, Tinubu stated that Adams richly deserved the title of *Ààrẹ Ọnà Kakañfò* and that the *Kakañfò*-designate had "never left anyone in doubt over his resolve to fight for the interest of Yoruba race."[90] The *Asiwaju* of Lagos added, "With this, you have joined the elite rank of generalissimos in Yorubaland. You deserve this honour. You have a heart of steel. You have never left anyone in doubt about your resolve and readiness to fight for and defend the interest of Yoruba race." Tinubu concluded that Adams's ascension to the title is significant because it "come(s) with an extra youth, vigour and vitality, which would be an added advantage."[91]

About three years later, as most Yorùbá in the Southwest states groaned under the siege of the constant destruction of crops by roaming herds of cattle, kidnapping, ransoming, and rape allegedly perpetrated by Fulani herdsmen, some accused Tinubu of silence because of his ambition to run for president in 2023. Against the backdrop of the long-running struggle for the restructuring or dissolution of the Nigerian federation championed by different groups in Yorubaland, the challenge posed by the herdsmen sharpened the calls. In light of this, Adams again attacked Tinubu during a TV interview. "Our elder brother [Tinubu]," he said, "is already gearing up to run for president but look at how he is handling his base, the South-West. . . . I don't think our brother is in sync with what the region stands for. I don't think he wants the concept of restructuring as well. I think what he wants is to be the President of Nigeria and 'chop up' as they do in Lagos."[92] Adams also accused Tinubu of being "a poor student of history" who "was only paying lip service to the concept of restructuring,"[93] adding that "first of all, he is supposed to settle rifts with all those he fought with in the South-West before you start running up and down to become president."[94]

A newspaper described what followed as "a free-for-all brawl between the loyalists of two prominent Yoruba sons, Asiwaju Bola Tinubu and *Aare* Gani Adams, over the subject of restructuring and 2023 presidency."[95] Media reports of this "brawl" must have served as a further confirmation for Adams that he was now an equal of the preeminent politician. The *Telegraph* reports: "In their own rights, the duo of *Asiwaju* Bola Tinubu and *Aare* Gani Adams are distinguished personalities who have made their marks in their various endeavours. In fact, they not only possess cult-like followership, they are, without doubt, astute and influential in the country, such that any action or inaction from them draws reactions from many quarters."[96]

Comparing the men further, the report described the *Asiwaju* as one who had "carved a niche for himself when it comes to the art of politics [and one who] has become a force and a voice of reckoning over the past 20 years," adding that "to call him a genius is [to say] the obvious because his footprints are everywhere." On the other hand, the report insisted that "the formidability of . . . the *Ààrẹ Ọ̀nà Kakañfò* of Yorubaland, is never negotiable." Adams "is a strategist . . . [who] has demonstrated courage and dedication in defence of the Yoruba race."[97]

In their response, a group called Bola Tinubu Disciples Organisation (BTDO), while dismissing Adams as "an ingrate,"[98] reminded him of his humble background. The group stated, "It is on record that the coming into the limelight of Adams, was an offshoot of the support he enjoyed from Tinubu."[99] They added,

> We are [embarrassed] that Adams could have easily forgotten the roles *Asiwaju* Tinubu played in his climb to the stardom. . . . *Asiwaju* played the father for Adams when he wedded. When he was declared wanted by then Lagos Police Commissioner, Mr Mike Okiro, it was the same *Asiwaju* that saved him. This ingrate would have been wasted by Okiro, but *Asiwaju* Tinubu rose up and stood firmly by him. . . . Gani Adams was one time prominent *Okada* rider on the streets of Mushin and became popular through his notorious activities. He graduated from Okada riding to a 'cut and nail carpenter' in Mushin.[100]

Adams's former comrades in the OPC joined the fray. Chief Maruff Olanrewaju, the national president of Oodua Progressives Care Initiative (OPCI), which broke away from Adams's OPC, condemned his former leader's "unguarded outbursts and vituperations . . . against . . . Tinubu," adding that "no responsible and reliable Yoruba will support Gani Adams on this unwarranted attack."[101] Razak Arogundade Balogun (Saddam), ex-member of the OPC's National Guard who now leads another faction called OPC New Era, also condemned Adams's "vitriolic and ill-advised attack" on Tinubu, suggesting that he "go for training and counselling on how a true *Omoluabi*[102] should relate and comport when addressing or dealing with elders."[103]

Figure 5.11. *Front row: Baba Oodua,* OPC New Era, Otunba Boye Mayeungbe (*left*); the author; the president of OPC New Era, Rasaq Arogundade Balogun (Saddam); the secretary-general (*left of Balogun*); and members of the group at the weekly NCC meeting in December 2021. Author's photo.

In November 2020, when I asked him for his reaction to the accusations by Balogun and others, Adams was very angry that I had raised anything relating to his erstwhile comrades. "When I was in detention in 2005 and 2006, they didn't want me to return," he said of the former members of the OPC National Guard. "So, after my return, I removed them when I heard about what they had done. Tinubu was using them. So I removed them and spread them out so they were no longer close to me. I had the biggest trouble when they were close to me."[104]

He added, "After the [anti-]Jega rally, Tinubu gave them N20 million to create the impression that they were a faction of the OPC. Tinubu will give money to all my children to say that they are not my children." Balogun and the others denied taking money from Tinubu to attack Adams.

On December 7, 2021, I attended the weekly NCC meeting of the OPC New Era faction to meet with the president of group, Rasaq Arogundade Balogun (Saddam) and his lieutenants. The meeting was hosted by the Kosofe Local Government chapter of the group at the Alapere area of Ketu, Lagos. It turned out that I was treated like an august guest, asked to sit at the table with leaders of the group, and elaborately introduced and asked to address the members. It felt as if my presence was regarded as a legitimation of the faction, as the leader told the members to beware of their actions because "people are watching from around the world."

Balogun told his comrades that he was particularly happy about my visit because it was a result of information provided to me indicating that the members of his faction were "the real men behind the OPC." He asked his comrades, "Where was Gani Adams when we faced the police?" He complained that the "real men" who fought the OPC battles were "written out" of Gani Adams's books on the OPC. He assured them that I was going to write a book that would reveal the contributions of people like him. While welcoming me before Balogun arrived, the *Baba Oodua* of the group, Otunba Boye Mayeungbe, used expletives in referring to Gani Adams, a signal of the nature of the enmity between the factions. One other significant thing happened while I was with them: some members of the group came forward to pay their monthly financial contributions. Whether or not this was prompted by my presence, I could not say. But Balogun pointed out that the group was sustained by such membership contributions, contrary to Adams's claims that they were sponsored by former Governor Tinubu.

The proxy war between the general and the generalissimo became "very messy," as a group claiming to be the *Ààrẹ Ọ̀nà Kakañfò* Strategic Intervention Group (ASIG) responded to the BTDO, while dismissing Tinubu as "a business man in politics with no ideology."[105] ASIG stated that the BTDO, "rather than addressing issues raised . . . decided to go haywire, raining insulting words on the personality of Gani Adams." The group added that Tinubu, whom the group reminded the public had been accused by Adams of having "no interest in the actualization of Oodua Republic and restructuring," is a politician whose "political background is alien to Yoruba ideology."[106] The group further accused Tinubu of having "a hand in the breakup of all the socio-cultural groups in Yorubaland [including the] OPC," thus bringing Tinubu into the internal crisis of the OPC. ASIG concluded by categorically accusing Tinubu of sponsoring "the [OPC] renegades in Somolu,[107] Ilorin[108] and Ibadan.[109] Now those groups have gone under and they are of no relevance at the moment."[110]

There is no doubt that Adams loathes the criticisms and sometimes vile disparagement he attracted from his clashes with Tinubu. In fact, in recent years, Adams finds the mention of Tinubu's name in a positive light or in relation to him extremely annoying. Yet, ultimately, the savvy accumulator of power and influence realizes that going head-to-head with Tinubu is a guarantor of his own eminence, even *preeminence,* as well as a way of purchasing legitimacy with an important faction of the regional and national elite formations that are opposed to Tinubu and his political ambition. Thus, such contention—that is, playing against a big man (Tinubu)—entrenches Adams in the vortex of Nigeria's unending ethno-regional competition for power with the attendant massive resources that flow from electoral politics.

—ʍ—

At exactly 4:10 a.m. on March 1, 2023, INEC declared Tinubu, the candidate of the APC in the February 28, 2023, presidential election, as the winner of the election, and therefore the president-elect. The former governor of Lagos State and long-term kingmaker defeated three of his closest rivals by polling 8,794,726 votes. The PDP candidate, Atiku Abubakar, won 6,984,520 votes; the Labour Party (LP) candidate, Peter Obi, won 6,101,533 votes; and the New Nigeria People's Party (NNPP) candidate, Rabiu Kwankwaso, won 1,496,687 votes.[111]

Although Adams did not publicly support any of the presidential candidates, LP's Obi, who was regarded as an antiestablishment candidate, particularly by the urban youth, visited Adams at his Omole Phase II, Lagos, home on February 13, 2023, during his campaign tour.[112] Adams was particularly touched by "the gesture and respect." He told Obi and his entourage that "by virtue of his title as well as leadership of the Oodua People's Congress (OPC) and Oodua Progressives Union (OPU), he is a major player and stakeholder in the South-West and Nigeria."[113] He added that "Obi's respect for the stool he occupies is a reflection of [the LP candidate's] understanding of Nigeria's problems."[114] However, Adams emphasized that Obi's presence in his house was not "an endorsement." While wishing Obi well in the 2023 presidential election, the *Kakañfò* told his guest that his "'beautiful ideas' will be difficult to implement if Nigeria is not restructured to regionalism"[115]—which is the long-held position of the core of the Yorùbá progressives, organized around *Afenifere*, a faction of which strongly supported Obi's candidacy.[116] Adams added, "Anybody that wants to be the Nigerian president should restructure the country into federating units where each region will develop at their own pace."[117]

However, when Tinubu was declared the president-elect, Adams issued a press release that same morning congratulating his old patron turned rival. In the press statement, the *Kakañfò* called Tinubu's victory "a reflection of his doggedness and consistency in Nigeria's politics."[118] He added that "by virtue of his position as the *Aare Ona Kakanfo* of Yoruba land and a citizen of Nigeria, it is . . . very important for him to congratulate the president-elect on his victory at the just concluded presidential polls."[119]

Figure 5.12. Labour Party presidential candidate Peter Obi during his visit to Adams's home in February 2023. Photo courtesy of *Nigerian Tribune*.

When I called him to ask why he had congratulated Tinubu despite their "cold war," he reminded me that the former Lagos governor had also congratulated him when he was announced as the *Kakaǹfò*-designate. Therefore, he added, he was only "returning the favor."[120]

What does the future hold for the relationship between the general of Nigerian politics and the Yorùbá generalissimo now that Tinubu has acquired the maximum power he has always longed for—and now that the *Kakaǹfò* is at the zenith of his own sociocultural power? Will the necessary potency of the politics of incumbency and the messiness of the potential politics of a battle for a second term in office force a compromise or uneasy conciliation between the cultural generalissimo and the political general turned president? Only time will tell.

A SYMBIOSIS: BETWEEN OGD AND OGA

Otunba Gbenga Daniel (popularly called OGD), the former governor of Ogun State (2003–11), said of Adams, "You are a determined personality who is highly

Figure 5.13. Gbenga Daniel pays a courtesy visit to Adams in the latter's home to seek his support for the PDP presidential candidate in the 2019 election, Abubakar Atiku. Photo courtesy of *Nigerian Tribune*.

principled and not after monetary gains but honour. *I am yet to see a greater Yoruba man of your generation* in the way you have carried and improved yourself with the resolve to move the Yoruba nation to higher levels."[121]

Otunba Gani Adams (OGA, as he was and is still sometimes called by members of the OPC), spoke just as kindly of Daniel: "As a sitting Governor, *Otunba* Daniel called us to a round table and settled the factional crisis within the movement *rescuing the region from bloodshed*. What he said on the occasion still remained indelible in my memory as he stated that he was not talking 'as a governor but as [a] *true son of Oduduwa*.'"[122]

The two men uttered these statements while *serenading* each other. Adams, who about two months earlier had been announced as the *Kakaǹfò*-designate, was meeting with Daniel on December 27, 2017, in his Sagamu home, on one of his visits to eminent Nigerians to canvass support for his impending installation. During the visit, he also described Daniel as an "asset to the Yoruba nation."[123] As observed in chapter 4, Adams visited the eminent Nigerians who, for one reason or another, could not or did not visit him at home after the announcement of his new title.

Daniel declared Adams as the "greatest Yoruba man" of his generation and pointed to Adams's transformation ("the way you have carried and improved yourself"),[124] while Adams celebrated Daniel's role in preventing "bloodshed" in Yorubaland as an example of the fact that the latter was a "true son of Oduduwa"[125] (the Yorùbá progenitor). Both were again displaying the sustained amity that has characterized their relationship—unlike the relationship between Adams and Daniel's erstwhile fellow contender for leadership in Yorùbá politics, Tinubu.[126] Indeed, Adams's relationship with Daniel has been as significant as his relationship with Tinubu in the last two decades. However, while the latter has been mostly contentious in the past decade, Adams's association with Daniel has remained harmonious. Greater symbiosis in the relationship between Daniel and Adams is evident.

It is important to note that Adams's relationships with the governors emerged partly as a result of the competition between Tinubu and Daniel, two politically ambitious men, to obtain primacy or supremacy in Yorùbá politics as leverage for their national ambitions. By 2001, the OPC had emerged as a powerful social force in urban Southwest Nigeria. Around the same time, political parties and politicians began to focus more closely on their plans for the 2003 general elections. Tinubu, as Lagos governor, was engaged in a two-pronged battle, one internal to his political party, the Alliance for Democracy (AD), and the other external, particularly in relation to warding off the planned onslaught by the PDP, on whose platform President Olusegun Obasanjo was hoping to capture the Southwest states. The Yoruba-dominated AD had won virtually every seat, both local and federal, in the 1999 elections that ushered in Nigeria's Fourth Republic. Therefore, though the PDP had a Yorùbá presidential candidate, Obasanjo, the party performed poorly in the six Yorùbá states. Though Obasanjo won the presidency, he suffered "electoral humiliation" in his home region, which he was hoping to reverse in 2003.

While Tinubu was aware of Obasanjo and the PDP's plan to defeat him in 2003, he was also eager to expand his influence in the region as a bargaining chip with his important political allies in the North (particularly Vice President Atiku Abubakar) in the hope of being on a presidential ticket (possibly as a running mate) in the near future, most probably in the 2007 presidential election. In this context, though he had limited leverage within the AD, which was then largely in the grip of the old grandees of the party,[127] Tinubu was hoping to support his own candidates in the other Yorùbá states, whose eventual victory would help to enlarge his influence in the region as a political king and kingmaker. In this bid, as some interlocutors who are close to both men told me, Tinubu was secretly supportive of Daniel. (In fact, one of Daniel's properties, I learned, was used as the office for the transition committee when Tinubu won the governorship in 1999.) In the course of time, when it became clear that, despite Tinubu's support, Daniel had no chance of wrestling the AD ticket from the incumbent governor, Segun Osoba, he left the AD and joined the PDP, where he picked up the governorship ticket. Some insisted that even as the candidate of an opposing party, Tinubu still backed his old ally against his own party's candidate, Osoba.

In an effort to ward off both his internal and external political enemies, Tinubu began courting the Adams faction of the OPC. During this period, Daniel began his own courting of the Adams faction. Like Aregbesola in the case of the Tinubu-Adams relationship, Wale Adedayo, a journalist, activist, and Adams's close adviser and strategist, facilitated the Daniel-Adams relationship. Adedayo—whose nickname in political circles is *Babalawo* (*Ifa* priest)[128]—was close to Adams and also knew how the group's huge membership, capacity for enforcement, and grassroots spread could be deployed by a political machine such as the one Daniel was building in the race for the governorship of Ogun State in 2003. Thus, when Daniel recruited Adedayo into his campaign team in 2001, Adedayo convinced his new principal to also befriend Adams.

Incidentally, around 2002, after his first arrest and detention, Adams was becoming aware of the potential political potency of the OPC and how it could be used to strengthen the group and transform his own fortunes. As members of the group revealed, this was when they decided to deploy their advertised nonpartisan stance in particular ways. Nonpartisanship meant that they could work with any politician or political party that approached them for "security services," particularly regarding electoral politics. It was a policy that the OPC leaders later described as "*a la'tan*" (keeping our options open). Though at this point Adams was already being courted by Tinubu, when a close strategic adviser such as Adedayo introduced him to Daniel, emerging policy (in the OPC) was meeting its experimental implementation (in the relationships with Tinubu, Daniel, and other politicians and political office seekers).

Over the years, I met with Adedayo, an old colleague in journalism, who gave me a rare insight into the relationship between Daniel and Adams.[129] He explained to me how Adams benefited greatly from the relationship with Daniel. First, it gave him an alternative to Tinubu and allowed him to exercise a measure of autonomy in his relationships with both—and with other politicians. However, according to those close to both men, while Daniel did not mind Adams's relationship with Tinubu, Tinubu grew increasingly uncomfortable with the Adams-Daniel association, particularly as the relationship between the two governors deteriorated. As Daniel, the self-styled "Lion of the West," started to create his own political empire while competing with Tinubu, who was called "the Lion of Bourdillon," for leadership,[130] Adams effectively maneuvered between the men while gaining maximum advantage from their competition. However, as Adams's relationship with Tinubu eventually deteriorated, his relationship with Daniel grew stronger. According to those close to Adams and Daniel, when Tinubu started vetting Adams's more excessive demands, Daniel indulged him. Even when both governors supported Adams, Daniel went beyond the call of duty. For instance, when Adams was detained for fourteen months between 2005 and 2006, both Tinubu and Daniel supported the group and Adams's family financially (some even suggested that Tinubu might have given more), but only Daniel visited Adams in detention in Abuja. Tinubu only sent his commissioner, Aregbesola, Adams's aides claimed. Also, while Daniel had visited Adams in his home, Tinubu never did.[131]

"The two governors [Tinubu and Daniel] supported us," Monsuru Akande told me.[132] "They *supported* us weekly. The two governors made us [the OPC Adams faction] into what we became. They gave us exposure and raised our standard. They changed our orientation."[133]

A few reasons may be adduced for the differences in how Tinubu and Daniel treated Adams in the long term—and vice versa. The first may be a difference in style, though a source who worked with Daniel stated that, "at the core," there is no significant difference in the men's attitudes toward power. As someone who is sensitive to any hint of condescension, perhaps Adams found Daniel more down-to-earth and more solicitous toward him than Tinubu. Beyond this may be the substantive needs of both men. It could be argued that, while Tinubu needed Adams as much as Daniel did, Tinubu, over the long term, had other possible sources of enforcement in Lagos, such as the National Union of Road Transport Workers (NURTW), which Daniel did not have. Thus, Daniel would have needed Adams more than Tinubu did. Also, Tinubu had a far bigger national constituency than Daniel and therefore a far greater network of provisioning to attend to, which might have tempered his willingness to accede to what a source close to Tinubu described as Adams's "incessant and huge" requests. Additionally, despite leaving office in 2007, Tinubu, unlike Daniel, has determined who became the governor of Lagos since then. Thus, his role of governor-general or governor emeritus allows him to continue to distribute a lot of largesse, which logically has secured him huge influence with countless people, groups, and institutions. If the cost became prohibitive while the subject became uncontrollable, Tinubu could do without the leader of a social movement (OPC), especially when such a leader wanted to eat his cake and have it too. As for Daniel, the two governors who succeeded him in Ogun State

Figure 5.14. *Left to right:* Chair, African Newspapers of Nigeria, Dr. Olatokunbo Awolowo Dosumu; Mojisola Adams; Adams; and former governor of Ogun State Chief Gbenga Daniel during the installation of twenty-one Aare Chiefs-in-Council by the *Ààrẹ Ọ̀nà Kakaǹfò*, in Lagos, Saturday, January 12, 2019. Photo courtesy of *Nigerian Tribune.*

have had no allegiance to him; in fact, they have been his political adversaries. Therefore, Daniel has had no influence with the state government. In this context, the leader of a social force such as Adams could help Daniel augment his influence, particularly since he left office in 2011. After 2011, Adams mostly needed Daniel to lend his august presence to the significance of his many public events and ceremonies. Daniel has obliged him on this score. For instance, he was one of the august guests—along with Mrs. Titi Atiku Abubakar, former second lady, and Dr. Mrs. Awolowo Dosumu, daughter of Chief Obafemi Awolowo—when Adams marked the first anniversary of his installation in January 2019 by constituting an advisory council.[134]

While he was still governor, to show his ascendancy in Yorùbá politics relative to Tinubu, Daniel convened a peace meeting—which Adams references above—between the two factions of the OPC, the Fasehun and Adams factions (see chap. 2). Wale Adedayo[135] and one of Daniel's commissioners, Niran Malaolu, a former newspaper editor, were the brains behind this initiative.

At the meeting, in March 2005, both Fasehun and Adams agreed to bury the hatchet and unite the two factions, with Fasehun taking the position of founder and spiritual leader and Adams becoming the national coordinator. Although subsequent meetings in Lagos to harmonize the positions of the two groups failed, the advertised success of this truce boosted Daniel's image as a peacemaker and political leader committed to the greater good of Yorubaland. Indeed, as leading members of the OPC on both sides confirmed, "the reconciliation stopped the intra-OPC clashes and killings," which had claimed more members' lives than other conflicts. This was a major victory for Daniel, especially given that an earlier effort endorsed by Tinubu had failed.

As Kayode Ogundamisi—former secretary-general of the OPC's Fasehun faction, former student leader, and activist—revealed, before the OGD effort, Tinubu had facilitated a reconciliation between the two groups that did not involve the two major gladiators.

"Myself and [Evangelist Kunle] Adesokan [then the secretary-general of the OPC's Adams faction] organised this," explained Ogundamisi.[136] "We had a couple of meetings, just the two of us. Later we brought in Alhaji Modiu. I briefed Fasehun about the effort, and Alhaji Modiu briefed Adams. Rotimi Obadofin, the president of OLM [Oodua Liberation Movement], also played a vital role. But the efforts collapsed on Adams's side. Adams treated everything with suspicion."[137]

Thus, Daniel had succeeded where others had failed.[138]

Because Daniel backed the OPC under Adams's leadership, the Ogun State wing of the congress thrived very well in the eight years that Daniel was in office.

"We had a very vibrant structure in Ogun State," one of the key leaders of the OPC told me.[139] "OGD was a grassroots politician. Therefore, he saw OPC as a grassroots organisation that he could rely on for his political ambition, for elections, to provide security, and other things. He even made the Ogun State chair of the OPC, Jimoh Adesina, the executive vice chairman of the Abeokuta South Local Government. Wale Adedayo negotiated the position for the OPC. Daniel wanted to give Adesina the chairmanship, but [a leading traditional ruler in Ogun State] asked for the chairmanship [for someone else]."[140]

Daniel is also often eager to defend Adams's honor and integrity in public. For instance, while Tinubu alleged in 2015 that Adams had been suborned by the ruling party, PDP, Daniel, when he received Adams in his home in 2017, told the *Kakañfò*-designate, "I have come to see you as a *very principled man who does not worship money*; I have seen you rubbish people with money over your principled stand."[141] Daniel strongly believed in Adams's ability to mobilize the

Figure 5.15. Seeking Votes. *Left to right: Akogun* Tola Adeniyi, former managing director of the *Daily Times*; Adams; and Governor Gbenga Daniel during the visit to Adams's home to solicit his support for the PDP presidential candidate, Atiku Abubakar, in November 2018. Photo courtesy of *Nigerian Tribune*.

members of the OPC and others to support any political candidate; therefore, as the director general of Atiku Abubakar's Presidential Campaign Organisation in 2019, he visited the *Kakaǹfò* at home in November 2018 to seek his support.[142]

The visit was as much an acknowledgment of the enormous influence Adams wielded, coming almost four years after the "disaster" of his public support for Jonathan, as it was a public acknowledgment of the abandonment of Adams and the OPC's initial position on partisan politics. Even during and after the anti-Jega rally, Adams insisted publicly that he was nonpartisan.[143] But publicly receiving the director general of a presidential campaign organization who came to canvass support in his home could only be interpreted as partisan. An online news site reported, "As the race to win Nigerians' hearts for votes in the February poll picks up, politicians are lobbying for support of influential persons across the country. Adams, formerly a controversial leader of the Oodua People's Congress (OPC), is regarded as having influence in some South-Western states. [Vice President] Atiku [Abubakar] will be seeking to gain sizeable endorsement in the region President Muhammadu Buhari dominated in the 2015 poll against [President] Goodluck Jonathan."[144]

Obviously, for Adams, whose group used to sing fervently in 1999 that "whoever asked us to vote, *Yemoja*[145] will kill him or her,"[146] the times have changed.

Elections were no longer anathema to the pursuit of self-determination for the Yorùbá and Adams.

PLAYING "PROPER" YORUBA: BETWEEN A "PROGRESSIVE" GENERALISSIMO AND A "RETROGRESSIVE" GENERAL

On Wednesday, December 2, 2020, Nigeria's two-time head of state and retired general, President Olusegun Obasanjo, was at the Lagos home of Chief Ayo Adebanjo, the ninety-two-year-old leader of the *Afenifere* (Awolowo political camp). Although Obasanjo and the *Afenifere* have spent the last three decades fighting a war of attrition, they have, on occasion, reached a measure of accommodation that often left one side (the *Afenifere*) gritting its teeth after being left in the lurch by the other. The last such "agreement" was reached over the 2003 elections, when the group and its political party arm, the AD, decided not to field a presidential candidate and to support their "son," Obasanjo, while the latter guaranteed a level playing ground for the AD's candidates in the other national and state elections. In the end, the group members believed that the mercurial general double-crossed them. In the massively rigged elections, Obasanjo's PDP defeated most of the AD's candidates in the national and state elections. Among the six AD governors in the Yorùbá (Southwest) states, only Governor Tinubu of Lagos State survived the tsunami to win a reelection bid.[147]

However, in their mutual opposition to the incompetent and ethnocentric administration of President Mohammadu Buhari (2015–23)[148] and to the national paralysis and crises inadequately addressed by the Buhari administration, Obasanjo and the *Afenifere* leaders again found common cause[149]—despite Obasanjo's initial support of Buhari. In fact, in the light of terrorism, farmer-herder conflict, and insecurity, including widespread kidnappings and rape, Obasanjo was, at this point, spearheading a summit where the Yorùbá would take a collective critical stance on the state of the nation. As someone close to Obasanjo told me, he did not want Gani Adams at the summit. Adams got wind of this and did not appreciate it. If a gathering of the most prominent Yorùbá did not include him, the *Kakaǹfò*, it would constitute a form of rejection through exclusion, a most humiliating experience. Two of those in charge of the secretariat of the planned summit, Akin Osuntokun, Obasanjo's former special adviser and former managing director of the News Agency of Nigeria, and Yinka Odumakin,[150] *Afenifere*'s spokesman, were also close to Adams. Adams installed Osuntokun as the *Ajugun'Nla Àárẹ Ọna Kakaǹfò* in January 2020, while Odumakin and his wife, Joe, had been close allies of Adams for more than two decades. Osuntokun and Odumakin asked Adebanjo to intervene in the long-running mutual hostility between the generalissimo and the retired general, Obasanjo.

Figure 5.16. President Olusegun Obasanjo shaking hands with Adams at the seventieth birthday ceremony of Dr. Tokunbo Awolowo Dosumu in 2018. Photo courtesy of *Nigerian Tribune*.

Interestingly, Adams and Obasanjo share comparable humble beginnings and are also known for their long memories. Obasanjo had ordered the police to shoot on sight at the height of the OPC clashes in Lagos. He even threatened to declare a state of emergency and remove the Lagos governor, Tinubu, whom he accused of not dealing with the crisis provoked by the OPC. He also gave marching orders to the police to arrest Adams. Apart from these actions, between 2005 and 2006, Obasanjo ordered Adams (along with Fasehun) to be detained for fourteen months. Adams has never forgotten his ordeal at the hands of Obasanjo.

Similarly, Adams had spent the last one and a half decades inveighing against Obasanjo, describing him in different ways as someone who is not a "true" or "proper" Yoruba, especially because he is not a "progressive." Obasanjo, who takes note of every slight and often avenges himself one way or another in his own time, must have been aware of the disparaging things Adams had said about him over the years. Obasanjo was also averse to the self-determination campaign of the OPC and other Yorùbá groups, as well as similar campaigns in other parts of Southern Nigeria. He had always presented himself as a nationalist who believed fervently in Nigeria. Therefore, his recent questioning of Nigeria's unity and his public statement accusing Buhari of "mismanagement of [Nigeria's] diversity and socio-economic development of [the] country,"[151] in addition to describing Buhari as "an agent of destabilisation, ethnic bigot and religious fanatic,"[152] was sweet music to the Yorùbá progressive establishment, including Adams.

Figure 5.17. President Olusegun Obasanjo (*third from left*); *Afenifere* leader Chief Ayo Adebanjo (*middle*); and Adams (*third from right*) at a meeting between Obasanjo and Adams at Adebanjo's home. Others at the meeting include Akin Osuntokun, former director general of the News Agency of Nigeria and member of the *Afenifere* caucus (*second from right*); Yinka Odumakin, publicity secretary of *Afenifere* (*second from left*); and two others. Photo courtesy of *Nigerian Tribune*.

To ensure a united front, Adebanjo felt that Obasanjo, the most prominent Yorùbá of this era, and Adams, the *Kakaǹfò*, should be reconciled to unite the Yorùbá in the struggle to restructure the Nigerian federation.

"Akin Osuntokun and Yinka Odumakin came to me to say I should intervene to resolve matters between Obasanjo and Adams," Adebanjo told me on the phone.[153] "I was at meeting with [Pastor Enoch Adejare] Adeboye [the general overseer of the Redeemed Christian Church of God, RCCG] where Gani Adams flared up and said he will never have anything to do with Obasanjo. I asked him to calm down. We are trying to resolve a bigger problem. If everyone is thinking about the past, we will not move forward. You cannot say you will not have anything to do with anyone. We want to bring everyone together. He [Adam] saw my point."

When the ninety-two-year-old Adebanjo called the eighty-three-year-old Obasanjo to inform him that he wanted to visit him about Adams, Obasanjo, in deference to Adebanjo's age, told the older man that he would rather visit the *Afenifere* leader in his home. Thus, Adebanjo asked Adams and some of the members of his caucus to meet Obasanjo in his Lekki Phase 1 home in Lagos. Adebanjo, as well as Osuntokun and Odumakin, told me that the meeting went well, with Obasanjo sharing jokes with Adams. However, in deference to Obasanjo's age and status, Adebanjo promised that he would ensure that Adams visited Obasanjo at home so that they could put the past behind them and work together in the interest of the Yoruba. The meeting at Adebanjo's house ended on a good note, and they even took a group photograph. Thereafter, Obasanjo left for his Abeokuta, Ogun State, home.[154]

Perhaps in the eagerness to announce another milestone in the process of uniting the Yorùbá (which was not unrelated to Adams's command of media relations in the context of the projection of his own status), Odumakin alerted some of his contacts in the media about the meeting. He followed up by issuing a press statement.[155] Reporters who did not get the statement but got wind of the meeting contacted Adebanjo, Odumakin, and Adams for confirmation. Odumakin emphasized that the meeting had been convened to discuss "the future of the Yoruba and the rising wave of insecurity in Nigeria"[156] and that it "took far-reaching decisions on major and critical issues affecting the Yoruba nation to be the basis of consultation with other leaders across the South-West."[157] Adebanjo added that "critical issues like restructuring [of the Nigerian federation], which is one of the factors that created the face-off between Obasanjo and Adams in the first instance, was discussed and other matters like security and a way forward for the country."[158] However, the initial reports in most of the online newspapers focused on the "15-year-old rift" and the "reconciliation" between Obasanjo and Adams.

On his part, Adams never mentioned the issue of "reconciliation" in his reactions when contacted by the media. He only said that "the meeting was a robust deliberation with particular interest in the state of the nation, including insecurity, unity, among others."[159] However, with headlines such as "Breaking: Obasanjo, Gani Adams Reconcile, Settle 15-Year Rift,"[160] "Afenifere Reconciles Obasanjo, Gani Adams,"[161] and "*Afenifere* reconciles Olusegun Obasanjo, Gani Adams, Settles 15-Year Rift,"[162] Obasanjo's associates were wondering what had happened. They called him. Obasanjo, who was caught up in traffic for several hours after he left the Lagos Island venue of the meeting, was caught off guard. He was furious. Obasanjo found the impression that the reports created—that he and Adams were *equals* who were at odds with each other and had now resolved their differences—demeaning. One of the reports stated that Adebanjo described Obasanjo and Adams as "two warring parties [who] expressed their grouses,"[163] though the newspaper did not directly quote the *Afenifere* leader. Even though Adams still had grudges against Obasanjo for incarcerating him,[164] in a sense, being on "equal" terms with a civil war hero, two-time head of state, and internationally respected statesman elevated him.

Obasanjo did not expect the confidential meeting to be reported in the media, particularly in the light in which it was presented. Though no one had said it was a secret meeting, at the same time, they had not discussed releasing the details to the media. Therefore, Obasanjo must also have felt that the other side had acted in bad faith.

"It was quite embarrassing for Obasanjo," Osuntokun, his former aide and *Afenifere* caucus member, told me. "There was no reason to release a statement to the media when we were still working secretly to arrange an important summit and smoothen the relationship between President Obasanjo and Adams."

Obasanjo's response—released the same day—also disappointed Adebanjo and his allies. The former president's statement essentially denied the rationale for the meeting in Adebanjo's house. "My attention has been drawn to some publications reporting an acclaimed reconciliation between Gani Adams and myself at the residence of Chief Ayo Adebanjo in Lagos today," the statement began. Obasanjo, in part, misrepresented what had happened. The former president said "he was not on a reconciliatory mission" in Adebanjo's house; rather, he said, "he paid a visit to Adebanjo, but met Adams there."[165] The host and those who organized the meeting disputed this. The meeting was not a coincidence. Obasanjo added that "he had no quarrel with . . . Adams" and that "he had refused to grant Adams' request to visit him when he was president and after he left office" because "he had *a reservation for Adams' past way of life*, which, he said, was not in accordance with his standards and principles."[166] In truth, Obasanjo, who loves to rebuke people, mentioned his objection to Adams's past at the meeting—to which Adams gave what seemed an adequate response.

However, Obasanjo's statement that "he had no quarrel with Adams" was almost a literal translation of a common saying in Yoruba: "*mi o ba' ja*." In the context of a difference, disagreement, or dispute, such a statement is meant to either dismiss the basis of the dispute; to indicate that the other person is not worthy of one's time and attention; or to suggest that the other party is of subordinate or lesser status. I suggest that Obasanjo was *thinking in Yorùbá* when he made the statement. This is borne out by the additional allegations he raised: first, that he had refused Adams's requests to visit him as president and after he left office, and second, that he had "a reservation for Adams' past way of life." Both not only expressed his disdain for Adams but, more importantly, attempted to establish and emphasize social (status) distance between Obasanjo and a "*lesser man.*" For Adams, it was yet another way for an accomplished Yorùbá man to (in)directly call him "a boy," or an "insignificant" person—as Tinubu did during the electioneering campaign in 2015.

My reading of Obasanjo's statement is further confirmed by the latter's position that "if at all anybody feels I have a quarrel with him or her that needs reconciliation, such reconciliation will, no doubt, take place in my residence in Abeokuta only."[167] Indeed, in Yorubaland, the settlement of a dispute between an older and a much younger person (usually in age, but also in status or rank), even if it takes place in the house of someone older than both, would still involve the younger person visiting the home of the older to signal that she or he has received that party's blessing as the final indication of reconciliation.

On this score, as Adebanjo confirmed to me, Adams was expected to visit Obasanjo in his home at a later date. It was only upon such a visit that, in cultural terms, a reconciliation could be declared.

However, Obasanjo's denial of the "reconciliatory effort" also irritated Adebanjo and Adams. But while Adebanjo felt insulted by Obasanjo's claim that he could not have been reconciled with Adams in Adebanjo's home, Adams was particularly incensed by Obasanjo's "reservation for Adams' past way of life." He saw it as a challenge to his honor, accomplishments, and status in society. Indeed, it was Obasanjo's way of demolishing the basis of Adams's claim to eminence—*his past*. While Obasanjo considered this past questionable, for Adams, it was one of self-sacrifice and suffering for the cause of the Yoruba, democracy, justice, freedom, and equity. As he saw it, most people's agreement with his reading of his past had earned him his sociocultural distinction. In fact, it was this past that had earned him a seat beside the former president at the home of the *Afenifere* leader. Adams thus felt he had to defend his honor against Obasanjo.

But Adebanjo, Osuntokun, and Odumakin persuaded Adams not to respond. When I spoke to him a few days after Obasanjo's rejoinder, Adebanjo clarified things further:

> I called Obasanjo to tell him I wanted to come and see him regarding Gani Adams. He said he would rather come to see me. So, Obasanjo knew why he came to my house, contrary to what he said in his statement. At the meeting, he was saying he didn't want to have anything to do with Adams because of his 'criminal' past. Adams responded, and we agreed that he was not convicted by any court. In fact, the courts dismissed the charges against him. Anyway, we eventually resolved matters, and I told Obasanjo that I will come with Gani Adams to see him in his home to finally resolve everything. We took a photograph together.[168]

However, with the benefit of hindsight, Adebanjo added, "Maybe we should have issued a statement that all parties would have agreed to. But we didn't do that. Yinka Odumakin made a mistake by issuing a statement saying that *Afenifere* had reconciled Obasanjo and Adams." The *Afenifere* leader added that when he heard that Obasanjo was very angry, he asked Yinka Odumakin to withdraw the statement. Odumakin promised to do so, but it was too late. It was all over social media.

But Adebanjo objected to Obasanjo's statement that if Adams wanted to be reconciled with him, it would not be in someone else's home, particularly since Adebanjo had already promised to take Adams to Obasanjo's home. "That was not fair to me," said the nonagenarian. He added that he had since contacted Obasanjo, who promised to see him in his home the next day, December 11, 2020.[169]

Incidentally, while Adams was outraged by Obasanjo's disparaging reference to his past, he was also disappointed that Adebanjo did not issue a statement to defend him against Obasanjo,[170] especially since he had already defended himself against the same charge to the satisfaction of the *Afenifere* leader at the meeting. However, the *Kakaǹfò* failed to appreciate the nonagenarian's no-win situation, particularly as a peacemaker, since Obasanjo had promised to return to see Adebanjo over the controversy.

Not a man to let any slight pass—despite the pleas from the Yorùbá elder and his associates—Adams fired his own shot at Obasanjo a few days later. He called a press conference and said, "My guardian angel will not forgive me if I reconcile with Obasanjo."[171] Describing Obasanjo as "not a progressive,"[172] Adams also "berated the former president who cast aspersion on his character."[173] As usual, Adams granted an extensive interview to *Vanguard*, the newspaper that reports his activities most frequently—and later followed up with another interview with *Punch*, in which he recalled his "horrible experiences" in "prisons under Obasanjo."[174]

It is significant that Adams conceded that there had been "no reconciliation" at Adebanjo's house. As explained above, the two men were not technically reconciled at the meeting. What happened was at best the start of a *reconciliation effort*. However, as Adams indicated in subsequent media interviews, his grouse with Obasanjo was the man's attack on his character. His explanation bears a long quotation because it reveals Adams's perpetual and passionate attention to anything that would affect his *public image*—in this case negatively:

> I think Obasanjo has the right to say there was no reconciliation on that day, but the only thing I do not like in that statement is someone *condemning my character*. I don't know what Obasanjo meant by my past way of life. But all

> I know is that we don't have the same character because I know Obasanjo *is not a progressive element*, either when he was in office and out of office, so we cannot share the same character. So, I can't be in accord with someone who is not a progressive. So, when he said he does not like my character, President Obasanjo *will not like the character of a progressive Nigerian*. . . . I agree, we don't share the same character of being progressive because he is not a progressive person. . . . You ask yourself which progressive organisation he belongs to. From his antecedent, tell me any credible organisation he belongs to. He has never been a member of any progressive organisation.[175]

By focusing on Obasanjo's lack of progressive credentials, which is akin to stating that the former president is not a "proper Yoruba,"[176] Adams presents himself as the "true Yoruba" and not an "aberration"—which he assumed the former president to be. Even though he did not mention Awolowo, Adams's response indirectly summoned the ghost of the late leader, the epitome of *progressive politics* in Yorubaland, to adjudicate between him and the "retrogressive" former president. Beyond this, and despite the wide age difference between them, Adams was particularly attentive to what he regarded as the condescension in Obasanjo's statement. He strongly repudiated the former president's claims—even stating that Obasanjo "crossed the line" by impugning his character—and indirectly reminded Obasanjo of his (Adams's) own eminence:

> Secondly, talking about the issue of reconciliation, *I've never requested any visit to his house*. I don't know where the information came from that I requested to meet him twice and he rejected it. I have never requested to meet Obasanjo, the meeting that was held at the home of Pa Adebanjo was at the request of Pa Adebanjo. Initially, I refused but Pa Adebanjo is one of those people I respect most in Yoruba land, and I had no option than to oblige him. We met, we had a discussion, and I was so shocked when the statement came out. Ordinarily, I would not have reacted, but for Obasanjo to talk about my character in a negative way, because it may affect me and my family. *The only thing I have in my life is my name*, I don't toy with it and I don't want anybody to assassinate my character . . . I will never go to his house. Assuming he did not talk about my character, I could consider going to meet him. . . . Though his press secretary called me the next day trying to defend that statement and I told him that such a statement would not help the unity of Yoruba land. He asked me when I was coming to visit *Baba* (Obasanjo), and I told him to forget about it. *I will never visit him for reconciliation and if I go, my guardian angel will be annoyed with me*.[177]

I could not confirm whether Obasanjo's assistant called Adams. If he did try to smooth things over, it would be a further confirmation of Adams's position that he was not one to be trifled with—even by a former president and civil war hero. He was a "hero" in his own right—a hero for democracy and self-determination.

Adebanjo, Osuntokun, and Odumakin were also disappointed with Adams's response to Obasanjo, given that they had persuaded him not to respond publicly so the matter could be resolved amicably. It surprised me that they all assumed that Adams would let things lie when it involved an attack against him in the media. Fortunately for the three, the former president ignored Adams's response. But those who know Obasanjo well believed that if there was any opportunity in the future, he would surely remind Adams of the affront. For now, they both had a common enemy to fight: President Buhari. Yet Adams had had the last say.

RESOURCE CONTROL AND EMPOWERMENT: ADAMS, JONATHAN, AND THE POLITICAL ECONOMY OF ELECTORAL POLITICS

"When Chief Olusegun Obasanjo was the president for eight years, *he never really looked at us*,"[178] Adams told a TV interviewer while explaining why he backed President Jonathan in the 2015 presidential election. "Instead, he was always antagonising us and always looked the other way. But when President Jonathan became the president, he called me to Abuja, spoke with me and we had a handshake *and ever since my life has not remained the same* and that was how our relationship began. He has since been supporting us (OPC) and our activities and that is one of the reasons we have been backing him."[179]

Adams added that he "has [since the handshake with the president] remained loyal to" Jonathan, who "solicited his support and advised that he should ensure that OPC remained peaceful" during his presidency.[180]

It can be argued that serendipity has played a minor but sometimes critical role in the consolidation of Adams's influence and power. As reflected in chapter 3, a chance meeting with the then vice president Jonathan at the anniversary of *TheNEWS* magazine in March 2008 meant that, when, two years later, Jonathan was elevated to the position of the Nigerian president after the death of President Umaru Musa Yar'Adua (2007–10), Adams was on the new president's radar.

Yet some perplexities of identity construction and identity struggles in Nigeria (the latter of which would ordinarily pit President Jonathan against Adams),[181] as well as Adams's search for personal (im)material certainties and Jonathan's own lust for power, led the men into a political alliance.

"President Jonathan invited me to the [Aso Rock Presidential] Villa two months after he became president," Adams revealed to me.[182] "He told me that if the police provoked me, I should let him know. He said all he wanted was I should let him have a peaceful government. I told him that we have reorganized the OPC."

One of the aides of the new president, a lawyer, (Niger Delta) environmental rights activist, and senior special adviser on research and strategy, Oronto Douglas, had known Adams during years of interactions among self-determination groups in Southern Nigeria. Therefore, it was easy for Jonathan to reach out to Adams through Douglas, as Adams told me. Douglas became the go-between for the president and the OPC leader.

As Adams stated, his relationship with Jonathan began when the president invited him to Abuja, spoke to him, and shared a "handshake" with him that transformed his life. In Nigeria, a "handshake" in this context would be regarded as a hefty financial inducement, although Adams regularly denied that he ever took money from Jonathan personally—even while admitting that the president "has been nice to [him]."[183]

In late 2017, when I asked him about the basis of their warm relationship, Adams told me that he supported Jonathan "for ideological reasons." He added, "[Jonathan] organized the most successful National Conference in Nigeria. The conference had 633 recommendations to move Nigeria forward. He promised to implement the recommendations. . . . I don't choose my friends based on material reasons."[184]

However, to his aides, comrades, and friends, it was evident that, in the Jonathan era (2010–15), particularly after the government gave "pipeline security" contracts to some of the militant groups in Southern Nigeria, including the OPC, Adams had entered a new period of enhanced personal prosperity. In Jonathan, Adams found a new patron and relationship that far transcended the rewards of his relationships with Tinubu and Daniel—especially the former. In another interview, Adams accused Tinubu of a "plot to destroy the OPC by denying it of *government patronage*," contrasting this with "President Goodluck Jonathan[, who] has been magnanimous, awarding pipeline protection contracts to leaders of the organisation and other militants across the country." He added that Tinubu "deliberately instructed" the governors in his home region not to "empower" the OPC.[185] For the OPC leader, if anyone in the government, especially a Yorùbá (such as Tinubu and Obasanjo), failed to empower him and his group, that constituted an attempt to destroy him and his organization.

In fact, Adams admitted that the Jonathan presidency ensured his personal (material) transformation ("ever since my life has not remained the same"), even while insisting that the benefits of his relationship with the president were (ethno-)national: "Everything we are doing is not just for the Yoruba race. We

Figure 5.18. Adams addressing the press after meeting with President Jonathan at the State House, Marina, Lagos, in March 2015. Behind him is Dr. Reuben Abati, the president's senior special adviser on media and publicity. Photo courtesy of *The-NEWS* magazine.

are saying all of these so that we can have a new Nigerian [*sic*] that we can be proud for [*sic*]."[186]

Adams met Jonathan at the old Marina State House in Lagos in March 2015 in the context of the impending general elections, in which the APC—a coalition of opposition parties and a faction of the ruling PDP, which Tinubu was instrumental in building—seemed poised to trounce the president and his party at the polls. The president had panicked a few weeks earlier and postponed the elections, originally scheduled to be held on February 14 and 28, until March 28 and April 11 because of a "lack of troops to protect the voters." Most Nigerians and the main opposition party, the APC, regarded this postponement as "foul play."[187] It was against this background that Adams became the convener of the Coalition of Concerned Nigerians (COCN), which organized a protest in Lagos to ask for the removal of the INEC chair, Attahiru Jega (see the praeludium).

Marruf Olanrewaju, then the OPC coordinator in Kwara State, told me that he accompanied Adams to the meeting.[188] He said Governor Gbenga Daniel and a few other PDP stalwarts, including the party chair, were also there. Olanrewaju, who has since left to form his own group, the OPCI, said, "We agreed with Jonathan, to support him. Adams told the president that OPC had six million members. He will deliver their votes to him. He claimed that the OPC was in thirty-four states. So Jonathan thought that if he won the Southwest and the Southeast [along with his own home region of South-South], he would win reelection."[189]

Emerging from his solidarity visit to Jonathan in Lagos a couple of weeks before the presidential elections, Adams announced that the OPC had endorsed Jonathan's candidacy for a second term. The first reason for the endorsement, according to Adams, was that "every elected president in the country was given a second chance and Jonathan should have his."[190] The second was personal for Adams; it was also a potshot at President Obasanjo. "The second main reason is that as an activist, for the past 20 years I have never witnessed any president who will be in power for four years without using the instrument of power to *harass an activist* or civil society."[191] The OPC leader also said that Jonathan's "humility and his love for Nigeria" was an additional reason "our dear organization [the OPC] support[s] him." Adams made it clear that the president's acknowledgment of his influence and eminence mattered a lot to him, reportedly adding that "the group's visit to the President was an honour to the group because the Yoruba cherished being honoured by leaders." He concluded: "Our coming here is to show the entire Nigerians that we are in full support of Mr President. We want him to finish the projects that he started in the first term during [his] second term."[192]

As Adams admitted, the relationship with Jonathan propelled his status in an unprecedented way. Not only was he no longer targeted for condemnation, arrests, and detentions as he was under President Obasanjo, or ignored as he was under President Yar'Adua, but he also, on a few occasions, had audience with President Jonathan. Additionally, apart from the fact that Jonathan was the first president to count him as a friend,[193] the administration's decision to award contracts to militant groups to protect the oil pipelines, which were being regularly attacked, leading to the loss of billions of naira, transformed Adams's access to petro-naira in an unprecedented way. This time, he was not *climbing through* the system; he bypassed a multilayered patronage system in the oil economy to reach the ur-patron. Since all his earlier patrons also owed their wealth to oil, Adams, at this point, could afford to owe no allegiance to any other patron than the *ultimate big man*, the president.

Did Adams receive money from Jonathan? Adams offered a categorical no,[194] even while acknowledging the pipeline protection contract that his group secured from the Nigerian National Petroleum Corporation (NNPC). On the contrary, Adesina Akinpelu alleged in a *Vanguard* interview that, during the meeting at the old State House in Marina, Lagos, Adams collected a huge sum of money from Jonathan.[195] "He collected the money in the morning and now invited the [OPC] members in the evening claiming that President Jonathan wanted to meet them. When the meeting was held in the evening, he [Adams] gave them about N21 million. The other money which was contained in [a] 'Ghana Must Go' bag was given to him in the morning. I have my intelligence report from Marina. I am an ex-military man. I have my colleagues around him. This man is a liar."[196] OPC's publicity secretary, Hakeen Ologunro, described Akinpelu and others as "shady characters" whose allegations against Adams were "indeed laughable."[197]

Being plugged into the politics of oil resources in a petro-state and the related struggle over what is called "resource control" ensured that Adams's insistence that political leaders and public officeholders *empower* him and his group collocated well with the subtext of the Jonathan era. President Jonathan was considered the first person from a "minority" group to serve as the head of state in Nigeria. Although this is not technically true, because General Yakubu Gowon (1966–75) was from the minority Angas in the North of Nigeria, it was repeated during Jonathan's presidency for two reasons. First, apart from the fact that most Southern Nigerians regard everyone from the North of Nigeria as Hausa (or Hausa-Fulani), Gowon (a Christian) never emphasized his non-Hausa identity in the context of a regime that came to power in 1966 through a coup led by northern (Muslim) soldiers. His actions ensured the popularity of this view in Southern Nigeria. Second, in the context of the political economy of oil in Nigeria, the minorities from the oil-rich Niger Delta region have become what might be called a globally idealized minority—a people occupying a resource-rich, environmentally devastated, and politically marginalized corner of the world who are, in addition, constant targets of violence and exclusion perpetrated by the majorities and the state. The oil-bearing states in Nigeria used the political slogan "resource control" to capture the campaign for a return to the centrality of the derivation principle in the revenue allocation formula, "particularly [in the case of] the allocation of the proceeds from mineral exploitation."[198] Constitutional law professor and senor advocate of Nigeria Itse Sagay describes *resource control* as another name for "fiscal federalism"—which "goes hand in hand with true federalism . . . [as] was recognised and implemented faithfully in the Independence and Republican Constitutions

(1960 and 1963)."[199] Adefemi V. Isumonah also explains the context of the principle: "During the formative years of Nigeria's fiscal federalism when their lands were the main sources of major revenue earners, the northern and western parts of Nigeria pushed for and got derivation principle, weighted 100%, and later 50%, inserted in Section 134 of the 1960, Independence Constitution and section 140 of the 1963, Republican Constitution."[200] Isumonah argues that as crude oil increasingly became the central source of revenue for the Nigerian federation, "derivation was progressively whittled down by the north and west-controlled federal governments."[201] Between 1966, when the military took over power, and 1979, when they handed that power to civilians, the derivation principle in the revenue allocation formula had decreased to 45 percent under General Yakubu Gowon (1966–75) and 20 percent under Generals Murtala Mohammed (1975–76) and Olusegun Obasanjo (1976–79). Under the North-led civilian government of Alhaji Shehu Shagari (1979–83), the principle was totally abolished.[202] In 1992, the Ibrahim Babangida regime, in response to agitation in the Niger Delta region, established the Oil Mineral Producing and Development Commission (OMPADEC), to be funded by 3 percent of proceeds from the sale of crude oil. OMPADEC was replaced by the Niger Delta Development Commission (NDDC) in 2000. The 1999 Constitution, decreed into law by the departing General Abdusalami Abubakar, fixed the derivation fund (called special funds) for the nine oil-bearing states at 13 percent. There is continued agitation in the Niger Delta for the percentage to be raised to twenty-five or fifty.

Against the backdrop of the struggle for resource control and the politics of consumption, Adams told the press that, because "the President came from the Niger Delta region, which produces the bulk of the nation's wealth, it was incumbent upon the citizens to support the minority to complete a second term through Jonathan." He added, "As a matter of fact for a person coming from the minority [from which] 85 percent of the resources used to run this country [is derived], we must use that opportunity to give him a second ticket so that this country can be run peacefully."[203]

Especially because it was accidental—due to the death of a majority president—Jonathan's emergence as president was depicted as the first opportunity for the minorities, who had been struggling for the control of their resources, to take the helm of affairs in the country. Therefore, given his limited political traction and his deep interest in empowering his own people, including the insurrectional groups in the Niger Delta region, Jonathan found the initiative to contract out the protection of oil pipelines to the militant groups appealing. This would allow him to legally disburse billions of dollars to his specific (Niger

Delta) and larger (Southern Nigeria) region of the country and ensure that he attracted political backing from the leading militants as well as the millions of young people who belonged to these groups.

In 2011, the Nigerian National Petroleum Corporation (NNPC) gave multi-billion-naira contracts to the leaders of militant groups, or ex-militants, as they were called in the Niger Delta region, to protect the oil pipelines, which were constantly being vandalized. They included the leaders of Niger Delta militant groups such as Government[204] Oweizide Ekpemupolo (popularly called Tompolo) of the Movement for the Emancipation of the Niger Delta (MEND), Mujaheedin Asari-Dokubo (formerly of the Ijaw Youth Council and later of the Niger Delta People's Volunteer Force), Chief Bipobiri Ajube (popularly known as General Shoot-at-Sight), and others. The contracts, which were for one year, were renewed in 2015 and extended to the Southwest states of Ondo, Ogun, Oyo, and Lagos[205]—OPC's territory. The Southwest contracts were shared among the Adams and Fasehun factions of the OPC and one Ajube in Ondo State. In announcing the renewal of the contracts in 2015, the NNPC stated: "The pipeline protection contract is part of our community engagement programme across our host communities. It aims at getting community members to help in the task of protecting the pipelines around their communities. The recent rise in the frequency and intensity of wilful attacks on our pipelines dictates that we step up our community engagement programme to help stem the tide of the pipeline vandalism scourge."[206]

Adams agreed with the rationale for the use of extrastate enforcement structures to police the pipelines. When a journalist asked him why a "self-determination" group was asking for a contract from the government, Adams explained that it was "purely business" and also an "empowerment" program for members of his group. According to the OPC leader,

> Securing the pipelines is an empowerment programme for members of an organisation that has been in existence since 1994. There is nothing wrong for leaders of such an organisation to apply for that because they have suffered detention and illegal arrests in the past and have been brutalised. For a group that has been doing a lot of things for the society free of charge, it is not too much to apply for a security job. Protecting pipelines is not a rosy job too because it involves lives. If OPC is offered the job, I don't think it is asking for too much. Most of the people in government have business connections that cut across party affiliations. . . . The pipeline security job is purely business; it is not as if we are asking for free money. OPC getting involved in pipeline protection is not a bad idea; for any organisation to be accepted, it needs empowerment.[207]

He added that it took three days of agonizing debate before his faction decided to make a bid for the contract, after he had also been persuaded to do so by some who were close to Jonathan following a similar bid by the Fasehun faction. More importantly, Adams provided what might seem a general ethical justification for collective empowerment and personal enrichment:

> We were just out to make a point that anything that will benefit the OPC from the federal government has to be shared. Although Dr. Fasehun applied for the contract first, some of his friends from the Niger Delta advised me that I should apply too. . . . Besides, there was pressure from my members that I should apply and it took three-day marathon meetings for us to agree. . . . The truth is that we are in a capitalist world and there is no way you can fight the capitalists without having the resources to do so. You cannot even try to change society without having capital or resources to do so. It might have been possible in the past, but not anymore. And when NADECO[208] was fighting its struggle, it had to raise money from different places, both locally and internationally. So there is nothing wrong if we get a legitimate job, not criminal, to repackage the organisation, empower our members and provide them with jobs.[209]

In another interview, Adams said that the contract given to his group would provide a total of fifteen thousand jobs: "Nigeria was losing more than N3 billion everyday [to] the activities of the vandals and the agitation of that contract started from Dr. Fredrick Fasehun one and a half years ago and you know the bureaucracy of Nigerian ministries. It was a long process and it was just granted and it will empower nothing less than 5,000 youths from my side. Altogether, that is about 15,000 jobs for Yoruba land. Will you deny Yoruba youths the opportunity of getting 15,000 jobs because of politics?"[210]

Although the actual amounts paid to the ex-militants were never publicly disclosed, the *Wall Street Journal*, which described the payments as "government cash" for "oil bandits,"[211] reported that the annual payment was US$9 million (N5.6 billion).[212] However, the money stemmed the spate of attacks on pipelines that, alongside bombings and kidnappings, had plummeted Nigeria's oil production to as low as 500,000 barrels per day. Production went up to 2.6 million barrels daily.[213] While pointing to the Jonathan government's advertisement of the initiative as a "success story," the *Wall Street Journal* commented that the message being sent to the young people was "that militancy promises more rewards than risks."[214]

In admitting that his group got the contract, Adams prevaricated about how much his faction of the OPC collected, even while defending the decision of the Jonathan administration:

> They alleged that some ethnic militia collected nine billion, what I know is that President Goodluck Jonathan gave us a contract to protect pipeline and in that pipeline contract, the analysis is that Nigeria is losing 1.3 trillion naira every year to vandals. And when you see how much they will pay us for a year, in six zones—we have three zones in south west, three in South-South. I have only one in South-West; Dr. Fasehun has one and another guy in Ondo has one. The entire money NNPC will spend for us to protect the pipeline is not up to four billion for the six zones. You know what happened[?] They intentionally wrote the propaganda to affect the rally of last Monday [the anti-Jega rally], and at the same time, they haven't given us a dime for the contract. President Jonathan has not given us money; we are just planning on how to start the job now.[215]

For Adams, this was his—and the OPC members'—share of "the nation's *commonwealth*," though he denied that he had been "bought over" through the contract. As if to emphasize that such empowerment gave him direct control of resources, ostensibly denied him by Tinubu (whom he held responsible for sponsoring the propaganda against him), Adams added: "As a Nigerian, we have *a right to share from the commonwealth and that does not mean they have induced us*. Tinubu is the Chairman of Oando,[216] and it's an oil company and hardly will you see any governor in Nigeria that does not have interest in oil business. Hardly will you see any minister that does not have interest in oil business. Look, the south-south has been benefiting from the Amnesty package from the past four or five years. We have never benefited from it."[217]

He employed more rousing rhetoric to defend his action and to show that, as a figure of past suffering, he had earned the right to benefit from the "national cake":

> We are not contesting elections with the politicians, so I see no reason why they should deny us the opportunity to benefit from the Federal Government. This is a country where some of the governors are involved in crude oil business, as well as owning construction companies, which they use to get contracts, but *someone who paid dearly* during the struggle *is being denied an opportunity to benefit from the national cake*. I have been to many detentions, police formations and about six different prisons. *There is nothing wrong with us benefitting from the system now*, but I will certainly not compromise our principles. The struggle is in the blood of my members, in their hearts, and it has become their lives.[218]

Given that the processes of these contracts were shrouded in secrecy, I could not confirm how much Adams's faction actually received from the NNPC. A source claimed that it had received "only the first installment"—a little over

N500 million. However, many people who condemned Adams for taking this contract did not know, as I gathered, that some highly placed people in the Southwest, including traditional rulers and politicians, sent him the names of unemployed young men around them or in their hometowns to employ for pipeline protection. Although the jobs were expected to be only for registered OPC members, some influential people saw the contract as an opportunity to get jobs for their own people.

The contract was reportedly canceled when Buhari replaced Jonathan in May 2015, but not before it became a matter of contention among the OPC members and Adams's ex-comrades. Added to the allegations that Jonathan previously gave Adams billions of naira to be used to empower the six million members the group claimed to have, Adams's adversaries accused the OPC leader of having lost focus and control of the group. They alleged that in Jonathan's bid to ensure electoral victory in 2015, he had conceded to Adams's request to empower the members of the OPC by providing a huge sum to help millions of young people in the OPC start small businesses. According to his ex-comrades, Adams allegedly proposed to Jonathan that, with a purported membership in thirty-three of the thirty-six states of the federation,[219] the OPC could massively mobilize its members and their families to support the president. If this was true, the claim would have been sweet music to Jonathan's ears.

However, Adams's accusers gave different figures and different purposes for the money. While some accused him of receiving N9 billion for the pipeline project, others alleged that the money was for the empowerment of OPC members, and others still said the money was for both.[220] Another report alleged that he collected N10.6 billion from Jonathan.[221] OPC Kwara State coordinator Maruff Olanrewaju[222] addressed a press conference in February 2016 on behalf of six other states' coordinators—including Oyo State coordinator Chief Adeagbo Musediq; Ondo State coordinator Mr. Rotimi Akinsonwon; Delta State coordinator Mr. Hakeem Agboola; Sokoto State coordinator Alhaji Yekini Salaudeen; Kaduna State coordinator Alhaji Rasaq Ogunsanwo; and Bayelsa State coordinator, Akeem Ologburo. Olanrewaju asked President Buhari and the Economic and Financial Crimes Commission (EFCC) "to investigate all Gani Adams' banks accounts," as well as the accounts of those he alleged to be Adams's fronts, from February to November 2015.[223]

While denying the allegations—particularly in response to a similar claim by Lai Muhammed, then the APC spokesperson and later the federal information minister—Adams stated categorically in 2016: "It is on record that we have not received any money from the government as payment for the pipeline

contract. Such allegation coming from a person who today occupies the office of the nation's Minister of Information is rather unfortunate and sad."[224]

In what some believed was a tactical move to discourage the new president from regarding him as an enemy while also opening the door to opportunities for himself, a day after the inauguration of Buhari, on May 30, 2015, Adams called a press conference in his Ilupeju, Lagos office. He was full of praise for the man he had tried to stop from becoming president, describing Buhari "as an incorruptible leader, who lived a decent life, even after years of occupying high office." But even then, he made a veiled reference to Tinubu, while expressing his anxiety about possible retribution against him: "From [Buhari's] statements, I think he's determined to change this country, but not with the calibre of people that surrounds him. He must ensure that he has grip of the government because we have people from his own party that will be pushing him to use the federal might against those who did not support him during the election."[225]

Adams was not prepared to risk everything for another spell in detention, given Buhari's penchant for detaining people without trial during his first coming as military head of state. By sending messages to the new president through the media, Adams signaled that he was ready to move on from the Jonathan era. He would need a new strategy to play with—or in the era of—the new Big Man in the country.

CONCLUSION

Central to Gani Adams's genius[226]—his practical wisdom—is the awareness of the need, as well as the capacity, to continually reinvent and reposition himself. In this chapter, I have explored how he performs this constant reinvention and repositioning in his relationships with big(ger) men, particularly within the context of the ethno-regional competition for power and national electoral politics. In these relationships, as Marshall Sahlins argues, Adams's every public action as a big man "is designed to make a competitive and invidious comparison with others" and to show his "standing above the masses."[227] In recent years, he has endeavored to show his (politically) moral and cultural standing *above* even some members of the superelite. For a man whose unique position or status in society is largely of his own creation,[228] the sustenance of that status depends on what produced it: high ambition and intense competition.[229]

Karin Barber has shown that, in the context of late nineteenth- and early twentieth-century Yorùbá society, to gain and keep sociocultural legitimacy and sustain ambition and competitiveness, a big man must display qualities

such as "toughness, unassailability, intransigence and power—often conceived in terms of the ability to perpetrate outrages with impunity."[230] For Andrew Apter, this implies that, because big men in Yorùbá society "pursue dangerous careers" and "occupy a liminal role on the margins of success and failure,"[231] they must be "ruthless competitors for public recognition."[232]

The public career of Gani Adams, as examined in this and the previous four chapters, illustrates, in new ways, the challenges of becoming and being a big man in late twentieth- and early twenty-first-century Yorùbá society—a society that encourages a certain pattern of individualism that leads to intense competition for power, especially for "those who are strong and old enough to seize it."[233]

Political parties in Nigeria are oftentimes based on an alliance among various levels (from the local to the national) of big men and women who have shared ambitions for power and resources. Thus, the outcome of politics is more often than not overdetermined by the management of the multilevel and multifarious relationships between these big men, whose relationships necessarily intersect with those of other big men and women outside the political party framework—including traditional rulers, religious leaders, leaders of ethnoregional groups, retired militariat, businesspeople, heads of corporations, top civil servants, and more. This pattern of doing politics has been accentuated by the nature of the transition programs that eventuated in Nigeria's Fourth Republic. As military rule was coming to an end between 1998 and 1999, the super-big men in the country, both the serving and retired military chiefs and their civilian counterparts, came together to anoint a retired general, Olusegun Obasanjo, as the safest bet to hold Nigeria together in the transition from the end of General Sani Abacha's autocracy (1993–98) to democratic rule. The emergent ruling party, the PDP, was an agglomeration of the most powerful and influential big men (with a few big women) from all parts of Nigeria, supported by the "nonpolitical" big men, including retired generals, powerful traditional rulers, influential retired top civil servants, and the richest businessmen. Thus, it took a similar group of big men (some of them exiles from the ruling party) to come together between 2014 and 2015 to dislodge President Jonathan and the PDP from power after sixteen years of PDP domination.

This chapter shows that Gani Adams's emergence did not simply mirror and mimic the national political template; the pattern of his relationships at the highest level of the sociopolitical class drew its logic from this template. Adams is therefore a prodigious exemplar of the age.

Whether he is contending with regional big men with national networks and ambitions, such as Tinubu and Daniel, or with national big men, such as (incumbent or former) Presidents Obasanjo and Jonathan, Adams has exemplified

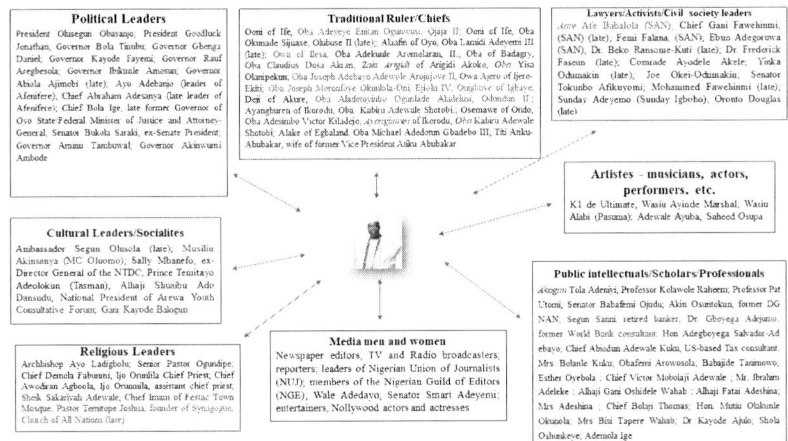

Figure 5.19. A snapshot of Adams's Network of Relationships of amity—and, in a few cases, enmity. This does not represent all of Adams's relationships; it only attempts to capture many of the relationships expressed in this book.

a disciplined and undeviating focus on his tactical and strategic interests, converting or mobilizing relations of both amity and enmity with all these big men to enhance his own status. Thus, ultimately, those who hoped to use (and perhaps dump) him are used (and even dumped, if necessary) in turn by Adams. In this way, Adams seems to simultaneously expend and yet retain his *use value*.[234] He always manages to retain a relative autonomy (see fig. 3.78) that might appear disproportional if not counterintuitive to his constant need for patronage.

Through these relationships of amity and enmity, Adams accumulates (social and material) power and (political and cultural) influence. By *playing*, *playing with*, or *playing against* these big men, Adams grows his own (big man) status. Also, by playing with or against people at the highest level of the political league in Nigeria, Adams displays his affinity, in the highest possible degree (in excelsis), with the regional and national elite. Whether these big men are courting or shunning him, whether they are praising or disparaging him, whether they are associating with him or disassociating themselves from him, they help, intentionally or inadvertently, in not just affirming but also enhancing his eminence. They help to acknowledge and actualize his *being a big man*. Thus, the contours of the different relations of amity and enmity between Adams and other big(ger) men examined in this chapter reflect Pareto's warning about what will happen if the governing elite does not "find ways to assimilate the exceptional individuals who come to the front in the subject classes."[235]

NOTES

1. Job Osazuwa, "Lagos Stand Still for Kalu's Daughter's Wedding," *Sun*, December 23, 2017, https://www.sunnewsonline.com/lagos-stands-still-for-kalus-daughters-wedding/.

2. Ibid.

3. Ibid.

4. I return to this below.

5. Richard Werbner, "Introduction: Postcolonial Subjectivities; The Personal, the Political and the Moral," in *Postcolonial Subjectivities in Africa*, ed. Richard Werbner (London: Zed Books, 2002), 2.

6. Ibid.

7. Michel Foucault, "The Subject and Power," in *Beyond Structuralism and Hermeneutics*, ed. H. Dreyfus and P. Rabinow (Chicago: University of Chicago Press, 1983), 220.

8. Francis Nyamnjoh, "'A Child Is One Person's Only in the Womb': Domestication, Agency and Subjectivity in the Cameroonian Grassfields," in Werbner, *Postcolonial Subjectivities in Africa*, 111.

9. Abner Cohen, *The Politics of Elite Culture: Explorations in the Dramaturgy of Power in a Modern African Society* (Berkeley: University of California Press, 1981), 60, 61.

10. Ibid., 60.

11. Ibid.

12. Ibid., 60–61.

13. In his concept of "figuration," Nobert Elias also argues that the "interdependence of players" in a field of action may be "of allies or of opponents." Elias, *What Is Sociology?* (New York: Columbia University Press, 1978), 130.

14. Karin Barber, introduction to *Readings in African Popular Culture*, ed. Karin Barber (Oxford: James Currey; Bloomington: Indiana University Press, 1987), 4; following Jean-Francois Bayart, *The State in Africa: The Politics of the Belly*, trans. Mary Harper, Chritopher Harrison, and Elizabeth Harrison (London: Longman, 1993), 218–27.

15. Karin Barber, "How Man Makes God in West Africa: Yoruba Attitudes towards the *Orisa*," *Africa: Journal of the International African Institute* 51, no. 3 (1981): 724.

16. Ranajit Guha and Gayatri Chakravorty Spivak, eds., *Selected Subaltern Studies* (1982, reprint, New York: Oxford University Press, 1988).

17. Frederick Cooper, *Decolonization and African Society: The Labor Question in French and British Africa* (Cambridge: Cambridge University Press, 1996), 9.

18. On the question of the elect as reflected in the initial theological sense of the concept and practice of élite in eighteenth-century Europe, see Gareth Williams, "Subalternity and the Neoliberal Habitus: Thinking Insurrection on the El Salvador/South Central Interface," *Nepantla: Views from South* 1, no. 1 (2000): 112–13; T. B.

Bottomore, *Elites and Society* (Middlesex: Penguin Books, 1966), 7; Wale Adebanwi, *Yoruba Elites and Ethnic Politics in Nigeria: Obafemi Awolowo and Corporate Agency* (Cambridge: Cambridge University Press, 2014), 8.

19. Andrew Apter, *Black Critics and Kings: The Hermeneutics of Power in Yoruba Society* (Chicago: University of Chicago Press, 1992), 93.

20. Nyamnjoh, "'A Child Is One Person's Only in the Womb,'" 111.

21. This position can be compared and contrasted with Thoden van Velzen's analysis of the "proponents of what he called the Big-Man paradigm—developed by people like Baily, Barth, and others." H. U. E. Thoden van Velzen, "Robinson Crusoe and Friday: Strength and Weakness of the Big Man Paradigm," *Man, Journal of the Royal Anthropological Institute*, n.s., 8, no. 4 (1973): 592–612. For van Velzen, as Trouwborst articulates it, "the elements most stressed are the 'Big Man' as a 'powerful individual,' as a 'cold and virile entrepreneur' or as a 'shrewd manipulator." Van Velzen, "Robinson Crusoe and Friday," 592, 596. See Albert A. Trouwborst, "The 'Big-Man': A Melanesian Model in Africa," in *Private Politics: A Multi-disciplinary Approach to "Big-Man" Systems*, ed. M. van Bakel, Renée R. Hagesteijn, and Pieter Van De Velde (Leiden: Brill, 1986), 50.

22. Since he acquired the traditional honorific title of *Asiwaju* (Leader) of Lagos, Governor Tinubu has preferred to be addressed by this title. He also loves to be hailed as the *Jagaban* (Borgu), his other title from the Borgu "Kingdom," in Northern Nigeria.

23. "Àlàáfíà" in Yorùbá is normally translated as "peace." But in this context, it refers to well-being. It could also mean good health.

24. See OVTV Online, "K1 De Ultimate Performance at Rasak Okoya 80th Birthday," YouTube, January 15, 2020, https://www.youtube.com/watch?v=qzG30bu5hNU&t=608s.

25. As I note later in the chapter, Tinubu eventually won election as president and was sworn in on May 29, 2023.

26. In what turned out to be a highly controversial—and later popular—statement in light of the "conspiracies" against his candidacy within the ruling party on the eve of the presidential primary election, Tinubu publicly said, "*emi l'okan*" (It is my turn, or I am next for the presidency). See Eniola Daniel, "Tinubu Says He Went to 'War' for Buhari to Be President," *Guardian*, June 2, 2022, https://guardian.ng/news/it-is-my-turn-to-be-president-says-tinubu/; Boluwatife Akinyemi, "It Is My Turn, It Is Yoruba's Turn—Tinubu," *Nigerian Tribune*, June 3, 2022, https://tribuneonlineng.com/it-is-my-turn-it-is-yorubas-turn-tinubu/; Macdonald Dzirutwe, "Tinubu Says It Is His Turn to Rule Nigeria in Election Appeal to Buhari," Reuters, June 3, 2022, https://www.reuters.com/world/africa/tinubu-says-it-is-his-turn-rule-nigeria-election-appeal-buhari-2022-06-03/; Ebunoluwa Olafusi, "Adebanjo: 'Emi lo kan' Doesn't Mean Turn of Yoruba—It's Tinubu-Buhari Agreement," *Cable*, February 11, 2023, https://www.thecable.ng/adebanjo-emi-lo-kan-doesnt-mean-turn-of-yoruba-its-tinubu-buhari-agreement; Olasunkanmi Akinlotan, "2023: 'Emi Lokan' Is Wrong

for Nigeria, Obasanjo Criticises Tinubu," *Premium Times*, January 2, 2023, https://www.premiumtimesng.com/news/top-news/573623-2023-emi-lokan-is-wrong-for-nigeria-obasanjo-criticises-tinubu.html.

27. For an example of Adams's affronts against Tinubu in the media, see Taiwo-Hassan Adebayo, "Tinubu Using Yoruba for Own Selfish Interest—Gani Adams," *Premium Times*, March 21, 2015, https://www.premiumtimesng.com/regional/ssouth-west/178876-tinubu-using-yoruba-for-own-selfish-interest-gani-adams.html.

28. For video of this, see GoldMyne TV, "Balikis and Musa's Wedding with K1 De Ultimate Dishing Out Brand New Tunes," YouTube, December 27, 2020, https://www.youtube.com/watch?v=fcZrQwddmaw.

29. For an attempt to locate Tinubu in the wider politics of (Southwestern) Nigeria, see Adebanwi, *Yoruba Elites and Ethnic Politics*, esp. chap. 7.

30. Frederick Fasehun, *OPC: Our History, Our Mission* (Lagos: Inspired Communications, 2005), 50.

31. Segun Akanni, telephone interview with the author, November 14, 2020. By the time of this interview, Akanni had moved to Canada.

32. Monsuru Akande, telephone interview with the author, November 17, 2020.

33. Tinubu provided financial assistance to many people, including, sometimes, rivals. For instance, while he was supporting Adams, according to Fasehun's former personal assistant, Taofik Adeyemi, Tinubu also paid for Fasehun's heart surgery in the United States. Adeyemi, interview with the author, April 1, 2021.

34. Ibid.

35. Akinwale Kasali, "Restructuring: Adams, Tinubu Rift Gets Messier, as Group Slams Tinubu, Call Him a Businessman in Politics without Ideology," *Source*, July 9, 2020, https://thesourceng.com/restructuring-adams-tinubu-rift-gets-messier-as-group-slams-tinubu-calls-him-a-businessman-in-politics-without-ideology.

36. Ibid.

37. Kemi Olaitan, "OPC Disowns Gani Adams over Attack on Tinubu," *ThisDay*, July 12, 2020, https://www.thisdaylive.com/index.php/2020/07/12/opc-disowns-gani-adams-over-attack-on-tinubu/.

38. Michael Abimboye, "Why Tinubu Starved Us, Jonathan Gave Us Multibillion Naira Pipeline Contracts—Gani Adams," *Premium Times*, March 24, 2015, https://www.premiumtimesng.com/news/headlines/179053-while-tinubu-starved-us-jonathan-gave-us-multibillion-naira-pipeline-contracts-gani-adams.html.

39. Wale Elegbede, "2023: Tinubu's Camp, Adams Throw Punches," *Telegraph*, July 10, 2020, https://www.newtelegraphng.com/2023-tinubus-camp-adams-throw-punches/.

40. A credible source also claimed that Adams had obtained a promise from Governor Segun Agagu to support him to be the PDP candidate for the Federal House of Representatives because of the support he offered while Agagu was running for a second term. Unfortunately, though Agagu was declared the winner of the election, the Court of Appeal later invalidated the results and awarded victory to Agagu's former

secretary to the state government, Dr. Olusegun Mimiko. This, the source claimed, scuttled Adams's ambition. However, when asked whether he had political ambitions, Adams told the *Sun*, "What am I aspiring to? I come from Ondo State. If I want to aspire to any position, it must be from my state. I don't have any political ambition, because, truly speaking, the system is not okay yet"(NBF News, "Gani Adams: My Name Rings Louder Bell than Some Governors," *The Nigerian Voice*, December 4, 2011, https://www.thenigerianvoice.com/news/76834/gani-adams-my-name-rings-louder-bell-than-some-governors.html).

41. Thompson, a retired judge, was one of the leaders of the Yoruba Council of Elders (YCE), a rival group to *Afenifere*. For more on YCE, see Adebanwi, *Yoruba Elites and Ethnic Politics*.

42. Adeola Balogun and Gbenro Adeoye, "Everybody Is in Politics for Selfish Interests—Adams, OPC National Coordinator," *Punch*, March 28, 2015, https://www.latestnigeriannews.com/news/1322644/everybody-is-in-politics-for-selfish-interestsadams-opc-national-coordinator.html (emphasis added).

43. Adams's former comrades rendered a different version of events concerning Obasanjo's attitude toward Adams. Although it is true that Obasanjo was initially displeased with Adams for his and his group's support for Tinubu, they alleged that Obasanjo ordered Adams's detention for several months in 2005–6 for a different reason. They said that Obasanjo told one of Adams's benefactors—a sitting senator who was close to the president and had tried to plead for Adams's release—that he received a security report about Adams's visit to a powerful retired general who was the president's political adversary. The retired general, Obasanjo reportedly alleged, gave Adams several millions of naira. I could not confirm this story or the allegation. Balogun and Adeoye, "Everybody Is in Politics for Selfish Interests."

44. Ibid. (emphasis added).

45. Ibid. (emphasis added).

46. This was at a time when the group had decided to "*la'tan*" (keep their options open) by financially supporting different political parties that sought their help.

47. Balogun and Adeoye, "Everybody Is in Politics for Selfish Interests" (emphasis added).

48. For the literature on godfathers in Nigeria, see Omobolaji Ololade Olarinmoye, "Godfathers, Political Parties and Electoral Corruption in Nigeria," *African Journal of Political Science and International Relations* 2, no. 4 (2008): 66–73; Leena Hoffmann, "Fairy Godfathers and Magical Elections: Understanding the 2003 Electoral Crisis in Anambra State, Nigeria," *Journal of Modern African Studies* 48, no. 2 (2010): 285–310; Isaac Olawale Albert, "Explaining 'Godfatherism' in Nigerian Politics," *African Sociological Review* 9, no. 2 (2005): 79–105; Gbemisola Animasawun, "Godfatherism in Nigeria's Fourth Republic: The Pyramid of Violence and Political Insecurity in Ibadan, Oyo State, Nigeria" (E-papers Series 27, IFRA-Nigeria, Ibadan, 2013); Chris Albin-Lackey, "Criminal Politics: Violence, 'Godfathers' and Corruption in Nigeria," *Human Rights Watch* 19, no. 16A (2007): 33–37; J. Shola Omotola,

"Godfathers and the 2007 Nigerian Elections," *Journal of African Elections* 2, no. 2 (2007): 134–54.

49. Larry Diamond, *Class, Ethnicity, and Democracy in Nigeria: The Failure of the First Republic* (Syracuse, NY: Syracuse University Press, 1988), 325.

50. While he conceded that he had considered what was to be done along with Akanni, Adedayo said he was not directly involved in contacting Aregbesola. Adedayo, telephone interview with the author, March 26, 2021.

51. One of Adams's aides, interview with the author, November 14, 2020.

52. Shola Oshunkeye, "People Who Ignore Me, Do So at Their Peril," *Sunday Sun*, December 4, 2011, 33.

53. This word is used in the social scene in Yorubaland to refer to a certain form of sociability, particularly social exuberance.

54. Oshunkeye, "People Who Ignore Me, Do So at Their Peril" (emphasis added).

55. Ibid.

56. Balogun and Adeoye, "Everybody Is in Politics for Selfish Interests" (emphasis added).

57. Akande, interview with the author, November 17, 2020.

58. Fasehun, *OPC*, 58, 62 (emphasis added).

59. Adebayo, "Tinubu Using Yoruba."

60. Ibid.

61. Ibid.

62. As mentioned earlier, Adams is often suspicious of everyone's intentions. In one moment of pique in 2020 during a telephone chat, he accused Tinubu of sponsoring the former members of OPC who were criticizing him over his latest attack against Tinubu and then said, "I know you talk to Tinubu regularly; you can tell him I said so."

63. See chap. 3 for a discussion of the policy of *l'atan*.

64. Obafemi Hamzat, "'Why Gani Adams Pushed Me out of APC' . . . Ex-P.A, Segun Akanni Tells His Attack Story," *Global Excellence*, June 20, 2020, https://globalexcellenceonline.com/why-gani-adams-pushed-me-out-of-apc-ex-p-a-segun-akanni-tells-his-attack-story/.

65. Ibid.

66. Ibid.

67. Segun Akanni, *The Volunteer of the Savannah: A True Picture of Gani Adams* (Lagos: Prince Genesis Concept, 2015), 26.

68. Ibid.

69. Ibid., 27.

70. Ibid.

71. Gani Adams, telephone interview with the author, November 30, 2020.

72. See Hamzat, "'Why Gani Adams Pushed Me out of APC"; *Elite*, "My Close Shave with Death—Segun Akanni, Ex- CoS to Gani Adams," June 20, 2020, https://www.theelitesng.com/my-close-shave-with-death-segun-akanni-ex-cos-to-gani

-adams/. See also Dapo Akinrefon, "I'm a Target of Assassination, Ex-Gani Adams' Aide Cries Out," *Vanguard*, June 7, 2019, https://www.vanguardngr.com/2019/06/im-a-target-of-assassination-ex-gani-adams-aide-cries-out/; Temidayo Akinsuyi, "How I Parted Ways with Aare Gani Adams—Akanni," *Independent*, June 24, 2020, https://independent.ng/how-i-parted-ways-with-aare-gani-adams-akanni/. For Adams's reaction, see Tajudeen Adebanjo, "Adams Not Involved in Attacks on Ex-aide," *Nation*, June 26, 2020, https://thenationonlineng.net/adams-not-involved-in-attacks-on-ex-aide/; Michael Adesanya, "Alleged Threat to Life: Lagos OPC Boss Defends Gani Adams, Chides Segun Akanni," *City Voice*, June 24, 2020, https://cityvoiceng.com/alleged-threat-to-life-lagos-opc-boss-defends-gani-adams-chides-segun-akanni/.

73. Akinsuyi, "How I Parted Ways with Aare Gani Adams—Akanni."

74. Gbenga Olarinoye, "Why OPC Supported Jonathan for 2nd Term, by Gani Adams," *Vanguard*, January 28, 2016, https://www.vanguardngr.com/2016/01/why-opc-supported-jonathan-for-2nd-term-by-gani-adams/.

75. See TV360 Nigeria, "Tinubu: 'Defend Yourself against OPC," YouTube, March 20, 2015, https://www.youtube.com/watch?v=cPbIakeYRWc.

76. Ibid. (emphasis added).

77. Wale Odunsi, "Elections: OPC Replies APC, Says, 'Nobody Can Kill Jonathan, Adams' Friendship," *Daily Post*, April 10, 2015, https://dailypost.ng/2015/04/10/elections-opc-replies-apc-says-nobody-can-kill-jonathan-adams-friendship/.

78. Dimeji Kayode-Adedeji, "Gani Adams Alleges Plot to Assassinate Him," *Premium Times*, May 15, 2015, http://www.premiumtimesng.com/regional/ssouth-west/183040-gani-adams-alleges-plot-to-assassinate-him.html.

79. Ibid.

80. Ibid.

81. Lekan Olanrewaju, "'Tinubu Did Not Give Me N10m to Kill Gani Adams': Wale Adedayo Releases Statement," YNaija, March 11, 2012, https://naija.yafri.ca/tinubu-did-not-give-me-n10m-to-kill-gani-adams-wale-adedayo-releases-statement/. See also Kayode Ogundamisi, "Asiwaju Bola Ahmed Tinubu, Did Not Give Me N10m to Kill Gani Adams—Wale Adedayo," Blogspot, March 10, 2012, http://kayodeogundamisi.blogspot.com/2012/03/asiwaju-bola-ahmed-tinubu-did-not-give.html.

82. Olanrewaju, "'Tinubu Did Not Give Me N10m to Kill Gani Adams."

83. When he eventually sacked Akanni in 2018, again, he accused Akanni of having been bribed by Tinubu to sabotage him. Akanni, interview with the author, November 14, 2020.

84. Others similarly accused included Adesina Akinpelu, Olayiwola Ogunsolu, Lateef Ogungbayi, Gbenga Egunlusi, Ranti Akande, Lateef Olawale Oshodi, Soji Folorunsho, Segun Olusanya Idowu Akintunde Sunday Bankole Kehinde Ogunyale, and Sunday Adebayo. Wale Odunsi, "Gani Adams Accused Expelled OPC Members of Begging Tinubu to Back His Removal," *Daily Post*, August 18, 2015, https://

dailypost.ng/2015/08/18/gani-adams-accuses-expelled-opc-members-of-begging-tinubu-to-back-his-removal/. Aee also Maina Maina, "APC Sponsoring Those Calling for Gani Adams' Resignation—OPC," *Daily Post*, March 21, 2015, https://dailypost.ng/2015/03/21/apc-sponsoring-those-calling-for-gani-adams-resignation-opc/.

85. Odunsi, "Gani Adams Accused Expelled OPC Members."

86. Ibid.

87. Dele Ogunyemi, "OPC Leaders Question Gani Adams over Jonathan's N1.6bn Campaign Fund," *Daily Trust*, April 7, 2015, https://dailytrust.com/opc-leaders-query-gani-adams-over-jonathan-s-n1-6bn-campaign-fund.

88. Ibid.

89. *Anthonia Soyingbe,* "2015—Gani Adams Denies Collecting Money from Jonathan," *Daily Independent, April 17, 2015,* https://allafrica.com/stories/201504171788.html.

90. *Premium Times,* "Aare Ona Kakanfo: Tinubu Congratulates Gani Adams," October 17, 2017, https://www.premiumtimesng.com/regional/ssouth-west/246429-aare-ona-kakanfo-tinubu-congratulates-gani-adams.html.

91. Ibid.

92. Elegbede, "2023."

93. Ibid.

94. Ibid.

95. Ibid.

96. Ibid.

97. Ibid.

98. The national publicity secretary of a breakaway group, OPC New Era, also once accused Adams of having "a foible of biting the fingers that had at one time or the other fed him. To mention just [a] few, Senator Bola Ahmed Tinubu, Senator Ogunwale and Pastor T.B. Joshua are living witnesses to Gani Adams ungrateful nature." *Nigerian Voice,* "How God Used Policemen to Rescue Me from Gani Adams' Killer Squad-OPC National PRO," November 8, 2017, https://www.thenigerianvoice.com/news/259540/how-god-used-policemen-to-rescue-me-from-gani-adams-killer.html.

99. Elegbede, "2023."

100. Ibid. See also Temidayo Akinsuyi, "Group Attacks Gani Adams over Statement on Tinubu," *Independent,* July 5, 2020, https://www.independent.ng/group-attacks-gani-adams-over-statement-on-tinubu/; Akinwale Kasali, "Restructuring: Tinubu Group Slams Gani Adams, Says He Is a Traitor, an Ingrate, Unfit to Lead Yoruba Race," *Source,* July 6, 2020, https://thesourceng.com/restructuring-tinubu-group-slams-gani-adams-says-he-is-a-traitor-an-ingrate-unfit-to-lead-yoruba-race/.

101. Stephen Olufemi Oni, "Gani Adams under Fire for Attacking Tinubu," *Telegraph,* July 13, 2020, https://www.newtelegraphng.com/gani-adams-under-fire-for-attacking-tinubu-2/. See also Akinwale Kasali, "Tinubu/Gani Rift: OPC Faction

Condemns Gani Adams over Tinubu," *Source*, July 12, 2020, https://thesourceng.com/tinubu-gani-rift-opc-faction-condemns-gani-adams-over-tinubu/.

102. Literally "child begotten by the god [of character]." This can be translated as "gentleman," but it has a deeper meaning for the Yoruba. It suggests someone of good breeding who possesses all the best qualities of human goodness—honor, integrity, character, dignity, empathy, diligence, uprightness, and respect for others. However, for the Yoruba, these qualities and their practices are also linked to the transcendent.

103. Olaitan, "OPC Disowns Gani Adams over Attack on Tinubu."

104. Adams, telephone interview with the author, November 30, 2020.

105. Kasali, "Restructuring: Adams, Tinubu Rift Gets Messier."

106. Ibid.

107. A reference to OPC New Era, led by Balogun.

108. A reference to OPCI, led by Olanrewaju.

109. This is also a reference to OPC New Era because Adeshina Akinpelu, the faction's national public relations officer, is based in Ibadan. There had been a clash between this faction and the Adams faction in 2018. Earlier, in 2017, Akinpelu had been attacked and suffered serious physical injuries, for which he was hospitalized. He later alleged that this was an "assassination attempt" by the Adams faction. See Olufemi Atoyebi, "Police Arrest 46 as OPC Factions Clash in Ibadan," *Punch*, January 29, 2018, https://punchng.com/police-arrest-46-as-opc-factions-clash-in-ibadan/; "How God Used Policemen."

110. Elegbede, "2023."

111. Dennis Erezi, "INEC Declares Bola Tinubu Winner of 2023 Presidential Election," *Guardian*, March 1, 2023, https://guardian.ng/news/inec-declares-bola-tinubu-winner-of-2023-presidential-election/.

112. Damilola Olufemi, "Peter Obi Meets Gani Adams," *Punch*, February 13, 2023, https://punchng.com/just-in-peter-obi-meets-gani-adams/.

113. Wale Odunsi, "Peter Obi, Gani Adams Meet in Lagos," *Daily Post*, February 13, 2023, https://dailypost.ng/2023/02/13/peter-obi-gani-adams-meet-in-lagos/ (emphasis added).

114. Ibid.

115. Ibid.

116. At the point of the presidential election, the apex Yorùbá political organization, *Afenifere*, was led by Chief Ayo Adebanjo. The former leader of the group, the ninety-five-year-old Chief Reuben Fasoranti, because of old age and failing health, had stepped down in March 2021 and asked Adebanjo to take over as the acting leader of the group. Seye Olumide and Oluwaseun Akingboye, "Fasoranti Steps Down as Afenifere Leader, Adebanjo Takes Over," *Guardian*, March 17, 2021, https://guardian.ng/politics/fasoranti-steps-down-as-afenifere-leader-adebanjo-takes-over/; Peter Dada, "Adebanjo Emerges Afenifere Leader as Fasoranti Steps Down over Old Age," *Punch*, March 17, 2021, https://punchng.com/adebanjo-emerges-afenifere-leader-as-fasoranti-steps-down-over-old-age/. However, with Adebanjo leading

the group into strong support for Obi, the Labour Party's candidate, some elements within the group who supported Tinubu asked Fasoranti to reaffirm his leadership and announce *Afenifere*'s endorsement of Tinubu's candidacy. Fasoranti did. This led to yet another crisis in the group, with Fasoranti and Adebanjo publicly contesting who was the "current" leader. Fasoranti later confirmed that Adebanjo remained the leader of the group. For more on this, see *Nation*, "Adebanjo No More Acting Afenifere Leader—Fasoranti," November 2, 2022, https://thenationonlineng.net/adebanjo-no-more-acting-afenifere-leader-fasoranti/; Seye Olumide, "Afenifere: I Remain Leader, Says Adebanjo as Fasoranti Returns,." *Guardian*, November 3, 2022, https://guardian.ng/news/afenifere-i-remain-leader-says-adebanjo-as-fasoranti-returns/; *Nigerian Tribune*, "I Never Said Adebanjo Is No Longer Afenifere Leader—Fasoranti," November 4, 2022, https://tribuneonlineng.com/i-never-said-adebanjo-is-no-longer-afenifere-leader-%E2%80%95-fasoranti/.

117. Olufemi, "Peter Obi Meets Gani Adams."

118. Temidayo Akinsuyi, "Presidential Polls: Gani Adams Congratulates Tinubu, Says Victory Reflects President-Elect's Doggedness," *Independent*, March 1, 2023, https://independent.ng/presidential-polls-gani-adams-congratulates-tinubu-says-victory-reflects-president-elects-doggedness/.

119. Ibid.

120. Adams, telephone communication, March 31, 2023.

121. *Topnews*, "Gani Adams Extols Gbenga Daniel, Calls Him 'Asset to Yoruba Nation,'" December 27, 2017, http://www.topnewsmagazines.com/gani-adams-extols-gbenga-daniel-calls-him-asset-to-yoruba-nation/ (emphasis added).

122. Ibid. (emphasis added).

123. Ibid.

124. Don Silas, "Gani Adams Is the Greatest Yoruba Man of His Generation—Gbenga Daniel," *Daily Post*, December 28, 2017, https://dailypost.ng/2017/12/28/gani-adams-greatest-yoruba-man-generation-gbenga-daniel/.

125. *Topnews*, "Gani Adams Extols Gbenga Daniel, Calls Him."

126. See Adebanwi, *Yoruba Elites and Ethnic Politics*, chap. 7.

127. For details, see ibid., esp. chap. 7 for Tinubu's ascendancy.

128. This is because many believe that he has "occult" powers. He also advertises this. See Wale Adedayo, *Micro-seconds Away from Death* (Ogun State: Journal Communications, 2010).

129. When I spoke to Adedayo on the phone even up to late 2020, he was still eager to discuss his knowledge and his opinion about Adams and Daniel, and he even provided me with me other crucial contacts within the OPC. However, when I called him on March 26, 2021, he said he had reconciled with Daniel and asked me to "forget about OPC." I told him I was finishing my book on the Adams faction and therefore could not forget about it. Shortly afterward, the phone went dead. I called back several times, but he did not answer. I sent him a WhatsApp message, and he responded that he did not want to get involved in an OPC matter again.

130. For further details, see Adebanwi, *Yoruba Elites and Ethnic Politics*, chap. 7.

131. As even Adams himself has acknowledged to close aides, whom one visits and who visits one's home are measures of a person's standing in society. A former governor who lived in Lagos once complained in my presence that Tinubu had never visited his home, though he went to Tinubu's home regularly. If Tinubu did not visit a fellow former governor in Lagos, it is hard to see why he would visit Adams's home.

132. Akande, telephone interview with the author, November 17, 2020.

133. That is, they gave them money weekly.

134. Bola Badmus and Olalekan Olabulo, "Restructuring Re-echoed as Aare Adams Inaugurates Advisory Council," *Nigerian Tribune*, January 13, 2019, https://tribuneonlineng.com/restructuring-re-echoed-as-aare-adams-inaugurates-advisory-council/.

135. Adedayo later left Daniel's administration and published a book, *Microseconds to Death*, where he alleges that Daniel had a price on his head with the help of Adams. Later in a statement denying Adams's allegation that Tinubu had paid him to eliminate Adams, Adedayo said: "Shortly after I left *Daani Elebo*'s [Daniel] Administration, the weekly National Coordinating Council (NCC) of the OPC under Gani Adams became a place he did everything possible to set the boys against me. He failed because they knew the truth. At a meeting held in Abeokuta, Gani Adams claimed I was 'chopping' certain sums of money meant for cadres of the OPC sent through me by OGD. Of course, it was a lie from the pit of hell. I am of the firm opinion that OGD still wants to take me out. They want to set the boys against me. But they have failed. A number of us risked everything in our lives and career for the OPC under Gani Adams when The Carpenter from Arigidi-Akoko was a NOBODY. The members know that. It was for that reason ALONE they refused to move against me. Even now, they are the ones pleading I should leave Gani Adams to his dementia in young age, swearing that The Carpenter from Arigidi Akoko has lost his mind because of crumbs from OGD's table." Ogundamisi, "Asiwaju Bola Ahmed Tinubu." In response to Adedayo's book, Raheem Ajayi, described as "a serving member of Ogun State Executive Council and a self-professed disciple of OGD," wrote a rejoinder entitled *Traitor Unmasked*, described as a book that "paints a vivid picture of political treachery and hypocrisy by otherwise trusted political aides with opportunistic tendencies." Curiously, the review was published without the name of the author. "Unmasking the Traitor," *Vanguard*, February 24, 2011, https://www.vanguardngr.com/2011/02/unmasking-the-traitor/.

136. Ogundamisi, telephone interview with the author, November 15, 2020.

137. Ibid.

138. There were earlier attempts by the *Ooni* of Ife, Oba Okunade Sijuade, Olbuse II, which collapsed into violence, and by Chief Abraham Adesanya, the leader of the *Afenifere*, the Yorùbá progressive political organization.

139. Interview with the author, November 14, 2020.

140. Ibid.

141. Don Silas, "Gani Adams Is the Greatest Yoruba Man of His Generation—Gbenga Daniel," *Daily Post*, December 28, 2017, https://dailypost.ng/2017/12/28/gani-adams-greatest-yoruba-man-generation-gbenga-daniel/.

142. Taofik Bankole, "2019 Election: Gbenga Daniel Pays Courtesy Visit to Aare Gani Adams, Seeks Support for Atiku," Nuesroom, November 26, 2018, https://neusroom.com/2019-election-gbenga-daniel-pays-courtesy-visit-to-aare-gani-adams-seeks-support-for-atiku/.

143. See Odunsi, "Elections."

144. Ibid.

145. River goddess.

146. Rasaq Arogundade Balogun reminded me about this song during a telephone interview on November 18, 2020.

147. For details, see Adebanwi, *Yoruba Elites and Ethnic Politics*.

148. At this point, Buhari was on his second term, scheduled to end in May 2023.

149. Obasanjo first met some Yorùbá leaders in the home of Chief Ayo Adebanjo in mid-2018 to mobilize them against Buhari's second-term bid. See Dapo Akinrefon, "2019: Obasanjo Holds Secret Talks with Yoruba Leaders in Lagos," June 23, 2018, https://www.vanguardngr.com/2018/06/2019-obasanjo-holds-secret-talks-yoruba-leaders-lagos/.

150. Sadly, Odumakin died on April 3, 2021.

151. "Presidency Replies Obasanjo, Says He's Nigeria's 'Divider-In-Chief,'" *Premium Times*, September 13, 2020, https://www.premiumtimesng.com/news/headlines/414283-presidency-replies-obasanjo-says-hes-nigerias-divider-in-chief.html.

152. Obasanjo claimed to be echoing an earlier statement by Tinubu, which the latter denied. See Eniola Akinkuotu, "Tinubu Was Right for Calling Buhari a Tribalist, Religious Fanatic, Says Obasanjo," *Punch*, January 21, 2019, https://punchng.com/tinubu-was-right-for-calling-buhari-a-tribalist-religious-fanatic-says-obasanjo/.

153. Adebanjo, telephone communication, December 10, 2020.

154. This account of the meeting is based on my telephone calls with Osuntokun, December 3, 2020; Adebanjo, December 10, 2020; and Odumakin, December 11, 2020.

155. See Seyi Olumide, "*Afenifere* Reconciles Olusegun Obasanjo, Gani Adams, Settles 15-Year Rift," *Guardian*, December 3, 2020.

156. Sahara Reporters, "Insecurity: Obasanjo, *Afenifere* Leaders Meet in Lagos, Discuss Way Forward for South-West," December 2, 2020, http://saharareporters.com/2020/12/02/insecurity-obasanjo-afenifere-leaders-meet-lagos-discuss-way-forward-south-west.

157. Olumide, "*Afenifere* Reconciles."

158. Ibid.

159. Ibid.

160. Eagle Online, "Breaking: Obasanjo, Gani Adams Reconcile, Settle 15-Year Rift," December 3, 2020, https://theeagleonline.com.ng/breaking-obasanjo-gani-adams-reconcile-settle-15-year-rift-photo/.

161. Temidayo Akinsuyi, "Afenifere Reconciles Obasanjo, Gani Adams," *Independent*, December 2, 2020, https://www.independent.ng/afenifere-reconciles-obasanjo-gani-adams/.

162. Dare Akinrefon, "Obasanjo, Adams Reconcile 15-Year Rift," *Vanguard*, December 2, 2020, https://www.vanguardngr.com/2020/12/obasanjo-adams-reconcile-15-year-rift/.

163. Olumide, "*Afenifere* Reconciles."

164. Although he had also told the media that Obasanjo's persecution had turned into a blessing for him.

165. Daud Olatunji, "Why I Rejected Gani Adams' Request to Visit Me—Obasanjo," *Punch*, December 2, 2020, https://punchng.com/why-i-rejected-gani-adams-request-to-visit-me-obasanjo/. See also Mojeed Alabi, "Why I've Refused to See Gani Adams—Obasanjo," *Premium Times*, December 2, 2020, https://www.premiumtimesng.com/news/more-news/429134-why-ive-refused-to-see-gani-adams-obasanjo.html.

166. Ibid. (emphasis added).

167. Ibid.

168. Adebanjo, telephone communication, December 10, 2020.

169. It might seem unusual that the former president, who was himself eighty-three at this point—although a very energetic octogenarian—was eager to make the rounds between Abeokuta and Lagos (a distance of more than one hundred kilometers, not minding the bad roads and heavy traffic) to see Adebanjo. The most important reason, I suggest, is that, as Obasanjo had done with virtually every head of state who succeeded him—either as military head of state or as civilian president—(with the exception of General Abdusalami Abubakar, who released him from jail and handed over power to him), he engaged in a campaign against President Buhari. He was always happy to work with anyone who was well positioned to support him in opposing the incumbent head of state. Adams agrees with this reading. In his response to Obasanjo, he said, "He is just looking for political space [by working with the *Afenifere*]. When Obasanjo is not allowed to have any influence in any government, he will be opposed to that government. That is his mission. If he cannot control the president, he will be the enemy of that president." See Dapo Akinrefon, "Gani Adams Attacks Obasanjo, Replies Omo-Agege," *Vanguard*, December 12, 2020, https://www.vanguardngr.com/2020/12/gani-adams-attacks-obasanjo-replies-omo-agege/ (emphasis added).

170. To show his disappointment with Adebanjo, Adams, I was told, failed to show up at the next scheduled meeting alongside Adebanjo with Pastor Adeboye.

171. Dapo Akinrefon, "My Guardian Angel Won't Forgive Me If I Reconcile with Obasanjo—Aare Adams," *Vanguard*, December 8, 2020, https://www.vanguardngr

.com/2020/12/my-guarding-angel-wont-forgive-me-if-i-reconcile-with-obasanjo-aare-adams/.

172. Gbenga Adeniyi, "I'm a Progressive, Obasanjo's Not, Says Gani Adams," *Punch*, December 9, 2020, https://punchng.com/im-a-progressive-obasanjos-not-says-gani-adams/.

173. Ibid.

174. Tobi Aworinde, "My Experiences in Prisons under Obasanjo Horrible—Gani Adams," *Punch*, December 26, 2020, https://punchng.com/my-experiences-in-prisons-under-obasanjo-horrible-gani-adams/.

175. Akinrefon, "Gani Adams Attacks Obasanjo" (emphasis added).

176. For more on this view of Obasanjo in Yorubaland, see Adebanwi, *Yoruba Elites and Ethnic Politics*, chap. 5.

177. Ibid. (emphasis added).

178. Adams was, at this point, obviously thinking in Yorùbá even though speaking in English. This is a literal translation of "*ko wo wa*," which properly translated means "he did not care about us," or more appropriately, "he did not *support* us."

179. Damilare Okunola, "Gani Adams: Jonathan Has Been Nice to Me," P.M. News, March 18, 2015, https://www.pmnewsnigeria.com/2015/03/18/gani-adams-jonathan-has-been-nice-to-me/ (emphasis added). See also Elegbede, "2023."

180. Okunola, "Gani Adams."

181. See Adefemi V. Isumonah's take on how the collaboration between Adams's West and the North contributed to the marginalization of Jonathan's oil-rich region in the allocation of federally distributable revenues on the basis of the derivation principle. Victor Adefemi Isumonah, "Minority Political Mobilization in the Struggle for Resource Control in Nigeria," *Extractive Industries and Society* 2, no. 4 (2015): 645–53.

182. Adams, interview with the author, December 14, 2017.

183. Okunola, "Gani Adams."

184. Adams, interview with the author, December 14, 2017.

185. Abimboye, "Why Tinubu Starved Us."

186. Ibid. The *sic* was added in the original story by *P.M. News*. This is significant because, since Adams became a big man (and even before then), few news reports pointed to syntax errors in his statements.

187. Will Ross, "Nigeria Postpones Presidential Vote over Security," BBC, February 8, 2015, https://www.bbc.co.uk/news/world-africa-31221545. See also Remi Adekoya, "Nigeria's Elections: Democracy Postponed," *Guardian* (London), February 8, 2015, https://www.theguardian.com/commentisfree/2015/feb/08/nigeria-elections-democracy-postponed-goodluck-jonathan.

188. Olanrewaju, telephone interview with the author, January 28, 2021.

189. Ibid.

190. *TheNEWS*, "Gani Adams Endorses Jonathan for Second Term," March 13, 2015, https://www.thenewsnigeria.com.ng/2015/03/13/gani-adams-endorses-jonathan-for-second-term/.

191. Ibid. (emphasis added). He gave yet another reason the following year at the second congress of the OPU.

192. Ibid.

193. See Odunsi, "Elections."

194. *Soyingbe, "2015."*

195. Ola Ajayi, Bukola Ifegbayi, and Fisayo Ogunwale, "OPC Crisis: Why Gani Adams Must Go—Akinpelu," *Vanguard*, April 26, 2015, https://www.vanguardngr.com/2015/04/opc-crisis-why-gani-adams-must-go-akinpelu/. See also Ola Ajayi, "Faction in OPC Asks Adams to Present Bank Account Statements," *Vanguard*, April 3, 2015, https://www.vanguardngr.com/2015/04/faction-in-opc-asks-adams-to-present-bank-account-statements/.

196. Ajayi, Ifegbayi, and Ogunwale, "OPC Crisis." When he escaped what he described as an "assassination attempt" during a clash between the OPC factions (Adams and New Era factions) in September 2017, Akinpelu alleged that Adams was responsible for his ordeal. He was seriously injured and subsequently hospitalized. Significantly, Akinpelu pointed to the cash that was flowing among the OPC factions when he told the press that the almost half a million naira in his car to be "disburse[d to] their members who traveled to Ibadan for the event" (a Yorùbá summit tagged Ibadan Declaration on the Yoruba Standpoint on Restructuring) had been stolen by his attackers. See Musliudeen Adebayo, "Police Arrest 2 Suspects over OPC Factional Clash in Ibadan as Victim, Adesina Akinpelu, Recounts Ordeal," *Daily Post*, September 9, 2017, https://dailypost.ng/2017/09/09/police-arrest-2-suspects-opc-factional-clash-ibadan-victim-adesina-akinpelu-recounts-ordeal-photos/. However, in September 2019, speaking on a radio program in Ibadan, Akinpelu said he had made up with Adams and that he and other were working toward bringing together all the factions of the OPC. See 32fm 94.9 Ibadan, "Com. Akinpelu Adesina (OPC) Live on Eto Oselu with Peter Olasupo (Captain P2)," YouTube, September 16, 2019, https://www.youtube.com/watch?v=3KlN9HQ_F9k.

197. Dapo Akinrefon, "Expelled Members behind Attack on Adams," *Vanguard*, March 19, 2015, https://www.vanguardngr.com/2015/03/expelled-members-behind-attack-on-adams/.

198. Victor Adefemi Isumonah, "Minority Political Mobilization in the Struggle for Resource Control in Nigeria," *Extractive Industries and Society* 2, no. 4 (2015): 647. See also Eghosa E. Osaghae et al., *Youths Militias, Self Determination and Resource Control Struggles in the Niger-delta Region of Nigeria*, CODESRIA Research Reports 5 (Dakar: CODESRIA, 2011).

199. Itse Sagay, "Nigeria: Federalism, the Constitution and Resource Control" (speech, Fourth Sensitisation Programme, Ibori Vanguard, Lagos, May 19, 2001), 10, https://unpub.wpb.tam.us.siteprotect.com/var/m_f/fa/fa2/22697/235469-nigeria_federalism_.pdf.

200. Isumonah, "Minority Political Mobilization," 647.

201. Ibid.

202. Ibid.

203. "Gani Adams Endorses Jonathan for Second Term."

204. His first name is actually Government; it is not an alias. In this part of Nigeria, some people bear interesting names, including one whose first and last names are London England.

205. David Oputah, "Tompolo, Asari Dokubo Get New Pipeline Deals," *Cable News*, March 12, 2015, https://www.thecable.ng/tompolo-asari-dokubo-get-new-pipeline-deals.

206. Ibid.

207. Adeola Balogun,"Fasehun and I Must Share S'West Pipeline Security Contract Equally—Gani Adams," *Punch*, April 20, 2013, https://jimidisu.com/fasehun-and-i-must-share-swest-pipeline-security-contract-equally-gani-adams-punch/.

208. The National Democratic Coalition, which fought against the General Abacha regime and for the actualization of the June 12, 1993, presidential election won by MKO Abiola.

209. Folarin Ademosu, "Fasehun Can Kill, Destroy for Power, Money and Women," *P.M. News*, August 21, 2013, https://www.pmnewsnigeria.com/2013/08/21/fasehun-can-kill-destroy-for-power-money-and-women/.

210. Eniola Akinkuotu, "Jonathan Deserves Praise for Giving OPC Contract," *Punch*, March 23, 2015, http://www.punchng.com/politics/jonathan-deserves-praise-for-giving-opc-contract-gani-adams/.

211. In its 2012 report, the *Journal* focused on the Niger Delta militants who had been accused of attacking the pipelines in the past. Therefore, the OPC leaders could not have been included among those described by the paper as "oil bandits."

212. Drew Hinshaw, "Nigeria's Former Oil Bandits Now Collect Government Cash," *Wall Street Journal*, August 22, 2012, https://www.wsj.com/articles/SB10001424052702304019404577420160886588518.

213. Ibid.

214. Ibid.

215. Abimboye, "Why Tinubu Starved Us."

216. Oando PLC is a Nigerian multinational energy company headed by Wale Tinubu, Bola Tinubu's relation. Even though Tinubu is often associated with the company, contrary to Adams's claims, Bola Tinubu was not the chairman of the company at that point.

217. Abimboye, "Why Tinubu Starved Us."

218. Ademosu, "Fasehun Can Kill" (emphasis added).

219. Some of Adams's erstwhile comrades claimed that the group is only present in twenty-three states. There is no way of confirming either claim. However, there is no doubt that the group has a presence in many states in Nigeria, as the number of state coordinators who are either regularly or occasionally reported show.

220. Ebun Sessou and Iyabo Aina, "I Never Collected Money from Ghaddafi, Jonathan, Obanikoro—Gani Adams. Asks Accusers to Show Proof," *Vanguard*, February 20, 2016, https://www.vanguardngr.com/2016/02/i-never-collected-money-from-ghaddafi-jonathan-obanikoro-gani-adams/. They made other wild allegations in the

same report, including that Adams collected "$22 million from late Libyan President, Muammar Gaddafi." Adams denied this strongly. He challenged his accusers: "They should explain what the money was meant for and how it was sent to me. Such huge amount of money could not be transferred to an individual secretly, so they need to explain how I received the money." A spokesman for the OPC Adams faction added, "They should provide details of the supposed relationship between Gaddafi and Adams, who I believe has never travelled to any North African country. This is not the first time we are hearing such. I recall how Otunba Adams wrote a petition to the Department of State Services (DSS), through his lawyer, Kehinde Oluwole, to investigate the story. Till now, nothing has been heard." See Wale Adunsi, "Publish the Account through Which Gaddafi Gave Adams $22m—OPC Dares Petitioners," *Daily Post*, March 16, 2016, https://dailypost.ng/2016/03/16/publish-the-account-through-which-gaddafi-gave-adams-22m-opc-dares-petitioners/.

221. Ameh Comrade Godwin, "OPC Want Gani Adams Arrested, Accuse Him of Collecting N10.6bn from Jonathan," *Daily Post*, February 15, 2016, https://dailypost.ng/2016/02/15/opc-want-gani-adams-arrested-accuse-him-of-collecting-n10-6bn-from-jonathan/.

222. The OPC Adams faction claimed to have expelled Olanrewaju, but Ilorin-based Olanrewaju has said that he left the faction to form his own group, OPCI.

223. Ibid.

224. Sessou and Aina, "I Never Collected Money."

225. Chuks Nwanne, "Learn from Jonathan's Mistakes, Gani Adams Cautions Buhari," *Guardian*, May 31, 2015, https://guardian.ng/news/learn-from-jonathans-mistakes-gani-adams-cautions-buhari.

226. The urban Yorùbá would call this *ogbon ori*—that is practical wisdom, or intense shrewdness—which is slightly different from *ogbon* (wisdom) qua *ogbon*.

227. Marshall Sahlins, "Poor Man, Rich Man, Big-Man, Chief: Political Types in Melanesia and Polynesia," *Comparative Studies in Society and History* 5, no. 3 (1963): 289.

228. Sahlins's favored phrase is "his own personal manufacture." Ibid.

229. Ibid.

230. Barber, "How Man Makes God," 729.

231. Apter, *Black Critics and Kings*, 90 (emphasis added).

232. Ibid., 89.

233. Ibid., 93.

234. I do not use this phrase in the political economy or Marxian sense, though I seek to mimic it. Here, *use value* means both Adams's actual and potential capacity to be serviceable (his *usefulness*) to particular persons' interests, needs, and purposes.

235. Vilfredo Pareto, *The Rise and Fall of the Elites*, with introduction by Hans L. Zetterberg (1968; reprint, Salem, NH: Ayer, 2017).

6 / The Liability of Status Sustenance

A "MESSIAH"[1] OR A NEW "GENERAL" ON THE HORIZON?

In late September 2020, at a small gathering of his supporters, Sunday Adeyemo, popularly called Sunday Igboho, charged the Yorùbá in Nigeria and the diaspora to join him in a peaceful protest to declare the creation of the Oduduwa Republic, a new nation-state for the Yoruba, on October 1, 2020. The chosen date for the declaration of what would have been the world's newest nation-state after South Sudan coincided with Nigeria's sixtieth anniversary as an independent state.

At this point, Igboho was a forty-eight-year-old former motorcycle repairer who later became an enforcer[2] and was now a businessman and activist. The man who was nicknamed after his hometown of Igboho—the sixteenth-century second capital of the Oyo Empire—stated at the gathering, "We are expecting the *Aare Ona Kakanfo* to lead us and we will follow. We are not waiting for the traditional rulers. I held a meeting with some traditional rulers but they are not forthcoming. But we will not ask traditional rulers to lead us, our *Aare Ona Kakanfo* is a brave warrior and we want him to lead us."[3]

But on the appointed date,[4] apart from Igboho's supporters, not many people showed up for the proposed announcement of a new republic. A disappointed Igboho told the few journalists at the event that the Yorùbá leaders who had agreed to show up were "afraid" to fulfill their promises. He reproached them, dismissing them as "cowards."[5] Because Igboho had called on Gani Adams as the *Ààrẹ Ọ̀nà Kakañfò* to lead the army of peaceful protesters for the proposed republic, many people took Igboho's statement as an indictment of the generalissimo. The *Kakañfò* did too. When asked for his reaction, he responded angrily to the journalist as well as to Igboho:

Figure 6.1. A banner calling for support for Oduduwa Republic with the images of Sunday Adeyemo (Igboho), Adams, and Oduduwa (*top left*), the Yorùbá progenitor. The proposed flag of the new nation-state is on the top right. Photo courtesy of *Nigerian Tribune*.

> What is he trying to insinuate? I don't understand. . . . He said I should lead, but he didn't call me. *He should have come to me respectfully* to ask me to lead. He didn't call me. . . . He was calling [on] me on the social media. By issuing such a call, he made the security agencies to focus on me, as if I was the one who asked him to do this. After making the call . . . even if he couldn't come to my house, he should have called me. The members of the OPC [Oodua People's Congress] in Ibadan [Oyo State] will be at least five hundred thousand. Even if I didn't show up, if I asked my followers to join him, at least he would have had ten thousand people behind him. *But he exposed us all.* He created an alarm, such that the security network started monitoring key leaders. That's not how it is done. *He shouldn't let the Yoruba suspect him*, that he is being used. . . . If we suspect him, we will avoid him. . . . *Government plant people in the struggle*; [such an informant] will speak as if he were bold, but they will bug you. He will get all [the] secrets and reveal them to the government. . . . I am not saying he is like that, but if he is talking too much, we might start suspecting him. . . . You just started the struggle, and then you start attacking leaders. . . . He should not insult our leaders. . . . He should be careful. *He is our son.* He just started a struggle. He used to buy and sell cars. If you are new to a struggle, you have to get training. . . . This is the [normal] *course of self-determination.*[6]

Why was Adams so peeved? His reaction is understandable, not just because of the specific challenge that Igboho threw at him but also because of the greater potential threat that Igboho represented to the *Kakaǹfò*'s status and public image. This is reflected in Adams's response. First, he raised the question of his elevated status in Yorubaland: (1) by demanding that Igboho should have consulted him "respectfully," by either calling him or visiting his house for a dialogue, and (2) by presenting himself as a veritable father or elder[7] (on the basis of his status as the *Kakaǹfò*) who regarded Igboho, though only two years younger, as "our son," one who ostensibly needed guidance from the father. Second, on the basis of Igboho's failure to respect existing seniority, Adams queried Igboho's bona fides: by probing the younger man's understanding of the complexity of what "the struggle" for self-determination entailed (given that, until recently, Igboho was only "buying and selling cars") and by raising (but, at the same time, dismissing) doubts about Igboho's authenticity and sincerity (because, according to Adams, Igboho could easily be mistrusted and "suspected" as a government spy).

There are other reasons for Adams to be wary of the otherwise deferential Igboho. Since he emerged as a potential leader within and beyond the OPC, particularly since he acquired fame and financial resources, Adams has faced challenges to his status, authority, and influence. The latest challenges have mainly come from his former close comrades in the OPC, including members of the National Guard who formed rival OPC factions: OPC New Era, OPC Reform, and Oodua Progressive Care Initiative (OPCI). In fact, the leader of OPCI, Marruf Olanrewaju, expressed disappointment in Adams's reaction to Igboho's emergence. In January 2021, a few months after Igboho challenged Adams about the Oduduwa Republic, Olanrewaju told me that, though Adams "always wanted to be *Ààrẹ Ọ̀nà Kakaǹfò*," he seemed not to know what to do about "all the crises" in Yorubaland and Nigeria:

> Where is the *Ààrẹ* now with all the crises? We can no longer see Adams because the real fighters [in the OPC] are gone. Now, he goes around with musicians so as to draw a crowd. And now that Sunday Igboho is out, he is saying that Igboho is an "illiterate." But Igboho is building on what he [Adams] did. Why is he not doing [what needs to be done]? He has turned OPC [in]to a political group. In 2019, he said he was warming up for a political party. Is he no longer interested in Yoruba cause? . . . He is [only] an *Ààrẹ* [*Ọ̀nà Kakaǹfò*] on paper.[8]

For several reasons, Igboho's challenge to Adams's position, role, status, and influence seemed to be more potent than that of his erstwhile comrades who had formed rival groups such as OPC New Era and OPCI. First, Igboho had never been a member of the OPC or one of Adams's followers. Second, unlike his former comrades, who might have an axe to grind with him (which could affect their credibility when he called them out), Igboho was directly addressing a matter that had greater resonance among the Yorùbá in light of the incompetence and, as many other groups in Nigeria saw it, the frontal ethnocentrism of President Mohammadu Buhari.[9] Though not all Yorùbá agree on secession, most Yorùbá agree that something ought to be done about the narrow-mindedness and ineptitude of the Buhari administration and about the structural fatalities of the Nigerian state that had made Buhari's worst excesses possible without redress. Therefore, whatever inspired the call for Yorùbá separation from the Nigerian state or for Yorùbá self-determination—such as Buhari's insularity and ineptitude and the criminal activities of some Fulani herdsmen, including farmland destruction, kidnapping, and rape—Igboho's activities were turning him into a hero in Yorubaland.

In addition, Igboho's trajectory seemed to replicate Adams's rise in a meaningful, although slightly altered, way. One of the most significant differences between the two is that Igboho lacked an organizational context, such as the OPC, for his rise. He burst into public consciousness at a time when the Yorùbá were, again, feeling threatened by what they regarded as a northern-dominated government that was intent on suppressing them. Under President Buhari, just as in the early to late 1990s, when the OPC was formed under the northern-dominated military regimes of Generals Ibrahim Babangida and Sani Abacha, there were agitations for the self-determination of the Yoruba, which were interpreted as either a push to reorder Nigeria to give greater autonomy to the Yorùbá region or a move to take the Yorùbá out of Nigeria. Those in the latter group had become loudest in the context of Buhari's kakistocracy.[10] Retired history professor Banji Akintoye later became the arrowhead of this group, while Igboho represented its sharpest edge. Under the umbrella of the Yoruba Self-Determination Movement (YSDM), in August 2022, Akintoye wrote to President Buhari seeking a "peaceful break away" of the Yorùbá from Nigeria because of their "worsening and painful plight."[11] Akintoye added, "Upon asserting this right of self-determination, we [of the] Yoruba nation shall be free to determine our political status, pursue our economic, social and cultural development according to policies chosen independently by us, and to live under the government independently chosen and ordered by us."[12]

Adams had emerged two decades earlier in a similar context. Though Igboho and Adams have followed different trajectories, their life histories seem to converge. Both started out poor and socially insignificant but have ended up with considerable material means and influence. Igboho too has become a fairly rich businessman with his own collection of high-end vehicles (including Mercedes Benz SUVs and a Range Rover), and his two wives and children live in Europe. Like Adams, Igboho is surrounded by stories of "metaphysical powers."[13] Yet there are significant differences. While Igboho became popular or notorious first through his role in the Ife-Modakeke communal clashes[14] and later through his support for, or efforts against, political godfathers,[15] Adams

Figure 6.2. Igboho (*far right*) and his supporters addressing the people of Igangan at the rally where he issued the ultimatum in January 2021. Beside him is Sunday Adebayo, Adams's former personal assistant and former member of the Adams OPC NCC, now a member of OPC New Era. Photo courtesy of Sunday Adebayo.

honed his skills as a prodemocracy activist before becoming a freedom fighter with wider Yorùbá ethno-nationalist aspirations.

Yet Adams realized that Igboho's rise and challenge—Igboho was now being called the "messiah" of the Yoruba—if unchecked, would not just lead to the ascendancy of the latter; he could also undermine the legitimacy of the *Kakaǹfò*, who swore to protect the Yorùbá and their interests in Nigeria. This potential was exacerbated in the context of the increasing spate of herdsmen-related criminal activities in Yorubaland.

On January 15, 2021, Igboho stormed the Igangan community in the Ibarapa Local Government Area of Oyo State to issue a seven-day ultimatum to the herdsmen to quit Yorubaland or be forced out.[16] This ultimatum sent shock waves through the country, with the federal and state government, as well as the leaders in the North, condemning it. Some argued that the ultimatum was unconstitutional and illegal because it was issued to Nigerians of a different ethnic group who enjoyed the constitutional protection of freedom of movement and freedom to be domiciled in any part of the federation. Igboho's defenders replied that the ultimatum was issued to "criminal herdsmen" and not the Fulani in general.

After the rally, Igboho and his supporters confronted the *Sarkin* (leader of the) Fulani in Igangan, Saliu Kadri, accusing him and his fellow Fulani of "killing Yoruba natives including Oyo businessman, Fatai Aborode, Alhaja Serifat Adisa, and her children, and an Igangan prince, among others, [adding] that his move and actions had the blessing of Yoruba traditional rulers."[17]

A couple of weeks later, some young men set houses and cars belonging to the *Sarkin* Fulani of the town, Saliu Abdulkadir, on fire. A resident told the press, "We were happy with what Sunday Igboho did. He is like a liberator. We need such action because we have not been sleeping with our two eyes closed. It's either somebody is kidnapped on his farm or somebody is robbed or killed. The government is also not helping because we don't see them taking any decisive step."[18] A former minister of aviation, Femi Fani-Kayode, tweeted that "*new leaders* are rising up in the SW [Southwest]. They are strong, fearless, radical and young."[19]

Fearing that the Fulani-led federal government would declare a state of emergency, the governor of Oyo State, Seyi Makinde, asked security men to arrest Igboho. The governor was, in turn, condemned by some Yorùbá leaders.[20] Given the state of helplessness in the Yorùbá states—and also in Southeast Nigeria—caused by security challenges, including those involving the herdsmen, Igboho's popularity shot up among the Yorùbá both at home and abroad. The Yorùbá and other southerners lit social media and blogs up with praise and support for Igboho's action, just as northerners and the federal and state governments condemned him.

This raised questions about the role of the *Kakañfò*, the man who was expected to defend the Yorùbá and Yorubaland.

Two years before the latest attacks by the herdsmen, which led to Igboho's response, Adams had announced publicly that he was "ready to lead battle against killer herdsmen."[21] After recent herdsmen-related killings and attacks and the Buhari administration's decision to create cattle ranches all over the country to stem the tide of herder-farmer clashes, Adams told the press in July 2018 that the "insecurity in the land is reaching an alarming peak." He added, "Thousands of lives have been lost to these killers, but it is strange that not even a single arrest or prosecution has been effected. . . . I find it difficult to comprehend this open insult that some killers, whose kinsmen live in our villages, towns, and cities, will invade Yorubaland at will, kidnap, rape and, in some bizarre situations, kill some of our sons and daughters."[22] A few months earlier, he had announced that the Yorùbá would "resist any conspiracy aimed at killing our people at will."[23]

However, the *Kakañfò*'s critics said he only "talked tough" but did not take any action. Therefore, by taking action, Igboho was not just throwing a challenge to Adams; he was throwing Adams's position and status into crisis. Beyond that, Igboho's emergence also throws into question what it means to be a Yorùbá and a person of consequence in Yorubaland in the twenty-first century. While Yorùbá identity faced significant challenges during the democratization struggle (particularly from around 1990–99), which was the context in which Adams emerged, that identity has been thrown into a similar but different crisis under democratic rule in the first two decades of the twenty-first century, particularly under President Buhari. The voices for the secession of the Yorùbá from Nigeria are drowning out the voices for the restructuring of the Nigerian federation. While Adams had become a strong voice for restructuring (even championing it when he attended the National Conference under President Jonathan), Igboho's action—in the context of the strong reactions to what some see as the "menace" of the Fulani herdsmen and the associated insecurity in the land—presses the struggle for eminence in Yorubaland into a significantly different direction. In the late 1990s and early 2000s when Adam emerged, the democratic question was assumed to be fused with the self-determination question in Nigeria. Now the self-determination question is fused with the question of the separatism or secession of the Yorùbá from Nigeria. And as one who is now seen as a member of the elite, Adams seems, initially, incapable of responding adequately to the emergent question.

Though Igboho himself had become a man of some means before this period, he is still regarded as closer to the grassroots than the rich and connected *Kakañfò*. Igboho looks like the new *authentic* subaltern leader. Adams was compelled to respond to this challenge. He therefore raised the decibel of his voice on Yorùbá self-determination or secession,[24] such that he even attracted the attention of John Campbell, the former US Ambassador to Nigeria and Ralph Bunche Senior Fellow for Africa Policy Studies at the Council on Foreign Relations (CFR). Campbell wrote a short piece on Adams's new position on the CFR blog.[25] At a gathering in mid-April 2021, Adams stated, "I support the popular view of the Yoruba that we have graduated from the restructuring that we have been clamouring for since 1991 to self-determination." He added, "Though the dominant elite in Nigeria are 'not ready for restructuring' . . . if Nigeria is not reorganized within the next three years, the future of the country is on the brink."[26] Campbell, who described Adams as "[having] long been involved in Yoruba cultural and political movements," noted that "the *Aare* seems be to advocating a form of governance similar to that of the Federal Republic of Germany—an example often cited in Nigeria of successful regional devolution."[27]

CHALLENGING ADAMS'S DOMINANCE

On February 28, 2021, Sunday Igboho and a few of his aides and friends visited Adams at home. Before this point, there had been several failed attempts at a meeting. The tension between the two Yorùbá warriors—one a culturally designated warrior, the other an emergent warrior—had become worrisome to the leadership of the *Afenifere*, the apex Yorùbá sociopolitical group. The deputy leader, Chief Ayo Adebanjo, decided to intervene by inviting both men to his home. Igboho did not show up. Unknown to Adebanjo, by this time, some of Adams's estranged comrades were now backing Igboho. Two splinter groups, one from the Fasehun faction (OPC Reform, led by Dare Adesope) and the other from the Adams faction (OPC New Era, led by Arogundade Rasaq Balogun), were working in concert with Igboho. In fact, Adams's estranged friend, former personal assistant, and former key member of his inner circle, Sunday Adebayo, was, by this time, one of the key people supporting Igboho. Adams's erstwhile comrades discouraged Igboho from reconciling with Adams, warning him that Adams would subsume him and profit from the association.

As the pressure from Adebanjo grew, Igboho relented and visited Adebanjo's home in Lekki, Lagos Island. However, because Igboho hadn't shown up when they were supposed to meet, Adams was not at Adebanjo's house when he arrived. Therefore, Adebanjo pleaded with Igboho to go to Adams's house on the mainland to resolve their differences. Present at Adebanjo's house were other Yorùbá leaders and a retired Yorùbá deputy inspector general (DIG) of the police. Adebanjo asked the retired DIG and two members of his kitchen cabinet in *Afenifere*—the group's national publicity secretary, Yinka Odumakin, and the former director general of the News Agency of Nigeria (NAN) and one of Adams's chiefs, Akin Osuntokun—to accompany Igboho to Adams's house. Adebanjo had to specially appeal to Sunday Adebayo, Adams's estranged friend and now Igboho's right-hand man, to join Igboho on the trip. When they got to Adams's house, according to Adebayo, he refused to go inside until Adams, in a show of magnanimity, personally came out to persuade his estranged boyhood friend to join the others in his home.

According to Adebayo and Osuntokun, both of whom I communicated with by telephone on that day, the meeting was convivial. Igboho was deferential, as was usual in private, acknowledging Adams's leadership. Adams, seated on the throne-like chair he had made for himself after his installation as *Kakańfò* (complete with the name of his office written in gold letters at the top of the baroque, high-back chair), sat Igboho to his right and one of the intervenors, Gboyega Adejumo (one of his chiefs), to his left. It was as if he were holding court.

Figure 6.3. Sunday Igboho (*left*) with Adams and one of Adams's chiefs, *Gbonka Ààrẹ Ọ̀nà Kakaǹfò*, Gboyega Adejumo (*right*), sitting at a peace meeting in Adams's house on February 28, 2021. Photo courtesy of *Nigerian Tribune.*

Adams insisted at the meeting that he could not lead a response to the herdsmen "invasion" unless he received a "mandate" from all the Yorùbá traditional rulers.[28] He asked that the traditional rulers be persuaded to authorize him, as the *Kakaǹfò*, and the OPC to take on the Fulani herdsmen who were behind the attacks in Yorubaland. Some at the meeting felt that this was Adams's way to avoid being targeted by the Buhari administration if people in Yorubaland took the law into their hands against the Fulani herdsmen and kidnappers—which was what Igboho favored. These critics felt that Adams had become too comfortable to risk another long spell in detention. But Adams believed that, without the publicly stated mandate by the leading traditional rulers, he would have no legitimacy or widespread support. Yet he felt that he, and not Igboho, had the legitimate cultural office and duty to take charge of a coordinated response. Igboho should be following his lead, not dictating the pace.

However, Adebayo saw Adams's move as a way of taking over Igboho's initiative. A few weeks before the meeting in Adams's house, Adebayo had told me on the telephone while he was in Igboho's home in Ibadan that Adams was privately opposed to Igboho's action in Igangan and only supported it publicly when he realized how popular it was among the Yorùbá at home and abroad. He accused Adams of trying to profit from the heightened agitation in Yorubaland against the incursion of the herdsmen.[29]

To seize the initiative, in March 2021, Adams embarked on a visit to the governors of the Southwest states to discuss the modalities for responding to

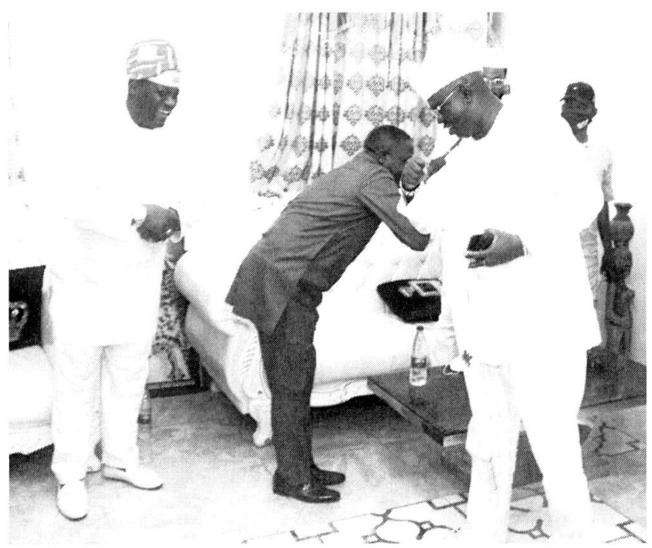

Figure 6.4. Adams greeting Igboho by bumping arms while others watch. This was during the COVID-19 pandemic. Though neither is masked, they are observing the safe greeting method of the era. Photo courtesy of *Nigerian Tribune*.

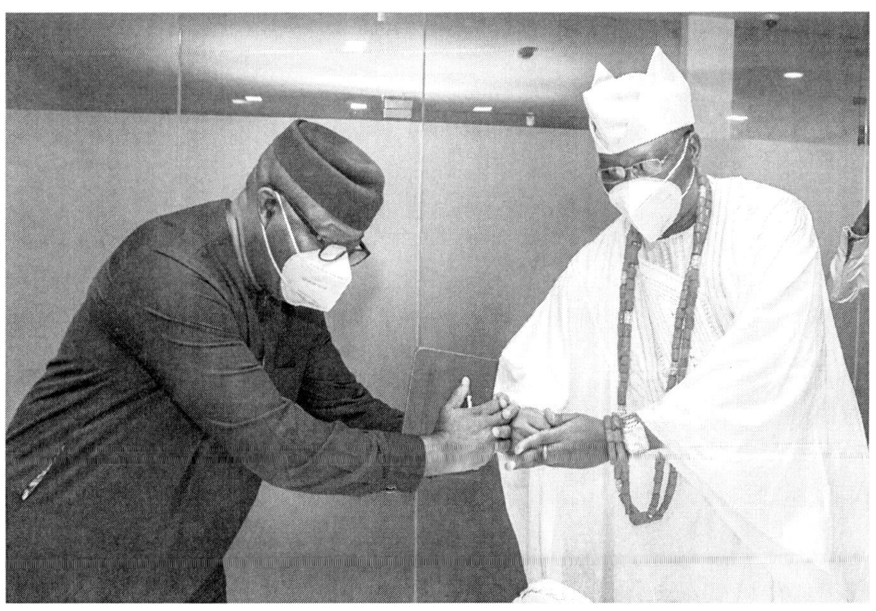

Figure 6.5. Governor Fayemi receiving Adams in his office in Ado-Ekiti in March 2021. Photo courtesy of *Nigerian Tribune*.

Figure 6.6. Adams and Governor Seyi Makinde of Oyo State exchange greetings in the COVID-era style in March 2021. Photo courtesy of *Nigerian Tribune*.

the insecurity in the region. When he met Governor Kayode Fayemi of Ekiti State, who was also the chair of the Nigerian Governors' Forum, Fayemi reportedly "appreciated Adams for his concern for peace, security and stability of the country, and assured him that peace will reign in the region and Nigeria in general."[30]

Adams also met Governor Seyi Makinde of Oyo State. After their meeting, he told the press, "I wrote all the South-West governors to meet them on security matters and [the] economy. I was happy that I have met two of them now. . . . It is very important that we should interface on prevalent issues within our region, especially security. What we have witnessed for the past three years is very alien to our history. So, I came here to discuss with the governor. . . . The outcome of the meeting is not something that I can divulge in the media. But I can assure you that we had a fruitful meeting."[31]

Despite the peace initiative in Adams's house, the emergent "general," Igboho, refused to yield to the generalissimo. He continued his campaign. On March 19, 2021, after the failed effort to declare a new republic in October, he again raised the flag of the Oduduwa Republic. Igboho, who had repeatedly ignored the invitation of the inspector general of the police,[32] reproached Yorùbá politicians who were preparing to run for the presidency of Nigeria in the approaching 2023 election. In what seemed like a replay of the Gani Adams of 1998–99, who was then opposed to Yorùbá participation in the transition to civil rule program, Igboho told the press, "You should know that you are not supposed to seek election to the office of the President, you should identify with our agitation and lead us in the secession struggle." He threatened the politicians: "I will not allow you to campaign because I will kill you all [Yorùbá politicians] before [the 2023] campaigns. I swear to God, we will shoot them with guns from the back."[33]

The same day, with Professor Banji Akintoye beside him, Igboho—who by this time was being described in the media as a "Yoruba freedom fighter"[34]—declared that there was no basis for the continued existence of Nigeria.[35] Akintoye, a Second Republic senator, a professor of history, and the author of the authoritative *A History of the Yoruba People*,[36] has been the leading advocate for the creation of a new Yorùbá nation-state in its current iteration. Igboho added in Yoruba, "We are taking back our territory. . . . This country is finished. We don't want Nigeria again. We want [a] Yoruba nation. . . . Akintoye, he [is] our leader. . . . I speak for all Yoruba leaders. We don't want the Fulani in our land. They are raping our sisters; they are killing our people."[37]

At the OPC National Coordinating Council (NCC) meeting on May 18, 2021, Adams took on Igboho again. Three days earlier, on May 15, 2021, Igboho had held a rally in Osogbo, Osun State, to mobilize the Yorùbá for the struggle to create an independent state. Like in all the other places he visited for his rallies, he was met by a mammoth crowd. Igboho's constituents believed that the success of the Osogbo rally, the first in a series, worried Adams. Adebayo, Adams's erstwhile friend, told me that Adams organized an NCC meeting of the OPC a few days later to halt Igboho's momentum.[38]

In a live-streamed speech at the NCC meeting, where he spoke in a fit of pique, Adams attacked Tinubu (though he did not mention his name),[39] whom he believed was funding all the activities that would directly or indirectly undermine him. He also took on Igboho in the address, which was uploaded to YouTube and widely shared.[40]

Adams described Tinubu's decision to celebrate his sixty-ninth birthday in the North of Nigeria—specifically Kano—as "pathetic," in that it turned him into a "football that the Fulani are kicking around" because he wanted to be president. He accused Tinubu of bribing many people to destroy his reputation, alleging that he is Tapa (Nupe) and not Yoruba. He also accused the former Lagos State governor of many unprintable things.

He then moved to Igboho, first indirectly and eventually directly: "It is easy to say you are fighting for [a] Yoruba nation[-state]. Those who are fighting for

[a] Yoruba nation, we are not subverting one another. Some are thinking that they will do it alone, someone who doesn't have capacity. Some are thinking, 'Let us exclude one particular person [meaning himself] from the equation.' [The person planning this] doesn't [even] have power. . . . Anyone who is scheming to wage war against me, before July, the earth will consume him [he will die]."[41] The crowd chorused "*Ase*!" (Amen!).

He added, "I want to advise our younger brother [àbúrò *wa*], Sunday Igboho, if he wants to fight this fight, if he wants to be one of those who will succeed, he has to be careful who he surrounds himself with. Because I see some people who our elder brother in Lagos [*egbon wa l'Eko*—meaning Tinubu] has bought over completely that surround him [Igboho]."[42] This was a reference to Adams's former comrades, particularly Sunday Adebayo, Rasaq Arogundade Balogun (both of the OPC New Era), and Taofeek Adeyemi (once Fasehun's personal assistant and now a member of OPC Reform), who are now with Igboho.

Adams continued, "It is dangerous for him [Igboho] to have people like that around himself. He should look for a good team. When I saw some pictures, I was left wondering whether Igboho was serious with this struggle. Because these ones, they have been bought and their *elédá*[43] [maker] has been bought too. Wherever *Lagbaja* in Lagos [meaning Tinubu] asked them to go, that's where they will go. You, who claim to be fighting for freedom, if *Lagbaja* asked them to perpetrate evil against you, they will. They only want money. They don't have power."[44]

He gave what might be regarded as a misogynist analogy about a woman who had been "used" or "climbed over" by several men and abandoned, only to be found by another man who would like to treat her as a "fresh bride." "People will laugh at you," he added. "And if they don't laugh at you, you will be brushed with eternal filth [*ìdòtí ayérayé*]."

Although Adams admitted that the rally held a few days earlier by Igboho constituted "part of the advocacy" needed for self-determination, he called Igboho, tongue in cheek, by his alias, "entertainer."

"My position as the *Ààrẹ Ọ̀nà Kakaǹfò* is to guide all freedom fighters [with] my experience and my spiritual potentials," Adams asserted.

> They are thinking, "If we invite him to a meeting, we will not be able to control him" . . . [We are talking about] someone who has not fought a battle and is already thinking of how to appropriate money. He is yet to fight a battle; he is still engaging in *entertainment*. He is still an *entertainer*. Because some are at the level of the struggle, he is an entertainer. He is still entertaining the Yoruba; he is yet to start a struggle. Only an empty barrel makes a lot of noise.

> You want to engage in a struggle, and you then surround yourself with our *used items* who have betrayed us, those we have *used* and *dumped*. . . . I looked at the picture, and I laughed. A traitor will always be a traitor.[45]

Igboho joined battle with the generalissimo the next day. His response was also live streamed,[46] and he also spoke in Yoruba. This time, the younger man, who had always been diffident toward Adams and restrained in his responses, was neither diffident nor restrained.

"I have been respecting you," he said without mentioning Adams's name. "But if I honor you and you don't stay in your place, if I disgrace you, you will hate yourself. Anyone I discredit will never amount to anything before God."[47] His supporters shouted "*Ase*!" (Amen!). He continued,

> God knows that I am doing this with all my heart. I am working for the Yoruba with all my heart. I am not looking for money. I just want my name in the history book. Those claiming that they are powerful, they have occult power, they can do battle, they are in the struggle for the money. I will be bold and say it. They have taken so much money over the years. They can't affirm that evil should happen to them if they took money from anyone in the past. But I can say that. I say that all the time. We have evidence of where they had taken money in the past. I will not mention anyone's name. But they should sleep and think deeply about what they say in public on the internet.[48]

He then responded to Adams's charge that he was a mere "entertainer":

> Yes, I am an entertainer. God gave me that [blessing]. I entertain the elderly; I entertain the old [a slip of the tongue—he must mean the young]. But I will use the entertainment to free the Yoruba from [the yoke of] Nigeria. Those who are angry . . . there is no going back. God has granted [the mission] to us. . . . Even though we are an 'empty barrel' [as Adams described him], making noise as an empty barrel, we will use that noise to take the Yoruba to the Promised Land. Let them come out and speak the same way we are speaking [about secession from Nigeria]. If they did, the politicians will ask them about the money they had given them in the past. All the empty-barrel noise that we are making, if they did that, the government would ask them for the money they had given them repeatedly in the past. Let them dare. . . . They have been compromised. Let them dare to hold rallies as we have been doing.

He also dismissed Adams's request at the NCC asking OPC members to contribute money to buy some cows for sacrifice. "We have Christians and Muslims in our midst," said Igboho, who is a Christian. "We can't ask them to make sacrifices [to the *orisa*]. . . . We will only call on God. God will lead us to the Promised Land.... Whoever is angry, who will not grant [leadership] to the one who is chosen by God, who says we will not have a Yoruba nation, we will be free after they have passed.... I am an entertainer.... An elder who does not exercise caution in speaking about a younger person, the younger person will also not exercise any caution in speaking about him."

Igboho's supporters hailed him.

Not done, Igboho's lieutenants—and Adams's former lieutenants, whom the *Kakañfò* had dismissed as "used and dumped"—including Sunday Adebayo, Taofeek Adeyemi, Ranti Akande (Otepa), Musa Kila (Warrior), and Omotoso Afolabi (the vice president of OPC Reform) also appeared on a live-stream channel, Isokan Omo Odua TV, to rebut Adams.[49] They spoke on behalf of OPC New Era, led by Balogun, and OPC Reform, led by Oludare Adesope. Taofeek Adeyemi, who spoke in Yorùbá for the team, said that, contrary to the picture that Adams painted in his address to the NCC, Igboho was carrying on the struggle for self-determination for the Yoruba. He repudiated Adams's claim that Tinubu was sponsoring Igboho: "We are not agents of politicians. We are standing with Igboho. Yoruba nation is a must. There is no going back. We appreciate the support of the [people in the] Diaspora. We have taken an oath. We can never betray Igboho. We thank Igboho who God raised. We are imploring Adams as *Aare* not to be a *domestic Aare*. He should come out to fight. We are here to liberate the Yoruba against Fulani incursion and Yoruba bastards."[50]

Adebayo also spoke, implying that Adams was no longer the arrowhead of the struggle for self-determination. "God has given Igboho leadership. We should all support him. *We know those who take contracts from politicians.*[51] Anyone who is serious should come and support Igboho. No one should be deceiving the Yoruba. He [implying Adams] is sitting in the corner of a room asking some people to contribute money.... We are not taking money from anyone. ... *Eni ba dale, a ba le lo* [literally, whoever betrays the land, will disappear into the land; meaning whoever betrays the Yorùbá cause will die a violent death]."[52]

Some Yorùbá in the diaspora, including YouTubers, Facebook broadcasters, and live-streamers, who were very happy with Igboho's activities regarding the herdsmen or his campaign for a sovereign Yorùbá state, also joined the fray. They called Adams all sorts of names online, accusing him of being "cowardly" while Igboho had shown "courage."[53]

It would appear that what may be described as *the Gani Adams franchise*—the trajectory of which I have traced in the preceding chapters—is being appropriated by Igboho and afforded a new lease on life in a repeated, even if slightly different, performance of the career of self-determination in contemporary Southwestern Nigeria. Whether Igboho succeeds or not in becoming the dominant big man / enforcer in Southwestern Nigeria, it is clear that Gani Adams's trajectory has become a compelling and attractive model for some subaltern young men in that region of Nigeria who also hope to become big in the future.

STATE REPRESSION, EXILE, AND A NEW "DOCTOR" ON THE HORIZON

On Thursday, July 1, 2021, shortly after 1:00 a.m., the Department of State Security (DSS; otherwise called State Security Service, SSS), the agency in charge of internal security in Nigeria, stormed the home of Sunday Igboho in Soka area, Ibadan, in what was reportedly "a bid to affect his arrest."[54] The raid was carried out seventy-two hours before Igboho's planned rally in Lagos to continue his campaign for a sovereign Yorùbá nation-state. The DSS claimed that there was a "hot gun duel between them and Igboho's guards," after which security operatives killed two of Igboho's men.

After subduing Igboho's men, the DSS arrested thirteen suspects, including a woman. Expensive automobiles belonging to Igboho, including his Mercedes Benz G-Wagen and Prado Jeep, valuable properties such as furniture, and parts of his home were reportedly destroyed. At a press conference held at DSS headquarters in Abuja, spokesman Peter Afunanya stated that a total of seven AK-47 rifles were recovered at the scene, alongside pump-action guns, thirty AK-47 magazines, five thousand rounds of ammunition, three locally made bulletproof jackets, other weapons, and Igboho's German residency permit (one of Igboho's wives and his children live in Germany and have European Union passports).[55] Footage from the incident revealed blood spatter in Igboho's living room and destroyed vehicles.[56]

The DSS also reportedly "arrested" Igboho's cat. Having failed to arrest Igboho despite the strong intelligence that he was in the house and their certainty that there was no "natural" way he could have escaped arrest, the security operates feared that the Igboho could have transformed himself into a cat. Such was their belief in Igboho's famed occult powers that they did not want to take any chances. They assumed that if they took the cat with them, by the time it transformed back into the wanted man, they would still have *it/him* in their custody.

The DSS spokesman, who asked Igboho to surrender himself to relevant authorities to face justice, claimed that the service acted "on intelligence that [Igboho] had stockpiled arms" in his house—though it was obvious that the attack was solely because of his separatist agitations, as the agency itself revealed. In the press statement, the service added that it wanted to "inform Nigerians and the world that Sunday Igboho and his group, *in the guise of campaign for self-determination*, have become well-armed and determined to undermine public order. . . . The arrests and seizures are, no doubt, a confirmation of a grand plan by Igboho and his cohorts to *wage a violent insurrection against the Nigerian State*."[57] Ostensibly, the DSS was overstating Igboho's capacity in order to excuse their hijack of what should have been police duty.[58] The items found in the house clearly showed that Igboho had little or no capacity to "wage a violent insurrection against" the state.

The security agencies had, in the past, publicly issued an invitation to him, which Igboho ignored. Even though he confirmed that he was in the house when the security men arrived, Igboho did not disclose how he "miraculously" escaped. However, the next day, he dismissed the DSS's claims that a cache of arms and ammunition had been recovered from his residence during the raid. He told the press that the Buhari-led federal government decided to frame him because they regarded him as a threat to "the Fulanisation agenda in Nigeria."[59] He also expressed surprised at the raid. "I did not kill or fight with anybody," he said. "What I'm doing is to fight for my people. I am fighting for my people because the Fulani bandits killed my family, kidnap and take ransom from them."[60] In a public statement, Igboho said,

> Of public knowledge, my intervention has not led to any loss of life or bloodshed. My means of curbing criminality is to chase the criminal Fulani herdsmen out of their hideouts in company with the people of the affected communities. . . . Nigerians, the security operatives and the presidency are aware that I have never moved against the peaceful Fulanis and other tribes living peacefully in the South West. My unjust persecution—for defending my people and community—is therefore surprising and unwarranted. After several unsuccessful attempts to link me to any crime, the Buhari regime desperately opted to forcefully silence me so that the criminal herdsmen who enjoy government's sympathy, protection and immunity can easily overrun the Southwest. . . . Yoruba people would not be demanding for a nation if the government had lived up to its responsibilities. Self-determination is not a crime and all efforts to silence us and acquire our ancestral land for local and foreign criminal herdsmen will fail.[61]

He subsequently fled Nigeria. In the meantime, he sued the DSS and was awarded N20 billion damages by Justice Ladiran Akintola of the Oyo State High Court, who also declared the raid on Igboho's house "illegal."[62] However, on Monday, July 19, 2021, while preparing to board a plane to Germany at the Cadjèhoun Airport, in Cotonou, the capital of the Republic of Benin, Igboho was arrested by the Beninese authorities. He was detained without any criminal charges or extradition request[63] but was reportedly accused of "illegal migration."[64]

"I started out with nothing, but I became very comfortable," Igboho told me in Yorùbá in his temporary home in Cotonou, Republic of Benin, when I visited him in March 2023. "Given how rich and comfortable I was, I would not have been fighting for the Yoruba. One of my two wives is in Canada with my kids. My other wife is in Germany with my kids. I moved them all out of Nigeria a few years ago. So, ordinarily, I have nothing at stake. But in 2021, I saw the suffering of my people and decided to intervene on their behalf."[65]

He told me about the circumstances of his arrest and the conditions of his detention. He claimed that the Beninese authorities would not have been able to arrest him in Cotonou but for his wife, who was traveling with him and was arrested after he had "escaped." He told me that he surrendered to the authorities only because of that. "They first detained me in a solitary underground cell for about two months, putting me in handcuffs and leg chains," he revealed.

After spending almost eight months in jail without trial, Igboho was released on March 7, 2022, and handed over to the leader of the Ilana Omo Oodua Worldwide, Professor Adebanji Akintoye, and his deputy and linguist, Professor Wale Adeniran, both of whom had also moved into exile in the Republic of Benin.[66] Adeniran has a wide network in Francophone West Africa, including the Republic of Benin, having worked for many years as a French language expert, linguist, and translator around the world, particularly in the subregion. Adeniran's network was useful in his role as deputy to Akintoye, whose own wider network in Nigeria and the Nigerian Diaspora across the world was critical for the support that was provided to Igboho. Akintoye described the release of Igboho, who had become the historian's protégé, as the "triumph of truth over darkness in Yoruba Land."[67] *Afenifere,* the leading Yorùbá political organization, stated in Lagos that Igboho's release "is not just for him and the Yoruba people, it is a victory indicator for all those who believe in personal liberty and the right of a given people to self-determination."[68]

In the aftermath of his release, the terms of which were not clear, Igboho remained in the Republic of Benin.[69] Nigeria's famous writer and Nobel laureate, Wole Soyinka, visited him in Cotonou, where he was received by Akintoye and Adeniran. Media reports indicated that the terms of his release, which some assumed were facilitated by Soyinka (Igboho's counsel, Yomi Alliyu, SAN, denied Soyinka's involvement),[70] included remaining in the small West African nation for some time.

Perhaps the assumption of Soyinka's involvement in Igboho's release was a result of the famous writer's public support for Igboho's activities concerning

Figure 6.7. *Left to right:* The leader of Ilana Omo Yoruba, Professor Banji Akintoye; Sunday Adeyemo (Igboho); and the deputy leader of Ilana Omo Yoruba, Professor Wale Adeniran, after Igboho's release from detention in Cotonou, March 7, 2022. Photo courtesy of *Nigerian Tribune*.

Figure 6.8. Wole Soyinka, Sunday Adeyemo (Igboho), and Banjo Akintoye during Soyinka's solidarity visit to Igboho in Cotonou on May 1, 2022. Photo courtesy of *Nigerian Tribune*.

insecurity in the Southwest and opposition to the attack on Igboho's house[71] and his detention in the Republic of Benin. The Nobel laureate's "solidarity visit"[72] to Igboho on May 1, 2022, after the latter's release, also fueled suspicion that he had been involved. Earlier, in August 2021, Soyinka had asked the Beninese authorities to release the Yorùbá agitator. Speaking with journalists during an interactive session in Lagos entitled "Sanctions on the Loose: Chasing the Gnat with a Sledgehammer," the literary icon said that Igboho had not committed any crime against Nigeria. "I refuse to believe that Igboho committed any offence except agitating against Fulani tyranny on his people. He peacefully demonstrated his position. I can't consider that to be decided a criminal. Agitating for secession is not a criminal act as long as it's done peacefully. You don't have to criminalise that," stated Soyinka.[73]

Sunday Adeyemo could not have craved a greater recognition than the kind offered him by the literary icon's visit. He described Soyinka as "baba mi" (literally "my father") during the visit. Being photographed with the Nobel laureate (who had also been photographed a few times with Gani Adams—see chap. 3), for Igboho, was a strong rebuttal to Gani Adams, who had publicly dismissed him, in an address to the OPC NCC on May 18, 2021, as someone who was not "serious with this struggle." Soyinka's visit therefore affirmed Igboho's legitimacy. If only Adams could see him now with perhaps the most famous and most accomplished living Yorùbá—Soyinka!

However, when Igboho's ordeal began, Gani Adams rallied Yorùbá leaders to his defense. He asked the Yorùbá governors and traditional rulers whom Igboho had "abused and insulted . . . to forgive and help him," while reminding them that Igboho had "insulted [Adams] too."[74] Stated Adams, "We must not allow this to consume him. . . . Either you support self-determination or not, anything that happens to Sunday Igboho will be a slap to the entire Yoruba race. If you allow this to consume Sunday Igboho, it will create an advantage for the criminals, who have already invaded our farms and communities to cause a security threat."[75] Again, when Igboho was arrested in Cotonou, Adams defended him. He described Igboho as someone "fighting for Yoruba liberation."[76] Igboho, he added, "never committed any crime. He was just expressing his displeasure under the ambit of law."[77] The *Kakaǹfò* described the detention of the beleaguered younger man without trial in Cotonou as a "misplacement of justice." He added, "It is evident that the Benin Republic has taken Igboho's case far beyond the normal legal procedures," while calling on the Yorùbá in the diaspora "to approach the African Union Court or International Court of Justice over the continuous detention."[78]

Six months after hosting Soyinka, on November 1, 2022, Igboho was presented with an honorary doctorate by a university based in the United States,

Figure 6.9. The New "Doctor" and the old Professor. Igboho and the eighty-seven-year-old Professor Adebanji Akintoye, leader of Ilana Omo Oodua, a Yorùbá self-determination group, after Igboho was presented with an honorary doctorate by the Nigerian campus of Triune Biblical University, North Bend, Washington, on November 2, 2022. Photo courtesy of *Nigerian Tribune*.

Triune Biblical University. Though it was the Nigerian campus of a hardly known theological university awarding the degree,[79] the conferment of the honorary doctorate was treated in Nigeria, both in the print media and online, as a stop press.[80]

One of the major newspapers in Nigeria, *Vanguard*, reported, "Yoruba Nation agitator, Chief Sunday Adeyemo, fondly called Sunday Igboho, has been conferred with honorary doctorate degree. Igboho was conferred with Doctor of peace and security management/international relations with specialization in war/conflict and peace studies by the Triune Biblical University USA. Reacting, the Yoruba nation agitator in a post on his Instagram said 'Congratulations to me as I was conferred Doctor of peace and security management/international relations with specialization in war/conflict and peace studies from TRIUNE BIBLICAL UNIVERSITY USA. It's such an honor to know that Yoruba Nation's efforts are not in vain.'"[81]

The conferment ceremony was held in a house in Cotonou, where the representatives of the university, decked out in academic regalia, complete with distinguishing hoods, stoles, and cords, were joined by Igboho, who also wore academic regalia. Distinguished scholars Akintoye and Adeniran, Igboho's elderly patrons, added legitimacy to the occasion with their presence as they felicitated the new "Dr. Sunday Adeyemo (Igboho)."

At an event reminiscent of Adams's conferment of an honorary doctorate about a decade earlier (though with far less ceremony, given that it was held in a residence rather than on a university campus), Igboho was eager to remind the audience—both those present and those watching online[82]—of what he had sacrificed to earn the honor. Grinning from ear to ear, he told his well-wishers, in what looked like an acceptance speech, that, even though he did not have much education, he had sufficient wisdom to lead the struggle of his people for freedom, justice, and self-determination.

By becoming a *Dr.* like Adams, in addition to having suffered a long spell of detention in the struggle for self-determination by the Yoruba, Igboho seemed not only to have completely embraced the Adams (sociocultural and political) *franchise* but to be threatening to appropriate it. Except that the *real* owner of the franchise was not about to surrender it.

NOTES

1. One of Igboho's admirers describes him as a "messiah" of the Yorùbá at the moment. See Gbedu WakaAbout, "(Serious Warning) from Gani Adams to people in Diaspora. Kidnapping story. Sunday Igboho replies," Facebook, May 20, 2021, https://www.facebook.com/100742798321881/videos/469317094144408/.

2. His critics dismissed him as a "political thug," but he described himself as someone who "fights against injustice" and a "businessman." He reportedly "rose to fame following his role in the Modakeke-Ife communal crisis in 1997, where he played an active part." See Adejumo Kabir, "Oyo Crisis: Who Is Sunday Igboho, Self-acclaimed Yoruba Warrior?," *Premium Times*, January 23, 2021, https://www.premiumtimesng.com/regional/ssouth-west/438195-yoruba-herders-clash-who-is-sunday-igboho-the-self-titled-yoruba-warrior.html.

3. Olufemi Makinde, "Oodua Republic: Yoruba Hunters' Group Vows to Arrest Secessionists," *The Whistler*, September 15, 2020, https://thewhistler.ng/oodua-republic-yoruba-hunters-group-vows-to-arrest-secessionists/.

4. Other groups either planned a rally or spoke about declaring a new republic on that day. See Dayo Johnson et al., "Oduduwa Republic Oct 1 Rally Divides Yoruba Leaders," *Vanguard*, September 7, 2020, https://www.vanguardngr.com/2020/09/oduduwa-republic-oct-1-rally-divides-yoruba-leaders/. See also Kazeem Olalekan Israel, "Sunday Igboho and the Farce of Oduduwa Republic," *Business Day*, March 24, 2021, https://businessday.ng/opinion/article/sunday-igboho-and-the-farce-of-oduduwa-republic/.

5. Facetv Africa, "We Want Oduduwa Republic. Sunday Igboho and His Loyal Boys Continue Peacful [*sic*] Rally in Ibadan," YouTube, October 1, 2020, https://www.youtube.com/watch?v=_nq75ncEajI.

6. This is my translation of the interview, which was conducted in Yoruba, "Wow!!! Aare Ona Kakanfo [Chief Gani Adams] Replies Sunday Igboho," January 19, 2021, https://www.youtube.com/watch?v=ElqWxpdEf8k (emphasis added). See also Olufemi Olaniyi, "Islamic Leaders Boycott Oduduwa Republic Rally, Gani Adams Tackles Igboho," *Punch*, October 4, 2020, https://punchng.com/islamic-leaders-boycott-oduduwa-republic-rally-gani-adams-tackles-igboho/ (emphasis added); Adejumo Kabir, "Yoruba Nation: Gani Adams Criticises Sunday Igboho's 'Wrong Methods,'" *Premium Times*, July 8, 2021, https://www.premiumtimesng.com/news/top-news/472326-yoruba-nation-gani-adams-criticises-sunday-igbohos-wrong-methods.html; Fikayo Olowolagba, "Why I Didn't Join Sunday Igboho for Yoruba Nation Rally—Gani Adams," *Daily Post*, July 13, 2021, https://dailypost.ng/2021/07/13/why-i-didnt-join-sunday-igboho-for-yoruba-nation-rally-gani-adams/.

7. Recall that a university teacher had described Adams, six years before he was installed as the *Kakanfò*, as "our father." See chap. 3.

8. Marruf Olanrewaju, telephone interview with the author, January 28, 2021.

9. Mike Ozekhome, "Is Buhari Really President of All and for No One?," *Sun*, September 19, 2018, https://www.sunnewsonline.com/is-buhari-really-president-of-all-and-for-no-one/; Chido Nwangwu, "Buhari's 'Animal Farm' and Terrorism at the NDA," *ThisDay*, August 27, 2021, https://www.thisdaylive.com/index.php/2021/08/27/buharis-animal-farm-and-terrorism-at-the-nda/; Adeshina Peter, "President Buhari's Ethnocentric Image Is His Fault," *Will*, October 15, 2017, https://thewillnigeria.com/opinion-president-buharis-ethnocentric-image-is-his-fault/.

10. A kakistocracy is a government in which the worst people are in charge. The earliest use of the word dates to the seventeenth century in Paul Gosnold's *A Sermon Preached at the Publique Fast the Ninth Day of Aug. 1644 at St. Marie.*

11. Olasunkanmi Akinlotan, "Why We Want to Break Away from Nigeria—Yoruba Group Writes Buhari," *Premium Times*, August 14, 2022, https://www.premiumtimesng.com/news/top-news/548638-why-we-want-to-break-away-from-nigeria-yoruba-group-writes-buhari.html.

12. Ibid. See also Dayo Johnson et al., "S/West Secession Letter to Buhari Divides Yoruba Leaders," *Vanguard*, September 4, 2022, https://www.vanguardngr.com/2022/09/s-west-secession-letter-to-buhari-divides-yoruba-leaders/.

13. Faruk Shuaibu, "The Untold Story of Controversial Yoruba Youth Leader Sunday Igboho," *Daily Trust*, January 26, 2021, https://dailytrust.com/the-untold-story-of-controversial-yoruba-youth-leader-sunday-igboho.

14. See Isaac Olawale Albert, "Ife-Modakeke Crisis," in *Community Conflict in Nigeria: Management, Resolution and Transformation*, ed. Onigu Otite and Isaac Olawale Albert (Ibadan: Spectrum Books, 1999), 12–22.

15. Presidential adviser Senator Babafemi Ojudu published a piece alleging that he organized a meeting between Igboho and Governor Bola Tinubu, who gave the former money to dissuade him from working with the PDP to cause trouble during the elections in Ekiti State. In response, Igboho denied ever meeting Ojudu or taking money from Tinubu. See Babafemi Ojudu, "ENCOUNTER: The Sunday Igboho I Knew," *Premium Times*, January 25, 2021, https://www.premiumtimesng.com/features-and-interviews/438570-encounter-the-sunday-igboho-i-knew-by-babafemi-ojudu.html; Jemilar Nasiru, "Ojudu Shares Details of Tinubu's 'Secret Meeting' with Sunday Igboho in 2009," *Cable News*, January 25, 2021, https://www.thecable.ng/ojudu-shares-details-of-tinubus-secret-meeting-with-sunday-igboho-in-2009; Samuel Oamen, "I Don't Know You, Sunday Igboho Disowns Ojudu," *Nation*, January 26, 2021, https://thenationonlineng.net/i-dont-know-you-sunday-igboho-disowns-ojudu/.

16. Adeola Badru, "Don't Demonize Sunday Igboho, Akintola Warns Makinde," *Vanguard*, March 1, 2021, https://www.vanguardngr.com/2021/03/dont-demonize-sunday-igboho-akintola-warns-makinde/. For videos of Igboho's rally at Igangan, see Kilarigbo Live, "Tension: Sunday Igboho Finally Chased Fulani Away as Promised from Ibarapa Land after 7-Days," YouTube, January 22, 2021, https://www.youtube.com/watch?v=XqwEE2CyWZA; Objectv Media, "Sunday Igboho Leads Crowd in Oyo to Protest against Fulani Invaders," YouTube, January 22, 2021, https://www.youtube.com/watch?v=tIhXhtoAxWE.

17. Badru, "Don't Demonize Sunday Igboho."

18. Bisi Oladele et al., "IGP under Fire over Sunday Igboho Arrest Order," *Nation*, January 24, 2021, https://thenationonlineng.net/igp-under-fire-over-sunday-igboho-arrest-order/.

19. Quoted in ibid. (emphasis added). For the tweet, see @realFFK, January 22, 2021, https://twitter.com/realFFK/status/1352639745160081412.

20. Badru, "Don't Demonize Sunday Igboho."

21. Dapo Akinrefon and Ola Ajayi, "I'm Ready to Lead Battle against Killer Herdsmen—Gani Adams," *Vanguard*, July 4, 2018, https://www.vanguardngr.com/2018/07/im-ready-lead-battle-killer-herdsmen-gani-adams/.

22. Ibid.

23. Friday Olokor, "Yoruba can Defend Themselves against Killer Herdsmen—Gani Adams," *Punch*, February 9, 2018, https://punchng.com/yoruba-can-defend-themselves-against-killer-herdsmen-gani-adams/.

24. Subsequently, Adams was louder about the popular calls for Yorùbá secession or self-determination. See Segun Kasali, "Yorubas Have Metamorphosed from Restructuring to Self-determination, Says Gani Adams," *Nigerian Tribune*, April 7, 2021, https://tribuneonlineng.com/yorubas-have-metamorphosed-from-restructuring-to-self-determination-says-gani-adams/; Dapo Akinrefon, "Secession: Clamour for Oodua Republic Is Long Overdue—Gani Adams," *Vanguard*, March 29, 2021, https://www.vanguardngr.com/2021/03/secession-clamour-for-oodua-republic-is-long-overdue-gani-adams/; Sahara Reporters, "Yoruba Nation: Gani Adams Says No Going Back on Call for Oduduwa Republic," April 1, 2021, http://saharareporters.com/2021/04/01/yoruba-nation-gani-adams-says-no-going-back-call-oduduwa-republic; Ifeoluwa Adediran, "Yorubas Have 'Graduated from Restructuring to Self-determination'—Gani Adams," *Premium Times*, April 14, 2021, https://www.premiumtimesng.com/news/top-news/455174-yorubas-have-graduated-from-restructuring-to-self-determination-gani-adams.html.

25. John Campbell, "Yoruba Debate 'Restructuring' of Nigeria or 'Autonomy,'" Council on Foreign Relations blog, April 16, 2021, https://www.cfr.org/blog/yoruba-debate-restructuring-nigeria-or-autonomy.

26. Adediran, "Yorubas Have 'Graduated.'"

27. Campbell, "Yoruba Debate."

28. Some members of Adams's OPC in Oyo State, in turn, announced their readiness to take on the alleged criminals if given a go-ahead by Adams. See Objectv Media, "Fulani Bandits: We're Everywhere & Ready, Only Need Aare Gani Adam's Orders—OPC Warriors, Feb 5, 2021," YouTube, February 5, 2021, https://www.youtube.com/watch?v=Rta482ecKlo.

29. Sunday Adebayo, telephone interview with the author, January 24, 2021.

30. Victor Ogunje, "Fayemi Meets Adams over South-West Security," *ThisDay*, March 17, 2021, https://www.thisdaylive.com/index.php/2021/03/17/fayemi-meets-adams-over-south-west-security/.

31. Rotimi Agboluaje, "Makinde, Gani Adams in Closed-Door Meeting over Insecurity," *Guardian*, March 19, 2021, https://guardian.ng/news/makinde-gani-adams-in-closed-door-meeting-over-insecurity/. See also Yinka Adeniran, "Makinde, Gani Adams in Closed Door Meeting," *Nation*, March 19, 2021, https://thenationonlineng.net/makinde-gani-adams-in-closed-door-meeting/.

32. Oamen Samuel, "Why I Didn't Accept IGP's Invitation Letters, by Sunday Igboho," *Nation*, April 2, 2021, https://thenationonlineng.net/why-i-didnt-accept-igps

-invitation-letters-by-sunday-igboho/; *Punch*, "IGP under Pressure to Arrest Igboho as Activist Snubs Police Invitation," April 3, 2021, https://punchng.com/ig-under-pressure-to-arrest-igboho-as-activist-snubs-police-invitation/.

33. Adejumo Kabir, "2023: Sunday Igboho Threatens Ambitious Yoruba Politicians in Video," *Premium Times*, March 1, 2021, https://www.premiumtimesng.com/news/top-news/445972-2023-sunday-igboho-threatens-ambitious-yoruba-politicians-in-video.html.

34. Adeola Badru, "We Don't Want One Nigeria Again, but Yoruba Nation—Sunday Igboho," *Vanguard*, March 17, 2021, https://www.vanguardngr.com/2021/03/we-dont-want-one-nigeria-again-but-yoruba-nation-sunday-igboho/.

35. Ibid.

36. Stephen Adebanji Akintoye, *The History of the Yoruba People* (Dakar: Amalion, 2010).

37. Kilarigbo Live, "Sunday Igboho Declares Yoruba Nation," YouTube, March 19, 2021, https://www.youtube.com/watch?v=hox22us3eLo. See also BBC, "Sunday Igboho: Nigerians React as Activist Call for 'Yoruba Nation,'" March 19, 2021, https://www.bbc.com/pidgin/tori-56453558.

38. Adebayo, telephone interview with the author, May 20, 2021.

39. He said that the *Aláàfin* of Oyo had instructed him not to "mention anyone's name." For more on the *Aláàfin*, see chap. 4.

40. See "High Tension in Bourdillon as Gani Adams Blasts & Expose Bola Tinubu Deadly Secrets and 2023 Ambition," YouTube, May 19, 2021, https://www.youtube.com/CN9BCw2riuk. Perhaps as a result of some peace initiatives, this YouTube link has been taken down. For others containing some parts of Adams's criticism of Tinubu and Igboho, see GistMediaTV, "IBA Gani Adams Reveals What Could Happen to Tinubu as He Expøses Those Who Betrayed MKO Abiola," June 3, 2021, https://www.youtube.com/watch?v=ZS3XrLz3Ojw. See also Kilarigbo Live, "Gani Adams Fires Back at Tinubu Endorses Oduduwa Nation," September 12, 2020, https://www.youtube.com/watch?v=wF89EtHH3ok&t=47s; OganlaTV, "Gani Adams Blast Bola Ahmed Tinubu for Not Supporting Oduduwa Republic," September 12, 2020, https://www.youtube.com/watch?v=wF89EtHH3ok.

41. Ibid. (my translation).

42. My translation.

43. *Elédà* is central to the Yorùbá concept of God as the "maker" or "creator" of human beings. Depending on the context, it could mean one's creator (i.e., *Olodumare*—God) or one's guardian spirit. It is also used interchangeably in some contexts with *orí* (head/creator). See Molefi Kete Asante, "Eleda," in *Encyclopedia of African Religion*, ed. Molefi Kete Asante and Ama Mazama (Thousand Oaks, CA: Sage, 2009). For a more complex interrogation of *orí* in relation to the concept of *àṣúwàdá*, see Olatunde Bayo Lawuyi, "Orí, Ayé and the Ontogeny of Society," *Journal of Contemporary African Studies* 39, no. 3 (2021): 353–63; A. Akiwowo, "Asuwada Eniyan," *Ife: Annals of the Institute of Cultural Studies* 1 (1986): 113–23; and Olatuni Bayo

Lawuyi and Olufemi Taiwo, "Towards an African Sociological Tradition: A Rejoinder to Akiwowo and Makinde," *International Sociology* 5, no. 1 (1990): 57–73.

44. My translation.

45. Italics added.

46. Kilarigbo Live, "Sunday Igboho Explains Why He's Angry," YouTube, May 20, 2021, https://www.youtube.com/watch?v=iDrNGIQjFXQ.

47. My translation.

48. Ibid.

49. See Isokan Omo Oodua TV, "Live Interview," Facebook, May 19, 2021, https://m.facebook.com/isokanomoooduatv/videos/403387390629022/.

50. Ibid.

51. See chap. 4 on Adams's relationships with President Jonathan and Governors Tinubu and Daniel.

52. Ibid.

53. For two examples, see Gbedu WakaAbout, "(Serious Warning)"; T.O.E Tv News 1, "Gani Adams Come Over Here. You're Too Jealous Kilode. Ani Adams Come," Facebook, May 20, 2021, https://www.facebook.com/watch/?v=295778231943589.

54. Adejumo Kabir and Nasir Ayitogo, "SSS Confirms Invading Sunday Igboho's House, Killing Two," *Premium Times*, July 1, 2021, https://www.premiumtimesng.com/news/top-news/471136-just-in-sss-confirms-invading-sunday-igbohos-house-killing-two.html.

55. Ibid.

56. See SaharaTV, "Sunday Igboho's House Attacked Again," YouTube, July 1, 2021, https://www.youtube.com/watch?v=6woFYgEVgZo.

57. Ibid.

58. The DSS has a pattern of either hijacking police and other security agencies' primary responsibilities or even committing acts of "impunity" (Iyobosa Uwugiaren et al., "Ending Impunity, Osinbajo Sacks DSS DG, Lawal Daura," *ThisDay*, August 8, 2018, https://www.thisdaylive.com/index.php/2018/08/08/ending-impunity-osinbajo-sacks-dss-dg-lawal-daura/), including illegal invasions and blockage—even of the National Assembly. This escalated under the Buhari administration, particularly under Lawal Daura and the leadership of the DSS. See also Sani Tukur, "Osinbajo Sacks Lawal Daura as SSS DG," *Premium Times*, August 7, 2018, https://www.premiumtimesng.com/news/headlines/279192-osinbajo-sacks-lawal-daura-as-sss-dg.html.

59. Oluwole Ige, "Igboho Accuses DSS of Planting Arms in His House, Says 'I Use Charms, Not Guns,'" *Nigerian Tribune*, July 3, 2021, https://tribuneonlineng.com/igboho-accuses-sss-of-planting-arms-in-his-house-says-i-use-charms-not-guns/.

60. Oyindamola Olubajo, "'I Was Indoors When Soldiers, SSS Attacked My Residence'—Sunday Igboho," *Peoples Gazette*, July 1, 2021, https://gazettengr.com/i-was-indoors-when-soldiers-sss-attacked-my-residence-sunday-igboho/.

61. Ige, "Igboho Accuses DSS."

62. Sodiq Oyeleke, "Court Awards N20bn Damages against DSS for Raiding Igboho's House," *Punch*, September 17, 2021, https://punchng.com/breaking-court-awards-n20bn-damages-against-dss-for-raiding-igbohos-house/.

63. Dapo Akinrefon, "Sunday Igboho to Spend 6 More Months in Benin Prison," *Vanguard*, February 7, 2022, https://www.vanguardngr.com/2022/02/sunday-igboho-to-spend-6-more-months-in-benin-prison/.

64. Nwokoye Mpi, "Nigeria-Benin: Sunday Igboho's Legal Woes Could Reignite Border Battle," *Africa Report*, August 26, 2021, https://www.theafricareport.com/118157/nigeria-benin-sunday-igbohos-legal-woes-could-reignite-border-battle/.

65. Igboho, personal communication, March 9, 2023, Cotonou, Republic of Benin.

66. Dapo Akinrefon, "Benin Republic 'Releases' Sunday Igboho," *Vanguard*, March 7, 2022, https://www.vanguardngr.com/2022/03/breaking-benin-republic-releases-sunday-igboho/. Adeniran later resigned from the Akintoye-led Ilana Omo Oodua, first in November 2022—he was later persuaded against it and elected the leader of the group in place of Akintoye, who voluntarily left the position—and again in January 2023. See Kunle Daramola, "Cracks in Yoruba Nation Movement as Akintoye's Deputy Resigns," *Cable*, November 7, 2022, https://www.thecable.ng/cracks-in-yoruba-nation-movement-as-akintoyes-deputy-resigns; Seye Olumide and Rotimi Agboluaje, "Second Ilana Omo Oodua Leader Resigns in 34 Days," *Guardian*, January 8, 2023, https://guardian.ng/news/second-ilana-omo-oodua-leader-resigns-in-34-days/; *Sahara Reporters*, "Prof Akintoye's Successor, Adeniran Resigns as Leader of Yoruba Self-Determination Organisation, Ilana Omo Oodua Amid Fraud Allegations," January 7, 2023, https://saharareporters.com/2023/01/07/breaking-prof-akintoyes-successor-adeniran-resigns-leader-yoruba-self-determination.

67. Akinrefon, "Benin Republic 'Releases' Sunday Igboho."

68. Dapo Akinrefon, "Sunday Igboho's Release, Victory for Self-determination—Afenifere," *Vanguard*, March 7, 2022, https://www.vanguardngr.com/2022/03/sunday-igbohos-release-victory-for-self-determination-afenifere/.

69. It appeared that the Beninese authorities were waiting for Nigeria's president, Buhari, to leave office on May 29, 2023, before allowing Igboho to leave the country. The Buhari administration had failed to secure his repatriation to Nigeria (Idowu Abdullahi, "Sunday Igboho Regains Freedom in Benin after Two Years," *Punch*, October 8, 2023, https://punchng.com/sunday-igboho-regains-freedom-in-benin-after-two-years/). Chief Ayo Adebanjo, the leader of the Yorùbá political group *Afenifere* told me during a visit to his home in Lagos in August 2023—where I first learned that Igboho would be allowed to leave Benin soon—that some prominent Yoruba, including a former head of state and an internationally respected writer, had persuaded the Beninese government against granting the request of the Buhari administration. The Yoruba-Beninese community also weighed in on this, as some of the people I met in Cotonou during my trip in March 2023 revealed. A source close to Igboho had told *Vanguard* in March 2022 that "it is in [Igboho's] best interest to remain in the Benin Republic for now because we don't trust the [Buhari] Government" (Dapo Akinrefon, "Why Sunday Igboho Can't Leave Benin Republic—Source," *Vanguard*, March

9, 2022). Five months after President Bola Tinubu succeeded Buhari, Igboho was allowed to leave the Republic of Benin to join his family in Germany. See Oluwole Ige, "I'm Now Free to Return Home—Sunday Igboho," *Nigerian Tribune*, October 8, 2023, https://tribuneonlineng.com/im-now-free-to-return-home-sunday-igboho/; Ebunoluwa Olafusi, "Lawyer: Igboho Released by Benin Republic, Now in Germany," *Cable*, October 9, 2023, https://www.thecable.ng/lawyer-igboho-released-by-benin-republic-now-in-germany#google_vignette.

70. Dapo Akinrefon, "Wole Soyinka Not Involved in Sunday Igboho's Release—Counsel," *Vanguard*, March 8, 2022, https://www.vanguardngr.com/2022/03/wole-soyinka-not-involved-in-sunday-igbohos-release-counsel/.

71. See Chiamaka Okafor, "Soyinka Advises Nigerian Govt on Sunday Igboho," *Premium Times*, July 6, 2021, https://www.premiumtimesng.com/regional/ssouth-west/471927-soyinka-advises-nigerian-govt-on-sunday-igboho.html.

72. Dapo Akinrefon and Olasunkanmi Akoni, "Why Soyinka Visited Sunday Igboho—Sources," *Vanguard*, May 3, 2022, https://www.vanguardngr.com/2022/05/why-soyinka-visited-sunday-igboho-sources/.

73. Gbenga Adeniji, "Release Igboho to Continue His Journey, Soyinka Tells Benin Republic," *Punch*, August 27, 2021, https://punchng.com/breaking-release-igboho-to-continue-his-journey-soyinka-tells-benin-republic/; Sahara Reporters, "Release Sunday Igboho to Continue His Journey—Soyinka Tells Benin Republic," New York, August 27, 2021. https://saharareporters.com/2021/08/27/release-sunday-igboho-continue-his-journey-%E2%80%93-soyinka-tells-benin-republic.

74. Sahara Reporters, "Let's Help Igboho Though He Abused Us—Gani Adams Appeals to South-West Governors, Ooni, Others," July 7, 2021, https://saharareporters.com/2021/07/07/lets-help-igboho-though-he-abused-us%E2%80%94gani-adams-appeals-south-west-governors-ooni-others.

75. Ibid.

76. Dapo Akinrefon, "Gani Adams to Beninese Govt: Allow Sunday Igboho Seek Proper Medical Treatment Abroad," *Vanguard*, March 8, 2022, https://www.vanguardngr.com/2022/03/gani-adams-to-beninese-govt-allow-sunday-igboho-seek-proper-medical-treatment-abroad/.

77. *Premium Times*, "How Sunday Igboho Can Be Released—Gani Adams," February 9, 2022, https://www.premiumtimesng.com/news/more-news/510521-how-sunday-igboho-can-be-released-gani-adams.html.

78. Ibid. See also Bola Badmus, "Gani Adams to Buhari: Effect Release of Sunday Igboho, Kanu from Detention," *Nigerian Tribune*, January 13, 2022, https://tribuneonlineng.com/gani-adams-to-buhari-effect-release-of-sunday-igboho-kanu-from-detention/.

79. An online search shows that Triune Biblical University is based in North Bend, Washington (though a Nigerian newspaper reported wrongly that it is based in Brooklyn, New York). Its main campus in Nigeria is based in Isolo/Okota in Lagos. However, the university has many satellite campuses in Nigeria, one in another part of Lagos (Badagry) and three in other states (Ekiti, Ondo, and Oyo States). The

Nigerian campus claims to offer "Worldwide Associate, Bachelor, Master and Doctorate degrees in Biblical Studies, Christian Education, Christian Counseling. Missiology and Divinity." See https://www.tbuworldwide.com/ and https://www.tbuworldwide.com/NigerianCampus.php.

80. See Henry Tyohemba, "Sunday Igboho Bags Honorary Degree from US Varsity," *Leadership*, November 3, 2022, https://leadership.ng/sunday-igboho-bags-honorary-degree-from-us-varsity/; Francis Ugwu, "Sunday Igboho Bags Honorary Doctorate Degree in War Studies from US Varsity," *Daily Post*, November 2, 2022, https://dailypost.ng/2022/11/02/sunday-igboho-bags-honorary-doctorate-degree-in-war-studies-from-us-varsity/.

81. *Vanguard*, "Sunday Igboho Bags Honorary Doctorate Degree in U.S.," November 3, 2022, https://www.vanguardngr.com/2022/11/sunday-igboho-bags-honorary-doctorate-degree-in-u-s/.

82. See SP Media Tv, "Chief Sunday Igboho Blow Hot after Receiving Doctorate Degree of Peace and Security Management," YouTube, November 2, 2022, https://www.youtube.com/watch?v=ums3phcoU5g; Super Media, "Dr. Igboho Congratulations Sir," YouTube, November 1, 2022, https://www.youtube.com/watch?v=2_oEoLoZ4Lo.

Coda

BECOMING AND BEING

No matter how long Gani Adams lasts as the key figure among the champions of the struggle for self-determination for the Yorùbá, and whether the Yorùbá succeed in creating a nation-state of their own outside the current Nigerian federation, there is no doubt that his status as an eminent person in (Southwest) Nigeria or in the imagined new nation and beyond is assured. He has successfully mobilized his initial subaltern agency and subjectivity, to paraphrase Francis Nyamnjoh, to manipulate himself into a position of abundance.[1] In part, the intensely sustained mediation and mediatization enfolding Adams's social biography reflect and are reflected in his current position of abundance—material, cultural, and aesthetic, among others.[2] This points to one of the important conclusions of the ultimate theorist of subalternity, Antonio Gramsci: in the end, "the subaltern becomes an individual subject [*il subelterno*]" because "to be 'subaltern' one must be 'leading' [*dirigente*], 'responsible' and a 'protagonist.'"[3]

A recent letter Adams sent to António Manuel de Oliveira Guterres, the secretary-general of the United Nations (UNSG), on his letterhead with his personal coat of arms as the fifteenth *Ààrẹ Ọ̀nà Kakaǹfò*, demonstrates how eminent Adams has become and how much of a "responsible leader" and "protagonist" he considers himself to be. The coat of arms is expected to indicate his "full heraldic achievements," as it did for the European nobility among whom the practice emerged in the twelfth century. Apart from the coat of arms, the letter also contains all the marks of Adams's distinction: "Bsc, DPA, FCIA, D.Litt, LFICWLS, WWCCA." In the letter, dated June 14, 2022, under the title "Avoiding a Replica of the Bosnian War in Nigeria," Adams greets the

UNSG, on behalf of "the more than 60 million Yoruba people in South-West Nigeria and across the world," as he alerts him to the fact that "things are no longer normal in Nigeria." He warned Guterres that "what happened in the defunct Yugoslavia that led to the balkanisation of that country is becoming like a child's play in Nigeria" because, among other reasons, "the Fulani in Northern Nigeria are now engaged in a war of attrition all over the country." He cautioned that, given that the Fulani are "gradually moving to down to the South" and the southerners are "determined to engage them," Nigeria might be consumed in a "full scale war." Adams added that "ironically, Nigeria's President [Mohammadu Buhari] is a Fulani." The four-page letter lists "evidence" of the "aggressive killing agenda" and concludes by asking the "United Nations to escalate this danger to a global concern."

The letter, containing some simplifications of the national crises in Nigeria and the security challenges that have overwhelmed the administration of President Buhari, was also Adams's way of reaffirming himself as the "supreme guardian" of Yorùbá interests and the "ultimate protector" of his people. It was also an affirmation of his power to take the concerns of the Yorùbá to the head of the global organization.

In December 2011, a journalist who later became one of his chiefs, Shola Oshunkeye, asked Adams, "When you started people were saying [']this *young boy, this illiterate*, what could he teach us[?'] But *before everybody's eyes, you became a phenomenon*. How did you do it?"[4]

I have tried to answer this important question in this book. It is apposite here, though, to reflect, again, on Adams's response to the specific question about the transformation of the life of "an unknown quantity,"[5] one dismissed as "a young boy [and] illiterate," to a life at the acme of power and influence. His response reflects his understanding of his own subjectivity in history, and his reflexivity—especially regarding his ascendancy—which, as Margaret S. Archer says, "mediate[s] the role that objective structural or cultural powers play in influencing social action." Adams said,

> I think that is the normal way of speaking for human beings. When Jesus Christ started his miracles, from when he was just 12, *people did not take him serious[ly]*. People only began to take him serious[ly] when he turned 30. Unfortunately, he died at 33 years. *I am not relating myself to Jesus Christ*. I'm just trying to make an example. Anthony Enahoro [late elder statesman] moved the motion for Nigeria's independence in 1954 at the age of 23 years. General Yakubu Gowon became Head of State at 29 in 1966. Even [President] Obasanjo became Head of States in 1976, he was just 39 years. Most of the governors . . . became governors at less than 40 years. . . . So, how can you see

> someone who joined the struggle at the age of 23, and you will not take him serious[ly]? I am 17 years in the struggle. . . . *Even if somebody were a dullard, his brain would have changed all this while to become brilliant* because we meet people everyday. We listen to many people everyday. We do research everyday. We have challenges everyday, and we solve them well. *All these things build you for future to become what you are.*[6]

This kind of narrative of the legitimacy of his belongingness to an *achieved status*, self-praise,[7] and his defense of why and how he has managed to maintain this status represent, to use Pamela J. Stewart and Andrew Strathern's words, "historical consciousness and its permutations, and therefore strongly affect, as well as reflect intensions and agency."[8] It also points to how he has successfully mobilized and combined the duality of public history ("concerning a whole ethnic group")[9] with his own personal history, a history that is not only "subject to distortions"[10] but also concerned chiefly with personal interests.

The preceding chapters address the journalist's lay question about how Adams became "a phenomenon" by rendering it as two related scholarly questions: (1) How can the subaltern transform themselves into the elite? and (2) What are the processes by which strategic improvisers in the lower classes (can potentially) maneuver themselves into the upper reaches of society (and the state)? The Gani Adams case, I think, provides a compelling example of how to address these questions—with potentials for comparative studies of similar cases in Nigeria, and in the African continent, particularly through the problematization of, as Richard Werbner puts it, "the personal, the political and the moral" during a period of remarkable postcolonial transformations.[11] This is especially so in the quest to understand how young people in Africa turn precarity into opportunity by, paradoxically, transforming the generalized "absence of conventional avenues for self-realization"[12] that they face in the late twentieth and early twenty-first centuries into a means of self-actualization.

Potential comparative examples in Nigeria would include the leading Niger Delta "retired" militants who, initially, through the agency of violence and the struggle for "resource control," became prominent and powerful actors at the state and federal levels, and are now superrich Big Men. For many years, these militants, including Mujahid Dokubo-Asari (Niger Delta People's Volunteer Force, NDPVF), Ateke Tom (Niger Delta Vigilante, NDV), Government Ekpemupolo Tompolo (Emancipation of the Niger Delta, MEND), Victor Ebikabowei Ben "Boyloaf" (Movement for the Emancipation of the Niger Delta, MEND), Bibopre Ajube "General Shoot-at-Sight" (Movement for the Emancipation of the Niger Delta, MEND), and 'General' John Togo (Niger Delta Liberation Force, NDLF), took up arms against the state, with the groups being involved in hostage taking, pipelines sabotage, and generally making it difficult for the Nigerian state and the multinational oil companies to extract oil from the Niger Delta region—with oil production at a point in 2011 well under half of the installed capacity of 2.5 million barrels per day.[13] For their acts of insurrection and sabotage, these men were hunted by the state and its agencies—and fought against one another.[14]

After accepting the amnesty offer by President Musa Yar'Adua in 2009, the Niger Delta militants—the "once . . . fearless warlord[s] in the creeks of the Niger Delta; . . . freedom fighter[s] and liberator[s] of [their] people"[15]—have all become truly Big Men and millionaire or even billionaires.[16] As *Daily Trust* reports, "Few years ago, they were seen as wanted men disrupting the flow of oil in the Niger Delta by attacking oil facilities, security personnel and other symbols of authority. But even then, [they] were seeing themselves as the champions of their marginalised people." Since then, they have acquired, though primarily through the contracts for the protection of oil pipelines, but also through other forms of political patronage and business opportunities. Like Adams, the ex-Niger Delta militants have also been involved in mobilizing for elections on behalf of politicians, while changing political patrons at will—depending on the political climate in their states and at the federal level.[17] To draw three illustrations of their transformation, Atake Tom has been crowned a king in his hometown,[18] Dokubo-Asari has established a private university in the Republic of Benin,[19] while Ajube "now commands the economy, wages war against poverty, fights unemployment and creates opportunities for jobless youths in the Niger Delta region."[20]

—~—

A comparative example outside of Nigeria is the case of Julius Malema, the South African activist turned politician, a man, who like Adams, "hurried his way to the top."[21] Malema is the former president of the African National Congress Youth League (ANCYL), a member of Parliament, and the president and commander in chief of the Economic Freedom Fighters, a South African political party, which he founded in July 2013. The use of the title of president and of martial titles (that is, commander in chief and generalissimo/field marshal) by both Adams and Malema is striking. Fiona Forde notes that in 2006, Malema "graduated from youth politics to the big league" without turning back. In this new status, Forde notes further, "[Malema] developed a sense of self-importance that far outweighed his station in life and an arrogance that cost many people their standing" in the party, as he became "a sharp political blade."[22]

There are other parallels between Adams's meteoric rise and Malema's. Malema, who was described as "tactically clever and politically street-smart when it comes to the disaffected youth,"[23] also experienced a rags-to-riches transformation from the poverty-stricken Masakaneng in Seshego township, where he was raised by a single parent, to the membership of the South African Parliament and considerable personal wealth. His mother was a domestic worker. He started out on his political journey as a kid removing the racist National Party posters on behalf of the African National Congress (ANC)[24] and was later elected chair of the Youth League branch in Seshego and, a few years later, the national president of the Congress of South African Students (COSAS). This was followed by his election as the president of the African ANCYL. Malema's charismatic leadership of the youth in the ANC under the patronage of President Jacob Zuma ultimately turned him into such a big man that he eventually clashed with his patron. With a rhetoric as fiery as Adams's, using the constant invocation of violence as an accepted way of settling social, economic, and political disputes,[25] Malema, who now wears a US$17,000 Breitling watch, later led his followers out of the ANC to form the Economic Freedom Fighters (EFF). From his subaltern status in Seshego to his home in upmarket Sandton, Johannesburg (one of two reported multimillion-rand homes where he holds court),[26] Malema lives a life of indulgence and abundance: "Parties are held at the trendiest clubs in Johannesburg, where there is no limit to the consumption of Johnnie Walker Black Label whisky and Veuve Clicquot French champagne. He . . . is always seen in expensive cars, from BMWs to Lexus's to Mercedes Benz's."[27]

The ways in which Gani Adams and Julius Malema creatively intertwine "the personal and the public, the moral and the political" constitute grounds for further comparative examination. This is particularly the case given both men's "newly acquired capacity to project, for a greater audience in a wider political arena, a consciousness—and conscience . . . of history,"[28] despite the controversial ways in which both have mobilized ethno-regional history (in the case of Adams) and ethno-racial history (in the case of Malema) in their political lives. Thus, between the transformations of the president of the Oodua People's Congress (OPC) and Yorùbá generalissimo and of the president and commander in chief of the EFF from subalterns to elites—which included their somewhat "playful self-fashioning" through titles[29]—lies important perspectives about aestheticized self-making, youth and social maturation, (*personalized*) social transformation, ethno-racial relations, and political mobilization around identities in contemporary Africa.

—ꟽ—

In examining how to *become*, as well as how to *be*, a big man in a contemporary African state and society, I have analyzed Adams's beginning as a "firebrand" who was committed to laying down his life for the cause of his people—what he described as a struggle for "self-determination," which included regional autonomy, justice, equity, democracy, good governance, and, possibly, separation of the Yorùbá country from the Nigerian state. This struggle consumed his everyday life. In the course of the endeavor, however, he was forced to reflect on and examine his own life and his location in the general order of things. This book argues that this process produced *ideological* self-examination and *material* (both in a critical sense and in financial terms) self-examination of his social circumstances. The conclusions Adams reached led to the morphing of the sociopolitical pursuit of collective self-determination for the Yorùbá people and personal *self*-determination that helped to propel him to the top of the social ladder. I follow Margaret S. Archer in suggesting that the questions raised about the whole range of Adams's actions in society cannot be answered without serious reference to his reflexivity because "*the subjective powers of reflexivity mediate the role that objective structural or cultural powers play in influencing social action and are thus indispensable to explaining social outcomes.*"[30]

By using his reflexivity to mediate the structural and cultural constraint and enablement of his age, the man *of* the people has emerged as the man *and* his people—a man who is both distinguished *among* his people (the Yorùbá) and distinguishable *from* his people (particularly the young and the subaltern). The man who has worked hard to create a paradise for the masses, has, in the process, also created a paradise for himself—thus becoming and being a man of high visibility and relative wealth.

The Adams case thus encourages us to deepen our reflection on action, agency, and reflexivity, particularly in the "context of uncertainty and disorder which characterise many parts of Africa—and elsewhere," as Boel Berner has argued.[31] This reflection, which Africanist scholars have engaged in, encourages an examination of a public anthropology of actually existing societies in Africa, particularly through the social biography of individuals or groups of individuals who constitute "special and vital parts of a greater whole."[32] In light of the foregoing analysis of Adams's combination of deliberate[33] and emergent strategies,[34] his personal and sociocultural projects provide us with a telling and potentially comparative case of how to be(come) a big man in the contemporary postcolony.

BE(COM)ING A BIG MAN IN AFRICA

Rather than merely being a social scientific gloss, the term *big man* (*eeyan nla*, or *eni nla*; also meaning important person—often man—or person of consequence) is a vernacular concept among the Yorùbá.[35] It is a word or phenomenon that lends itself to easy translation. Beyond Yorubaland, in most parts of Africa, the word, phrase, or concept is part of everyday vocabulary.

In this section, I engage the extant literature on the big man in order to draw out my take on the concept both in the context of the purchase it has on the Yorùbá case and in terms of its value for understanding the Adams phenomenon.

The genealogy of the popularity of the concept of "big man" in the literature is often traced to Marshall Sahlins.[36] Though Sahlins did not invent the concept, his clarification and elaboration of the big man as a heuristic device for understanding observed social phenomenon in Melanesian societies popularized it in the discipline of anthropology. While I will not go into too much detail about the rich and interesting literature on the big man in anthropology[37]—particularly in relation to more recent literature on the same in Africanist political science and sociology[38]—it is important to briefly elaborate Sahlins's original articulation of this conceptual model or ideal type in his landmark work, given the way in which contemporary Africanist political science and sociology have turned it into a tool of caricature in their analysis of the postcolonial socioeconomic and political process. In fact, I would suggest that the concept seems to have reached an intellectual cul-de-sac in its usage in Africanist political science as a means to dismiss political leaders (as corrupt, prebendal, clientelist, patrimonial, etc.) rather than to explain the complicated and nuanced relationships between a wide range of leaders and their constituents.[39] Here, partly because I am using the concept of Big Man to describe not a political leader but a cultural leader—and his processes of social achievement and personal transformation—I think I avoid the pathologizing limitations of this term's use in contemporary Africanist political science. If this take legitimizes the usage, I will go as far as to wager that Gani Adams himself will agree with me that he is a "big man."

I further suggest that much of the contemporary Africanist political and sociological literature embraces the approach to the Big Man exemplified by M. Godelier,[40] who argued that "typical for the 'Big-Man' is . . . his participation in the competition for wealth and his renown based on his success in it."[41] This is a departure from the core spirit of the definition and reality captured by Sahlins. As I show in this book, the concept, as articulated by Sahlins, is still useful in understanding the social process, especially when stripped of its negative and heavily judgmental overtones that Africanist political science and sociology[42] have since imposed on it in the enthusiastic drive to pathologize African politics. In the original formulation, based on what ethnographers observed in Melanesian societies, the Big Man is a self-made man "who created [or achieved] his power, and does not accumulate wealth or ritual power to be inherited by a successor."[43] Therefore, the Big Man is regarded as "egalitarian" and thus distinguishable from ascribed chiefs.[44]

Sahlins's description bears a long quotation here. I will use it, first, to extract its core meaning for my analysis of Adams's case and, second, to reemphasize its basic comparative value beyond the Melanesia context (including in Western—as Sahlins himself admitted—and African contexts):

> The Melanesian big-man seems so thoroughly bourgeois, so *reminiscent of the free enterprising rugged individual of our own* [Western] *heritage*. He combines with an ostensible interest in the general welfare a more profound measure of self-interested cunning and economic calculation. His gaze, as Veblen might have put it, is fixed unswervingly to the main chance. . . . *But the indicative quality of big-man authority is everywhere the same: it is personal power*. Big-men do not come to office; they do not succeed to, nor are they installed in, existing positions of leadership over political groups. The attainment of big-man status is rather the outcome *of a series of acts which elevate a person above the common herd and attract about him a coterie of loyal, lesser men.*[45]

Since Sahlins offered his elaboration and clarifications, the concept has been applied beyond Melanesia, and in other disciplines,[46] "when achievement rather than ascribed leader status is under discussion"[47]—that is, when describing "a person who by means of personal skills and abilities achieves a position of renown and power."[48] Close to when Sahlins was writing, Joan Vincent[49] and H. U. E. Thoden van Velzen[50] found parallels in Africa "in situations of changing political structure and new opportunities."[51] Following Max Weber,[52] Pamela Brown adds that "Such labels have the generality of a reference to charisma, wherever a leader is defined as exceptional and attractive to followers."

I argue that Sahlins invites us to pay attention to the contradictory elements that make a man a Big Man: "interest in general welfare" and "self-interested cunning and economic calculation." Returning to these original (anthropological) ideas of what it means to be a big man, as I show in this book, refreshes our understanding of this concept as well as the practical reality it captures and reveals how this illuminates *original* African (specifically, Yorùbá) ideas and practices of what it means to be a big man—prior to postcolonial state practices and the heuristic devices imposed on them by Africanist political science and sociology. As processes, the elements that make a Big Man can be translated into personal transformation (achievement) only if the agent fixes his gaze "unswervingly to the main chance." Ultimately, the most crucial quality of the authority of the big man is "personal power," which is attained as a result of "a series of acts" and not as a result of being in "office."[53] In fact, Sahlins goes further to state that "it is not accurate to speak of 'big-man' as a political title, for it is but an acknowledged standing in interpersonal relations—a 'prince among men' so to speak, as opposed to 'The Prince of Danes.'" The phrases Melanesian groups use to describe such men resonate with the Yorùbá case: *man of importance* or *man of renown*, *generous rich-man*, or *center-man*, as well as *big-man*.[54] Yorùbá equivalents are *eniyan pataki* (important person), *eni nla* (big man or eminent person), or even *awon baba wa* (our father), as a university teacher once described Adams at a public event.[55]

Sahlins also observed that a man's "bigness" is "normally set by competition with other ambitious men," given that "little or no authority is given by social ascription."[56] In Adams's case, as he competed—and collaborated, sometimes tactically and at other times strategically—with other ambitious men within and beyond Yorubaland (see chap. 5), he received further acknowledgments of his bigness because the media began to report him as being among dignitaries at events while seeking his opinion on the most pressing public, regional, and national issues. Therefore, the status of Big Man, in this context, is both a way of expressing a concept as well as a social reality. The concept of the Big Man, as this book shows, captures social experiences of leadership, achievement, and agency in specific contexts.[57]

However, it is important to state that I am not merely transposing the Melanesian context to the African (Yorùbá) context. I use the concept comparatively but with the consciousness that there are similarities and dissimilarities in the two widely different contexts. I am arguing that, as initially elaborated in the Melanesian context, examining the Big Man in a specific context in which the status arises from personal power attained as a result of "a series of acts," without the explicit assumptions of, or exclusive focus on, corruption, abuse of power, or other faults (which now dominate the Africanist literature on the Big Man), could provide us with greater illumination on ethnic as well as cultural politics. This is true, I argue, even in a context where a peculiar "notion of individuality and instrumentality . . . is central to politics."[58] Two leading scholars of modern Yorùbá society, Karin Barber and Andrew Apter, have provided penetrating perspectives on the Yorùbá concept and practices of the Big Man that form an excellent background for this study. Karin Barber, in her influential 1981 essay,[59] compares the "self-made man" in Yorùbá society to the Big Man of New Guinea. On the basis of her study of Okuku town, she argues that the Yorùbá "live in a kind of society where it is very clear that the *human* individual's power depends in the long run on the attention and acknowledgement of his fellow-men."[60] Against this backdrop, she contends,

> The dynamic impulse in political life is the rise of self-made men. Individuals compete to make a position for themselves by recruiting supporters willing to

> acknowledge their greatness. Titles are positions of power, but they are not hereditary; they are achieved by men who must first have established themselves. The title system itself is quite flexible, allowing a man in a small position to enlarge it by his own efforts; and it is also possible for men to by-pass the title system and become important in the town in a variety of other ways. There is, then, a lot of scope for self-aggrandizement, but the self-made man . . . is only "big" if other people think so.[61]

Thus, for the Yorùbá, the self-made man (often a male) who recruits supporters or followers who acknowledge his greatness is a big man.

On his part, Andrew Apter, using his work in Ayede, a small Yorùbá town, examines the historical context of the phenomenon of the Big Man in Yorùbá society, which was, in the late nineteenth and early twentieth centuries, based on the accumulation of wives, children, slaves, land, farms, and great wealth, reflecting what he describes as a "military pattern of self-aggrandizement."[62] However, being a Big Man in late nineteenth- and early twentieth-century Yorùbá society took more than an accumulation of wealth. As Apter notes, "A man became big by *attracting followers*, expanding his household with matrilineal kin and clients who became associated with his lineage . . . and by *exchanging his influence for loyalty and support*."[63] Apter identifies other essential conditions for becoming a big man in that era, which are critical for understanding contemporary conditions for becoming a big man in late twentieth- and early twenty-first-century Yorùbá society. A man became big by "a variety of agencies," including "*his own special genius*" and "a good head (*ori*), or personal destiny . . . *which raises their fortunes to uncommon heights*." In some cases, bigness can also be a function of "a special relation to an *orisa* [god] or to the possession of powerful *juju* medicines [magic]."[64] Apter makes a critical point about the two contradictory implications of these "assets" for the big man: they enhance his "extraordinary status" but also expose him to "special vulnerability." Thus, the status of a big man ensures security but portends danger, particularly in a "competitive and individualistic Yoruba society, where social status is largely achieved, and fortunes can change dramatically overnight"—as the Gani Adams case examined in this book reflects. It is for this reason that the big man is always consumed with maintaining and expanding his estate (including his wealth, power, and influence) and, more crucially, devoted to identifying, containing, incorporating, or neutralizing potential competitors.

Furthermore, this book responds to one of the earliest critiques of the big man concept, which I think has not yet been sufficiently addressed—at least not in the Africanist literature. In an illuminating article, H. U. E. Thoden van Velzen argues that "Big Man anthropology is mainly *elite anthropology*; it concentrates too exclusively on a few powerful individuals, their manoeuvres, recruitment procedures and strategies."[65] He adds that extant literature on the big man "neglects the study of *anti-establishment forces* as these manifest themselves in antagonistic classes, levelling coalitions and smaller units of contradiction and protest." He concludes, "If my reading of the Big Man literature is right, it would mean that we need to pose new questions. For example, *what chances do the 'weak' have to restructure the distribution of resources*?"[66] This book is an attempt to address this question and the noted lacuna in the literature in the context of an ethnographic study of a big man who was initially an antiestablishment force reflecting the tensions of antagonistic classes through protests and violent clashes and who, starting from a position of weakness, has managed to use violence and other cultural resources to "restructure the distribution of resources" in his own favor.

In examining the role that "personal uniqueness, volition, and achievement play"[67] in contemporary Nigerian history, I reflect on the processes through which, as a cultural agent, Gani Adams became a big man in his own rights—thus achieving one of the important conditions of being a big man: *personally creating his own power*.[68] Yet he only became a big man through the primary institutional apparatus and activities of the OPC and other institutional processes that he built around himself.[69] Unlike the case of the Melanesian big man, who lacks "institutional affiliation" but "gains prominence solely through charisma and unusual ability to attract followers,"[70] Adams's power, influence, and prominence are tied to institutional affiliation, particularly with the OPC, and to specific modes of intervention with key institutions and key agents within the larger Yorùbá context and Nigerian polity. These institutional affiliations are a reflection of the ways in which he mobilizes history (past)[71] and contemporary dynamics (present) in the creation of a new cultural—and also social and political—ethos to realize both his personal and ethnocultural ambitions (future).

In the preceding chapters, I examine the various (agential and institutional) dimensions of Gani Adams's public life to understand "not just the workings of power" but also, as Sherry B. Ortner states, "the attempt of subalterns (in the Gramscian sense) to attain to the privilege of becoming subjects in the first place."[72]

THE ACTIVE AGENT AND THE HUMAN PROJECT: WAY MAKING IN THE WORLD

While I have argued that Gani Adams's project raises interesting and significant sociological questions, I am minded in this concluding chapter to reemphasize its immersion in continental (African) and global (human) processes. Despite its manifold manifestations in different sociocultural contexts around the world, Margaret S. Archer has alerted us to the ubiquity of what she describes as the "human project"—that is, "any course of action intentionally engaged upon a human being."[73] Crucial to this human project, she argues, is the internal conversation that all active agents have with themselves that constitutes the "manner in which we reflexively make our way through the world."[74] "Being an 'active agent,'" she argues, "hinges on the fact that individuals develop and define their ultimate concerns: those internal goods that they care about most, the precise constellation of which makes for their concrete singularity."[75] Though Archer has some serious disagreements with the theorists who conflate agency with structure, such as Giddens,[76] Archer, Giddens, and Ortner appear to agree on the role of reflexivity in agency, particularly in relation to structure. As Ortner articulates the consensus among the three theorists, "At the individual level I will assume, with Giddens, that actors are always at least partially 'knowing subjects,' that they have some degree of reflexivity about themselves and their desires, and that they have some 'penetration' into the ways in which they are formed by their circumstances."[77]

As evident in this book, in developing, defining, and doggedly pursuing his personal and sociocultural projects against the backdrop of the circumstances in which he was formed, Adams reflects the characteristics of an active agent even when his "concrete singularity" is evident in the particular ways in which he has pursued the things he cares most about. And because human projects are a universal phenomenon, Archer identifies three implications for the relationship between the active agent and the context/structure, which includes the social order. I find the third implication[78] particularly crucial for illuminating the relationship between the active agent and human projects, which I have examined in this book. In the interaction between the causal power of human beings and the different parts of the world around us, the outcome is not merely a matter of the "primary congruence or incongruence." The fact that human beings are reflexive implies that our internal deliberations about the constraints or enablements presented by the structural or cultural environment determine how we respond to that environment. Therefore, our success depends on our ability to not just *reconcile* ourselves with the constraints or enablements confronting us in the environment but leverage those same constraints and enablements.[79]

The capacity and success of the active agent, based on the agent's reflexivity, to reconcile him or herself with the constraints or enablements of the environment—by circumventing or renouncing constraints or by embracing and accepting, or even leveraging, enablements—manifests in the "adaptive ingenuity"[80] of each agent. This book shows that Adams's reflexivity, signaled by his "adaptive genius," allowed him to combine different efforts to realize his personal and sociocultural project. This reflexivity continues to help him maintain and augment his present status.[81]

Against this backdrop, Archer, in her review of extant social theory on structure and agency, concludes that the literature has fully and robustly confronted the analysis of cultural and structural properties that determine or constrain the social contexts in which agents act, while appreciating "people's natal social world context and its associated life chances."[82] Yet there is a need for a greater emphasis on "a second causal power [that] is *necessarily at play*, namely the personal power to reflect subjectively upon one's circumstances and to decide what to do in them or to do about them."[83]

As students of society, we do not have to agree with or endorse the modes of reflexivity and the consequent actions of agents such as Adams. What is important for social analysis is that we identify and explain what they do, how and why they do what they do, and what implications these actions have for society. To throw intelligent light on the actions of agents such as Adams, we need to focus on their reflexivity—as much as we are able to penetrate that. Rather than "*imputing subjective motives*" to important social agents such as Gani Adams, we can, as I have tried to do in this book, examine the agents' own "reflexively defined reasons, aims and concerns"[84]—even when the agents attempt to obscure, confuse, or obfuscate their reasons, aims, and concerns in public. Ethnographers—particularly those working within environments in which they are insiders[85]—who have exceptional access to such active agents are well placed to use the agents' reflexivity in the study of their social location within the larger social dynamics.

Thus, the underlying purpose of the foregoing analysis of "the attempt of subalterns (in the Gramscian sense) to attain the privilege of becoming subjects," to use Sherry B. Ortner's phrase,[86] is to place "the human" and agency (the *acting* subject) at the center of the social along the lines of practice theory—as already championed by many theorists and ethnographers, including Pierre Bourdieu,[87] Antony Giddens,[88] Marshall Sahlins,[89] William H. Sewell,[90] Sherry B. Ortner,[91] and Richard Werbner.[92]

THE ELITE ECLIPSES THE SUBALTERN?

I have used Adams's transformation from a subaltern to an elite—through the process of being *a subaltern of the elite*, then *an elite of subalterns*, and eventually *an elite* in his own right—to interrogate subalternity, elites, and ethnocultural politics in a contemporary postcolonial context. Adams's trajectory and present status reveal that, while the fundamental claim to legitimacy of a subaltern who has been transformed into an elite remains his link to the subaltern, he must not only maintain that link but *be seen* to maintain the link. The account here is very Gramscian in the way it analyzes Adams's initial subalternity as historically determined—within particular economic, political, social, and cultural contexts.[93] This then forms the basis of exploring how he, at the outset, survived at the margins and eventually succeeded in his "ascent from a subordinate social position to a dominant one."[94] Gramsci encourages us "to understand how the conditions and relations of the past influence the present and future development of the subaltern's lived experience,"[95] including the possibility of that person's transition from a subordinate position to a dominant one.

In Adams's case, while past political agendas predisposed his group to violence, his current social status (as an eminent Yorùbá and Nigerian) leads him to abjure violence. However, paradoxically, his current cultural office (*Kakaǹfò*/generalissimo) implies violence, or at least the willingness to fight for self-determination for the Yorùbá in the context of the ethno-regional challenges of contemporary Nigeria. In light of this, he uses his constant rhetoric and particular forms of action (such as challenging Igboho concerning what to do about the challenge of banditry, kidnapping, and the clashes between farmers and herders or meeting governors to discuss regional security) to highlight his "unbroken" link to the subalterns who form the ready "army" needed to defend Yorùbá interests and Yorubaland. An example of this is the rhetorical question Adams asked when reaffirming the role of the OPC in his transformed life and in relation to his current status: "I don't want to become an honorary *Ààrẹ Ọ̀nà Kakaǹfò*. . . . No matter the position I hold, I will be grateful to God and to the OPC. . . . OPC made me and I will never forsake the OPC. The *Ààrẹ Ọ̀nà Kakaǹfò* is the generalissimo, OPC members are freedom fighters when the generalissimo forgets his rank and file, how will he be a general?"[96] Yet, as one who has become a *proper* elite, Adams needs to constantly distinguish himself from the subaltern to maintain his eminence. As a matter of fact, as he steps up the social ladder, Adams moves further away from the subalterns in the objective material circumstances of his life. But despite this, he maintains a delicate balance by attempting to reconcile his personal material transformation with his politics—or more crucially, by ensuring that his rhetoric remains *subaltern-like*, or at least *subaltern-lite*, particularly in the link to the larger cultural (ethnonationalist) project of self-determination. As he once told me during a casual discussion, "You need capital to fight capitalism."

In reflecting on subalternity in contemporary Africa through Gani Adams's life story, following Achille Mbembe, in this book I have tried to "complicate the concept of agency" by showing the paradoxes inherent in the actions of subalterns[97] while also distancing myself "from the false dualism between a victim vision and a hero vision of subalternity."[98] I do so "in the interest of a true critique of responsibility,"[99] to throw into crisis individual, corporate, and shared notions and practices of ethnocultural responsibility in a contemporary postcolonial formation.

ADAMS'S MATHÉMATIQUES

How to Become a Big Man in Africa is an effort toward a public anthropology of subalterns and elites through long-term ethnography, thick description, interpretive history, political analysis, iconography, and media analysis. I hope to contribute to one of the traditions of the study of Africa that, as Mbembe argues, "have become powerful examples of how we should think and write about human agency, as well as what analytical strategies we should deploy in order to describe and interpret specific forms of social life in particular settings."[100]

The book uses Adams's public life as a means of tracking the trajectory of strategic improvisers and cultural agents in contemporary Africa. This particular improviser and agent mobilized youth anger, even angst, and morphed it into ethno-nationalist agitation and frustration, which he eventually converted into a platform for *self-determination* (in both a personal and a collective sense) in an attempt to transform his and his group's relations with others and other groups. Adams is presented as a big man in whose life story many of the challenges of the African state and society are reflected: access to and the distribution of power, the precaritization of young people, their frustrations and aspirations, ethno-regional conflict, state and extrastate violence, cultural transformation, economic anxieties, and social mobility, among others. It is evident that Adams is as much a skillful victim and beneficiary of the vacuity of the Nigerian state—in terms of its capacity to command legitimacy and allegiance—as he is a victim and beneficiary of the ephemerality of a society that lacks the capacity to develop and deepen productive and sustainable (nonviolent) means of social achievement. Paradoxically, Adams is also both a warrior against and a structurally tame(d) spectator in a society that lacks an egalitarian and generalized process for self-actualization for most young people.

This case shows that, though there is a useful general pattern that can facilitate comparative work, the specific manifestations and dimensions of what it means to be a Big Man differ among societies and contexts.[101] Ethnographers therefore need to immerse themselves in the context to provide the necessary illumination about particular manifestations of the phenomenon of the Big Man in contemporary Africa without starting out, as is common, with a negative view of the phenomenon. Yet we can discern in Adams's story a wider narrative about the transformations in and of personal agency and subjectivity that starts with marginalization, dispossession, and exploitation and ends up on the other side of the material divide in society. Thus, Adams's story and this book suggest that, ultimately, it is the (generalized and generalizable) *tactics* (and, I will add, *strategies*) by which individuals advance themselves[102] that is of comparative value, and not just a specific manifestation of personal advancement—as is also evident in the case of Malema in South Africa. Malema has sought and won a position within the state as a member of Parliament on the platform of the EFF. This constitutes an opportunity to consolidate his personal, sociocultural, economic, and political projects. Also, while Adams focuses on ethno-regional differences between the Yorùbá and others (particularly the Hausa-Fulani), Malema focuses on racial differences between Black South Africans and others—particularly white South Africans.[103]

However, it is important to note that I do not assume a linearity to Adams's life or take it for granted that his personal project had a guaranteed end—that is, becoming a big man—despite his mastery of a particular kind of *mathématiques*—"extreme (mental and physical) flexibility as well as . . . tricky skills of improvisation"[104]—necessary for his transformation. As the moments when he escaped death show, sometimes he depended on luck. While he was a genius at what he did, his survival and ascendancy were not absolutely a function of that genius. There were no guarantees that he would be successful in the end. This is often true of the *transformed* lives that evolve through precarious engagements but develop a measure of stability. While people who live such lives, to use Filip de Boeck's words, "are, of course, conscious actors and participants in their own lives, struggling, to some extent, to stay in control and therefore continuously seizing and capturing the moment and the opportunity to reinvent and reimagine their lives in different ways,"[105] in totality, there is no *steady* advance planning. However, as De Boeck brilliantly and poignantly notes on the basis of his examination of the lives of the Congolese, which "consist of constant stops and starts directed by the tricky and unforeseeable processes of seizure and capture":[106] "Indeed, to steer your life unharmed through all the pitfalls, all the possible parameters of your daily existence, seems to demand an advanced knowledge of higher mathematics and of topics such as chaos, fractals, mobility, and dynamics."[107] What De Boeck describes as "higher mathematics," Achille Mbembe, in a similar context, calls "a system of intelligibility" that "determine[s] the logic of effective action."[108] Mbembe argues that by examining the *causality, possibility,* and *efficacy* (as I have done here) that undergird or result from the actions of particular agents in society, we can account for "the rationalities at work."

The introductory parts of this book examine Gani Adams's initial (deprived) position in "relation to the distributions of resources"[109] in society (which belies the ultimate outcome) and trace his evolution through his reflections on this relation, the structural and cultural constraints he confronted and overcame, and the enablements he embraced and leveraged. These are then linked to the processes through which he tapped into the existing systems of resource distribution to become a resource distributor himself—that is, a veritable big man. By laying out and explaining the different aspects and stages of this trajectory and connecting them analytically, I hope I have accounted for the transformation of a particular strategic improviser—especially one for whom the *I* (the individual) and the *we* (the OPC and the Yorùbá) often collocate—while also presenting a robust ethnography of subjectivity in an African context. I also hope that I have provided a template for a comparative ethnography of the transformation of a particular subject (subaltern) into elite status.

In reflecting on this case, I close by suggesting that, in such projects of *self-making* or self-actualization as Adams's, the *I* and the *we*[110] (i.e., individual and collective subjectivities) can both be *pronouncedly personalized* pronouns. Such personalized pronouns are most acutely reflected in the trajectory of a man who "lived through times of acute social disturbances."[111] Even while he epitomized these disturbances, Adams ensured that, unlike most of his youthful followers, he was not one of the "casualties of history."

NOTES

1. Francis Nyamnjoh argues that among the Bum in the Cameroon Grassfields, using one's agency in this way "while everyone else is barely struggling to get by" is considered "destructive for others and ultimately for the accumulating individual." This is not so in the larger Yorùbá context. See Nyamnjoh, "'A Child Is One Person's Only in the Womb': Domestication, Agency and Subjectivity in the Cameroonian Grassfields," in *Postcolonial Subjectivities in Africa*, ed. Richard Werbner (London: Zed Books, 2002), 120.

2. I thank one of the readers of the manuscript for urging me to clarify this and providing the language to do so.

3. Antonio Gramsci, *Selections from Prison Notebooks*, 336–7, and Gramsci, *Qauderni*, vol. II, Q11, 12, 1388–89, quoted in Guido Liguori, "Conceptions of Subalternity in Gramsci," in *Antonio Gramsci*, ed. Mark McNally (London: Palgrave-Macmillan, 2015), 128.

4. Shola Oshunkeye, "People Who Ignore Me, Do so at Their Peril," *Sunday Sun*, December 4, 2011, 32 (emphasis added). See also NBF News, "Gani Adams: My Name Rings Louder Bell than Some Governors," *Nigerian Voice*, December 4, 2011, https://www.thenigerianvoice.com/news/76834/gani-adams-my-name-rings-louder-bell-than-some-governors.html.

5. Temitayo Odunlami and Nurudeen Oyewole, "I Can't Be a Warrior in Time of Peace—Gani Adams," *Daily Trust*, January 13, 2018, https://dailytrust.com/i-cant-be-a-warrior-in-time-of-peace-gani-adams/.

6. Oshunkeye, "People Who Ignore Me, Do so at Their Peril," 44 (emphasis added).

7. On self-praise as a form of strategic self-presentation, see Yaping Guo and Wei Ren, "Managing Image: The Self-praise of Celebrities on Social Media," *Discourse, Context & Media* 38 (2020): 1.

8. Pamela J. Stewart and Andrew Strathern, *Violence: Theory and Ethnography* (London: Continuum, 2002), 17.

9. Georges Balandier, *Political Anthropology* (New York: Vantage Books, 1970), 20.

10. Ibid.

11. Richard Werbner, "Introduction: Postcolonial Subjectivities; The Personal, the Political and the Moral," in Werbner, *Postcolonial Subjectivities in Africa*, 3.

12. Adeline Masquelier, *Fada: Boredom and Belonging in Niger* (Chicago: University of Chicago Press, 2019), 6.

13 *Africa Confidential*, "Abuja Buys a Delta amnesty," 50, no. 22 (November 2009), https://www.africa-confidential.com/article-preview/id/3305/Abuja_buys_a_Delta_amnesty.

14. *Africa Confidential*, "The Hunt for Tompolo," 50, no. 12 (June 12, 2009), https://www.africa-confidential.com/article-preview/id/3131/The_hunt_for_Tompolo; *Africa Confidential*, "General John Togo and All His Enemies," 51, no. 25 (December 17, 2010), https://www.africa-confidential.com/article-preview/id/3786/General_John_Togo_and_all_his_enemies.

15. Mike Odiegwu, "SHOOT-AT-SIGHT: From Niger Delta Agitator to Successful Entrepreneur," *Nation*, July 24, 2021, https://thenationonlineng.net/shoot-at-sight-from-niger-delta-agitator-to-successful-entrepreneur/.

16. See Shehu Abubakar and Solomon Chung, "Lifestyles of Billionaire Militants," *Daily Trust*, September 15, 2012, https://dailytrust.com/lifestyles-of-billionaire-militants/.

17. See *Africa Confidential*, "All the President's Militias," 51, no. 24 (December 3, 2010), https://www.africa-confidential.com/article-review/id/3763/All_the_President%27s_militias; *Africa Confidential*, "Lots of Gunboats, Little Diplomacy," 56, no. 3 (February 6, 2015), https://www.africa-confidential.com/article-preview/id/5997/Lots_of_gunboats%2c_little_diplomacy; *Africa Confidential*, "Militants Pick Their Party," 59 (June 15, 2018), https://www.africa-confidential.com/article-preview/id/12351/Militants_pick_their_party; *Africa Confidential*, "A Fight for the President's Base," 52, no. 4 (February 18, 2011), https://www.africa-confidential.com/article-preview/id/3853/A_fight_for_the_President%e2%80%99s_base; Eniola Akinkuotu, "Nigeria: Ex-militant Asari Dokubo Wants to Build Tinubu an Army," *The Africa Report*, July 27, 2023, https://www.theafricareport.com/317151/nigeria-ex-militant-asari-dokubo-wants-to-build-tinubu-army/.

18. Wale Odunsi, "Ateke Tom, Ex-militant Leader Crowned King of Okochiri in Rivers," *Daily Post*, November 26, 2017, https://dailypost.ng/2017/11/26/ateke-tom-ex-militant-leader-crowned-king-okochiri-rivers-photos/.

19. Aderonke Ogunleye, "EXCLUSIVE: Asari-Dokubo Establishes Own University, Names It after King Amachree," *Premium Times*, October 11, 2013, https://www.premiumtimesng.com/news/146438-exclusive-asari-dokubo-establishes-university-names-king-amachree.html?tztc=1.

20. Odiegwu, "SHOOT-AT-SIGHT."

21. Fiona Forde, *An Inconvenient Youth: Julius Malema and the "New" ANC* (Johannesburg: Jonathan Ball Publishers, 2011; Edinburgh: Portobello Books, 2012), xviii.

22. Ibid., 69. See also Fiona Forde's update on Malema's public career, *Still an Inconvenient Youth: Julius Malema Carries* (London: Picador, 2014). For a more sympathetic view of Malema and the EFF, see Janet Smith and Floyd Shivambu, *The Coming Revolution: Julius Malema and the Fight for Economic Freedom* (Johannesburg: Jacana Media, 2004).

23. Max Du Preez and Mandy Rossouw, *The World according to Julius Malema* (Cape Town: NB, 2010).

24. Interestingly enough, Adams, according to one of the activist-journalists who knew him well in the early days, Babafemi Ojudu (who later became a senator), Adams started out in the prodemocracy movement by coordinating the pasting of antimilitary/prodemocracy posters around urban areas at the behest of Dr. Beko Ransome-Kuti, the late prodemocracy activist and chair of the Campaign for Democracy. Ojudu, telephone conversation, April 9, 2023.

25. Siyamtanda Capa, "'Revolutionaries Must Be Willing to Kill,' Malema Tells EFF Delegates," IOL, October 15, 2022, https://www.iol.co.za/weekend-argus/news/revolutionaries-must-be-willing-to-kill-malema-tells-eff-delegates-d15b971e-3893-411a-b57f-cc87496ed721.

26. He reportedly owns another mansion in Limpopo. Charleyne Hunter-Gault, "South African Official's Luxe Lifestyle Raises Doubts," NPR, March 10, 2010, https://www.npr.org/templates/story/story.php?storyId=124458077; Marida Fitzpatrick, "Malema 'Misses' R3m," News24, February 23, 2010, https://www.news24.com/News24/Malema-misses-R3m-20100223.

27. Fitzpatrick, "Malema 'Misses' R3m." See also Hunter-Gault, "South African Official's Luxe Lifestyle Raises Doubts."

28. To paraphrase Richard Werbner's reflection on the case of self-fashioning of Nuriaty in Mayotte—a small French-controlled island in the Comoro Archipelago of the western Indian Ocean—examined by Michael Lambek. Werbner, "Introduction," 4; Michael Lambek, "Nuriaty, the Saint, and the Sultan," in Werbner, *Postcolonial Subjectivities in Africa*, 25–43.

29. Werbner, "Introduction," 3.

30. Margaret S. Archer, *Making Our Way through the World: Human Reflexivity and Social Mobility* (Cambridge: Cambridge University Press, 2007), 5 (emphasis in original). In his own reflections on agency, Andrew Apter would seem to reverse Archer's

emphasis on the agent's reflexivity in relation to the "external world" when he argues that "With some degree of autonomy, agents are always implicated in webs of sociality because their actions are evaluated by others, implying forms of recognition and reflexivity." Apter, *Beyond Words: Discourse and Critical Agency in Africa* (Chicago: University of Chicago Press, 2007), 4.

31. Boel Berner, "Manoeuvring in Uncertainty: On Agency, Strategies and Negotiations," in *Manoeuvring in an Environment of Uncertainty: Structural Change and Social Action in Sub-Saharan Africa*, ed. Boel Berner and Per Trulsson (Aldershot: Ashgate, 2000), 279.

32. Richard Werbner, *Anthropology after Gluckman: The Manchester School, Colonial and Postcolonial Transformations* (Manchester: Manchester University Press, 2020), 164. Werbner's book is a fascinating account of his own reflexivity—based on over six decades of study and research—as well as reflections on the reflexivity evident in the work of the leading members of the Manchester School and other anthropologists.

33. Graham Crow, "The Use of the Concept of 'Strategy' in Recent Sociological Literature," *Sociology* 24 (1989): 2.

34. Berner, "Manoeuvring in Uncertainty," 279.

35. Cf. Lamont Lindstrom, "'Big Man': A Short Terminological History," *American Anthropologist* 83, no. 4 (1981): 902. Lindstrom writes, "The term 'big man' appears in other early ethnographic work although as a vernacular rather than scientific gloss." He states further that "the undoubted reason big man won through, at last, as the scientific label of the newly defined types of leader" in Melanesia was because "the term is often a direct translation of leadership status labels in a wide range of Melanesian languages." For example, *nema asori* in the Kwamera language of Tanna means "big, grand, or important men."

36. Marshall Sahlins, "Poor Man, Rich Man, Big-Man, Chief: Political Types in Melanesia and Polynesia," *Comparative Studies in Society and History* 5, no. 3 (1963). There have been "all kinds of shades and some corrections have gradually been introduced" to Sahlins's "clear-cut picture" of the Melanesian big man, as Albert A. Trouwborst states. Trouwborst, "The 'Big-Man': A Melanesian Model in Africa," in *Private Politics: A Multi-disciplinary Approach to 'Big-Man' Systems*, ed. M. van Bakel, Renée R. Hagesteijn, and Pieter Van De Velde (Leiden: Brill, 1986), 49.

37. For a review of the anthropological literature on *big man* until 1980, see Lindstrom, "'Big Man,'" 900–905. Brown also points to early references to big men in coastal and island Melanesia. See Paula Brown, "Big Man, Past and Present: Model, Person, Hero, Legend," *Ethnology* 29, no. 2 (1990): 97.

38. The concept eventually "[escaped] the bounds of the anthropological community" as "its audience widen[ed]." Lindstrom, "'Big Man,'" 903. It became a favored concept in Africanist political science and sociology and even African literature. For an example of the latter, see Chinua Achebe, *A Man of the People*. See also Deborah Nyangulu, "Big Men and Performances of Sovereignty in Contemporary African Novels," *Research in African Literatures* 49, no. 3 (2018): 101–15. For a few examples of

works in Africanist political science and anthropology, see Crow, "Use of the Concept," 2.

39. For a critique of the neopatrimonialism literature in Africa, see Thandika Mkandiwire, "Neopatrimonialism and the Political Economy of Economic Performance in Africa: Critical Reflections," *World Politics* 67, no. 3 (2015): 563–612.

40. M. Godelier, "Social Hierarchies among the Baruya of New Guinea," in *Inequality in New Guinea Highland Societies*, ed. A. Strathern (Cambridge: Cambridge University Press, 1982), 30–32.

41. See Trouwborst, "'Big-Man,'" 49.

42. This paradigm, as Daniel Posner and Daniel Young stated in 2007, "has dominated the study of African politics for the past thirty-years." Daniel N. Posner and Daniel J. Young, "The Institutionalization of Political Power in Africa," *Journal of Democracy* 18, no. 3 (2007): 126–27. Examples include Jean-Pascal Daloz, "'Big Men' in Sub-Saharan Africa: How Elites Accumulate Positions and Resources," *Comparative Sociology* 2, no. 1 (2003): 271–85; Jean-Francois Bayart, *The State in Africa: The Politics of the Belly*, trans. Mary Harper, Christopher Harrison, and Elizabeth Harrison (London: Longman, 1993); Goran Hyden, *African Politics in Comparative Perspective* (Cambridge: Cambridge University Press, 2006); Roger Southall and H. Melber, *A New Scramble for Africa: Imperialism, Investment and Development* (Scottsville: University of KwaZulu-Natal Press, 2006); Mimmi Söderberg Kovacs and Jesper Bjarnesen, *Violence in African Elections: Between Democracy and Big Man* (London: Zed Books, 2018); Nikkie Wiegink, "'It Will Be Our Time to Eat': Former Renamo Combatants and Big-Man Dynamics in Central Mozambique," *Journal of Southern African Studies* 41, no. 4 (2015): 869–85; Elisabete Azevedo-Harman, "Parliaments in Africa: Representative Institutions in the Land of the 'Big Man,'" *Journal of Legislative Studies* 17, no. 1 (2011): 65–85; Johan De Smedt, "'No Raila, No Peace!': Big Man Politics and Election Violence at the Kibera Grassroots," *African Affairs* 108, no. 433 (October 2009): 581–98; Larry Diamond, "Progress and Retreat in Africa: The Rule of Law versus the Big Man," *Journal of Democracy* 19, no. 2 (April 2008): 138–49; Gabrielle Lynch, "Moi: The Making of an African 'Big-Man,'" *Journal of Eastern African Studies* 2, no. 1 (2008): 18–43. Even in this generally grim picture of the Big Man in Africa, Jean-Pascal Daloz stands out. Daloz, in his rather dismissive view of African politics, posits that his "'Big Man' model applies to '*all* types of elites including other important categories in sub-Saharan Africa, like 'traditional rulers,' some religious and even top military leaders." Daloz, "'Big Men,'" 271 (emphasis added). The problem with this maximalist view is that, by exaggerating a concept that captures a significant phenomenon, it trivializes the genuine work of social transformation by many famous and not-so-famous leaders in Africa, like Nelson Mandela, Kwame Nkrumah, Thabo Mbeki, Julius Nyerere, Nnamdi Azikiwe, Obafemi Awolowo, Seretse Khama, and Masisi Mokgweetsi.

Also, "Big-Manship" is a universal phenomenon. See van Bakel, Hagesteijn, and Van De Velde, introduction to *Private Politics*, 5. It is "essentially . . . found everywhere on earth." H. J. M. Claessen, *Politieke Antropogie: Enn terrreinverkenning* (Assen: Van

Gorcum, 1974), 102. Trouwborst qualifies this by stating that "we find *elements* of *aspects* of 'Big-Manship' all over the world"—which is truer. Trouwborst, "'Big-Man,'" 52. However, Daloz's position is that "leaders usually aim at posing as Big Men, controlling as many fields of activities and networks as possible. They endeavour to be surrounded by the greatest possible number of supporters and clients." Daloz, "'Big Men,'" 271. While this may be true of Mobutu Sese Seko, Teodoro Obiang Nguema Mbasogo, Ali Bongo Ondimba or even Jacob Zuma, it will constitute a false and ridiculous description of Mandela, Thabo Mbeki, Ellen Johnson Sirleaf, or John Atta Mills. The refusal to recognize exceptions to this rule does damage to the genuine analysis of contemporary African social formations. However, I do not question the recognition of bureaucratic rationality as central to the embrace of modernity in Africa. See Olúfemi Táíwò, *How Colonialism Preempted Modernity in Africa* (Bloomington: Indiana University Press, 2010); Táíwò, *Africa Must Be Modern* (Bloomington: Indiana University Press, 2014). However, Daloz's conclusion that "sub-Saharan Africa is overflowing with illustrations demonstrating that the elites from this part of the world have never been *completely Westernized*" is preposterous. Daloz, "'Big Men,'" 277 (emphasis added). The domestication of the Enlightenment in Africa, which I examine in an ongoing work (and which Táíwò has explained with much elegance in *How Colonialism Preempted Modernity*, as well as his latest work), does not mean an absolute embrace of "Westernization." It means a full embrace of the key tenets of the Enlightenment, including progress, rationality, subjectivity, and rule by consent. See Táíwò, *Against Decolonisation: Taking African Agency Seriously* (London: Hurst, 2022). Because of the exclusive focus on politics, Daloz's "Big Man" can be, in part, challenging for understanding Big Men who are cultural entrepreneurs—like Adams. Still, I will admit that Daloz's take sheds useful light on the dynamics of Big Men in Africa. For instance, he is spot-on in noting that "supporters expect [the Big Man] to display external signs of wealth with regard to those representing other networks. They revel in the idea that he possesses more prestigious and impressive goods for these are in some way a credit to the whole community or of the faction which identifies with it. The absence of eminence would be disappointing and would be a factor of delegitimization for the Big Man." Daloz, "'Big Men,'" 281. Interestingly enough, Daloz preaches against formulaic approaches—or what he described as "undue extrapolation" or "ethnocentrism" (Daloz, xi)—in the study of elites in his other important books, *The Sociology of Elite Distinction* (2010) and *Rethinking Social Distinction* (2013).

43. Brown, "Big Man, Past and Present," 97.

44. Though this view was based solely and exclusively on the "achieved" status. Brown reminds us about scholars who hold contrary views, such as M. Jolly, "The Chimera of Equality in Melanesia," *Mankind* 17 (1987): 168–83; L. Josephides, *The Production of Inequality: Gender and Exchange Among the Kewa* (London: Routledge, 1985); Strathern, *Inequality in New Guinea Highland Societies*; and N. Thomas, "The Force of Ethnology: Origins and Significance of the Melanesia/Polynesia Division," *Current Anthropology* 30 (1989): 27–34. See Brown, "Big Man, Past and Present," 97.

As Thoden van Velzen reminds us, in the early literature, big men were "powerful individuals" known for "their role in social change and contribution to the functioning of society." H. U. E. Thoden van Velzen, "Robinson Crusoe and Friday: Strength and Weakness of the Big Man Paradigm," *Man*, n.s., 8, no. 4 (1973): 609.

45. Sahlins, "Poor Man, Rich Man," 289 (emphasis added).

46. See also the introduction and contributions by scholars—working in different disciplines and different parts of the world—to the volume edited by van Bakel, Hagesteijn, and Van De Velde, *Private Politics*.

47. Brown, "Big Man, Past and Present," 100.

48. Van Bakel, Hagesteijn, and Van De Velde, introduction, 3.

49. Joan Vincent, *African Elite: The Big Men of a Small Town* (New York: Columbia University Press, 1971), 232–55.

50. Thoden van Velzen, "Robinson Crusoe and Friday."

51. Brown, "Big Man, Past and Present," 100.

52. M. Weber, *The Theory of Social and Economic Organization* (New York: Free Press, 1947), 358–63; in Brown, "Big Man, Past and Present," 100.

53. Again, this is contrary contemporary Africanist literature's emphasis on big men's occupation of, or access to, public offices, which they use for personal enrichment and clientelist and patrimonial purposes.

54. Sahlins, "Poor Man, Rich Man," 289.

55. This description is particularly important because it was stated in Lagos in 2012 (by a lady who was a university lecturer at the Obafemi Awolowo University, Nigeria) to welcome Adams, who was then forty-two, to the presentation of a book authored by Harvard professor Jacob K. Olupona, an event attended by the most important Yorùbá monarch, the *Ooni* of Ife, *Oba* Okunade Sijuade, and other elderly Yorùbá. See chap. 3 for details.

56. Sahlins, "Poor Man, Rich Man," 290.

57. For a comparative Indian case, see Mattison Mines and Vijayalakshmi Gourishankar, "Leadership and Individuality in South Asia: The Case of the South Indian Big-Man," *Journal of Asian Studies* 49, no. 4 (1990): 761–86.

58. Ibid., 761.

59. Karin Barber, "How Man Makes God in West Africa: Yoruba Attitudes towards the *Orisa*," *Africa: Journal of the International African Institute* 51, no. 3 (1981): 724–45.

60. Ibid., 724.

61. Ibid.

62. Andrew Apter, *Black Critics and Kings: The Hermeneutics of Power in Yoruba Society* (Chicago: University of Chicago Press, 1992), 88–89.

63. Ibid., 89 (emphasis added).

64. In preceding chapters, I show how Adams reflects the "variety of agencies" in the "new" context of later twentieth- and early twenty-first-century Yorubaland.

65. Thoden van Velzen, "Robinson Crusoe and Friday," 609.

66. Ibid. (emphasis added).

67. Cf. Mines and Gourishankar, "Leadership and Individuality in South Asia," 761.

68. As Paula Brown states, "A big man has personally created his power." Brown, "Big Man, Past and Present," 97.

69. Such as OPU and festivals.

70. Cf. Douglas L. Oliver, *A Solomon Island Society: Kinship and Leadership among the Siuai of Bougainville* (Cambridge, MA: Harvard University Press, 1955); Sahlins, "Poor Man, Rich Man"; Maurice Godelier, *The Making of Great Men: Male Domination and Power among the New Guinea Baruya* (Cambridge: Cambridge University Press, 1986),, 163–64; Mines and Gourishankar, "Leadership and Individuality in South Asia," 762. As Mines and Gourishankar note, the distinction between the big man's charisma/ability to attract followers and his institutional affiliation "can be overstated." They added, correctly, in my view, that in the South Indian context, "institutional position is a necessary condition of the viability of the . . . big-man, but it is not sufficient." Yet I will argue that this is less true in Adams's case. But it is important to note that since his installation as the *Aare,* he has been working through reducing or reconstructing his "institutional affiliation" with the OPC, now that he has gained a far more powerful status. However, since this new status also carries the duty of leading an army of sorts, he can ill afford to give the impression that he has separated himself from the OPC vanguard.

71. For instance, his actions recall the tradition of warriors in nineteenth- and early twentieth-century Yorubaland, such as that of *omo ogun* (war boys) and *olori ogun* (war general). See chaps. 2 and 5 for the elaboration of the *omo ogun* and *olori ogun,* respectively.

72. Sherry B. Ortner, *Anthropology and Social Theory: Culture, Power, and the Acting Subject* (Durham, NC: Duke University Press, 2006), 109.

73. Archer, *Making Our Way through the World,* 64.

74. Ibid., 6.

75. Ibid., 6–7.

76. For instance, Margert S. Archer argues that "the basic reason for avoiding [conflation] is that the 'parts' and the 'people' are *not* co-existent through time and therefore any approach which amalgamates them wrongly foregoes the possibility of examining the interplay between them over time." See Margaret S. Archer, *Culture and Agency: The Place of Culture in Social Theory,* rev. ed. (Cambridge: Cambridge University Press, 1996), xiv. See also Archer, *Being Human: The Problem of Agency* (Cambridge: Cambridge University Press, 2000).

77. Ortner, *Anthropology and Social Theory,* 111.

78. The first is that "the pursuit of any human project entails the attempt to exercise our causal powers as human beings," while the second is that, once our own causal power and that of the natural reality are activated, they "work in entirely different ways." Archer, *Making Our Way through the World,* 8.

79. Cf. Archer, *Making Our Way through the World,* 8–9. I have rendered Archer's argument in this specific way to illuminate my argument in this book.

80. Ibid., 10.

81. This necessarily returns me to the argument about agency that I developed in *Yoruba Elites and Ethnic Politics in Nigeria*, particularly concerning how the agent can mobilize, manipulate, and sidestep structural constraint to attain particular personal projects. Writing in the context of Ghana, Stephan F. Miescher also reflects on some men as "gendered actors, engaged creatively with historical opportunities embedded in structural constraints that reflected West Africa's transformations over the last hundred years." Miescher, *Making Men in Ghana* (Bloomington: Indiana University Press, 2005), 16.

82. Archer, *Making Our Way through the World*, 10.

83. Ibid., 11.

84. Ibid., 13.

85. See Wale Adebanwi, "Elites, Ethnographic Encounters and the 'Native' Ethnographer in Contemporary Africa," in *Contemporary African Ethnographies*, ed. Rosabelle Boswell and Francis Nyamnjoh (Pretoria: Human Sciences Research Council Press, 2017), 149–76.

86. Ortner, *Anthropology and Social Theory*, 109.

87. Bourdieu's argument about habitus, referenced in chap. 1, is particularly useful because it can be read as an aspect of subjectivity, though, as Ortner notes, "the main emphasis of Bourdieu's arguments about habitus is on the ways in which it established a range of options and limits for the social actor." Ibid. See Pierre Bourdieu, *Outline of the Theory of Practice*, trans. R. Nice (Stanford, CA: Stanford University Press, 1977); Bourdieu, *The Logic of Practice*, trans. R. Nice (Stanford, CA: Stanford University Press, 1990); Bourdieu, *Pascalian Medications*, trans. R. Nice (Stanford, CA: Stanford University Press, 2000).

88. Ortner states that Sahlins's subject is similar to Bourdieu's because the actor is "structurally driven," though the historical actors the former focuses on are "subjectively more complex." Ortner, *Anthropology and Social Theory*, 110. See Marshall Sahlins, *Islands of History* (Chicago: University of Chicago Press, 1985).

89. Giddens, even while recognizing that the subject is produced from a cultural and structural context, also places emphasis on the agency of subjects who can "sometime [act] against the structures that made them." Ortner, *Anthropology and Social Theory*, 110. See Anthony Giddens, *Central Problems in Social Theory: Action, Structure and Contradiction in Social Analysis* (Berkeley: University of California Press, 1979).

90. Sewell posits that "in the world of human struggle and stratagems, plenty thoughts, perceptions, and actions consistent with the reproduction of existing social patterns fail to occur, and inconsistent ones occur all the time." William H. Sewell, "A Theory of Structure: Duality, Agency, and Transformation," *American Journal of Sociology* 98, no. 1 (1992): 15.

91. Ortner concludes that Bourdieu, Sahlins, Giddens, and Sewell "have in one way or another brought back the acting subject to social theory." Ortner, *Anthropology and Social Theory*, 110. See also Ortner, "Theory in Anthropology since the

Sixties," *Comparative Studies in Society and History* 26, no. 1 (1984): 126–66; Ortner, *Life and Death on Mt. Everest: Sherpas and Himalayan Mountaineering* (Princeton, NJ: Princeton University Press, 1999).

92. Richard Werbner, *Reasonable Radicals and Citizenship in Botswana: The Public Anthropology of Kalanga Elites* (Bloomington: Indiana University Press, 2004).

93. Marcus Green, "Gramsci Cannot Speak: Presentations and Interpretations of Gramsci's Concept of the Subaltern," *Rethinking Marxism* 14, no. 3 (2002): 8.

94. Ibid.

95. Ibid.

96. Dapo Akinrefon, "With 52 Titles Already, I Didn't Think I Would Become the *Aare Ona Kakanfo*—Gani Adams," *Vanguard*, October 22, 2017, https://www.vanguardngr.com/2017/10/52-titles-already-didnt-think-become-ona-kakanfo-gani-adams/.

97. Achille Mbembe, *Out of the Dark Night: Essays on Decolonization* (New York: Columbia University Press, 2021), 126.

98. Ibid.

99. Ibid.

100. Ibid., 26.

101. Cf. Trouwborst, "'Big-Man,'" 48.

102. F. G. Bailey, *Stratagems and Spoils: A Social Anthropology of Politics* (Cambridge, MA: Westview, 2001), 5.

103. Interestingly enough, Malema, like Adams, also pursued tertiary education later in life. He is currently studying for a master's degree at the University of Witwatersrand.

104. Filip de Boeck, "Local Futures and the Future of the Local," in *African Futures: Essays on Crisis, Emergence, and Possibility*, ed. Brian Goldstone and Juan Obarrio (Chicago: University of Chicago Press, 2017), 165.

105. Ibid., 165.

106. Ibid.

107. Ibid.

108. Achille Mbembe, "Everything Can Be Negotiated: Ambiguities and Challenges in Time of Uncertainty," in Berner and Per Trulsson, *Manoeuvring in an Environment of Uncertainty*, 272.

109. To borrow Archer's phrase in *Making Our Way through the World*, 13.

110. For an examination of a different project of uniting the *I* and the *we*, see Adebanwi, *Yoruba Elites and Ethnic Politics*, especially the introduction.

111. Interestingly enough, E. P. Thompson makes this important observation about the working class in England in his attempt to "rescue" them from the "enormous condescension of posterity." Thompson, *The Making of the English Working Class* (New York: Vintage Books, 1963), 12.

BIBLIOGRAPHY

BOOKS, BOOK CHAPTERS, AND JOURNAL ARTICLES

Abbink, J., and I. van Kessel, eds. *Vanguard or Vandals: Youth, Politics and Conflict in Africa*. Leiden: Brill, 2004.

Abbink, Jon, and Tijo Salverda, eds. *The Anthropology of Elites: Power, Culture, and the Complexities of Distinction*. New York: Palgrave Macmillan, 2013.

Abrahams, R. G. "Sungusungu: Village Vigilante Groups in Tanzania." *African Affairs* 86, no. 343 (1987): 179–96.

———. "Vigilantism: Order and Disorder on the Frontiers of the State." In *Inside and Outside the Law: Anthropological Studies of Authority and Ambiguity*, edited by Olivia Harris, 33–44. London: Routledge, 1987.

Abrams, Jerold J. "Aesthetics of Self-fashioning and Cosmopolitanism: Foucault and Rorty on the Art of Living." *Philosophy Today* 46, no. 2 (2002): 185–92.

Achebe, Chinua. *A Man of the People*. London: Heinemann, 1966.

Adams, Gani. *Leadership Challenge: Gani Adams and the Oodua People's Congress*. Edited by Michael M. Ogbeidi. Laos: Publishers Express, 2005.

———. *My Life and Struggle*. Lagos: Publishers Express, 2007.

———. "Politics and Agenda of Ethnic Militias: The Case of OPC." In *Urban Violence, Ethnic Militias and the Challenge of Democratic Consolidation in Nigeria*, edited by T. Babawale, 97–100. Lagos: Malthouse, 2003.

Adebanwi, Wale. *Authority Stealing: Anti-corruption War and Democratic Politics in Post-military Nigeria*. Durham, NC: Carolina Academic Press, 2012.

———. "The Carpenter's Revolt: Youth, Violence and the Reinvention of Culture in Nigeria." *Journal of Modern African Studies* 43, no. 3 (2005): 339–65.

———. "Comparative Politics of Austerity in Nigeria." Background paper for the World Bank Group, June 2017.

———. "Elites, Ethnographic Encounters and the 'Native' Ethnographer in Contemporary Africa." In *Contemporary African Ethnographies*, edited by Rosabelle Boswell and Francis Nyamnjoh, 149–76. Pretoria: Human Sciences Research Council Press, 2017.

———. *Trials and Triumphs*. Lagos: West African Book, 2008.

———. *Yoruba Elites and Ethnic Politics in Nigeria: Obafemi Awolowo and Corporate Agency*. Cambridge: Cambridge University Press, 2014.

Adebanwi, Wale, and Obadare Ebenezer, eds. *Encountering the Nigerian State*. New York: Palgrave Macmillan, 2010.

Adedayo, Wale. *Micro-seconds Away from Death*. Ogun State: Journal Communications, 2010.

Adélékè, Adélékè. *Arts of Being Yorùbá: Divination, Allegory, Tragedy, Proverb, Panegyric*. Bloomington: Indiana University Press, 2017.

Aderibigbe, J. O. "The Current Austerity Measures and Their Impact on the Nigerian Economy." *African Development* 10, no. 1–2 (1985): 217–35.

Adogame, Afe. "*Aiye loja, orun nile*: The Appropriation of Ritual Space-Time in the Cosmology of the Celestial Church of Christ." *Journal of Religion in Africa* 30, no. 1 (2000): 3–29.

Agamben, Giorgio. *State of Exception*. Translated by Kevin Attell. Chicago: University of Chicago Press, 2005.

Agbaje, Adigun A. B., Larry Diamond, and Ebere Onwudiwe, eds. *Nigeria's Struggle for Democracy and Good Governance: A Festschrift for Oyeleye Oyediran*. Ibadan: Ibadan University Press, 2004.

Agbaje, Adigun A. B., and Oyeyele Oyediran, eds. *Nigeria: Politics of Transition and Governance, 1986–1996*. Dakar: CODESRIA, 1999.

Akanni, Segun. *The Volunteer of the Savannah: A True Picture of Gani Adams*. Lagos: Prince Genesis Concept, 2015.

Akintoye, Stephen Adebanji. *The History of the Yoruba People*. Dakar: Amalion, 2010.

Akinyele, R. T. "Ethnic Militancy and National Stability in Nigeria: A Case Study of the Oodua People's Congress." *African Affairs* 100, no. 401 (2001): 623–40.

———. "The Involvement of the Oodua People's Congress in Crime Control in Southwestern Nigeria." In *Gouverner les villes d'Afrique. Etat, gouvernement local et acteurs privés*, edited by Laurent Fourchard, 139–60. Paris: Karthala, 2007.

Akiwowo, A. "Asuwada Eniyan." *Ife: Annals of the Institute of Cultural Studies* 1 (1986): 113–23.

Albert, Isaac Olawale. "Explaining 'Godfatherism' in Nigerian Politics." *African Sociological Review* 9, no. 2 (2005): 79–105.

———. "Ife-Modakeke crisis." In *Community Conflict in Nigeria: Management, Resolution and Transformation*, edited by Onigu Otite and Isaac Olawale Albert, 12–22. Ibadan: Spectrum Books, 1999.

Albert, Isaac Olawale, T. Awe, G. Hérault, and W. Omitoogun. *Informal Channels for Conflict Resolution in Ibadan, Nigeria*. Ibadan: IFRA, 1995.

Anderson, Benedict. *Imagined Communities: Reflections on the Origin and Spread of Nationalism*. London: Verso, 1991.

Anderson, David M. "Vigilantes, Violence and the Politics of Public Order in Kenya." *African Affairs* 101, no. 405 (2002): 531–55.

Anifowose, Remi. *Violence and Politics in Nigeria: The Tiv and Yoruba Experience*. New York: NOK, 1982.

Animasawun, Gbemisola. "Godfatherism in Nigeria's Fourth Republic: The Pyramid of Violence and Political Insecurity in Ibadan, Oyo State, Nigeria." E-papers Series 27, IFRA-Nigeria, Ibadan, 2013.

Apter, Andrew. *Beyond Words: Discourse and Critical Agency in Africa*. Chicago: University of Chicago Press, 2007.

———. *Black Critics and Kings: The Hermeneutics of Power in Yoruba Society*. Chicago: University of Chicago Press, 1992.

———. "The Historiography of Yoruba Myth and Ritual." *History in Africa* 14 (1987): 1–25.

Apter, David. *Oduduwa's Chain: Locations and Culture in the Yoruba Atlantic*. Chicago: University of Chicago Press, 2018.

———. "Yoruba Ethnogenesis from Within." *Comparative Studies in Society and History* 55, no. 2 (2013): 356–87.

Archer, Margaret S. *Being Human: The Problem of Agency*. Cambridge: Cambridge University Press, 2000.

———. *Culture and Agency: The Place of Culture in Social Theory*. 1988. Reprint, Cambridge: Cambridge University Press, 1996.

———. *Making Our Way through the World: Human Reflexivity and Social Mobility*. Cambridge: Cambridge University Press, 2007.

Asante, Molefi Kete. "Eleda." In *Encyclopedia of African Religion*, edited by Molefi Kete Asante and Ama Mazama, 238–39. Thousand Oaks, CA: Sage, 2009.

Askari, Eva Krapf. Review of *History of an African Independent Church*, by H. W. Turner, and *Aladura: A Religious Movement among the Yoruba*, by J. D. Y. Peel. *Bulletin of the School of Oriental and African Studies, University of London* 32, no. 3 (1969): 661–63.

Awofeso, Bimbo. *Abiola: To Make Whole Again*. Lagos: Update, 1990.

Awolowo, Obafemi. *Awo: The Autobiography of Chief Obafemi Awolowo*. Cambridge: Cambridge University Press, 1960.

Ayandele, Emmanuel A. *The Missionary Impact on Modern Nigeria, 1842–1914: A Political and Social Analysis*. London: Longman, 1966.

Azevedo-Harman, Elisabete. "Parliaments in Africa: Representative Institutions in the Land of the 'Big Man.'" *Journal of Legislative Studies* 17, no. 1 (2011): 65–85.

Babarinsa, Dare. *House of War: The Story of Awo's Followers*. Ibadan: Spectrum Books, 2003.

Bailey, F. G. *Stratagems and Spoils: A Social Anthropology of Politics*. Cambridge, MA: Westview, 2001.

Bakaari, Farah, Vincent Benlloch, and Barry Driscoll. "Political Scientists Talk about African 'Big Men' Inconsistently." LSE Blog, March 22, 2021.

Baker, Bruce. "When the Bakassi Boys Came: Eastern Nigeria Confronts Vigilantism." *Journal of Contemporary African Studies* 20, no. 2 (2002): 223–44.

Baker, Victoria J. "Elders in the Shadow of the Big Man." *Bijdragen tot de Taal-, Land- en Volkenkunde* Deel 139, *1ste Afl., Anthropologica* 25 (1983): 1–17.

Balandier, Georges. *Political Anthropology*. New York: Vantage, 1970.

Bangura, Yusuf. *Crisis, Adjustment and Politics in Nigeria*. Uppsala: AKUT, 1989.

Banks, Marcus. *Ethnicity: Anthropological Constructions*. London: Routledge, 1996.

Banks, Marcus, and Richard Vokes. "Introduction: Anthropology, Photography and the Archive." *History and Anthropology* 21, no. 4 (2010): 337–49.

Barber, Karin. "How Man Makes God in West Africa: Yoruba Attitudes towards the *Orisa*." *Africa: Journal of the International African Institute* 51, no. 3 (1981): 724–45.

———. Introduction to *Readings in African Popular Culture*, edited by Karin Barber, 1–11. Oxford: James Currey; Bloomington: Indiana University Press, 1987.

———. "When People Cross Thresholds." *African Studies Review* 50, no. 2 (2007): 111–23.

Barnes, Sandra T. *Patrons and Power: Creating a Political Community in Metropolitan Lagos*. Manchester: Manchester University Press, 1986.

Bayart, Jean-Francois. *The State in Africa: The Politics of the Belly*. Translated by Mary Harper, Christopher Harrison, and Elizabeth Harrison. London: Longman, 1993.

Beck, Ulrick. *Risk Society*. London: Sage, 1992.

Becker, H. *Sociological Work: Method and Substance*. Chicago: Aldine, 1970.

Behrend, Heike. "'I Am Like a Movie Star in My Street': Photographic Self-creation in Postcolonial Kenya." In *Postcolonial Subjectivities in Africa*, edited by Richard Werbner, 44–62. London: Zed Books, 2002.

Berner, Boel. "Manoeuvring in Uncertainty: On Agency, Strategies and Negotiations." In *Manoeuvring in an Environment of Uncertainty: Structural Change and Social Action in Sub-Saharan Africa*, edited by Boel Berner and Per Trulsson, 277–309. Aldershot: Ashgate, 2000.

Berry, Sara. "Questions of Ownership: Proprietorship and Control in a Changing Rural Terrain—a Case Study from Ghana." *Africa* 83, no. 1 (2013): 36–56.

Beverly, John. *Subalternity and Representation: Arguments in Cultural Theory*. Durham, NC: Duke University Press, 1999.

Blatterer, Harry. *Coming of Age in Times of Uncertainty*. New York: Berghahn Books, 2007.

Boltanski, Luc. "Les usages sociaux de l'automobile: concurrence pour l'espace et accidents." *Actes de la recherché en sciences sociales* 1, no. 2 (1975): 25–49.

Bottomore, T. B. *Elites and Society*. Middlesex: Penguin, 1966.

Bourdieu, Pierre. *Distinction: Social Critique and the Judgement of Taste*. Translated by Richard Nice. Cambridge, MA: Harvard University Press, 1984.

———. *The Logic of Practice*. Translated by Richard Nice. Stanford, CA: Stanford University Press, 1990.

———. *Outline of the Theory of Practice*. Translated by R. Nice. Stanford, CA: Stanford University Press, 1977.
———. *Pascalian Meditations*. Translated by Richard Nice. Stanford, CA: Stanford University Press, 2000.
Brown, Paula. "Big Man, Past and Present: Model, Person, Hero, Legend." *Ethnology* 29, no. 2 (1990): 97–115.
Buur, Lars. "Democracy & Its Discontents: Vigilantism, Sovereignty and Human Rights in South Africa." *Review of African Political Economy* 35, no. 118 (2008): 571–84.
Buur, Lars, and Steffen Jensen. "Introduction: Vigilantism and the Policing of Everyday Life in South Africa." *African Studies* 63, no. 2 (2004): 139–52.
Casey, Conerly. "Policing through Violence: Fear, Vigilantism, and the Politics of Islam in Northern Nigeria." In *Global Vigilantes: Perspectives on Justice and Violence*, edited by David Pratten and A. Sen, 90–119. London: Hurst, 2007.
Chabal, Patrick, and J.-P. Daloz. *African Works: Disorder as Political Instrument*. Oxford: James Currey, 1999.
Claessen, H. J. M. *Politieke Antropogie: Enn terrreinverkenning*. Assen: Van Gorcum, 1974.
Clark, Graham. *Symbols of Excellence*. Cambridge: Cambridge University Press, 1986.
Clark, John E., and M. Blake. "The Power of Prestige: Competitive Generosity and the Emergence of Rank Society in Lowland Mesoamerica." In *Factional Competition and Politics Development in the New World*, edited by E. M. Brumfiel and J. W. Fox, 17–30. Cambridge: Cambridge University Press, 1994.
Clayton, Daniel. "Subaltern Space." In *Handbook of Geographical Knowledge*, edited by J. Agnew and D. Livingstone, 246–60. London: Sage, 2010.
Clifford, James. *Routes: Travel and Translation in the Late Twentieth Century*. Cambridge, MA: Harvard University Press, 1997.
Clothey, Fred W. "Towards a Comprehensive Interpretation of Ritual." *Journal of Ritual Studies* 2, no. 2 (1988): 147–61.
Cohen, Abner. *The Politics of Elite Culture: Explorations in the Dramaturgy of Power in a Modern African Society*. Berkeley: University of California Press, 1981.
———. *Urban Ethnicity*. London: Routledge, 2001.
Coleman, James S. *Nigeria: Background to Nationalism*. Berkeley: University of California Press, 1958.
Comaroff, Jean, and John Comaroff. Introduction to *Modernity and Its Malcontents. Ritual and Power in Postcolonial Africa*, edited by Jean Comaroff and John Comaroff, xi–xxxiii. Chicago: The Chicago University Press, 1993.
———. "Reflections on Youth: From the Past to the Postcolony." In *Frontiers of Capital: Ethnographic Reflections on the New Economy*, edited by Melissa S. Fisher and Greg Downey, 267–81. Durham: Duke University Press, 2006.
Comaroff, John L., and Jean Comaroff. "Chief, Capital, and the State in Contemporary Africa: An Introduction." In *The Politics of Custom: Chiefship, Capital, and the*

State in Contemporary Africa, edited by John L. Comaroff and Jean Comaroff, 1–48. Chicago: University of Chicago Press, 2018.

———. *The Politics of Custom: Chiefship, Capital, and the State in Contemporary Africa*. Chicago: University of Chicago Press, 2018.

Cooper, Frederick. *Decolonization and African Society: The Labor Question in French and British Africa*. Cambridge: Cambridge University Press, 1996.

Cote, James E., and Anton Allahar. *Generation on Hold: Coming of Age in the Late Twentieth Century*. New York: New York University, 1994.

Crehan, Kate. *Gramsci, Culture and Anthropology*. London: Pluto, 2002.

Crow, Graham. "The Use of the Concept of 'Strategy' in Recent Sociological Literature." *Sociology* 23, no. 1 (1989): 1–24.

Cruise O'Brien, D. B. "A Lost Generation? Youth Identity and State Decay in West Africa." In *Postcolonial Identities in Africa*, edited by R. Werbner and T. Ranger, 55–74. London: Zed Books, 1996.

Daloz, Jean-Pascal. "'Big Men' in Sub-Saharan Africa: How Elites Accumulate Positions and Resources." *Comparative Sociology* 2, no. 1 (2003): 271–85.

———. *Rethinking Social Distinction*. New York: Palgrave Macmillan, 2013.

———. *The Sociology of Elite Distinction: From Theoretical to Comparative Perspectives*. New York: Palgrave Macmillan, 2010.

———. "Voitures et prestige au Nigeria" [Cars and prestige in Nigeria]. *Politique Africaine* 38 (1990): 148–53.

de Boeck, Filip. "Local Futures and the Future of the Local." In *African Futures: Essays on Crisis, Emergence, and Possibility*, edited by Brian Goldstone and Juan Obarrio, 151–66. Chicago: University of Chicago Press, 2017.

de Certeau, Michel. *The Practice of Everyday Life*. Berkeley: University of California Press, 1984.

Demirović, Alex. "The Politics of Truth: For a Different Way of Life." In *Gramsci and Foucault: A Reassessment*, edited by David Kreps, 11–30. London: Routledge, 2015.

De Smedt, Johan. "'No Raila, No Peace!': Big Man Politics and Election Violence at the Kibera Grassroots." *African Affairs* 108, no. 433 (2009): 581–98.

De St. Jorre, John. *The Nigerian Civil War*. London: Hodder and Stoughton, 1972.

Diamond, Larry. *Class, Ethnicity, and Democracy in Nigeria: The Failure of the First Republic*. Syracuse, NY: Syracuse University Press, 1988.

———. "Progress and Retreat in Africa: The Rule of Law versus the Big Man." *Journal of Democracy* 19, no. 2 (2008): 138–49.

Diamond, Larry, Anthony Kirk-Greene, and Oyeleye Oyediran, eds. *Transition without End: Nigerian Politics and Civil Society under Babangida*. Boulder, CO: Lynne Rienner, 1997.

Diouf, Mamadou. "Engaging Postcolonial Cultures: African Youth and Public Space." *African Studies Review* 46, no. 2 (2003): 1–12.

Douglas, Mary. *Purity and Danger: An Analysis of Concepts of Pollution and Taboo*. Abingdon: Routledge, 1966.

Drewal, Margaret Thompson. *Yoruba Rituals: Performers, Play, Agency.* Bloomington: Indiana University Press, 1992.

Driscoll, Barry. "Big Man or Boogey Man? The Concept of the Big Man in Political Science." *Journal of Modern African Studies* 58, no. 4 (2021): 521–50.

Dulani, Boniface, and John Tengatenga. "Big Man Rule in Africa: Are Africans Getting the Leadership They Want?" *African Review* 46 (2019): 275–91.

Du Preez, Max, and Mandy Rossouw. *The World according to Julius Malema.* Cape Town: NB, 2010.

Durham, Deborah. "Uncertain Citizens: Herero and the New Intercalary Subject in Postcolonial Botswana." In *Postcolonial Subjectivities in Africa,* edited by Richard Werbner, 139–70. London: Zed Books, 2002.

———. "Youth and the Social Imagination in Africa: Introduction to Parts 1 and 2." *Anthropological Quarterly* 73, no. 3 (2000): 113–20.

Edwards, Elizabeth. "Anthropology and Photography: A Long History of Knowledge and Affect." *Photographies* 8, no. 3 (2015): 235–52.

Elias, Nobert. *What Is Sociology?* New York: Columbia University Press, 1978.

Eriksen, T. H. *Ethnicity and Nationalism: Anthropological Perspectives.* London: Pluto, 1993.

Fadipe, N. A. *The Sociology of the Yoruba.* Edited by Francis Olu Okediji and Oladejo O. Okediji. Ibadan: Ibadan University Press, 1970.

Falola, Toyin, and G. O. Oguntomisin. *Yoruba Warlords of the Nineteenth Century.* Trenton, NJ: Africa World Press, 2001.

Fasehun, Frederick. *Frederick Fasehun: The Son of Oodua.* Lagos: Inspired Communications, 2002.

———. *OPC: Our History, Our Mission.* Lagos: Inspired Communications, 2005.

Fayemi, J. Kayode. *Out of the Shadows: Exile and the Struggle for Freedom & Democracy in Nigeria.* Ibadan: Amandla Consulting, 2005.

Ferguson, James. *Global Shadows: Africa in the Neoliberal World Order.* Durham, NC: Duke University Press, 2006.

Forde, Fiona. *An Inconvenient Youth: Julius Malema and the "New" ANC.* Johannesburg: Jonathan Ball Publishers, 2011; Edinburgh: Portobello Books, 2012.

———. *Still an Inconvenient Youth: Julius Malema Carries.* London: Picador, 2014.

Fortes, Meyer. "Ritual and Office in Tribal Society." In *Essays on the Ritual of Social Relations,* edited by Max Gluckman, 53–88. Manchester: University of Manchester Press, 1962.

Foucault, Michel. "The Subject and Power." In *Beyond Structuralism and Hermeneutics,* edited by H. Dreyfus and P. Rabinow, 208–26. Chicago: University of Chicago Press, 1983.

Fourchard, Laurent. "A New Name for an Old Practice: Vigilantes in South-Western Nigeria." *Africa* 78, no. 1 (2008): 535–58.

Frank, Gelya. "Anthropology and Individual Lives: The Story of the Life History and the History of the Life Story." *American Anthropologist* 97, no. 1 (1995): 145–48.

Friedman, Jonathan. *Consumption and Identity*. London: Routledge, 2004.

Fumanti, Mattia. *The Politics of Distinction: African Elites from Colonialism to Liberation in a Namibian Frontier Town*. Canon Pyon: Sean Kingston, 2016.

———. "'Showing-Off Aesthetics': Looking Good, Making Relations and 'Being in the World' in the London Akan Diaspora." *Ethnos: Journal of Anthropology* 78, no. 2 (2013): 200–25.

Gana, Aaron T., and Yakubu B. C. Omelle, eds. *Democratic Rebirth in Nigeria*. Vol. 1, *1999–2003*. Abuja: African Centre for Democratic Governance, 2005.

Geertz, Clifford. "Deep Play: Notes on the Balinese Cockfight." In *Interpretation of Cultures*. New York: Basic Books, 1972.

Gellner, Ernest. *Nations and Nationalism*. Oxford: Blackwell, 1983.

Geschiere, Peter. "African Chiefs and the Post–Cold War Moment: Millennial Capitalism and the Struggle over Moral Authority." In *The Politics of Custom: Chiefship, Capital, and the State in Contemporary Africa*, edited by John L. Comaroff and Jean Comaroff, 49–78. Chicago: University of Chicago Press, 2018.

Gibbs, Tim. "Becoming a 'Big Man' in Neo-liberal South Africa: Migrant Masculinities in the Minibus-Taxi Industry." *African Affairs* 113, no. 452 (2014): 431–48.

Giddens, Anthony. *Central Problems in Social Theory: Action, Structure and Contradiction in Social Analysis*. Berkeley: University of California Press, 1979.

———. *Modernity and Self-identity*. Cambridge: Polity, 1991.

Gluckman, Max. "Les Rites de Passage." In *Essays on the Ritual of Social Relations*, edited by Max Gluckman, 1–52. Manchester: Manchester University Press, 1962.

Godelier, Maurice. *The Making of Great Men: Male Domination and Power among the New Guinea Baruya*. Cambridge: Cambridge University Press, 1986.

———. "Social Hierarchies among the Baruya of New Guinea." In *Inequality in New Guinea Highland Societies*, edited by A. Strathern, 3–34. Cambridge: Cambridge University Press, 1982.

Goffman, Erving. *The Presentation of Self in Everyday Life*. New York: Doubleday Anchor Books, 1959.

Goodson, Ivor. "The Story of Life History." In *The Routledge International Handbook on Narrative and Life History*, edited by Ivor Goodson, Ari Antikainen, Pat Sikes, and Molly Andrews, 23–34. New York: Routledge, 2016.

Gore, Charles, and David Pratten. "The Politics of Plunder: The Rhetoric of Order and Disorder in Southern Nigeria." *African Affairs* 102, no. 407 (2003): 211–40.

Gore, Charles D. "Commemoration, Memory and Ownership: Some Social Contexts of Contemporary Photography in Benin City, Nigeria." *Visual Anthropology* 14, no. 3 (2001): 321–42.

Gramsci, Antonio. *Prison Notebooks*. Vol. 2, No. 3, §14. Edited and translated by Joseph A. Buttigieg. 1971. Reprint, New York: Columbia University Press, 1996.

———. *The Southern Question*. New York: Bordighera Press, 1995.

Green, Marcus E. "Gramsci and Subaltern Struggles Today: Spontaneity, Political Organization and Occupy Wall Street." In *Antonio Gramsci*, edited by Mark McNally, 156–78. London: Palgrave-Macmillan, 2015.

Guichaoua, Yvan. "How Do Ethnic Militias Perpetuate in Nigeria? A Micro-level Perspective on the Oodua People's Congress." *World Development* 38, no. 11 (2010): 1657–66.

———. "The Making of an Ethnic Militia: The Oodua People's Congress in Nigeria." CRISE Working Paper 26, University of Oxford, November 2006.

———. "Self-determination Group or Extra-legal Governance Agency? Multifaceted Nature of the Oodua People's Congress in Nigeria." *Journal of International Development* 21 (2009): 520–33.

———. "Who Joins Ethnic Militias? A Survey of the Oodua People's Congress in Southwestern Nigeria." CRISE Working Paper 44, University of Oxford, March 2007.

Guha, Ranajit, and Gayatri Chakravorty Spivak, eds. *Selected Subaltern Studies*. 1982. Reprint, New York: Oxford University Press, 1988.

Guo, Yaping, and Wei Ren. "Gramsci Cannot Speak: Presentations and Interpretations of Gramsci's Concept of the Subaltern." *Rethinking Marxism* 14, no. 3 (2002): 1–24.

———. "Managing Image: The Self-praise of Celebrities on Social Media." *Discourse, Context & Media* 38 (2020): 1–9.

Guya, Ranajit. "On Some Aspects of the Historiography of Colonial India." In *Selected Subaltern Studies*, edited by Ranajit Guya and Gayatri Chakravorty Spivak, 37–44. Oxford: Oxford University Press, 1988.

Guyer, Jane I. "Wealth in People, Wealth in Things: Introduction." *Journal of African History* 36, no. 1 (1995): 83–90.

Guyer, Jane I., and Samuel M. Eno Belinga. "Wealth in People as Wealth in Knowledge: Accumulation and Composition in Equatorial Africa." *Journal of African History* 36, no. 1 (1995): 91–120.

Hansen, Karen T. "Getting Stuck in the Compound: Some Odds against Social Adulthood in Lusaka, Zambia." *Africa Today* 51, no. 4 (2005): 3–16.

Hardiman, David. "'Subaltern Studies' at Crossroads." *Economic and Political Weekly* 21, no. 7 (February. 15, 1986): 288–90.

Harnischfeger, Johannes. "The Bakassi Boys: Fighting Crime in Nigeria." *Journal of Modern African Studies* 41, no. 1 (2003): 23–49.

———. *Democratization and Islamic Law: The Sharia Conflict in Nigeria*. Frankfurt: Campus, 2008.

Harrison, Simon. "From Prestige Goods to Legacies: Property and the Objectification of Culture in Melanesia." *Comparative Studies in Society and History* 42, no. 3 (2000): 662–79.

Higazi, Adam. "Social Mobilization and Collective Violence: Vigilantes and Militias in the Lowlands of Plateau State, Central Nigeria." *Africa: Journal of the International African Institute* 78, no. 1 (2008): 107–35.

Higley, John, and Michael Burton. *Elite Foundations of Liberal Democracy*. Lanham, MD: Rowman and Littlefield, 2006.

Higley, John, and Richard Gunther, eds. *Elites and Democratic Consolidation in Latin America and Southern Europe*. New York: Cambridge University Press, 1991.

Hirst, Fred. *Social Limits to Growth*. London: Routledge, 1977.

Hjarvard, Stig. "The Mediatization of Society: A Theory of the Media as Agents of Social and Cultural Change." *Nordicom Review* 29, no. 2 (2008): 105–34.

Hobsbawm, Eric, and Terence Ranger. *The Invention of Tradition*. Cambridge: Cambridge University Press, 1992.

Hoffman, Danny. "Disagreement: Dissent Politics and the War in Sierra Leone." *Africa Today* 52, no. 3 (2006): 3–22.

Hoffmann, Leena. "Fairy Godfathers and Magical Elections: Understanding the 2003 Electoral Crisis in Anambra State, Nigeria." *Journal of Modern African Studies* 48, no. 2 (2010): 285–310.

Honwana, Alcinda. *The Time of Youth: Work, Social Change, and Politics in Africa*. Boulder, CO: Kumarian Press, 2012.

———. "'Waithood': Youth Transitions and Social Change." In *Development and Equity: An Interdisciplinary Exploration by Ten Scholars from Africa, Asia and Latin America*, edited by Dick Foeken, Ton Dietz, Leo de Haan, and Linda Johnson, 28–40. Leiden: Brill, 2014.

Honwana, Alcinda, and Fillip de Boeck, eds. *Makers and Breakers: Children and Youth in Postcolonial Africa*. Oxford: James Currey, 2005.

Horton, Robin. "Ritual Man in Africa." *Africa: Journal of the International African Institute* 35, no. 2 (1964): 85–103.

Hucks, Tracey E. *Yoruba Traditions and African American Religious Nationalism*. Albuquerque: University of New Mexico Press, 2012.

Human Rights Watch. "The O'odua People's Congress: Fighting Violence with Violence." *Human Rights Watch* 15, no. 4A (February 28, 2003). https://www.hrw.org/node/255663/printable/print.

Huntington, Samuel. *The Third Wave: Democratization in the Late Twentieth Century*. Norman: University of Oklahoma Press, 1991.

Hyden, Goran. *African Politics in Comparative Perspective*. Cambridge: Cambridge University Press, 2006.

Ibeanu, Okechukwu. "Ethnicity and Transition to Democracy in Nigeria: Explaining the Passing of Authoritarian Rule in a Multi-ethnic Society." *African Journal of Political Science/Revue Africaine de Science Politique* 5, no. 2 (2000): 45–65.

Ihonvbere, Julius O. "Economic Crisis, Structural Adjustment and Social Crisis in Nigeria." *World Development* 21, no. 1 (1991): 141–53.

———. "Where Is the Third Wave? A Critical Evaluation of Africa's Non-transition to Democracy." *Africa Today* 43, no. 4 (1996): 343–67.

International IDEA. *Democracy in Nigeria: Continuing Dialogue(s) for Nation-Building*. Stockholm: International IDEA, 2000.

Ismail, Olawale. "From 'Area-Boyism' to 'Junctions and Bases': Youth Social Formation and the Micro-structures of Violence in Lagos Island." In *State Fragility, State*

Formation, and Human Security in Nigeria, edited by Mojubaola O. Okome, 87–109. New York: Palgrave Macmillan, 2013.

Isumonah, Victor Adefemi. "Minority Political Mobilization in the Struggle for Resource Control in Nigeria." *Extractive Industries and Society* 2, no. 4 (2015): 645–53.

Jega, Attahiru. "General Introduction: Identity Transformation and the Politics of Identity under Crisis and Adjustment." In *Identity Transformation and Identity Politics under Structural Adjustment in Nigeria*, edited by Attahiru Jega, 11–23. Uppsala: Nordic Africa Institute, 2000.

———, ed. *Identity Transformation and Identity Politics under Structural Adjustment in Nigeria*. Uppsala: Nordic Africa Institute, 2000.

Johnson, A. W., and T. K. Earle. *The Evolution of Human Societies: From Foraging Group to Agrarian State*. Stanford, CA: Stanford University Press, 2000.

Johnson, Samuel. *The History of the Yorubas: From the Earliest Times to the Beginning of the British Protectorate*. Lagos: CMS Nigeria Bookshop, 1921.

Jolly, M. "The Chimera of Equality in Melanesia." *Mankind* 17 (1987): 168–83.

Joseph, Richard. *Democracy and Prebendal Politics in Nigeria: The Rise and Fall of the Second Republic*. Cambridge: Cambridge University Press, 1987.

Josephides, Lisette. *The Production of Inequality: Gender and Exchange among the Kewa*. London: Routledge, 1985.

Kandeh, Jimmy D. "Ransoming the State: Elite Origins of Subaltern Terror in Sierra Leone." *Review of African Political Economy* 26, no. 81 (1999): 349–66.

Kapferer, Bruce. "Beyond Symbolic Representation: Victor Turner and Variations on the Themes of Ritual Process and Liminality." *Suomen Antropologi: Journal of the Finnish Anthropological Society* 33, no. 4 (2008): 2–25.

Karl, Terry Lynn. "The Perils of the Petro-State: Reflections on the Paradox of Plenty." *Journal of International Affairs* 53, no. 1 (1999): 31–48.

Keane, John. *Violence and Democracy*. Cambridge: Cambridge University Press, 2004.

Kenghammer, Brandon. *Muslims Talking Politics: Framing Islam, Democracy, and Law in Northern Nigeria*. Chicago: University of Chicago Press, 2016.

Kifordu, Henry Ani. "Ethnic Politics, Political Elite, and Regime Change in Nigeria." *Studies in Ethnicity and Nationalism* 11, no. 3 (2011): 427–50.

Kovacs, Mimmi Söderberg, and Jesper Bjarnesen. *Violence in African Elections: Between Democracy and Big Man*. London: Zed Books, 2018.

Králová, Jana. "What Is Social Death?" *Contemporary Social Science* 10, no. 3 (2015): 235–48.

Laitin, David D. *Hegemony and Culture: Politics and Religious Change among the Yoruba*. Chicago: University of Chicago Press, 1986.

Lambek, Michael. "Nuriaty, the Saint, and the Sultan." In *Postcolonial Subjectivities in Africa*, edited by Richard Werbner, 25–43. London: Zed Books, 2002.

Lasswell, Harold D., Daniel Lerner, and Easton C. Rothwell. *The Comparative Study of Elites*. Stanford, CA: Hoover Institute Studies Series, 1952.

Law, Robin C. C. *The Oyo Empire, c. 1600–c. 1836*. Oxford: Oxford University Press, 1977.

Lawuyi, Olatunde Bayo. "Orí, Ayé and the Ontogeny of Society." *Journal of Contemporary African Studies* 39, no. 3 (2021): 353–63.

Lawuyi, Olatunji Bayo, and Olufemi Taiwo. "Towards an African Sociological Tradition: A Rejoinder to Akiwowo and Makinde." *International Sociology* 5, no. 1 (1990): 57–73.

Leach, Edmund. *The Essential Edmund Leach: Anthropology of Society*. New Haven, CT: Yale University Press, 2001.

Lefebvre, Henri. *Everyday Life in the Modern World*. London: Allen Lane, 1971.

LeVan, Carl A. *Contemporary Nigerian Politics: Competition in a Time of Transition and Terror*. Cambridge: Cambridge University Press, 2019.

Liebau, E., and L. Chisholm. "Youth, Social Change and Education: Issue and Problems." *Journal of Educational Policy* 8, no. 1 (1993): 3–8.

Liguori, Guido. "Conceptions of Subalternity in Gramsci." In *Antonio Gramsci*, edited by Mark McNally, 118–33. London: Palgrave-Macmillan, 2015.

Linde, Charlotte. *Life Stories: The Creation of Coherence*. New York: Oxford University Press, 1993.

Lindstrom, Lamont. "'Big Man': A Short Terminological History." *American Anthropologist* 83, no. 4 (1981): 900–905.

Lynch, Gabrielle. "Moi: The Making of an African 'Big-Man.'" *Journal of Eastern African Studies* 2, no. 1 (2008): 18–43.

Machiavelli, Niccolò. *The Prince*. Translated by George Bull. London: Penguin, 1961.

Mafeje, Archie. "South Africa: The Dynamics of a Beleaguered State." *African Journal of Political Economy/Revue Africaine d'Economie Politique* 1, no. 1 (1986): 95–119.

Mains, Daniel. *Hope Is Cut: Youth, Unemployment, and the Future in Urban Ethiopia*. Philadelphia: Temple University Press, 2012.

———. "Too Much Time: Changing Conceptions of Boredom, Progress, and the Future among Young Men in Urban Ethiopia, 2003–2015." *Focaal: Journal of Global and Historical Anthropology* 78 (2017): 38–51.

Makinde, Olufemi. "Oodua Republic: Yoruba Hunters' Group Vows to Arrest Secessionists." *The Whistler*, September 15, 2020. https://thewhistler.ng/oodua-republic-yoruba-hunters-group-vows-to-arrest-secessionists/.

Malinowski, Bronislaw. *Magic, Science and Religion and Other Essays*. Introduction by Robert Redfield. Glencore, IL: Free Press, 1948.

Malkki, Lissa A. *Purity and Exile: Violence, Memory, and National Cosmology among Hutu Refugees in Tanzania*. Chicago: University of Chicago Press, 1995.

Mann, Kristin. *Marrying Well: Marriage, Status and Educated Elites in Colonial Lagos*. Cambridge: Cambridge University Press, 1985.

Marcus, George E., ed. *Elites: Ethnographic Issues*. Albuquerque: School of American Research, University of New Mexico Press, 1983.

Marks, Monique. *Young Warriors: Youth Politics, Identity and Violence in South Africa*. Johannesburg: Witwatersrand University Press, 2001.

Masquelier, Adeline. *Fada: Boredom and Belonging in Niger.* Chicago: University of Chicago Press, 2019.

———. "The Scorpion's Sting: Youth, Marriage and the Struggle for Social Maturity in Niger." *Journal of the Royal Anthropological Institute* 11 (2005): 59–83.

———. "Teatime: Boredom and the Temporalities of Young Men in Niger." *Africa* 83, no. 3 (2013): 470–91.

Matory, Lorand J. *Black Atlantic Religion: Tradition, Transnationalism, and Matriarchy in the Afro-Brazilian Candomblé.* Princeton, NJ: Princeton University Press, 2005.

———. "The English Professors of Brazil: On the Diasporic Roots of the Yoruba Nation." *Comparative Studies in Society and History* 41, no. 1 (1999): 72–103.

Mbembe, Achille. "Everything Can Be Negotiated: Ambiguities and Challenges in Time of Uncertainty." In *Manoeuvring in an Environment of Uncertainty: Structural Change and Social Action in Sub-Saharan Africa,* edited by Boel Berner and Per Trulsson, 265–75. Aldershot: Ashgate, 2000.

———. Foreword to *An Inconvenient Youth: Julius Malema and the "New" ANC,* by Fiona Forde. Johannesburg: Picador Africa, 2011.

———. *Out of the Dark Night: Essays on Decolonization.* New York: Columbia University Press, 2021.

McNamara, Kim. "Publicising Private Lives: Celebrities, Image Control and the Reconfiguration of Public Space." *Social & Cultural Geography* 10, no. 1 (2009): 9–23.

Meagher, Kate. "Hijacking Civil Society: The Inside Story of the Bakassi Boys Vigilante Group of South-eastern Nigeria." *Journal of Modern African Studies* 45, no. 1 (2007): 89–115.

Meyer, Birgit. "Mediation and Immediacy: Sensational Forms, Semiotic Ideologies and the Question of the Medium." *Social Anthropology/Anthropologie sociale* 19, no. 1 (2011): 23–39.

Miescher, Stephan F. *Making Men in Ghana.* Bloomington: Indiana University Press, 2005.

Milchman, Alan, and Alan Rosenberg. "The Aesthetic and Ascetic Dimensions of an Ethics of Self-fashioning: Nietzsche and Foucault." *Perrhesia,* no. 2(2007): 44–65.

Miller, Paul Allen. "The Art of Self-fashioning, or Foucault on Plato and Derrida." *Foucault Studies,* no. 2 (2005): 54–74.

Mines, Mattison, and Vijayalakshmi Gourishankar. "Leadership and Individuality in South Asia: The Case of the South Indian Big-Man." *Journal of Asian Studies* 49, no. 4 (1990): 761–86.

Mkandiwire, Thandika. "Neopatrimonialism and the Political Economy of Economic Performance in Africa: Critical Reflections." *World Politics* 67, no. 3 (2015): 563–612.

Momoh, Abubakar. "Youth Culture and Area Boys in Lagos." In *Identity Transformation and Identity Politics under Structural Adjustment in Nigeria,* edited by A. Jega, 181–203. Uppsala: Nordiska Afrikainstitutet, 2000.

Momoh, Abubakar, and Said Adejumobi. *The Nigerian Military and the Crisis of Democratic Transition: A Study in the Monopoly of Power.* Lagos: CLO, 1999.

Moncada, Eduardo. "Varieties of Vigilantism: Conceptual Discord, Meaning and Strategies." *Global Crime* 18, no. 4 (2017): 403–23.

Morris, Rosalind C. Introduction to *Reflections on the History of an Idea: Can the Subaltern Speak?*, edited by Rosalind C. Morris, 1–20. New York: Columbia University Press, 2010.

Mosca, Gaetano. *The Ruling Class*. New York: McGraw-Hill, 1939.

Munro, P. *Subject to Fiction: Women Teachers' Life History Narratives and the Cultural Politics of Resistance*. Buckingham: Open University Press, 1998.

Mustapha, Abdul Raufu, and Kate Meagher. *Overcoming Boko Haram: Faith, Society & Islamic Radicalization in Northern Nigeria*. Woodbridge: James Currey, 2020.

Nnoli, Okwudiba. "Ethnic Conflicts in Africa: A Comparative Analysis." In *Ethnic Conflicts in Africa*, edited by O. Nnoli, 287–310. Dakar: CODESRIA, 1998.

———. *Ethnicity and Development in Nigeria*. Aldershot: Avebury, 1995.

Nolte, Insa. "Ethnic Vigilantes and the State: The Oodua People's Congress in South-Western Nigeria." *International Relations* 21, no. 2 (2007): 217–35.

———. "Identity and Violence: The Politics of Youth in Ijebu-Remo, Nigeria." *Journal of Modern African Studies* 42, no. 1 (2004): 61–90.

———. "'Without Women, Nothing Can Succeed': Yoruba Women in the Oodua People's Congress (OPC), Nigeria." *Africa* 78, no. 1 (2008): 84–106.

Nugent, Stephen, and Cris Shore, eds. *Elite Cultures: Anthropological Perspectives*. London: Routledge, 2002.

Nwankwo, Nkem. *My Mercedes Is Bigger Than Yours*. Ibadan: Heinemann, 1975.

Nwokedi, Emeka. "Nigeria's Democratic Transition: Explaining the Annulled 1993 Presidential Election." *Round Table* 83, no. 330 (1994): 189–204.

Nyamnjoh, Francis. "'A Child Is One Person's Only in the Womb': Domestication, Agency and Subjectivity in the Cameroonian Grassfields." In *Postcolonial Subjectivities in Africa*, edited by Richard Werbner, 111–38. London: Zed Books, 2002.

Nyangulu, Deborah. "Big Men and Performances of Sovereignty in Contemporary African Novels." *Research in African Literatures* 49, no. 3 (2018): 101–15.

Obadare, Ebenezer. "Being Adedibu: On Contracting (Out) the State in Nigeria." Translated by Vincent Foucher. *Politique Africaine* 106, no. 2 (2007): 110–27.

———. *Pastoral Power, Clerical State: Pentecostalism, Gender, and Sexuality in Nigeria*. Notre Dame, IN: University of Notre Dame Press, 2022.

Ogundiran, Akinwumi. *The Yoruba: A New History*. Bloomington: Indiana University Press, 2020.

Oguntomisin, Dare. *Kurunmi of Ijaye, 1831–1862: A Biography of a Militant Yoruba Ruler*. Ikeja: John West, 1986.

Ojo, Bamidele A., ed. *Nigeria's Third Republic: The Problems and Prospects of Political Transition to Civil Rule*. New York: Nova Science, 1998.

Okeke, Okechukwu. *Hausa-Fulani Hegemony: The Dominance of the Muslim North in Contemporary Nigerian Politics*. Enugu: Acena, 1992.

Olarinmoye, Omobolaji Ololade. "Godfathers, Political Parties and Electoral Corruption in Nigeria." *African Journal of Political Science and International Relations* 2, no. 4 (2008): 66–73.

———. "The Subaltern Encounters the State: OPC-State Relations 1999–2003." In *Encountering the Nigerian State*, edited by Wale Adebanwi and Obadare Ebenezer, 139–54. New York: Palgrave Macmillan, 2010.

Oliver, Douglas L. *A Solomon Island Society: Kinship and Leadership among the Siuai of Bougainville*. Cambridge, MA: Harvard University Press, 1955.

Olukoshi, Adebayo O. "Introduction: From Crisis to Adjustment in Nigeria." In *The Politics of Structural Adjustment*, edited by Adebayo Olukoshi. London: James Currey, 1993.

Olupona, Jacob K. "Bonds, Boundaries, and Bondage of Faith." *Harvard Divinity Bulletin* 41, no. 2 (2013). https://wcfia.harvard.edu/publications/bonds-boundaries-and-bondage-faith.

———. *City of 201 Gods: Ilé-Ifè* in Time, Space, and the Imagination. Berkeley: University of California Press, 2011.

———. *Kingship, Religion, and Rituals in a Nigerian Community: A Phenomenological Study of Ondo Yoruba Festivals*. Stockholm: Almqvist and Wiksell International, 1991.

Olupona, Jacob Kẹhinde, and Terry Rey, eds. Òrìṣà *Devotion as World Religion: The Globalization of Yorùbá Religious Culture*. Madison: University of Wisconsin Press, 2008.

Omobowale, Ayokunle Olumuyiwa, and Akinpelu Olanrewaju Olutayo. "Chief Lamidi Adedibu and Patronage Politics in Nigeria." *Journal of Modern African Studies* 45, no. 3 (2007): 425–46.

Omoruyi, Omo. *The Tale of June 12: The Betrayal of the Democratic Rights of Nigerians (1993)*. London: Press Alliance Network, 1999.

Omotola, J. Shola. "Godfathers and the 2007 Nigerian Elections." *Journal of African Elections* 2, no. 2 (2007): 134–54.

Onimode, Bade. "Game Theory and the Politics of Transformation in Nigeria." In *Governance and Development in Nigeria: Essays in Honour of Professor Billy J. Dudley*, edited by Oyeleye Oyediran, 64–92. Ibadan: Oyediran Consult International, 1996.

Onwudiwe, Ebere. "Geopolitical Zones and the Consolidation of Democracy." In *Nigeria's Struggle for Democracy and Good Governance: A Festschrift for Oyeleye Oyediran*, edited by Adigun Agbaje, Larry Diamond, and Ebere Onwudiwe, 267–76. Ibadan: University of Ibadan Press, 2004.

Ortner, Sherry B. *Anthropology and Social Theory: Culture, Power, and the Acting Subject*. Durham, NC: Duke University Press, 2006.

———. *Life and Death on Mt. Everest: Sherpas and Himalayan Mountaineering*. Princeton, NJ: Princeton University Press, 1999.

———. "Theory in Anthropology since the Sixties." *Comparative Studies in Society and History* 26, no. 1 (1984): 126–66.

Osaghae, Eghosa E. "Explaining the Changing Patterns of Ethnic Politics in Nigeria." *Nationalism and Ethnic Politics* 9, no. 3 (2003): 54–73.

———. *Structural Adjustment and Ethnicity in Nigeria*. Research Report 98. Uppsala: Nordiska Afrikainstitutet, 1995.

Osaghae, Eghosa E., Augustine Ikelegbe, Omobolaji O. Olarinmoye, and Stephen I. Okhomina. *Youths Militias, Self Determination and Resource Control Struggles in the Niger-delta Region of Nigeria*. CODESRIA Research Reports 5. Dakar: CODESRIA, 2011.

Osaghae, Eghosa E., and Rotimi T. Suberu. "A History of Identities, Violence, and Stability in Nigeria." CRISE Working Paper 6, Queen Elizabeth House, University of Oxford, 2005.

Oshun, Olawale. *Clapping with One Hand: June 12 and the Crisis of a State Nation*. Lagos: Josel, 1999.

———. *The Open Grave: NADECO and the Struggle for Democracy in Nigeria*. Lagos: Josel, 2002.

Pareto, Vilfredo. *The Mind and Society*. London: Jonathan Cape, 1935.

———. *The Rise and Fall of the Elites*. With an introduction by Hans L. Zetterberg. 1968. Reprint, Salem, NH: Ayer, 2017.

Patterson, Orlando. *Slavery and Social Death: A Comparative Study*. Cambridge, MA: Harvard University Press, 1982.

Peatrik, Anne-Marie. "Towards an Anthropology of Youth in Africa." Translated by Matthew Cunningham. *Ateliers d'anthropologie* 47 (2020). https://doi.org/10.4000/ateliers.12620.

Peel, J. D. Y. *Aladura: A Religious Movement among the Yoruba*. London: Oxford University Press, 1968.

———. *Christianity, Islam, and Orisa Religion: Three Traditions in Comparison and Interaction*. Berkeley: University of California Press, 2015.

———. *Ijeshas and Nigerians: The Incorporation of a Yoruba Kingdom, 1890s–1970s*. Cambridge: Cambridge University Press, 1983.

———. "Olaju: A Yoruba Concept of Development." *Journal of Development Studies* 14, no. 2 (1978): 135–65.

———. *Religious Encounter and the Making of the Yoruba*. Bloomington: Indiana University Press, 2000.

Pina-Cabral, João. Introduction to *Elites: Choice, Leadership and Succession*, edited by João Pina-Cabral and Antonia Pedroso de Lima, 1–8. Oxford: Berg, 2000.

Plourde, Aimée M. "The Origins of Prestige Goods as Honest Signals of Skill and Knowledge." *Human Nature* 19, no. 4 (2008): 374–88.

———. "Prestige Goods and the Formation of Political Hierarchy: A Costly Signalling Model." In *Patterns and Process of Cultural Evolution*, edited by Stephen Shennan, 265–76. Berkeley: University of California Press, 2009.

Posner, Daniel N., and Daniel J. Young. "Institutionalization of Political Power in Africa." *Journal of Democracy* 18, no. 3 (2007): 126–40.

Post, Kenneth W. J., and George D. Jenkins. *The Price of Liberty: Personality and Politics in Colonial Nigeria*. Cambridge: Cambridge University Press, 1973.

Prakash, Gyan. "The Impossibility of Subaltern History." *Nepantla: Views from South* 1, no. 2 (2000): 287–94.

Pratten, David. "Introduction: The Politics of Protection; Perspectives on Vigilantism in Nigeria." *Africa: Journal of the International African Institute* 78, no. 1 (2008): 1–15.

Probst, Peter. "Matter of Mimicry: Visual Publics." *Critical Interventions* 2, no. 1–2 (2008): 7–10.

———. "Picturing the Past: Heritage, Photography, and the Politics of Appearance in a Yoruba City." In *Reclaiming Heritage: Alternative Imaginaries of Memory in West Africa*, edited by Ferdinand de Jong and Michael Rowlands, 99–126. London: Routledge, 2007.

Rancière, Jacques. *Dissensus: On Politics and Aesthetics*. Edited and translated by Steven Corcoran. London: Bloomsbury Academic, 2010.

———. "The Thinking of Dissensus: Politics and Aesthetics." In *Reading Ranciere*, edited by Richard Stamp and Paul Bowman, 1–17. London: Continuum International, 2011.

Rapport, Roy. *Ritual and Religion in the Making of Humanity*. New York: Cambridge University Press, 1999.

Riach, Graham. *An Analysis of Gayatri Chakravorty Spivak's "Can the Subaltern Speak?"* London: Macat International, 2017.

Riches, David. "The Phenomenon of Violence." In *The Anthropology of Violence*, edited by David Riches, 1–27. Oxford: Basil Blackwell, 1986.

Roscoe, Paul B. "Before Elites: The Political Capacities of Big Men." In *Before Elites: Alternatives to Hierarchical Systems in Modelling Social Formations*, edited by Tobias L. Kienlin and Andreas Zimmerman, 41–54. Bonn: Rudolph Habelt, 2012.

Rotimi, Kemi. *The Police in a Federal State: The Nigerian Experience*. Ibadan: College Press, 2001.

Sahlins, Marshall. *Islands of History*. Chicago: University of Chicago Press, 1985.

———. "Poor Man, Rich Man, Big-Man, Chief: Political Types in Melanesia and Polynesia." *Comparative Studies in Society and History* 5, no. 3 (1963): 285–303.

Said, Edward W. Foreword to *Selected Subaltern Studies*, edited by Ranajit Guha and Gayatri C. Spivak, v–x. 1982. Reprint, New York: Oxford University Press, 1988.

Salverda, Tijo, and Jon Abbink. "Introduction: An Anthropological Perspective on Elite Power and the Cultural Politics of Elites." In *The Anthropology of Elites: Power, Culture, and the Complexities of Distinction*, edited by Jon Abbink and Tijo Salverda, 1–28. New York: Palgrave Macmillan, 2013.

Sarker, Sonita. "Subalternity In and Out of Time, In and Out of History." In *Gramsci and Foucault: A Reassessment*, edited by David Kreps, 91–110. London: Routledge, 2015.

Schatzberg, Michael. *Political Legitimacy in Middle Africa: Father, Family, Food*. Bloomington: Indiana University Press, 2001.

Schmidt, Bettina, and Ingo Schroeder, eds. *Anthropology of Violence and Conflict*. London: Routledge, 2001.

Sewell, William H. "A Theory of Structure: Duality, Agency, and Transformation." *American Journal of Sociology* 98, no. 1 (1992): 1–29.

Shore, Cris. "Introduction: Towards an Anthropology of the Elites." In *Elite Cultures: Anthropological Perspectives*, edited by Stephen Nugent and Cris Shore, 1–21. London: Routledge, 2002.

Simone, AbdouMaliq. "Some Reflections on Making Popular Culture in Urban Africa." *African Studies Review* 51, no. 3 (2008): 75–89.

Skeggs, Beverley. "Exchange, Value and Affect: Bourdieu and 'the Self.'" *Sociological Review* 52, no. 2, Supplement (2004): 75–95.

Smith, Daniel Jordan. "The Bakassi Boys: Vigilantism, Violence and Political Imagination in Nigeria." *Current Anthropology* 19, no. 3 (2004): 429–55.

———. *To Be a Man Is Not a One-Day Job: Masculinity, Money, and Intimacy in Nigeria*. Chicago: University of Chicago Press, 2017.

Smith, Janet, and Floyd Shivambu. *The Coming Revolution: Julius Malema and the Fight for Economic Freedom*. Johannesburg: Jacana Media, 2004.

Smith, Nicholas Rush. *Contradictions of Democracy: Vigilantism and Rights in Post-Apartheid South Africa*. Oxford: Oxford University Press, 2019.

Smith, Robert. "The *Alafin* in Exile: A Study of the Igboho Period in Oyo History." *Journal of African History* 6, no. 1 (1965): 57–77.

Sontag, Susan. *On Photography*. New York: Picador, 1973.

Southall, Roger, and H. Melber, eds. *A New Scramble for Africa: Imperialism, Investment and Development*. Scottsville: University of KwaZulu-Natal Press, 2006.

Spencer, Jonathan. *Anthropology, Politics and the State: Democracy and Violence in South Asia*. Cambridge: Cambridge University Press, 2007.

Spivak, Gayatri Chakravorty. "Can the Subaltern Speak?" In *Marxism and the Interpretation of Culture*, edited by Cary Nelson and Lawrence Grossberg, 271–313. Urbana: University of Illinois Press, 1988.

———. *The Postcolonial Critic: Interviews, Strategies, Dialogues*. Edited by Sarah Harasym. London: Routledge, 1990.

———. "Scattered Speculations on the Subaltern and the Popular." *Postcolonial Studies* 8, no. 4 (2005): 475–76.

———. "Theory in the Margin: Coetzee's 'Foe Reading Defoe's Crusoe/Roxana.'" In *Consequences of Theory: Selected Papers of the English Institute, 1987–1988*, edited by Jonathan Arac and Barbara Johnson, 154–80. Baltimore: Johns Hopkins University Press, 1991.

———. "The Trajectory of the Subaltern in My Work." Lecture, University of California, Santa Barbara, 2004. Aired September 13, 2004, on UCTV, 88 min. http://www.uctv.tv/search-details.aspx?showID=8840.

Sprague, Stephen. "How I See the Yoruba See Themselves." *Studies in the Anthropology of Visual Communication* 5, no. 1 (1978): 9–29.

Stasik, Michael, Valerie Hänsch, and Daniel Mains. "Temporalities of Waiting in Africa." *Critical African Studies* 12, no. 1 (2020): 1–9.

Stephenson, Barry. *Ritual: A Very Short Introduction*. Oxford: Oxford University Press, 2015.

Stewart, Pamela J., and Andrew Strathern. *Violence: Theory and Ethnography*. London: Continuum, 2002.
Strathern, Andrew, ed. *Inequality in New Guinea Highland Societies*. Cambridge: Cambridge University Press, 1982.
Swidler, Ann. "Culture in Action: Symbols and Strategies." *American Sociological Review* 51 (1986): 273–86.
Táíwò, Olúfemi. *Africa Must Be Modern*. Bloomington: Indiana University Press, 2014.
———. *Against Decolonisation: Taking African Agency Seriously*. London: Hurst, 2022.
———. *How Colonialism Preempted Modernity in Africa*. Bloomington: Indiana University Press, 2010.
Tallroth, Nils Borje. "Structural Adjustment in Nigeria." *Finance and Development* 24, no. 3 (1987): 20–22.
Thoden van Velzen, H. U. E. "Robinson Crusoe and Friday: Strength and Weakness of the Big Man Paradigm." *Man, Journal of the Royal Anthropological Institute*, n.s., 8, no. 4 (1973): 592–612.
Thomas, N. "The Force of Ethnology: Origins and Significance of the Melanesia/Polynesia Division." *Current Anthropology* 30 (1989): 27–34.
Thompson, E. P. *The Making of the English Working Class*. New York: Vintage Books, 1963.
Tilman, Rick. *Thorstein Veblen and His Critics, 1891–1963: Conservative, Liberal and Radical Perspectives*. Princeton, NJ: Princeton University Press, 1992.
Tonkin, Elizabeth. "Zik's Story: Autobiography as Political Exemplar." In *Self-assertion and Brokerage: Early Cultural Nationalism in West Africa*, edited by P. F. de Moraes Farias and Karin Barber, 35–54. Birmingham: Centre of West African Studies, 1990.
Travers, Martin. "Fascism and Aesthetic Self-fashioning: Politics and the Ritualised Body in the Poetry of Stefan George." *Culture, Theory, and Critique* 42, no. 1 (1999): 20–35.
Trouwborst, Albert A. "The 'Big-Man': A Melanesian Model in Africa." In *Private Politics: A Multi-disciplinary Approach to 'Big-Man' Systems*, edited by M. van Bakel, Renée R. Hagesteijn, and Pieter Van De Velde, 48–53. Leiden: Brill, 1986.
Turner, H. W. *History of the African Independent Church*. 2 Vols. Oxford: Clarendon, 1967.
———. "A Typology for Modern African Religious Movements." *Journal of Religion in Africa* 1, no. 1 (1967): 1–34.
Turner, Victor. *The Forest of Symbols: Aspects of Ndembu Ritual*. Ithaca, NY: Cornell University Press, 1967.
———. *The Ritual Process*. London: Routledge, 1969.
Ukiwo, Ukoha. "Deus Ex Machina or Frankenstein Monster: The Changing Roles of Bakassi Boys in Eastern Nigeria." *Democracy and Development: A Journal of West African Affairs* 3, no. 1 (2002): 39–51.

———. "The Study of Ethnicity in Nigeria." *Oxford Development Studies* 33, no. 1 (2005): 7–23.

Ungar, Mark, Sally Avery Bermanzohn, and Kenton Worcester. "Introduction: Violence and Politics." In *Violence and Politics: Globalization's Paradox*, edited by Mark Ungar, Sally Avery Bermanzohn, and Kenton Worcester, 1–12. New York: Routledge, 2002.

Usman, Aribidesi, and Toyin Falola. *The Yoruba from Prehistory to the Present*. Cambridge: Cambridge University Press, 2019.

Utas, Mats, ed. *African Conflicts and Informal Power: Big Men and Networks*. London: Zed Books, 2012.

van Bakel, M., Renée R. Hagesteijn, and Pieter Van De Velde, eds. *Private Politics: A Multi-disciplinary Approach to 'Big-Man' Systems*. Leiden: Brill, 1986.

van Gennep, Arnold. *The Rites of Passage*. London: Routledge, 1960.

Vaughan, Olufemi. *Nigerian Chiefs: Traditional Power in Modern Politics, 1980s–1990s*. Rochester, NY: University of Rochester Press, 2000.

Vigh, Henrik. "Youth Mobilisation as Social Navigation: Reflections on the Concept of Dubriagem." *Cadernos de Estudos Aricanos* 18, no. 19 (2010): 139–64.

Vincent, Joan. *African Elite: The Big Men of a Small Town*. New York: Columbia University Press, 1971.

Vokes, Richard, and Darren Newbury. "Photography and African Futures." *Visual Studies* 33, no. 1 (2018): 1–10.

Weber, M. *The Theory of Social and Economic Organization*. New York: Free Press, 1947.

Werbner, Richard. *Anthropology after Gluckman: The Manchester School, Colonial and Postcolonial Transformations*. Manchester: Manchester University Press, 2020.

———. "Beyond Oblivion: Confronting Memory Crisis." In *Memory and the Postcolony: African Anthropology and the Critique of Power*, edited by R. Werbner, 1–17. London: Zed Books, 1998.

———. "Introduction: Postcolonial Subjectivities; the Personal, the Political and the Moral." In *Postcolonial Subjectivities in Africa*, edited by Richard Werbner, 1–21. London: Zed Books, 2002.

———. "The Poetics of Wisdom Divination: Renewing the Moral Imagination." *Journal of the Royal Anthropological Institute* 23, no. 1 (2017): 81–102.

———. *Reasonable Radicals and Citizenship in Botswana: The Public Anthropology of Kalanga Elites*. Bloomington: Indiana University Press, 2004.

Wiegink, Nikkie. "'It Will Be Our Time to Eat': Former Renamo Combatants and Big-Man Dynamics in Central Mozambique." *Journal of Southern African Studies* 41, no. 4 (2015): 869–85.

Williams, Gareth. "Subalternity and the Neoliberal Habitus: Thinking Insurrection on the El Salvador/South Central Interface." *Nepantla: Views from South* 1, no. 1 (2000): 139–70.

Wyn, Johanna, and Ron White. *Rethinking Youth*. London: Sage, 1997.

NEWSPAPERS, NEWS MAGAZINES, PERIODICALS, ONLINE NEWS, OTHERS

Abdullahi, Idowu. "Sunday Igboho Regains Freedom in Benin after Two Years." *Punch*, October 8, 2023. https://punchng.com/sunday-igboho-regains-freedom-in-benin-after-two-years/.

Abimboye, Michael. "Sack Jega Now, Gani Adams Tells Jonathan." *Premium Times*, March 8, 2015. https://www.premiumtimesng.com/news/top-news/178158-sack-jega-now-gani-adams-tells-jonathan.html.

———. "Why Tinubu Starved Us, Jonathan Gave Us Multibillion Naira Pipeline Contracts—Gani Adams." *Premium Times*, March 24, 2015. https://www.premiumtimesng.com/news/headlines/179053-while-tinubu-starved-us-jonathan-gave-us-multibillion-naira-pipeline-contracts-gani-adams.html.

Abubakar, Shehu, and Solomon Chung. "Lifestyles of Billionaire Militants." *Daily Trust*, September 15, 2012. https://dailytrust.com/lifestyles-of-billionaire-militants/.

Adams, Gani. "I'm Not in Hiding." Interview. *TheNEWS*, January 31, 2000.

Adebanjo, Adegbenro, and Yemi Olowolabi. "End of the Manhunt." *TELL*, September 3, 2001.

Adebanjo, Tajudeen. "Adams Not Involved in Attacks on Ex-aide." *Nation*, June 26, 2020. https://thenationonlineng.net/adams-not-involved-in-attacks-on-ex-aide/.

Adebayo, Musliudeen. "Police Arrest 2 Suspects over OPC Factional Clash in Ibadan as Victim, Adesina Akinpelu, Recounts Ordeal." *Daily Post*, September 9, 2017. https://dailypost.ng/2017/09/09/police-arrest-2-suspects-opc-factional-clash-ibadan-victim-adesina-akinpelu-recounts-ordeal-photos/.

Adebayo, Taiwo Hassan. "Tinubu Using Yoruba for Own Selfish Interest—Gani Adams." *Premium Times*, March 21, 2015. https://www.premiumtimesng.com/regional/ssouth-west/178876-tinubu-using-yoruba-for-own-selfish-interest-gani-adams.html.

Adebisi, Yemi. "Nigeria: As Gani Adams Joins the 'Jega Must Go' Campaigners." *Daily Independent*, March 21, 2015. https://allafrica.com/stories/201503230794.html.

Adedayo, Festus. "Gani Adams: Fly Perched on Our Balls." *Sunday Tribune*, August 26, 2001.

———. "Oluomo, Bayo Success and the Curse of Lagos Motor Park Kingpins." *Cable News*, January 20, 2019. https://www.thecable.ng/mc-oluomo-bayo-success-and-the-curse-of-lagos-motor-park-kingpins.

Adediran, Ifeoluwa. "Yorubas Have 'Graduated from Restructuring to Self-determination' Gani Adams." *Premium Times*, April 14, 2021. https://www.premiumtimesng.com/news/top-news/455174-yorubas-have-graduated-from-restructuring-to-self-determination-gani-adams.html.

Adedoyin, Wole Adegoke. "Before MC Oluomo, There Was Lawani Asani Oluwo Alias Omo Pupa ni Mushin." *Opera News*. Accessed May 8, 2021. https://ng.opera.news/ng/en/crime/9edaaa31b32c08fb40d4ad83e70e7c0c.

Adegbamigbe, Ademola. "The OPC Bogey." *TheNEWS*, January 31, 2000.
Adekoya, Remi. "Nigeria's Elections: Democracy Postponed." *Guardian*, February 8, 2015. https://www.theguardian.com/commentisfree/2015/feb/08/nigeria-elections-democracy-postponed-goodluck-jonathan.
Ademosu, Folarin. "Fasehun Can Kill, Destroy for Power, Money and Women." *P.M. News*, August 21, 2013. https://www.pmnewsnigeria.com/2013/08/21/fasehun-can-kill-destroy-for-power-money-and-women/.
Adeniji, Gbenga. "Release Igboho to Continue His Journey, Soyinka Tells Benin Republic." *Punch*, August 27, 2021. https://punchng.com/breaking-release-igboho-to-continue-his-journey-soyinka-tells-benin-republic/.
Adeniran, Yinka. "Makinde, Gani Adams in Closed Door Meeting." *Nation*, March 19, 2021. https://thenationonlineng.net/makinde-gani-adams-in-closed-door-meeting/.
Adeniyi, Gbenga. "I'm a Progressive, Obasanjo's Not, Says Gani Adams." *Punch*, December 9, 2020. https://punchng.com/im-a-progressive-obasanjos-not-says-gani-adams/.
Adeoye, Oba. "Nigeria: Celebrating Gani Adams' Day of Honour." *Daily Independent*, May 4, 2009.
Adepoju, Femi. "Gani Adams' Wedding: The Role of Masquerades." *P.M. News*, December 3, 2003.
Adesanya, Michael. "Alleged Threat to Life: Lagos OPC Boss Defends Gani Adams, Chides Segun Akanni." *City Voice*, June 24, 2020. https://cityvoiceng.com/alleged-threat-to-life-lagos-opc-boss-defends-gani-adams-chides-segun-akanni/.
Adeshina, Akinpelu. "Gani Adams: Two Years on the Road of Infamy." *Nigerian Voice*. Accessed April 12, 2021. https://www.thenigerianvoice.com/news/247428/gani-adams-two-years-on-the-road-of-infamy.html.
Adewale, Femi. "Ojudu Visits Gani Adams." *Freedom Online*, December 8, 2017. https://freedomonline.com.ng/ojudu-visits-gani-adams/.
Adeyemo, Segun. "Confusion as OPC Leader, Gani Adams, Becomes C&S Ordained Apostle." *City People*, December 16, 2020. https://citynewsng.com/opc-leader-gani-adams-becomes-c-s-ordained-priest/.
Adunsi, Wale. "Publish the Account through Which Gaddafi Gave Adams $22m—OPC Dares Petitioners." *Daily Post*, March 16, 2016. https://dailypost.ng/2016/03/16/publish-the-account-through-which-gaddafi-gave-adams-22m-opc-dares-petitioners/.
Africa Confidential. "Abuja Buys a Delta Amnesty." *Africa Confidential* 50, no. 22 (November 2009). https://www.africa-confidential.com/article-preview/id/3305/Abuja_buys_a_Delta_amnesty.
———. "All the President's Militias." *Africa Confidential* 51, no. 24 (December 3, 2010). https://www.africa-confidential.com/article-review/id/3763/All_the_President%27s_militias.
———. "A Fight for the President's Base." *Africa Confidential* 52, no. 4 (February 18, 2011). https://www.africa-confidential.com/article-preview/id/3853/A_fight_for_the_President%e2%80%99s_base.

———. "General John Togo and All His Enemies." *Africa Confidential* 51, no. 25 (December 17, 2010). https://www.africa-confidential.com/article-preview/id/3786/General_John_Togo_and_all_his_enemies.

———. "The Hunt for Tompolo." *Africa Confidential* 50, no. 12 (June 12, 2009). https://www.africa-confidential.com/article-preview/id/3131/The_hunt_for_Tompolo.

———. "Lots of Gunboats, Little Diplomacy." *Africa Confidential* 56, no. 3 (February 6, 2015). https://www.africa-confidential.com/article-preview/id/5997/Lots_of_gunboats%2c_little_diplomacy.

———. "Militants Pick Their Party." *Africa Confidential* 59 (June 15, 2018). https://www.africa-confidential.com/article-preview/id/12351/Militants_pick_their_party.

Agakameh, Dele. "His Offence Is Heinous . . . Okiro." Interview. *TELL*, September 3, 2001.

Agbo, Anayochukwu. "Who Knows Him from Adam?" *TELL*, September 3, 2001.

Agboluaje, Rotimi. "Makinde, Gani Adams in Closed-Door Meeting over Insecurity." *Guardian*, March 19, 2021. https://guardian.ng/news/makinde-gani-adams-in-closed-door-meeting-over-insecurity/.

Agomuo, Zebulon. "96 Hours of *Madness*." *Post Express*, October 21, 2000.

Aimienmwona, Joseph. "OPC: The Pains of Insanity." *Post Express*, October 22, 2000.

Ajai, Sunday O. "Politicians and Thuggery in Nigeria." *Daily Trust*, June 6, 2017. https://dailytrust.com/politicians-and-thuggery-in-nigeria.

Ajani, Jide. "Regional Govt Tops Yoruba Agenda for Confab." *Vanguard*, February 11, 2005.

Ajayi, Ola. "Faction in OPC Asks Adams to Present Bank Account Statements." *Vanguard*, April 3, 2015. https://www.vanguardngr.com/2015/04/faction-in-opc-asks-adams-to-present-bank-account-statements/.

Ajayi, Ola, Bukola Ifegbayi, and Fisayo Ogunwale. "OPC Crisis: Why Gani Adams Must Go—Akinpelu." *Vanguard*, April 26, 2015. https://www.vanguardngr.com/2015/04/opc-crisis-why-gani-adams-must-go-akinpelu/.

Akinkuotu, Eniola. "Jonathan Deserves Praise for Giving OPC Contract." *Punch*, March 23, 2015. http://www.punchng.com/politics/jonathan-deserves-praise-for-giving-opc-contract-gani-adams/.

———. "Nigeria: Ex-militant Asari Dokubo wants to build Tinubu an army." *The Africa Report*, July 27, 2023. https://www.theafricareport.com/317151/nigeria-ex-militant-asari-dokubo-wants-to-build-tinubu-army/.

———. "Tinubu Was Right for Calling Buhari a Tribalist, Religious Fanatic, Says Obasanjo." *Punch*, January 21, 2019. https://punchng.com/tinubu-was-right-for-calling-buhari-a-tribalist-religious-fanatic-says-obasanjo/.

Akinlotan, Olasunkanmi. "2023: 'Emi Lokan' Is Wrong for Nigeria, Obasanjo Criticises Tinubu." *Premium Times*, January 2, 2023. https://www.premiumtimesng.com/news/top-news/573623-2023-emi-lokan-is-wrong-for-nigeria-obasanjo-criticises-tinubu.html.

———. "Why We Want to Break Away from Nigeria—Yoruba Group Writes Buhari." *Premium Times*, August 14, 2022. https://www.premiumtimesng.com/news/top-news/548638-why-we-want-to-break-away-from-nigeria-yoruba-group-writes-buhari.html.

Akinola, Wale, and Emma Nnadozie. "Lagos Bloodbath: Fasehun, Gani Adams, 9 Other OPC Leaders Held. Flown to Abuja." *Vanguard*, October 23, 2005.

Akinrefon, Dapo. "Aare Gani Adams' Wife Gives Birth to Twins." *Vanguard*, May 27, 2020. https://www.vanguardngr.com/2020/05/aare-gani-adams-wife-gives-birth-to-twins/.

———. "Benin Republic 'Releases' Sunday Igboho." *Vanguard*, March 7, 2022. https://www.vanguardngr.com/2022/03/breaking-benin-republic-releases-sunday-igboho/.

———. "Buhari Lacks Courage to Tackle Insecurity—Gani Adams." *Vanguard*, December 13, 2020. https://www.vanguardngr.com/2020/12/buhari-lacks-the-courage-to-tackle-insecurity-in-nigeria-%E2%80%95-gani-adams/.

———. "Daystar Pastor, Sam Adeyemi Congratulates Him." *Vanguard*, January 9, 2018. https://www.vanguardngr.com/2018/01/aare-ona-kakanfo-final-rites-gani-adams-installation-begins/.

———. "Expelled Members behind Attack on Adams." *Vanguard*, March 19, 2015. https://www.vanguardngr.com/2015/03/expelled-members-behind-attack-on-adams/.

———. "Gani Adams Attacks Obasanjo, Replies Omo-Agege." *Vanguard*, December 12, 2020. https://www.vanguardngr.com/2020/12/gani-adams-attacks-obasanjo-replies-omo-agege/.

———. "Gani Adams to Beninese Govt: Allow Sunday Igboho Seek Proper Medical Treatment Abroad." *Vanguard*, March 8, 2022. https://www.vanguardngr.com/2022/03/gani-adams-to-beninese-govt-allow-sunday-igboho-seek-proper-medical-treatment-abroad/.

———. "IG Parleys Aare Adams on Security." *Vanguard*, June 19, 2019. https://www.vanguardngr.com/2019/06/ig-parleys-aare-adams-on-security/.

———. "I'm a Target of Assassination, Ex-Gani Adams' Aide Cries Out." *Vanguard*, June 7, 2019. https://www.vanguardngr.com/2019/06/im-a-target-of-assassination-ex-gani-adams-aide-cries-out/.

———. "My Guardian Angel Won't Forgive Me If I Reconcile with Obasanjo—Aare Adams." *Vanguard*, December 8, 2020. https://www.vanguardngr.com/2020/12/my-guarding-angel-wont-forgive-me-if-i-reconcile-with-obasanjo-aare-adams/.

———. "No Comparison between Alaafin, Aare Ona Kakanfo Chiefs—Gani Adams; Installs New Chiefs." *Vanguard*, January 16, 2020. https://www.vanguardngr.com/2020/01/between-alaafins-chiefs-and-that-of-aare-onakakanfo-%E2%80%95gani-adams/.

———. "Ooni of Ife, Aare Adams Task INEC on Credible Polls." *Vanguard*, January 29, 2019. https://www.vanguardngr.com/2019/01/ooni-of-ife-aare-adams-task-inec-on-credible-polls-2/.

———. "Secession: Clamour for Oodua Republic Is Long Overdue—Gani Adams." *Vanguard*, March 29, 2021. https://www.vanguardngr.com/2021/03/secession-clamour-for-oodua-republic-is-long-overdue-gani-adams/.

———. "Sunday Igboho's Release, Victory for Self-determination—Afenifere." *Vanguard*, March 7, 2022. https://www.vanguardngr.com/2022/03/sunday-igbohos-release-victory-for-self-determination-afenifere/.

———. "Sunday Igboho to Spend 6 More Months in Benin Prison." *Vanguard*, February 7, 2022. https://www.vanguardngr.com/2022/02/sunday-igboho-to-spend-6-more-months-in-benin-prison/.

———. "25 People Contested for Aare Ona Kakanfo Title—Gani Adams." *Vanguard*, January 22, 2018. https://www.vanguardngr.com/2018/01/25-people-contested-aare-ona-kakanfo-title-gani-adams/.

———. "2019: Obasanjo Holds Secret Talks with Yoruba Leaders in Lagos." *Vanguard*, June 23, 2018. https://www.vanguardngr.com/2018/06/2019-obasanjo-holds-secret-talks-yoruba-leaders-lagos/.

———. "Why I Picked Gani Adams as New Aare Ona Kakanfo—Alaafin." *Vanguard*, October 17, 2017. https://www.vanguardngr.com/2017/10/picked-gani-adams-new-aare-ona-kakanfo-alaafin/.

———. "With 52 Titles Already, I Didn't Think I Would Become the *Ààrẹ Ọ̀nà Kakañfò*—Gani Adams." *Vanguard*, October 22, 2017. https://www.vanguardngr.com/2017/10/52-titles-already-didnt-think-become-ona-kakanfo-gani-adams/.

———. "Wole Soyinka Not Involved in Sunday Igboho's Release—Counsel." *Vanguard*, March 8, 2022. https://www.vanguardngr.com/2022/03/wole-soyinka-not-involved-in-sunday-igbohos-release-counsel/.

Akinrefon, Dapo. "Why Sunday Igboho Can't Leave Benin Republic—Source." *Vanguard*, March 9, 2022. https://www.vanguardngr.com/2022/03/why-sunday-igboho-cant-leave-benin-republic-source-2/.

Akinrefon, Dapo, and Ola Ajayi. "I'm Ready to Lead Battle against Killer Herdsmen—Gani Adams." *Vanguard*, July 4, 2018. https://www.vanguardngr.com/2018/07/im-ready-lead-battle-killer-herdsmen-gani-adams/.

Akinrefon, Dapo, and Olasunkanmi Akoni. "Why Soyinka Visited Sunday Igboho—Sources." *Vanguard*, May 3, 2022. https://www.vanguardngr.com/2022/05/why-soyinka-visited-sunday-igboho-sources/.

Akinrefon, Dapo, and Gbenga Olarinoye. "Courage, Commitment Earned Adams *Aare Ona Kakanfo* Title—Alaafin." *Vanguard*, January 16, 2018. https://www.vanguardngr.com/2018/01/courage-commitment-earned-adams-aare-ona-kakanfo-title-alaafin/.

Akinrefon, Dare. "Obasanjo, Adams Reconcile 15-Year Rift." *Vanguard*, December 2, 2020. https://www.vanguardngr.com/2020/12/obasanjo-adams-reconcile-15-year-rift/.

Akinsuyi, Temidayo. "Afenifere Reconciles Obasanjo, Gani Adams." *Independent*, December 2, 2020. https://www.independent.ng/afenifere-reconciles-obasanjo-gani-adams/.

———. "Gani Adams' Wife, Ayaba Mojisola Gives Birth to Twins." *Independent,* May 27, 2020. https://www.independent.ng/gani-adams-wife-ayinba-mojisola-givers-birth-to-twins/.

———. "Group Attacks Gani Adams over Statement on Tinubu." *Independent,* July 5, 2020. https://www.independent.ng/group-attacks-gani-adams-over-statement-on-tinubu/.

———. "How I Parted Ways with Aare Gani Adams—Akanni." *Independent,* June 24, 2020. https://independent.ng/how-i-parted-ways-with-aare-gani-adams-akanni/.

———. "Presidential Polls: Gani Adams Congratulates Tinubu, Says Victory Reflects President-Elect's Doggedness." *Independent,* March 1, 2023. https://independent.ng/presidential-polls-gani-adams-congratulates-tinubu-says-victory-reflects-president-elects-doggedness/.

Akinsuyi, Yemi. "12 Killed, 30 Vehicles Burnt in OPC Rival Clash." *ThisDay,* October 23, 2005.

Akintunde, Muyiwa. "Dr Frederick Faseun: 'Give a Dog a Bad Name.'" *Africa Today,* February 2000. http://archive.africatoday.com/secret/feb00/feb00intervwdrfred.htm.

———. "Obasanjo Is Not bias." *Africa Today,* February 2002. http://archive.africatoday.com/secret/feb02/feb02obasanjoisnot.htm.

———. "The Rimi Interview." *Africa Today,* February 2002. http://archive.africatoday.com/secret/feb02/feb02therimiinterview.htm.

Akinyemi, Boluwatife. "It Is My Turn, It Is Yoruba's Turn—Tinubu." *Nigerian Tribune,* June 3, 2022. https://tribuneonlineng.com/it-is-my-turn-it-is-yorubas-turn-tinubu/.

Alabi, Mojeed. "Why I've Refused to See Gani Adams—Obasanjo." *Premium Times,* December 2, 2020. https://www.premiumtimesng.com/news/more-news/429134-why-ive-refused-to-see-gani-adams-obasanjo.html.

Albin-Lackey, Chris. "Criminal Politics: Violence, 'Godfathers' and Corruption in Nigeria." *Human Rights Watch* 19, no. 16A (2007): 33–37.

Aneasoronye, Modestus. "Five Things You Need to Know about Operation Amotekun." *Business Day,* March 4, 2020. https://businessday.ng/news/article/five-things-you-need-to-know-about-operation-amotekun/.

Anonymous. "Unmasking the Traitor." *Vanguard,* February 24, 2011. https://www.vanguardngr.com/2011/02/unmasking-the-traitor/.

Atoyebi, Olufemi. "Police Arrest 46 as OPC Factions Clash in Ibadan." *Punch,* January 29, 2018. https://punchng.com/police-arrest-46-as-opc-factions-clash-in-ibadan/.

Aworinde, Tobi. "My Experiences in Prisons under Obasanjo Horrible—Gani Adams." *Punch,* December 26, 2020. https://punchng.com/my-experiences-in-prisons-under-obasanjo-horrible-gani-adams/.

Badmus, Bola. "Gani Adams Celebrates 2nd Anniversary, Installs New Chiefs." *Nigerian Tribune,* January 16, 2020. https://tribuneonlineng.com/gani-adams-celebrates-2nd-anniversary-installs-new-chiefs/.

———. "Gani Adams to Buhari: Effect Release of Sunday Igboho, Kanu from Detention." *Nigerian Tribune*, January 13, 2022. https://tribuneonlineng.com/gani-adams-to-buhari-effect-release-of-sunday-igboho-kanu-from-detention/.

Badmus, Bola, and Olalekan Olabulo. "Restructuring Re-echoed as Aare Adams Inaugurates Advisory Council." *Nigerian Tribune*, January 13, 2019. https://tribuneonlineng.com/restructuring-re-echoed-as-aare-adams-inaugurates-advisory-council/.

Badru, Adeola. "Don't Demonize Sunday Igboho, Akintola Warns Makinde." *Vanguard*, March 1, 2021. https://www.vanguardngr.com/2021/03/dont-demonize-sunday-igboho-akintola-warns-makinde/.

———. "We Don't Want One Nigeria Again, but Yoruba Nation-Sunday Igboho." *Vanguard*, March 17, 2021. https://www.vanguardngr.com/2021/03/we-dont-want-one-nigeria-again-but-yoruba-nation-sunday-igboho/.

Badru, Adeola, Dayo Johnson, Adeola Badru, Rotimi Ojomoyela, Shina Abubakar, and James Ogunnaike. "How South West Gave Legal Teeth to Amotekun." *Vanguard*, March 7, 2020. https://www.vanguardngr.com/2020/03/how-south-west-gave-legal-teeth-to-amotekun/.

Balogun, Adeola. "Fasehun and I Must Share S'West Pipeline Security Contract Equally—Gani Adams." *Punch*, April 20, 2013. https://jimidisu.com/fasehun-and-i-must-share-swest-pipeline-security-contract-equally-gani-adams-punch/.

Balogun, Adeola, and Gbenro Adeoye. "Everybody Is in Politics for Selfish Interests—Adams, OPC National Coordinator." *Punch*, March 28, 2015. https://www.latestnigeriannews.com/news/1322644/everybody-is-in-politics-for-selfish-interestsadams-opc-national-coordinator.html.

Bankole, Taofik. "2019 Election: Gbenga Daniel Pays Courtesy Visit to Aare Gani Adams, Seeks Support for Atiku." Nuesroom, November 26, 2018. https://neusroom.com/2019-election-gbenga-daniel-pays-courtesy-visit-to-aare-gani-adams-seeks-support-for-atiku/.

BBC. "MC Oluomo Book: Di Book *My Service to Humanity* Na about Im Life." February 2, 2021. https://www.bbc.com/pidgin/tori-55910593.

———. "Nigerian Vigilante Leader Arrested." August 22, 2001. http://news.bbc.co.uk/1/hi/world/africa/1505010.stm.

———. "Nigerian Vigilante Leader Charged." August 24, 2001. http://news.bbc.co.uk/1/hi/world/africa/1507846.stm.

———. "Sunday Igboho: Nigerians React as Activist Call for 'Yoruba Nation.'" March 19, 2021. https://www.bbc.com/pidgin/tori-56453558.

BBC News. "Nigeria: More Divided Than United?" November 26, 1999. http://news.bbc.co.uk/2/hi/africa/538133.stm.

Benson, Dayo. "Fasehun is not the leader of OPC—Fawehinmi." *Vanguard*, September 19, 1999.

Campbell, John. "Yoruba Debate 'Restructuring' of Nigeria or 'Autonomy.'" Council on Foreign Relations blog, April 16, 2021. https://www.cfr.org/blog/yoruba-debate-restructuring-nigeria-or-autonomy.

Capa, Siyamtanda. "'Revolutionaries Must Be Willing to Kill,' Malema Tells EFF Delegates." IOL, October 15, 2022. https://www.iol.co.za/weekend-argus/news/revolutionaries-must-be-willing-to-kill-malema-tells-eff-delegates-d15b971e-3893-411a-b57f-cc87496ed721.

Chukwumba, Obiora. "An Eye for an Eye." *TELL*, December 13, 1999.

Dada, Peter. "Adebanjo Emerges Afenifere Leader as Fasoranti Steps Down Over Old Age." *Punch*, March 17, 2021. https://punchng.com/adebanjo-emerges-afenifere-leader-as-fasoranti-steps-down-over-old-age/.

Daily Champion. "OPC Not Murderers—Afenifere." *Daily Champion*, March 9, 2006.

Daily Independent. "Why I'm Celebrating My Birthday—Aare Gani Adams." April 30, 2018. https://www.independent.ng/why-im-celebrating-my-birthday-aare-gani-adams/.

Daily Times. "OPC Cries Out over Police Attack on Members." *Daily Times*, September 26, 2001.

Daily Trust. "I Will Support Military Strike—Ex-Minister." February12, 2002.

Daniel, Eniola. "Tinubu Says He Went to 'War' for Buhari to Be President." *Guardian*, June 2, 2022. https://guardian.ng/news/it-is-my-turn-to-be-president-says-tinubu/.

Daramola, Kunle. "Cracks in Yoruba Nation Movement as Akintoye's Deputy Resigns." *Cable*, November 7, 2022. https://www.thecable.ng/cracks-in-yoruba-nation-movement-as-akintoyes-deputy-resigns.

Dzirutwe, Macdonald. "Tinubu Says It Is His Turn to Rule Nigeria in Election Appeal to Buhari." Reuters, June 3, 2022. https://www.reuters.com/world/africa/tinubu-says-it-is-his-turn-rule-nigeria-election-appeal-buhari-2022-06-03/.

Eagle Online. "Breaking: Obasanjo, Gani Adams Reconcile, Settle 15-Year Rift." December 3, 2020. https://theeagleonline.com.ng/breaking-obasanjo-gani-adams-reconcile-settle-15-year-rift-photo/.

Egbas, Jude. "This Is the Full Story of How MC Oluomo Was Stabbed with a Poisoned Knife at Lagos APC Campaign Rally." Pulse Ng, January 9, 2019. https://www.pulse.ng/news/politics/mc-oluomo-how-notorious-nurtw-official-was-stabbed-with-poisoned-knife/1gh9279.

Egede, Prisca, and Emmanuel Onwubiko. "Labour May Invite OPC for Picketing. 500 Lawyers to Defend Detained Labour Men." *Guardian*, October 18, 2003.

Eghaghe, Richard. "I Am a Man of Peace—Gani Adams." *Daily Independent*, February 18, 2004.

———. "Pastor Adeboye Salutes Adams on Installation as Aare Ona Kakanfo, Regrets Inability to Attend." January 22, 2018. https://theeagleonline.com.ng/pastor-adeboye-salutes-adams-on-installation-as-aare-ona-kakanfo-regrets-inability-to-attend/.

Ehigiator, Kenneth, and Bukola Oduyoye. "OPC Members Besiege MMA as Gani Adams Returns to Lagos." *Vanguard*, December 21, 2006. https://allafrica.com/stories/200612210313.html.

Elegbede, Wale. "2023: Tinubu's Camp, Adams Throw Punches." *Telegraph,* July 10, 2020. https://www.newtelegraphng.com/2023-tinubus-camp-adams-throw-punches/.

Elesho, Richard, and Bamidele Adebayo. "Divided It Stands." *TheNEWS,* July 19, 1999.

Elites. "My Close Shave with Death—Segun Akanni, Ex-CoS to Gani Adams." June 20, 2020. https://www.theelitesng.com/my-close-shave-with-death-segun-akanni-ex-cos-to-gani-adams/.

EnviroNews Nigeria. "Why Gani Adams Was Chosen out of 25 Shortlisted as Aare Ona Kakanfo, by Alaafin." January 15, 2018. https://www.environewsnigeria.com/gani-adams-chosen-25-shortlisted-aare-ona-kakanfo-alaafin/.

Ezeamalu, Ben, and Michael Abimboye. "OPC Factions Clash after Anti-Jega Protest." *Premium Times,* March 17, 2015. https://www.premiumtimesng.com/news/top-news/178602-opc-factions-clash-after-anti-jega-protest.html.

Ezekiel123. "Shrine to Church; Checkout Photos of Gani Adams Installation & Ordination in 2017 and 2012." Accessed November 3, 2020. https://ng.opera.news/ng/en/religion/97484e2c9f6e6e4b379f120cc719fde2.

Fabiyi, Olusola. "My Stay in Prison Taught Me That One Can Actually Stay Off Women." *Saturday Punch,* December 23, 2006.

FeelrightNews TV. "Sunday Igboho and Gani Adams Fight!!" Seriously, May 23, 2021. https://www.youtube.com/watch?v=yzQwft5NUpI&t=6s.

Festac News Online. "Festac Mosque Hosts Special Jumat Service for Gani Adams." Accessed November 3, 2020. https://festaconline.com.ng/festac-mosque-jumat-service-gani-adams/.

Fitzpatrick, Marida. "Malema 'misses' R3m." *TimesLIVE,* February 23, 2010. https://www.news24.com/news24/malema-misses-r3m-20100223.

Folarin, Samson. "Fasehun: My Father, Mentor Is Gone, Says Gani Adams." *Punch,* December 1, 2018. https://punchng.com/faseun-my-father-mentor-is-gone-says-gani-adams/.

Francis, Juliana, and Kelechi Ngboji. "Blood Flows as Area Boys, OPC Clash." *Sun,* May 24, 2005.

Gbadamosi, Abisoye. "Biography of Otunba (Dr.) Gani Adams." *Otunba Gani Adams Cares for Nigerians* (blog), July 2011. http://otunbaganicares.blogspot.com/2011/07/biography-of-otunba-dr-gani-adams.html.

Gbedu WakaAbout. "(Serious Warning) from Gani Adams to people in Diaspora. Kidnapping Story. Sunday Igboho replies." Facebook, May 20, 2021. https://www.facebook.com/100742798321881/videos/469317094144408/.

Gbeminiyi, Saka. ". . . Our Men Slept with Women—OPC." *Sunday Tribune,* January 20, 2002.

GistMediaTV. "IBA Gani Adams Reveals What Could Happen to Tinubu as He Expøses Those Who Betrayed MKO Abiola." June 3, 2021. https://www.youtube.com/watch?v=ZS3XrLz3Ojw.

Godwin, Ameh Comrade. "OPC Want Gani Adams Arrested, Accuse Him of Collecting N10.6bn from Jonathan." *Daily Post*, February 15, 2016. https://dailypost.ng/2016/02/15/opc-want-gani-adams-arrested-accuse-him-of-collecting-n10-6bn-from-jonathan/.

Guardian. "Panel Urges Police to Stop Indiscriminate Arrests." February 8, 2000.

Hamzat. "'Why Gani Adams Pushed Me out of APC' . . . Ex-P.A, Segun Akanni Tells His Attack Story." *Global Excellence*, June 20, 2020. https://globalexcellenceonline.com/why-gani-adams-pushed-me-out-of-apc-ex-p-a-segun-akanni-tells-his-attack-story/.

Hinshaw, Drew. "Nigeria's Former Oil Bandits Now Collect Government Cash." *Wall Street Journal*, August 22, 2012. https://www.wsj.com/articles/SB10000872396390444184704577587220160886588518.

Hunter-Gault, Charleyne. "South African Official's Luxe Lifestyle Raises Doubts." NPR, March 10, 2010. https://www.npr.org/templates/story/story.php?storyId=124458077.

Ige, Ise-Oluwa. "FG Accuses OPC of Killing 10,000 People." *Vanguard*, March 8, 2006.

Ige, Oluwole. "Igboho Accuses DSS of Planting Arms in His House, Says 'I Use Charms, Not Guns.'" *Nigerian Tribune*, July 3, 2021. https://tribuneonlineng.com/igboho-accuses-sss-of-planting-arms-in-his-house-says-i-use-charms-not-guns/.

———. "I'm Now Free to Return Home—Sunday Igboho." *Nigerian Tribune*, October 8, 2023. https://tribuneonlineng.com/im-now-free-to-return-home-sunday-igboho/.

Iheamnachor, Davies. "Gani Adams Divinely Chosen to Save, Strengthen Yoruba Nation—SS/SE Communities." *Vanguard*, December 24, 2017. https://www.vanguardngr.com/2017/12/gani-adams-divinely-chosen-save-strengthen-yoruba-nation-ssse-communities/.

Iroanusi, Queen Esther. "Amotekun: Don't Back Down, Nigerians Tell South-West Governors." *Premium Times*, January 26, 2020. https://www.premiumtimesng.com/regional/ssouth-west/374375-amotekun-dont-back-down-nigerians-tell-south-west-governors.html.

James, Segun. "Gani Adams Installs 16 New Chiefs." *ThisDay*, January 17, 2020. https://www.thisdaylive.com/index.php/2020/01/17/gani-adams-installs-16-new-chiefs/.

John, Igbokwe. "Aare Ona Kakanfo, Otunba Gani Adams Rolls on the Floor during Thanksgiving Service." *City People*, January 22, 2018. http://www.citypeopleonline.com/aare-ona-kakanfo-otunba-gani-adams-rolls-floor-thanksgiving-service/.

Johnson, Bamidele. "Nigeria: Horror! Tales From Kano Killing Fields." *Tempo*, August 11, 1999. https://allafrica.com/stories/199908110228.html.

———. "The Plot against Lagos." *Tempo*, January 21, 2000. https://allafrica.com/stories/200001210303.html.

Johnson, Dayo, Dapo Akinrefon, Jimitota Onoyume, Adeola Badru, Demola Akinyemi, Olayinka Ajayi, Ola Ajayi, Shina Abubakar, James Ogunnaike, and

Rotimi Ojomoyela. "Oduduwa Republic Oct 1 Rally Divides Yoruba Leaders." *Vanguard*, September 7, 2020. https://www.vanguardngr.com/2020/09/oduduwa-republic-oct-1-rally-divides-yoruba-leaders/.

Johnson, Dayo, Nnamdi Ojiego, Rotimi Ojomoyela, and James Ogunnaike. "S/West Secession Letter to Buhari Divides Yoruba Leaders." *Vanguard*, September 4, 2022. https://www.vanguardngr.com/2022/09/s-west-secession-letter-to-buhari-divides-yoruba-leaders/.

Jonathan, Zovoe. "Photos: Aare Ona Kakanfo Rolls on Floor during Church Thanksgiving Service." *Punch*, January 22, 2018. https://punchng.com/photos-aare-ona-kakanfo-rolls-on-floor-during-church-thanksgiving-service/.

Joseph, Richard. *"Nigeria: 1993; The Way Forward," Testimony before the Subcommittee on Africa, House Committee on Foreign Affairs, August 4, 1993*. 103rd Congr. 1993.

Kabir, Adejumo. "Growing Insecurity in Nigeria Shows Buhari Has Failed—Gani Adams." *Premium Times*, December 14, 2020. https://www.premiumtimesng.com/news/more-news/431112-growing-insecurity-in-nigeria-shows-buhari-has-failed-gani-adams.html.

———. "Oyo Crisis: Who Is Sunday Igboho, Self-acclaimed Yoruba Warrior?" *Premium Times*, January 23, 2021. https://www.premiumtimesng.com/regional/ssouth-west/438195-yoruba-herders-clash-who-is-sunday-igboho-the-self-titled-yoruba-warrior.html.

———. "2023: Sunday Igboho Threatens Ambitious Yoruba Politicians in Video." *Premium Times*, March 1, 2021. https://www.premiumtimesng.com/news/top-news/445972-2023-sunday-igboho-threatens-ambitious-yoruba-politicians-in-video.html.

———. "Yoruba Nation: Gani Adams Criticises Sunday Igboho's 'Wrong Methods.'" *Premium Times*, July 8, 2021. https://www.premiumtimesng.com/news/top-news/472326-yoruba-nation-gani-adams-criticises-sunday-igbohos-wrong-methods.html.

Kabir, Adejumo, and Nasir Ayitogo. "SSS Confirms Invading Sunday Igboho's House, Killing Two." *Premium Times*, July 1, 2021. https://www.premiumtimesng.com/news/top-news/471136-just-in-sss-confirms-invading-sunday-igbohos-house-killing-two.html.

Kasali, Akinwale. "Restructuring: Adams, Tinubu Rift Gets Messier, as Group Slams Tinubu, Calls Him a Businessman in Politics without Ideology." *Source*, July 9, 2020. https://thesourceng.com/restructuring-adams-tinubu-rift-gets-messier-as-group-slams-tinubu-calls-him-a-businessman-in-politics-without-ideology/.

———. "Restructuring: Tinubu Group Slams Gani Adams, Says He Is a Traitor, an Ingrate, Unfit to Lead Yoruba Race." *Source*, July 6, 2020. https://thesourceng.com/restructuring-tinubu-group-slams-gani-adams-says-he-is-a-traitor-an-ingrate-unfit-to-lead-yoruba-race/.

———. "Tinubu/Gani Rift: OPC Faction Condemns Gani Adams over Tinubu." *Source*, July 12, 2020. https://thesourceng.com/tinubu-gani-rift-opc-faction-condemns-gani-adams-over-tinubu/.

Kasali, Segun. "Eledumare Festival: Gani Adams Urges Southwest Governors to Declare 2 Days Holiday." *Nigerian Tribune*, March 12, 2020. https://tribuneonlineng.com/eledumare-festival-gani-adams-urges-southwest-governors-to-declare-2-days-holiday/.

———. "Yorubas Have Metamorphosed from Restructuring to Self-determination, Says Gani Adams." *Nigerian Tribune*, April 7, 2021. https://tribuneonlineng.com/yorubas-have-metamorphosed-from-restructuring-to-self-determination-says-gani-adams/.

Kayode-Adedeji, Dimeji. "Gani Adams Alleges Plot to Assassinate Him." *Premium Times*, May 15, 2015. http://www.premiumtimesng.com/regional/ssouth-west/183040-gani-adams-alleges-plot-to-assassinate-him.html.

———. "Nigeria Police Made Me Famous—Gani Adams." *Premium Times*, June 27, 2015. https://www.premiumtimesng.com/news/more-news/185751-nigeria-police-made-me-famous-gani-adams.html.

Kehinde, Ronke. "Jewel behind the Lion." *Compass*, May 21, 2011.

Kilarigbo Live. "Gani Adams Fires Back at Tinubu Endorses Oduduwa Nation." September 12, 2020. https://www.youtube.com/watch?v=wF89EtHH30k&t=47s.

Lanre, Wale-Ojo. "Why We Sponsored 18 Festivals in Yoruba Land—Gani Adams." *Nigerian Tribune*, October 25, 2017. https://tribuneonlineng.com/sponsored-18-festivals-yoruba-land-gani-adams/.

Lasisi, Akeem. *Aare Ona Kakanfo* [For Aare Gani Adams]. December 18, 2017. Published in the program of the installation, Oyo, January 2018.

Maina, Maina. "APC Sponsoring Those Calling for Gani Adams' Resignation—OPC." *Daily Post*, March 21, 2015. https://dailypost.ng/2015/03/21/apc-sponsoring-those-calling-for-gani-adams-resignation-opc/.

McGreal, Chris. "Nigeria's Ethnic Hatreds Turn Lethal." *Guardian*, October 19, 2000. https://www.theguardian.com/world/2000/oct/20/chrismcgreal.

Monitor. "Police Hold 22 OPC Men." September 26, 2001.

Mpi, Nwokoye. "Nigeria-Benin: Sunday Igboho's Legal Woes Could Reignite Border Battle." *Africa Report*, August 26, 2021. https://www.theafricareport.com/118157/nigeria-benin-sunday-igbohos-legal-woes-could-reignite-border-battle/.

Nasiru, Jemilar. "Ojudu Shares Details of Tinubu's 'Secret Meeting' with Sunday Igboho in 2009." *Cable News*, January 25, 2021. https://www.thecable.ng/ojudu-shares-details-of-tinubus-secret-meeting-with-sunday-igboho-in-2009.

Nation. "Adams Holds Thanksgiving at Ijo Orunmila." February 7, 2018. https://thenationonlineng.net/adams-holds-thanksgiving-ijo-orunmila/.

———. "Adebanjo No More Acting Afenifere Leader—Fasoranti." November 2, 2022. https://thenationonlineng.net/adebanjo-no-more-acting-afenifere-leader-fasoranti/.

———. "Adeboye Salutes Adams on Installation as *Aare Ona Kakanfo*." January 23, 2018. https://thenationonlineng.net/adeboye-salutes-adams-installation-aare-ona-kakanfo/.

———. "Varsity Packed as OPC's Adams Gets Doctorate Degree." June 1, 2007.

National Insight. "We're Partners in Progress, Gani Adams Tells Lagos CP." September 22, 2019. https://nationalinsightnews.com/were-partners-in-progress-gani-adams-tells-lagos-cp/.

National Mirror. "Abiola's Death: Yoruba Leaders Were Induced, Gani Adams." August 5, 2011.

NBF News. "Gani Adams: My Name Rings Louder Bell Than Some Governors." *Nigerian Voice*, December 4, 2011. https://www.thenigerianvoice.com/news/76834/gani-adams-my-name-rings-louder-bell-than-some-governors.html.

Ndujihe, Clifford. "National Conference: Glimpses of a Likely Yoruba Agenda." *Guardian*, January 24, 2005. https://www.dawodu.com/articles/national-conference-glimpses-of-a-likely-yoruba-agenda-681.

New Humanitarian. "Abducted Policeman Murdered." January 11, 2000. https://www.thenewhumanitarian.org/report/11648/nigeria-abducted-policeman-murdered.

New Nigerian. "OPC Activities: The North Is Watching." December 14, 1999.

New Nigerian on Sunday. "No Peace Agenda for Nigeria." February 20, 2000.

Nigerian Tribune. "I'm Not Satisfied with the State of the Yoruba Nation—Gani Adams." April 29, 2010.

———. "I Never Said Adebanjo Is No longer Afenifere leader—Fasoranti." November 4, 2022. https://tribuneonlineng.com/i-never-said-adebanjo-is-no-longer-afenifere-leader-%E2%80%95-fasoranti/.

———. "The OPC and the Rest of Us." (Editorial). October 25, 2000.

———. "We'll Leverage on Past Successes to Reinvent Glorious Days of South-West, Yoruba Race—Gani Adams." January 16, 2022. https://tribuneonlineng.com/well-leverage-on-past-successes-to-reinvent-glorious-days-of-south-west-yoruba-race-%E2%80%95-gani-adams/.

Nigerian Voice. "How God Used Policemen to Rescue Me from Gani Adams' Killer Squad-OPC National PRO." November 8, 2017. https://www.thenigerianvoice.com/news/259540/how-god-used-policemen-to-rescue-me-from-gani-adams-killer.html.

Nnadozie, Emma, Albert Akpor, and Olasunkanmi Akoni. "Gani Adams: YCE, Gani, Others Seek Fair Hearing OPC Members Protest Arrest in Lagos, Demand Release." *Vanguard*, August 24, 2001.

Nwangwu, Chido. "Buhari's 'Animal Farm' and Terrorism at the NDA." *ThisDay*, August 27, 2021. https://www.thisdaylive.com/index.php/2021/08/27/buharis-animal-farm-and-terrorism-at-the-nda/.

Nwanne, Chuks. "Learn from Jonathan's Mistakes, Gani Adams Cautions Buhari." *Guardian*, May 31, 2015. https://guardian.ng/news/learn-from-jonathans-mistakes-gani-adams-cautions-buhari.

Oamen, Samuel. "I Don't Know You, Sunday Igboho Disowns Ojudu." *Nation*, January 26, 2021. https://thenationonlineng.net/i-dont-know-you-sunday-igboho-disowns-ojudu/.

Obassa, Shittu. "OPC, Fasehun: Our Stand." *New Nigerian*, January 27, 2001.
Obia, Vincent. "Hate Thy Neighbour." *TheWeek*, February 18, 2002.
Ode, Sunday. "Return of the Evil Days." *New Nigerian*, July 22, 2000.
Odiegwu, Mike. "SHOOT-AT-SIGHT: From Niger Delta Agitator to Successful Entrepreneur." *Nation*, July 24, 2021. https://thenationonlineng.net/shoot-at-sight-from-niger-delta-agitator-to-successful-entrepreneur/.
Odunlami, Tayo. "The Road to War." *TheNEWS*, January 31, 2000.
———. "Unending Mayhem." *TheNEWS*, January 24, 2000.
Odunlami, Temitayo, and Nurudeen Oyewole. "I Can't Be a Warrior in Time of Peace—Gani Adams." *Daily Trust*, January 13, 2018. https://dailytrust.com/i-cant-be-a-warrior-in-time-of-peace-gani-adams/.
Odunsi, Wale. "Ateke Tom, Ex-militant Leader Crowned King of Okochiri in Rivers." *Daily Post*, November 26, 2017. https://dailypost.ng/2017/11/26/ateke-tom-ex-militant-leader-crowned-king-okochiri-rivers-photos/.
———. "Elections: OPC Replies APC, Says, 'Nobody Can Kill Jonathan, Adams' Friendship.'" *Daily Post*, April 10, 2015. https://dailypost.ng/2015/04/10/elections-opc-replies-apc-says-nobody-can-kill-jonathan-adams-friendship/.
———. "Gani Adams Accused Expelled OPC Members of Begging Tinubu to Back His Removal." *Daily Post*, August 18, 2015. https://dailypost.ng/2015/08/18/gani-adams-accuses-expelled-opc-members-of-begging-tinubu-to-back-his-removal/.
———. "Gani Adams Restates Plan for Southwest, Yoruba Race." *Daily Post*, January 16, 2022. https://dailypost.ng/2022/01/16/gani-adams-restates-plan-for-southwest-yoruba-race/.
———. "Security in Lagos: Details of OPC Leader Gani Adams' Meeting with Police Boss." *Daily Post*, September 22, 2019. https://dailypost.ng/2019/09/22/security-lagos-details-opc-leader-gani-adams-meeting-police-boss/.
Offi, Stepp. "An Eye for an Eye." *TELL*, January 24, 2000.
OganlaTV. "Gani Adams Blast Bola Ahmed Tinubu for Not Supporting Oduduwa Republic." September 12, 2020. https://www.youtube.com/watch?v=wF89EtHH30k.
Ogbonnikan, Femi. "OPC: An Organisation Shooting Itself in the Foot." *Daily Independent*, November 11, 2005.
Ogunbiyi, Tayo. "Gani Adams and the Preservation of Indigenous Culture." *Business Day*, January 6, 2019. https://businessday.ng/analysis/article/gani-adams-and-the-preservation-of-indigenous-culture/.
Ogundadegbe, Alex. "The Evolution, the Revolution." *TheWeek*, February 18, 2002.
Ogundamisi, Kayode. "'Asiwaju Bola Ahmed Tinubu, Did Not Give Me N10m to Kill Gani Adams'—Wale Adedayo." Blogspot, March 10, 2012. http://kayodeogundamisi.blogspot.com/2012/03/asiwaju-bola-ahmed-tinubu-did-not-give.html.
Ogunje, Victor. "Fayemi Meets Adams over South-West Security." *ThisDay*, March 17, 2021. https://www.thisdaylive.com/index.php/2021/03/17/fayemi-meets-adams-over-south-west-security/.

Ogunleye, Aderonke. "EXCLUSIVE: Asari-Dokubo establishes own university, names it after King Amachree." *Premium Times*, October 11, 2013. https://www.premiumtimesng.com/news/146438-exclusive-asari-dokubo-establishes-university-names-king-amachree.html?tztc=1.

Ogunsakin, Mustapha. "Adams: 'I'm a Freedom Fighter.'" *Guardian*, August 25, 2001.

Ogunyemi, Dele. "OPC Leaders Question Gani Adams over Jonathan's N1.6bn Campaign Fund." *Daily Trust*, April 7, 2015. https://dailytrust.com/opc-leaders-query-gani-adams-over-jonathan-s-n1-6bn-campaign-fund.

Ojo, Oluseye. "IGP to Partner Gani Adams to Tackle Rising Insecurity." *Sun*, June 18, 2019. https://www.sunnewsonline.com/igp-to-partner-gani-adams-to-tackle-rising-insecurity/.

Ojudu, Babafemi. "ENCOUNTER: The Sunday Igboho I Knew." *Premium Times*, January 25, 2021. https://www.premiumtimesng.com/features-and-interviews/438570-encounter-the-sunday-igboho-i-knew-by-babafemi-ojudu.html.

Okafor, Chiamaka. "Soyinka Advises Nigerian Govt on Sunday Igboho." *Premium Times*, July 6, 2021. https://www.premiumtimesng.com/regional/ssouth-west/471927-soyinka-advises-nigerian-govt-on-sunday-igboho.html.

Okegbile, Deji. "Archbishop Ayo Ladigbolu at 80: A Prince and a Muslim Evangelist to a Methodist Archbishop." *Deji Okegbile Blog*, June 27, 2018. http://dejiokegbile.com/archbishop-ayo-ladigbolu-80-a-prince-and-a-muslim-evangelist-to-a-methodist-archbishop/.

Okunola, Damilare. "Gani Adams: Jonathan Has Been Nice to Me." *P.M. News*, March 18, 2015. https://www.pmnewsnigeria.com/2015/03/18/gani-adams-jonathan-has-been-nice-to-me/.

Oladele, Bisi, Yinka Adeniran, Alao Abiodun, and Gbenga Omokhunu. "IGP under Fire over Sunday Igboho Arrest Order." *Nation*, January 24, 2021. https://thenationonlineng.net/igp-under-fire-over-sunday-igboho-arrest-order/.

Oladele, Kayode, and Sina Loremikan. "Good Night, Comrade Ayodele Akele—the Bridge Builder of the 'Have Nots.'" Sahara Reporters, June 26, 2020. http://saharareporters.com/2020/06/26/good-night-comrade-ayodele-akele-bridge-builder-%E2%80%9Chave-nots%E2%80%9D-kayode-oladele-and-sina.

Oladinni, Victor. "Fury of the Men of War." *TheNEWS*, November 15, 1999.

Oladipo, Tunde. "Carnage in Ibadan." *TheNEWS*, January 24, 2000.

Olafusi, Ebunoluwa. "Adebanjo: 'Emi lo kan' Doesn't Mean Turn of Yoruba—It's Tinubu-Buhari Agreement." *Cable*, February 11, 2023. https://www.thecable.ng/adebanjo-emi-lo-kan-doesnt-mean-turn-of-yoruba-its-tinubu-buhari-agreement.

———. "Lawyer: Igboho Released by Benin Republic, Now in Germany." *Cable*, October 9, 2023. https://www.thecable.ng/lawyer-igboho-released-by-benin-republic-now-in-germany#google_vignette.

Olaitan, Kemi. "OPC Disowns Gani Adams over Attack on Tinubu." *ThisDay*, July 12, 2020. https://www.thisdaylive.com/index.php/2020/07/12/opc-disowns-gani-adams-over-attack-on-tinubu/.

Olaiya, Adeyinka. "Aare Gani Adams in Brazil, Set to Address Parliament, Holds Convention." *Ancestral News*, December 9, 2022. https://ancestrals.com.ng/2022/12/09/aare-gani-adams-in-brazil-set-to-address-parliament/.

———. "Gani Adams in Brazil Bar Association, Grace OPU Summit, Task Parliament." *Ancestral News*, December 15, 2022. https://ancestrals.com.ng/2022/12/15/gani-adams-address-brazil-bar-association-grace-opu-summit-task-parliament/.

———. "Gani Adams in Pele's Santos, Appoints Chief, Applauds Brazil." *Ancestral News*, December 12, 2022. https://ancestrals.com.ng/2022/12/12/gani-adams-in-peles-santos-appoints-chief-applauds-brazil/.

Olalekan Israel, Kazeem. "Sunday Igboho and the Farce of Oduduwa Republic." *Business Day*, March 24, 2021. https://businessday.ng/opinion/article/sunday-igboho-and-the-farce-of-oduduwa-republic/.

Olaniyi, Olufemi. "Islamic Leaders Boycott Oduduwa Republic Rally, Gani Adams Tackles Igboho." *Punch*, October 4, 2020. https://punchng.com/islamic-leaders-boycott-oduduwa-republic-rally-gani-adams-tackles-igboho/.

Olanrewaju, Lekan. "'Tinubu Did Not Give Me N10m to Kill Gani Adams': Wale Adedayo Releases Statement." YNaija, March 11, 2012. https://naija.yafri.ca/tinubu-did-not-give-me-n10m-to-kill-gani-adams-wale-adedayo-releases-statement/.

Olanrewaju, Sulaimon, and Saka Gbeminiyi. "Why the Police Do Not Want OPC's Assistance in Providing Security—Gani Adams." *Nigerian Tribune*, April 30, 2008.

Olarinoye, Gbenga. "Why OPC Supported Jonathan for 2nd Term, by Gani Adams." *Vanguard*, January 28, 2016. https://www.vanguardngr.com/2016/01/why-opc-supported-jonathan-for-2nd-term-by-gani-adams/.

Olarinoye, Gbenga, and Ola Ajayi. "Ooni Visit Alaafin, as Monarchs End 79-Yr Old Supremacy Battle." *Vanguard*, January 18, 2016. https://www.vanguardngr.com/2016/01/ooni-visits-alaafin-as-monarchs-end-79-yr-old-supremacy-battle/.

Olatunji, Daud. "Why I Rejected Gani Adam's Request to Visit Me—Obasanjo." *Punch*, December 2, 2020. https://punchng.com/why-i-rejected-gani-adams-request-to-visit-me-obasanjo/.

Olatuyi, Oluseto, Kunle Adeyemi, and Semiu Okanlawon. "OPC Withdraws Vigilance Services." *Punch*, December 28, 2005.

Olawale, Gabriel. "Insecurity Preventing Nigerians in Diaspora from Coming Home—Gani Adams." *Vanguard*, February 7, 2022. https://www.vanguardngr.com/2022/02/insecurity-preventing-nigerians-in-diaspora-from-coming-home-gani-adams/.

Olawoyin, Oladehinde. "Why I Made Gani Adams Aare Ona Kakanfo—Alaafin." *Premium Times*, October 19, 2017. https://www.premiumtimesng.com/regional/ssouth-west/246600-i-made-gani-adams-aare-ona-kakanfo-alaafin.html.

Olofintila, Tunde. "Between Aare Baamofin and *Ààrẹ Ọ̀nà Kakaǹfò* of Yorubaland." *Vanguard*, November 21, 2017. https://www.vanguardngr.com/2017/11/aare-baamofin-aare-ona-kakanfo-yorubaland/.

Olokor, Friday. "Adeboye Hails Gani Adams, Regrets Absence from Installation." *Punch*, January 23, 2018. https://punchng.com/adeboye-hails-gani-adams-regrets-absence-from-installation/.

———. "Gani Adams Is Prayer Warrior, Says Chief of Staff." *Punch*, January 25, 2018. https://punchng.com/gani-adams-is-prayer-warrior-says-chief-of-staff/.

———. "Yoruba Can Defend Themselves against Killer Herdsmen—Gani Adams." *Punch*, February 9, 2018. https://punchng.com/yoruba-can-defend-themselves-against-killer-herdsmen-gani-adams/.

Olowolagba, Fikayo. "Why I Didn't Join Sunday Igboho for Yoruba Nation Rally—Gani Adams." *Daily Post*, July 13, 2021. https://dailypost.ng/2021/07/13/why-i-didnt-join-sunday-igboho-for-yoruba-nation-rally-gani-adams/.

Olubajo, Oyindamola. "'I Was Indoors When Soldiers, SSS Attacked My Residence'—Sunday Igboho." *Peoples Gazette*, July 1, 2021. https://gazettengr.com/i-was-indoors-when-soldiers-sss-attacked-my-residence-sunday-igboho/.

Olukoya, Olayinka, Adebayo Waheed, and Olalekan Olabulo. "Declare MKO Ex-president, Family Tells FG." *Nigerian Tribune*, June 13, 2012.

Oluku, Esther. "Insecurity: IG Sends Emissaries to Gani Adams over OPC's Threats to Herdsmen." *ThisDay*, June 19, 2019. https://www.thisdaylive.com/index.php/2019/06/19/insecurity-ig-sends-emissaries-to-gani-adams-over-opcs-threats-to-herdsmen/.

Olumide, Seye. "Afenifere: I Remain Leader, Says Adebanjo as Fasoranti Returns." *Guardian*, November 3, 2022. https://guardian.ng/news/afenifere-i-remain-leader-says-adebanjo-as-fasoranti-returns/.

———. "*Afenifere* Reconciles Olusegun Obasanjo, Gani Adams, Settles 15-Year Rift." *Guardian*, December 3, 2020.

———. "Utomi, Adams Task FG on Corruption, Security." *Guardian*, November 12, 2019. https://guardian.ng/news/utomi-adams-task-fg-on-corruption-security/.

Olumide, Seye, and Rotimi Agboluaje. "Second Ilana Omo Oodua Leader Resigns in 34 Days." *Guardian*, January 8, 2023. https://guardian.ng/news/second-ilana-omo-oodua-leader-resigns-in-34-days/.

Olumide, Seye, and Oluwaseun Akingboye. "Fasoranti Steps Down as Afenifere Leader, Adebanjo Takes Over." *Guardian*, March 17, 2021. https://guardian.ng/politics/fasoranti-steps-down-as-afenifere-leader-adebanjo-takes-over/.

Omonijo, Bolade. "Afenifere Berates FG over Comments on OPC." *Vanguard*, March 9, 2006.

Oni, Stephen Olufemi. "Gani Adams under Fire for Attacking Tinubu." *Telegraph*, July 13, 2020. https://www.newtelegraphng.com/gani-adams-under-fire-for-attacking-tinubu-2/.

Oputah, David. "Tompolo, Asari Dokubo Get New Pipeline Deals." *Cable News*, March 12, 2015. https://www.thecable.ng/tompolo-asari-dokubo-get-new-pipeline-deals.

Orok, Gabriel, and Moses Uchendu. "War in Lagos as OPC Loses 50 Men in Police Execution." *P.M. News*, July 17, 2000. https://allafrica.com/stories/200007170472.html.

Osaigbovo, Nosa. "The Outlaw as Hero." Friday, April 23, 2010. http://www.tribune.com.ng/index.php/mosaic/4427-the-outlaw-as-hero.

Osazuwa, Job. "Lagos Stand Still for Kalu's Daughter's Wedding." *Sun*, December 23, 2017. https://www.sunnewsonline.com/lagos-stands-still-for-kalus-daughters-wedding/.

Oshunkeye, Shola. "People Who Ignore Me, Do So at Their Peril." *Sunday Sun*, December 4, 2011.

Oyeleke, Sodiq. "Court Awards N20bn Damages against DSS for Raiding Igboho's House." *Punch*, September 17, 2021. https://punchng.com/breaking-court-awards-n20bn-damages-against-dss-for-raiding-igbohos-house/.

Oyeniyi, Emmanuel Femi. "Gani Adams Becomes Apostle." Facebook, December 17, 2020. https://www.facebook.com/2328403104051034/posts/aare-gani-adams-ordination-as-an-apostle-an-abomination-on-the-altar-emmanuel-fe/3430714593819874/.

Ozekhome, Mike. "Is Buhari Really President of All and for No One?" *Sun*, September 19, 2018. https://www.sunnewsonline.com/is-buhari-really-president-of-all-and-for-no-one/.

Payne, Julia. "Nigeria Postpones Feb. 14 Presidential Election to March 28." Reuters, February 8, 2015. https://www.reuters.com/article/us-nigeria-election/nigeria-postpones-feb-14-presidential-election-to-march-28-inec-idUSKBN0LB0TL20150208.

Peter, Adeshina. "President Buhari's Ethnocentric Image Is His Fault." *Will*, October 15, 2017. https://thewillnigeria.com/opinion-president-buharis-ethnocentric-image-is-his-fault/.

Phillips, Barnaby. "Africa: Kano 'Tense' after Ethnic Riots." BBC News, July 23, 1999. http://news.bbc.co.uk/2/hi/africa/401888.stm.

Premium Times. "Aare Ona Kakanfo: Tinubu Congratulates Gani Adams." October 17, 2017. https://www.premiumtimesng.com/regional/ssouth-west/246429-aare-ona-kakanfo-tinubu-congratulates-gani-adams.html.

———. "How Sunday Igboho Can Be Released—Gani Adams." February 9, 2022. https://www.premiumtimesng.com/news/more-news/510521-how-sunday-igboho-can-be-released-gani-adams.html.

———. "Presidency Replies Obasanjo, Says He's Nigeria's 'Divider-In-Chief.'" September 13, 2020. https://www.premiumtimesng.com/news/headlines/414283-presidency-replies-obasanjo-says-hes-nigerias-divider-in-chief.html.

———. "What Gani Adams Said during Installation as Aare Ona Kakanfo." January 14, 2018. https://www.premiumtimesng.com/regional/ssouth-west/255466-%E2%80%8Ewhat-gani-adams-said-installation-aare-ona-kakanfo-full-speech.html.

———. "Why We Can't Proceed with Elections—Jega." February 8, 2015. https://www.premiumtimesng.com/news/headlines/176422-cant-proceed-election-jega.html.

Punch. "IGP under Pressure to Arrest Igboho as Activist Snubs Police Invitation." April 3, 2021. https://punchng.com/ig-under-pressure-to-arrest-igboho-as-activist-snubs-police-invitation/.

———. "Lagos Clashes: Scores of Youths Still in Detention." November 5, 2000.

Ross, Will. "Nigeria Postpones Presidential Vote over Security." BBC, February 8, 2015. https://www.bbc.co.uk/news/world-africa-31221545.

Sahara Reporters. "Insecurity: Obasanjo, Afenifere Leaders Meet in Lagos, Discuss Way Forward for South-West." New York, December 2, 2020. http://saharareporters.com/2020/12/02/insecurity-obasanjo-afenifere-leaders-meet-lagos-discuss-way-forward-south-west.

———. "Let's Help Igboho Though He Abused Us—Gani Adams Appeals to South-West Governors, Ooni, Others." July 7, 2021. https://saharareporters.com/2021/07/07/lets-help-igboho-though-he-abused-us%E2%80%94gani-adams-appeals-south-west-governors-ooni-others.

———. "Nigerians in Diaspora Don't Want to Come Home Because of Insecurity—Gani Adams." February 6, 2022. http://saharareporters.com/2022/02/06/nigerians-diaspora-dont-want-come-home-because-insecurity%E2%80%93gani-adams.

———. "Prof Akintoye's Successor, Adeniran Resigns as Leader of Yoruba Self-Determination Organisation, Ilana Omo Oodua Amid Fraud Allegations." January 7, 2023. https://saharareporters.com/2023/01/07/breaking-prof-akintoyes-successor-adeniran-resigns-leader-yoruba-self-determination.

———. "Release Sunday Igboho to Continue His Journey—Soyinka Tells Benin Republic." New York, August 27, 2021. https://saharareporters.com/2021/08/27/release-sunday-igboho-continue-his-journey-%E2%80%93-soyinka-tells-benin-republic.

———. "Yoruba Nation: Gani Adams Says No Going Back on Call for Oduduwa Republic." April 1, 2021. http://saharareporters.com/2021/04/01/yoruba-nation-gani-adams-says-no-going-back-call-oduduwa-republic.

Samuel, Oamen. "Why I Didn't Accept IGP's Invitation Letters, by Sunday Igboho." *Nation*, April 2, 2021. https://thenationonlineng.net/why-i-didnt-accept-igps-invitation-letters-by-sunday-igboho/.

Sani, Lekan, Ben Akparanta, Eno Bassey, and Tunde Alao. "Suspected OPC Members Re-launch War on Bandits, Behead Four." *Guardian* (Lagos), August 17, 2001.

Saturday Tribune. "Obasanjo Presidency Was a Disaster to the S/West—Gani Adams." October 27, 2007.

———. "OPC Will Reject OBJ's Third Term Agenda—Gani Adams." August 30, 2005.

Schuhr, Alexander. "Notes on the African Big Man." Good Men Project, November 14, 2017. https://goodmenproject.com/featured-content/notes-african-big-man-phtz/.

Sessou, Ebun, and Iyabo Aina. "I Never Collected Money from Ghaddafi, Jonathan, Obanikoro—Gani Adams. Asks Accusers to Show Proof." *Vanguard*, February 20, 2016. https://www.vanguardngr.com/2016/02/i-never-collected-money-from-ghaddafi-jonathan-obanikoro-gani-adams/.

Shariff, Ujudud. "OPC: The Limis of Tolerance." *Daily Trust*, February 12, 2002.

Shuaibu, Faruk. "The Untold Story of Controversial Yoruba Youth Leader Sunday Igboho." *Daily Trust*, January 26, 2021. https://dailytrust.com/the-untold-story-of-controversial-yoruba-youth-leader-sunday-igboho.

Silas, Don. "Gani Adams Is the Greatest Yoruba Man of His Generation—Gbenga Daniel." *Daily Post*, December 28, 2017. https://dailypost.ng/2017/12/28/gani-adams-greatest-yoruba-man-generation-gbenga-daniel/.

Soyingbe, Anthonia. "2015—Gani Adams Denies Collecting Money from Jonathan." *Daily Independent*, April 17, 2015. https://allafrica.com/stories/201504171788.html.

Suleiman, Tajudeen. "Nigeria: Massacre in Kano." *TheNews*, August 2, 1999. https://allafrica.com/stories/199908020234.html.

Suleiman, Toba. "OPC to Provide Security for Bonnke." *ThisDay*, February 13, 2004.

The New Humanitarian. "OPC faction to stop vigilante activity." September 5, 2001. https://www.thenewhumanitarian.org/report/25930/nigeria-opc-faction-stop-vigilante-activity.

TheNEWS. "Gani Adams Endorses Jonathan for Second Term." March 13, 2015. https://www.thenewsnigeria.com.ng/2015/03/13/gani-adams-endorses-jonathan-for-second-term/.

———. "I'm Invincible: 'No One Can Arrest Me'—Gani Adams." *TheNEWS*, January 31, 2000.

ThisDay. "At OPU World Congress 2019, It Was Glitz and Glamour in Akure." February 3, 2019. https://www.thisdaylive.com/index.php/2019/02/03/at-opu-world-congress-2019-it-was-glitz-and-glamour-in-akure/.

Thomas, Tunde, and Henry Omafode. "How We Toppled Fasehun—Gani Adams." *Spectator*, December 16–22, 2009.

Tijani, Taju. "Banjo Akintoye: Beyond Yoruba triumphalism as UNPO Member." *Guardian*, May 29, 2020. https://guardian.ng/opinion/banji-akintoye-beyond-yoruba-triumphalism-as-unpo-member/.

———. "Hard Talk on Yoruba Race." *TT Soundings*, August 13, 2011. https://tajutijani.wordpress.com/2011/08/13/hard-talk-on-yoruba-race/.

TimesLIVE. "Malema's Mystery Millions." February 19, 2012. https://www.timeslive.co.za/news/south-africa/2010-02-19-malemas-mystery-millions/.

Topnews. "Gani Adams Extols Gbenga Daniel, Calls Him 'Asset to Yoruba Nation.'" December 27, 2017. http://www.topnewsmagazines.com/gani-adams-extols-gbenga-daniel-calls-him-asset-to-yoruba-nation/.

Tukur, Sani. "Osinbajo Sacks Lawal Daura as SSS DG." *Premium Times*, August 7, 2018. https://www.premiumtimesng.com/news/headlines/279192-osinbajo-sacks-lawal-daura-as-sss-dg.html.

Tyohemba, Henry. "Sunday Igboho Bags Honorary Degree from US Varsity." *Leadership*, November 3, 2022. https://leadership.ng/sunday-igboho-bags-honorary-degree-from-us-varsity/.

Ugbolue, Henry. "Balance of Terror." *TheNEWS*, January 10, 2000.

Uguru, Okorie. "Gani Adams: Interview." ("Weekend Treat"). *Nation*, September 11, 2009.

Ugwu, Francis. "Sunday Igboho Bags Honorary Doctorate Degree in War Studies from US Varsity." *Daily Post*, November 2, 2022. https://dailypost.ng/2022/11/02/sunday-igboho-bags-honorary-doctorate-degree-in-war-studies-from-us-varsity/.

Uwugiaren, Iyobosa, Deji Elumoye, Omololu Ogunmade, Onyebuchi Ezigbo, Olawale Olaleye, Shola Oyeyipo, and James Sowole. "Ending Impunity, Osinbajo Sacks DSS DG, Lawal Daura." *ThisDay*, August 8, 2018. https://www.thisdaylive.com/index.php/2018/08/08/ending-impunity-osinbajo-sacks-dss-dg-lawal-daura/.

Uzendu, Malachy. "OPC Kills 10,000—FG." *Daily Champion*, March 8, 2006.

Vanguard. "Aare Ona Kakanfo Cap Fits Adams—Fayose." October 18, 2017. https://www.vanguardngr.com/2017/10/aare-ona-kakanfo-cap-fits-adams-fayose/.

———. "Aare Ona Kakanfo Instals 21 Chiefs across Yoruba Land." January 12, 2019. https://www.vanguardngr.com/2019/01/aare-onakakanfo-instals-21-chiefs-across-yoruba-land/.

———. "Aare Ona Kakanfo: Tinubu Congratulates Gani Adams." October 17, 2017. https://www.vanguardngr.com/2017/10/aare-ona-kakanfo-tinubu-congratulates-gani-adams/.

———. "Buhari Congratulates Aare Ona Kakanfo, Gani Adams, Tasks Him on National Unity." January 12, 2018. https://www.vanguardngr.com/2018/01/buhari-congratulates-aare-ona-kakanfo-gani-adams-tasks-national-unity/.

———. "Conferment of Aare Ona Kakanfo of Yorubaland on Adams God-Ordained—Daniel." October 20, 2017. https://www.vanguardngr.com/2017/10/conferment-aare-ona-kakanfo-yorubaland-adams-god-ordained-daniel/.

———. "Declare 2 Days Holiday for Eledumare Festival, Gani Adams Urges Governors." March 13, 2020. https://www.vanguardngr.com/2020/03/declare-2-days-holiday-for-eledumare-festival-gani-adams-urges-governors/.

———. "How South-West Gave Legal Teeth to Amotekun." March 7, 2020. https://www.vanguardngr.com/2020/03/how-south-west-gave-legal-teeth-to-amotekun/.

———. "Obasanjo Orders Clampdown on OPC." November 26, 1999.

———. "Sunday Igboho Bags Honorary Doctorate Degree in U.S." November 3, 2022. https://www.vanguardngr.com/2022/11/sunday-igboho-bags-honorary-doctorate-degree-in-u-s/.

———. "Why Obasanjo Should Not Be Allowed to Kill Labour, by Gani Adams." October 8, 2004.

INDEX

Numbers in italics indicate figures.

Wale Adebanwi is Presidential Penn Compact Professor of Africana Studies with secondary appointment in the Department of Political Science, and Director of Center for Africana Studies, University of Pennsylvania. He is a research associate at the African Studies Center, Oxford University; author of *Yorùbá Elites and Ethnic Politics in Nigeria: Ọbáfemi Awólówò and Corporate Agency* (2004); and editor of *Everyday State and Democracy in Africa: Ethnographic Encounters* (2022).

FOR INDIANA UNIVERSITY PRESS

Tony Brewer *Artist and Book Designer*

Anna Francis *Assistant Acquisitions Editor*

Anna Garnai *Editorial Assistant*

Brenna Hosman *Production Coordinator*

Katie Huggins *Production Manager*

David Miller *Lead Project Manager/Editor*

Bethany Mowry *Acquisitions Editor*

Dan Pyle *Online Publishing Manager*

Stephen Williams *Marketing and Publicity Manager*

Jennifer Witzke *Senior Artist and Book Designer*